Get Connected.

Interactive Applications

Connect Business' **Interactive Applications** offer students a variety of tools to help engage students in application level thinking about the core contents. Interactive Application exercises include: Drag and Drops, Case Analyses, Sequencing, Video Cases, and Decision Generators, which are all auto-gradable. After completing an activity, students receive immediate feedback and can track their progress through a personalized report, while instructors are provided detailed results on how each student in their course is performing.

Student Progress Tracking

Connect keeps instructors informed about how each student, section, and class is performing, allowing for more productive use of lecture and office hours. The progress tracking function enables instructors to:

- View scored work immediately and track individual or group performance with assignment and grade reports.

- Access an instant view of student or class performance relative to learning objectives.

- Collect data and generate reports required by many accreditation organizations, such as AACSB.

assignment statistics

View score statistics on submitted assignments.

show: Assignment Statistics

▶ show report options & settings

Scores below are **averages across attempts.**

assignment statistics: mwf 9am (Chris Nowack)

report created: 07/27/2012 5:04 PM CDT

assignment type: Homework, LearnSmart, Practice, Quiz, Exam

Click on an assignment name to view **attempt details.**

expand all | collapse all   export to excel

assignment	mean score	highest score	lowest score	# students submitted	# times submitted
▶ comprehension case (3 attempts, 10 points)	0	0	0	1	1
▶ exam 1 (1 attempts, 30 points)	10	10	10	1	1
▶ Homework 1 (3 attempts, 40 points)	18.7	18.7	18.7	1	1

Get Engaged.

eBooks

Connect Plus includes a media-rich eBook that allows you to share your notes with your students. Your students can insert and review their own notes, highlight the text, search for specific information, and interact with media resources. Using an eBook with *Connect Plus* gives your students a complete digital solution that allows them to access their materials from any computer.

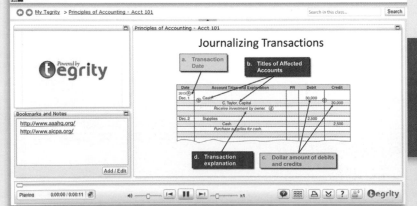

Intro to Business — connect

switch section

home | **library** | reports

library

» show library menu ◄ ► [ ] Go 🖨 A A A | 🔍 Search eBook... | Go

ebook

Business eBook

Content

Chapter 13 ▾

Chapter Opener

Introduction

What Is Digital Market...

Growth and Benefits of...

Using Digital Media...

Digital Media and the ...

Types of Consumer-Gene...

Using Digital Media to...

Using Digital Media to...

Legal and Social Issue...

Digital Media's Impact...

Review Your Understand...

Revisit the World of B...

Chapter13: Digital Marketing and Social Networking

Using Digital Media in Business

p. 404   The phenomenal growth of digital media has provided new ways of conducting business. Given almost instant communication with precisely defined consumer groups, firms can use real-time exchanges to create to stimulate interactive communication, forge closer relationships, and learn more accurately about consumer and supplier needs. With \$19.2 billion in annual revenue, Amazon.com is one of the most successful e-businesses, ranked 130th on the *Fortune* 500 list in 2009. Amazon is a true global e-business, and was one of the early success stories in the industry, getting 50 percent of its revenue from international sales. The United Kingdom, Japan, and Germany each account for 10 percent.[3] Many of you may not remember a world before Amazon because it has completely transformed how many people shop. Previously, consumers had to travel store to store in order to find goods and compare prices.

   Because it is fast and inexpensive, digital communication is making it easier for businesses to conduct marketing research, provide and obtain price and product information, and advertise, as well as to fulfill their business goals by selling goods and services online. Even the U.S. government engages in digital marketing activities—marketing everything from Treasury bonds and other financial instruments to oil-drilling leases and wild horses. Procter & Gamble uses the Internet as a fast, cost-effective means for marketing research, judging consumer demand for potential new products by inviting online consumers to sample

Lecture Capture

Make your classes available anytime, anywhere. With simple, one-click recording, students can search for a word or phrase and be taken to the exact place in your lecture that they need to review.

Business

A Changing World

ninth edition

O.C. Ferrell
University of New Mexico

Geoffrey A. Hirt
DePaul University

Linda Ferrell
University of New Mexico

McGraw-Hill Irwin

McGraw-Hill
Irwin

BUSINESS: A CHANGING WORLD, NINTH EDITION
Published by McGraw-Hill/Irwin, a business unit of The McGraw-Hill Companies, Inc., 1221 Avenue of the Americas, New York, NY, 10020. Copyright © 2014 by The McGraw-Hill Companies, Inc. All rights reserved. Printed in the United States of America. Previous editions © 2011, 2009, and 2008. No part of this publication may be reproduced or distributed in any form or by any means, or stored in a database or retrieval system, without the prior written consent of The McGraw-Hill Companies, Inc., including, but not limited to, in any network or other electronic storage or transmission, or broadcast for distance learning.

Some ancillaries, including electronic and print components, may not be available to customers outside the United States.

This book is printed on acid-free paper.

1 2 3 4 5 6 7 8 9 0 DOW/DOW 1 0 9 8 7 6 5 4 3

ISBN 978-0-07-802313-2
MHID 0-07-802313-0

Senior Vice President, Products & Markets: *Kurt L. Strand*
Vice President, General Manager, Products & Markets: *Brent Gordon*
Vice President, Content Production & Technology Services: *Kimberly Meriwether David*
Managing Director: *Paul Ducham*
Senior Brand Manager: *Anke Braun Weekes*
Executive Director of Development: *Ann Torbert*
Development Editor: *Gabriela Gonzalez*
Executive Marketing Manager: *Michael Gedatus*
Content Project Manager: *Angela Norris*
Buyer II: *Debra R. Sylvester*
Designer: *Debra Kubiak*
Cover/Interior Designer: *Pam Verros*
Cover Image: *Yuji Sakai/Getty Images*
Content Licensing Specialist: *Joanne Mennemeier*
Photo Researcher: *Danny Meldung/Photo Affairs, Inc.*
Media Project Manager: *Ron Nelms*
Typeface: *10.5/12 Minion*
Compositor: *Laserwords Private Limited*
Printer: *R. R. Donnelley*

All credits appearing on page or at the end of the book are considered to be an extension of the copyright page.

Library of Congress Cataloging-in-Publication Data

Ferrell, O. C.
    Business : a changing world / O. C. Ferrell, University of New Mexico, Geoffrey A. Hirt,
DePaul University, Linda Ferrell, University of New Mexico.—ninth edition.
        pages cm
    Includes index.
    ISBN 978-0-07-802313-2 (alk. paper)—ISBN 0-07-802313-0 (alk. paper)
    1. Business. 2. Management—United States. I. Hirt, Geoffrey A. II. Ferrell, Linda. III. Title.
HF1008.F47 2014
650—dc23   2012042692

The Internet addresses listed in the text were accurate at the time of publication. The inclusion of a website does not indicate an endorsement by the authors or McGraw-Hill, and McGraw-Hill does not guarantee the accuracy of the information presented at these sites.

www.mhhe.com

Dedication

To James Ferrell

To Linda Hirt

To George Ferrell

Authors

O.C. Ferrell

O.C. Ferrell is Distinguished Professor of Marketing, Bill Daniels Professor of Business Ethics in the Anderson School of Management at the University of New Mexico. He served as the Bill Daniels Distinguished Professor of Business Ethics at the University of Wyoming and the Chair of the Department of Marketing at Colorado State University. He also has held faculty positions at the University of Memphis, University of Tampa, Texas A&M University, Illinois State University, and Southern Illinois University, as well as visiting positions at Queen's University (Ontario, Canada), University of Michigan (Ann Arbor), University of Wisconsin (Madison), and University of Hannover (Germany). He has served as a faculty member for the Master's Degree Program in Marketing at Thammasat University (Bangkok, Thailand). Dr. Ferrell received his B.A. and M.B.A. from Florida State University and his Ph.D. from Louisiana State University. His teaching and research interests include business ethics, corporate citizenship, and marketing.

Dr. Ferrell is widely recognized as a leading teacher and scholar in business. His articles have appeared in leading journals and trade publications. In addition to *Business: A Changing World,* he has two other textbooks, *Marketing* and *Business Ethics: Ethical Decision Making and Cases,* that are market leaders in their respective areas. He also has co-authored other textbooks for marketing, management, business and society, and other business courses, as well as a trade book on business ethics. He chaired the American Marketing Association (AMA) ethics committee that developed its current code of ethics. He is past president of the Academic Council for the AMA. Currently he is vice president of publications for the Academy of Marketing Science and a distinguished Fellow.

Dr. Ferrell's major focus is teaching and preparing learning materials for students. He has taught the introduction to business course using this textbook. This gives him the opportunity to develop, improve, and test the book and ancillary materials on a firsthand basis. He has traveled extensively to work with students and understands the needs of instructors of introductory business courses. He lives in Albuquerque, New Mexico, and enjoys skiing, golf, and international travel.

Geoffrey A. Hirt

Geoffrey A. Hirt is currently Professor of Finance at DePaul University and a Mesirow Financial Fellow. From 1987 to 1997, he was Chairman of the Finance Department at DePaul University. He teaches investments, corporate finance, and strategic planning. He developed and was director of DePaul's M.B.A. program in Hong Kong and has taught in Poland, Germany, Thailand, and Hong Kong. He received his Ph.D. in Finance from the University of Illinois at Champaign–Urbana, his M.B.A. from Miami University of Ohio, and his B.A. from Ohio-Wesleyan

University. Dr. Hirt has directed the Chartered Financial Analysts Study program for the Investment Analysts Society of Chicago since 1987.

Dr. Hirt has published several books, including *Foundations of Financial Management* published by McGraw-Hill/Irwin. Now in its fourteenth edition, this book is used at more than 600 colleges and universities worldwide. It has been used in more than 31 countries and has been translated into more than 13 different languages. Additionally, Dr. Hirt is well known for his text, *Fundamentals of Investment Management*, also published by McGraw-Hill/Irwin, and now in its tenth edition. He plays tennis and golf, is a music lover, and enjoys traveling with his wife, Linda.

Linda Ferrell

Dr. Linda Ferrell is Professor of Marketing and Bill Daniels Professor of Business Ethics in the Anderson School of Management at the University of New Mexico. She completed her Ph.D. in Business Administration, with a concentration in management, at the University of Memphis. She has taught at the University of Tampa, Colorado State University, University of Northern Colorado, University of Memphis, and the University of Wyoming. She also team teaches a class at Thammasat University in Bangkok, Thailand, as well as an online Business Ethics Certificate course through the University of New Mexico.

Her work experience as an account executive for McDonald's and Pizza Hut's advertising agencies supports her teaching of advertising, marketing management, marketing ethics, and marketing principles. She has published in the *Journal of Public Policy & Marketing, Journal of Business Research, Journal of the Academy of Marketing Science, Journal of Business Ethics, AMS Review, Journal of Academic Ethics, Journal of Marketing Education, Marketing Education Review, Journal of Teaching Business Ethics, Case Research Journal, and is co-author of Business Ethics: Ethical Decision Making and Cases* (9th edition) *and Business and Society* (4th edition). She co-leads the Daniels Fund business ethics initiative at the University of New Mexico.

Dr. Ferrell is the President Elect for the Academy of Marketing Science and a past president for the Marketing Management Association. She is a member of the college advisory board for Cutco Vector. She is on the NASBA Center for the Public Trust Board of Directors, University of Central Florida-Nicholson School of Communication Board of Visitors, University of Tampa-Sykes College of Business, Board of Fellows, and the Direct Selling Education Foundation Board of Directors. She frequently speaks to organizations on "Teaching Business Ethics," including the Direct Selling Education Foundation's training programs, Ethics & Compliance Officer Association, NASBA Center for the Public Trust Ethical Leadership Conference, as well as others. She has served as an expert witness in cases related to advertising, business ethics, and consumer protection.

Welcome

This new edition reflects many dynamic changes in the business environment related to how managers make decisions. It is important for students to understand how the functional areas of business have to be coordinated as changes in the economy, technology, global competition, and consumer decision making continues to evolve. All of these changes are presented in concepts that entry-level students can understand. Our book contains all of the essentials that most students should learn in a semester. *Business: A Changing World* has, since its inception, been a concise presentation of the essential material needed to teach introduction to business. From our experience in teaching the course, we know that the most effective way to engage a student is by making business exciting, relevant, and up to date. Our teachable, from-the-ground-up approach involves a variety of media, application exercises, and subject matter, including up-to-date content supplements, boxed examples, video cases, PowerPoints, and testing materials that work for entry-level business students. We have worked hard to make sure that the content of this edition is as up to date as possible in order to best reflect today's dynamic world of business. We cover major changes in our economy related to sustainability, digital marketing, and social networking.

The Ninth Edition

The ninth edition represents one of our most thorough revisions. This is because so many recent events and changes in the environment relate to the foundational concepts in business. The most recent recession, high unemployment rates, and the financial instability in Europe have resulted in an economy sometimes called the New Normal. This means that an Introduction to Business textbook has to provide adequate coverage of these changes as they relate to traditional business concepts. Businesses must adapt to be successful. Therefore, we have listened to your feedback and incorporated needed changes in content, boxes, cases, exercises, and other features.

This is our second edition with a chapter on digital marketing and social networking in business. Since launching this chapter in the eighth edition, this dynamic area continues to change the face of business. Entrepreneurs and small businesses have to be able to increase sales and reduce costs by using social networking to communicate and develop relationships with customers. Because this area is a moving target, we have made substantial changes to the ninth edition of Chapter 13, Digital Marketing and Social Networking.

While the title of our book remains *Business: A Changing World,* we could have changed the title to *Business: A Green World.* Throughout the book, we recognize the importance of sustainability and "green" business. By using the philosophy *reduce, reuse, and recycle,* we believe every business can be more profitable and contribute to a better world through green initiatives. There is a new "Going Green" box in each chapter that covers these environmental changes. Our "Entrepreneurship in Action" boxes also discuss many innovations and opportunities to use green business for success.

We have been careful to continue our coverage of global business, ethics and social responsibility, and information technology as it relates to the foundations important in an introduction to business course. Our co-author team has a diversity of expertise in these important areas. O.C. Ferrell and Linda Ferrell have been recognized as leaders in business ethics education, and their insights are reflected in every chapter and in the "Consider Ethics and Social Responsibility" boxes. In addition, they maintain a website, www.e-businessethics.com, that provides free resources such as PowerPoints and cases that can be used in the classroom. Geoff Hirt has a strong background in global business development, especially world financial markets and trade relationships.

The foundational areas of introduction to business, entrepreneurship, small business management, marketing, accounting, and finance have been completely revised. Examples have been provided to which students can easily relate. An understanding of core functional areas of business is presented so students get a holistic view of the world of business. Box examples related to "Responding to Business Challenges," "Entrepreneurship in Action," "Going Green," and "Consider Ethics and Social Responsibility" help provide real-world examples in these areas.

Our goal is to make sure that the content and teaching package for this book are of the highest quality possible. We wish to seize this opportunity to gain your trust, and we appreciate any feedback to help us continually improve these materials. We hope that the real beneficiary of all of our work will be well-informed students who appreciate the role of business in society and take advantage of the opportunity to play a significant role in improving our world. As students understand how our free enterprise system operates and how we fit into the global competitive environment, they will develop the foundation for creating their own success and improving our quality of life.

O.C. Ferrell
Geoffrey Hirt
Linda Ferrell

Built from the Ground Up to be Exciting, Applicable, and Happening!

The best-selling integrated text and digital resource package on the market, *Business: A Changing World* was built from the ground up—that is, developed and written expressly for faculty and students who value a brief, flexible, and affordable resource that is exciting, applicable, and happening!

What sets this fastest growing learning program apart from the competition? An unrivaled mixture of exciting content and resources, application-focused text and activities, and fresh topics and examples that show students what is happening in the world of business today!

Built from the Ground Up
It's easy for students taking their first steps into business to become overwhelmed. Longer books try to solve this problem by chopping out examples or topics to make ad hoc shorter editions. *Business: A Changing World* carefully builds just the right mix of coverage and applications to give your students a firm grounding in business principles. Where other books have you sprinting through the semester to get everything in, Ferrell/Hirt/Ferrell allows you the breathing space to explore topics and incorporate other activities that are important to you and your students. The exceptional resources and the *Active Classroom Resource Manual* support you in this effort every step of the way.

Exciting
It's exciting to see students succeed! It's exciting to see more As and Bs in a course without grade inflation. Ferrell/Hirt/Ferrell makes these results possible for your course with its integrated learning package that is proven effective, tailored to each individual student, and easy to use.

Applicable
When students see how content applies to them, their life, their career, and the world around them, they are more engaged in the course. *Business: A Changing World* helps students maximize their learning efforts by setting clear objectives; delivering interesting cases and examples; focusing on core issues; and providing engaging activities to apply concepts, build skills, and solve problems.

Happening!
Because it isn't tied to the revision cycle of a larger book, *Business: A Changing World* inherits no outdated or irrelevant examples or coverage. Everything in the ninth edition reflects the very latest developments in the business world—from the recent recession, high unemployment rates, and the financial instability in Europe, to the growth of digital marketing and social networking. In addition, ethics continues to be a key issue, and Ferrell/Hirt/Ferrell use "Consider Ethics and Social Responsibility" boxes to instill in students the importance of ethical conduct in business. To ensure you always know what's happening, join the author-led Facebook group page supporting this text.

EXCITING

McGraw-Hill *Connect®* is the leading online assignment and assessment solution that connects students with the tools and resources they need to achieve success while providing instructors with tools to quickly pick content and assignments according to the learning objectives they want to emphasize.

Connect improves student learning and retention with engaging activities that prepare students for class, help them master concepts, and review for exams.

TAILORED TO YOU

Connect's rich content, abundant assignment types, and flexible policy options can be customized, while its powerful study tools adapt to individual student understanding and need. Simply put, Connect offers everything you need to reach your goals, your way.

EASY TO USE

"I quickly learned how easy it was to get going with Connect!"

–Dr. Jason Overby, College of Charleston

Please visit **www.mcgrawhillconnect.com** to learn more.

LearnSmart within *Connect* is an adaptive learning system designed to help students learn faster, study more efficiently, and retain more knowledge for greater success. *LearnSmart* adaptively

assesses students' skill levels to determine which topics students have mastered and which require further practice. Then it delivers customized learning content based on their strengths and weaknesses. The result: Students learn faster and more efficiently because they get the help they need, right when they need it—instead of getting stuck on lessons, or being continually frustrated with stalled progress.

Interactive Applications within *Connect* offer students a variety of tools to help them assess their understanding. All *Interactive Applications* require students to APPLY what they have learned from the text to these assignments and, other than the Comprehension Cases, are all auto-graded. Some of the *Interactive Application* exercises include: video cases, decision generators, and comprehensive cases.

Click and Drag exercises allow students to reinforce key models/processes by requiring students to label key illustrations and models from the text or build a process, and then demonstrate application-level knowledge.

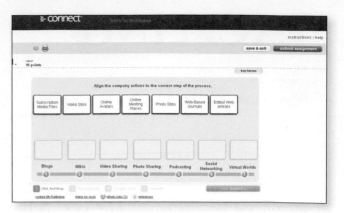

Video cases give students the opportunity to watch case videos and apply chapter concepts to a real-world business scenario as the scenario unfolds.

Decision generators require students to make real business decisions based on specific real-world scenarios and cases.

Integrated Media-Rich eBook

- A web-optimized eBook is seamlessly integrated within *Connect Plus*.
- Students can highlight, take notes, or even access shared instructors' notations to learn course material.
- The integrated eBook provides students with a cost-saving alternative to the traditional textbook.

Facilitate Learning and Measure Results

McGraw-Hill *Connect* strengthens the link between faculty, students, and coursework, helping everyone accomplish more in less time.

Student Progress Tracking

Connect keeps instructors informed about how each student, section, and class is performing, allowing for more productive use of lecture and office hours. For details, see the front inside cover.

Exciting News on the Industry's Best Video Program

iSee it! Video Clips

What's the difference between *leadership* and *management?* What are line vs. staff employees? Topics such as these are often confused by students learning the language of business for the first time. What if you were able to convey important concepts in a fun, animated, and memorable way that explains the topic in a way students will quickly understand and remember? What if students could quickly access the clip while they are reading their book right on their smart phone or computer? *iSee it!* video clips are the solution! Students simply scan the QR Code in their text or type in the URL to access these hot new video clips!

End-of-Chapter "*See for Yourself Videocase* " Clips

Videocases at the end of every chapter are supported by a stimulating mix of clips providing topical reinforcement and real-world insight to help students master the most challenging business topics—segments such as "Redbox Succeeds by Identifying Market Need" or "Groupon Masters Promotion to Become a Popular Daily Deal Site" or "Should Employees Use Social Media Sites at Work?" The videos can be found in the *Connect* Library resources, as well as the Instructor Edition of the Online Learning Center.

Manager's Hotseat

(*Connect* Library)—short video cases that show 15 real managers applying their years of experience in confronting certain management and organizational behavior issues. Students assume the role of the manager as they watch the video and answer multiple choice questions that pop up during the segment, forcing them to make decisions on the spot. Students learn from the managers' unscripted mistakes and successes, and then do a report critiquing the managers' approach by defending their reasoning.

HAPPENING

QR Codes QR codes are happening. Companies are using them on direct mail pieces, in-store displays, and catalogs, and the authors have included them in *Business: A Changing World*. These codes bring the text to life by creating the direct link to our brand new *iSee it!* video clips, which visually explain the most challenging or confusing topics to students in a fun, animated, and memorable way.

Facebook Stay up to date! A lot changes in the business world, and on a daily basis, which is why the authors have created a Facebook page to stay connected with their readers from around the world and update them with relevant current events, study tips for students, and more. To join the community, please visit **www.bit.ly/FerrellFacebook.**

Unique Chapter on Digital Marketing and Social Networking—Chapter 13
Digital media and digital marketing are recognized for their increasing value in strategic planning while adding new methods to the traditional marketing mix. Marketers' new ability to convert all types of communications into digital media has created efficient, inexpensive ways of connecting businesses and consumers and improves the flow and the usefulness of information. Additionally, this chapter describes how businesses use different types of social media and legal and ethical considerations marketers need to make.

New to This Edition
As always, when revising this material for the current edition, all examples, figures, and statistics have been updated to incorporate the most recently published data and discuss any recent developments that affect the world of business. Additionally, content was updated to ensure the most pertinent topical coverage is provided. Here are the highlights for each chapter:

Chapter 1: The Dynamics of Business and Economics
- New content on socially responsible companies
- New *See for Yourself Videocase*—Redbox

Chapter 2: Business Ethics and Social Responsibility
- New content on highly ethical cultures
- New section on misuse of company resources
- New section on unemployment
- New "Consider Ethics and Social Responsibility" box in the appendix
- New information about the Dodd-Frank Act

Chapter 3: Business in a Borderless World
- Updated information on the European financial crisis and bailouts
- New section on the Association of Southeast Asian Nations (ASEAN)

Chapter 4: Options for Organizing Business
- Additional information on Sarbanes-Oxley effectiveness and director compensation
- New *See for Yourself Videocase*—PODS

Chapter 5: Small Business, Entrepreneurship, and Franchising
- Updated content on retailing and wholesaling
- Expanded coverage on the role of small business in the American economy

Chapter 6: The Nature of Management
- Updated information on managerial compensation
- New *See for Yourself Videocase*—Zappos

Chapter 7: Organization, Teamwork, and Communication
- New section on improving communication effectiveness

Chapter 8: Managing Service and Manufacturing Operations
- New section on integrating operations and supply chain management
- New *See for Yourself Videocase*—Toyota

Chapter 9: Motivating the Workforce
- Updated information on the best places to start a career
- New *See for Yourself Videocase*—Container Store

Chapter 10: Managing Human Resources
- New section on trends in management of the workforce
- New *See for Yourself Videocase*—Hollywood Labor

Chapter 11: Customer-Driven Marketing
- Expanded coverage on customer relationship management
- Information about the rise in digital surveys and Internet research
- New section on the importance of marketing to society

Chapter 12: Dimensions of Marketing Strategy
- New section on the importance of marketing strategy
- New *See for Yourself Videocase*—Groupon

Chapter 13: Digital Marketing and Social Networking
- Significant restructuring and rearrangement of material
- New information on types of mobile marketing
- New section on apps and widgets
- More in-depth information on consumer privacy and online piracy

Chapter 14: Accounting and Financial Statements
- Updated information on the financial information and ratios of Starbucks and McDonald's
- Significant updates to industry analysis section
- New information about compliance to accounting principles
- New *See for Yourself Videocase*—Goodwill

Chapter 15: Money and the Financial System
- Additional information on deflation

Chapter 16: Financial Management and Securities Markets
- Expanded coverage concerning capital budgeting for Apple products

Appendix D: Personal Financial Planning
- New information on changes to health insurance due to new legislation

TEACHING AND LEARNING RESOURCES

Instructor's Resource CD (IRCD) ISBN 0077506618

This CD contains the Instructor's Manual, a Test Bank, and PowerPoint presentations.

Connect Instructor Library and Online Learning Center

www.mhhe.com/ferrell9e Access everything you need to teach a great course through our convenient online resource. A secured Instructor Library/Resource Center stores your essential course materials to save you prep time before class.

- **Instructor's Manual** The Instructor's Manual to accompany this text is an all-inclusive resource designed to support instructors in effectively teaching the Introduction to Business course. It includes learning objectives, lecture outlines, PowerPoint notes, supplemental lecture, answers to discussion questions and end-of-chapter exercises, notes for video cases, term paper and project topics, suggestions for guest speakers, and roles and options for implementing role-playing exercises.

- **Test Bank and EZ Test Online** The Test Bank offers more than 2,000 questions, which are categorized by topic, level of learning (knowledge, comprehension, or application), Learning Objectives, Bloom's Taxonomy, and accreditation standards (AACSB).

- **PowerPoint Presentations** The PowerPoint presentations feature slides that can be used and personalized by instructors to help present concepts to the students effectively. Each set of slides contains additional figures and tables from the text.

- **Videos** McGraw-Hill provides industry-leading video support to help students understand concepts and see how they apply in the real world.

- ***A Guide for Introducing and Teaching Ethics in Introduction to Business*** Written by O.C. Ferrell and Linda Ferrell, this is your one-stop guide for integrating this important issue into all aspects of your course. It helps you to demonstrate how business ethics lead to business success and offers a wide range of business ethics resources, including university centers, government resources, and corporate ethics programs.

- **Active Classroom Resource Guide** An additional collection of team projects, cases, and exercises that instructors can choose from to be used in class or out.

TEACHING OPTIONS AND SOLUTIONS

McGraw-Hill Higher Education and Blackboard have teamed up. What does this mean for you?

The **Best** of **Both Worlds**

1. **Your life, simplified. Single Sign-On:** A single login and single environment provide seamless access to all course resources—all McGraw-Hill's resources are available within the Blackboard Learn™ platform.

2. **Deep integration of content and tools. Deep Integration:** One-click access to a wealth of McGraw-Hill content and tools—all from within Blackboard Learn.

3. **Seamless Gradebooks. One Gradebook:** Automatic grade synchronization with Blackboard gradebook. All grades for McGraw-Hill *Connect* assignments are recorded in the Blackboard gradebook automatically.

4. **A solution for everyone. Openness:** Unique in Higher Education, the partnership of McGraw-Hill Higher Education and Blackboard preserves the spirit of academic freedom and openness. Blackboard remains publisher independent, and McGraw-Hill remains LMS independent. The result makes our content, engines, and platform more usable and accessible, with fewer barriers to adoption and use.

5. **100% FERPA**-compliant solution protects student privacy.

6. **McGraw-Hill and Blackboard** can now offer you easy access to industry-leading technology and content, whether your campus hosts it, or we do. Be sure to ask your local McGraw-Hill representative for details.

Campus McGraw-Hill Campus™ is a new one-stop teaching and learning experience available to users of any learning management system. This institutional service allows faculty and students to enjoy single sign-on (SSO) access to all McGraw-Hill Higher Education materials, including the award-winning McGraw-Hill *Connect* platform, from directly within the institution's website. McGraw-Hill Campus™ provides faculty with instant access to all McGraw-Hill Higher Education teaching materials (e.g., eTextbooks, test banks, PowerPoint slides, animations, and learning objects, etc.) allowing them to browse, Search, and use any instructor ancillary content in our vast library at no additional cost to instructor or students. Students enjoy SSO access to a variety of free content (e.g., quizzes, flash cards, narrated presentations . . . etc.) and subscription-based products (e.g. McGraw-Hill *Connect*). With this program enabled, faculty and students will never need to create another account to access McGraw-Hill products and services. Learn more at **www.mhcampus.com.**

  McGraw-Hill reinvents the textbook-learning experience for today's students with *Connect Plus Business.* A seamless integration of an eBook and *Connect* provides all of the *Connect* features plus the following:

- An integrated eBook, allowing for anytime, anywhere online access to the textbook.
- Dynamic links between the problems or questions assigned to students and the location in the eBook where that problem or question is covered.
- Powerful search function to pinpoint and connect key concepts in a snap.

For more information about *Connect,* go to **connect.mcgraw-hill.com**, or contact your local McGraw-Hill sales representative.

 Learn Smart. Choose Smart.
CourseSmart is a new way for faculty to find and review eTextbooks. It's also a great option for students who are interested in accessing their course materials digitally and saving money.

CourseSmart offers thousands of the most commonly adopted textbooks across hundreds of courses from a wide variety of higher-education publishers. It is the only place for faculty to review and compare the full text of a textbook online, providing immediate access without the environmental impact of requesting a print exam copy.

With the CourseSmart eTextbook, students can save up to 45 percent off the cost of a printed book, reduce their impact on the environment, and access powerful web tools for learning. CourseSmart is an online eTextbook, which means users access and view their textbook online when connected to the Internet. Students can also print sections of the book for maximum portability. CourseSmart eTextbooks are available in one standard online reader with full text search, notes, and highlighting and e-mail tools for sharing notes between classmates. For more information on CourseSmart, go to **http://www.coursesmart.com.**

Mc Graw Hill create Instructors can now tailor their teaching resources to match the way they teach! With McGraw-Hill Create, **www.mcgrawhillcreate.com**, instructors can easily rearrange chapters, combine material from other content sources, and quickly upload and integrate their own content, like course syllabi or teaching notes. Find the right content in Create by searching through thousands of leading McGraw-Hill textbooks. Arrange the material to fit your teaching style. Order a Create book and receive a complimentary print review copy in 3–5 business days or a complimentary electronic review copy (echo) via e-mail within one hour. Go to **www.mcgrawhillcreate.com** today and register.

 Tegrity Campus is a service that makes class time available 24/7 by automatically capturing every lecture in a searchable format for students to review when they study and complete assignments. With a simple one-click start-and-stop process, you capture all computer screens and corresponding audio. Students can replay any part of any class with easy-to-use browser-based viewing on a PC or Mac. Educators know that the more students can see, hear, and experience class resources, the better they learn. In fact, studies prove it. With patented Tegrity "search anything" technology, students instantly recall key class moments for replay online, or on iPods and mobile devices. Instructors can help turn all their students' study time into learning moments immediately supported by their lecture. To learn more about Tegrity, watch a 2-minute Flash demo at **http://tegritycampus.mhhe.com.**

Assurance of Learning Ready

Many educational institutions today are focused on the notion of *assurance of learning,* an important element of some accreditation standards. *Business: A Changing World* is designed specifically to support instructors' assurance of learning initiatives with a simple yet powerful solution.

Each test bank question for *Business: A Changing World* maps to a specific chapter learning outcome/objective listed in the text. Instructors can use our test bank software, EZ Test and EZ Test Online, to easily query for learning outcomes/objectives that directly relate to the learning objectives for their course. Instructors can then use the reporting features of EZ Test to aggregate student results in similar fashion, making the collection and presentation of assurance of learning data simple and easy.

The McGraw-Hill Companies is a proud corporate member of AACSB International. Understanding the importance and value of AACSB accreditation, *Business: A Changing World* recognizes the curricula guidelines detailed in the AACSB standards for business accreditation by connecting selected questions in the text and the test bank to the six general knowledge and skill guidelines in the AACSB standards. The statements contained in *Business: A Changing World* are provided only as a guide for the users of this textbook. The AACSB leaves content coverage and assessment within the purview of individual schools, the mission of the school, and the faculty. While the *Business: A Changing World* teaching package makes no claim of any specific AACSB qualification or evaluation, we have within *Business: A Changing World* labeled selected questions according to the six general knowledge and skills areas.

McGraw-Hill Customer Experience Group Contact Information

At McGraw-Hill, we understand that getting the most from new technology can be challenging. That's why our services don't stop after you purchase our products. You can e-mail our Product Specialists 24 hours a day to get product training online. Or you can search our knowledge bank of Frequently Asked Questions on our support website. For Customer Support, call **800-331-5094,** e-mail **hmsupport@mcgraw hill.com,** or visit **www.mhhe.com/support.** One of our Technical Support Analysts will be able to assist you in a timely fashion.

Acknowledgments

The ninth edition of *Business: A Changing World* would not have been possible without the commitment, dedication, and patience of Jennifer Sawayda and Harper Baird. Jennifer Sawayda provided oversight for editing and developing text content, cases, boxes, and the supplements. Harper Baird assisted with editing, and Alexi Sherrill assisted in developing some of the boxes in this edition. Brett Nafziger developed the PowerPoints, Gwyneth Walters developed the Test Bank, and Jennifer Sawayda developed the Instructor's Manual. Anke Weekes, Brand Manager, provided leadership and creativity in planning and implementing all aspects of the ninth edition. Gabriela Gonzalez, Development Editor, did an outstanding job of coordinating all aspects of the development and production process. Angela Norris was the Content Project Manager. Ron Nelms managed the technical aspects of the Online Learning Center. Others important in this edition include Michael Gedatus (Marketing Manager) and Debra Kubiak (Designer). Michael Hartline developed the Personal Career Plan in Appendix C. Vickie Bajtelsmit developed Appendix D on personal financial planning. Eric Sandberg of Interactive Learning assisted in developing the interactive exercises found on the OLC. Many others have assisted us with their helpful comments, recommendations, and support throughout this and previous editions. We'd like to express our thanks to the reviewers who helped us shape the ninth edition:

NaRita Gail Anderson
University of Central Oklahoma

Brenda Anthony
Delta College

Harvey S. Bronstein
Oakland Community College

Colin Brooks
University of New Orleans

Diana Carmel
Golden West College

Mark Lee Clark
Collin College

Dr. Deshaun H. Davis
Northern Virginia Community College

Bob Farris
Mt. San Antonio College

Connie Golden
Lakeland Community College

Terri Gonzales-Kreisman
Phoenix College

Carol Gottuso
Metropolitan Community College

Maurice P. Greene
Monroe College

Selina Andrea Griswold
University of Toledo

MaryAnne Holcomb
Antelope Valley College

Sandra Kana
Mid-Michigan Community College

Regina Korossy
Pepperdine University

Chris Mcnamara
Fingers Lake Community College

Lauren Paisley
Genesee Community College

Michael Quinn
James Madison University

Gregory J. Rapp
Portland Community College

Carol Rowey
Surry Community College

Greg Simpson
Blinn College

Lisa Strusowski
Tallahassee Community College

Bruce Yuille
Cornell University-Ithaca

We extend special appreciation to the following people who reviewed previous editions:

Linda Anglin, *Mankato State University*

Brenda Anthony, *Tallahassee Community College*

Phyllis Alderdice, *Jefferson Community College*

Vondra Armstrong, *Pulaski Tech College*

John Bajkowski, *American Association of Individual Investors*

Gene Baker, *University of North Florida*

Lia Barone, *Norwalk Community College*

James Bartlett, *University of Illinois*

Ellen Benowitz, *Mercer County Community College*

Stephanie Bibb, *Chicago State University*

Barbara Boyington, *Brookdale County College of Monmouth*

Suzanne Bradford, *Angelina College*

Alka Bramhandkar, *Ithaca College*

Dennis Brode, *Sinclair Community College*

Eric Brooks, *Orange County Community College*

Nicky Buenger, *Texas A&M University*

Anthony Buono, *Bentley College*

Tricia Burns, *Boise State University*

William Chittenden, *Texas Tech University*

Michael Cicero, *Highline Community College*

M. Lou Cisneros, *Austin Community College*

Margaret Clark, *Cincinnati State Tech & Community College*

Debbie Collins, *Anne Arundel Community College—Arnold*

Karen Collins, *Lehigh University*

Katherine Conway, *Borough of Manhattan Community College*

Rex Cutshall, *Vincennes University*

Dana D'Angelo, *Drexel University*

Laurie Dahlin, *Worcester State College*

Peter Dawson, *Collin County Community College—Plano*

John DeNisco, *Buffalo State College*

Tom Diamante, *Adelphi University*

Joyce Domke, *DePaul University*

Michael Drafke, *College of DuPage*

John Eagan, *Erie Community College/City Campus SUNY*

Glenda Eckert, *Oklahoma State University*

Thomas Enerva, *Lakeland Community College*

Robert Ericksen, *Craven Community College*

Donna Everett, *Santa Rosa Junior College*

Joe Farinella, *DePaul University*

Gil Feiertag, *Columbus State Community College*

James Ferrell, *R. G. Taylor, P.C.*

Art Fischer, *Pittsburg State University*

Jackie Flom, *University of Toledo*

Toni Forcino, *Montgomery College—Germantown*

Jennifer Friestad, *Anoka—Ramsey Community College*

Chris Gilbert, *Tacoma Community College/ University of Washington*

Ross Gittell, *University of New Hampshire*

Frank Godfrey, *St. Augustine's College*

Kris Gossett, *Ivy Tech Community College of Indiana*

Bob Grau, *Cuyahoga Community College—Western Campus*

Gary Grau, *Northeast State Tech Community College*

Jack K. Gray, *Attorney-at-Law, Houston, Texas*

Catherine Green, *University of Memphis*

Claudia Green, *Pace University*

Phil Greenwood, *University of St. Thomas*

David Gribbin, *East Georgia College*

Peggy Hager, *Winthrop University*

Michael Hartline, *Florida State University*

Neil Herndon, *University of Missouri*

James Hoffman, *Borough of Manhattan Community College*

Joseph Hrebenak, *Community College of Allegheny County—Allegheny Campus*

Stephen Huntley, *Florida Community College*

Rebecca Hurtz, *State Farm Insurance Co.*

Roger Hutt, *Arizona State University—West*

Verne Ingram, *Red Rocks Community College*

Scott Inks, *Ball State University*

Steven Jennings, *Highland Community College*

Carol Jones, *Cuyahoga Community College—Eastern Campus*

Gilbert "Joe" Joseph, *University of Tampa*

Norm Karl, *Johnson County Community College*

Janice Karlan, *LaGuardia Community College*

Eileen Kearney, *Montgomery County Community College*

Craig Kelley, *California State University—Sacramento*

Susan Kendall, *Arapahoe Community College*

Ina Midkiff Kennedy, *Austin Community College*

Arbrie King, *Baton Rouge Community College*

John Knappenberger, *Mesa State College*

Gail Knell, *Cape Cod Community College*

Anthony Koh, *University of Toledo*

Velvet Landingham, *Kent State University—Geauga*

Daniel LeClair, *AACSB*

Frank Lembo, *North Virginia Community College*

Richard Lewis, *East Texas Baptist College*

Corinn Linton, *Valencia Community College*

Corrine Livesay, *Mississippi College*

Thomas Lloyd, *Westmoreland Community College*

Terry Loe, *Kennerow University*

Kent Lutz, *University of Cincinnati*

Scott Lyman, *Winthrop University*

Dorinda Lynn, *Pensacola Junior College*

Isabelle Maignan, *ING*

Larry Martin, *Community College of Southern Nevada—West Charles*

Therese Maskulka, *Youngstown State University*

Kristina Mazurak, *Albertson College of Idaho*

Debbie Thorne McAlister, *Texas State University—San Marcos*

John McDonough, *Menlo College*

Tom McInish, *University of Memphis*

Noel McDeon, *Florida Community College*

Mary Meredith, *University of Louisiana at Lafayette*

Michelle Meyer, *Joliet Junior College*

George Milne, *University of Massachusetts—Amherst*

Daniel Montez, *South Texas College*

Glynna Morse, *Augusta College*

Stephanie Narvell, *Wilmington College—New Castle*

Fred Nerone, *International College of Naples*

Laura Nicholson, *Northern Oklahoma College*

Stef Nicovich, *University of New Hampshire*

Michael Nugent, *SUNY—Stony Brook University New York*

Mark Nygren, *Brigham Young University—Idaho*

Wes Payne, *Southwest Tennessee Community College*

Dyan Pease, *Sacramento City College*

Constantine G. Petrides, *Borough of Manhattan Community College*

John Pharr, *Cedar Valley College*

Shirley Polejewski, *University of St. Thomas*

Daniel Powroznik, *Chesapeake College*

Krista Price, *Heald College*

Larry Prober, *Rider University*

Stephen Pruitt, *University of Missouri—Kansas City*

Kathy Pullins, *Columbus State Community College*

Charles Quinn, *Austin Community College*

Victoria Rabb, *College of the Desert*

Tom Reading, *Ivy Tech State College*

Delores Reha, *Fullerton College*

Susan Roach, *Georgia Southern University*

Dave Robinson, *University of California—Berkely*

Marsha Rule, *Florida Public Utilities Commission*

Carol A. Rustad, *Sylvan Learning*

Martin St. John, *Westmoreland Community College*

Don Sandlin, *East Los Angeles College*

Nick Sarantakes, *Austin Community College*

Andy Saucedo, *Dona Ana Community College—Las Cruces*

Elise "Pookie" Sautter, *New Mexico State University*

Dana Schubert, *Colorado Springs Zoo*

Marianne Sebok, *Community College of Southern Nevada—West Charles*

Jeffery L. Seglin, *Seglin Associates*

Daniel Sherrell, *University of Memphis*

Morgan Shepherd, *University of Colorado Elaine Simmons, Guilford Technical Community College*

Nicholas Siropolis, *Cuyahoga Community College*

Robyn Smith, *Pouder Valley Hospital*

Kurt Stanberry, *University of Houston Downtown*

Cheryl Stansfield, *North Hennepin Community College*

Ron Stolle, *Kent State University—Kent*

Jeff Strom, *Virginia Western Community College*

Scott Taylor, *Moberly Area Community College*

Wayne Taylor, *Trinity Valley Community College*

Ray Tewell, *American River College*

Evelyn Thrasher, *University of Mass—Dartmouth*

Steve Tilley, *Gainesville College*

Jay Todes, *Northlake College*

Amy Thomas, *Roger Williams University*

Kristin Trask, *Butler Community College*

Ted Valvoda, *Lakeland Community College*

Sue Vondram, *Loyola University*

Elizabeth Wark, *Springfield College*

Emma Watson, *Arizona State University—West*

Jerry E. Wheat, *Indiana University Southeast*

Frederik Williams, *North Texas State University*

Richard Williams, *Santa Clara University*

Pat Wright, *Texas A&M University*

Timothy Wright, *Lakeland Community College*

Lawrence Yax, *Pensacola Junior College—Warrington*

Brief Contents

Contents

Chapter 7

Organization, Teamwork, and Communication 208

Chapter 8

Managing Service and Manufacturing Operations 238

part 1

Business in a Changing World

Chapter Outline

The Dynamics of Business and Economics

Learning Objectives

After reading this chapter, you will be able to:

LO 1-1   Define basic concepts such as business, product, and profit.

LO 1-2   Identify the main participants and activities of business and explain why studying business is important.

LO 1-3   Define economics and compare the four types of economic systems.

LO 1-4   Describe the role of supply, demand, and competition in a free-enterprise system.

LO 1-5   Specify why and how the health of the economy is measured.

LO 1-6   Trace the evolution of the American economy and discuss the role of the entrepreneur in the economy.

LO 1-7   Evaluate a small-business owner's situation and propose a course of action.

Apple Stores: The Future of Retail?

In 2011, Apple surpassed Google as the most valuable global brand at more than $153 billion. Much of Apple's success can be attributed to its innovative products such as the iPad. However, Apple has also made a profound mark in the world of retailing. Its stores, which were first opened in 2001, are the fastest growing retail stores in history. An obvious draw is store design—modern and spacious, creating a relaxed, low-pressure atmosphere. The stores are like showrooms that allow customers to test products and take educational classes.

To truly understand Apple's retail success, it is important to look beneath the surface. According to *Forbes* contributor Steve Denning, two keys to Apple's success are *delight the customer* and *avoid selling.* Apple focuses extensively on meeting customer needs and wants. This focus significantly alters employee behavior and complements the *avoid selling* mantra. Rather than pushing products on consumers, Apple store employees are asked to listen and assist. Employees have been trained to speak with customers within two minutes of them entering the store. Apple executives are also constantly looking for new innovative ways to enhance customer service. The company recently began installing iPad stations equipped with a customer service app designed to answer customer questions. If the customer requires additional assistance, he or she can press a help button on the app.

Apple has been so successful in the retail arena that other stores are looking to adopt its retail strategies. Microsoft and Sony have opened some of their own stores,

continued

and other industries are using Apple products to enhance their businesses. Apple's blend of exceptional products, appealing stores, and knowledgeable and dedicated employees creates a top-notch customer experience and is having enormous repercussions for the retail industry as a whole.[1]

Introduction

We begin our study of business in this chapter by examining the fundamentals of business and economics. First, we introduce the nature of business, including its goals, activities, and participants. Next, we describe the basics of economics and apply them to the United States economy. Finally, we establish a framework for studying business in this text.

LO 1-1

business
individuals or organizations who try to earn a profit by providing products that satisfy people's needs

product
a good or service with tangible and intangible characteristics that provide satisfaction and benefits

The Nature of Business

A **business** tries to earn a profit by providing products that satisfy people's needs. The outcome of its efforts are **products** that have both tangible and intangible characteristics that provide satisfaction and benefits. When you purchase a product, you are buying the benefits and satisfaction you think the product will provide. A Subway sandwich, for example, may be purchased to satisfy hunger, while a Chevrolet Camaro may be purchased to satisfy the need for transportation and the desire to present a certain image.

Most people associate the word *product* with tangible goods—an automobile, computer, phone, coat, or some other tangible item. However, a product can also be a service, which occurs when people or machines provide or process something of value to customers. Dry cleaning, a checkup by a doctor, a performance by a basketball player—these are examples of services. Some services, such as Flickr, an online photo management and sharing application, do not charge a fee for use but obtain revenue from ads on their sites. A product can also be an idea. Accountants and attorneys, for example, generate ideas for solving problems.

The Goal of Business

profit
the difference between what it costs to make and sell a product and what a customer pays for it

The primary goal of all businesses is to earn a **profit,** the difference between what it costs to make and sell a product and what a customer pays for it. If a company spends $8.00 to manufacture, finance, promote, and distribute a product that it sells for $10.00, the business earns a profit of $2.00 on each product sold. Businesses have the right to keep and use their profits as they choose—within legal limits—because profit is the reward for the risks they take in providing products. Earning profits contributes to society by providing employment, which in turn provides money that is reinvested in the economy. In addition, profits must be earned in a responsible manner. Not all organizations are businesses, however. **Nonprofit organizations,** such as the Red Cross, Special Olympics, and other charities and social causes, do not have the fundamental purpose of earning profits, although they may provide goods or services and engage in fund raising.

nonprofit organizations
organizations that may provide goods or services but do not have the fundamental purpose of earning profits

To earn a profit, a person or organization needs management skills to plan, organize, and control the activities of the business and to find and develop employees so that it can make products consumers will buy. A business also needs marketing expertise to learn what products consumers need and want and to develop, manufacture, price, promote, and distribute those products. Additionally, a business needs financial resources and skills to fund, maintain, and expand its operations. Other challenges for businesspeople include abiding by laws and government regulations; acting in an ethical and socially responsible manner; and adapting to economic, technological, political, and social changes. Even nonprofit organizations engage in management, marketing, and finance activities to help reach their goals.

To achieve and maintain profitability, businesses have found that they must produce quality products, operate efficiently, and be socially responsible and ethical in dealing with customers, employees, investors, government regulators, and the community. Because these groups have a stake in the success and outcomes of a business, they are sometimes called **stakeholders.** Many businesses, for example, are concerned about how the production and distribution of their products affect the environment. Concerns about landfills becoming high-tech graveyards plague many electronics firms. Best Buy offers recycling of electronics at all of its stores. The stores take cell phones, wide-screen TVs, and most other electronic products in their green program, regardless of where they were purchased. Other businesses are concerned about the quality of life in the communities in which they operate. For example, Charlotte Street Computers in Asheville, North Carolina, has created a refurbishing center for old computers. The center refurbishes the computers and then donates them to those in need.[2] Others are concerned with promoting business careers among African American, Hispanic, and Native American students. The Diversity Pipeline Alliance is a network of national organizations that work toward preparing students and professionals of color for leadership and management in the 21st-century workforce. The Pipeline assists individuals in getting into the appropriate college, pursuing a career in business, or earning an advanced degree in business.[3] Other companies, such as Home Depot, have a long history of supporting natural disaster victims, relief efforts, and recovery.

Seventh Generation is a leading brand of environmentally friendly household products. Its Natural 4X Laundry Detergent is packed in a bottle made from 100 percent recycled fiber.

stakeholders
groups that have a stake in the success and outcomes of a business

The People and Activities of Business

Figure 1.1 shows the people and activities involved in business. At the center of the figure are owners, employees, and customers; the outer circle includes the primary business activities—management, marketing, and finance. Owners have to put up resources—money or credit—to start a business. Employees are responsible for the work that goes on within a business. Owners can manage the business themselves or hire employees to accomplish this task. The president, CEO, and chairman of the board of Procter & Gamble, Robert A. McDonald, does not own P&G, but is

LO 1-2

of interesting and challenging career opportunities throughout the world, such as marketing, human resources management, information technology, finance, production and operations, wholesaling and retailing, and many more.

Studying business can also help you better understand the many business activities that are necessary to provide satisfying goods and services—and that these activities carry a price tag. For example, if you buy a new compact disk, about half of the price goes toward activities related to distribution and the retailer's expenses and profit margins. The production (pressing) of the CD represents about $1, or a small percentage of its price. Most businesses charge a reasonable price for their products to ensure that they cover their production costs, pay their employees, provide their owners with a return on their investment, and perhaps give something back to their local communities. Bill Daniels founded Cablevision, building his first cable TV system in Casper, Wyoming, in 1953, and is now considered "the father of cable television." Prior to Daniels' passing in 2000, he had established a foundation that currently has funding of $1.1 billion and supports a diversity of causes from education to business ethics. During his career, Daniels created the Young American Bank, where children could create bank accounts and learn about financial responsibility, and this remains the world's only charter bank for young people. He created the Daniels College of Business through a donation of $20 million to the University of Denver. During his life, he affected many individuals and organizations, and his business success has allowed his legacy to be one of giving and impacting communities throughout the United States.[9] Thus, learning about business can help you become a well-informed consumer and member of society.

Business activities help generate the profits that are essential not only to individual businesses and local economies but also to the health of the global economy. Without profits, businesses find it difficult, if not impossible, to buy more raw materials, hire more employees, attract more capital, and create additional products that in turn make more profits and fuel the world economy. Understanding how our free-enterprise economic system allocates resources and provides incentives for industry and the workplace is important to everyone.

The Economic Foundations of Business

LO 1-3

To continue our introduction to business, it is useful to explore the economic environment in which business is conducted. In this section, we examine economic systems, the free-enterprise system, the concepts of supply and demand, and the role of competition. These concepts play important roles in determining how businesses operate in a particular society.

economics
the study of how resources are distributed for the production of goods and services within a social system

natural resources
land, forests, minerals, water, and other things that are not made by people

Economics is the study of how resources are distributed for the production of goods and services within a social system. You are already familiar with the types of resources available. Land, forests, minerals, water, and other things that are not made by people are **natural resources. Human resources,** or labor, refers to the physical and mental abilities that people use to produce goods and services. **Financial resources,** or capital, are the funds used to acquire the natural and human resources needed to provide products. Because natural, human, and financial resources are used to produce goods and services, they are sometimes called *factors of production*. The firm can also have intangible resources such as a good reputation for quality products or being socially responsible. The goal is to turn the factors of production and intangible resources into a competitive advantage.

Economic Systems

An **economic system** describes how a particular society distributes its resources to produce goods and services. A central issue of economics is how to fulfill an unlimited demand for goods and services in a world with a limited supply of resources. Different economic systems attempt to resolve this central issue in numerous ways, as we shall see.

Although economic systems handle the distribution of resources in different ways, all economic systems must address three important issues:

1. What goods and services, and how much of each, will satisfy consumers' needs?
2. How will goods and services be produced, who will produce them, and with what resources will they be produced?
3. How are the goods and services to be distributed to consumers?

Communism, socialism, and capitalism, the basic economic systems found in the world today (Table 1.1), have fundamental differences in the way they address these issues. The factors of production in command economies are controlled by government planning. In many cases, the government owns or controls the production of goods and services. Communism and socialism are, therefore, considered command economies.

Communism.   Karl Marx (1818–1883) first described **communism** as a society in which the people, without regard to class, own all the nation's resources. In his ideal political-economic system, everyone contributes according to ability and receives benefits according to need. In a communist economy, the people (through the government) own and operate all businesses and factors of production. Central government planning determines what goods and services satisfy citizens' needs, how the goods and services are produced, and how they are distributed. However, no true communist economy exists today that satisfies Marx's ideal.

On paper, communism appears to be efficient and equitable, producing less of a gap between rich and poor. In practice, however, communist economies have been marked by low standards of living, critical shortages of consumer goods, high prices, corruption, and little freedom. Russia, Poland, Hungary, and other eastern European nations have turned away from communism and toward economic systems governed by supply and demand rather than by central planning. However, their experiments with alternative economic systems have been fraught with difficulty and hardship. Cuba continues to apply communist principles to its economy, but Cuba is also experiencing economic and political change. Countries such as Venezuela are trying to incorporate communist economic principles. Hugo Chavez, Venezuela's president, has developed a partnership with Cuba.[10] However, communism is declining and its future as an economic system is uncertain. When Fidel Castro stepped down as president of Cuba, his younger brother Raul formally assumed the role and eliminated many of the bans, including allowing the purchase of electric appliances, microwaves, computers, and cell phones. The communist country appears more open to free enterprise now.[11] There is a plan to shift hundreds of thousands of Cuban workers from the public sector to the private sector. Similarly, China has become the first communist country to make strong economic gains by adopting capitalist approaches to business. The Chinese state is the largest shareholder among China's

human resources
the physical and mental abilities that people use to produce goods and services; also called labor

financial resources
the funds used to acquire the natural and human resources needed to provide products; also called capital

economic system
a description of how a particular society distributes its resources to produce goods and services

communism
first described by Karl Marx as a society in which the people, without regard to class, own all the nation's resources

Need help understanding the basic Economic Systems?

http://bit.ly/FerrellQR1-2

Can't Scan? Try ScanLife at your app store.

TABLE 1.1

Comparison of Communism, Socialism, and Capitalism

	Communism	Socialism	Capitalism
Business ownership	Most businesses are owned and operated by the government.	The government owns and operates major industries; individuals own small businesses.	Individuals own and operate all businesses.
Competition	None. The government owns and operates everything.	Restricted in major industries; encouraged in small business.	Encouraged by market forces and government regulations.
Profits	Excess income goes to the government.	Profits earned by small businesses may be reinvested in the business; profits from government-owned industries go to the government.	Individuals are free to keep profits and use them as they wish.
Product availability and price	Consumers have a limited choice of goods and services; prices are usually high.	Consumers have some choice of goods and services; prices are determined by supply and demand.	Consumers have a wide choice of goods and services; prices are determined by supply and demand.
Employment options	Little choice in choosing a career; most people work for government-owned industries or farms.	Some choice of careers; many people work in government jobs.	Unlimited choice of careers.

Source: "Gross Domestic Product or Expenditure, 1930–2002," *InfoPlease* (n.d.), www.infoplease.com/ipa/A0104575.html (accessed February 16, 2004).

150 largest companies and influences thousands of other businesses.[12] Economic prosperity has advanced in China with the government claiming to ensure market openness, equality, and fairness.[13]

socialism
an economic system in which the government owns and operates basic industries but individuals own most businesses

Socialism.   **Socialism** is an economic system in which the government owns and operates basic industries—postal service, telephone, utilities, transportation, health care, banking, and some manufacturing—but individuals own most businesses. For example, in France the postal service industry La Posta is fully owned by the French government and makes a profit. Central planning determines what basic goods and services are produced, how they are produced, and how they are distributed. Individuals and small businesses provide other goods and services based on consumer demand and the availability of resources. Citizens are dependent on the government for many goods and services.

Most socialist nations, such as Sweden, India, and Israel, are democratic and recognize basic individual freedoms. Citizens can vote for political offices, but central government planners usually make decisions about what is best for the nation. People are free to go into the occupation of their choice, but they often work in government-operated organizations. Socialists believe their system permits a higher standard of living than other economic systems, but the difference often applies to the nation as a whole rather than to its individual citizens. Socialist economies profess egalitarianism—equal distribution of income and social services. They believe their economics are more stable than those of other nations. Although this may be true, taxes and unemployment are generally higher in socialist countries. Perhaps as a result, many socialist countries have also experienced economic difficulties.

Capitalism.   **Capitalism,** or **free enterprise,** is an economic system in which individuals own and operate the majority of businesses that provide goods and services. Competition, supply, and demand determine which goods and services are produced, how they are produced, and how they are distributed. The United States, Canada, Japan, and Australia are examples of economic systems based on capitalism.

There are two forms of capitalism: pure capitalism and modified capitalism. In pure capitalism, also called a **free-market system,** all economic decisions are made without government intervention. This economic system was first described by Adam Smith in *The Wealth of Nations* (1776). Smith, often called the father of capitalism, believed that the "invisible hand of competition" best regulates the economy. He argued that competition should determine what goods and services people need. Smith's system is also called *laissez-faire* ("let it be") *capitalism* because the government does not interfere in business.

Modified capitalism differs from pure capitalism in that the government intervenes and regulates business to some extent. One of the ways in which the United States and Canadian governments regulate business is through laws. Laws such as the Federal Trade Commission Act, which created the Federal Trade Commission to enforce antitrust laws, illustrate the importance of the government's role in the economy. In the most recent recession, the government provided loans and took ownership positions in banks such as Citigroup, AIG (an insurance company), and General Motors. These actions were thought necessary to keep these firms from going out of business and creating a financial disaster for the economy.

Mixed Economies.   No country practices a pure form of communism, socialism, or capitalism, although most tend to favor one system over the others. Most nations operate as **mixed economies,** which have elements from more than one economic system. In socialist Sweden, most businesses are owned and operated by private individuals. In capitalist United States, an independent federal agency operates the postal service and another independent agency operates the Tennessee Valley Authority, an electric utility. In Great Britain and Mexico, the governments are attempting to sell many state-run businesses to private individuals and companies. In Germany, the Deutsche Post is privatized and trades on the stock market. In once-communist Russia, Hungary, Poland, and other eastern European nations, capitalist ideas have been implemented, including private ownership of businesses.

Countries such as China and Russia have used state capitalism to advance the economy. State capitalism tries to integrate the powers of the state with the advantages of capitalism. It is led by the government but uses capitalistic tools such as listing state-owned companies on the stock market and embracing globalization.[14] State capitalism includes some of the world's largest companies such as Russia's Gazprom, which is the largest natural gas company. China's ability to make huge investments to the point of creating entirely new industries puts many private industries at a disadavantage.[15]

capitalism (free enterprise) an economic system in which individuals own and operate the majority of bucinoccoc that provido goods and services

free-market system pure capitalism, in which all economic decisions are made without government intervention

mixed economies economies made up of elements from more than one economic system

Entrepreneurship in Action
Warby Parker Brings Prescription Eyewear Online

David Gilboa, Neil Blumenthal, Andrew Hunt, and Jeffrey Raider
Business: Warby Parker
Founded: February 2010
Success: Warby Parker bested its projected annual sales goal in just 21 days. The company sold more than 20,000 pairs of eyeglasses in its first year.

Warby Parker allows customers to order prescription eyeglasses online. This is a unique concept because glasses are a higher-risk item that consumers prefer to try on before purchasing. Warby Parker sells eyeglass frames and prescription lenses for under $100—about half the price of many other companies' eyeware—by cutting out licensing and retail markups. For those nervous about ordering such a personal item online, the company offers two features to reduce risk. Using facial recognition software, customers can upload pictures of themselves and virtually try on various frames. Warby Parker will also mail out up to five sample frames per customer, allowing individuals to try different styles in person.

Warby Parker's four founders created the company while in college, thinking they would ease into business by testing it on their family and friends. Much to their surprise, the site took off. They met their first-year goal in 21 days and were able to hire additional employees. In addition to its successful business concept, Warby Parker engages in philanthropy by donating a pair of glasses to someone in need for each pair sold.[26]

The free-enterprise system provides the conditions necessary for entrepreneurs to succeed. In the past, entrepreneurs were often inventors who brought all the factors of production together to produce a new product. Thomas Edison, whose inventions include the record player and lightbulb, was an early American entrepreneur. Henry Ford was one of the first persons to develop mass assembly methods in the automobile industry. Other entrepreneurs, so-called captains of industry, invested in the country's growth. John D. Rockefeller built Standard Oil out of the fledgling oil industry, and Andrew Carnegie invested in railroads and founded the United States Steel Corporation. Andrew Mellon built the Aluminum Company of America and Gulf Oil. JP Morgan started financial institutions to fund the business activities of other entrepreneurs. Although these entrepreneurs were born in another century, their legacy to the American economy lives on in the companies they started, many of which still operate today. Milton Hershey began producing chocolate in 1894 in Lancaster, Pennsylvania. In 1900, the

TABLE 1.4		
Popular Internet Activities	**Activity**	**Internet Users Performing Each Activity (%)**
	Send or read e-mail	92
	Use a search engine	92
	Get news online	76
	Buy a product online	71
	Visit social network sites	65

Source: The Pew Research Center's Internet & American Life Project tracking surveys, 2002–2011, http://pewinternet.org.

company was mass producing chocolate in many forms, lowering the cost of chocolate and making it more affordable to the masses, where it had once been a high-priced, luxury good. Early advertising touted chocolate as "a palatable confection and most nourishing food." Today, the Hershey Company employs more than 13,000 employees and sells almost $5 billion in chocolates and candies annually throughout the world.[27]

Entrepreneurs are constantly changing American business practices with new technology and innovative management techniques. Bill Gates, for example, built Microsoft, a software company whose products include Word and Windows, into a multibillion-dollar enterprise. Frederick Smith had an idea to deliver packages overnight, and now his FedEx Company plays an important role in getting documents and packages delivered all over the

ABC's *Shark Tank* allows potential entrepreneurs to receive funding for their businesses—but only if they receive approval from the panel of "sharks," self-made millionaires who choose whether to fund the projects.

world for businesses and individuals. Steve Jobs co-founded Apple and turned the company into a successful consumer electronics firm that revolutionized many different industries, with products such as the iPod, iPhone, Mac computers, and iPad. The company went from near bankruptcy in the 1990s to become one of the most valuable brands in the entire world. Entrepreneurs have been associated with such uniquely American concepts as Dell Computers, Ben & Jerry's, Levi's, McDonald's, Dr Pepper, Apple, Google, Facebook, and Walmart. Walmart, founded by entrepreneur Sam Walton, was the first retailer to reach $100 billion in sales in one year and now routinely passes that mark, with more than $419 billion in 2011.[28] Sam Walton's heirs own about 40 percent of the company.[29] We will examine the importance of entrepreneurship further in Chapter 5.

The Role of Government in the American Economy

The American economic system is best described as modified capitalism because the government regulates business to preserve competition and protect consumers and employees. Federal, state, and local governments intervene in the economy with laws and regulations designed to promote competition and to protect consumers, employees, and the environment. Many of these laws are discussed in Appendix B.

Additionally, government agencies such as the U.S. Department of Commerce measure the health of the economy (GDP, productivity, etc.) and, when necessary, take steps to minimize the disruptive effects of economic fluctuations and reduce unemployment. When the economy is contracting and unemployment is rising, the federal government through the Federal Reserve Board (see Chapter 15) tries to spur growth so that consumers will spend more money and businesses will hire more employees. To accomplish this, it may reduce interest rates or increase its own spending for goods and services. When the economy expands so fast that inflation results, the government may intervene to reduce inflation by slowing down economic growth. This can be accomplished by raising interest rates to discourage spending by businesses and consumers. Techniques used to control the economy are discussed in Chapter 15.

The Role of Ethics and Social Responsibility in Business

In the past few years, you may have read about a number of scandals at a number of well-known corporations, including Enron, Countrywide Financial, BP, and even leading banks such as Bank of America and Citigroup. In many cases, misconduct by individuals within these firms had an adverse effect on current and retired employees, investors, and others associated with these firms. In some cases, individuals went to jail for their actions. Top executives like Enron's Jeffrey Skilling and Tyco's Dennis Kozlowski received long prison sentences for their roles in corporate misconduct. These scandals undermined public confidence in corporate America and sparked a new debate about ethics in business. Business ethics generally refers to the standards and principles used by society to define appropriate and inappropriate conduct in the workplace. In many cases, these standards have been codified as laws prohibiting actions deemed unacceptable.

Society is increasingly demanding that businesspeople behave ethically and socially responsibly toward not only their customers but also their employees, investors, government regulators, communities, and the natural environment. No area is more debated as online privacy. Software, music, and film executives want to defend their intellectual property. On the other hand, companies such as Google are concerned that strict laws would stifle innovation and enable censorship.[30] When actions are heavily criticized, a balance is usually required to support and protect various stakeholders.

While one view is that ethics and social responsibility are a good supplement to business activities, there is an alternative viewpoint. Research has shown that ethical behavior can not only enhance a company's reputation but can also drive profits.[31] The ethical and socially responsible conduct of companies such as Whole Foods, Starbucks, and the hotel chain Marriott provides evidence that good ethics is good business. There is growing recognition that the long-term value of conducting business in an ethical and socially responsible manner that considers the interests of all stakeholders creates superior financial performance.[32]

To promote socially responsible and ethical behavior while achieving organizational goals, businesses can monitor changes and trends in society's values. Businesses should determine what society wants and attempt to predict the long-term effects of their decisions. While it requires an effort to address the interests of all stakeholders, businesses can prioritize and attempt to balance conflicting demands. The goal is to develop a solid reputation of trust and avoid misconduct to develop effective workplace ethics.

Can You Learn Business in a Classroom?

Obviously, the answer is yes, or there would be no purpose for this textbook! To be successful in business, you need knowledge, skills, experience, and good judgment. The topics covered in this chapter and throughout this book provide some of the knowledge you need to understand the world of business. The opening vignette at the beginning of each chapter, boxes, examples within each chapter, and the case at the end of each chapter describe experiences to help you develop good business judgment. The "Build Your Skills" exercise at the end of each chapter and the "Solve the Dilemma" box will help you develop skills that may be useful in your future career. However, good judgment is based on knowledge and experience plus personal insight and understanding. Therefore, you need more courses in business, along with some practical experience in the business world, to help you develop the special insight necessary to put your personal stamp on knowledge as you apply it. The challenge in business is in the area of judgment, and judgment does not develop from memorizing an introductory business text-book. If you are observant in your daily experiences as an employee, as a student, and as a consumer, you will improve your ability to make good business judgments.

Figure 1.5 is an overview of how the chapters in this book are linked together and how the chapters relate to the participants, the activities, and the environmental factors found in the business world. The topics presented in the chapters that follow are those that will give you the best opportunity to begin the process of understanding the world of business.

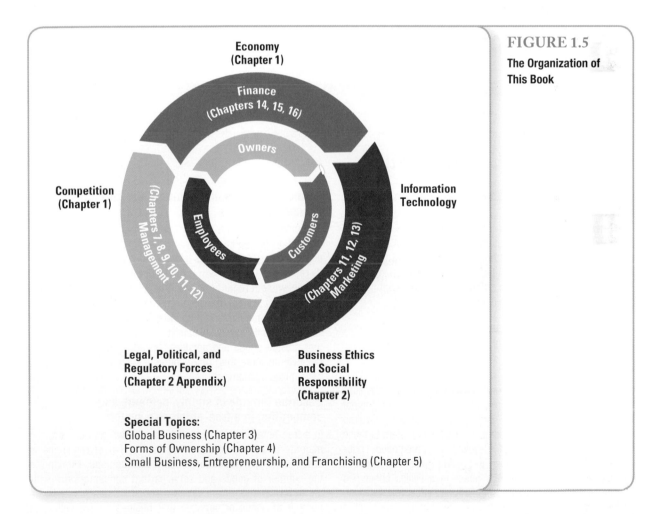

FIGURE 1.5

The Organization of This Book

So You Want a Job in the Business World

When most people think of a career in business, they see themselves entering the door to large companies and multinationals that they read about in the news and that are discussed in class. In a national survey, students indicated they would like to work for Google, Walt Disney, Apple, and Ernst & Young. In fact, most jobs are not with large corporations, but are in small companies, nonprofit organizations, government, and even self-employed individuals. There are 20 million individuals that the Small Business Administration says own their businesses and have no employees. In addition, there are nearly 5 million small businesses which employ 10 or fewer workers. With more than 75 percent of the economy based on services, there are jobs available in industries, such as health care, finance, education, hospitality, entertainment and transportation. The world is changing quickly and large corporations replace the equivalent of their entire workforce every four years.

The fast pace of technology today means that you have to be prepared to take advantage of emerging job opportunities and markets. You must also become adaptive and recognize that business is becoming more global, with job opportunities around the world. If you want to obtain such a job, you shouldn't miss a chance to spend some time overseas. To get you started on the path to thinking about job opportunities, consider all of the changes in business today that might affect your possible long-term track and that could bring you lots of success. You may want to stay completely out of large organizations and corporations and put yourself in a position for an entrepreneurial role as a self-employed contractor or small-business owner. However, there are many who feel that experience in larger businesses is helpful to your success later as an entrepreneur.

You're on the road to learning the key knowledge, skills, and trends that you can use to be a star in business. Business's impact on our society, especially in the area of sustainability and improvement of the environment, is a growing challenge and opportunity. Green businesses and green jobs in the business world are provided to give you a glimpse at the possibilities. Along the way, we will introduce you to some specific careers and offer advice on developing your own job opportunities. Research indicates that you won't be that happy with your job unless you enjoy your work and feel that it has a purpose. Since you spend most of your waking hours every day at work, you need to seriously think about what is important to you in a job.[33]

Review Your Understanding

Define basic concepts such as business, product, and profit.

A business is an organization or individual that seeks a profit by providing products that satisfy people's needs. A product is a good, service, or idea that has both tangible and intangible characteristics that provide satisfaction and benefits. Profit, the basic goal of business, is the difference between what it costs to make and sell a product and what a customer pays for it.

Identify the main participants and activities of business and explain why studying business is important.

The three main participants in business are owners, employees, and customers, but others—government regulators, suppliers, social groups, etc.—are also important. Management involves planning, organizing, and controlling the tasks required to carry out the work of the company. Marketing refers to those activities—research, product development, promotion, pricing, and distribution—designed to provide goods and services that satisfy customers. Finance refers to activities concerned with funding a business and using its funds effectively. Studying business can help you prepare for a career and become a better consumer.

Define economics and compare the four types of economic systems.

Economics is the study of how resources are distributed for the production of goods and services within a social system; an economic system describes how a particular society distributes its resources. Communism is an economic system in which the people, without regard to class, own all the nation's resources. In a socialist system, the government owns and operates basic industries, but individuals own most businesses. Under capitalism, individuals own and operate the majority of businesses that provide goods and services. Mixed economies have elements from more than one economic system; most countries have mixed economies.

Describe the role of supply, demand, and competition in a free-enterprise system.

In a free-enterprise system, individuals own and operate the majority of businesses, and the distribution of resources is determined by competition, supply, and demand. Demand is the number of goods and services that consumers are willing to buy at different prices at a specific time. Supply is the number of goods or services that businesses are willing to sell at different prices at a specific time. The price at which the supply of a product equals demand at a specific point in time is the equilibrium price. Competition is the rivalry among businesses to convince consumers to buy goods or services. Four types of competitive environments are pure competition, monopolistic competition, oligopoly, and monopoly. These economic concepts determine how businesses may operate in a particular society and, often, how much they can charge for their products.

Specify why and how the health of the economy is measured.

A country measures the state of its economy to determine whether it is expanding or contracting and whether the country needs to take steps to minimize fluctuations. One commonly used measure is gross domestic product (GDP), the sum of all goods and services produced in a country during a year. A budget deficit occurs when a nation spends more than it takes in from taxes.

Trace the evolution of the American economy and discuss the role of the entrepreneur in the economy.

The American economy has evolved through several stages: the early economy, the Industrial Revolution, the manufacturing economy, the marketing economy, and the service and Internet-based economy of today. Entrepreneurs play an important role because they risk their time, wealth, and efforts to develop new goods, services, and ideas that fuel the growth of the American economy.

Evaluate a small-business owner's situation and propose a course of action.

"Solve the Dilemma" on page 29 presents a problem for the owner of the firm. Should you, as the owner, raise prices, expand operations, or form a venture with a larger company to deal with demand? You should be able to apply your newfound understanding of the relationship between supply and demand to assess the situation and reach a decision about how to proceed.

Revisit the World of Business

Revisit the World of Business Questions

1. Why is Apple having such a profound impact on the retail store experience?

2. How is Apple integrating its products into the retail store experience?

3. Describe Apple's approach to customer service.

Learn the Terms

budget deficit 17
business 4
capitalism, or free enterprise 11
communism 9
competition 14
demand 12
depression 16
economic contraction 16
economic expansion 15
economic system 9
economics 8

entrepreneur 21
equilibrium price 13
financial resources 9
free-market system 11
gross domestic product (GDP) 17
human resources 9
inflation 15
mixed economies 11
monopolistic competition 14
monopoly 15
natural resources 8

nonprofit organizations 4
oligopoly 14
product 4
profit 4
pure competition 14
recession 16
socialism 10
stakeholders 5
supply 13
unemployment 16

Check Your Progress

1. What is the fundamental goal of business? Do all organizations share this goal?

2. Name the forms a product may take and give some examples of each.

3. Who are the main participants of business? What are the main activities? What other factors have an impact on the conduct of business in the United States?

4. What are four types of economic systems? Can you provide an example of a country using each type?

5. Explain the terms *supply, demand, equilibrium price,* and *competition.* How do these forces interact in the American economy?

6. List the four types of competitive environments and provide an example of a product of each environment.

7. List and define the various measures governments may use to gauge the state of their economies. If unemployment is high, will the growth of GDP be great or small?

8. Why are fluctuations in the economy harmful?

9. How did the Industrial Revolution influence the growth of the American economy? Why do we apply the term *service economy* to the United States today?

10. Explain the federal government's role in the American economy.

Get Involved

1. Discuss the economic changes occurring in Russia and eastern European countries, which once operated as communist economic systems. Why are these changes occurring? What do you think the result will be?

2. Why is it important for the government to measure the economy? What kinds of actions might it take to control the economy's growth?

3. Is the American economy currently expanding or contracting? Defend your answer with the latest statistics on GDP, inflation, unemployment, and so on. How is the federal government responding?

Build Your Skills

THE FORCES OF SUPPLY AND DEMAND

Background

WagWumps are a new children's toy with the potential to be a highly successful product. WagWumps are cute and furry, and their eyes glow in the dark. Each family set consists of a mother, a father, and two children. Wee-Toys' manufacturing costs are about $6 per set, with $3 representing marketing and distribution costs. The wholesale price of a WagWump family for a retailer is $15.75, and the toy carries a suggested retail price of $26.99.

Task

Assume you are a decision maker at a retailer, such as Target or Walmart, that must determine the price the stores in your district

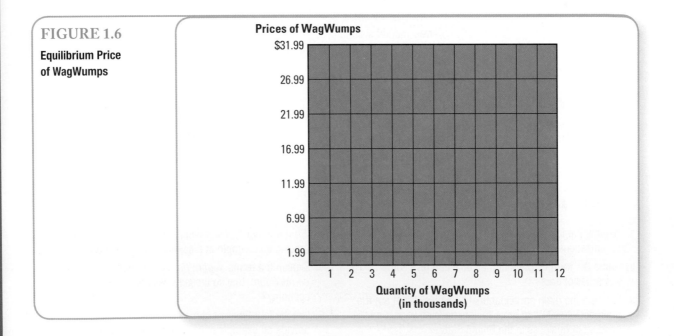

FIGURE 1.6

Equilibrium Price of WagWumps

Prices of WagWumps

(y-axis: $31.99, 26.99, 21.99, 16.99, 11.99, 6.99, 1.99)

Quantity of WagWumps (in thousands) (x-axis: 1 2 3 4 5 6 7 8 9 10 11 12)

should charge customers for the WagWump family set. From the information provided, you know that the SRP (suggested retail price) is $26.99 per set and that your company can purchase the toy set from your wholesaler for $15.75 each. Based on the following assumptions, plot your company's supply curve on the graph provided in Figure 1.6 and label it "supply curve."

Quantity	Price
3,000	$16.99
5,000	21.99
7,000	26.99

Using the following assumptions, plot your customers' demand curve on Figure 1.6 and label it "demand curve."

Quantity	Price
10,000	$16.99
6,000	21.99
2,000	26.99

For this specific time, determine the point at which the quantity of toys your company is willing to supply equals the quantity of toys the customers in your sales district are willing to buy and label that point "equilibrium price."

Solve the Dilemma   LO 1-7

MRS. ACRES HOMEMADE PIES

Shelly Acres, whose grandmother gave her a family recipe for making pies, loved to cook, and she decided to start a business she called Mrs. Acres Homemade Pies. The company produces specialty pies and sells them in local supermarkets and select family restaurants. In each of the first six months, Shelly and three part-time employees sold 2,000 pies for $4.50 each, netting $1.50 profit per pie. The pies were quite successful and Shelly could not keep up with demand. The company's success results from a quality product and productive employees who are motivated by incentives and who enjoy being part of a successful new business.

To meet demand, Shelly expanded operations, borrowing money and increasing staff to four full-time employees. Production and sales increased to 8,000 pies per month, and profits soared to $12,000 per month. However, demand for Mrs. Acres Homemade Pies continues to accelerate beyond what Shelly can supply. She has several options: (1) maintain current production levels and raise prices; (2) expand the facility and staff while maintaining the current price; or (3) contract the production of the pies to a national restaurant chain, giving Shelly a percentage of profits with minimal involvement.

Discussion Questions

1. Explain and demonstrate the relationship between supply and demand for Mrs. Acres Homemade Pies.
2. What challenges does Shelly face as she considers the three options?
3. What would you do in Shelly's position?

Build Your Business Plan

THE DYNAMICS OF BUSINESS AND ECONOMICS

Have you ever thought about owning your business? If you have, how did your idea come about? Is it your experience with this particular field? Or might it be an idea that evolved from your desires for a particular product or service not being offered in your community? For example, perhaps you and your friends have yearned for a place to go have coffee, relax, and talk. Now is an opportunity to create the café bar you have been thinking of!

Whether you consider yourself a visionary or a practical thinker, think about your community. What needs are not being met? While it is tempting to suggest a new restaurant (maybe even one near campus), easier-to-implement business plans can range from a lawn care business or a designated driver business to a placement service agency for teenagers.

Once you have an idea for a business plan, think about how profitable this idea might be. Is there sufficient demand for this business? How large is the market for this particular business? What about competitors? How many are there?

To learn about your industry, you should do a thorough search of your initial ideas of a product/service on the Internet.

See for Yourself Videocase

REDBOX SUCCEEDS BY IDENTIFYING MARKET NEED

Just a few short years ago, you probably didn't even know that Redbox existed. Today, you can find the tell-tale bright red kiosks in stores and fast-food restaurants across the country. As one of the top rental companies in the United States, Redbox is a true entrepreneurial success story.

Building Redbox into a successful firm was not easy, however. It was fraught with challenges, including an inability to secure funding from venture capitalists. Like most successful companies, Redbox started out by identifying a need. It recognized that consumers could not often find the movies they wanted in convenient locations. But like all good ideas, Redbox required funding to get started. This proved to be a major difficulty. Realizing that customers did not want to pay much for renting movies, Redbox decided to charge only one dollar. Yet the kiosks, which contain more than 800 components, required a large amount of capital.

"Capital was always a struggle for us," said Mark Achler, senior vice president of new business development. "We have a capital-intensive business that required lots of people and high inventory costs, and we were only charging a dollar. Not one venture capitalist wanted to give us money."

However, Redbox was certain that demand for its product offerings and services would exceed the costs. The company finally found a partner in the more established Coinstar, which already had partnerships with many different retailers. The alliance with Coinstar opened the way for Redbox to begin installing kiosks at the front of stores.

Redbox did not immediately expand across the country. Instead, it took a cautious approach toward its business model. "The way we built this model was, to start with, can you make a single kiosk profitable? Then can you make a region of kiosks profitable, and then the country full of kiosks profitable? We never took the next step until we could prove the previous one," said Gary Cohen, senior vice president of marketing and customer experience. In this way, Redbox was able to test its concept without taking the risk of widespread failure.

Even though it was expanding, it was some time before Redbox was able to earn a profit. Like all entrepreneurs, the founders of Redbox had to take many risks if they wanted

the company to succeed. "The risks for starting Redbox were significant," Achler said. "The first couple years we had some red ink. It took us a while before we turned profitable." Yet with persistence and continual relationship building with retailers, Redbox has been able to secure 37 percent of the DVD-rental market.

One way that Redbox has been able to secure such a large share of the market is by meeting the needs of a variety of stakeholders. Redbox views its customers as its first priority and has developed its kiosks and database to meet their needs. For instance, customers can reserve movies online and pick them up at their nearest kiosk. If a kiosk happens to be out of a particular movie, customers can search the Redbox database to locate the movie at a nearby kiosk. This combination of convenience and low prices has attracted customers who desire a simplified process to renting movies.

Additionally, Redbox has created a process that also benefits the needs of its retail partners. Redbox kiosks help attract consumers to the store, where they may purchase additional products. Customers must come back the next day to return their movie, where they may once again purchase more products from the retailer. In this way, Redbox creates a win–win situation for both itself and its partners.

This is not to say that everything is easy for Redbox. For instance, it must continually safeguard against allowing underage children to rent inappropriate (rated-R) movies. Competition from rivals like Netflix and new technology such as Internet streaming are potent threats to Redbox. Yet if Redbox approaches this changing and dynamic marketplace as proactively as it approached its business model, the company could have a bright future ahead of it.[34]

DISCUSSION QUESTIONS

1. Why are consumers so willing to rent from Redbox?
2. How was Redbox able to overcome some of its earliest challenges?
3. What are some recommendations for ways that Redbox can maintain its high market share?

Remember to check out our Online Learning Center at www.mhhe.com/ferrell9e.

Team Exercise

Major economic systems, including capitalism, socialism, and communism, as well as mixed economies, were discussed in this chapter. Assuming that you want an economic system that is best for the majority, not just a few members

of society, defend one of the economic systems as the best system. Form groups and try to reach agreement on one economic system. Defend why you support the system that you advance.

Appendix A

Guidelines for the Development of the Business Plan

These guidelines are for students to create a hypothetical business plan for a product/service/business of their choice. Students should assume to have $25,000 to start this new business in their community.

At the end of every chapter, there will be a section entitled "Build Your Business Plan" to assist you in the development of the business plan.

Phase 1: Development of the Business Proposal

You are encouraged to submit your idea for approval to your instructor as soon as possible. This will eliminate wasted effort on an idea that is not feasible in the instructor's view. Business plan proposals will be evaluated based on their thoroughness and your ability to provide support for the idea.

The business proposal consists of the following elements.

Business Description. This consists of an overview of the existing product/service or the product/service/business you will be starting (manufacturer, merchandiser, or service provider). This includes developing a mission (reason for existence; overall purpose of the firm) and a rationale for why you believe this business will be a success. What is your vision for this proposed product/business?

Brief Marketing Plan. (The marketing plan will be further developed as the plan evolves.) A description of your business/product/service is required. Identify the target market and develop a strategy for appealing to it. Justify your proposed location for this business. Describe how you will promote the new business and provide a rationale for your pricing strategy. Select a name for this business. The name should be catchy yet relate to the competencies of the business.

Competitive Analysis. Identify the competition as broadly as possible. Indicate why this business will be successful given the market.

Phase 2: Final Written Business Plan

Executive Summary. The executive summary appears first but should be written last.

Business Description. This section requires fleshing out the body of the business plan, including material from your revised preliminary proposal with more data, charts, and appendices. Include a description of the proposed form of organization, either a partnership or corporation, and the rationalization of the form chosen.

Industry and Market Analysis. An analysis of the industry including the growth rate of the industry and number of new entrants into this field is necessary. Identify uncontrollable variables within the industry. Determine an estimate of the proposed realistic size of the potential market. This will require interpretation of statistics from the U.S. census as well as from local sources such as the Chamber of Commerce.

Competitive Analysis. Include an exhaustive list of the primary and secondary competition, along with the competitive advantage of each.

Marketing Strategy. Target market specifics need to be developed.

Decisions on the marketing mix variables need to be made:

- Price (at the market, below market, above market)
- Promotion (sales associates, advertising budget, use of sales promotions, and publicity/goodwill)
- Distribution—Rationale of choice and level of distribution
- Product/Service—A detailed rationale of the perceived differential advantage of your product/service offering

Operational Issues. How will you make or provide your product/service? Location rationale, facility type, leasing considerations, and sources of suppliers need to be detailed. Software/hardware requirements necessary to maintain operations must be determined.

Human Resources Requirement. Number and description of personnel needed, including realistic required education and skills.

Financial Projections. Statement of cash flows must be prepared for the first twelve months of the business. This must include startup costs, opening expenses, estimation of cash inflows and outflows. A breakeven analysis should be included and an explanation of all financial assumptions.

Appendixes

Phase 3: Oral Presentation

Specific separate guidelines on the oral presentation will be provided.

2

Business Ethics and Social Responsibility

Learning Objectives

After reading this chapter, you will be able to:

LO 2-1   Define business ethics and social responsibility and examine their importance.

LO 2-2   Detect some of the ethical issues that may arise in business.

LO 2-3   Specify how businesses can promote ethical behavior.

LO 2-4   Explain the four dimensions of social responsibility.

LO 2-5   Debate an organization's social responsibilities to owners, employees, consumers, the environment, and the community.

LO 2-6   Evaluate the ethics of a business's decision.

News Corporation's Corporate Culture: An Accident Waiting to Happen

Rupert Murdoch and his company News Corp. seemed invincible. As the owner of such media as Fox News and *The Wall Street Journal,* the company commanded the respect of politicians and public. Now the conglomerate faces the biggest challenge in its history after a phone hacking scandal was unveiled at company-owned tabloid *News of the World.*

In 2007, a reporter at *News of the World* was arrested for phone hacking. An investigation concluded that only one person at the company was guilty.

Scandal Grows at News Corp.

Former Senior Executive Is Arrested in Hacking Probe; Top Police Official Resigns

By Cassell Bryan-Low, Sara Schaefer Muñoz and Alistair MacDonald

LONDON—The head of Scotland Yard stepped down on Sunday and Rebekah Brooks—a close confidante of News Corp.'s top executive, Rupert Murdoch—was arrested as a convulsive phone hacking scandal raced into the loftiest ranks of Britain's business and law-enforcement worlds.

The surprise resignation of Metropolitan Police Commissioner Paul Stephenson came amid a spreading onslaught of allegations that some members of his force were corrupt and had forged too-close ties with the discredited newspaper at the heart of the scandal, News

Corp.'s now-defunct News of the World.

Ms. Brooks is at the center of a web of political and media elite that has come under intense scrutiny as details have spilled out about the lengths to which British newspapers have gone to get scoops and the cozy ties that may have protected their actions.

She was arrested Sunday in connection with the central allegations.

Please turn to page A8

Rebekah Brooks, right, with former boss, Rup...
See related stories on pages A8-A9

Japanese Women Squeak Past U.S. in World Cup Th...

ENTER THE WORLD OF BUSINESS

However, new findings reveal that hacking was more widespread. The resulting outrage forced deputy chief operating officer James Murdoch to close the 167-year-old *News of the World,* and both Rupert and James Murdoch testified before the U.K. Parliament. Additionally, suggestions that the police had accepted bribes from *News of the World* led the Metropolitan police examiner to resign.

Although James Murdoch had received an e-mail in 2008 alluding to more widespread hacking, he claims that he did not read the entire e-mail. It has been alleged that he might have purposely avoided knowledge of the misconduct, similar to what may have happened with the leaders at Enron.

How did such widespread misconduct go unchecked? In the United Kingdom, newspapers like *News of the World* connect authority figures and the general public. Because *News of the World* held such sway, politicians courted News Corp. officials. Additionally, the Murdoch family owns 40 percent of the company's voting stock. If board members

continued

displeased him, Murdoch could choose new directors. Shareholders even sued Murdoch in 2011 after News Corp. acquired his daughter's company. Murdoch's aggressive strategies could have reduced oversight and created a culture of winning at any cost.

With leadership problems and a lack of internal controls, a disaster was inevitable. Preliminary investigations have alleged that *News of the World* engaged in "serious criminality," including massive bribery. It is likely that several key officials at *News of the World* will face scrutiny and potential charges.[1]

Introduction

Any organization, including nonprofits, has to manage the ethical behavior of employees and participants in the overall operations of the organization. Misconduct can take on many forms within the business environment, including deceptive business practices and the withholding of important information from investors or consumers. Wrongdoing by some businesses has focused public attention and government involvement on encouraging more acceptable business conduct. Any organizational decision may be judged as right or wrong, ethical or unethical, legal or illegal.

In this chapter, we take a look at the role of ethics and social responsibility in business decision making. First we define business ethics and examine why it is important to understand ethics' role in business. Next we explore a number of business ethics issues to help you learn to recognize such issues when they arise. Finally, we consider steps businesses can take to improve ethical behavior in their organizations. The second half of the chapter focuses on social responsibility and unemployment. We survey some important issues and detail how companies have responded to them.

LO 2-1

business ethics
principles and standards that determine acceptable conduct in business

Business Ethics and Social Responsibility

In this chapter, we define **business ethics** as the principles and standards that determine acceptable conduct in business organizations. Personal ethics, on the other hand, relates to an individual's values, principles, and standards of conduct. The acceptability of behavior in business is determined by not only the organization but also stakeholders such as customers, competitors, government regulators, interest groups, and the public, as well as each individual's personal principles and values. The publicity and debate surrounding highly visible legal and ethical issues at a number of well-known firms, including Diamond Foods, Bank of America, and Citigroup, highlight the need for businesses to integrate ethics and responsibility into all business decisions. The most recent global financial crisis took a toll on consumer trust of financial services companies. Words used to describe these companies in a survey were "greedy," "impersonal," "opportunistic," and "distant." Most unethical activities within organizations are supported by an organizational culture that encourages employees to bend the rules. On the other hand, trust in business is the glue that holds relationships together. In Figure 2.1, you can see that trust in banks is lower than in other industries.

Organizations that exhibit a high ethical culture encourage employees to act with integrity and adhere to business values. Many experts agree that ethical leadership,

The R[...]

You have o[...]
the growing[...]
Fargo & Co[...]
aging borro[...]
many were[...]
ers are gen[...]
However, be[...]
company, W[...]
lower rates[...]
unethical ar[...]
to subprime[...]
America Co[...]
group Inc., [...]
foreclosure [...]
a particular[...]
whether cor[...]
zation's abili[...]

Well-pub[...]
ranging fron[...]
person's cre[...]
and diet pro[...]
software inc[...]
the level of[...]
mented, "An[...]
committing[...]
investors, ri[...]
more."[9] Ofte[...]
when coope[...]
scandals like[...]
create ethica[...]
of Citigroup[...]
founder and[...]
reaped lavish[...]
ing associate[...]
over executi[...]
they compei[...]
Group cut it[...]
year in profi[...]

However,[...]
issues. Ethica[...]
which valida[...]
and confider[...]
ing unethica[...]
about compa[...]
pany would [...]
about sometl[...]

Ethical is[...]
include all ai[...]

Entrepreneurship in Action
Local Philanthropist Provides Compassion on Wheels

The Bike Clinic

Peter Sprunger-Froese

Business: The Bike Clinic

Founded: 1993, in Colorado Springs

Success: Through the actions of The Bike Clinic and its sister organization, The Bike Clinic Too, people in need receive help and old bikes are given new life.

In the early 1990s, Peter Sprunger-Froese's shop was located on the roadside, where he repaired bicycles at no charge for those unable to afford bike shop services. After bicycle shop owner Kay Liggett discovered what Sprunger-Froese was doing, she offered to donate funds from her business to pay the rent for a shop along with $200 in parts each month. Sprunger-Froese began operating The Bike Clinic out of a one-room tin shack. The Bike Clinic repaired bikes and provided a second life to discarded bikes and parts. Sprunger-Froese gave the bicycles to homeless and mentally disabled people. Although The Bike Clinic earned no money, it helped others contribute meaningfully to their community. During and after the 2008–2009 recession, demand for bikes exploded. Sprunger-Froese was so backed up that a friend and bike aficionado opened The Bike Clinic Too. Recently, Sprunger-Froese has struggled both with fewer donations and the loss of his thumb. However, his vision endures through the philanthropy of The Bike Clinic Too.[2]

ethical values, and compliance are important in creating good business ethics. To truly create an ethical culture, however, managers must show a strong commitment to ethics and compliance. This "tone at the top" requires top managers to acknowledge their own role in supporting ethics and compliance, create strong relationships with the general counsel and the ethics and compliance department, clearly communicate company expectations for ethical behavior to all employees, educate all managers and supervisors in the business about the company's ethics policies, and train managers and employees on what to do if an ethics crisis occurs.[3]

Many consumers and social advocates believe that businesses should not only make a profit but also consider the social implications of their activities. We define **social responsibility** as a business's obligation to maximize its positive impact and minimize its negative impact on society. Although many people use the terms *social responsibility* and *ethics* interchangeably, they do not mean the same thing. Business ethics relates to an *individual's* or a *work group's* decisions that society evaluates as right or wrong, whereas social responsibility is a broader concept that concerns

social responsibility
a business's obligation to maximize its positive impact and minimize its negative impact on society

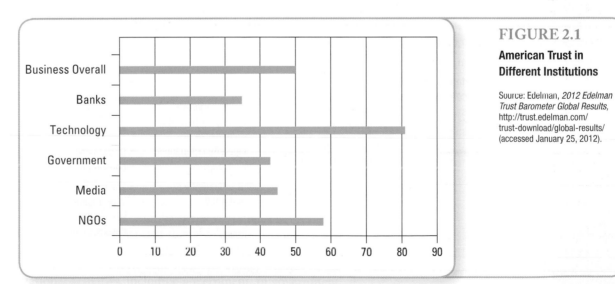

FIGURE 2.1

American Trust in Different Institutions

Source: Edelman, *2012 Edelman Trust Barometer Global Results*, http://trust.edelman.com/trust-download/global-results/ (accessed January 25, 2012).

The show "Undercover Boss" gives managers and business owners the chance to understand how their subordinates feel as they take on the responsibilities of their employees. Many bosses develop a stronger appreciation for their employees' challenging jobs, as Todd Rickets, co-owner of the Chicago Cubs, did after spending time undercover working as part of the janitorial staff and grounds crew.

TABLE 2

1960s
• Environme issues
• Civil rights
• Increased employee- tension
• Honesty
• Changing ethic
• Rising dru

Source: Adapte

employees spend an average of one hour each day using social networking sites or watching YouTube. In this case, the employee is not only misusing time but also company resources by using the company's computer and Internet access for personal use.[16] Time theft costs can be difficult to measure but are estimated to cost companies hundreds of billions of dollars annually. It is widely believed that the average employee "steals" 4.5 hours a week with late arrivals, leaving early, long lunch breaks, inappropriate sick days, excessive socializing, and engaging in personal activities such as online shopping and watching sports while on the job. All of these activities add up to lost productivity and profits for the employer—and relate to ethical issues in the area of time theft.

Abusive and Intimidating Behavior.   Abusive or intimidating behavior is the second most common ethical problem for employees. These concepts can mean anything from physical threats, false accusations, profanity, insults, yelling, harshness, and unreasonableness to ignoring someone or simply being annoying; and the meaning of these words can differ by person—you probably have some ideas of your own. Abusive behavior can be placed on a continuum from a minor distraction to a disruption of the workplace. For example, what one person may define as yelling might be another's definition of normal speech. Civility in our society is a concern, and the workplace is no exception. The productivity level of many organizations has been diminished by the time spent unraveling abusive relationships.

Abusive behavior is difficult to assess and manage because of diversity in culture and lifestyle. What does it mean to speak profanely? Is profanity only related to specific words or other such terms that are common in today's business world? If you are using words that are normal in your language but that others consider to be profanity, have you just insulted, abused, or disrespected them?

Within the concept of abusive behavior, intent should be a consideration. If the employee was trying to convey a compliment but the comment was considered abusive, then it was probably a mistake. The way a word is said (voice inflection) can be important. Add to this the fact that we now live in a multicultural environment—doing business and working with many different cultural groups—and the businessperson soon realizes the depth of the ethical and legal issues that may arise. There are problems of word meanings by age and within cultures. For example, an expression such as "Did you guys hook up last night?" can have various meanings, including some that could be considered offensive in a work environment.

Bullying is associated with a hostile workplace when a person or group is targeted and is threatened, harassed, belittled, verbally abused, or overly criticized. Bullying may create what some consider a hostile environment, a term generally associated with sexual harassment. Although sexual harassment has legal recourse, bullying has little legal recourse at this time. Bullying is a widespread problem in the United States, and can cause psychological damage that can result in health-endangering consequences to the target. Surveys indicate that approximately one in three adults have experienced bullying in the workplace, and one in seven workers witness bullying. Many victims and bystanders do not report bullying for fear of reprisals.[17] As Table 2.3 indicates, bullying can use a mix of verbal, nonverbal, and manipulative threatening expressions to damage workplace

TABLE 2.3

Actions Associated with Bullies

1. Spreading rumors to damage others
2. Blocking others' communication in the workplace
3. Flaunting status or authority to take advantage of others
4. Discrediting others' ideas and opinions
5. Use of e-mails to demean others
6. Failing to communicate or return communication
7. Insults, yelling, and shouting
8. Using terminology to discriminate by gender, race, or age
9. Using eye or body language to hurt others or their reputation
10. Taking credit for others' work or ideas

Source: © O. C. Ferrell, 2011.

productivity. One may wonder why workers tolerate such activities. The problem is that 81 percent of workplace bullies are supervisors. A top officer at Boeing cited an employee survey indicating 26 percent had observed abusive or intimidating behavior by management.[18]

Misuse of Company Resources.   Misuse of company resources has been identified by the Ethics Resource Center as a leading issue in observed misconduct in organizations. Issues might include spending an excessive amount of time on personal e-mails, submitting personal expenses on company expense reports, or using the company copier for personal use. While serious resource abuse can result in firing, some abuse can have legal repercussions. For example, one lawyer was found guilty of tax evasion after charging personal expenses through the law firm's bank account and manipulating the firm's ledgers to hide the misconduct.[19]

The most common way that employees abuse resources is by using company computers for personal use. Typical examples of using a computer for personal use include shopping on the Internet, downloading music, doing personal banking, surfing the Internet for entertainment purposes, or visiting Facebook. Some companies have chosen to block certain sites such as YouTube or Pandora from employees. However, other companies choose to take a more flexible approach. For example, many have instituted policies that allow for some personal computer use as long as the use does not detract significantly from the workday.

No matter what approach a business chooses to take, it must have policies in place to prevent company resource abuse. Because misuse of company resources is such a widespread problem, many companies, like Boeing, have implemented official policies delineating acceptable use of company resources. Boeing's policy states that use of company resources is acceptable when it does not result in "significant added costs, disruption of business processes, or any other disadvantage to the company." The policy further states that use of company resources for noncompany purposes is only acceptable when an employee receives explicit permission to do so.

This kind of policy is in line with that of many companies, particularly large ones that can easily lose millions of dollars and thousands of hours of productivity to these activities.[20]

Conflict of Interest. A conflict of interest, one of the most common ethical issue identified by employees, exists when a person must choose whether to advance his or her own personal interests or those of others. For example, a manager in a corporation is supposed to ensure that the company is profitable so that its stockholder-owners receive a return on their investment. In other words, the manager has a responsibility to investors. If she instead makes decisions that give her more power or money but do not help the company, then she has a conflict of interest—she is acting to benefit herself at the expense of her company and is not fulfilling her responsibilities as an employee. To avoid conflicts of interest, employees must be able to separate their personal financial interests from their business dealings. In the wake of the 2008 meltdown on Wall Street, stakeholders and legislators pushed for reform of the credit rating industry. Many cited rampant conflicts of interest between financial firms and the companies that rate them as part of the reason no one recognized the impending financial disaster. Conflict of interest has long been a serious problem in the financial industry because the financial companies pay the credit raters money in order to be rated. Because different rating companies exist, financial firms can also shop around for the best rating. There is no third-party mediator who oversees the financial industry and how firms are rated.[21]

Insider trading is an example of a conflict of interest. Insider trading is the buying or selling of stocks by insiders who possess material that is still not public. The Justice Department has taken an aggressive stance toward insider trading. For instance, Rajat Gupta, director of Goldman Sachs and Procter & Gamble, was arrested after being accused of passing insider information to his friend Raj Rajaratnam, former director of the hedge fund The Galleon Group. Rajaratnam himself was sentenced to 11 years in prison.[22] Until recently, however, it was not illegal for members of Congress to trade on nonpublic information. A new bill was passed to ban Congress members from engaging in insider trading and require them to provide more disclosure on their stock trades.[23] Bribery can also be a conflict of interest. While bribery is an increasing issue in many countries, it is more prevalent in some countries than in others. Transparency International has developed a Corruption Perceptions Index (Table 2.4). Note that there are 23 countries perceived as less corrupt than the United States.[24]

Fairness and Honesty

Fairness and honesty are at the heart of business ethics and relate to the general values of decision makers. At a minimum, business persons are expected to follow all applicable laws and regulations. But beyond obeying the law, they are expected not to harm customers, employees, clients, or competitors knowingly through deception, misrepresentation, coercion, or discrimination. Honesty and fairness can relate to how the employees use the resources of the organization. In contrast, dishonesty is usually associated with a lack of integrity, lack of disclosure, and lying. One common example of dishonesty is theft of office supplies. Approximately 35 percent of shrinkage—inventory losses due to shoplifting, employee theft, or errors—is a result of employee theft.[25] Although the majority of office supply thefts involve small things such as pencils or Post-it Notes, some workers admit to stealing more expensive equipment such as laptops, PDAs, and cell phones. Employees

Rank	Country	CPI Score*	TABLE 2.4
1.	New Zealand	9.5	**Least Corrupt Countries**
2.	Denmark/Finland	9.4	
4.	Sweden	9.3	
5.	Singapore	9.2	
6.	Norway	9.0	
7.	Netherlands	8.9	
8.	Australia/Switzerland	8.8	
10.	Canada	8.7	
11.	Luxembourg	8.5	
12.	Hong Kong	8.4	
13.	Iceland	8.3	
14.	Germany/Japan	8.0	
16.	Austria/Barbados/United Kingdom	7.8	
19.	Belgium/Ireland	7.5	
21.	Bahamas	7.3	
22.	Chile/Qatar	7.2	
24.	United States	7.1	

*Corruption Perceptions Index (CPI) score relates to perceptions of the degree of public sector corruption as seen by businesspeople and country analysts, and ranges between 0 (highly corrupt) to 10 (very clean)

Source: *Corruption Perceptions Index 2011.* Copyright Transparency International 2011. Reproduced with permission. For more information visit http://cpi.transparency.org/cpi2011/.

should be aware of policies on taking items and recognize how these decisions relate to ethical behavior.

One aspect of fairness relates to competition. Although numerous laws have been passed to foster competition and make monopolistic practices illegal, companies sometimes gain control over markets by using questionable practices that harm competition. Bullying can also occur between companies that are intense competitors. For example, Pool Corporation, the largest U.S. distributor of pool products, was accused by the Federal Trade Commission of using anticompetitive tactics to bar new distributors from entering the market.[26] In many cases, the alleged misconduct can have not only monetary and legal implications but can threaten reputation, investor confidence, and customer loyalty. In the case of Pool Corporation, the company had allegedly bullied pool manufacturers by threatening to refuse to distribute their products if they did business with other pool distributors. Such behavior is unacceptable. At the minimum, a business found guilty of anticompetitive practices will be forced to stop such conduct. However, many companies end up paying millions in penalties to settle allegations.[27]

sources for drugs to treat a variety of illnesses and conditions. However, research suggests that a significant percentage of these imported pharmaceuticals may not actually contain the labeled drug, and the counterfeit drugs could even be harmful to those who take them.[32]

Another important aspect of communications that may raise ethical concerns relates to product labeling. This becomes an even greater concern with potentially harmful products like cigarettes. In Europe, at least 30 percent of the front side of cigarette packaging and 40 percent of the back needs to be taken up by the warning. The Food and Drug Administration passed similar rules for the United States, but its ruling was blocked until the lawsuit between the FDA and cigarette companies is resolved.[33] However, labeling of other products raises ethical questions when it threatens basic rights, such as freedom of speech and expression. This is the heart of the controversy surrounding the movement to require warning labels on movies and videogames, rating their content, language, and appropriate audience age. Although people in the entertainment industry claim that such labeling violates their First Amendment right to freedom of expression, other consumers—particularly parents—believe that labeling is needed to protect children from harmful influences. Similarly, alcoholic beverage and cigarette manufacturers have argued that a total ban on cigarette and alcohol advertisements violates the First Amendment. Internet regulation, particularly that designed to protect children and the elderly, is on the forefront in consumer protection legislation. Because of the debate surrounding the acceptability of these business activities, they remain major ethical issues.

Business Relationships.   The behavior of businesspersons toward customers, suppliers, and others in their workplace may also generate ethical concerns. Ethical behavior within a business involves keeping company secrets, meeting obligations and responsibilities, and avoiding undue pressure that may force others to act unethically.

Managers in particular, because of the authority of their position, have the opportunity to influence employees' actions. For example, a manager might influence employees to use pirated computer software to save costs. The use of illegal software puts the employee and the company at legal risk, but employees may feel pressured to do so by their superior's authority. The National Business Ethics Survey found that employees who feel pressured to compromise ethical standards view top and middle managers as the greatest source of such pressure.[34]

It is the responsibility of managers to create a work environment that helps the organization achieve its objectives and fulfill its responsibilities. However, the methods that managers use to enforce these responsibilities should not compromise employee rights. Organizational pressures may encourage a person to engage in activities that he or she might otherwise view as unethical, such as invading others' privacy or stealing a competitor's secrets. The firm may provide only vague or lax supervision on ethical issues, creating the opportunity for misconduct. Managers who offer no ethical direction to employees create many opportunities for manipulation, dishonesty, and conflicts of interest.

plagiarism
the act of taking someone else's work and presenting it as your own without mentioning the source

Plagiarism—taking someone else's work and presenting it as your own without mentioning the source—is another ethical issue. As a student, you may be familiar with plagiarism in school, for example, copying someone else's term paper or quoting from a published work or Internet source without acknowledging it. In business, an ethical issue arises when an employee copies reports or takes the work or ideas of others and presents it as his or her own. A manager attempting to take credit for a subordinate's ideas is engaging in another type of plagiarism.

TABLE 2.5	
Questions to Consider in Determining Whether an Action Is Ethical	Are there any potential legal restrictions or violations that could result from the action?
	Does your company have a specific code of ethics or policy on the action?
	Is this activity customary in your industry? Are there any industry trade groups that provide guidelines or codes of conduct that address this issue?
	Would this activity be accepted by your co-workers? Will your decision or action withstand open discussion with co-workers and managers and survive untarnished?
	How does this activity fit with your own beliefs and values?

Making Decisions about Ethical Issues

Although we've presented a variety of ethical issues that may arise in business, it can be difficult to recognize specific ethical issues in practice. Whether a decision maker recognizes an issue as an ethical one often depends on the issue itself. Managers, for example, tend to be more concerned about issues that affect those close to them, as well as issues that have immediate rather than long-term consequences. Thus, the perceived importance of an ethical issue substantially affects choices. However, only a few issues receive scrutiny, and most receive no attention at all.[35]

Table 2.5 lists some questions you may want to ask yourself and others when trying to determine whether an action is ethical. Open discussion of ethical issues does not eliminate ethical problems, but it does promote both trust and learning in an organization.[36] When people feel that they cannot discuss what they are doing with their co-workers or superiors, there is a good chance that an ethical issue exists. Once a person has recognized an ethical issue and can openly discuss it with others, he or she has begun the process of resolving that issue.

Improving Ethical Behavior in Business

LO 2-3

Understanding how people make ethical choices and what prompts a person to act unethically may reverse the current trend toward unethical behavior in business. Ethical decisions in an organization are influenced by three key factors: individual moral standards, the influence of managers and co-workers, and the opportunity to engage in misconduct (Figure 2.2). While you have great control over your personal ethics outside the workplace, your co-workers and superiors exert significant control over your choices at work through authority and example. In fact, the activities and examples set by co-workers, along with rules and policies established by the firm, are critical in gaining consistent ethical compliance in an organization. If the company fails to provide good examples and direction for appropriate conduct,

FIGURE 2.2					
Three Factors That Influence Business Ethics	Individual Standards and Values	+	Managers' and Co-workers' Influence	+	Opportunity: Codes and Compliance Requirements	=	Ethical/Unethical Choices in Business

Employee Relations.   Another issue of importance to a business is its responsibilities to employees. Without employees, a business cannot carry out its goals. Employees expect businesses to provide a safe workplace, pay them adequately for their work, and keep them informed of what is happening in their company. They want employers to listen to their grievances and treat them fairly. In an effort to make Ford more competitive with foreign car companies, the United Auto Workers union agreed to allow the company to hire new workers at half the pay and with reduced benefits. This was a major concession on the part of the union, but was deemed a necessary step in keeping the company afloat. However, hiring new workers to do the same job as established ones for half the pay can result in dissatisfied employees and low morale.[54]

Congress has passed several laws regulating safety in the workplace, many of which are enforced by the Occupational Safety and Health Administration (OSHA). Labor unions have also made significant contributions to achieving safety in the workplace and improving wages and benefits. Most organizations now recognize that the safety and satisfaction of their employees are critical ingredients in their success, and many strive to go beyond what is legally expected of them. Healthy, satisfied employees also supply more than just labor to their employers. Employers are beginning to realize the importance of obtaining input from even the lowest-level employees to help the company reach its objectives.

A major social responsibility for business is providing equal opportunities for all employees regardless of their sex, age, race, religion, or nationality. Women and minorities have been slighted in the past in terms of education, employment, and advancement opportunities; additionally, many of their needs have not been addressed by business. The Equal Employment Opportunity Commission (EEOC) found Bass Pro Shops guilty of racial discrimination in its hiring practices. According to the EEOC, managers at multiple Bass Pro Shops retailers would not hire nonwhite employees despite their qualifications.[55] Women, who continue to bear most child-rearing responsibilities, often experience conflict between those responsibilities and their duties as employees. Consequently, day care has become a major employment issue for women, and more companies are providing day care facilities as part of their effort to recruit and advance women in the workforce. In addition, companies are considering alternative scheduling such as flex-time and job sharing to accommodate employee concerns. Telecommuting has grown significantly over the past 5 to 10 years as well. Many Americans today believe business has a social obligation to provide special opportunities for women and minorities to improve their standing in society.

Consumer Relations.   A critical issue in business today is business's responsibility to customers, who look to business to provide them with satisfying, safe products and to respect their rights as consumers. The activities that independent individuals, groups, and organizations undertake to protect their rights as consumers are known as **consumerism.** To achieve their objectives, consumers and their advocates write letters to companies, lobby government agencies, make public service announcements, and boycott companies whose activities they deem irresponsible.

Many of the desires of those involved in the consumer movement have a foundation in John F. Kennedy's 1962 consumer bill of rights, which highlighted four rights. The *right to safety* means that a business must not knowingly sell anything that could result in personal injury or harm to consumers. Defective or dangerous products erode public confidence in the ability of business to serve society. They also result in expensive litigation that ultimately increases the cost of products for

consumerism
the activities that independent individuals, groups, and organizations undertake to protect their rights as consumers

all consumers. The right to safety also means businesses must provide a safe place for consumers to shop.

The *right to be informed* gives consumers the freedom to review complete information about a product before they buy it. This means that detailed information about ingredients, risks, and instructions for use are to be printed on labels and packages. The *right to choose* ensures that consumers have access to a variety of products and services at competitive prices. The assurance of both satisfactory quality and service at a fair price is also a part of the consumer's right to choose. Some consumers are not being given this right. For instance, investigations by the Senate Commerce Committee found that phone-bill "cramming" has become a major issue. Cramming occurs when the phone company or a third party puts additional charges on the customer's bill. Officials believe that many of these charges are not authorized and that consumers remain unaware of them because they do not check their phone bills carefully enough.[56] The *right to be heard* assures consumers that their interests will receive full and sympathetic consideration when the government formulates policy. It also ensures the fair treatment of consumers who voice complaints about a purchased product.

The role of the Federal Trade Commission's Bureau of Consumer Protection exists to protect consumers against unfair, deceptive, or fraudulent practices. The bureau, which enforces a variety of consumer protection laws, is divided into five divisions. The Division of Enforcement monitors legal compliance and investigates violations of laws, including unfulfilled holiday delivery promises by online shopping sites, employment opportunities fraud, scholarship scams, misleading advertising for health care products, and more.

Sustainability Issues. Most people probably associate the term *environment* with nature, including wildlife, trees, oceans, and mountains. Until the 20th century, people generally thought of the environment solely in terms of how these resources could be harnessed to satisfy their needs for food, shelter, transportation, and recreation. As the earth's population swelled throughout the 20th century, however, humans began to use more and

Values

The Home Depot's values guide the beliefs and actions of all associates on a daily basis. Our values are the fabric of the Company's unique culture and are central to our success. In fact, they are our competitive advantage in the marketplace. Associate pride and our "orangeblooded" entrepreneurial spirit are distinctive hallmarks of our culture.

1. **Taking care of our people:**
   The key to our success is treating people well. We do this by encouraging associates to speak up and take risks, by recognizing and rewarding good performance and by leading and developing people so they may grow.

2. **Giving back to our communities:**
   An important part of the fabric of The Home Depot is giving our time, talents, energy and resources to worthwhile causes in our communities and society.

3. **Doing the right thing:**
   We exercise good judgment by "doing the right thing" instead of just "doing things right." We strive to understand the impact of our decisions, and we accept responsibility for our actions.

4. **Excellent customer service:**
   Along with our quality products, service, price and selection, we must go the extra mile to give customers knowledgeable advice about merchandise and to help them use those products to their maximum benefit.

5. **Creating shareholder value:**
   The investors who provide the capital necessary to allow our company to grow need and expect a return on their investment. We are committed to providing it.

6. **Building strong relationships:**
   Strong relationships are built on trust, honesty and integrity. We listen and respond to the needs of customers, associates, communities and vendors, treating them as partners.

7. **Entrepreneurial spirit:**
   The Home Depot associates are encouraged to initiate creative and innovative ways of serving our customers and improving the business and to spread best practices throughout the company.

8. **Respect for all people:**
   In order to remain successful, our associates must work in an environment of mutual respect, free of discrimination and harassment where each associate is regarded as a part of The Home Depot team.

Home Depot has adopted eight core values as the foundation for its ethical culture, including a strong emphasis on sustainability.

more of these resources and, with technological advancements, to do so with ever-greater efficiency. Although these conditions have resulted in a much-improved standard of living, they come with a cost. Plant and animal species, along with wildlife habitats, are disappearing at an accelerated rate, while pollution has rendered the atmosphere of some cities a gloomy haze. How to deal with these issues has become a major concern for business and society in the 21st century.

Although the scope of the word *sustainability* is broad, in this book we discuss the term from a strategic business perspective. Thus, we define **sustainability** as conducting activities in such a way as to provide for the long-term well-being of the natural environment, including all biological entities. Sustainability involves the interaction among nature and individuals, organizations, and business strategies and includes the assessment and improvement of business strategies, economic sectors, work practices, technologies, and lifestyles, so that they maintain the health of the natural environment. In recent years, business has played a significant role in adapting, using, and maintaining the quality of sustainability.

Environmental protection emerged as a major issue in the 20th century in the face of increasing evidence that pollution, uncontrolled use of natural resources, and population growth were putting increasing pressure on the long-term sustainability of these resources. Governments around the globe responded with environmental protection laws during the 1970s. In recent years, companies have been increasingly incorporating these issues into their overall business strategies. Some nonprofit organizations have stepped forward to provide leadership in gaining the cooperation of diverse groups in responsible environmental activities. For example, the Coalition for Environmentally Responsible Economies (CERES)—a union of businesses, consumer groups, environmentalists, and other stakeholders—has established a set of goals for environmental performance.

In the following section, we examine some of the most significant sustainability and environmental health issues facing business and society today, including animal rights, pollution, and alternative energy.

Pollution.   Another major issue in the area of environmental responsibility is pollution. Water pollution results from dumping toxic chemicals and raw sewage into rivers and oceans, oil spills, and the burial of industrial waste in the ground where it may filter into underground water supplies. Fertilizers and insecticides used in farming and grounds maintenance also run off into water supplies with each rainfall. Water pollution problems are especially notable in heavily industrialized areas. Medical waste—such as used syringes, vials of blood, and HIV-contaminated materials—has turned up on beaches in New York, New Jersey, and Massachusetts, as well as other places. Society is demanding that water supplies be clean and healthful to reduce the potential danger from these substances.

Air pollution is usually the result of smoke and other pollutants emitted by manufacturing facilities, as well as carbon monoxide and hydrocarbons emitted by motor vehicles. In addition to the health risks posed by air pollution, when some chemical compounds emitted by manufacturing facilities react with air and rain, acid rain results. Acid rain has contributed to the deaths of many forests and lakes in North America as well as in Europe. Air pollution may also contribute to global warming; as carbon dioxide collects in the earth's atmosphere, it traps the sun's heat and prevents the earth's surface from cooling. It is indisputable that the global surface temperature has been increasing over the past 35 years. Worldwide passenger vehicle ownership has been growing due to rapid industrialization and

sustainability
conducting activities in a way that allows for the long-term well-being of the natural environment, including all biological entities. Sustainability involves the assessment and improvement of business strategies, economic sectors, work practices, technologies, and lifestyles so that they maintain the health of the natural environment.

consumer purchasing power in China, India, and other developing countries with large populations. The most important way to contain climate change is to control carbon emissions. The move to green buildings, higher-mileage cars, and other emissions reductions resulting from better efficiency have the potential to generate up to 50 percent of the reductions needed to keep warming at no more than 28°C above present temperatures—considered the "safe" level.[57] The 2007 U.S. Federal Energy bill raised average fuel economy (CAFE) standards to 35 mpg for cars by 2020, while Europe has the goal of a 40 mpg standard by the same deadline. Because buildings create half of U.S. greenhouse emissions, there is tremendous opportunity to develop conservation measures. For example, some utilities charge more for electricity in peak demand periods, which encourages behavioral changes that reduce consumption. On the positive side, there are more than 100 million bicycles produced annually worldwide, more than double the passenger vehicles produced.[58] More and more consumers are recognizing the need to protect the planet. Figure 2.4 shows some of the most common ways that consumers conserve resources.

Land pollution is tied directly to water pollution because many of the chemicals and toxic wastes that are dumped on the land eventually work their way into the water supply. A study conducted by the Environmental Protection Agency found residues of prescription drugs, soaps, and other contaminants in virtually every waterway in the United States. Effects of these pollutants on humans and wildlife are uncertain, but there is some evidence to suggest that fish and other water-dwellers are starting to suffer serious effects.[59] Land pollution results from the dumping of residential and industrial waste, strip mining, forest fires, and poor forest conservation. In Brazil and other South American countries, rain forests are being destroyed—to make way for farms and ranches, at a cost of the extinction of the many animals and plants (some endangered species) that call the rain forest home. For example, annual deforestation in the Brazilian rainforest encompasses an area about the size of Delaware. The good news is that deforestation rates in Brazil

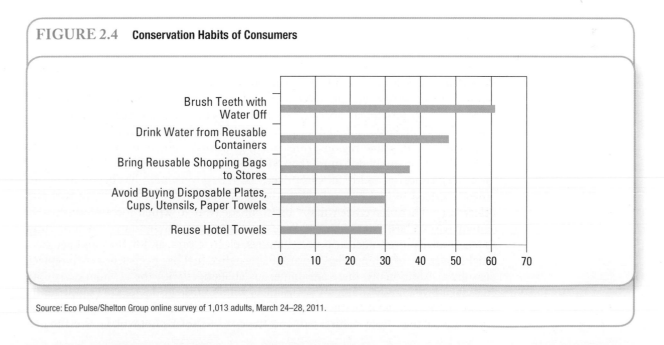

FIGURE 2.4   **Conservation Habits of Consumers**

Source: Eco Pulse/Shelton Group online survey of 1,013 adults, March 24–28, 2011.

Hydraulic fracturing, known as fracking, has the potential to reduce the United States' dependence on foreign oil. Fracking forces water, sand, and chemicals into underground tunnels of shale rock, bringing natural gas to the surface. Natural gas releases half the carbon dioxide of oil, and the United States has the potential to produce more than 30 percent more fuel than currently consumed. Lower-income towns have benefited economically from fracking because the drilling creates jobs and inserts money into the community.

However, fracking does have a dark side. There have been instances where fracking chemicals have contaminated drinking water and increased levels of methane in water wells. Currently, fracking is exempt from elements of the Safe Drinking Water Act. Gas companies can declare their chemical formulas as proprietary; therefore, few know what's going into the drilling wells. The Environmental Protection Agency has therefore begun examining the ramifications of fracking in response to concerns.

Many fear that the energy crisis and economic benefits will overshadow environmental concerns. Natural gas is a critical component of the government's plan for the country to run on 80 percent clean energy by 2035. Yet other countries have not been so accepting of fracking. France has temporarily banned fracking and drilling for shale rock until the government has conclusive environmental information. New York has enacted a moratorium as well. Stakeholders must try balancing the economic benefits with the potential costs of environmental degradation.[60]

Discussion Questions

1. What is the ethical issue involved with fracking, and why is it so hard to resolve?
2. Examine this issue from the perspective of the gas company as well as from the perspective of concerned stakeholders.
3. Why might the government want to support fracking?

may be decreasing due to new laws against illegal logging.[61] Large-scale deforestation also depletes the oxygen supply available to humans and other animals.

Related to the problem of land pollution is the larger issue of how to dispose of waste in an environmentally responsible manner. Americans use 102 billion plastic bags each year. It takes 1,000 years for the bags to decompose. San Francisco has banned plastic bags; Ireland is now charging a nationwide tax of 15 cents on all supermarket shopping bags; and India will fine those caught handing out plastic bags.[62] Whole Foods, the nation's leading natural and organic supermarket, ended its use of plastic bags on Earth Day 2008.[63] Whole Foods estimates that this move will keep 150 million new plastic grocery bags out of the environment each year.

Alternative Energy. With ongoing plans to reduce global carbon emissions, countries and companies alike are looking toward alternative energy sources. Traditional fossil fuels are problematic because of their emissions, but also because stores have been greatly depleted. Foreign fossil fuels are often imported from politically and economically unstable regions, often making it unsafe to conduct business there. The United States spends more than $1 billion a day on foreign oil.[64] With global warming concerns and rising gas prices, the U.S. government has begun to recognize the need to look toward alternative forms of energy as a source of fuel and electricity. There have been many different ideas as to which form of alternative energy would best suit the United States' energy needs. These sources include wind power, solar power, nuclear power, biofuels, electric cars, and hydro- and geothermal power. As of yet, no "best" form of alternative fuel has been selected to replace gasoline. Additionally, there are numerous challenges with the economic viability of alternative energy sources. For instance, wind and solar power cost significantly more than traditional energy; watts from wind power are estimated to be 290 percent higher than from natural gas, and the costs of solar photovoltaic is estimated be 230 percent more expensive. Alternative energy will likely require government subsidies to make any significant strides. The bankruptcy scandal of the solar company Solyndra, which was granted a $527 million federally funded loan despite signs that the company was in trouble, has added fuel to the debate of whether alternative energy ventures should be subsidized.[65]

Response to Environmental Issues.   Partly in response to federal legislation such as the National Environmental Policy Act of 1969 and partly due to consumer concerns, businesses are responding to environmental issues. Many small and large companies, including Walt Disney Company, Chevron, and Scott Paper, have created an executive position—a vice president of environmental affairs—to help them achieve their business goals in an environmentally responsible manner. Some companies are finding that environmental consciousness can save them money. For instance, Walmart estimates that it has saved $1 million in electricity costs by installing solar panels on some of its stores.[66]

Many firms are trying to eliminate wasteful practices, the emission of pollutants, and/or the use of harmful chemicals from their manufacturing processes. Other companies are seeking ways to improve their products. Utility providers, for example, are increasingly supplementing their services with alternative energy sources, including solar,

Wind power is growing in popularity as an alternative to traditional fuel sources.

wind, and geothermal power. Environmentalists are concerned that some companies are merely *greenwashing*, or "creating a positive association with environmental issues for an unsuitable product, service, or practice."

In many places, local utility customers can even elect to purchase electricity from green sources—primarily wind power—for a few extra dollars a month. Austin Energy of Austin, Texas, has an award-winning GreenChoice program that includes many small and large businesses among its customers.[68] Indeed, a growing number of businesses and consumers are choosing green power sources where available. New Belgium Brewing, the third-largest craft brewer in the United States, is the first all-wind-powered brewery in the country. Many businesses have turned to *recycling*, the reprocessing of

DID YOU KNOW? In one year, Americans generated 230 million tons of trash and recycled 23.5 percent of it.[67]

materials—aluminum, paper, glass, and some plastic—for reuse. Such efforts to make products, packaging, and processes more environmentally friendly have been labeled "green" business or marketing by the public and media. New Belgium, for instance, started selling aluminum cans of its beers because aluminum is easily recyclable and creates less waste. Lumber products at The Home Depot may carry a seal from the Forest Stewardship Council to indicate that they were harvested from sustainable forests using environmentally friendly methods.[69] Likewise, most Chiquita bananas are certified through the Better Banana Project as having been grown with more environmentally and labor-friendly practices.[70]

It is important to recognize that, with current technology, environmental responsibility requires trade-offs. Society must weigh the huge costs of limiting or eliminating pollution against the health threat posed by the pollution. Environmental responsibility imposes costs on both business and the public. Although people certainly do not want oil fouling beautiful waterways and killing wildlife, they insist on low-cost, readily available gasoline and heating oil. People do not want to contribute to the growing garbage-disposal problem, but they often refuse to pay more for "green" products packaged in an environmentally friendly manner, to recycle as much of their own waste as possible, or to permit the building of additional waste-disposal facilities (the "not in my backyard," or NIMBY, syndrome). Managers must coordinate environmental goals with other social and economic ones.

Community Relations.   A final, yet very significant, issue for businesses concerns their responsibilities to the general welfare of the communities and societies in which they operate. Many businesses simply want to make their communities better places for everyone to live and work. The most common way that businesses exercise their community responsibility is through donations to local and national charitable organizations. For example, Safeway, the nation's fourth-largest grocer, has donated millions of dollars to organizations involved in medical research, such as Easter Seals and the Juvenile Diabetes Research Foundation International. The company's employees have also raised funds to support social causes of interest.[71] California-based clothing company Patagonia donates 1 percent of its sales toward environmental preservation and restoration.[72] Even small companies participate in philanthropy through donations and volunteer support of local causes and national charities, such as the Red Cross and the United Way.

Volunteers at Habitat for Humanity construct a house in Winnipeg. Many companies encourage their employees to volunteer for charitable organizations such as Habitat for Humanity.

Unemployment

After realizing that the current pool of prospective employees lacks many basic skills necessary to work, many companies have become concerned about the quality of education in the United States. Unemployment has become a significant problem since the onset of the financial crisis in 2008. In the years following, unemployment reached as high as 10 percent in the United States. Although it has fallen to about 8.3 percent since then, many consumers remain unemployed.[73]

Although most would argue that unemployment is an economic issue, it also carries ethical implications. Consider the Occupy Wall Street protests. In the United States and other parts of the world, consumers got together to protest what they saw as the growing gap between the rich and the poor. One of the major issues was the fact that executives of Wall Street firms—some of them implicated in the misconduct leading up to the financial crisis—received high wages and bonuses while many employees were laid off or remained unemployed.[74] Although the protests eventually died down, this issue continues to be an ethical concern for many stakeholders.

Factory closures are another ethical issue because factories usually employ hundreds of workers. Sometimes it is necessary to close a plant due to economic reasons. However, when Caterpillar Inc. announced it was closing a Canadian factory, many questioned the ethics of the action. Workers of the factory had been locked out after they went on strike for higher wages. Critics believed the closure was retaliation for the problems caused by the strikes.[75]

Another criticism levied against companies involves hiring standards. Studies appear to show that while there are plenty of people unemployed, approximately 35 percent of companies cite employees' lack of experience as to why there are so many unfilled positions. Yet only about 28 percent are investing in more training and development for new hires. While it is important for employees to have certain skills, many feel that businesses must be willing to train employees if they want to fill their vacancies and decrease the unemployment rate.[76]

On the other hand, several businesses are working to reduce unemployment. After realizing that the current pool of prospective employees lacks many basic skills necessary to work, Target made a commitment to donate $1 billion in its ongoing efforts to improve education. Through the retailer's Take Charge of Education program, customers using a Target REDcard can select a specific school to which Target will contribute 1 percent of their total purchase. The company also provides funds for building new school libraries.[77]

Additionally, businesses are beginning to take more responsibility for the hard-core unemployed. These are people who have never had a job or who have been unemployed for a long period of time. Some are mentally or physically handicapped; some are homeless. Organizations such as the National Alliance of Businessmen fund programs to train the hard-core unemployed so that they can find jobs and support themselves. Also, while numerous businesses laid off employees during the last recession, others were praised for their refusal to lay off workers. Boston Consulting Group (BCG), for instance, avoided laying off employees during the recession and even hired its largest number of recruits in 2010. As a result, employees at BCG are highly motivated and voted BCG as one of the best companies to work for.[78] Such commitment enhances self-esteem and helps people become productive members of society.

So You Want a Job in Business Ethics and Social Responsibility

In the words of Kermit the Frog, "It's not easy being green." It may not be easy, but green business opportunities abound. A popular catch phrase, "Green is the new black," indicates how fashionable green business is becoming. Consumers are more in tune with and concerned about green products, policies, and behaviors by companies than ever before. Companies are looking for new hires to help them see their business creatively and bring insights to all aspects of business operations. The American Solar Energy Society estimates that the number of green jobs could rise to 40 million in the United States by 2030. Green business strategies not only give a firm a commercial advantage in the marketplace, but help lead the way toward a greener world. The fight to reduce our carbon footprint in an attempt against climate change has opened up opportunities for renewable energy, recycling, conservation, and increasing overall efficiency in the way resources are used. New businesses that focus on hydro, wind, and solar power are on the rise and will need talented business people to lead them. Carbon emissions' trading is gaining popularity as large corporations and individuals alike seek to lower their footprints. A job in this growing field could be similar to that of a stock trader, or you could lead the search for carbon-efficient companies in which to invest.

In the ethics arena, current trends in business governance strongly support the development of ethics and compliance departments to help guide organizational integrity. This alone is a billion-dollar business, and there are jobs in developing organizational ethics programs, developing company policies, and training employees and management. An entry-level position might be as a communication specialist or trainer for programs in a business ethics department. Eventually there's an opportunity to become an ethics officer that would have typical responsibilities of meeting with employees, the Board of Directors, and top management to discuss and provide advice about ethics issues in the industry, developing and distributing a code of ethics, creating and maintaining an anonymous, confidential service to answer questions about ethical issues, taking actions on possible ethics code violations, and reviewing and modifying the code of ethics of the organization.

There are also opportunities to help with initiatives to help companies relate social responsibility to stakeholder interests and needs. These jobs could involve coordinating and implementing philanthropic programs that give back to others important to the organization or developing a community volunteering program for employees. In addition to the human relations function, most companies develop programs to assist employees and their families to improve their quality of life. Companies have found that the healthier and happier employees are the more productive they will be in the workforce.

Social responsibility, ethics, and sustainable business practices are not a trend, they are good for business and the bottom line. New industries are being created and old ones are adapting to the new market demands, opening up many varied job opportunities that will lead to not only a paycheck, but to the satisfaction of making the world a better place.[79]

Review Your Understanding

Define business ethics and social responsibility and examine their importance.

Business ethics refers to principles and standards that define acceptable business conduct. Acceptable business behavior is defined by customers, competitors, government regulators, interest groups, the public, and each individual's personal moral principles and values. Social responsibility is the obligation an organization assumes to maximize its positive impact and minimize its negative impact on society. Socially responsible businesses win the trust and respect of their employees, customers, and society and, in the long run, increase profits. Ethics is important in business because it builds trust and confidence in business relationships. Unethical actions may result in negative publicity, declining sales, and even legal action.

Detect some of the ethical issues that may arise in business.

An ethical issue is an identifiable problem, situation, or opportunity requiring a person or organization to choose from among several actions that must be evaluated as right or wrong. Ethical issues can be categorized in the context of their relation with conflicts of interest, fairness and honesty, communications, and business associations.

Specify how businesses can promote ethical behavior by employees.

Businesses can promote ethical behavior by employees by limiting their opportunity to engage in misconduct. Formal codes of ethics, ethical policies, and ethics training programs reduce the incidence of unethical behavior by informing employees what is expected of them and providing punishments for those who fail to comply.

Explain the four dimensions of social responsibility.

The four dimensions of social responsibility are economic (being profitable), legal (obeying the law), ethical (doing what is right, just, and fair), and voluntary (being a good corporate citizen).

Debate an organization's social responsibilities to owners, employees, consumers, the environment, and the community.

Businesses must maintain proper accounting procedures, provide all relevant information about the performance of the firm to investors, and protect the owners' rights and investments. In relations with employees, businesses are expected to provide a safe workplace, pay employees adequately for their work, and treat them fairly. Consumerism refers to the activities undertaken by independent individuals, groups, and organizations to protect their rights as consumers. Increasingly, society expects businesses to take greater responsibility for the environment, especially with regard to animal rights, as well as water, air, land, and noise pollution. Many businesses engage in activities to make the communities in which they operate better places for everyone to live and work.

Evaluate the ethics of a business's decision.

"Solve the Dilemma" on page 67 presents an ethical dilemma at Checkers Pizza. Using the material presented in this chapter, you should be able to analyze the ethical issues present in the dilemma, evaluate Barnard's plan, and develop a course of action for the firm.

Revisit the World of Business

1. Why has the News Corp. scandal become such an issue?

2. What are some of the alleged ethical issues that News Corp. faced? Describe these issues.

3. Why would Rupert Murdoch's influence over the board be a problem?

Learn the Terms

bribes   40

business ethics   36

codes of ethics   50

consumerism   56

corporate citizenship   53

ethical issue   40

plagiarism   48

social responsibility   37

sustainability   58

whistleblowing   51

Check Your Progress

1. Define business ethics. Who determines whether a business activity is ethical? Is unethical conduct always illegal?

2. Distinguish between ethics and social responsibility.

3. Why has ethics become so important in business?

4. What is an ethical issue? What are some of the ethical issues named in your text? Why are they ethical issues?

5. What is a code of ethics? How can one reduce unethical behavior in business?

6. List and discuss the arguments for and against social responsibility by business (Table 2.8). Can you think of any additional arguments (for or against)?

7. What responsibilities does a business have toward its employees?

8. What responsibilities does business have with regard to the environment? What steps have been taken by some responsible businesses to minimize the negative impact of their activities on the environment?

9. What are a business's responsibilities toward the community in which it operates?

Get Involved

1. Discuss some recent examples of businesses engaging in unethical practices. Classify these practices as issues of conflict of interest, fairness and honesty, communications, or business relationships. Why do you think the businesses chose to behave unethically? What actions might the businesses have taken?

2. Discuss with your class some possible methods of improving ethical standards in business. Do you think that business should regulate its own activities or that the federal government should establish and enforce ethical standards? How do you think businesspeople feel?

3. Find some examples of socially responsible businesses in newspapers or business journals. Explain why you believe their actions are socially responsible. Why do you think the companies chose to act as they did?

Build Your Skills

MAKING DECISIONS ABOUT ETHICAL ISSUES

Background

The merger of Lockheed and Martin Marietta created Lockheed Martin, the number-one company in the defense industry—an industry that includes such companies as McDonnell Douglas and Northrop Grumman.

You and the rest of the class are managers at Lockheed Martin Corporation, Orlando, Florida. You are getting ready to do the group exercise in an ethics training session. The training instructor announces you will be playing *Gray Matters: The Ethics Game.* You are told that *Gray Matters,* which was prepared for your company's employees, is also played at 41 universities, including Harvard University, and at 65 other companies. Although there are 55 scenarios in *Gray Matters,* you will have time during this session to complete only the four scenarios that your group draws from the stack of cards.[80]

Task

Form into groups of four to six managers and appoint a group leader who will lead a discussion of the case, obtain a consensus answer to the case, and be the one to report the group's answers to the instructor. You will have five minutes to reach each decision, after which time, the instructor will give the point values and rationale for each choice. Then you will have five minutes for the next case, etc., until all four cases have been completed. Keep track of your group's score for each case; the winning team will be the group scoring the most points.

Since this game is designed to reflect life, you may believe that some cases lack clarity or that some of your choices are not as precise as you would have liked. Also, some cases have only one solution, while others have more than one solution. Each choice is assessed to reflect which answer is the most correct. **Your group's task is to select only one option in each case.**

4

Mini-Case

For several months now, one of your colleagues has been slacking off, and you are getting stuck doing the work. You think it is unfair. What do you do?

Potential Answers

A. Recognize this as an opportunity for you to demonstrate how capable you are.

B. Go to your supervisor and complain about this unfair workload.

C. Discuss the problem with your colleague in an attempt to solve the problem without involving others.

D. Discuss the problem with the human resources department.

7

Mini-Case

You are aware that a fellow employee uses drugs on the job. Another friend encourages you to confront the person instead of informing the supervisor. What do you do?

Potential Answers

A. You speak to the alleged user and encourage him to get help.

B. You elect to tell your supervisor that you suspect an employee is using drugs on the job.

C. You confront the alleged user and tell him either to quit using drugs or you will "turn him in."

D. Report the matter to employee assistance.

36

Mini-Case

You work for a company that has implemented a policy of a smoke-free environment. You discover employees smoking in the restrooms of the building. You also smoke and don't like having to go outside to do it. What do you do?

Potential Answers

A. You ignore the situation.

B. You confront the employees and ask them to stop.

C. You join them, but only occasionally.

D. You contact your ethics or human resources representative and ask him or her to handle the situation.

40

Mini-Case

Your co-worker is copying company-purchased software and taking it home. You know a certain program costs $400, and you have been saving for a while to buy it. What do you do?

Potential Answers

A. You figure you can copy it too since nothing has ever happened to your co-worker.

B. You tell your co-worker he can't legally do this.

C. You report the matter to the ethics office.

D. You mention this to your supervisor.

Solve the Dilemma   LO 2-6

CUSTOMER PRIVACY

Checkers Pizza was one of the first to offer home delivery service, with overwhelming success. However, the major pizza chains soon followed suit, taking away Checkers's competitive edge. Jon Barnard, Checkers's founder and co-owner, needed a new gimmick to beat the competition. He decided to develop a computerized information database that would make Checkers the most efficient competitor and provide insight into consumer buying behavior at the same time. Under the system, telephone customers were asked their phone number; if they had ordered from Checkers before, their address and previous order information came up on the computer screen.

After successfully testing the new system, Barnard put the computerized order network in place in all Checkers outlets. After three months of success, he decided to give an award to the family that ate the most Checkers pizza. Through the tracking system, the company identified the biggest customer, who had ordered a pizza every weekday for the past three months (63 pizzas). The company put together a program to surprise the family with an award, free-food certificates, and a news story announcing the award. As Barnard began to plan for the event, however, he began to think that maybe the family might not want all the attention and publicity.

Discussion Questions

1. What are some of the ethical issues in giving customers an award for consumption behavior without notifying them first?
2. Do you see this as a potential violation of privacy? Explain.
3. How would you handle the situation if you were Barnard?

Build Your Business Plan

BUSINESS ETHICS AND SOCIAL RESPONSIBILITY

Think about which industry you are considering competing in with your product/service. Is there any kind of questionable practices in the way the product has been traditionally sold? Produced? Advertised? Have there been any recent accusations regarding safety within the industry? What about any environmental concerns?

For example, if you are thinking of opening a lawn care business, you need to be thinking about what possible effects the chemicals you are using will have on the client and the environment. You have a responsibility to keep your customers safe and healthy. You also have the social responsibility to let the community know of any damaging effect you may be directly or indirectly responsible for.

See for Yourself Videocase

REBUILDING AMERICA'S TRUST IN BUSINESS

Corporate scandals, a growing awareness of environmental issues, and the most recent global recession have greatly altered the public's perspective of corporate America. Gone are the days in which consumers blindly trusted company publicity and rhetoric. The public's trust in business has been shattered, and many companies have a long way to go to earn it back.

The Arthur Page Society and the Business Roundtable Institute for Corporate Ethics are dedicated to corporate accountability and ethics. The organizations released a study addressing Americans' mistrust of business and how corporations can begin to win back the hearts and minds of consumers. The study, entitled "The Dynamics of Public Trust in Business— Emerging Opportunities for Leaders," shows that public trust in business has reached a low point. As the economy begins to recover, trust in business has increased slightly. However, trust of business continues to be a serious challenge for businesses to overcome. This presents major difficulties for businesses as trust is the glue that holds relationships together.

A major issue appears to be the imbalance of power. The public is angry over corporate bailouts and rising unemployment while corporate management still makes huge profits. The government defended corporate bailouts as a way to keep large companies from failing (which could have worsened the recession). Most of the money has since been paid back, and the government has made a profit. Still, the Occupy Wall Street protests in 2011 revealed how outraged many consumers felt toward what they believed was a failure to hold executives accountable and the disparity between employee and executive pay. This distrust of business is not limited to the United States. Financial services institutions and banks have the lowest rankings in consumer trust worldwide. According to the Edelman Trust Barometer, only 45 percent of global consumers trust financial services institutions, and 47 percent of global consumers trust banks. More recent scandals at JP Morgan Chase, Peregrine Financial, and British financial services firm Barclays continue to keep trust in this sector low.

Although the Arthur Page Society and the Business Roundtable see their report as a way to start a national dialogue, the report does offer a series of suggestions for businesses. First and foremost, the balance of power must be equalized. Companies must focus on creating mutual value and leaders must try to gain and retain trust. The study also suggests that corporations create quality products/services, sell products/services at fair prices, create and maintain positive employment practices, give investors a fair return, remain active in social responsibility, and create transparency.

Companies can use these suggestions to change their policies and behavior, but in order to be truly successful, companies must embrace these values. Perhaps the most important step companies can take is to align business interests with public interests. For example, it's no longer enough that businesses earn money for their shareholders; people want to know exactly how that money is being earned. Another example involves the growing public concern regarding how businesses affect the environment—investors want details on a business's impact and what that business is doing to be more sustainable. As the public fights to make its desires known regarding business behavior,

businesses that sincerely want to help the world are receiving some help. Maryland, Vermont, New York, California, and three other states have made "benefit corporations" legal. These corporations must make their values public, report yearly on their socially beneficial behavior, and agree to third-party audits of their social responsibility actions. Acquiring this designation requires the approval of more than half a company's shareholders. Companies can establish themselves as B corporations (more than 30,000 companies hold this designation), which certifies their socially responsible focus. It is entirely possible for businesses to regain public trust, but it means a change in values for many businesses in today's corporate America.[81]

DISCUSSION QUESTIONS

1. What are some of the reasons cited in the Arthur Page Society and the Business Roundtable Institute for Corporate Ethics report for public distrust of corporations?

2. What are some of the recommendations made by the report? Can you think of any other recommendations to give companies on how to behave more ethically?

3. What are the benefits of being perceived as an ethical company? What are the downsides of having a reputation for ethical misconduct?

Remember to check out our Online Learning Center at www.mhhe.com/ferrell9e.

Team Exercise

Sam Walton, founder of Walmart, had an early strategy for growing his business related to pricing. The "Opening Price Point" strategy used by Walton involved offering the introductory product in a product line at the lowest point in the market. For example, a minimally equipped microwave oven would sell for less than anyone else in town could sell the same unit. The strategy was that if consumers saw a product, such as the microwave, and saw it as a good value, they would assume that all of the microwaves were good values. Walton also noted that most people don't buy the entry-level product; they want more features and capabilities and often trade up.

Form teams and assign the role of defending this strategy or casting this strategy as an unethical act. Present your thoughts on either side of the issue.

Appendix B

The Legal and Regulatory Environment

Business law refers to the rules and regulations that govern the conduct of business. Problems in this area come from the failure to keep promises, misunderstandings, disagreements about expectations, or, in some cases, attempts to take advantage of others. The regulatory environment offers a framework and enforcement system in order to provide a fair playing field for all businesses. The regulatory environment is created based on inputs from competitors, customers, employees, special interest groups, and the public's elected representatives. Lobbying by pressure groups who try to influence legislation often shapes the legal and regulatory environment.

Sources of Law

Laws are classified as either criminal or civil. *Criminal law* not only prohibits a specific kind of action, such as unfair competition or mail fraud, but also imposes a fine or imprisonment as punishment for violating the law. A violation of a criminal law is thus called a crime. *Civil law* defines all the laws not classified as criminal, and it specifies the rights and duties of individuals and organizations (including businesses). Violations of civil law may result in fines but not imprisonment. The primary difference between criminal and civil law is that criminal laws are enforced by the state or nation, whereas civil laws are enforced through the court system by individuals or organizations.

Criminal and civil laws are derived from four sources: the Constitution (constitutional law), precedents established by judges (common law), federal and state statutes (statutory law), and federal and state administrative agencies (administrative law). Federal administrative agencies established by Congress control and influence business by enforcing laws and regulations to encourage competition and protect consumers, workers, and the environment. The Supreme Court is the ultimate authority on legal and regulatory decisions for appropriate conduct in business.

Courts and the Resolution of Disputes

The primary method of resolving conflicts and business disputes is through **lawsuits,** where one individual or organization takes another to court using civil laws. The legal system, therefore, provides a forum for businesspeople to resolve disputes based on our legal foundations. The courts may decide when harm or damage results from the actions of others.

Because lawsuits are so frequent in the world of business, it is important to understand more about the court system where such disputes are resolved. Both financial restitution and specific actions to undo wrongdoing can result from going before a court to resolve a conflict. All decisions made in the courts are based on criminal and civil laws derived from the legal and regulatory system.

A businessperson may win a lawsuit in court and receive a judgment, or court order, requiring the loser of the suit to pay monetary damages. However, this does not guarantee the victor will be able to collect those damages. If the loser of the suit lacks the financial resources to pay the judgment—for example, if the loser is a bankrupt business—the winner of the suit may not be able to collect the award. Most business lawsuits involve a request for a sum of money, but some lawsuits request that a court specifically order a person or organization to do or to refrain from doing a certain act, such as slamming telephone customers.

Workers exit a Chrysler truck plant. Because it could not come to an agreement with its debt holders by a prescribed deadline, Chrysler was forced to file for bankruptcy during the recession. Chrysler managed to survive bankruptcy, paid back its loans to the U.S. government, and became profitable once more.

The Court System

Jurisdiction is the legal power of a court, through a judge, to interpret and apply the law and make a binding decision in a particular case. In some instances, other courts will not enforce the decision of a prior court because it lacked jurisdiction. Federal courts are granted jurisdiction by the Constitution or by Congress. State legislatures and constitutions determine which state courts hear certain types of cases. Courts of general jurisdiction hear all types of cases; those of limited jurisdiction hear only specific types of cases. The Federal Bankruptcy Court, for example, hears only cases involving bankruptcy. There is some combination of limited and general jurisdiction courts in every state.

In a **trial court** (whether in a court of general or limited jurisdiction and whether in the state or the federal system), two tasks must be completed. First, the court (acting through the judge or a jury) must determine the facts of the case. In other words, if there is conflicting evidence, the judge or jury must decide who to believe. Second, the judge must decide which law or set of laws is pertinent to the case and must then apply those laws to resolve the dispute.

An **appellate court,** on the other hand, deals solely with appeals relating to the interpretation of law. Thus, when you hear about a case being appealed, it is not retried, but rather reevaluated. Appellate judges do not hear witnesses but instead base their decisions on a written transcript of the original trial. Moreover, appellate courts do not draw factual conclusions; the appellate judge is limited to deciding whether the trial judge made a mistake in interpreting the law that probably affected the outcome of the trial. If the trial judge made no mistake (or if mistakes would not have changed the result of the trial), the appellate court will let the trial court's decision stand. If the appellate court finds a mistake, it usually sends the case back to the trial court so that the mistake can be corrected. Correction may involve the granting of a new trial. On occasion, appellate courts modify the verdict of the trial court without sending the case back to the trial court.

Alternative Dispute Resolution Methods

Although the main remedy for business disputes is a lawsuit, other dispute resolution methods are becoming popular. The schedules of state and federal trial courts are often crowded; long delays between the filing of a case and the trial date are common. Further, complex cases can become quite expensive to pursue. As a result, many businesspeople are turning to alternative methods of resolving business arguments: mediation and arbitration, the mini-trial, and litigation in a private court.

Mediation is a form of negotiation to resolve a dispute by bringing in one or more third-party mediators, usually chosen by the disputing parties, to help reach a settlement. The mediator suggests different ways to resolve a dispute between the parties. The mediator's resolution is nonbinding— that is, the parties do not have to accept the mediator's suggestions; they are strictly voluntary.

Arbitration involves submission of a dispute to one or more third-party arbitrators, usually chosen by the disputing parties, whose decision usually is final. Arbitration differs from mediation in that an arbitrator's decision must be followed, whereas a mediator merely offers suggestions and facilitates negotiations. Cases may be submitted to arbitration because a contract—such as a labor contract—requires it or because the parties agree to do so. Some consumers are barred from taking claims to court by agreements drafted by banks, brokers, health plans, and others. Instead, they are required to take complaints to mandatory arbitration. Arbitration can be an attractive alternative to a lawsuit because it is often cheaper and quicker, and the parties frequently can choose arbitrators who are knowledgeable about the particular area of business at issue.

A method of dispute resolution that may become increasingly important in settling complex disputes is the **mini-trial,** in which both parties agree to present a summarized version of their case to an independent third party. That person then advises them of his or her impression of the probable outcome if the case were to be tried. Representatives of both sides then attempt to negotiate a settlement based on the advisor's recommendations. For example, employees in a large corporation who believe they have muscular or skeletal stress injuries caused by the strain of

Need help understanding Mediation vs Arbitration?

http://bit.ly/FerrellQR10-2

Can't Scan? Try ScanLife at your app store.

repetitive motion in using a computer could agree to a mini-trial to address a dispute related to damages. Although the mini-trial itself does not resolve the dispute, it can help the parties resolve the case before going to court. Because the mini-trial is not subject to formal court rules, it can save companies a great deal of money, allowing them to recognize the weaknesses in a particular case.

In some areas of the country, disputes can be submitted to a private nongovernmental court for resolution. In a sense, a **private court system** is similar to arbitration in that an independent third party resolves the case after hearing both sides of the story. Trials in private courts may be either informal or highly formal, depending on the people involved. Businesses typically agree to have their disputes decided in private courts to save time and money.

Regulatory Administrative Agencies

Federal and state administrative agencies (listed in Table B.1) also have some judicial powers. Many administrative agencies, such as the Federal Trade Commission, decide disputes that involve their regulations. In such disputes, the resolution process is usually called a "hearing" rather than a trial. In these cases, an administrative law judge decides all issues.

Federal regulatory agencies influence many business activities and cover product liability, safety, and the regulation or deregulation of public utilities. Usually, these bodies have the power to enforce specific laws, such as the Federal Trade Commission Act, and have some discretion in establishing

TABLE B.1   The Major Regulatory Agencies

Agency	Major Areas of Responsibility
Federal Trade Commission (FTC)	Enforces laws and guidelines regarding business practices; takes action to stop false and deceptive advertising and labeling.
Food and Drug Administration (FDA)	Enforces laws and regulations to prevent distribution of adulterated or misbranded foods, drugs, medical devices, cosmetics, veterinary products, and particularly hazardous consumer products.
Consumer Product Safety Commission (CPSC)	Ensures compliance with the Consumer Product Safety Act, protects the public from unreasonable risk of injury from any consumer product not covered by other regulatory agencies.
Interstate Commerce Commission (ICC)	Regulates franchises, rates, and finances of interstate rail, bus, truck, and water carriers.
Federal Communications Commission (FCC)	Regulates communication by wire, radio, and television in interstate and foreign commerce.
Environmental Protection Agency (EPA)	Develops and enforces environmental protection standards and conducts research into the adverse effects of pollution.
Federal Energy Regulatory Commission (FERC)	Regulates rates and sales of natural gas products, thereby affecting the supply and price of gas available to consumers; also regulates wholesale rates for electricity and gas, pipeline construction, and U.S. imports and exports of natural gas and electricity.
Equal Employment Opportunity Commission (EEOC)	Investigates and resolves discrimination in employment practices.
Federal Aviation Administration (FAA)	Oversees the policies and regulations of the airline industry.
Federal Highway Administration (FHA)	Regulates vehicle safety requirements.
Occupational Safety and Health Administration (OSHA)	Develops policy to promote worker safety and health and investigates infractions.
Securities and Exchange Commission (SEC)	Regulates corporate securities trading and develops protection from fraud and other abuses; provides an accounting oversight board.

operating rules and regulations to guide certain types of industry practices. Because of this discretion and overlapping areas of responsibility, confusion or conflict regarding which agencies have jurisdiction over which activities is common.

Of all the federal regulatory units, the **Federal Trade Commission (FTC)** most influences business activities related to questionable practices that create disputes between businesses and their customers. Although the FTC regulates a variety of business practices, it allocates a large portion of resources to curbing false advertising, misleading pricing, and deceptive packaging and labeling. When it receives a complaint or otherwise has reason to believe that a firm is violating a law, the FTC issues a complaint stating that the business is in violation.

If a company continues the questionable practice, the FTC can issue a cease-and-desist order, which is an order for the business to stop doing whatever has caused the complaint. In such cases, the charged firm can appeal to the federal courts to have the order rescinded. However, the FTC can seek civil penalties in court—up to a maximum penalty of $10,000 a day for each infraction—if a cease-and-desist order is violated. In its battle against unfair pricing, the FTC has issued consent decrees alleging that corporate attempts to engage in price fixing or invitations to competitors to collude are violations even when the competitors in question refuse the invitations. The commission can also require companies to run corrective advertising in response to previous ads considered misleading.

The FTC also assists businesses in complying with laws. New marketing methods are evaluated every year. When general sets of guidelines are needed to improve business practices in a particular industry, the FTC sometimes encourages firms within that industry to establish a set of trade practices voluntarily. The FTC may even sponsor a conference bringing together industry leaders and consumers for the purpose of establishing acceptable trade practices.

Unlike the FTC, other regulatory units are limited to dealing with specific products, services, or business activities. The Food and Drug Administration (FDA) enforces regulations prohibiting the sale and distribution of adulterated, misbranded, or hazardous food and drug products. For example, the FDA outlawed the sale and distribution of most over-the-counter hair-loss remedies after research indicated that few of the products were effective in restoring hair growth.

The Environmental Protection Agency (EPA) develops and enforces environmental protection standards and conducts research into the adverse effects of pollution. The Consumer Product Safety Commission recalls about 300 products a year, ranging from small, inexpensive toys to major appliances. The Consumer Product Safety Commission's website provides details regarding current recalls.

The Consumer Product Safety commission has fallen under increasing scrutiny in the wake of a number of product safety scandals involving children's toys. The most notable of these issues was lead paint discovered in toys produced in China. Other problems have included the manufacture of toys that include small magnets that pose a choking hazard, and lead-tainted costume jewelry.[82]

Important Elements of Business Law

To avoid violating criminal and civil laws, as well as discouraging lawsuits from consumers, employees, suppliers, and others, businesspeople need to be familiar with laws that address business practices.

The Uniform Commercial Code

At one time, states had their own specific laws governing various business practices, and transacting business across state lines was difficult because of the variation in the laws from state to state. To simplify commerce, every state—except Louisiana—has enacted the Uniform Commercial Code (Louisiana has enacted portions of the code). The **Uniform Commercial Code (UCC)** is a set of statutory laws covering several business law topics. Article II of the Uniform Commercial Code, which is discussed in the following paragraphs, has a significant impact on business.

Sales Agreements.   Article II of the Uniform Commercial Code covers sales agreements for goods and services such as installation but does not cover the sale of stocks and bonds, personal services, or real estate. Among its many provisions, Article II stipulates that a sales agreement can be enforced even though it does not specify the selling price or the time or place of delivery. It also requires that a buyer pay a reasonable price for goods at the time of delivery if the buyer and seller have not reached an agreement on price. Specifically, Article II addresses the rights of buyers and sellers, transfers of ownership, warranties, and the legal placement of risk during manufacture and delivery.

Article II also deals with express and implied warranties. An **express warranty** stipulates the specific terms the seller will honor. Many automobile manufacturers, for example, provide three-year or 36,000-mile warranties on their vehicles, during which period they will fix any and all defects specified in the warranty. An **implied warranty** is imposed on the producer or seller by law, although it may not be a written document provided at the time of sale. Under Article II, a consumer may assume that the product for sale has a clear title (in other words, that it is not stolen) and that the product will both serve the purpose for which it was made and sold as well as function as advertised.

The Law of Torts and Fraud

A **tort** is a private or civil wrong other than breach of contract. For example, a tort can result if the driver of a Domino's Pizza delivery car loses control of the vehicle and damages property or injures a person. In the case of the delivery car accident, the injured persons might sue the driver and the owner of the company—Domino's in this case—for damages resulting from the accident.

Fraud is a purposefully unlawful act to deceive or manipulate in order to damage others. Thus, in some cases, a tort may also represent a violation of criminal law. Health care fraud has become a major issue in the courts.

An important aspect of tort law involves **product liability**—businesses' legal responsibility for any negligence in the design, production, sale, and consumption of products. Product liability laws have evolved from both common and statutory law. Some states have expanded the concept of product liability to include injuries by products whether or not the producer is proven negligent. Under this strict product liability, a consumer who files suit because of an injury has to prove only that the product was defective, that the defect caused the injury, and that the defect made the product unreasonably dangerous. For example, a carving knife is expected to be sharp and is not considered defective if you cut your finger using it. But an electric knife could be considered defective and unreasonably dangerous if it continued to operate after being switched off.

Reforming tort law, particularly in regard to product liability, has become a hot political issue as businesses look for relief from huge judgments in lawsuits. Although many lawsuits are warranted—few

would disagree that a wrong has occurred when a patient dies because of negligence during a medical procedure or when a child is seriously injured by a defective toy, and that the families deserve some compensation—many suits are not. Because of multimillion-dollar judgments, companies are trying to minimize their liability, and sometimes they pass on the costs of the damage awards to their customers in the form of higher prices. Some states have passed laws limiting damage awards and some tort reform is occurring at the federal level. Table B.2 lists the state courts systems the U.S. Chamber of Commerce's Institute for Legal Reform has identified as being "friendliest" and "least friendly" to business in terms of juries' fairness, judges' competence and impartiality, and other factors.

The Law of Contracts

Virtually every business transaction is carried out by means of a **contract,** a mutual agreement between two or more parties that can be enforced in a court if one party chooses not to comply with the terms of the contract. If you rent an apartment or house, for example, your lease is a contract. If you have

---

TABLE B.2   State Court Systems' Reputations for Supporting Business

Most Friendly to Business	Least Friendly to Business
Delaware	Mississippi
Nebraska	West Virginia
Virginia	Alabama
Iowa	Louisiana
Idaho	California
Utah	Texas
New Hampshire	Illinois
Minnesota	Montana
Kansas	Arkansas
Wisconsin	Missouri

Source: U.S. Chamber of Commerce Institute for Legal Reform, in Martin Kasindorf, "Robin Hood Is Alive in Court, Say Those Seeking Lawsuit Limits," *USA Today*, March 8, 2004, p. 4A

borrowed money under a student loan program, you have a contractual agreement to repay the money. Many aspects of contract law are covered under the Uniform Commercial Code.

A "handshake deal" is in most cases as fully and completely binding as a written, signed contract agreement. Indeed, many oil-drilling and construction contractors have for years agreed to take on projects on the basis of such handshake deals. However, individual states require that some contracts be in writing to be enforceable. Most states require that at least some of the following contracts be in writing:

- Contracts involving the sale of land or an interest in land
- Contracts to pay somebody else's debt
- Contracts that cannot be fulfilled within one year
- Contracts for the sale of goods that cost more than $500 (required by the Uniform Commercial Code)

Only those contracts that meet certain requirements—called *elements*—are enforceable by the courts. A person or business seeking to enforce a contract must show that it contains the following elements: voluntary agreement, consideration, contractual capacity of the parties, and legality.

For any agreement to be considered a legal contract, all persons involved must agree to be bound by the terms of the contract. *Voluntary agreement* typically comes about when one party makes an offer and the other accepts. If both the offer and the acceptance are freely, voluntarily, and knowingly made, the acceptance forms the basis for the contract. If, however, either the offer or the acceptance are the result of fraud or force, the individual or organization subject to the fraud or force can void, or invalidate, the resulting agreement or receive compensation for damages.

The second requirement for enforcement of a contract is that it must be supported by *consideration*—that is, money or something of value must be given in return for fulfilling a contract. As a general rule, a person cannot be forced to abide by the terms of a promise unless that person receives a consideration. The something of value could be money, goods, services, or even a promise to do or not to do something.

Contractual capacity is the legal ability to enter into a contract. As a general rule, a court cannot enforce a contract if either party to the agreement lacks contractual capacity. A person's contractual capacity may be limited or nonexistent if he or she is a minor (under the age of 18), mentally unstable, retarded, insane, or intoxicated.

Legality is the state or condition of being lawful. For an otherwise binding contract to be enforceable, both the purpose of and the consideration for the contract must be legal. A contract in which a bank loans money at a rate of interest prohibited by law, a practice known as usury, would be an illegal contract, for example. The fact that one of the parties may commit an illegal act while performing a contract does not render the contract itself illegal, however.

Breach of contract is the failure or refusal of a party to a contract to live up to his or her promises. In the case of an apartment lease, failure to pay rent would be considered breach of contract. The breaching party—the one who fails to comply—may be liable for monetary damages that he or she causes the other person.

The Law of Agency

An **agency** is a common business relationship created when one person acts on behalf of another and under that person's control. Two parties are involved in an agency relationship: The **principal** is the one who wishes to have a specific task accomplished; the **agent** is the one who acts on behalf of the principal to accomplish the task. Authors, movie stars, and athletes often employ agents to help them obtain the best contract terms.

An agency relationship is created by the mutual agreement of the principal and the agent. It is usually not necessary that such an agreement be in writing, although putting it in writing is certainly advisable. An agency relationship continues as long as both the principal and the agent so desire. It can be terminated by mutual agreement, by fulfillment of the purpose of the agency, by the refusal of either party to continue in the relationship, or by the death of either the principal or the agent. In most cases, a principal grants authority to the agent through a formal *power of attorney,* which is a legal document authorizing a person to act as someone else's agent. The power of attorney can be used for any agency relationship, and its use is not limited to lawyers. For instance, in real estate transactions, often a lawyer or real estate agent is given power of attorney with the authority to purchase real estate for the buyer. Accounting firms often give employees agency relationships in making financial transactions.

Both officers and directors of corporations are fiduciaries, or people of trust, who use due care and loyalty as an agent in making decisions on behalf of the organization. This relationship creates a duty of care, also called duty of diligence, to make informed decisions. These agents of the corporation are not held responsible for negative outcomes if they are informed and diligent in their decisions. The duty of loyalty means that all decisions should be in the interests of the corporation and its stakeholders. Many people believe that executives at financial firms such as Countrywide Financial, Lehman Brothers, and Merrill Lynch failed to carry out their fiduciary duties. Lawsuits from shareholders called for the officers and directors to pay large sums of money from their own pockets.

The Law of Property

Property law is extremely broad in scope because it covers the ownership and transfer of all kinds of real, personal, and intellectual property. **Real property** consists of real estate and everything permanently attached to it; **personal property** basically is everything else. Personal property can be further subdivided into tangible and intangible property. *Tangible property* refers to items that have a physical existence, such as automobiles, business inventory, and clothing. *Intangible property* consists of rights and duties; its existence may be represented by a document or by some other tangible item. For example, accounts receivable, stock in a corporation, goodwill, and trademarks are all examples of intangible personal property. **Intellectual property** refers to property, such as musical works, artwork, books, and computer software, that is generated by a person's creative activities.

Copyrights, patents, and trademarks provide protection to the owners of property by giving them the exclusive right to use it. *Copyrights* protect the ownership rights on material (often intellectual property) such as books, music, videos, photos, and computer software. The creators of such works, or their heirs, generally have exclusive rights to the published or unpublished works for the creator's lifetime, plus 50 years. *Patents* give inventors exclusive rights to their invention for 20 years. The most intense competition for patents is in the pharmaceutical industry. Most patents take a minimum of 18 months to secure.

A *trademark* is a brand (name, mark, or symbol) that is registered with the U.S. Patent and Trademark Office and is thus legally protected from use by any other firm. Among the symbols that have been so protected are McDonald's golden arches and Coca-Cola's distinctive bottle shape. It is estimated that large multinational firms may have as many as 15,000 conflicts related to trademarks. Companies are diligent about protecting their trademarks both to avoid confusion in consumers' minds and because a term that becomes part of everyday language can no longer be trademarked. The names *aspirin* and *nylon,* for example, were once the exclusive property of their creators but became so widely used as product names (rather than brand names) that now anyone can use them.

As the trend toward globalization of trade continues, and more and more businesses trade across national boundaries, protecting property rights, particularly intellectual property such as computer software, has become an increasing challenge. While a company may be able to register as a trademark a brand name or symbol in its home country, it may not be able to secure that protection abroad. Some countries have copyright and patent laws that are less strict than those of the United States; some countries will not enforce U.S. laws. China, for example, has often been criticized for permitting U.S. goods to be counterfeited there. Such counterfeiting harms not only the sales of U.S. companies but also their reputations if the knockoffs are of poor quality. Thus, businesses engaging in foreign trade may have to take extra steps to protect their property because local laws may be insufficient to protect them.

The Law of Bankruptcy

Although few businesses and individuals intentionally fail to repay (or default on) their debts, sometimes they cannot fulfill their financial obligations. Individuals may charge goods and services beyond their ability to pay for them. Businesses may take on too much debt in order to finance growth, or business events such as an increase in the cost of commodities can bankrupt a company. An option of last resort in these cases is bankruptcy, or legal insolvency. Some well-known companies that have declared bankruptcy include Hostess, American Airlines, and Eastman Kodak.

Individuals or companies may ask a bankruptcy court to declare them unable to pay their debts and thus release them from the obligation of repaying those debts. The debtor's assets may then be sold to pay off as much of the debt as possible. In the case of a personal bankruptcy, although the individual is released from repaying debts and can start over with a clean slate, obtaining credit after bankruptcy proceedings is very difficult. About 2 million households in the United States filed for bankruptcy in 2005, the most ever. However, a new, more restrictive law went into effect in late 2005, allowing fewer consumers to use bankruptcy to eliminate their debts. The law makes it harder for consumers to prove that they should be allowed to clear their debts for what is called a "fresh start" or Chapter 7 bankruptcy. Although the person or company in debt usually initiates bankruptcy proceedings, creditors may also initiate them. The subprime mortgage crisis of early 2008 caused a string of bankruptcies among individuals, and Chapter 7 and 11 bankruptcies among banks and other businesses as well. Tougher bankruptcy laws and a slowing economy converged on the subprime crisis to create a situation in which bankruptcy filings skyrocketed. Table B.3 describes the various levels of bankruptcy protection a business or individual may seek.

Laws Affecting Business Practices

One of the government's many roles is to act as a watchdog to ensure that businesses behave in accordance with the wishes of society. Congress has enacted a number of laws that affect business practices; some of the most important of these are summarized in Table B.4. Many state legislatures have enacted similar laws governing business within specific states.

The **Sherman Antitrust Act,** passed in 1890 to prevent businesses from restraining trade and monopolizing markets, condemns "every contract, combination, or conspiracy in restraint of trade." For example, a request that a competitor agree to fix prices or divide markets would, if accepted, result in a violation of the Sherman Act. AT&T faced serious resistance from the U.S. Justice Department after it announced its bid to acquire T-Mobile. Because there are only a few dominant cell phone carriers in the market, the Justice Department believed that the merger would make AT&T too powerful. Critics feared that the merger would lead to higher prices for consumers. Due to increased pressure from the Justice Department, AT&T dropped its bid to acquire T-Mobile—a move that cost it a $4 billion charge.[83] The Sherman Antitrust Act, still highly relevant 100 years after its passage, is being copied throughout the world as the basis for regulating fair competition.

Because the provisions of the Sherman Antitrust Act are rather vague, courts have not always interpreted it as its creators intended. The Clayton Act was passed in 1914 to limit specific activities that can reduce competition. The **Clayton Act** prohibits price discrimination, tying and exclusive agreements, and the acquisition of stock in another corporation where the effect may be to substantially lessen competition or tend to create a monopoly. In addition, the Clayton Act prohibits members of one company's board of directors from holding seats on the boards of competing corporations. The act also

TABLE B.3	**Types of Bankruptcy**
Chapter 7	Requires that the business be dissolved and its assets liquidated, or sold, to pay off the debts. Individuals declaring Chapter 7 retain a limited amount of exempt assets, the amount of which may be determined by state or federal law, at the debtor's option. Although the type and value of exempt assets varies from state to state, most states' laws allow a bankrupt individual to keep an automobile, some household goods, clothing, furnishings, and at least some of the value of the debtor's residence. All nonexempt assets must be sold to pay debts.
Chapter 11	Temporarily frees a business from its financial obligations while it reorganizes and works out a payment plan with its creditors. The indebted company continues to operate its business during bankruptcy proceedings. Often, the business sells off assets and less-profitable subsidiaries to raise cash to pay off its immediate obligations.
Chapter 13	Similar to Chapter 11 but limited to individuals. This proceeding allows an individual to establish a three- to five-year plan for repaying his or her debt. Under this plan, an individual ultimately may repay as little as 10 percent of his or her debt.

TABLE B.4   **Major Federal Laws Affecting Business Practices**

Act (Date Enacted)	Purpose
Sherman Antitrust Act (1890)	Prohibits contracts, combinations, or conspiracies to restrain trade; establishes as a misdemeanor monopolizing or attempting to monopolize.
Clayton Act (1914)	Prohibits specific practices such as price discrimination, exclusive dealer arrangements, and stock acquisitions in which the effect may notably lessen competition or tend to create a monopoly.
Federal Trade Commission Act (1914)	Created the Federal Trade Commission; also gives the FTC investigatory powers to be used in preventing unfair methods of competition.
Robinson-Patman Act (1936)	Prohibits price discrimination that lessens competition among wholesalers or retailers; prohibits producers from giving disproportionate services of facilities to large buyers.
Wheeler-Lea Act (1938)	Prohibits unfair and deceptive acts and practices regardless of whether competition is injured; places advertising of foods and drugs under the jurisdiction of the FTC.
Lanham Act (1946)	Provides protections and regulation of brand names, brand marks, trade names, and trademarks.
Celler-Kefauver Act (1950)	Prohibits any corporation engaged in commerce from acquiring the whole or any part of the stock or other share of the capital assets of another corporation when the effect substantially lessens competition or tends to create a monopoly.
Fair Packaging and Labeling Act (1966)	Makes illegal the unfair or deceptive packaging or labeling of consumer products.
Magnuson-Moss Warranty (FTC) Act (1975)	Provides for minimum disclosure standards for written consumer product warranties; defines minimum consent standards for written warranties; allows the FTC to prescribe interpretive rules in policy statements regarding unfair or deceptive practices.
Consumer Goods Pricing Act (1975)	Prohibits the use of price maintenance agreements among manufacturers and resellers in interstate commerce.
Antitrust Improvements Act (1976)	Requires large corporations to inform federal regulators of prospective mergers or acquisitions so that they can be studied for any possible violations of the law.
Trademark Counterfeiting Act (1980)	Provides civil and criminal penalties against those who deal in counterfeit consumer goods or any counterfeit goods that can threaten health or safety.
Trademark Law Revision Act (1988)	Amends the Lanham Act to allow brands not yet introduced to be protected through registration with the Patent and Trademark Office.
Nutrition Labeling and Education Act (1990)	Prohibits exaggerated health claims and requires all processed foods to contain labels with nutritional information.
Telephone Consumer Protection Act (1991)	Establishes procedures to avoid unwanted telephone solicitations; prohibits marketers from using automated telephone dialing system or an artificial or prerecorded voice to certain telephone lines.
Federal Trademark Dilution Act (1995)	Provides trademark owners the right to protect trademarks and requires relinquishment of names that match or parallel existing trademarks.
Digital Millennium Copyright Act (1998)	Refined copyright laws to protect digital versions of copyrighted materials, including music and movies.

continued

TABLE B.4   continued

Act (Date Enacted)	Purpose
Children's Online Privacy Protection Act (2000)	Regulates the collection of personally identifiable information (name, address, e-mail address, hobbies, interests, or information collected through cookies) online from children under age 13.
Sarbanes-Oxley Act (2002)	Made securities fraud a criminal offense; stiffened penalties for corporate fraud; created an accounting oversight board; and instituted numerous other provisions designed to increase corporate transparency and compliance.
Do Not Call Implementation Act (2003)	Directs FCC and FTC to coordinate so their rules are consistent regarding telemarketing call practices, including the Do Not Call Registry.
Dodd-Frank Wall Street Reform and Consumer Protection Act (2010)	Increases accountability and transparency in the financial industry, protects consumers from deceptive financial practices, and establishes the Bureau of Consumer Financial Protection.

exempts farm cooperatives and labor organizations from antitrust laws.

In spite of these laws regulating business practices, there are still many questions about the regulation of business. For instance, it is difficult to determine what constitutes an acceptable degree of competition and whether a monopoly is harmful to a particular market. Many mergers were permitted that resulted in less competition in the banking, publishing, and automobile industries. In some industries, such as utilities, it is not cost effective to have too many competitors. For this reason, the government permits utility monopolies, although recently, the telephone, electricity, and communications industries have been deregulated. Furthermore, the antitrust laws are often rather vague and require interpretation, which may vary from judge to judge and court to court. Thus, what one judge defines as a monopoly or trust today may be permitted by another judge a few years from now. Businesspeople need to understand what the law says on these issues and try to conduct their affairs within the bounds of these laws.

The Internet: Legal and Regulatory Issues

Our use and dependence on the Internet is increasingly creating a potential legal problem for businesses. With this growing use come questions of maintaining an acceptable level of privacy for consumers and proper competitive use of the medium. Some might consider that tracking individuals who visit or "hit" their website by attaching a "cookie" (identifying you as a website visitor for potential recontact and tracking your movement throughout the site) is an improper use of the Internet for business purposes. Others may find such practices acceptable and similar to the practices of non-Internet retailers who copy information from checks or ask customers for their name, address, or phone number before they will process a transaction. There are few specific laws that

Whether you like it or not, Google, like Yahoo! and AOL, tracks people's Web browsing patterns. By tracking the sites you visit, the companies' advertisers can aim ads targeted closer to your interests.

regulate business on the Internet, but the standards for acceptable behavior that are reflected in the basic laws and regulations designed for traditional businesses can be applied to business on the Internet as well. One law aimed specifically at advertising on the internet is the CAN-SPAM Act of 2004. The law restricts unsolicited e-mail advertisements by requiring the consent of the recipient. Furthermore, the CAN-SPAM Act follows the "opt-out" model wherein recipients can elect to not receive further emails from a sender simply by clicking on a link.[85]

The central focus for future legislation of business conducted on the Internet is the protection of personal privacy. The present basis of personal privacy protection is the U.S. Constitution, various Supreme Court rulings, and laws such as the 1971 Fair Credit Reporting Act, the 1978 Right to Financial Privacy Act, and the 1974 Privacy Act, which deals with the release of government records. With few regulations on the use of information by businesses, companies legally buy and sell information on customers to gain competitive advantage. Sometimes existing laws are not enough to protect people, and the ease with which information on customers can be obtained becomes a problem. For example, identity theft has increased due to the proliferation of the use of the Internet. A disturbing trend is how many children have had their identities stolen. One study of 40,000 children revealed that more than 10 percent have had their Social Security numbers stolen. The rates of child identity theft have risen since the advent of the Internet.[86] It has been suggested that the treatment of personal data as property will ensure privacy rights by recognizing that customers have a right to control the use of their personal data.

Internet use is different from traditional interaction with businesses in that it is readily accessible, and most online businesses are able to develop databases of information on customers. Congress has restricted the development of databases on children using the Internet. The Children's Online Privacy Protection Act of 2000 prohibits website and Internet providers from seeking personal information from children under age 13 without parental consent. Companies are still running afoul of COPPA. Playdom, a Disney-owned online game company, was forced to pay $3 million to settle allegations that it had collected and disclosed the personal information of children under 13 years of age.[87]

The Internet has also created a copyright dilemma for some organizations that have found that the web addresses of other online firms either match or are very similar to their company trademark. "Cybersquatters" attempt to sell back the registration of these matching sites to the trademark owner. Companies such as Taco Bell, MTC, and KFC have paid thousands of dollars to gain control of domain names that match or parallel company trademarks. The Federal Trademark Dilution Act of 1995 helps companies address this conflict. The act provides trademark owners the right to protect trademarks, prevents the use of trademark-protected entities, and requires the relinquishment of names that match or closely parallel company trademarks. The reduction of geographic barriers, speed of response, and memory capability of the Internet will continue to create new challenges for the legal and regulatory environment in the future.

Legal Pressure for Responsible Business Conduct

To ensure greater compliance with society's desires, both federal and state governments are moving toward increased organizational accountability for misconduct. Before 1991, laws mainly punished those employees directly responsible for an offense. Under new guidelines established by the Federal Sentencing Guidelines for Organizations (FSGO), however, both the responsible employees and the firms that employ them are held accountable for violations of federal law. Thus, the government now places responsibility for controlling and preventing misconduct squarely on the shoulders of top management. The main objectives of the federal guidelines are to train employees, self-monitor and supervise employee conduct, deter unethical acts, and punish those organizational members who engage in illegal acts.

A 2004 amendment to the FSGO requires that a business's governing authority be well informed about its ethics program with respect to content, implementation, and effectiveness. This places the responsibility squarely on the shoulders of the firm's leadership, usually the board of directors. The board must ensure that there is a high-ranking manager accountable for the day-to-day operational oversight of the ethics program. The board must provide for adequate authority, resources, and access to the board or an appropriate subcommittee of the board. The board must ensure that there are confidential mechanisms available so that the organization's employees and agents may report or seek guidance about potential or actual misconduct without fear of retaliation. Finally, the board is required to oversee the discovery of risks and to design, implement, and modify approaches to deal with those risks.

If an organization's culture and policies reward or provide opportunities to engage in misconduct through lack of managerial concern or failure to comply with the seven minimum requirements of the FSGO (provided in Table B.5), then the organization may incur not only penalties but also the loss of customer trust, public confidence, and other intangible assets. For this reason, organizations cannot succeed solely through a legalistic approach to compliance with the sentencing guidelines; top management must cultivate high ethical standards that will

---

TABLE B.5   Seven Steps to Compliance

1. Develop standards and procedures to reduce the propensity for criminal conduct.

2. Designate a high-level compliance manager or ethics officer to oversee the compliance program.

3. Avoid delegating authority to people known to have a propensity to engage in misconduct.

4. Communicate standards and procedures to employees, other agents, and independent contractors through training programs and publications.

5. Establish systems to monitor and audit misconduct and to allow employees and agents to report criminal activity.

6. Enforce standards and punishments consistently across all employees in the organization.

7. Respond immediately to misconduct and take reasonable steps to prevent further criminal conduct.

Source: United States Sentencing Commission, *Federal Sentencing Guidelines for Organizations,* 1991.

serve as barriers to illegal conduct. The organization must want to be a good citizen and recognize the importance of compliance to successful workplace activities and relationships.

The federal guidelines also require businesses to develop programs that can detect—and that will deter employees from engaging in—misconduct. To be considered effective, such compliance programs must include disclosure of any wrongdoing, cooperation with the government, and acceptance of responsibility for the misconduct. Codes of ethics, employee ethics training, hotlines (direct 800 phone numbers), compliance directors, newsletters, brochures, and other communication methods are typical components of a compliance program. The ethics component, discussed in Chapter 2, acts as a buffer, keeping firms away from the thin line that separates unethical and illegal conduct.

Despite the existing legislation, a number of ethics scandals in the early 2000s led Congress to pass—almost unanimously—the **Sarbanes-Oxley Act,** which criminalized securities fraud and strengthened penalties for corporate fraud. It also created an accounting oversight board that requires corporations to establish codes of ethics for financial reporting and to develop greater transparency in financial reports to investors and other interested parties. Additionally, the law requires top corporate executives to sign off on their firms' financial reports, and they risk fines and jail sentences if they misrepresent their companies' financial position. Table B.6 summarizes the major provisions of the Sarbanes-Oxley Act.

The Sarbanes Oxley Act has created a number of concerns and is considered burdensome and expensive to corporations. Large corporations report spending more than $4 million each year to comply

TABLE B.6   Major Provisions of the Sarbanes-Oxley Act

1. Requires the establishment of a Public Company Accounting Oversight Board in charge of regulations administered by the Securities and Exchange Commission.

2. Requires CEOs and CFOs to certify that their companies' financial statements are true and without misleading statements.

3. Requires that corporate boards of directors' audit committees consist of independent members who have no material interests in the company.

4. Prohibits corporations from making or offering loans to officers and board members.

5. Requires codes of ethics for senior financial officers; code must be registered with the SEC.

6. Prohibits accounting firms from providing both auditing and consulting services to the same client without the approval of the client firm's audit committee.

7. Requires company attorneys to report wrongdoing to top managers and, if necessary, to the board of directors; if managers and directors fail to respond to reports of wrongdoing, the attorney should stop representing the company.

8. Mandates "whistleblower protection" for persons who disclose wrongdoing to authorities.

9. Requires financial securities analysts to certify that their recommendations are based on objective reports.

10. Requires mutual fund managers to disclose how they vote shareholder proxies, giving investors information about how their shares influence decisions.

11. Establishes a 10-year penalty for mail/wire fraud.

12. Prohibits the two senior auditors from working on a corporation's account for more than five years; other auditors are prohibited from working on an account for more than seven years. In other words, accounting firms must rotate individual auditors from one account to another from time to time.

Source: O. C. Ferrell, John Fraedrich, and Linda Ferrell, *Business Ethics: Ethical Decision Making and Cases,* 8th ed. (Mason, OH: South-Western Cengage Learning, 2011), pp. 108–109.

with the Act according to Financial Executives International. The Act has caused more than 500 public companies a year to report problems in their accounting systems. Additionally, Sarbanes-Oxley failed to prevent and detect the widespread misconduct of financial institutions that led to the financial crisis.

On the other hand, there are many benefits, including greater accountability of top managers and boards of directors, that improve investor confidence and protect employees, especially their retirement plans. It is believed that the law has more benefits than drawbacks—with the greatest benefit being that boards of directors and top managers are better informed. Some companies such as Cisco and Pitney

Bowes report improved efficiency and cost savings from better financial information.

In spite of the benefits Sarbanes-Oxley offers, it did not prevent widespread corporate corruption from leading to the most recent recession. The resulting financial crisis prompted the Obama administration to create new regulation to reform Wall Street and the financial industry. In 2010, the Dodd-Frank Wall Street Reform and Consumer Protection Act was passed. In addition to new regulations for financial institutions, the legislation created a Consumer Financial Protection Bureau (CFPB) to protect consumers from complex or deceptive financial products. Table B.7 highlights some of the major provisions of the Dodd-Frank Act.

TABLE B.7   Major Provisions of the Dodd-Frank Wall Street Reform and Consumer Protection Act

1. Enhances stability of the finance industry through the creation of two new financial agencies, the Financial Oversight Stability Council and the Office of Financial Research.

2. Institutes an orderly liquidation procedure for the Federal Deposit Insurance Corporation to liquidate failing companies.

3. Eliminates the Office of Thrift Supervision and transfers its powers to the Comptroller of the Currency.

4. Creates stronger regulation and greater oversight of hedge funds.

5. Establishes the Federal Insurance Agency to gather information and oversee the insurance industry for risks.

6. Requires regulators to have regulations in place for banks. Also prohibits and/or limits proprietary trading, hedge fund sponsorship and private equity funds, and relationships with hedge funds and private equity funds.

7. Regulates derivatives and complex financial instruments by limiting where they can be traded and ensuring that traders have the financial resources to meet their responsibilities.

8. Provides a framework for creating risk-management standards for financial market utilities and the payment, clearing, and settlement activities performed by institutions.

9. Improves investor protection through acts such as creating a whistleblower bounty program and increasing consumer access to their credit scores.

10. Institutes the Bureau of Consumer Financial Protection to educate consumers and protect them from deceptive financial products.

11. Attempts to reform the Federal Reserve in ways that include limiting the Federal Reserve's lending authority, reevaluating methods for Federal Reserve regulations and the appointment of Federal Reserve Bank directors, and instituting additional disclosure requirements.

12. Reforms mortgage activities with new provisions that include increasing the lender's responsibility to ensure the borrower can pay back the loan, prohibiting unfair lending practices, requiring additional disclosure in the mortgage loan process, and imposing penalties against those found guilty of noncompliance with the new standards.

Source: *Brief Summary of the Dodd-Frank Wall Street Reform and Consumer Protection Act,* http://banking.senate.gov/public/_files/070110_Dodd_Frank_Wall_Street_Reform_comprehensive_summary_Final.pdf (accessed March 17, 2011).

The Dodd-Frank Act contains 16 titles meant to increase consumer protection, enhance transparency and accountability in the financial sector, and create new financial agencies. In some ways, Dodd-Frank is attempting to improve upon provisions laid out in the Sarbanes-Oxley Act. For instance, Dodd-Frank takes whistleblower protection a step further by offering additional incentives to whistleblowers for reporting misconduct. If whistleblowers report misconduct that results in penalties of more than $1 million, the whistleblower will be entitled to a percentage of the settlement.[88] Another provision, the Durbin Amendment, limits the swipe fees that debit card issuers are allowed to charge merchants.[89] Additionally, complex financial instruments must now be made more transparent so that consumers will have a better understanding of what these instruments involve.

The act also created three new agencies: the Consumer Financial Protection Bureau (CFPB), the Office of Financial Research, and the Financial Stability Oversight Council. While the CFPB was created to protect consumers, the other two agencies work to maintain stability in the financial industry so such a crisis will not recur in the future.[90] Although it is too early to tell whether these regulations will serve to create widescale positive financial reform, the Dodd-Frank Act is certainly leading to major changes on Wall Street and in the financial sector.

3

Business in a Borderless World

Learning Objectives

After reading this chapter, you will be able to:

LO 3-1   Explore some of the factors within the international trade environment that influence business.

LO 3-2   Investigate some of the economic, legal-political, social, cultural, and technological barriers to international business.

LO 3-3   Specify some of the agreements, alliances, and organizations that may encourage trade across international boundaries.

LO 3-4   Summarize the different levels of organizational involvement in international trade.

LO 3-5   Contrast two basic strategies used in international business.

LO 3-6   Assess the opportunities and problems facing a small business that is considering expanding into international markets.

P&G Steps Up Its International Expansion

Four billion global customers may seem like a lot, but for Procter & Gamble CEO Bob McDonald, it's just the beginning. McDonald intends to raise this number to 5 billion by 2015. The key to this growth is through targeting emerging economies like India and the Philippines. While P&G has built its profits on offering premium products in developed markets, economies in which income is as low as $1 per day require P&G to adapt its marketing strategy. To work within this constraint, P&G has begun offering no frills packages to low-income global consumers.

Of the countries targeted by P&G, India stands out for its 1.2 billion consumers. To expand, it is focusing on needs-based innovation and products

ENTER THE WORLD OF BUSINESS

new to the country. For example, P&G sells single-serving packets of many products to accommodate lower incomes. It is also working to change the lifestyles of Indian consumers. After recognizing that most Indians go to the barber for shaves, P&G introduced the "Women Against Lazy Stubble" campaign. The campaign indicated that women prefer clean shaves and introduced Gillette's Mac3 razor as an alternative to the barber. P&G gained nearly half of the Indian razor market in two years.

The second challenge for P&G is finding a way to get its innovative products onto shelves. With few large retailers in India, small stores with limited space can easily stock P&G items like razors and toothbrushes. Disposable diapers, however, take up more room. Competition is another problem. In India, P&G must fight against major competitors like Unilever and Colgate-Palmolive. P&G's Indian sales have been growing steadily, but it lags behind Unilever with sales of $800 million versus $3.8 billion. The trick for P&G will be to balance its products with the needs of its Indian customers—both retailers and end-users.[1]

Introduction

Consumers around the world can drink Coca-Cola and Pepsi; eat at McDonald's and Pizza Hut; see movies from Mexico, England, France, Australia, and China; and watch CNN and MTV on Samsung and Panasonic televisions. It may surprise you that the Japanese firm Komatsu sells earth-moving equipment to China that is manufactured in Peoria, Illinois.[2] The products you consume today are just as likely to have been made in China, Korea, or Germany as in the United States. Likewise, consumers in other countries buy Western electrical equipment, clothing, rock music, cosmetics, and toiletries, as well as computers, robots, and earth-moving equipment.

Many U.S. firms are finding that international markets provide tremendous opportunities for growth. Accessing these markets can promote innovation while intensifying global competition spurs companies to market better and less expensive products. Today, the nearly 7 billion people that inhabit the earth comprise one tremendous marketplace.

In this chapter, we explore business in this exciting global marketplace. First, we look at the nature of international business, including barriers and promoters of trade across international boundaries. Next, we consider the levels of organizational involvement in international business. Finally, we briefly discuss strategies for trading across national borders.

> **DID YOU KNOW?** Subway has surpassed McDonald's as the largest global restaurant chain with over 36,000 units.[3]

> **international business** the buying, selling, and trading of goods and services across national boundaries

> **LO 3-1**

The Role of International Business

International business refers to the buying, selling, and trading of goods and services across national boundaries. Falling political barriers and new technology are making it possible for more and more companies to sell their products overseas as well as at home. And, as differences among nations continue to narrow, the trend toward the globalization of business is becoming increasingly important. Starbucks serves millions of global customers at more than 5,500 shops in more than 50 countries.[4] The Internet provides many companies easier entry to access global markets than opening bricks-and-mortar stores.[5] Amazon.com, an online retailer, has distribution centers from Nevada to Germany that fill millions of orders a day and ship them to customers in every corner of the world. Procter & Gamble's Febreze brand passed the $1 billion mark partially due to its strong growth overseas. While U.S. sales of air fresheners have fallen in recent years, global sales have seen an increase.[6] Indeed, most of the world's population and two-thirds of its total purchasing power are outside the United States.

When McDonald's sells a Big Mac in Moscow, Sony sells a stereo in Detroit, or

American companies such as KFC have become widely popular in China. Some have more sales in China than they have in the United States.

a small Swiss medical supply company sells a shipment of orthopedic devices to a hospital in Monterrey, Mexico, the sale affects the economies of the countries involved. The U.S. market, with 311 million consumers, makes up only a small part of the nearly 7 billion people elsewhere in the world to whom global companies must consider marketing. Global marketing requires balancing your global brand with the needs of local consumers.[7] To begin our study of international business, we must first consider some economic issues: why nations trade, exporting and importing, and the balance of trade.

Why Nations Trade

Nations and businesses engage in international trade to obtain raw materials and goods that are otherwise unavailable to them or are available elsewhere at a lower price than that at which they themselves can produce. A nation, or individuals and organizations from a nation, sell surplus materials and goods to acquire funds to buy the goods, services, and ideas its people need. Poland and Hungary, for example, want to trade with Western nations so that they can acquire new technology and techniques to revitalize their formerly communist economies. Which goods and services a nation sells depends on what resources it has available.

Some nations have a monopoly on the production of a particular resource or product. Such a monopoly, or **absolute advantage,** exists when a country is the only source of an item, the only producer of an item, or the most efficient producer of an item. Because South Africa has the largest deposits of diamonds in the world, one company, De Beers Consolidated Mines Ltd., controls a major portion of the world's diamond trade and uses its control to maintain high prices for gem-quality diamonds. The United States, until recently, held an absolute advantage in oil-drilling equipment. But an absolute advantage not based on the availability of natural resources rarely lasts, and Japan and Russia are now challenging the United States in the production of oil-drilling equipment.

absolute advantage
a monopoly that exists when a country is the only source of an item, the only producer of an item, or the most efficient producer of an item

Most international trade is based on **comparative advantage,** which occurs when a country specializes in products that it can supply more efficiently or at a lower cost than it can produce other items. The United States has a comparative advantage in producing agricultural commodities such as corn and wheat. The United States at one time had a comparative advantage in manufacturing automobiles, heavy machinery, airplanes, and weapons; other countries now hold the comparative advantage for many of these products. Other countries, particularly India and Ireland, are also gaining a comparative advantage over the United States in the provision of some services, such as call-center operations, engineering, and software programming. As a result, U.S. companies are increasingly **outsourcing,** or transferring manufacturing and other tasks to countries where labor and supplies are less expensive. Outsourcing has become a controversial practice in the United States because many jobs have moved overseas where those tasks can be accomplished for lower costs. For example, the Philippines has surpassed India as the popular choice for call-center jobs. Call-center jobs are appealing to many Filipinos because the pay is almost as much as the average family income within the country. English is also one of the country's official languages, which makes it easier to communicate with English-speaking customers.[8]

comparative advantage
the basis of most international trade, when a country specializes in products that it can supply more efficiently or at a lower cost than it can produce other items

outsourcing
the transferring of manufacturing or other tasks—such as data processing—to countries where labor and supplies are less expensive

Trade between Countries

To obtain needed goods and services and the funds to pay for them, nations trade by exporting and importing. **Exporting** is the sale of goods and services to foreign markets. The United States exported more than $2.1 trillion in goods and services

exporting
the sale of goods and services to foreign markets

importing
the purchase of goods
and services from foreign
sources

balance of trade
the difference in value
between a nation's exports
and its imports

trade deficit
a nation's negative balance
of trade, which exists when
that country imports more
products than it exports

Need help
understanding
Balance of Trade?

http://bit.ly/FerrellQR3-1

balance of payments
the difference between the
flow of money into and out
of a country

in 2011.[9] In China, General Motors is targeting wealthier customers with the Cadillac, middle management with the Buick Excelle, office workers with the Chevrolet Spark, and rural consumers with the Wuling minivan.[10] U.S. companies that view China as both a growth market for exports and a market for lower-cost labor for imports and can strategically integrate these into their operations enjoy significantly higher profits than companies who only focus on one of these opportunities.[11] U.S. businesses export many goods and services, particularly agricultural, entertainment (movies, television shows, etc.), and technological products. **Importing** is the purchase of goods and services from foreign sources. Many of the goods you buy in the United States are likely to be imports or to have some imported components. Sometimes, you may not even realize they are imports. The United States imported more than $2.6 trillion in goods and services in 2011.[12]

Balance of Trade

You have probably read or heard about the fact that the United States has a trade deficit, but what is a trade deficit? A nation's **balance of trade** is the difference in value between its exports and imports. Because the United States (and some other nations as well) imports more products than it exports, it has a negative balance of trade, or **trade deficit.** Table 3.1 shows the trade deficit for the United States. In 2011, the United States had a trade deficit of around $558 billion, more than 10 percent higher than it was in 2010.[13] The trade deficit fluctuates according to such factors as the health of the United States and other economies, productivity, perceived quality, and exchange rates. In 2011, the United States had a $295.5 million trade deficit with China.[14] As Figure 3.1 indicates, U.S. exports to China have been rapidly increasing but not fast enough to offset the imports from China. Trade deficits are harmful because they can mean the failure of businesses, the loss of jobs, and a lowered standard of living.

Of course, when a nation exports more goods than it imports, it has a favorable balance of trade, or trade surplus. Until about 1970, the United States had a trade surplus due to an abundance of natural resources and the relative efficiency of its manufacturing systems. Table 3.2 shows the top 10 countries with which the United States has a trade deficit and a trade surplus.

The difference between the flow of money into and out of a country is called its **balance of payments.** A country's balance of trade, foreign investments, foreign aid, loans, military expenditures, and money spent by tourists comprise its balance

TABLE 3.1   U.S. Trade Deficit, 1990–2011 (in billions of dollars)

	1990	2000	2005	2006	2007	2008	2009	2010	2011
Exports	$535.2	1,072.8	1,287.4	1,459.8	$1,654.6	$1,842.7	$1,575.0	$2,837.6	$2,103.1
Imports	616.1	1,449.5	1,996.1	2,213.1	2,351.3	2,541.0	1,956.3	$2,337.6	2,661.1
Trade surplus/deficit	−80.9	−376.7	−708.6	−753.3	−696.7	−698.3	−381.3	−500.0	−558.0

Sources: U.S. Bureau of the Census, Foreign Trade Division, *U.S. Trade in Goods and Services—Balance of Payments (BOP) Basis,* February 10, 2012, www.census.gov/foreign-trade/statistics/historical/gands.pdf (accessed February 27, 2012).

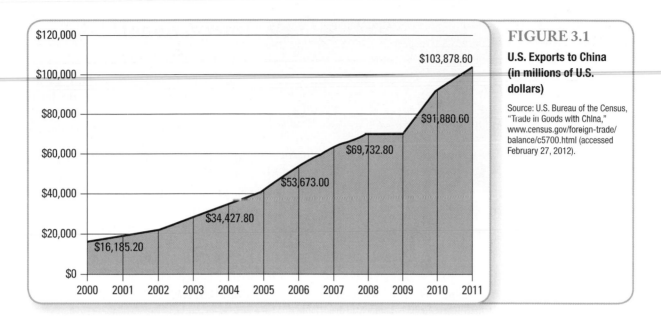

FIGURE 3.1

U.S. Exports to China (in millions of U.S. dollars)

Source: U.S. Bureau of the Census, "Trade in Goods with China," www.census.gov/foreign-trade/balance/c5700.html (accessed February 27, 2012).

Chart values: $16,185.20 (2000); $34,427.80; $53,673.00; $69,732.80; $91,880.60; $103,878.60 (2011)

TABLE 3.2

Top Ten Countries with which United States has Trade Deficits/Surpluses

Trade Deficit	Trade Surplus
1. China	Hong Kong
2. Japan	Australia
3. Mexico	Belgium
4. Germany	Netherlands
5. Saudi Arabia	United Arab Emirates
6. Canada	Singapore
7. Ireland	Panama
8. Russia	Chile
9. Nigeria	Turkey
10. Venezuela	Brazil

Sources: "Top Ten Countries with which the U.S. has a Trade Deficit," November 2011, www.census.gov/foreign-trade/top/dst/current/deficit.html (accessed January 25, 2012); "Top Ten Countries with which the U.S. has a Trade Surplus," November 2011, www.census.gov/foreign-trade/top/dst/current/surplus.html (accessed January 25, 2012).

of payments. As you might expect, a country with a trade surplus generally has a favorable balance of payments because it is receiving more money from trade with foreign countries than it is paying out. When a country has a trade deficit, more money flows out of the country than into it. If more money flows out of the country than into it from tourism and other sources, the country may experience declining production and higher unemployment, because there is less money available for spending.

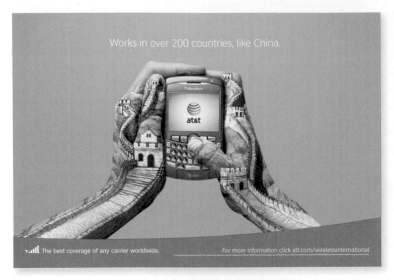

Works in over 200 countries, like China.

at&t

📶 The best coverage of any carrier worldwide.   For more information click att.com/wirelessinternational

The infrastructure of countries—their transportation, communication, and other systems—differs around the world. AT&T has used the opportunity to make inroads with consumers who don't want their cell phones to stop working when they go abroad.

International Trade Barriers

Completely free trade seldom exists. When a company decides to do business outside its own country, it will encounter a number of barriers to international trade. Any firm considering international business must research the other country's economic, legal, political, social, cultural, and technological background. Such research will help the company choose an appropriate level of involvement and operating strategies, as we will see later in this chapter.

Economic Barriers

When looking at doing business in another country, managers must consider a number of basic economic factors, such as economic development, infrastructure, and exchange rates.

LO 3-2

Economic Development.   When considering doing business abroad, U.S. business people need to recognize that they cannot take for granted that other countries offer the same things as are found in *industrialized nations*—economically advanced countries such as the United States, Japan, Great Britain, and Canada. Many countries in Africa, Asia, and South America, for example, are in general poorer and less economically advanced than those in North America and Europe; they are often called *less-developed countries* (LDCs). LDCs are characterized by low per-capita income (income generated by the nation's production of goods and services divided by the population), which means that consumers are less likely to purchase nonessential products. Nonetheless, LDCs represent a potentially huge and profitable market for many businesses because they may be buying technology to improve their infrastructures, and much of the population may desire consumer products. For example, automobile manufacturers are looking toward LDCs as a way to expand their customer base. The rising middle class has caused many consumers in India and China to desire their own vehicles. Companies such as General Motors are partnering with domestic manufacturers to create electric vehicles for the Chinese market.[15]

A country's level of development is determined in part by its **infrastructure,** the physical facilities that support its economic activities, such as railroads, highways, ports, airfields, utilities and power plants, schools, hospitals, communication systems, and commercial distribution systems. When doing business in LDCs, for example, a business may need to compensate for rudimentary distribution and communication systems, or even a lack of technology.

infrastructure
the physical facilities that support a country's economic activities, such as railroads, highways, ports, airfields, utilities and power plants, schools, hospitals, communication systems, and commercial distribution systems

exchange rate
the ratio at which one nation's currency can be exchanged for another nation's currency

Exchange Rates.   The ratio at which one nation's currency can be exchanged for another nation's currency is the **exchange rate.** Exchange rates vary daily and can be found in newspapers and through many sites on the Internet. Familiarity with exchange rates is important because they affect the cost of imports and exports. When the value of the U.S. dollar declines relative to other currencies, such as the

Going Green

China Faces Growing Concerns over Pollution

China has made great strides in sustainability. The country has become the largest producer of wind turbines worldwide and has captured more than half of the market for solar technology. However, with 1.3 billion consumers and a growing middle class, pollution in China has also grown—with sometimes catastrophic results. The Ministry of Environmental Protection in Beijing has estimated that one-sixth of China's river water is dangerously polluted. Acid rain is also common in China, and less than one-fifth of its hazardous waste is properly treated each year. Perhaps most tragically, many cities located near factories have reported high incidences of cancer and other diseases.

The situation has prompted the Chinese government to take action. The government is closing many of the country's worst-polluting factories, adopting stringent environmental laws, and has announced its intention of implementing a cap-and-trade system. Although most people would applaud China's attempt to reduce pollution, serious economic disadvantages come with better environmental enforcement. The loss of jobs that occurs when factories close is a major drawback. For example, one older steel mill employed 6,000 workers, many of whom were laid off when the factory closed. Additionally, because the majority of China is still powered by coal (a dirtier source of energy), the nation is opening up new power plants even as it is closing less efficient older ones. Finally, although China releases the most greenhouse gas emissions, each person in China gives off one-third of the carbon emissions of the average American. Therefore, China's pollution problem not only involves the clash between economics and the environment but also brings up the issue of fairness.[16]

Discussion Questions

1. Describe the environmental issues that China is facing.
2. Describe the clash between China's economic situation and the environment. Why is this such a major concern?
3. Do you feel that it is fair for China to receive attention for green gas emissions when U.S. citizens emit more gas emissions per person?

euro, the price of imports becomes relatively expensive for U.S. consumers. On the other hand, U.S. exports become relatively cheap for international markets—in this example, the European Union.

Occasionally, a government may intentionally alter the value of its currency through fiscal policy. Devaluation decreases the value of currency in relation to other currencies. If the U.S. government were to devalue the dollar, it would lower the cost of American goods abroad and make trips to the United States less expensive for foreign tourists. Thus, devaluation encourages the sale of domestic goods and tourism. Mexico has repeatedly devalued the peso for this reason. Revaluation, which increases the value of a currency in relation to other currencies, occurs rarely.

Ethical, Legal, and Political Barriers

A company that decides to enter the international marketplace must contend with potentially complex relationships among the different laws of its own nation, international laws, and the laws of the nation with which it will be trading; various trade restrictions imposed on international trade; changing political climates; and different ethical values. Legal and ethical requirements for successful business are increasing globally. For instance, India has strict limitations on foreign retailers that want to operate within the country. Until recently, foreign retailers were required to partner with a domestic firm if they wanted to do business within India. Walmart partnered with Bharti Enterprises in order to gain entry into the country. India has now reduced the restrictions slightly. Single-brand retailers like Nike can now own their own stores in India without a partner, but multibrand retailers like Walmart are still limited by the former restrictions. Although India represents a lucrative market for retailers, many multibrand retailers such as IKEA are avoiding doing business within India because of the legal barriers.[17]

The watch on the right, a knockoff developed by Digital Time Co., Ltd. in Thailand, received a special award for falsification. The dubious honor is given to the "best" product knockoffs by the organization Action Plagiarius in an effort to shame their makers. (The real watch was created by FORTIS Uhren AG in Grenchen, Switzerland.)

Laws and Regulations.   The United States has a number of laws and regulations that govern the activities of U.S. firms engaged in international trade. For example, the Webb-Pomerene Export Trade Act of 1918 exempts American firms from anti-trust laws if those firms are acting together to enter international trade. This law allows selected U.S. firms to form monopolies to compete with foreign monopolistic organizations, although they are not allowed to limit free trade and competition within the United States or to use unfair methods of competition in international trade. The United States also has a variety of friendship, commerce, and navigation treaties with other nations. These treaties allow business to be transacted between citizens of the specified countries. For example, Belgium is a gateway to European markets and has lowered its taxes to give U.S. companies greater reason to locate their European operations there. Belgium has the lowest patent income tax and has 0 percent withholding tax on corporate dividends and interest from a U.S. company. This prevents a company from paying both U.S. and Belgian tax, or double taxation.[18]

Once outside U.S. borders, businesspeople are likely to find that the laws of other nations differ from those of the United States. Many of the legal rights that Americans take for granted do not exist in other countries, and a firm doing business abroad must understand and obey the laws of the host country. Some countries have strict laws limiting the amount of local currency that can be taken out of the country and the amount of currency that can be brought in; others forbid foreigners from owning real property outright.

In Mexico, for example, foreigners cannot directly own property in what is known as the "Restricted Zone." The Restricted Zone includes land within 100 kilometers of Mexico's international borders along with land within 50 kilometers of Mexico's oceans and beaches. Foreigners who wish to use property in these areas must obtain a title through a bank title transfer or through a corporation.[19]

Some countries have copyright and patent laws that are less strict than those of the United States, and some countries fail to honor U.S. laws. Because copying is a tradition in China and Vietnam and laws protecting copyrights and intellectual property are weak and minimally enforced, those countries are flooded with counterfeit videos, movies, CDs, computer software, furniture, and clothing. Companies are angry because the counterfeits harm not only their sales, but also their reputations if the knockoffs are of poor quality. Such counterfeiting is not limited to China or Vietnam. It is estimated that nearly half of all software installed on personal computers worldwide is illegally pirated or copied, amounting to more than $50 billion in global revenue losses annually.[20] In countries where these activities occur, laws against them may not be sufficiently enforced if counterfeiting is deemed illegal. Thus, businesses engaging in foreign trade may have to take extra steps to protect their products because local laws may be insufficient to do so.

Tariffs and Trade Restrictions.   Tariffs and other trade restrictions are part of a country's legal structure but may be established or removed for political reasons. An

import tariff is a tax levied by a nation on goods imported into the country. A *fixed tariff* is a specific amount of money levied on each unit of a product brought into the country, while an *ad valorem tariff* is based on the value of the item. Most countries allow citizens traveling abroad to bring home a certain amount of merchandise without paying an import tariff. A U.S. citizen may bring $200 worth of merchandise into the United States duty free. After that, U.S. citizens must pay an ad valorem tariff based on the cost of the item and the country of origin. Thus, identical items purchased in different countries might have different tariffs.

import tariff
a tax levied by a nation on goods imported into the country

Countries sometimes levy tariffs for political reasons, as when they impose sanctions against other countries to protest their actions. However, import tariffs are more commonly imposed to protect domestic products by raising the price of imported ones. Such protective tariffs have become controversial, as Americans become increasingly concerned over the U.S. trade deficit. Protective tariffs allow more expensive domestic goods to compete with foreign ones. For example, the United States has lost a significant number of steelworks over the past few decades to foreign competition in places such as China. Other markets can produce steel more cheaply than the United States. Many people and special interest groups in the United States, such as unions, would like to see tariffs placed on Chinese steel, which is significantly less expensive, in order to protect remaining U.S. steel production. The United States has also imposed tariffs on imported sugar for almost two centuries. The European Union levies tariffs on many products, including some seafood imports.

Critics of protective tariffs argue that their use inhibits free trade and competition. Supporters of protective tariffs say they insulate domestic industries, particularly new ones, against well-established foreign competitors. Once an industry matures, however, its advocates may be reluctant to let go of the tariff that protected it. Tariffs also help when, because of low labor costs and other advantages, foreign competitors can afford to sell their products at prices lower than those charged by domestic companies. Some Americans argue that tariffs should be used to keep domestic wages high and unemployment low.

Exchange controls restrict the amount of currency that can be bought or sold. Some countries control their foreign trade by forcing businesspeople to buy and sell foreign products through a central bank. If John Deere, for example, receives payments for its tractors in a foreign currency, it may be required to sell the currency to that nation's central bank. When foreign currency is in short supply, as it is in many less-developed countries, the government uses foreign currency to purchase necessities and capital goods and produces other products locally, thus limiting its need for foreign imports.

exchange controls
regulations that restrict the amount of currency that can be bought or sold

A **quota** limits the number of units of a particular product that can be imported into a country. A quota may be established by voluntary agreement or by government decree. The United States imposes quotas on certain goods, such as garments produced in Vietnam and China. Quotas are designed to protect the industries and jobs of the country imposing the quota.

quota
a restriction on the number of units of a particular product that can be imported into a country

An **embargo** prohibits trade in a particular product. Embargoes are generally directed at specific goods or countries and may be established for political, economic, health, or religious reasons. While the United States maintains a trade embargo with Cuba, European hotel chains are engaged in a building boom on the Caribbean island, where tourism is the number-one industry. U.S. hotel chains are eager to build in Cuba but have no opportunity until the embargo is lifted. Until recently, U.S. tourists were forbidden by the U.S. government to vacation in Cuba because of the embargo. However, the government has begun to allow more

embargo
a prohibition on trade in a particular product

Americans to visit Cuba with certain restrictions.[21] It may be surprising to know that U.S. farmers export hundreds of millions of dollars worth of commodities to Cuba each year, based on a 2000 law that provided permission for some trade to the embargoed country.[22] Health embargoes prevent the importing of various pharmaceuticals, animals, plants, and agricultural products. Muslim nations forbid the importation of alcoholic beverages on religious grounds.

dumping
the act of a country or business selling products at less than what it costs to produce them

One common reason for setting quotas or tariffs is to prohibit **dumping,** which occurs when a country or business sells products at less than what it costs to produce them. For example, in 2012 the U.S. Commerce Department began an investigation over whether businesses from China and Vietnam were dumping wind turbine parts by charging extremely low prices.[23] A company may dump its products for several reasons. Dumping permits quick entry into a market. Sometimes dumping occurs when the domestic market for a firm's product is too small to support an efficient level of production. In other cases, technologically obsolete products that are no longer salable in the country of origin are dumped overseas. Dumping is relatively difficult to prove, but even the suspicion of dumping can lead to the imposition of quotas or tariffs.

Political Barriers.   Unlike legal issues, political considerations are seldom written down and often change rapidly. Nations that have been subject to economic sanctions for political reasons in recent years include Cuba, Iran, Syria, and North Korea. While these were dramatic events, political considerations affect international business daily as governments enact tariffs, embargoes, or other types of trade restrictions in response to political events.

Businesses engaged in international trade must consider the relative instability of countries such as Iraq, Haiti, and Venezuela. Political unrest in countries such as Pakistan, Somalia, and the Democratic Republic of the Congo may create a hostile or even dangerous environment for foreign businesses. Natural disasters, like the Haitian or Chilean earthquakes in 2010, can cripple a country's government, making the region even more unstable. Even a developed country such as Japan had

Dumping can spark trade wars. After the Obama administration imposed stiff tariffs on Chinese-made tires it alleged were being dumped on the U.S. market, China retaliated by slapping tariffs on U.S. chicken products exported to China.

its social, economic, and political institutions stressed by the 2011 earthquake and tsunamis. Finally, a sudden change in power can result in a regime that is hostile to foreign investment. Some businesses have been forced out of a country altogether, as when Hugo Chávez conducted a socialist revolution in Venezuela to force out or take over American oil companies. Whether they like it or not, companies are often involved directly or indirectly in international politics.

Political concerns may lead a group of nations to form a **cartel,** a group of firms or nations that agrees to act as a monopoly and not compete with each other, to generate a competitive advantage in world markets. Probably the most famous cartel is OPEC, the Organization of Petroleum Exporting Countries, founded in the 1960s to increase the price of petroleum throughout the world and to maintain high prices. By working to ensure stable oil prices, OPEC hopes to enhance the economies of its member nations.

cartel
a group of firms or nations that agrees to act as a monopoly and not compete with each other, in order to generate a competitive advantage in world markets

Social and Cultural Barriers

Most businesspeople engaged in international trade underestimate the importance of social and cultural differences; but these differences can derail an important transaction. For example, when Big Boy opened a restaurant in Bangkok, it quickly became popular with European and American tourists, but the local Thais refused to eat there. Instead, they placed gifts of rice and incense at the feet of the Big Boy statue (a chubby boy holding a hamburger) because it reminded them of Buddha. In Japan, customers tiptoed around a logo painted on the floor at the entrance to an Athlete's Foot store because in Japan it is considered taboo to step on a crest.[24] And in Russia, consumers found the American-style energetic happiness of McDonald's employees insincere and offensive when the company opened its first stores there.[25] Unfortunately, cultural norms are rarely written down, and what is written down may well be inaccurate.

Cultural differences include differences in spoken and written language. Although it is certainly possible to translate words from one language to another, the true meaning is sometimes misinterpreted or lost. Consider some translations that went awry in foreign markets:

- Scandinavian vacuum manufacturer Electrolux used the following in an American campaign: "Nothing sucks like an Electrolux."
- The Coca-Cola name in China was first read as "Ke-kou-ke-la," meaning "bite the wax tadpole."
- In Italy, a campaign for Schweppes Tonic Water translated the name into Schweppes Toilet Water.[26]

Translators cannot just translate slogans, advertising campaigns, and website language; they must know the cultural differences that could affect a company's success.

Differences in body language and personal space also affect international trade. Body language is nonverbal, usually unconscious communication through gestures, posture, and facial expression. Personal space is the distance at which one person feels comfortable talking to another. Americans tend to stand a moderate distance away from the person with whom they are speaking. Arab businessmen tend to stand face-to-face with the object of their conversation. Additionally, gestures vary from culture to culture, and gestures considered acceptable in American society—pointing, for example—may be considered rude in others. Table 3.3 shows some of the behaviors considered rude or unacceptable in other countries. Such cultural

TABLE 3.3

Cultural Behavioral Differences

Region	Gestures Viewed as Rude or Unacceptable
Japan, Hong Kong, Middle East	Summoning with the index finger
Middle and Far East	Pointing with index finger
Thailand, Japan, France	Sitting with soles of shoes showing
Brazil, Germany	Forming a circle with fingers (the "O.K." sign in the United States)
Japan	Winking means "I love you"
Buddhist countries	Patting someone on the head

Source: Adapted from Judie Haynes, "Communicating with Gestures," *EverythingESL* (n.d.), http://www.everythingesl.net/inservices/body_language.php (accessed March 8, 2010).

differences may generate uncomfortable feelings or misunderstandings when business people of different countries negotiate with each other.

Family roles also influence marketing activities. Many countries do not allow children to be used in advertising, for example. Advertising that features people in nontraditional social roles may or may not be successful either. One airline featured advertisements with beautiful hostesses serving champagne on a flight. The ad does not seem unusual in Western markets, but there was a major backlash in the Middle East. Saudi Arabia even considered restricting the airline from flights in that country. Not only is alcohol usage forbidden among Muslims, unveiled women are not allowed to interact with men—especially without their husbands around. Some in Saudi Arabia saw the airline as being insensitive to their religious beliefs and customs.[27]

The people of other nations quite often have a different perception of time as well. Americans value promptness; a business meeting scheduled for a specific time seldom starts more than a few minutes late. In Mexico and Spain, however, it is not unusual for a meeting to be delayed half an hour or more. Such a late start might produce resentment in an American negotiating in Spain for the first time.

Companies engaged in foreign trade must observe the national and religious holidays and local customs of the host country. In many Islamic countries, for example, workers expect to take a break at certain times of the day to observe religious rites. Companies also must monitor their advertising to guard against offending customers. In Thailand and many other countries, public displays of affection between the sexes are unacceptable in advertising messages; in many Middle Eastern nations, it is unacceptable to show the soles of one's feet.[28] In Russia, smiling is considered appropriate only in private settings, not in business.

With the exception of the United States, most nations use the metric system. This lack of uniformity creates problems for both buyers and sellers in the international marketplace. American sellers, for instance, must package goods destined for foreign markets in liters or meters, and Japanese sellers must convert to the English system if they plan to sell a product in the United States. Tools also must be calibrated in the correct system if they are to function correctly. Hyundai and Honda service technicians need metric tools to make repairs on those cars.

The literature dealing with international business is filled with accounts of some-times humorous but often costly mistakes that occurred because of a lack of under-standing of the social and cultural differences between buyers and sellers. Such problems cannot always be avoided, but they can be minimized through research on the cultural and social differences of the host country.

Technological Barriers

Many countries lack the technological infrastructure found in the United States, and some marketers are viewing such barriers as opportunities. For instance, market-ers are targeting many countries such as India and China and some African coun-tries where there are few private phone lines. Citizens of these countries are turning instead to wireless communication through cell phones. Technological advances are creating additional global marketing opportunities. Along with opportunities, changing technologies also create new challenges and competition. The U.S. market share of the personal computer market is dropping as new competitors emerge that are challenging U.S. PC makers. In fact, out of the top five global PC companies—Hewlett-Packard, Dell, Acer, Lenovo, and Toshiba—three are from Asian countries. On the other hand, Apple Inc.'s iPad and other tablet computer makers have already begun eroding the market share of traditional personal computers, leading many to believe that personal computers have hit the maturity stage of the product life cycle.[29]

Trade Agreements, Alliances, and Organizations

LO 3-3

Although these economic, political, legal, and sociocultural issues may seem like daunting barriers to international trade, there are also organizations and agreements—such as the General Agreement on Tariffs and Trade, the World Bank, and the Inter-national Monetary Fund—that foster international trade and can help companies get involved in and succeed in global markets. Various regional trade agreements, such as the North American Free Trade Agreement and the European Union, also promote trade among member nations by eliminating tariffs and trade restrictions. In this sec-tion, we'll look briefly at these agreements and organizations.

General Agreement on Tariffs and Trade

During the Great Depression of the 1930s, nations established so many protective tariffs covering so many products that international trade became virtually impos-sible. By the end of World War II, there was considerable international momentum to liberalize trade and minimize the effects of tariffs. The **General Agreement on Tariffs and Trade (GATT),** originally signed by 23 nations in 1947, provided a forum for tariff negotiations and a place where international trade problems could be discussed and resolved. More than 100 nations abided by its rules. GATT spon-sored rounds of negotiations aimed at reducing trade restrictions. The most recent round, the Uruguay Round (1988–1994), further reduced trade barriers for most products and provided new rules to prevent dumping.

The **World Trade Organization (WTO),** an international organization deal-ing with the rules of trade between nations, was created in 1995 by the Uruguay Round. Key to the World Trade Organization are the WTO agreements, which are the legal ground rules for international commerce. The agreements were negotiated

General Agreement on Tariffs and Trade (GATT) a trade agreement, originally signed by 23 nations in 1947, that provided a forum for tariff negotiations and a place where international trade problems could be discussed and resolved

World Trade Organization (WTO) international organization dealing with the rules of trade between nations

Entrepreneurship in Action
Entrepreneurs Make Money in an Unusual Way

David Auerbach, Ani Vallabhaneni, and Lindsay Stradley
Business: Sanergy
Founded: 2011, in Kenya
Success: The idea for Sanergy won the three student entrepreneurs the $100,000 grand prize in MIT's annual Business Plan Competition, enabling them to start their Kenyan business.

Making money off human waste seems like an unusual (and disgusting) idea. But for recent MBA graduate David Auerbach, it is an opportunity to make money and meet critical needs in developing countries. According to the World Health Organization, 2.6 billion people lack proper sanitation facilities, a situation Auerbach witnessed when visiting China. Auerbach partnered with fellow students Ani Vallabhaneni and Lindsay Stradley to submit a business plan for a sanitation business in Kenya. They won MIT's annual Business Plan Competition and received $100,000 to start Sanergy.

Sanergy involves a four-step process. First, it builds the sanitation facilities, which include showers and toilets. The centers are then franchised to other entrepreneurs, who charge five cents for each use. The waste is collected daily and finally converted into electricity and fertilizer and sold. In this way, Sanergy can make a profit, create clean sanitation facilities for Kenyans, and generate jobs simultaneously.[30]

and signed by most of the world's trading nations and ratified by their parliaments. The goal is to help producers of goods and services and exporters and importers conduct their business. In addition to administering the WTO trade agreements, the WTO presents a forum for trade negotiations, monitors national trade policies, provides technical assistance and training for developing countries, and cooperates with other international organizations. Based in Geneva, Switzerland, the WTO has also adopted a leadership role in negotiating trade disputes among nations.[31] For example, the WTO investigated allegations that China was unfairly placing restrictions on the export of nine raw materials. The WTO eventually ruled that China was violating international trade rules.[32]

The North American Free Trade Agreement

The **North American Free Trade Agreement (NAFTA),** which went into effect on January 1, 1994, effectively merged Canada, the United States, and Mexico into one market of nearly 440 million consumers. NAFTA virtually eliminated all tariffs on goods produced and traded among Canada, Mexico, and the United States to create a free trade area. The estimated annual output for this trade alliance is more than $14 trillion. NAFTA makes it easier for U.S. businesses to invest in Mexico and Canada; provides protection for intellectual property (of special interest to high-technology and entertainment industries); expands trade by requiring equal treatment of U.S. firms in both countries; and simplifies country-of-origin rules, hindering Japan's use of Mexico as a staging ground for further penetration into U.S. markets.

Canada's more than 34 million consumers are relatively affluent, with a per capita GDP of $39,400.[33] Trade between the United States and Canada totals approximately $430 billion. About 80 percent of Canada's exports go to the United States, including gold, oil, and uranium.[34] In fact, Canada is the single largest trading partner of the United States.[35]

With a per capita GDP of $13,900, Mexico's more than 113 million consumers are less affluent than Canadian consumers.[36] However, trade with the United States and Mexico has tripled since NAFTA was initiated. Trade between the United States and Mexico totals more than $450 billion.[37] Millions of Americans cite their heritage as Mexican, making them the most populous Hispanic group in the country. These individuals often have close ties to relatives in Mexico and assist in Mexican–U.S. economic development and trade. Mexico is on a course of a market economy, rule of law, respect for human rights, and responsible public policies. There is also a commitment to the environment and sustainable human development. Many U.S. companies have taken advantage of Mexico's low labor costs and proximity to the United States to set up production facilities, sometimes called *maquiladoras*. Mexico is also attracting major technological

The WTO facilitates trade between nations through the development of trade policies.

industries, including electronics, software, and aerospace. Mexicali, for example, has attracted such companies as Skyworks Solutions, a maker of cell phone and PDA semiconductors; Gulfstream, a maker of executive jets; and Honeywell. Engineering in Mexicali is booming, with the enrollment of the engineering department at Mexicali's Universidad Autonoma de Baja California growing rapidly. Other companies that have an interest in Mexico include Eurocopter and Lenovo, which has a plant in Monterrey. With the maquiladoras and the influx of foreign technological industries, Mexico became the world's 12th-largest economy.[38]

However, there is great disparity within Mexico. The country's southern states cannot seem to catch up with the more affluent northern states on almost any socioeconomic indicator. For example, 47 percent of rural Mexicans in the south are considered extremely poor, compared with just 12 percent in the north. The disparities are growing, as can be seen comparing the south to the northern industrial capital of Monterrey, which is beginning to seem like south Texas.[39] However, drug gang wars threaten the economic stability of Mexico, especially in the northern states close to the U.S. border.

Despite its benefits, NAFTA has been controversial, and disputes continue to arise over the implementation of the trade agreement. For example, a trucking dispute between the United States and Mexico resulted in a ban on Mexican trucks operating within the U.S. border. In retaliation, Mexico instituted a punitive tariff on U.S. imports, claiming that the ban violated NAFTA. Americans in support of the ban felt it was necessary to protect the jobs of U.S. truck and warehouse workers. The dispute was eventually resolved, with President Obama agreeing to lift the ban in exchange for tougher standards for Mexican trucks crossing the border.[40] While many Americans feared the agreement would erase jobs in the United States, Mexicans have been disappointed that the agreement failed to create more jobs. Moreover, Mexico's rising standard of living has increased the cost of doing business there; many hundreds of *maquiladoras* have closed their doors and transferred work to China and other nations where labor costs are cheaper. Indeed, China has become the United States' second-largest importer.[41] On the other hand, high transportation costs, intellectual property theft, quality failures, and the difficulty management often incurs in controlling a business so far away and under a communist regime are now causing some manufacturers to reconsider opting for Mexican factories over China, even going so far as to relocate from China back to Mexico.[42]

Although NAFTA has been controversial, it has become a positive factor for U.S. firms wishing to engage in international marketing. Because licensing requirements have been relaxed under the pact, smaller businesses that previously could not afford to invest in Mexico and Canada will be able to do business in those markets without having to locate there. NAFTA's long phase-in period provided time for adjustment by those firms affected by reduced tariffs on imports. Furthermore, increased competition should lead to a more efficient market, and the long-term prospects of including most countries in the Western Hemisphere in the alliance promise additional opportunities for U.S. marketers.

The European Union

European Union (EU)
a union of European nations established in 1958 to promote trade among its members; one of the largest single markets today

The **European Union (EU),** also called the *European Community* or *Common Market,* was established in 1958 to promote trade among its members, which initially included Belgium, France, Italy, West Germany, Luxembourg, and the Netherlands. East and West Germany united in 1991, and by 1995 the United Kingdom, Spain, Denmark, Greece, Portugal, Ireland, Austria, Finland, and Sweden had joined as well. The Czech Republic, Estonia, Hungary, Latvia, Lithuania, Poland, Slovakia, and Slovenia joined in 2004. In 2007, Bulgaria and Romania also became members, Cyprus and Malta joined in 2008, and Croatia joined in 2013, which brought total membership to 28. Macedonia, Iceland, and Turkey are candidate countries that hope to join the European Union in the near future.[43] Until 1993, each nation functioned as a separate market, but at that time members officially unified into one of the largest single world markets, which today has nearly half a billion consumers with a GDP of more than $14 trillion.[44]

To facilitate free trade among members, the EU is working toward standardization of business regulations and requirements, import duties, and value-added taxes; the elimination of customs checks; and the creation of a standardized currency for use by all members. Many European nations (Austria, Belgium, Finland, France, Germany, Greece, Ireland, Italy, Luxembourg, the Netherlands, Portugal, Spain, and Slovenia) link their exchange rates to a common currency, the *euro;* however, several EU members have rejected use of the euro in their countries. Although the common currency requires many marketers to modify their pricing strategies and will subject them to increased competition, the use of a single currency frees companies that sell goods among European countries from the nuisance of dealing with complex exchange rates.[45] The long-term goals are to eliminate all trade barriers within the EU, improve the economic efficiency of the EU nations, and stimulate economic growth, thus making the union's economy more competitive in global markets, particularly against Japan and other Pacific Rim nations, and North America. However, several disputes and debates still divide the member nations, and many barriers to completely free trade remain. Consequently, it may take many years before the EU is truly one deregulated market.

The EU has also enacted some of the world's strictest laws concerning antitrust issues, which have had unexpected consequences for some non-European firms. For example, European antitrust regulators resisted the New York Stock Exchange's proposed merger with German marketplace organizer Deutsche Börse. They believed the merger would give the combined companies too much market power, thus decreasing competition.[46]

Less visible Pacific I
and Hong Kong, have
Vietnam, with one of th
government with priva
poor infrastructure. In
namese firms now com
country one of the wo
increase its presence in
production facilities in

Association of S

The **Association of !**
promotes trade and eco
including Malaysia, the
nam, Laos, Myanmar,
million people with a G
free trade, peace, and co
reduce or phase out tar
This elimination of tarif
be beneficial to busines:

However, ASEAN is
members of the Europ
quite different, with pc
racies (Philippines and
bodia), and communis
member-nations. For i:
over disputed territory

Despite these challer
but unlike the Europear
flows between member
falls that occurred amoi

World Bank

The **World Bank,** mor
tion and Development,
United States, in 1946 t

It loans its own func
ects ranging from road
cational facilities. The V
with international supp
source of advice and as
ment Association and t
World Bank and provid

International M

The **International M**
trade among member
cial cooperation. It als

The prosperity of the EU has suffered in recent years. EU members experienced a severe economic crisis in 2010 that required steep bailouts from the International Monetary Fund (IMF). The first country to come to the forefront was Greece, which had so much debt that it risked default. With an increase in Greek bond yields and credit risks—along with a severe deficit and other negative economic factors—the country's economy plummeted. Because Greece uses the euro as its currency, the massive downturn decreased the euro's value. This had a profound effect on other countries in the Euro zone. (The Euro zone refers collectively to European member countries that have adopted the euro as their form of currency.) Ireland and Portugal were particularly vulnerable because they had some of the region's largest deficits.[47] Ireland began experiencing problems similar to Greece, including a debt crisis, failing economic health, and rising bond yields.[48] Both Ireland and Portugal required bailout packages. In 2012, Spain and Cyprus also requested bailouts.

Greece continued to struggle even after the initial bailout because it did not have enough funds to repay its bondholders. Greece was forced to default. A default by one nation in the EU negatively affects the rest of the members by making them appear riskier as well.[49] In early 2012, the credit rating agency Standard & Poor's downgraded the sovereign debt of France, Austria, Spain, Portugal, Italy, Malta, Slovakia, Slovenia, and Cyprus. This means that these countries are perceived as riskier in terms of paying off their debt. Such downgrades could dissuade investors from investing in these countries.[50] Germany, on the other hand, has largely avoided the economic woes plaguing other countries. Germany has many exporting companies and has a smaller budget deficit and smaller household debt, which has enabled it to weather the crisis better than other EU members.[51] It was not downgraded but maintained its high ratings.[52]

Asia-Pacific Economic Cooperation

The **Asia-Pacific Economic Cooperation (APEC),** established in 1989, promotes open trade and economic and technical cooperation among member nations, which initially included Australia, Brunei Darussalam, Canada, Indonesia, Japan, Korea, Malaysia, New Zealand, the Philippines, Singapore, Thailand, and the United States. Since then, the alliance has grown to include China, Hong Kong, Chinese Taipei, Mexico, Papua New Guinea, Chile, Peru, Russia, and Vietnam. The 21-member alliance represents approximately 41 percent of the world's population, 44 percent of world trade, and 54 percent of world GDP. APEC differs from other international trade alliances in its commitment to facilitating business and its practice of allowing the business/private sector to participate in a wide range of APEC activities.[53]

Companies of the APEC have become increasingly competitive and sophisticated in global business in the past three decades. The Japanese and South Koreans in particular have made tremendous inroads on world markets for automobiles, cameras, and audio and video equipment. Products from Samsung, Sony, Sanyo, Toyota, Daewoo, Mitsubishi, Suzuki, and Toshiba are sold all over the world and have set standards of quality by which other products are often judged. The People's Republic of China, a country of 1.3 billion people, has launched a program of economic reform to stimulate its economy by privatizing many industries, restructuring its banking system, and increasing public spending on infrastructure (including railways and telecommunications). As a result, China has become

Asia-Pacific Economic Cooperation (APEC) an international trade alliance that promotes open trade and economic and technical cooperation among member nations

Respo[nsibility]

Starbuc[ks]

In 2008, Howard Schultz re[turned to Star]bucks after years of expan[sion, closing]
stores and cutting expenses[. Since then, the]
company has become more [careful in how]
to expand by focusing on its [core market.]

Starbucks operates in m[any countries. Its pri]mary focus is on expansion [into]
China in 1999. It now runs a[bout 570 stores and hopes]
to 1,500 by 2015. Finding th[e right locations is chal]lenging. Some have complai[ned that Starbucks]
was invasive and accused [the chain of forcing its]
culture along with its produ[cts. Critics seized on]
its Forbidden City location a[nd forced it to close]
out the media.

This time around, Schu[ltz hopes to incorpo]rate Chinese cultural expec[tations such as Chinese-]
inspired food items and mo[re.]

balance-of-payment deficits and provides foreign currencies to member nations. The International Monetary Fund tries to avoid financial crises and panics by alerting the international community about countries that will not be able to repay their debts. The IMF's Internet site provides additional information about the organization, including news releases, frequently asked questions, and members.

The IMF is the closest thing the world has to an international central bank. If countries get into financial trouble, they can borrow from the World Bank. However, the global economic crisis created many challenges for the IMF as it was forced to significantly increase its loans to both emerging economies and more developed nations. The usefulness of the IMF for developed countries is limited because these countries use private markets as a major source of capital.[66] Yet the European debt crisis changed this somewhat. Greece, Ireland, and Portugal required billions of dollars in bailouts from the IMF to keep their economies afloat.

Getting Involved in International Business

Businesses may get involved in international trade at many levels—from a small Kenyan firm that occasionally exports African crafts to a huge multinational corporation such as Shell Oil that sells products around the globe. The degree of commitment of resources and effort required increases according to the level at which a business involves itself in international trade. This section examines exporting and importing, trading companies, licensing and franchising, contract manufacturing, joint ventures, direct investment, and multinational corporations.

Exporting and Importing

Many companies first get involved in international trade when they import goods from other countries for resale in their own businesses. For example, a grocery store chain may import bananas from Honduras and coffee from Colombia. A business may get involved in exporting when it is called upon to supply a foreign company with a particular product. Such exporting enables enterprises of all sizes to participate in international business. Exporting to other countries becomes a necessity for established countries that seek to grow continually. Products often have higher sales growth potential in foreign countries than they have in the parent country. For instance, General Motors and YUM Brands! sell more of their products in China than in the United States. Walmart experienced sales growth in international markets even as domestic sales were falling. Table 3.4 shows the number of U.S. exporters and the export value by company size, while Figure 3.2 shows some of the world's largest exporting countries.

countertrade agreements foreign trade agreements that involve bartering products for other products instead of for currency

Exporting sometimes takes place through **countertrade agreements,** which involve bartering products for other products instead of for currency. Such arrangements are fairly common in international trade, especially between Western companies and eastern European nations. An estimated 40 percent or more of all international trade agreements contain countertrade provisions.

Although a company may export its wares overseas directly or import goods directly from their manufacturer, many choose to deal with an intermediary, commonly called an *export agent*. Export agents seldom produce goods themselves; instead, they usually handle international transactions for other firms. Export agents either purchase products outright or take them on consignment. If they purchase them outright, they generally mark up the price they have paid and attempt

The ship *Cosco Ran* transports [goods.]

	Number of Exporters	Percentage	Value (millions of dollars)	Percentage
Unknown	99,305	36	83,161	8.9
Small (<100 employees)	153,667	55.8	138,565	14.8
Medium (100–499)	16,297	5.9	86,297	9.2
Large (>500)	6,574	2.4	630,770	67.2

TABLE 3.4

U.S. Exporters and Value by Company Size

Source: "A Profile of U.S. Exporting Companies, 2008–2009," Bureau of the Census, www.census.gov/foreign trade/Press Release/edb/2009/exh1a.pdf (accessed January 25, 2012).

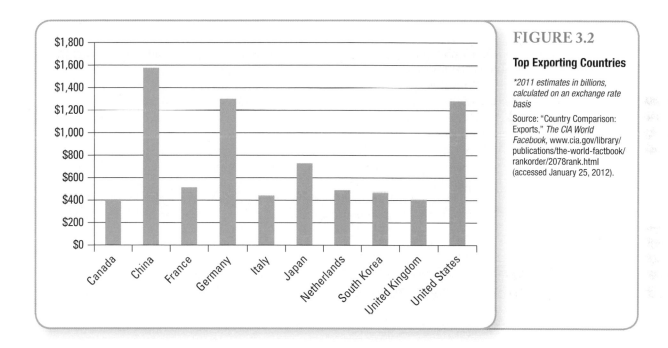

FIGURE 3.2

Top Exporting Countries

2011 estimates in billions, calculated on an exchange rate basis

Source: "Country Comparison: Exports," *The CIA World Factbook,* www.cia.gov/library/publications/the-world-factbook/rankorder/2078rank.html (accessed January 25, 2012).

to sell the product in the international marketplace. They are also responsible for storage and transportation.

An advantage of trading through an agent instead of directly is that the company does not have to deal with foreign currencies or the red tape (paying tariffs and handling paperwork) of international business. A major disadvantage is that, because the export agent must make a profit, either the price of the product must be increased or the domestic company must provide a larger discount than it would in a domestic transaction.

Trading Companies

A **trading company** buys goods in one country and sells them to buyers in another country. Trading companies handle all activities required to move products from one country to another, including consulting, marketing research, advertising, insurance,

trading company
a firm that buys goods in one country and sells them to buyers in another country

licensing
a trade agreement in
which one company—the
licensor—allows another
company—the licensee—
to use its company name,
products, patents, brands,
trademarks, raw materials,
and/or production processes
in exchange for a fee or
royalty

franchising
a form of licensing in
which a company—the
franchiser—agrees to
provide a franchisee a name,
logo, methods of operation,
advertising, products, and
other elements associated
with a franchiser's business
in return for a financial
commitment and the
agreement to conduct
business in accordance with
the franchiser's standard of
operations

product research and design, warehousing, and foreign exchange services to companies interested in selling their products in foreign markets. Trading companies are similar to export agents, but their role in international trade is larger. By linking sellers and buyers of goods in different countries, trading companies promote international trade. The best-known U.S. trading company is Sears World Trade, which specializes in consumer goods, light industrial items, and processed foods.

Licensing and Franchising

Licensing is a trade arrangement in which one company—the *licensor*—allows another company—the *licensee*—to use its company name, products, patents, brands, trademarks, raw materials, and/or production processes in exchange for a fee or royalty. The Coca-Cola Company and PepsiCo frequently use licensing as a means to market their soft drinks, apparel, and other merchandise in other countries. Licensing is an attractive alternative to direct investment when the political stability of a foreign country is in doubt or when resources are unavailable for direct investment. Licensing is especially advantageous for small manufacturers wanting to launch a well-known brand internationally. Yoplait is a French yogurt that is licensed for production in the United States.

Franchising is a form of licensing in which a company—the *franchiser*—agrees to provide a *franchisee* the name, logo, methods of operation, advertising, products, and other elements associated with the franchiser's business, in return for a financial commitment and the agreement to conduct business in accordance with the franchiser's standard of operations. Wendy's, McDonald's, Pizza Hut, and Holiday Inn are well-known franchisers with international visibility. Table 3.5 lists some of the top global franchises.

Licensing and franchising enable a company to enter the international marketplace without spending large sums of money abroad or hiring or transferring

TABLE 3.5
Top Global Franchises

Franchise	Country	Ranking
Subway	United States	1
McDonald's	United States	2
InterContinental Hotels Group	United Kingdom	11
DIA	Spain	21
Europcar	France	27
Kumon North America Inc.	Japan	33
Cartridge World	Australia	37
Yogen Fruz	Canada	44
Engel & Völkers	Germany	83
Schlotzsky's	United States	95

Source: "Top 100 Global Franchises—Ranking," *Franchise Direct*, www.franchisedirect.com/top100globalfranchises/rankings/ (accessed January 25, 2012).

personnel to handle overseas affairs. They also minimize problems associated with shipping costs, tariffs, and trade restrictions, and they allow the firm to establish goodwill for its products in a foreign market, which will help the company if it decides to produce or market its products directly in the foreign country at some future date. However, if the licensee (or franchisee) does not maintain high standards of quality, the product's image may be hurt; therefore, it is important for the licensor to monitor its products overseas and to enforce its quality standards.

Contract Manufacturing

Contract manufacturing occurs when a company hires a foreign company to produce a specified volume of the firm's product to specification; the final product carries the domestic firm's name. Spalding, for example, relies on contract manufacturing for its sports equipment; Reebok uses Korean contract manufacturers to manufacture many of its athletic shoes.

Outsourcing

Earlier, we defined outsourcing as transferring manufacturing or other tasks (such as information technology operations) to companies in countries where labor and supplies are less expensive. Many U.S. firms have outsourced tasks to India, Ireland, Mexico, and the Philippines, where there are many well-educated workers and significantly lower labor costs. Services, such as taxes or customer service, can also be outsourced.

Although outsourcing has become politically controversial in recent years amid concerns over jobs lost to overseas workers, foreign companies transfer tasks and jobs to U.S. companies—sometimes called *insourcing*—far more often than U.S. companies outsource tasks and jobs abroad.[67] However, some firms are bringing their outsourced jobs back after concerns that foreign workers were not adding enough value. For example, some of the bigger banks are now choosing to set up offshore operations themselves rather than outsource. This has to do with increased regulations in foreign countries and concerns over data security. One instance of fraud at the Indian outsourcer Satyam amounted to more than $1 billion.

Offshoring

Offshoring is the relocation of a business process by a company, or a subsidiary, to another country. Offshoring is different than outsourcing: the company retains control of the process because it is not subcontracting to a different company. Companies may choose to offshore for a number of reasons, ranging from lower wages, skilled labor, or taking advantage of time zone differences in order to offer services around the clock. Some banks have chosen not to outsource because of concerns about data security in other countries. These institutions may

contract manufacturing
the hiring of a foreign company to produce a specified volume of the initiating company's product to specification; the final product carries the domestic firm's name

offshoring
The relocation of business processes by a company or subsidiary to another country. Offshoring is different than outsourcing because the company retains control of the offshored processes.

In addition to catering to customers' local taste preferences with menu items like the Shaka Shaka Chicken from McDonald's Japan, the company also offers core menu items that are present in its restaurants throughout the world.

instead engage in offshoring, which allows a company more control over international operations because the offshore office is an extension of the company. Barclays Bank, for instance, has an international offshore banking unit called Barclays Wealth International. This branch helps the company better serve wealthy clients with international banking needs.[68]

Joint Ventures and Alliances

joint venture
the sharing of the costs and operation of a business between a foreign company and a local partner

Many countries, particularly LDCs, do not permit direct investment by foreign companies or individuals. A company may also lack sufficient resources or expertise to operate in another country. In such cases, a company that wants to do business in another country may set up a **joint venture** by finding a local partner (occasionally, the host nation itself) to share the costs and operation of the business. For example, Brazilian conglomerate Odebrecht created a joint venture with state-owned oil company Petroleos de Venezuela. Odebrecht paid $50 million, or a 40 percent stake, to search for oil in the Venezuelan state of Zulia. Because the oil industry is nationalized in Venezuela, foreign oil companies must enter into joint ventures if they want to explore for and drill oil in the country.[69]

strategic alliance
a partnership formed to create competitive advantage on a worldwide basis

In some industries, such as automobiles and computers, strategic alliances are becoming the predominant means of competing. A **strategic alliance** is a partnership formed to create competitive advantage on a worldwide basis. In such industries, international competition is so fierce and the costs of competing on a global basis are so high that few firms have the resources to go it alone, so they collaborate with other companies. An example of a strategic alliance is the partnership between Australian airlines Virgin Blue and Skywest. By forming an alliance, the two airlines hope to tap into the increased demand from the mining industry for flights to distant mining sites. As part of the agreement, Skywest can use as many as 18 Virgin Blue turbo-prop aircraft for 10 years. In addition to penetrating a lucrative market, Virgin Blue hopes the alliance will help it to extend its influence into regional markets and steal market share from its competitor, QantasLink.[70]

direct investment
the ownership of overseas facilities

Walmart has chosen to directly invest in China. However, it must still make adjustments to fit with the local culture. For instance, Walmart, which is normally against trade unions, was pressured to allow its Chinese employees to unionize.

Direct Investment

Companies that want more control and are willing to invest considerable resources in international business may consider **direct investment,** the ownership of overseas facilities. Direct investment may involve the development and operation of new facilities—such as when Starbucks opens a new coffee shop in Japan—or the purchase of all or part of an existing operation in a foreign country. India's Tata Motors purchased Jaguar and Land Rover from Ford Motor Company. Tata, a maker of cars and trucks, is attempting to broaden its global presence, including manufacturing these vehicles in the United Kingdom.[71]

The highest level of international business involvement is the **multinational corporation (MNC),** a corporation, such as IBM or ExxonMobil, that operates on a worldwide scale, without significant ties to any one nation or region. Table 3.6 lists the 10 largest multinational corporations. MNCs are more than simple corporations. They often have greater assets than some of the countries in which they do business. Nestlé, with headquarters in Switzerland, operates more than 400 factories around the world and receives revenues from Europe; North, Central, and South America; Africa; and Asia.[72] The Royal Dutch/Shell Group, one of the world's major oil producers, is another MNC. Its main offices are located in The Hague and London. Other MNCs include BASF, British Petroleum, Matsushita, Mitsubishi, Siemens, Texaco, Toyota, and Unilever. Many MNCs have been targeted by antiglobalization activists at global business forums, and some protests have turned violent. The activists contend that MNCs increase the gap between rich and poor nations, misuse and misallocate scarce resources, exploit the labor markets in LDCs, and harm their natural environments.[73]

multinational corporation (MNC)
a corporation that operates on a worldwide scale, without significant ties to any one nation or region

International Business Strategies

Planning in a global economy requires businesspeople to understand the economic, legal, political, and sociocultural realities of the countries in which they will operate. These factors will affect the strategy a business chooses to use outside its own borders.

multinational strategy
a plan, used by international companies, that involves customizing products, promotion, and distribution according to cultural, technological, regional, and national differences

Developing Strategies

Companies doing business internationally have traditionally used a **multinational strategy,** customizing their products, promotion, and distribution according to cultural, technological, regional, and national differences. To succeed in India,

LO 3-5

TABLE 3.6
Top 10 Largest Corporations

Company	Revenue (in millions)	Country
1. Royal Dutch Shell	$484,489	Netherlands
2. ExxonMobil	452,926	United States
3. Wal-Mart	446,950	United States
4. BP	386,463	Britain
5. Sinopec Group	375,214	China
6. China National Petroleum	352,338	China
7. State Grid	259,141.8	China
8. Chevron	245,621	United States
9. ConocoPhillips	237,272	United States
10. Toyota Motor	235,364	Japan

Source: "Global 500: The World's Largest Corporations," July 23, 2012, *Fortune,* F-1.

for example, McDonald's had to adapt its products to respect religious customs. McDonald's India does not serve beef or pork products and has vegetarian dishes for its largely vegetarian consumer base. Many soap and detergent manufacturers have adapted their products to local water conditions, washing equipment, and washing habits. For customers in some less-developed countries, Colgate-Palmolive Co. has developed an inexpensive, plastic, hand-powered washing machine for use in households that have no electricity. Even when products are standardized, advertising often has to be modified to adapt to language and cultural differences. Also, celebrities used in advertising in the United States may be unfamiliar to foreign consumers and thus would not be effective in advertising products in other countries.

**global strategy
(globalization)**
a strategy that involves
standardizing products
(and, as much as possible,
their promotion and
distribution) for the whole
world, as if it were a
single entity

More and more companies are moving from this customization strategy to a **global strategy (globalization),** which involves standardizing products (and, as much as possible, their promotion and distribution) for the whole world, as if it were a single entity. Examples of globalized products are American clothing, movies, music, and cosmetics. As it has become a global brand, Starbucks has standardized its products and stores. Starbucks was ranked as the world's most engaged brand in terms of online activities, even surpassing Coca-Cola, which is another global brand.

Before moving outside their own borders, companies must conduct environmental analyses to evaluate the potential of and problems associated with various markets and to determine what strategy is best for doing business in those markets. Failure to do so may result in losses and even negative publicity. Some companies rely on local managers to gain greater insights and faster response to changes within a country. Astute businesspeople today "think globally, act locally." That is, while constantly being aware of the total picture, they adjust their firms' strategies to conform to local needs and tastes.

Managing the Challenges of Global Business

As we've pointed out in this chapter, many past political barriers to trade have fallen or been minimized, expanding and opening new market opportunities. Managers who can meet the challenges of creating and implementing effective and sensitive business strategies for the global marketplace can help lead their companies to success. For example, the Commercial Service is the global business solutions unit of the U.S. Department of Commerce that offers U.S. firms wide and deep practical knowledge of international markets and industries, a unique global network, inventive use of information technology, and a focus on small and mid-sized businesses. Another example is the benchmarking of best international practices that benefits U.S. firms, which is conducted by the network of CIBERs (Centers for International Business Education and Research) at leading business schools in the United States. These CIBERs are funded by the U.S. government to help U.S. firms become more competitive globally. A major element of the assistance that these governmental organizations can provide firms (especially for small and medium-sized firms) is knowledge of the internationalization process.[74] Small businesses, too, can succeed in foreign markets when their managers have carefully studied those markets and prepared and implemented appropriate strategies. Being globally aware is therefore an important quality for today's managers and will become a critical attribute for managers of the 21st century.

So You Want a Job in Global Business

Have you always dreamt of traveling the world? Whether backpacking your way through Central America or sipping espressos at five-star European restaurants is your style, the increasing globalization of business might just give you your chance to see what the world has to offer. Most new jobs will have at least some global component, even if located within the United States, so being globally aware and keeping an open mind to different cultures is vital in today's business world. Think about the 1.3 billion consumers in China that have already purchased 500 million mobile phones. In the future, some of the largest markets will be in Asia.

Many jobs discussed in chapters throughout this book tend to have strong international components. For example, product management and distribution management are discussed as marketing careers in Chapter 12. As more and more companies sell products around the globe, their function, design, packaging, and promotions need to be culturally relevant to many different people in many different places. Products very often cross multiple borders before reaching the final consumer, both in their distribution and through the supply chain to produce the products.

Jobs exist in export and import management, product and pricing management, distribution and transportation, and advertising. Many "born global" companies such as Google operate virtually and consider all countries their market. Many companies sell their products through eBay and other Internet sites and never leave the U.S. Today communication and transportation facilitates selling and buying products worldwide with delivery in a few days. You may have sold or purchased a product on eBay outside the U.S. without thinking about how easy and accessible international markets are to business. If you have, welcome to the world of global business.

To be successful you must have an idea not only of differing regulations from country to country, but of different language, ethics, and communication styles and varying needs and wants of international markets. From a regulatory side, you may need to be aware of laws related to intellectual property, copyrights, antitrust, advertising, and pricing in every country. Translating is never only about translating the language. Perhaps even more important is ensuring that your message gets through. Whether on a product label or in advertising or promotional materials, the use of images and words varies widely across the globe.

Review Your Understanding

Explore some of the factors within the international trade environment that influence business.

International business is the buying, selling, and trading of goods and services across national boundaries. Importing is the purchase of products and raw materials from another nation; exporting is the sale of domestic goods and materials to another nation. A nation's balance of trade is the difference in value between its exports and imports; a negative balance of trade is a trade deficit. The difference between the flow of money into a country and the flow of money out of it is called the balance of payments. An absolute or comparative advantage in trade may determine what products a company from a particular nation will export.

Investigate some of the economic, legal-political, social, cultural, and technological barriers to international business.

Companies engaged in international trade must consider the effects of economic, legal, political, social, and cultural differences between nations. Economic barriers are a country's level of development (infrastructure) and exchange rates. Wide-ranging legal and political barriers include differing laws (and enforcement), tariffs, exchange controls, quotas, embargoes, political instability, and war. Ambiguous cultural and social barriers involve differences in spoken and body language, time, holidays and other observances, and customs.

Specify some of the agreements, alliances, and organizations that may encourage trade across international boundaries.

Among the most important promoters of international business are the General Agreement on Tariffs and Trade, the World Trade Organization, the North American Free Trade Agreement, the European Union, the Asia-Pacific Economic Cooperation, the Association of Southeast Asian Nations, the World Bank, and the International Monetary Fund.

Summarize the different levels of organizational involvement in international trade.

A company may be involved in international trade at several levels, each requiring a greater commitment of resources and effort, ranging from importing/exporting to multinational corporations. Countertrade agreements occur at the import/export level and involve bartering products for other products instead of currency. At the next level, a trading company links buyers and sellers in different countries to foster trade. In licensing and franchising, one company agrees to allow a foreign company the use of its company name, products, patents, brands, trademarks, raw materials, and production processes in exchange for a flat fee or royalty. Contract manufacturing occurs when a company hires a foreign company to produce a specified volume of the firm's product to specification; the final product carries the domestic firm's name. A joint venture is a partnership in which companies from different countries agree to share the costs and operation of the business. The purchase of overseas production and marketing facilities is direct investment. Outsourcing, a form of direct investment, involves transferring manufacturing to countries where labor and supplies are cheap. A multinational corporation is one that operates on a worldwide scale, without significant ties to any one nation or region.

Contrast two basic strategies used in international business.

Companies typically use one of two basic strategies in international business. A multinational strategy customizes products, promotion, and distribution according to cultural, technological, regional, and national differences. A global strategy (globalization) standardizes products (and, as much as possible, their promotion and distribution) for the whole world, as if it were a single entity.

Assess the opportunities and problems facing a small business that is considering expanding into international markets.

"Solve the Dilemma" on page 114 presents a small business considering expansion into international markets. Based on the material provided in the chapter, analyze the business's position, evaluating specific markets, anticipating problems, and exploring methods of international involvement.

Revisit the World of Business

1. Why is Procter & Gamble expanding into places such as India and the Philippines?

2. How is Procter & Gamble tailoring its products to meet the needs of Indian consumers?

3. What are some of the social and economic barriers P&G is facing in its expansion into India?

Learn the Terms

absolute advantage   87
Asia-Pacific Economic Cooperation (APEC)   101
Association of Southeast Asian Nations (ASEAN)   103
balance of payments   88
balance of trade   88
cartel   95
comparative advantage   87
contract manufacturing   107
countertrade agreements   104
direct investment   108
dumping   94
embargo   93
European Union (EU)   100
exchange controls   93
exchange rate   90
exporting   87
franchising   106
General Agreement on Tariffs and Trade (GATT)   97
global strategy (globalization)   110

import tariff   93
importing   88
infrastructure   90
international business 86
International Monetary Fund (IMF)   103
joint venture   108
licensing   106
multinational corporation (MNC)   109
multinational strategy   109
North American Free Trade Agreement (NAFTA)   98
offshoring   107
outsourcing   87
quota   93
strategic alliance   108
trade deficit   88
trading company   105
World Bank   103
World Trade Organization (WTO)   97

Check Your Progress

1. Distinguish between an absolute advantage and a comparative advantage. Cite an example of a country that has an absolute advantage and one with a comparative advantage.

2. What effect does devaluation have on a nation's currency? Can you think of a country that has devaluated or revaluated its currency? What have been the results?

3. What effect does a country's economic development have on international business?

4. How do political issues affect international business?

5. What is an import tariff? A quota? Dumping? How might a country use import tariffs and quotas to control its balance of trade and payments? Why can dumping result in the imposition of tariffs and quotas?

6. How do social and cultural differences create barriers to international trade? Can you think of any additional social or cultural barriers (other than those mentioned in this chapter) that might inhibit international business?

7. Explain how a countertrade agreement can be considered a trade promoter. How does the World Trade Organization encourage trade?

8. At what levels might a firm get involved in international business? What level requires the least commitment of resources? What level requires the most?

9. Compare and contrast licensing, franchising, contract manufacturing, and outsourcing.

10. Compare multinational and global strategies. Which is best? Under what circumstances might each be used?

Get Involved

1. If the United States were to impose additional tariffs on cars imported from Japan, what would happen to the price of Japanese cars sold in the United States? What would happen to the price of American cars? What action might Japan take to continue to compete in the U.S. automobile market?

2. Although NAFTA has been controversial, it has been a positive factor for U.S. firms desiring to engage in international business. What industries and specific companies have the greatest potential for opening stores in Canada and Mexico? What opportunities exist for small businesses that cannot afford direct investment in Mexico and Canada?

3. Identify a local company that is active in international trade. What is its level of international business involvement and why? Analyze the threats and opportunities it faces in foreign markets, as well as its strengths and weaknesses in meeting those challenges. Based on your analysis, make some recommendations for the business's future involvement in international trade. (Your instructor may ask you to share your report with the class.)

Build Your Skills

GLOBAL AWARENESS

Background

As American businesspeople travel the globe, they encounter and must quickly adapt to a variety of cultural norms quite different from the United States. When encountering individuals from other parts of the world, the best attitude to adopt is "Here is my way. Now what is yours?" The more you see that you are part of a complex world and that your culture is different from, not better than, others, the better you will communicate and the more effective you will be in a variety of situations. It takes time, energy, understanding, and tolerance to learn about and appreciate other cultures. Naturally you're more comfortable doing things the way you've always done them. Remember, however, that this fact will also be true of the people from other cultures with whom you are doing business.

Task

You will "travel the globe" by answering questions related to some of the cultural norms that are found in other countries. Form groups of four to six class members and determine the answers to the following questions. Your instructor has the answer key, which will allow you to determine your group's Global Awareness IQ, which is based on a maximum score of 100 points (10 points per question).

Match the country with the cultural descriptor provided.

A. Saudi Arabia   F. China
B. Japan   G. Greece
C. Great Britain   H. Korea
D. Germany   I. India
E. Venezuela   J. Mexico

_____ **1.** When people in this country table a motion, they want to discuss it. In America, "to table a motion" means to put off discussion.

_____ **2.** In this country, special forms of speech called *keigo* convey status among speakers. When talking with a person in this country, one should know the person's rank. People from this country will not initiate a conversation without a formal introduction.

_____ **3.** People from this country pride themselves on enhancing their image by keeping others waiting.

_____ **4.** When writing a business letter, people in this country like to provide a great deal of background information and detail before presenting their main points.

_____ **5.** For a man to inquire about another man's wife (even a general question about how she is doing) is considered very offensive in this country.

_____ **6.** When in this country, you are expected to negotiate the price on goods you wish to purchase.

_____ **7.** While North Americans want to decide the main points at a business meeting and leave the details for later, people in this country need to have all details decided before the meeting ends to avoid suspicion and distrust.

_____ **8.** Children in this country learn from a very early age to look down respectfully when talking to those of higher status.

_____ **9.** In this country the husband is the ruler of the household, and the custom is to keep the women hidden.

_____ **10.** Many businesspeople from the United States experience frustration because yes does not always mean the same thing in other cultures. For example, the word *yes* in this country means, "OK, I want to respect you and not offend you." It does not necessarily show agreement.

Solve the Dilemma   LO 3-6

GLOBAL EXPANSION OR BUSINESS AS USUAL?

Audiotech Electronics, founded in 1959 by a father and son, currently operates a 35,000-square-foot factory with 75 employees. The company produces control consoles for television and radio stations and recording studios. It is involved in every facet of production—designing the systems, installing the circuits in its computer boards, and even manufacturing and painting the metal cases housing the consoles. The company's products are used by all the major broadcast and cable networks. The firm's newest products allow television correspondents to simultaneously hear and communicate with their counterparts in different geographic locations. Audiotech has been very successful meeting its customers' needs efficiently.

Audiotech sales have historically been strong in the United States, but recently, growth is stagnating. Even though Audiotech is a small, family-owned firm, it believes it should evaluate and consider global expansion.

Discussion Questions

1. What are the key issues that need to be considered in determining global expansion?

2. What are some of the unique problems that a small business might face in global expansion that larger firms would not?

3. Should Audiotech consider a joint venture? Should it hire a sales force of people native to the countries it enters?

Build Your Business Plan

BUSINESS IN A BORDERLESS WORLD

Think about the product/service you are contemplating for your business plan. If it is an already established product or service, try to find out if the product is currently being sold internationally. If not, can you identify opportunities to do so in the future? What countries do you think would respond most favorably to your product? What problems would you encounter if you attempted to export your product to those countries?

If you are thinking of creating a new product or service for your business plan, think about the possibility of eventually marketing that product in another country. What countries or areas of the world do you think would be most responsive to your product?

Are there countries the U.S. has trade agreements or alliances with that would make your entry into the market easier? What would be the economic, social, cultural, and technological barriers you would have to recognize before entering the prospective country(ies)? Think about the specific cultural differences that would have to be taken into consideration before entering the prospective country.

See for Yourself Videocase

WALT DISNEY AROUND THE GLOBE

Mickey Mouse has been a beloved American icon since the 1930s. The success of this and other Disney characters helped to build Disney theme parks, first in Anaheim, California, in 1955 and then in Orlando, Florida, 16 years later. For decades, tourists from all over the globe traveled in droves to California or Florida to experience the "happiest place on earth." What could be more natural for Disney than to introduce Mickey around the globe with international parks?

Disneyland first opened on the international front in Tokyo, Japan, in 1983. Ten years later, Disney brought the magic to Paris, France. Finally, in 2005, Disneyland opened its gates in Hong Kong, China. Global expansion is tricky for any business. There are many challenges to overcome, such as economic, legal, political, social, and cultural barriers. While Mickey may be recognized and loved around the world, this does not mean that duplicating American parks in other countries would be a success.

Perhaps the greatest challenge for Disney when entering new international markets has been how to handle cultural differences. Euro Disney (later renamed Disneyland Resort Paris) opened near Paris, France, in 1992 to fanfare and problems. Many well-known French citizens and labor unions vocally opposed the park because they felt that it was wrong to allow a symbol of American culture to become a focal point in France. Attendance for the first three years was well below expectations, causing grave financial difficulties. Finally, in 1995, the park experienced a turnaround. Financial restructuring helped the park achieve profitability. New attractions, lower admission prices, renaming the park, and a marketing campaign increased attendance. The park, now the number-one tourist attraction in Europe with 15 million visitors per year, continues to expand

in anticipation of future growth. The theme park has attracted more than 250 million visitors in its 20-year history.

Having learned from its experience in France, The Walt Disney Company entered its venture in Hong Kong with an eye to embracing and honoring local culture. The company had learned to be sensitive to cultural variations in events, trends, and cuisine. The parks must embrace local culture while staying true to the Disney message. To this end, Disney hired a feng shui consultant to assist with the layout of the Hong Kong park. The fourth floor was eliminated at all hotels because of the cultural belief that the number four is bad luck. One of the Hong Kong Disneyland ballrooms measures 888 square meters, because eight signifies wealth in Chinese culture. Even with this attention to detail, Hong Kong Disneyland's first years have been rough, with attendance far below projections and protestors raising cultural and social objections. A major complaint among guests has been that the park is small. Over the next decade, the company plans to invest half a billion dollars in expansion efforts. Disney is also building a theme park in Shanghai, China. This park will be two to three times as large as Hong Kong Disney and is set to be completed in 2016.

While some locals continue to protest Disney's presence, there are benefits to allowing a global company like Disney to enter foreign markets. Disney theme parks attract both local and global tourists, which can be a major stimulus to the local economy. For example, Hong Kong expects that Hong Kong Disneyland will bring more than 50,000 jobs to the city between 2005 and 2025. Experts predict that the park will bring $19 billion (U.S.) to the local economy during the park's first 40 years. It is likely that with expansion and further refinement, Hong Kong Disneyland will be a success in the long run. Problems in France and Hong Kong have not deterred The

Walt Disney Company from further global expansion. Hopefully, the company has learned that it must pay close attention to cultural and social variances in global markets in order to succeed.[75]

DISCUSSION QUESTIONS

1.   What led The Walt Disney Company to believe that its theme parks would be successful internationally?

2.   What stumbling blocks did Disney encounter at its France and Hong Kong theme parks?

3.   What are some of the factors complicating international expansion of a brand like Disney? What can a multinational corporation do to mitigate these issues?

Remember to check out our Online Learning Center at www.mhhe.com/ferrell9e.

Team Exercise

Visit Transparency International's Country Corruption Index website: http://cpi.transparency.org/cpi2011/results/. Form groups and select two countries. Research some of the economic, ethical, legal, regulatory, and political barriers that would have an impact on international trade. Be sure to pair a fairly ethical country with a fairly unethical country (Sweden with Myanmar, Australia with Haiti). Report your findings.

part 2

Starting and Growing a Business

REI is also a favorite with employees. Employees at REI receive many benefits, including steep discounts on products and yearly gifts of REI gear. To ascertain the satisfaction of its employees, REI solicits feedback through annual employee surveys. As a result of its emphasis on employees, REI has been elected to *Fortune* magazine's "100 Best Companies to Work For" every year since 1998.[1]

Introduction

Need help understanding the Various Forms of Business Ownership?

http://bit.ly/FerrellQR4-1

The legal form of ownership taken by a business is seldom of great concern to you as a customer. When you eat at a restaurant, you probably don't care whether the restaurant is owned by one person (a sole proprietorship), has two or more owners who share the business (a partnership), or is an entity owned by many stockholders (a corporation); all you want is good food. If you buy a foreign car, you probably don't care whether the company that made it has laws governing its form of organization that are different from those for businesses in the United States. You are buying the car because it is well made, fits your price range, or appeals to your sense of style. Nonetheless, a business's legal form of ownership affects how it operates, how much taxes it pays, and how much control its owners have.

This chapter examines three primary forms of business ownership—sole proprietorship, partnership, and corporation—and weighs the advantages and disadvantages of each. These forms are the most often used whether the business is a traditional bricks and mortar company, an online-only one, or a combination of both. We also take a look at S corporations, limited liability companies, and cooperatives and discuss some trends in business ownership. You may wish to refer to Table 4.1 to compare the various forms of business ownership mentioned in the chapter.

TABLE 4.1   **Various Forms of Business Ownership**

Structure	Ownership	Taxation	Liability	Use
Sole Proprietorship	1 owner	Individual income taxed	Unlimited	Owned by a single individual and is the easiest way to conduct business.
Partnership	2 or more owners	Individual owners' income taxed	Somewhat limited	Easy way for two individuals to conduct business
Corporation	Any number of shareholders	Corporate and shareholder taxed	Limited	A legal entity with shareholders or stockholders
S Corporation	Up to 75 shareholders	Taxed as a partnership	Limited	A legal entity with tax advantages for restricted number of shareholders
Limited Liability Company	Unlimited number of shareholders	Taxed as a partnership	Limited	Avoid personal lawsuits

Sole Proprietorships

Sole proprietorships, businesses owned and operated by one individual, are the most common form of business organization in the United States. Common examples include many restaurants, hair salons, flower shops, dog kennels, and independent grocery stores. Many sole proprietors focus on services—small retail stores, financial counseling, appliance repair, child care, and the like—rather than on the manufacture of goods, which often requires large sums of money not available to most small businesses. As you can see in Figure 4.1, proprietorships far outnumber corporations, but they net far fewer sales and less income.

sole proprietorships businesses owned and operated by one individual; the most common form of business organization in the United States

Sole proprietorships are typically small businesses employing fewer than 50 people. (We'll look at small businesses in greater detail in Chapter 5.) Sole proprietorships constitute approximately three-fourths of all businesses in the United States. It is interesting to note that men are twice as likely as women to start their own business.[2] In many areas, small businesses make up the vast majority of the economy.

Advantages of Sole Proprietorships

Sole proprietorships are generally managed by their owners. Because of this simple management structure, the owner/manager can make decisions quickly. This is just one of many advantages of the sole proprietorship form of business.

Ease and Cost of Formation.   Forming a sole proprietorship is relatively easy and inexpensive. In some states, creating a sole proprietorship involves merely announcing the new business in the local newspaper. Other proprietorships, such as barber shops and restaurants, may require state and local licenses and permits because of the nature of the business. The cost of these permits may run from $25 to $100. No lawyer is needed to create such enterprises, and the owner can usually take care of the required paperwork without outside assistance.

Of course, an entrepreneur starting a new sole proprietorship must find a suitable site from which to operate the business. Some sole proprietors look no farther than their garage or a spare bedroom when seeking a workshop or office. Among the more famous businesses that sprang to life in their founders' homes are Google, Walt Disney, Dell, eBay, Hewlett-Packard, Apple, and Mattel.[3] Computers, personal

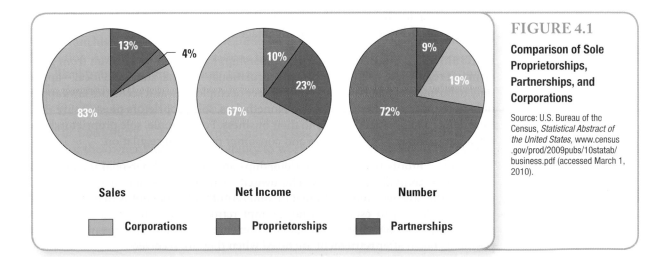

FIGURE 4.1

Comparison of Sole Proprietorships, Partnerships, and Corporations

Source: U.S. Bureau of the Census, *Statistical Abstract of the United States,* www.census .gov/prod/2009pubs/10statab/ business.pdf (accessed March 1, 2010).

TABLE 4.3

Issues and Provisions in Articles of Partnership

1. Name, purpose, location
2. Duration of the agreement
3. Authority and responsibility of each partner
4. Character of partners (i.e., general or limited, active or silent)
5. Amount of contribution from each partner
6. Division of profits or losses
7. Salaries of each partner
8. How much each partner is allowed to withdraw
9. Death of partner
10. Sale of partnership interest
11. Arbitration of disputes
12. Required and prohibited actions
13. Absence and disability
14. Restrictive covenants
15. Buying and selling agreements

Source: Adapted from "Partnership Agreement Sample," State of New Jersey, www.state.nj.us/njbusiness/starting/basics/partnership_agreement_sample.shtml (accessed March 15, 2010).

not required, it makes good sense for partners to draw them up. Articles of partnership usually list the money or assets that each partner has contributed (called *partnership capital*), state each partner's individual management role or duty, specify how the profits and losses of the partnership will be divided among the partners, and describe how a partner may leave the partnership as well as any other restrictions that might apply to the agreement. Table 4.3 lists some of the issues and provisions that should be included in articles of partnership.

In 1996 Stanford students Sergey Brin and Larry Page partnered to form the search engine Google as part of a research project. The company was incorporated in 1998 and is now the world's top search engine.

Advantages of Partnerships

Law firms, accounting firms, and investment firms with several hundred partners have partnership agreements that are quite complicated in comparison with the partnership agreement among two or three people owning a computer repair shop. The advantages must be compared with those offered by other forms of business organization, and not all apply to every partnership.

Ease of Organization.   Starting a partnership requires little more than drawing up articles of partnership. No legal charters have to be granted, but the name of the business should be registered with the state.

Availability of Capital and Credit.   When a business has several partners, it has the benefit of a combination of talents and skills and pooled financial resources. Partnerships tend to be larger than sole proprietorships and therefore have greater earning power and better credit ratings. Because many limited partnerships have been formed for tax purposes rather than for economic profits, the combined income of all U.S. partnerships is quite low, as shown in Figure 4.1. Nevertheless, the professional partnerships of many lawyers, accountants, and banking firms make quite large profits. For instance, the partners in the international law firm Davis Polk & Wardwell LLP take home an average of more than $2 million a year.[7]

Combined Knowledge and Skills.   Partners in the most successful partnerships acknowledge each other's talents and avoid confusion and conflict by specializing in a particular area of expertise such as marketing, production, accounting, or service. The diversity of skills in a partnership makes it possible for the business to be run by a management team of specialists instead of by a generalist sole proprietor. Co-founders Barry Nalebuff and Seth Goldman credit this diversity as being a key component to the success of their company Honest Tea. In less than a decade, Honest Tea went from $250,000 to $13.5 million in sales and attracted the attention of Coca-Cola. Coca-Cola bought a 40 percent stake in the company.[8] Service-oriented partnerships in fields such as law, financial planning, and accounting may attract customers because clients may think that the service offered by a diverse team is of higher quality than that provided by one person. Larger law firms, for example, often have individual partners who specialize in certain areas of the law—such as family, bankruptcy, corporate, entertainment, and criminal law.

Decision Making.   Small partnerships can react more quickly to changes in the business environment than can large partnerships and corporations. Such fast reactions are possible because the partners are involved in day-to-day operations and can make decisions quickly after consultation. Large partnerships with hundreds of partners in many states are not common. In those that do exist, decision making is likely to be slow. However, some partnerships have been successful despite their large size. The accounting firm Baird, Kurtz & Dodson is the 10th largest accounting and advisory firm in the United States, with approximately 250 partners and principals and 2,000 personnel. The company has gross revenues of more than $400 million. Some have attributed BKD's success to its strong diversification techniques and ability to operate in different market niches.[9]

Regulatory Controls.   Like a sole proprietorship, a partnership has fewer regulatory controls affecting its activities than does a corporation. A partnership does not have to file public financial statements with government agencies or send out quarterly financial statements to several thousand owners, as do corporations such as Apple and Ford Motor Co. A partnership does, however, have to abide by all laws relevant to the industry or profession in which it operates as well as state and federal laws relating to hiring and firing, food handling, and so on, just as the sole proprietorship does.

Disadvantages of Partnerships

Partnerships have many advantages compared to sole proprietorships and corporations, but they also have some disadvantages. Limited partners have no voice in the management of the partnership, and they may bear most of the risk of the business while the general partner reaps a larger share of the benefits. There may be a change in the goals and objectives of one partner but not the other, particularly when the partners are multinational organizations. This can cause friction, giving rise to an enterprise that fails to satisfy both parties or even forcing an end to the partnership. Many partnership disputes wind up in court or require outside mediation. A partnership can be jeopardized when two business partners cannot resolve disputes. For instance, Steve Wynn, CEO of Wynn Resorts, had a lawsuit filed against his company by long-time business partner Kazuo Okada. Okada claims that Wynn blocked him from viewing financial records of a $135 million donation that the company gave to the University of Macau. Okada believed the donation might not have constituted an appropriate use of the company's funds.[10] In some cases, the ultimate solution may be dissolving the partnership. Major disadvantages of partnerships include the following.

Unlimited Liability.   In general partnerships, the general partners have unlimited liability for the debts incurred by the business, just as the sole proprietor has unlimited liability for his or her business. Such unlimited liability can be a distinct disadvantage to one partner if his or her personal financial resources are greater than those of the others. A potential partner should check to make sure that all partners have comparable resources to help the business in time of trouble. This disadvantage is eliminated for limited partners, who can lose only their initial investment.

Business Responsibility.   All partners are responsible for the business actions of all others. Partners may have the ability to commit the partnership to a contract without approval of the other partners. A bad decision by one partner may put the other partners' personal resources in jeopardy. Personal problems such as a divorce can eliminate a significant portion of one partner's financial resources and weaken the financial structure of the whole partnership.

Life of the Partnership.   A partnership is terminated when a partner dies or withdraws. In a two-person partnership, if one partner withdraws, the firm's liabilities would be paid off and the assets divided between the partners. Obviously, the partner who wishes to continue in the business would be at a serious disadvantage. The business could be disrupted, financing would be reduced, and the management skills of the departing partner would be lost. The remaining partner would have to find another or reorganize the business as a sole proprietorship. In very large partnerships such as those found in law firms and investment banks, the continuation of the partnership may be provided for in the articles of partnership. The provision may simply state the terms for a new partnership agreement among the remaining partners. In such cases, the disadvantage to the other partners is minimal.

Selling a partnership interest has the same effect as the death or withdrawal of a partner. It is difficult to place a value on a partner's share of the partnership. No public value is placed on the partnership, as there is on publicly owned corporations. What is a law firm worth? What is the local hardware store worth? Coming up with a fair value that all partners can agree to is not easy. Selling a partnership interest is easier if the articles of partnership specify a method of valuation. Even if there is not a procedure for selling one partner's interest, the old partnership must still be dissolved and a new one created. In contrast, in the corporate form of business, the departure of owners has little effect on the financial resources of the business, and the loss of managers does not cause long-term changes in the structure of the organization.

Distribution of Profits.   Profits earned by the partnership are distributed to the partners in the proportions specified in the articles of partnership. This may be a disadvantage if the division of the profits does not reflect the work each partner puts into the business. You may have encountered this disadvantage while working on a student group project: You may have felt that you did most of the work and that the other students in the group received grades based on your efforts. Even the perception of an unfair profit-sharing agreement may cause tension between the partners, and unhappy partners can have a negative effect on the profitability of the business.

Limited Sources of Funds.   As with a sole proprietorship, the sources of funds available to a partnership are limited. Because no public value is placed on the business (such as the current trading price of a corporation's stock), potential partners do not know what one partnership share is worth. Moreover, because partnership shares cannot be bought and sold easily in public markets, potential owners may not want to tie up their money in assets that cannot be readily sold on short notice. Accumulating enough funds to operate a national business, especially a business requiring intensive investments in facilities and equipment, can be difficult. Partnerships also may have to pay higher interest rates on funds borrowed from banks than do large corporations because partnerships may be considered greater risks.

Taxation of Partnerships

Partnerships are quasi-taxable organizations. This means that partnerships do not pay taxes when submitting the partnership tax return to the Internal Revenue Service. The tax return simply provides information about the profitability of the organization and the distribution of profits among the partners. Partners must report their share of profits on their individual tax returns and pay taxes at the income tax rate for individuals.

Corporations

LO 4-3

When you think of a business, you probably think of a huge corporation such as General Electric, Procter & Gamble, or Sony because a large portion of your consumer dollars go to such corporations. A **corporation** is a legal entity, created by the state, whose assets and liabilities are separate from its owners. As a legal entity, a corporation has many of the rights, duties, and powers of a person, such as the right to receive, own, and transfer property. Corporations can enter into contracts with individuals or with other legal entities, and they can sue and be sued in court.

corporation
a legal entity, created by the state, whose assets and liabilities are separate from its owners

Corporations account for the majority of all U.S. sales and income. Thus, most of the dollars you spend as a consumer probably go to incorporated businesses (see Figure 4.1). Most corporations are not mega-companies like General Mills or Ford Motor Co.; even small businesses can incorporate. As we shall see later in the chapter, many smaller firms elect to incorporate as "S Corporations," which operate under slightly different rules and have greater flexibility than do traditional "C Corporations" like General Mills.

stock
shares of a corporation that may be bought or sold

dividends
profits of a corporation that are distributed in the form of cash payments to stockholders

Corporations are typically owned by many individuals and organizations who own shares of the business, called **stock** (thus, corporate owners are often called *shareholders* or *stockholders*). Stockholders can buy, sell, give or receive as gifts, or inherit their shares of stock. As owners, the stockholders are entitled to all profits that are left after all the corporation's other obligations have been paid. These profits may be distributed in the form of cash payments called **dividends.** For example, if a corporation earns $100 million after expenses and taxes and decides to pay the owners $40 million in dividends, the stockholders receive 40 percent of the profits in cash dividends. However, not all after-tax profits are paid to stockholders in dividends. Some corporations may retain profits to expand the business. For example, Berkshire Hathaway has always retained its earnings and reinvested them for the shareholders. This has resulted in an average 20 percent increase in per share investment over a 40-year period.[11]

Creating a Corporation

A corporation is created, or incorporated, under the laws of the state in which it incorporates. The individuals creating the corporation are known as *incorporators.* Each state has a specific procedure, sometimes called *chartering the corporation,* for incorporating a business. Most states require a minimum of three incorporators; thus, many small businesses can be and are incorporated. Another requirement is that the new corporation's name cannot be similar to that of another business. In most states, a corporation's name must end in "company," "corporation," "incorporated," or "limited" to show that the owners have limited liability. (In this text, however, the word *company* means any organization engaged in a commercial enterprise and can refer to a sole proprietorship, a partnership, or a corporation.)

The incorporators must file legal documents generally referred to as *articles of incorporation* with the appropriate state office (often the secretary of state). The articles of incorporation contain basic information about the business. The following 10 items are found in the Model Business Corporation Act, issued by the American Bar Association, which is followed by most states:

1. Name and address of the corporation.
2. Objectives of the corporation.
3. Classes of stock (common, preferred, voting, nonvoting) and the number of shares for each class of stock to be issued.
4. Expected life of the corporation (corporations are usually created to last forever).
5. Financial capital required at the time of incorporation.
6. Provisions for transferring shares of stock between owners.
7. Provisions for the regulation of internal corporate affairs.
8. Address of the business office registered with the state of incorporation.
9. Names and addresses of the initial board of directors.
10. Names and addresses of the incorporators.

corporate charter
a legal document that the state issues to a company based on information the company provides in the articles of incorporation

Based on the information in the articles of incorporation, the state issues a **corporate charter** to the company. After securing this charter, the owners hold an organizational meeting at which they establish the corporation's bylaws and elect a board of directors. The bylaws might set up committees of the board of directors and describe the rules and procedures for their operation.

Types of Corporations

If the corporation does business in the state in which it is chartered, it is known as a *domestic corporation*. In other states where the corporation does business, it is known as a *foreign corporation*. If a corporation does business outside the nation in which it is incorporated, it is called an *alien corporation*. A corporation may be privately or publicly owned.

A **private corporation** is owned by just one or a few people who are closely involved in managing the business. These people, often a family, own all the corporation's stock, and no stock is sold to the public. Many corporations are quite large, yet remain private, including Cargill, a farm products business. It is the nation's largest private corporation with annual revenues of well over $100 billion. Founded at the end of the Civil War, descendents of the original founder have owned equity in the company for more than 140 years.[12] The third-largest privately held company in the United States is Mars, founded by Forrest Mars Sr., who spent time in Switzerland learning to create chocolate confectionaries. Mars recently grew significantly through the acquisition of the Wm. Wrigley Jr. Company. Founded in Tacoma, Washington, in 1911, Mars is now the world's leading confectionary company and a leader in pet care products with Pedigree and Whiskas.[13] The business was successful early on because it paid employees three times the normal wage for the time. The company remains successful to this day, largely because of its established brands, such as M&Ms, and healthy snack lines for kids, like Generation Max.[14] Other well-known privately held companies include Chrysler, Publix Supermarkets, Dollar General, and MGM Entertainment. Privately owned corporations are not required to disclose financial information publicly, but they must, of course, pay taxes.

A **public corporation** is one whose stock anyone may buy, sell, or trade. Table 4.4 lists the largest U.S. corporations by revenues. Despite its high revenue, Fannie Mae had negative profits in 2011.[15] Thousands of smaller public corporations in the United States have sales under $10 million. In large public corporations such as AT&T, the stockholders are often far removed from the management of the company. In other public corporations, the managers are often the founders and the major shareholders. NASCAR, for example, was founded by William France in 1948, and ever since then his descendents have manned the helm as CEO. Grandson Brian France currently fills the post.[16] *Forbes* Global 2000 companies generate around $36 trillion in revenues, $2.64 trillion in profits, and $149 trillion in assets. They are worth $37 trillion in market value. The United States still has the majority of the Global 2000 companies, but other nations are catching up. The rankings of the Global 2000 span across 62 countries.[17] Publicly owned corporations must disclose financial information to the public under specific laws that regulate the trade of stocks and other securities.

The snack and food company Mars is privately owned by the Mars family. The company became one of the world's largest candy makers when Mars purchased chewing-gum company Wm. Wrigley Jr. Co. in 2008.

private corporation
a corporation owned by just one or a few people who are closely involved in managing the business

public corporation
a corporation whose stock anyone may buy, sell, or trade

TABLE 4.4

The Largest U.S. Corporations, Arranged by Revenue

Rank	Company	Revenues (in millions of $)
1.	ExxonMobil	$452,926.0
2.	Wal-Mart Stores	446,950.0
3.	Chevron	245,621.0
4.	ConocoPhillips	237,272.0
5.	General Motors	150,276.0
6.	General Electric	147,616.0
7.	Berkshire Hathaway	143,688.0
8.	Fannie Mae	137,451.0
9.	Ford Motor	136,264.0
10.	Hewlett-Packard	127,245.0
11.	AT&T	126,723.0
12.	Valero Energy	125,095.0
13.	McKesson	122,734.0
14.	Bank of America Corp.	115,074.0
15.	Verizon Communications	110,875.0
16.	JP Morgan Chase & Co.	110,838.0
17.	Apple	108,249.0
18.	CVS Caremark	107,750.0
19.	IBM	106,916.0
20.	Citigroup	102,939.0

Source: "Global 500: The World's Largest Corporations," *Fortune*, July 23, 2012, F-1.

initial public offering (IPO) selling a corporation's stock on public markets for the first time

A private corporation that needs more money to expand or to take advantage of opportunities may have to obtain financing by "going public" through an **initial public offering (IPO),** that is, becoming a public corporation by selling stock so that it can be traded in public markets. Digital media companies are leading a surge in initial public offerings. Pandora, Zynga, LinkedIn, and Groupon all released IPOs in 2011, followed by Facebook the following year.[18]

Also, privately owned firms are occasionally forced to go public with stock offerings when a major owner dies and the heirs have large estate taxes to pay. The tax payment may only be possible with the proceeds of the sale of stock. This happened to the brewer Adolph Coors Inc. After Adolph Coors died, the business went public and his family sold shares of stock to the public in order to pay the estate taxes.

On the other hand, public corporations can be "taken private" when one or a few individuals (perhaps the management of the firm) purchase all the firm's stock so that it can no longer be sold publicly. Taking a corporation private may be desirable when new owners want to exert more control over the firm or they want to avoid the necessity of public disclosure of future activities for competitive reasons. For example, RCN Corporation, a broadband provider, was purchased by a private equity group, Abry Partners LLC, for about $535 million in cash. Abry's goal with the purchase is to expand its companies offering broadband and cable service in New York, Boston, and Philadelphia.[19] Taking a corporation private is also one technique for avoiding a takeover by another corporation.

Quasi-public corporations and nonprofits are two types of public corporations. **Quasi-public corporations** are owned and operated by the federal, state, or local government. The focus of these entities is to provide a service to citizens, such as mail delivery, rather than earning a profit. Indeed, many quasi-public corporations operate at a loss. Examples of quasi-public corporations include the National Aeronautics and Space Administration (NASA) and the U.S. Postal Service.

Like quasi-public corporations, **nonprofit corporations** focus on providing a service rather than earning a profit, but they are not owned by a government entity. Organizations such as the Sesame Workshop, the Elks Clubs, the American Lung Association, the American Red Cross, museums, and private schools provide services without a profit motive. To fund their operations and services, nonprofit organizations solicit donations from individuals and companies and grants from the government and other charitable foundations.

quasi-public corporations corporations owned and operated by the federal, state, or local government

nonprofit corporations corporations that focus on providing a service rather than earning a profit but are not owned by a government entity

Elements of a Corporation

The Board of Directors.   A **board of directors,** elected by the stockholders to oversee the general operation of the corporation, sets the long-range objectives of the corporation. It is the board's responsibility to ensure that the objectives are achieved on schedule. Board members are legally liable for the mismanagement of the firm or for any misuse of funds. An important duty of the board of directors is to hire corporate officers, such as the president and the chief executive officer (CEO), who are responsible to the directors for the management and daily operations of the firm. The role and expectations of the board of directors took on greater significance after the accounting scandals of the early 2000s and the passage of the Sarbanes-Oxley Act.[20] As a result, most corporations have restructured how they compensate board directors for their time and expertise.

However, some experts now speculate that Sarbanes-Oxley did little to motivate directors to increase company oversight. One notable case of alleged director misconduct involves a lawsuit filed by the SEC against three directors of DHB Industries. The SEC accused these directors of purposefully ignoring red flags that indicated company misconduct. However, such lawsuits are the exception to the norm. If it cannot be proven that directors did not act in good faith, it is hard for the SEC to develop a case against them.[21] At the same time, the pay rate of directors is rising. In 2011, median pay for directors at the 500 largest companies was estimated to be about $234,000. At Apple, it is even higher at $984,000. Although such pay is meant to attract top-quality directors, concerns exist over whether excessive pay will have unintended consequences. Some believe that pay greater than $200,000

board of directors a group of individuals, elected by the stockholders to oversee the general operation of the corporation, who set the corporation's long-range objectives

Lionsgate is a diversified entertainment corporation that provides excellent documentation on its corporate governance and financial performance.

will cause directors to be more complacent and overlook potential misconduct in order to keep their positions.[22]

Directors can be employees of the company *(inside directors)* or people unaffiliated with the company *(outside directors).* Inside directors are usually the officers responsible for running the company. Outside directors are often top executives from other companies, lawyers, bankers, even professors. Directors today are increasingly chosen for their expertise, competence, and ability to bring diverse perspectives to strategic discussions. Outside directors are also thought to bring more independence to the monitoring function because they are not bound by past allegiances, friendships, a current role in the company, or some other issue that may create a conflict of interest. Many of the corporate scandals uncovered in recent years might have been prevented if each of the companies' boards of directors had been better qualified, more knowledgeable, and more independent.

There is a growing shortage of available and qualified board members. Boards are increasingly telling their own CEOs that they should be focused on serving their company, not serving on outside boards. Because of this, the average CEO sits on less than one outside board. This represents a decline from a decade ago when the average was two. Because many CEOs are turning down outside positions, many companies have taken steps to ensure that boards have experienced directors. They have increased the mandatory retirement age to 72 or older, and some have raised it to 75 or even older. Minimizing the amount of overlap between directors sitting on different boards helps to limit conflicts of interest and provides for independence in decision making.

preferred stock
a special type of stock whose owners, though not generally having a say in running the company, have a claim to profits before other stockholders do

common stock
stock whose owners have voting rights in the corporation, yet do not receive preferential treatment regarding dividends

Stock Ownership.   Corporations issue two types of stock: preferred and common. Owners of **preferred stock** are a special class of owners because, although they generally do not have any say in running the company, they have a claim to profits before any other stockholders do. Other stockholders do not receive any dividends unless the preferred stockholders have already been paid. Dividend payments on preferred stock are usually a fixed percentage of the initial issuing price (set by the board of directors). For example, if a share of preferred stock originally cost $100 and the dividend rate was stated at 7.5 percent, the dividend payment will be $7.50 per share per year. Dividends are usually paid quarterly. Most preferred stock carries a cumulative claim to dividends. This means that if the company does not pay preferred-stock dividends in one year because of losses, the dividends accumulate to the next year. Such dividends unpaid from previous years must also be paid to preferred stockholders before other stockholders can receive any dividends.

Although owners of **common stock** do not get such preferential treatment with regard to

Owners of preferred stock have first claim to company profits.

dividends, they do get some say in the operation of the corporation. Their ownership gives them the right to vote for members of the board of directors and on other important issues. Common stock dividends may vary according to the profitability of the business, and some corporations do not issue dividends at all, but instead plow their profits back into the company to fund expansion.

Common stockholders are the voting owners of a corporation. They are usually entitled to one vote per share of common stock. During an annual stockholders' meeting, common stockholders elect a board of directors. Some boards find it easier than others to attract high profile individuals. For example, the board of Procter & Gamble consists of Ernesto Zedillo, former president of Mexico; Kenneth I. Chenault, CEO of the American Express Company; Scott Cook, founder of Intuit Inc.; as well as the CEO of Archer Daniels Midland; the CEO of Boeing; and the CEO of Hewlett-Packard.[23] Because they can choose the board of directors, common stockholders have some say in how the company will operate. Common stockholders may vote by *proxy,* which is a written authorization by which stockholders assign their voting privilege to someone else, who then votes for his or her choice at the stockholders' meeting. It is a normal practice for management to request proxy statements from shareholders who are not planning to attend the annual meeting. Most owners do not attend annual meetings of the very large companies, such as Westinghouse or Boeing, unless they live in the city where the meeting is held.

Common stockholders have another advantage over preferred shareholders. In most states, when the corporation decides to sell new shares of common stock in the marketplace, common stockholders have the first right, called a *preemptive right,* to purchase new shares of the stock from the corporation. A preemptive right is often included in the articles of incorporation. This right is important because it allows stockholders to purchase new shares to maintain their original positions. For example, if a stockholder owns 10 percent of a corporation that decides to issue new shares, that stockholder has the right to buy enough of the new shares to retain the 10 percent ownership.

Advantages of Corporations

Because a corporation is a separate legal entity, it has some very specific advantages over other forms of ownership. The biggest advantage may be the limited liability of the owners.

Limited Liability.   Because the corporation's assets (money and resources) and liabilities (debts and other obligations) are separate from its owners', in most cases the stockholders are not held responsible for the firm's debts if it fails. Their liability or potential loss is limited to the amount of their original investment. Although a creditor can sue a corporation for not paying its debts, even forcing the corporation into bankruptcy, it cannot make the stockholders pay the corporation's debts out of their personal assets. Occasionally, the owners of a private corporation may pledge personal assets to secure a loan for the corporation; this would be most unusual for a public corporation.

Ease of Transfer of Ownership.   Stockholders can sell or trade shares of stock to other people without causing the termination of the corporation, and they can do this without the prior approval of other shareholders. The transfer of ownership (unless it is a majority position) does not affect the daily or long-term operations of the corporation.

Perpetual Life. A corporation usually is chartered to last forever unless its articles of incorporation stipulate otherwise. The existence of the corporation is unaffected by the death or withdrawal of any of its stockholders. It survives until the owners sell it or liquidate its assets. However, in some cases, bankruptcy ends a corporation's life. Bankruptcies occur when companies are unable to compete and earn profits. Eventually, uncompetitive businesses must close or seek protection from creditors in bankruptcy court while the business tries to reorganize.

External Sources of Funds. Of all the forms of business organization, the public corporation finds it easiest to raise money. When a corporation needs to raise more money, it can sell more stock shares or issue bonds (corporate "IOUs," which pledge to repay debt), attracting funds from anywhere in the United States and even overseas. The larger a corporation becomes, the more sources of financing are available to it. We take a closer look at some of these in Chapter 15.

Expansion Potential. Because large public corporations can find long-term financing readily, they can easily expand into national and international markets. And, as a legal entity, a corporation can enter into contracts without as much difficulty as a partnership.

With revenues surpassing $452 billion, Exxon Mobil is one of the world's largest corporations.

Disadvantages of Corporations

Corporations have some distinct disadvantages resulting from tax laws and government regulation.

Double Taxation. As a legal entity, the corporation must pay taxes on its income just like you do. When after-tax corporate profits are paid out as dividends to the stockholders, the dividends are taxed a second time as part of the individual owner's income. This process creates double taxation for the stockholders of dividend paying corporations. Double taxation does not occur with the other forms of business organization.

Forming a Corporation. The formation of a corporation can be costly. A charter must be obtained, and this usually requires the services of an attorney and payment of legal fees. Filing fees ranging from $25 to $150 must be paid to the state that awards the corporate charter, and certain states require that an annual fee be paid to maintain the charter. Today, a number of Internet services such as LegalZoom.com and Business.com make it easier, quicker, and less costly to form a corporation. However, in making it easier for people to form businesses without expert consultation, these services have increased the risk that people will not choose the kind of organizational form that is right for them. Sometimes, one form works better than another. The business's founders may fail to take into account disadvantages, such as double taxation with corporations.

Disclosure of Information.   Corporations must make information available to their owners, usually through an annual report to shareholders. The annual report contains financial information about the firm's profits, sales, facilities and equipment, and debts, as well as descriptions of the company's operations, products, and plans for the future. Public corporations must also file reports with the Securities and Exchange Commission (SEC), the government regulatory agency that regulates securities such as stocks and bonds. The larger the firm, the more data the SEC requires. Because all reports filed with the SEC are available to the public, competitors can access them. Additionally, complying with securities laws takes time.

DID YOU KNOW? The first corporation with a net income of more than $1 billion in one year was General Motors, with a net income in 1955 of $1,189,477,082.[24]

Employee–Owner Separation.   Many employees are not stockholders of the company for which they work. This separation of owners and employees may cause employees to feel that their work benefits only the owners. Employees without an ownership stake do not always see how they fit into the corporate picture and may not understand the importance of profits to the health of the organization. If managers are part owners but other employees are not, management–labor relations take on a different, sometimes difficult, aspect from those in partnerships and sole proprietorships. However, this situation is changing as more corporations establish employee stock ownership plans (ESOPs), which give shares of the company's stock to its employees. Such plans build a partnership between employee and employer and can boost productivity because they motivate employees to work harder so that they can earn dividends from their hard work as well as from their regular wages.

Other Types of Ownership

In this section we take a brief look at joint ventures, S corporations, limited liability companies, and cooperatives—businesses formed for special purposes.

Joint Ventures

A **joint venture** is a partnership established for a specific project or for a limited time. The partners in a joint venture may be individuals or organizations, as in the case of the international joint ventures discussed in Chapter 3. Control of a joint venture may be shared equally, or one partner may control decision making. Joint ventures are especially popular in situations that call for large investments, such as extraction of natural resources and the development of new products. For example, TEMCO LLC is a joint venture between Cargill and wholesale agricultural products company CHS Inc. The two companies are using the joint venture to capitalize on global opportunities for grain exporting. The joint venture was later expanded to export food grains to markets in Asia and other Pacific countries.[25]

joint venture
a partnership established for a specific project or for a limited time

S Corporations

An **S corporation** is a form of business ownership that is taxed as though it were a partnership. Net profits or losses of the corporation pass to the owners, thus eliminating double taxation. The benefit of limited liability is retained. Formally known as Subchapter S Corporations, they have become a popular form of business ownership for entrepreneurs and represent almost half of all corporate filings.[26] Vista Bank Texas is an S Corporation, and the owners get the benefits of tax advantages and limited liability. Advantages of S corporations include the simple method of

S corporation
corporation taxed as though it were a partnership with restrictions on shareholders

taxation, the limited liability of shareholders, perpetual life, and the ability to shift income and appreciation to others. Disadvantages include restrictions on the number (75) and types (individuals, estates, and certain trusts) of shareholders and the difficulty of formation and operation.

Limited Liability Companies

limited liability company (LLC)
form of ownership that provides limited liability and taxation like a partnership but places fewer restrictions on members

A **limited liability company (LLC)** is a form of business ownership that provides limited liability, as in a corporation, but is taxed like a partnership. Although relatively new in the United States, LLCs have existed for many years abroad. Professionals such as lawyers, doctors, and engineers often use the LLC form of ownership. Many consider the LLC a blend of the best characteristics of corporations, partnerships, and sole proprietorships. One of the major reasons for the LLC form of ownership is to protect the members' personal assets in case of lawsuits. LLCs are flexible, simple to run, and do not require the members to hold meetings, keep minutes, or make resolutions, all of which are necessary in corporations. For example, Segway, which markets the Segway Human Transporter, is a limited liability company.

Cooperatives

cooperative (co-op)
an organization composed of individuals or small businesses that have banded together to reap the benefits of belonging to a larger organization

Another form of organization in business is the **cooperative** or **co-op,** an organization composed of individuals or small businesses that have banded together to reap the benefits of belonging to a larger organization. Oglethorpe Power Corp., for example, is a power cooperative based in the suburbs of Atlanta;[28] Ocean Spray is a cooperative of cranberry farmers. REI operates a bit differently because it is owned by consumers rather than farmers or small businesses. A co-op is set up not to make money as an entity but so that its members can become more profitable or save money. Co-ops are generally expected to operate without profit or to create only enough profit to maintain the co-op organization.

Many cooperatives exist in small farming communities. The co-op stores and markets grain; orders large quantities of fertilizer, seed, and other supplies at discounted prices; and reduces costs and increases efficiency with good management. A co-op can purchase supplies in large quantities and pass the savings on to its members. It also can help distribute the products of its members more efficiently than each could on an individual basis. A cooperative can advertise its members' products and thus generate demand. Ace Hardware, a cooperative of independent hardware store owners, allows its members to share in the savings that result from buying supplies in large quantities; it also provides advertising, which individual members might not be able to afford on their own.

Trends in Business Ownership: Mergers and Acquisitions

LO 4-4

Companies large and small achieve growth and improve profitability by expanding their operations, often by developing and selling new products or selling current products to new groups of customers in different geographic areas. Such growth, when carefully planned and controlled, is usually beneficial to the firm and ultimately helps it reach its goal of enhanced profitability. But companies also grow by merging with or purchasing other companies.

A **merger** occurs when two companies (usually corporations) combine to form a new company. An **acquisition** occurs when one company purchases another, generally by buying most of its stock. The acquired company may become a subsidiary of the buyer, or its operations and assets may be merged with those of the buyer. The government sometimes scrutinizes mergers and acquisitions in an attempt to protect customers from monopolistic practices. For example, the decision to authorize Whole Foods' acquisition of Wild Oats was carefully analyzed, as was the merger of Sirius and XM Satellite Radio. In 2011, Google paid $151 million for restaurant review rating site Zagat. The company was just one of many that Google acquired during the year. While these acquisitions have the potential to diversify Google's service offerings and benefit it financially, some believe that Google might be investing in companies of which it has little knowledge. In these cases, acquisitions could end up harming the acquiring company.[29] Acquisitions sometimes involve the purchase of a division or some other part of a company rather than the entire company. The late 1990s saw a merger and acquisition frenzy, which is slowing in the 21st century (see Table 4.5).

When firms that make and sell similar products to the same customers merge, it is known as a *horizontal merger,* as when Martin Marietta and Lockheed, both defense contractors, merged to form Lockheed Martin. Horizontal mergers, however, reduce the number of corporations competing within an industry, and for this reason they are usually reviewed carefully by federal regulators before the merger is allowed to proceed.

When companies operating at different but related levels of an industry merge, it is known as a *vertical merger.* In many instances, a vertical merger results when one corporation merges with one of its customers or suppliers. For example, if Burger King were to purchase a large Idaho potato farm—to ensure a ready supply of potatoes for its french fries—a vertical merger would result.

A *conglomerate merger* results when two firms in unrelated industries merge. For example, the purchase of Sterling Drug, a pharmaceutical firm, by Eastman Kodak, best-known for its films and cameras, represents a conglomerate merger because

merger
the combination of two companies (usually corporations) to form a new company

acquisition
the purchase of one company by another, usually by buying its stock

Responding to Business Challenges
Can Microsoft Succeed in its Acquisition of Skype?

Do you Skype? If you do, you likely use its free video calling feature. Thanks to this feature, Skype has approximately 150 million monthly users. Sensing its potential, eBay purchased Skype in 2005 for $2.5 billion. Four years later, venture capitalists purchased 70 percent of the company. Despite changes in ownership, Skype has flourished, prompting Microsoft to purchase it for $8.5 billion. However, this acquisition has created concern over Skype's future.

Analysts are skeptical that Skype can survive being consumed by such a large corporation. Many question why Microsoft would want a video-conferencing site when it already provides video/voice software on two platforms. Skype's 8 million customers who use its pay-based services do not seem to justify Microsoft's willingness to pay more than $8 billion for the company. Additionally, major acquisitions often fail because stock prices tend to decrease due to investor uncertainty over whether the venture will succeed. Microsoft's decision to pay so much for Skype without a seemingly logical explanation concerns analysts and investors. Although new opportunities for Skype are emerging, such as its integration into school curriculums, are these market opportunities enough to quell investor fears and create a successful acquisition?[30]

Discussion Questions

1. Why do you think Microsoft decided to purchase Skype?
2. Why do analysts appear unsure about the success of the acquisition?
3. What are some of the risks involved with acquiring a new company?

TABLE 4.5   **Major Mergers and Acquisitions Worldwide 2000–2010**

Rank	Year	Acquirer	Target	Transaction Value (in millions of U.S. dollars)
1	2000	America Online Inc. (AOL) (*Merger*)	Time Warner	$164,747
2	2000	Glaxo Wellcome Plc.	SmithKline Beecham Plc.	75,961
3	2004	Royal Dutch Petroleum Co.	Shell Transport & Trading Co.	74,559
4	2006	AT&T Inc.	BellSouth Corporation	72,671
5	2001	Comcast Corporation	AT&T Broadband & Internet Svcs.	72,041
6	2004	JP Morgan Chase & Co.	Bank One Corporation	58,761
7	2010	Kraft	Cadbury	19,500
8	2008	Bank of America	Countrywide	4,000
9	2008	JP Morgan Chase & Co.	Bear Stearns Companies Inc.	1,100
10	2011	Southwest Airlines	AirTran Holdings	1,000

Unless noted, deal was an acquisition.

Sources: Institute of Mergers, Acquisitions and Alliances Research, *Thomson Financial,* www.imaa-institute.org/en/publications+mergers+acquisitions+m&a. php#Reports (accessed March 16, 2010); "JPMorgan Chase Completes Bear Stearns Acquisition," JPMorganChase News Release, May 31, 2008, www.bearstearns.com/ includes/pdfs/PressRelease_BSC_31May08.pdf (accessed March 1, 2010); David Mildenberg and Guy Beaudin, "Kraft Acquires Cadbury," *Bloomberg Businessweek* January 3, 2010, www.businessweek.com/managing/content/feb2010/ca2010028_928488.htm; "Southwest Completes Purchase of Orlando-Based AirTran," *Orlando Sentinel,* May 2, 2011, http://articles.orlandosentinel.com/2011-05-02/business/os-southwest-airtran-reuters-update2-20110502_1_southwest-executive-vice-president-southwest-brand-airtran-holdings (accessed January 27, 2012).

the two companies are of different industries. (Kodak later sold Sterling Drug to a pharmaceutical company.)

When a company (or an individual), sometimes called a *corporate raider,* wants to acquire or take over another company, it first offers to buy some or all of the other company's stock at a premium over its current price in a *tender offer.* Most such offers are "friendly," with both groups agreeing to the proposed deal, but some are "hostile," when the second company does not want to be taken over. OpenWave Systems Inc. adopted a poison pill plan to discourage hostile takeovers. (A poison pill is an attempt to make a takeover less attractive to a potential acquirer.) OpenWave's plan is set to go off if an outside company acquires 4.99 percent of OpenWave's stock. In that case, shareholders would be given the ability to gain more shares, which in turn would dilute the stock ownership of the acquiring company.[31]

Duke CEO Jim Rogers, left, and former Progress CEO Bill Johnson agreed to merge the two companies, with Bill Johnson leading the newly merged Duke Energy. However, shortly after, the board, consisting mostly of Duke board members, ousted Mr. Johnson and re-installed Mr. Rogers as CEO. Duke Energy suffered damage to its reputation.

To head off a hostile takeover attempt, a threatened company's managers may use one or more of several techniques. They may ask stockholders not to sell to the raider; file a lawsuit in an effort to abort the takeover; institute a *poison pill* (in which the firm allows stockholders to buy more shares of stock at prices lower than the current market value) or *shark repellant* (in which management requires a large majority of stockholders to approve the takeover); or seek a *white knight* (a more acceptable firm that is willing to acquire the threatened company). In some cases, management may take the company private or even take on more debt so that the heavy debt obligation will "scare off" the raider.

In a **leveraged buyout (LBO),** a group of investors borrows money from banks and other institutions to acquire a company (or a division of one), using the assets of the purchased company to guarantee repayment of the loan. In some LBOs, as much as 95 percent of the buyout price is paid with borrowed money, which eventually must be repaid.

Because of the explosion of mergers, acquisitions, and leveraged buyouts in the 1980s and 1990s, financial journalists coined the term *merger mania.* Many companies joined the merger mania simply to enhance their own operations by consolidating them with the operations of other firms. Mergers and acquisitions enabled these companies to gain a larger market share in their industries, acquire valuable assets such as new products or plants and equipment, and lower their costs. Mergers also represent a means of making profits quickly, as was the case during the 1980s when many companies' stock was undervalued. Quite simply, such companies represent a bargain to other companies that can afford to buy them. Additionally, deregulation of some industries has permitted consolidation of firms within those industries for the first time, as is the case in the banking and airline industries.

Some people view mergers and acquisitions favorably, pointing out that they boost corporations' stock prices and market value, to the benefit of their stockholders. In many instances, mergers enhance a company's ability to meet foreign competition in an increasingly global marketplace. Additionally, companies that are victims of hostile takeovers generally streamline their operations, reduce unnecessary staff,

leveraged buyout (LBO) a purchase in which a group of investors borrows money from banks and other institutions to acquire a company (or a division of one), using the assets of the purchased company to guarantee repayment of the loan

cut costs, and otherwise become more efficient with their operations, which benefits their stockholders whether or not the takeover succeeds.

Critics, however, argue that mergers hurt companies because they force managers to focus their efforts on avoiding takeovers rather than managing effectively and profitably. Some companies have taken on a heavy debt burden to stave off a takeover, later to be forced into bankruptcy when economic downturns left them unable to handle the debt. Mergers and acquisitions also can damage employee morale and productivity, as well as the quality of the companies' products.

Many mergers have been beneficial for all involved; others have had damaging effects for the companies, their employees, and customers. No one can say whether mergers will continue to slow, but many experts say the utilities, telecommunications, financial services, natural resources, computer hardware and software, gaming, managed health care, and technology industries are likely targets.

So You'd Like to Start a Business

If you have a good idea and want to turn it into a business, you are not alone. Small businesses are popping up all over the United States, and the concept of entrepreneurship is hot. Entrepreneurs seek opportunities and creative ways to make profits. Business emerges in a number of different organizational forms, each with its own advantages and disadvantages. Sole proprietorships are the most common form of business organization in the U.S. They tend to be small businesses and can take pretty much any form—anything from a hair salon to a scuba shop, from an organic produce provider to a financial advisor. Proprietorships are everywhere serving consumers' wants and needs. Proprietorships have a big advantage in that they tend to be simple to manage—decisions get made quickly when the owner and the manager are the same person and they are fairly simple and inexpensive to set up. Rules vary by state, but at most all you will need is a license from the state.

Many people have been part of a partnership at some point in their life. Group work in school is an example of a partnership. If you ever worked as a DJ on the weekend with your friend and split the profits, then you have experienced a partnership. Partnerships can be either general or limited. General partners have unlimited liability and share completely in the management, debts, and profits of the business. Limited partners, on the other hand, consist of at least one general partner and one or more limited partners who do not participate in the management of the company but share in the profits. This form of partnership is used more often in risky investments where the limited partner stands only to lose his or her initial investment. Real estate limited partnerships are an example

of how investors can minimize their financial exposure, given the poor performance of the real estate market in recent years. Although it has its advantages, partnership is the least utilized form of business. Part of the reason is that all partners are responsible for the actions and decisions of all other partners, whether or not all of the partners were involved. Usually, partners will have to write up an Articles of Partnership that outlines respective responsibilities in the business. Even in states where it is not required, it is a good idea to draw up this document as a way to cement each partner's role and hopefully minimize conflict. Unlike a corporation, proprietorships and partnerships both expire upon the death of one or more of those involved.

Corporations tend to be larger businesses, but do not need to be. A corporation can consist of nothing more than a small group of family members. In order to become a corporation, you will have to file in the state under which you wish to incorporate. Each state has its own procedure for incorporation, meaning there are no general guidelines to follow. You can make your corporation private or public, meaning the company issues stocks, and shareholders are the owners. While incorporating is a popular form of organization because it gives the company an unlimited lifespan and limited liability (meaning that if your business fails, you cannot lose personal funds to make up for losses), there is a downside. You will be taxed as a corporation and as an individual, resulting in double taxation. No matter what form of organization suits your business idea best, there is a world of options out there for you if you want to be or experiment with being an entrepreneur.

Review Your Understanding

Define and examine the advantages and disadvantages of the sole proprietorship form of organization.

Sole proprietorships—businesses owned and managed by one person—are the most common form of organization. Their major advantages are the following: (1) They are easy and inexpensive to form, (2) they allow a high level of secrecy, (3) all profits belong to the owner, (4) the owner has complete control over the business, (5) government regulation is minimal, (6) taxes are paid only once, and (7) the business can be closed easily. The disadvantages include: (1) The owner may have to use personal assets to borrow money, (2) sources of external funds are difficult to find, (3) the owner must have many diverse skills, (4) the survival of the business is tied to the life of the owner and his or her ability to work, (5) qualified employees are hard to find, and (6) wealthy sole proprietors pay a higher tax than they would under the corporate form of business.

Identify two types of partnership and evaluate the advantages and disadvantages of the partnership form of organization.

A partnership is a business formed by several individuals; a partnership may be general or limited. Partnerships offer the following advantages: (1) They are easy to organize, (2) they may have higher credit ratings because the partners possibly have more combined wealth, (3) partners can specialize, (4) partnerships can make decisions faster than larger businesses, and (5) government regulations are few. Partnerships also have several disadvantages: (1) General partners have unlimited liability for the debts of the partnership, (2) partners are responsible for each others' decisions, (3) the death or termination of one partner requires a new partnership agreement to be drawn up, (4) it is difficult to sell a partnership interest at a fair price, (5) the distribution of profits may not correctly reflect the amount of work done by each partner, and (6) partnerships cannot find external sources of funds as easily as can large corporations.

Describe the corporate form of organization and cite the advantages and disadvantages of corporations.

A corporation is a legal entity created by the state, whose assets and liabilities are separate from those of its owners. Corporations are chartered by a state through articles of incorporation. They have a board of directors made up of corporate officers or people from outside the company. Corporations, whether private or public, are owned by stockholders. Common stockholders have the right to elect the board of directors. Preferred stockholders do not have a vote but get preferential dividend treatment over common stockholders.

Advantages of the corporate form of business include: (1) The owners have limited liability, (2) ownership (stock) can be easily transferred, (3) corporations usually last forever, (4) raising money is easier than for other forms of business, and (5) expansion into new businesses is simpler because of the ability of the company to enter into contracts. Corporations also have disadvantages: (1) The company is taxed on its income, and owners pay a second tax on any profits received as dividends; (2) forming a corporation can be expensive; (3) keeping trade secrets is difficult because so much information must be made available to the public and to government agencies; and (4) owners and managers are not always the same and can have different goals.

Define and debate the advantages and disadvantages of mergers, acquisitions, and leveraged buyouts.

A merger occurs when two companies (usually corporations) combine to form a new company. An acquisition occurs when one company buys most of another company's stock. In a leveraged buyout, a group of investors borrows money to acquire a company, using the assets of the purchased company to guarantee the loan. They can help merging firms to gain a larger market share in their industries, acquire valuable assets such as new products or plants and equipment, and lower their costs. Consequently, they can benefit stockholders by improving the companies' market value and stock prices. However, they also can hurt companies if they force managers to focus on avoiding takeovers at the expense of productivity and profits. They may lead a company to take on too much debt and can harm employee morale and productivity.

Propose an appropriate organizational form for a startup business.

After reading the facts in "Solve the Dilemma" on page 145 and considering the advantages and disadvantages of the various forms of business organization described in this chapter, you should be able to suggest an appropriate form for the startup nursery.

Revisit the World of Business

1. How has REI's consumer cooperative structure contributed to its success?

2. What are some of the ways that REI is a customer-oriented retailer?

3. Why do you think employee satisfaction is important to REI's success?

Learn the Terms

acquisition 139

articles of partnership 125

board of directors 133

common stock 134

cooperative (co-op) 138

corporate charter 130

corporation 129

dividends 130

general partnership 125

initial public offering (IPO) 132

joint venture 137

leveraged buyout (LBO) 141

limited liability company (LLC) 138

limited partnership 125

merger 139

nonprofit corporations 133

partnership 124

preferred stock 134

private corporation 131

public corporation 131

quasi-public corporations 133

S corporation 137

sole proprietorships 121

stock 130

Check Your Progress

1. Name five advantages of a sole proprietorship.

2. List two different types of partnerships and describe each.

3. Differentiate among the different types of corporations. Can you supply an example of each type?

4. Would you rather own preferred stock or common stock? Why?

5. Contrast how profits are distributed in sole proprietorships, partnerships, and corporations.

6. Which form of business organization has the least government regulation? Which has the most?

7. Compare the liability of the owners of partnerships, sole proprietorships, and corporations.

8. Why would secrecy in operating a business be important to an owner? What form of organization would be most appropriate for a business requiring great secrecy?

9. Which form of business requires the most specialization of skills? Which requires the least? Why?

10. The most common example of a cooperative is a farm co-op. Explain the reasons for this and the benefits that result for members of cooperatives.

Get Involved

1. Select a publicly owned corporation and bring to class a list of its subsidiaries. These data should be available in the firm's corporate annual report, *Standard & Poor's Corporate Records,* or *Moody Corporate Manuals.* Ask your librarian for help in finding these resources.

2. Select a publicly owned corporation and make a list of its outside directors. Information of this nature can be found in several places in your library: the company's annual report, its list of corporate directors, and various financial sources. If possible, include each director's title and the name of the company that employs him or her on a full-time basis.

Build Your Skills   LO 4-5

SELECTING A FORM OF BUSINESS

Background

Ali Bush sees an opportunity to start her own website development business. Ali has just graduated from the University of Mississippi with a master's degree in computer science. Although she has many job opportunities outside the Oxford area, she wishes to remain there to care for her aging parents. She already has most of the computer equipment necessary to start the business, but she needs additional software. She is considering the purchase of a server to maintain websites for small businesses. Ali feels she has the ability to take this start-up firm and create a long-term career opportunity for herself and others. She knows she can hire Ole Miss students to work on a part-time basis to support her business. For now, as she starts the business, she can work out of the extra bedroom of her apartment. As the business grows, she'll hire the additional full- and/or part-time help needed and reassess the location of the business.

Task

1. Using what you've learned in this chapter, decide which form of business ownership is most appropriate for Ali. Use the tables provided to assist you in evaluating the advantages and disadvantages of each decision

Sole Proprietorships	
Advantages	Disadvantages
•	•
•	•
•	•
•	•
•	•
•	•
•	

Corporation	
Advantages	Disadvantages
•	•
•	•
•	•
•	•
•	•
•	•
•	•

Limited Liability Company	
Advantages	Disadvantages
•	•
•	•
•	•
•	•
•	•
•	•
•	•

Solve the Dilemma

TO INCORPORATE OR NOT TO INCORPORATE

Thomas O'Grady and Bryan Rossisky have decided to start a small business buying flowers, shrubs, and trees wholesale and reselling them to the general public. They plan to contribute $5,000 each in startup capital and lease a 2.5-acre tract of land with a small, portable sales office.

Thomas and Bryan are trying to decide what form of organization would be appropriate. Bryan thinks they should create a corporation because they would have limited liability and the image of a large organization. Thomas thinks a partnership would be easier to start and would allow them to rely on the combination of their talents and financial resources. In addition, there might be fewer reports and regulatory controls to cope with.

keep the preparation process simple. Five Guys also has no drive-thru service and refuses to deliver—even to the Pentagon.

Rather than dissuading customers, Five Guys' simplicity has made it successful. Five Guys relies on word-of-mouth communication rather than advertising, and customers give the restaurant rave reviews. The company continues to grow and is considering expanding into Europe. Five Guys is carving out its own niche among burger chains.[1]

Introduction

Although many business students go to work for large corporations upon graduation, others may choose to start their own business or to find employment opportunities in small organizations with 500 or fewer employees. Small businesses employ more than half of all private-sector employees.[2] Each small business represents the vision of its owners to succeed through providing new or better products. Small businesses are the heart of the U.S. economic and social system because they offer opportunities and demonstrate the freedom of people to make their own destinies. Today, the entrepreneurial spirit is growing around the world, from Russia and China to India, Germany, Brazil, and Mexico. For instance, even though China remains a communist country, private companies employ more than 90 percent of the country's workers. However, the state owns shares in many of these businesses.[3]

This chapter surveys the world of entrepreneurship and small business. First we define entrepreneurship and small business and examine the role of small business in the American economy. Then we explore the advantages and disadvantages of small-business ownership and analyze why small businesses succeed or fail. Next, we discuss how an entrepreneur goes about starting a business and the challenges facing small businesses today. Finally, we look at entrepreneurship in larger organizations.

LO 5-1

The Nature of Entrepreneurship and Small Business

In Chapter 1, we defined an entrepreneur as a person who risks his or her wealth, time, and effort to develop for profit an innovative product or way of doing something. **Entrepreneurship** is the process of creating and managing a business to achieve desired objectives. Many large businesses you may recognize (Levi Strauss and Co., Procter & Gamble, McDonald's, Dell Computers, Microsoft, and Google) all began as small businesses based on the visions of their founders. Some entrepreneurs who start small businesses have the ability to see emerging trends; in response, they create a company to provide a product that serves customer needs. For example, rather than inventing a major new technology, an innovative company may take advantage of technology to create new markets, such as Amazon.com. Or they may offer a familiar product that has been improved or placed in a unique retail environment, such as Starbucks and its coffee shops. A company may innovate by focusing on a particular market segment and delivering a combination of features

enterpreneurship
the process of creating and managing a business to achieve desired objectives

150

Rank	Entrepreneur	Company
1	Steve Jobs	Apple
2	Bill Gates	Microsoft
3	Fred Smith	FedEx
4	Jeff Bezos	Amazon
5	Larry Page and Sergey Brin	Google
6	Howard Schultz	Starbucks
7	Mark Zuckerberg	Facebook
8	John Mackey	Whole Foods
9	Herb Kelleher	Southwest Airlines
10	Narayana Murthy	Infosys
11	Sam Walton	Walmart
12	Muhammad Yunus	Grameen Bank

TABLE 5.1

Great Entrepreneurs of Our Time

Sources: John A. Byrne, "Greatest Entrepreneurs of Our Time," *Fortune,* April 9, 2012, pp. 68–86.

that consumers in that segment could not find anywhere else. Patagonia, a company that uses many organic materials in its clothing, has pledged 1 percent of sales to the preservation and restoration of the natural environment. For example, customers can return their worn-out Capilene® Performance Baselayers to Patagonia for recycling.[4]

Of course, smaller businesses do not have to evolve into such highly visible companies to be successful, but those entrepreneurial efforts that result in rapidly growing businesses gain visibility along with success. Entrepreneurs who have achieved success, like Michael Dell (Dell Computers), Bill Gates (Microsoft), Larry Page and Sergey Brin (Google), and the late Steve Jobs (Apple) are some of the most well known. Table 5.1 lists some of the greatest entrepreneurs of the past few decades.

The entrepreneurship movement is accelerating, and many new, smaller businesses are emerging. Technology once available only to the largest firms can now be obtained by a small business. Websites, podcasts, online videos, social media, cellular phones, and even expedited delivery services enable small businesses to be more competitive with today's giant corporations. Small businesses can also form alliances with other companies to produce and sell products in domestic and global markets.

What Is a Small Business?

This question is difficult to answer because smallness is relative. In this book, we will define a **small business** as any independently owned and operated business that is not dominant in its competitive area and does not employ more than 500 people. A local Mexican restaurant may be the most patronized Mexican restaurant in your community, but because it does not dominate the restaurant industry as a

small business

any independently owned and operated business that is not dominant in its competitive area and does not employ more than 500 people

TABLE 5.4		
10 Successful Traits of Young Entrepreneurs	Intuitive	Persistent
	Creative	Innovative
	Productive	Frugal
	Patient	Friendly
	Charismatic	Fearless

Source: Yan Susanto, "10 Successful Traits of Young Entrepreneurs," *Retire @ 21*, April 10, 2009, www.retireat21.com/blog/10-successful-traits-of-young-entrepreneurs (accessed March 17, 2011).

innovate or identify new markets in the fields of computers, biotechnology, genetic engineering, robotics, and other markets have become today's high-tech giants. Mark Zuckerberg, the CEO of Facebook (a social networking website), for instance, has created a company that is one of the fastest growing dot-coms in history. Facebook is approaching 1 billion monthly active users, and more than half of all active users log on to the site on any given day. Facebook has also contributed to the global economy through employment opportunities and support for businesses. A Deloitte study estimates that Facebook added approximately $20 billion in value to the European economy alone.[18] In general, high-technology businesses require greater capital and have higher initial startup costs than do other small businesses. Many of the biggest, nonetheless, started out in garages, basements, kitchens, and dorm rooms.

Advantages of Small-Business Ownership

LO 5-3

There are many advantages to establishing and running a small business. These can be categorized into personal advantages and business advantages. Table 5.4 lists some of the traits that can help entrepreneurs succeed.

Independence

Independence is probably one of the leading reasons that entrepreneurs choose to go into business for themselves. Being a small-business owner means being your own boss. Many people start their own businesses because they believe they will do better for themselves than they could do by remaining with their current employer or by changing jobs. They may feel stuck on the corporate ladder and that no business would take them seriously enough to fund their ideas. Sometimes people who venture forth to start their own small business are those who simply cannot work for someone else. Such people may say that they just do not fit the "corporate mold."

More often, small-business owners just want the freedom to choose whom they work with, the flexibility to pick where and when to work, and the option of working in a family setting. The availability of the computer, copy machine, fax,

Some of the advantages of small businesses include flexibility, lower start-up costs, and perhaps most desirable, the ability to be your own boss.

and Internet has permitted many people to work at home. In the past, most of them would have needed the support that an office provides.

Costs

As already mentioned, small businesses often require less money to start and maintain than do large ones. Obviously, a firm with just 25 people in a small factory spends less money on wages and salaries, rent, utilities, and other expenses than does a firm employing tens of thousands of people in several large facilities. Rather than maintain the expense of keeping separate departments for accounting, advertising, and legal counseling, small businesses often hire other firms (sometimes small businesses themselves) to supply these services as they are needed. Additionally, small-business owners can sometimes rely on friends and family members to help them save money by volunteering to work on a difficult project.

Flexibility

With small size comes the flexibility to adapt to changing market demands. Small businesses usually have only one layer of management—the owners. Decisions therefore can be made and executed quickly. In larger firms, decisions about even routine matters can take weeks because they must pass through multiple levels of management before action is authorized. When Taco Bell introduces a new product, for example, it must first research what consumers want, then develop the product and test it before introducing it nationwide—a process that sometimes takes years. An independent snack shop, however, can develop and introduce a new product (perhaps to meet a customer's request) in a much shorter time.

Focus

Small firms can focus their efforts on a precisely defined market niche—that is, a specific group of customers. Many large corporations must compete in the mass market or for large market segments. Smaller firms can develop products for particular groups of customers or to satisfy a need that other companies have not addressed. For example, Fatheadz, based in Indianapolis, Indiana, focuses on producing sunglasses for people with big heads. To be an official "fathead," you need a ball cap size of at least 7⅝ and a head circumference above the ear of at least 23.5 inches. The idea arose when Rico Elmore was walking down the Las Vegas strip with his brother and realized that he had lost his sunglasses. He went to a nearby sunglass shop, and out of 300 pairs of glasses, he could not find one that fit. He decided to start a company addressing this need, and Fatheadz now distributes its designs in Walmart optical stores throughout the country.[19] By targeting small niches or product needs, small businesses can sometimes avoid competition from larger firms, helping them to grow into stronger companies.

Reputation

Small firms, because of their capacity to focus on narrow niches, can develop enviable reputations for quality and service. A good example of a small business with a formidable reputation is W. Atlee Burpee and Co., which has the country's premier bulb and seed catalog. Burpee has an unqualified returns policy (complete satisfaction or your money back) that demonstrates a strong commitment to customer satisfaction.

LO 5-4 # Disadvantages of Small-Business Ownership

The rewards associated with running a small business are so enticing that it's no wonder many people dream of it. However, as with any undertaking, small-business ownership has its disadvantages.

High Stress Level

A small business is likely to provide a living for its owner, but not much more (although there are exceptions as some examples in this chapter have shown). There are ongoing worries about competition, employee problems, new equipment, expanding inventory, rent increases, or changing market demand. In addition to other stresses, small-business owners tend to be victims of physical and psychological stress. The small-business person is often the owner, manager, sales force, shipping and receiving clerk, bookkeeper, and custodian. Having to multitask can result in long hours for most small-business owners. Many creative persons fail, not because of their business concepts, but rather because of difficulties in managing their business.

High Failure Rate

Despite the importance of small businesses to our economy, there is no guarantee of success. Half of all new employer firms fail within the first five years.[20] Restaurants

Entrepreneurs experience a great deal of independence but also a great deal of stress. Many fail.

1. Overestimating the enthusiasm for their product or service.	**TABLE 5.5**
	10 Common Mistakes That Startup and Small Companies Make
2. Not validating demand and interest in the product.	
3. Starting to work with customers only when the product is ready for sale.	
4. Underestimating the difficulty in penetrating the market.	
5. Overestimating the product's uniqueness and underestimating the competition.	
6. Underestimating the effort needed to build the product.	
7. Hiring "big-company types" who are used to having a support staff.	
8. Not focusing on the main product and being tempted by side projects.	
9. Under- or over-pricing the product.	
10. Not having a vision for long-term growth.	

Source: David Lavenda, "10 Common Mistakes That Startup and Small Companies Make," FC Expert Blog (*Fast Company*), September 8, 2009, www.fastcompany.com/blog/david-lavenda/whatever-it-takes/10-common-mistakes-startupsmall-companies-make (accessed March 17, 2011).

are a case in point. Look around your own neighborhood, and you can probably spot the locations of several restaurants that are no longer in business.

Small businesses fail for many reasons (see Table 5.5). A poor business concept—such as insecticides for garbage cans (research found that consumers are not concerned with insects in their garbage)—will produce disaster nearly every time. Expanding a hobby into a business may work if a genuine market niche exists, but all too often people start such a business without identifying a real need for the goods or services. Other notable causes of small-business failure include the burdens imposed by government regulation, insufficient funds to withstand slow sales, and vulnerability to competition from larger companies. However, three major causes of small-business failure deserve a close look: undercapitalization, managerial inexperience or incompetence, and inability to cope with growth.

Undercapitalization.   The shortest path to failure in business is **undercapitalization**, the lack of funds to operate a business normally. Too many entrepreneurs think that all they need is enough money to get started, that the business can survive on cash generated from sales soon thereafter. But almost all businesses suffer from seasonal variations in sales, which make cash tight, and few businesses make money from the start. Many small rural operations cannot obtain financing within their own communities because small rural banks often lack the necessary financing expertise or assets sizable enough to counter the risks involved with small-business loans. Without sufficient funds, the best small-business idea in the world will fail.

undercapitalization the lack of funds to operate a business normally

Managerial Inexperience or Incompetence.   Poor management is the cause of many business failures. Just because an entrepreneur has a brilliant vision for a small business does not mean he or she has the knowledge or experience to manage a growing business effectively. A person who is good at creating great product ideas and marketing them may lack the skills and experience to make good management decisions in hiring, negotiating, finance, and control. Moreover, entrepreneurs may neglect those areas of management they know little about or find tedious, at the expense of the business's success.

Inability to Cope with Growth. Sometimes, the very factors that are advantages for a small business turn into serious disadvantages when the time comes to grow. Growth often requires the owner to give up a certain amount of direct authority, and it is frequently hard for someone who has called all the shots to give up control. It has often been said that the greatest impediment to the success of a business is the entrepreneur. Similarly, growth requires specialized management skills in areas such as credit analysis and promotion—skills that the founder may lack or not have time to apply. The founders of many small businesses, including Dell Computers, found that they needed to bring in more experienced managers to help manage their companies through growing pains.

Poorly managed growth probably affects a company's reputation more than anything else, at least initially. And products that do not arrive on time or goods that are poorly made can quickly reverse a success. The principal immediate threats to small and mid-sized businesses include rising inflation, energy and other supply shortages or cost escalations, and excessive household and/or corporate debt.

LO 5-5

Starting a Small Business

We've told you how important small businesses are, and why they succeed and fail, but *how do you go about* starting your own business in the first place? To start any business, large or small, you must have some kind of general idea. Sam Walton, founder of Walmart stores, had a vision of a discount retailing enterprise that spawned the world's largest retailing empire and changed the way companies look at business. Next, you need to devise a strategy to guide planning and development in the business. Finally, you must make decisions about form of ownership, the financial resources needed, and whether to acquire an existing business, start a new one, or buy a franchise.

The Business Plan

A key element of business success is a **business plan**—a precise statement of the rationale for the business and a step-by-step explanation of how it will achieve its goals. The business plan should include an explanation of the business, an analysis of the competition, estimates of income and expenses, and other information. It should also establish a strategy for acquiring sufficient funds to keep the business going. Many financial institutions decide whether to loan a small business money based on its business plan. A good business plan should act as a guide and reference document—not a shackle that limits the business's flexibility and decision making ability. The business plan must be revised periodically to ensure that the firm's goals and strategies adapt to changes in the environment. Business plans allow companies to assess market potential, determine price and manufacturing requirements, identify optimal distribution channels, and refine product selection. Former Patriots football linebacker Matt Chatham developed an innovative idea for a crepe franchise operation. Chatham wanted to create a franchise that would sell bigger, bolder, more Americanized crepes. These franchises would be located in mall food courts and other high-traffic areas. Chatham's idea won him first place at the 2011 business-plan competition at Babson College. He received $60,000 to launch his business concept. His first Skycrepers shop opened in August of that year.[22] The Small Business Administration website provides an overview of a plan for small businesses to use to gain financing. Appendix A presents a comprehensive business plan.

business plan
a precise statement of the rationale for a business and a step-by-step explanation of how it will achieve its goals

Forms of Business Ownership

After developing a business plan, the entrepreneur has to decide on an appropriate legal form of business ownership—whether it is best to operate as a sole proprietorship, partnership, or corporation—and to examine the many factors that affect that decision, which we explored in Chapter 4.

Financial Resources

The expression "it takes money to make money" holds especially true in developing a business enterprise. To make money from a small business, the owner must first provide or obtain money (capital) to get started and to keep it running smoothly. Even a small retail store will probably need at least $50,000 in initial financing to rent space, purchase or lease necessary equipment and furnishings, buy the initial inventory, and provide working capital. Often, the small-business owner has to put up a significant percentage of the necessary capital. Few new business owners have a large amount of their own capital and must look to other sources for additional financing.

Need help understanding How an Entrepreneur Can Secure Financing?

http://bit.ly/FerrellQR5-1

Equity Financing.   The most important source of funds for any new business is the owner. Many owners include among their personal resources ownership of a home, the accumulated value in a life-insurance policy, or a savings account. A new business owner may sell or borrow against the value of such assets to obtain funds to operate a business. Additionally, the owner may bring useful personal assets—such as a computer, desks and other furniture, a car or truck—as part of his or her ownership interest in the firm. Such financing is referred to as *equity financing* because the owner uses real personal assets rather than borrowing funds from outside sources to get started in a new business. The owner can also provide working capital by reinvesting profits into the business or simply by not drawing a full salary.

Small businesses can also obtain equity financing by finding investors for their operations. They may sell stock in the business to family members, friends, employees, or other investors. For example, Alexa Andrzejewski created photo-sharing site Foodspotting after realizing that while there are many reviews online about specific restaurants, there were none about favorite meals or dishes. In 2010, the Foodspotting iPhone app was released that allows food lovers to recommend or bookmark their favorite foods and look up these "best options" at restaurants. The company initially raised $750,000 in seed funding and raised $3 million more from investors interested in the concept.[23] **Venture capitalists** are persons or organizations that agree to provide some funds for a new business in exchange for an ownership interest or stock. Venture capitalists hope to purchase the stock of a small business at a low price and then sell the stock for a profit after the business has grown successful. The renewable energy industry has recently become a popular investment option among venture capitalists, who invested $4.9 billion in "cleantech," or renewable energy startups in 2010.[24] Although these forms of equity financing have helped many small businesses, they require that the small-business owner share the profits of the business—and sometimes control, as well—with the investors.

venture capitalists
persons or organizations that agree to provide some funds for a new business in exchange for an ownership interest or stock

Debt Financing. New businesses sometimes borrow more than half of their financial resources. Banks are the main suppliers of external financing to small businesses. On the federal level, the Small Business Administration offers financial assistance to qualifying businesses. They can also look to family and friends as sources for long-term loans or other assets, such as computers or an automobile, that are exchanged for an ownership interest in a business. In such cases, the business owner can usually structure a favorable repayment schedule and sometimes negotiate an interest rate below current bank rates. If the business goes bad, however, the emotional losses for all concerned may greatly exceed the money involved. Anyone lending a friend or family member money for a venture should state the agreement clearly in writing before any money changes hands.

The amount a bank or other institution is willing to loan depends on its assessment of the venture's likelihood of success and of the entrepreneur's ability to repay the loan. The bank will often require the entrepreneur to put up *collateral,* a financial interest in the property or fixtures of the business, to guarantee payment of the debt. Additionally, the small-business owner may have to provide personal property as collateral, such as his or her home, in which case the loan is called a *mortgage.* If the small business fails to repay the loan, the lending institution may eventually claim and sell the collateral or mortgage to recover its loss.

Banks and other financial institutions can also grant a small business a *line of credit*—an agreement by which a financial institution promises to lend a business a predetermined sum on demand. A line of credit permits an entrepreneur to take quick advantage of opportunities that require external funding. Small businesses may obtain funding from their suppliers in the form of a *trade credit*—that

Franson Nwaeze and Paula Merrell wanted to open a restaurant, but most lenders were skeptical about their lack of experience and money. When the husband-and-wife team learned that banks were much more willing to loan them money to buy a gas station, they purchased a Conoco station in Watauga, Texas, and opened up a successful restaurant in one-half of it. The business's motto is "fill'er-up outside, fill'er-up inside."

is, suppliers allow the business to take possession of the needed goods and services and pay for them at a later date or in installments. Occasionally, small businesses engage in *bartering*—trading their own products for the goods and services offered by other businesses. For example, an accountant may offer accounting services to an office supply firm in exchange for office supplies and equipment.

Additionally, some community groups sponsor loan funds to encourage the development of particular types of businesses. State and local agencies may guarantee loans, especially to minority business people or for development in certain areas.

Yogurtland, founded in 2006 by founder Philip Chang, is a successful franchise operation with more than 190 locations.

Approaches to Starting a Small Business

Starting from Scratch versus Buying an Existing Business.   Although entrepreneurs often start new small businesses from scratch much the way we have discussed in this section, they may elect instead to buy an existing business. This has the advantage of providing a built-in network of customers, suppliers, and distributors and reducing some of the guesswork inherent in starting a new business from the ground up. However, an entrepreneur who buys an existing business also takes on any problems the business already has.

Franchising.   Many small-business owners find entry into the business world through franchising. A license to sell another's products or to use another's name in business, or both, is a **franchise.** The company that sells a franchise is the **franchiser.** Dunkin' Donuts, Subway, and Jiffy Lube are well-known franchisers with national visibility. The purchaser of a franchise is called a **franchisee.**

The franchisee acquires the rights to a name, logo, methods of operation, national advertising, products, and other elements associated with the franchiser's business in return for a financial commitment and the agreement to conduct business in accordance with the franchiser's standard of operations. The initial fee to join a franchise varies greatly. In addition, franchisees buy equipment, pay for training, and obtain a mortgage or lease. The franchisee also pays the franchiser a monthly or annual fee based on a percentage of sales or profits. In return, the franchisee often receives building specifications and designs, site recommendations, management and accounting support, and perhaps most importantly, immediate name recognition. Visit the website of the International Franchise Association to learn more on this topic.

The practice of franchising first began in the United States in the 19th century when Singer used it to sell sewing machines. The method of goods distribution soon became commonplace in the automobile, gasoline, soft drink, and hotel industries. The concept of franchising grew especially rapidly during the 1960s, when it expanded to diverse industries. Table 5.6 shows the 10 fastest growing franchises and the top 10 new franchises.

franchise
a license to sell another's products or to use another's name in business, or both

franchiser
the company that sells a franchise

franchisee
the purchaser of a franchise

TABLE 5.6

Fastest Growing and Hottest New Franchises

Top 10 Fastest Growing Franchises	Top 10 New Franchises
Stratus Building Solutions	No Mas Vello
Subway	Complete Nutrition
CleanNet USA Inc.	Yogurtland Franchising Inc.
Vanguard Cleaning Systems	ShelfGenie Franchise Systems LLC
H&R Block	The Senior's Choice Inc.
Dunkin' Donuts	CPR-Cell Phone Repair
Chester's	Get In Shape For Women
Liberty Tax Service	Signal 88 Security
7-Eleven Inc.	Menchie's
Anytime Fitness	Smashburger Franchising LLC

Sources: "2011 Fastest-Growing Franchises," *Entrepreneur,* www.entrepreneur.com/franchises/rankings/fastestgrowing-115162/2012,-1.html (accessed February 2, 2012); "2012 New Franchise Rankings," *Entrepreneur,* www.entrepreneur.com/franchises/rankings/topnew-115520/2012,-1.html (accessed February 2, 2012).

The entrepreneur will find that franchising has both advantages and disadvantages. Franchising allows a franchisee the opportunity to set up a small business relatively quickly, and because of its association with an established brand, a franchise outlet often reaches the break-even point faster than an independent business would. Franchisees commonly report the following advantages:

- Management training and support.
- Brand-name appeal.
- Standardized quality of goods and services.
- National and local advertising programs.
- Financial assistance.
- Proven products and business formats.
- Centralized buying power.
- Site selection and territorial protection.
- Greater chance for success.[25]

However, the franchisee must sacrifice some freedom to the franchiser. Some shortcomings experienced by franchisees include:

- Franchise fees and profit sharing with the franchiser.
- Strict adherence to standardized operations.
- Restrictions on purchasing.
- Limited product line.
- Possible market saturation.
- Less freedom in business decisions.[26]

Strict uniformity is the rule rather than the exception. Entrepreneurs who want to be their own bosses are often frustrated with the restrictions of a franchise.

Help for Small-Business Managers

Because of the crucial role that small business and entrepreneurs play in the U.S. economy, a number of organizations offer programs to improve the small-business owner's ability to compete. These include entrepreneurial training programs and programs sponsored by the Small Business Administration. Such programs provide small-business owners with invaluable assistance in managing their businesses, often at little or no cost to the owner.

Entrepreneurs can learn critical marketing, management, and finance skills in seminars and college courses. In addition, knowledge, experience, and judgment are necessary for success in a new business. While knowledge can be communicated and some experiences can be simulated in the classroom, good judgment must be developed by the entrepreneur. Local chambers of commerce and the U.S. Department of Commerce offer information and assistance helpful in operating a small business. National publications such as *Inc.* and *Entrepreneur* share statistics, advice, tips, and success/failure stories. Additionally, most urban areas have weekly business journal/newspapers that provide stories on local businesses as well as on business techniques that a manager or small business can use.

The Small Business Administration offers many types of management assistance to small businesses, including counseling for firms in difficulty, consulting on improving operations, and training for owner/managers and their employees. Among its many programs, the SBA funds Small Business Development Centers (SBDCs). These are business clinics, usually located on college campuses, that provide counseling at no charge and training at only a nominal charge. SBDCs are often the SBA's principal means of providing direct management assistance.

The Service Corps of Retired Executives (SCORE) and the Active Corps of Executives (ACE) are volunteer agencies funded by the SBA to provide advice for owners of small firms. Both are staffed by experienced managers whose talents and experience the small firms could not ordinarily afford. SCORE has 12,400 volunteers at nearly 400 locations in the United States and has served more than 8.5 million small businesses.[28] The SBA also has organized Small Business Institutes (SBIs) on almost 500 university and college campuses in the United States. Seniors, graduate students, and faculty at each SBI provide onsite management counseling.

Finally, the small-business owner can obtain advice from other small-business owners, suppliers, and even customers. A customer may approach a small business it frequents with a request for a new product, for example, or a supplier may offer suggestions for improving a manufacturing process. Networking—building relationships and sharing information with colleagues—is vital for any businessperson, whether you work for a huge corporation or run your own small business. Communicating with other business owners is a great way to find ideas for dealing with employees and government regulation, improving processes, or solving problems. New technology is making it easier to network. For example, some states are establishing social networking sites for the use of their businesses to network and share ideas.

LO 5-6

The Future for Small Business[29]

Although small businesses are crucial to the economy, their size and limited resources can make them more vulnerable to turbulence and change in the marketplace than large businesses. Next, we take a brief look at the demographic, technological, and economic trends that will have the most impact on small business in the future.

Demographic Trends

America's baby boom started in 1946 and ended in 1964. Many boomers are over 50, and in the next few years, millions more will pass that mark. The baby boomer generation represents 27 percent of Americans.[30] This segment of the population is wealthy, but many small businesses do not actively pursue it. Some exceptions, however, include Gold Violin, which sells designer canes and other products online and through a catalog, and LifeSpring, which delivers nutritional meals and snacks directly to the customer. Industries such as travel, financial planning, and health care will continue to grow as boomers age. Many experts believe that the boomer demographic is the market of the future.

Another market with huge potential for small business is the echo boomers, also called millennials or Generation Y. Millennials number around 75 million and possess a number of unique characteristics. Born between 1977 and 1994, this cohort is not solely concerned about money. Those that fall into this group are also concerned with advancement, recognition, and improved capabilities. They need direct, timely feedback and frequent encouragement and recognition. Millennials do well when training sessions combine entertainment with learning. Working remotely is more acceptable to this group than previous generations, and virtual communication may become as important as face-to-face meetings.[31]

Yet another trend is the growing number of immigrants living in the United States, who now represent about 16 percent of the population. If this trend continues, by 2050 nearly one in five Americans will be classified as immigrants. The Latino population, the nation's largest minority group, is expected to triple in size by 2050.[32]

The Latino population is the biggest and fastest growing minority segment in the United States—and a lucrative market for businesses looking for ways to meet the segment's many needs.

This vast group provides still another greatly untapped market for small businesses. Retailers who specialize in ethnic products, and service providers who offer bi- or multilingual employees, will find a large amount of business potential in this market. Table 5.7 ranks top cities in the United States for small businesses and startups.

Technological and Economic Trends

Advances in technology have opened up many new markets to small businesses. Undoubtedly, the Internet will continue to provide new opportunities for small businesses. Arianna Huffington launched the popular *Huffington Post,* a news and blogging website, in 2005. The site has broken a number of important news stories. Partly because of its accessible format and the way it agglomerates news stories from many sites, HuffPo attracts approximately 25 million views a month. In 2011, AOL agreed to acquire the *Huffington Post* for $315 million.[33]

Technological advances and an increase in service exports have created new opportunities for small companies to expand their operations abroad. Changes in communications and technology can allow small companies to

Jack Dorsey founded the idea for Twitter on a sketchpad. Dorsey says the idea was based on how dispatched vehicles, such as cabs, communicate with one another. Via radio, they are constantly squawking to each other about where they are and what they are doing.

customize their services quickly for international customers. Also, free trade agreements and trade alliances are helping to create an environment in which small businesses have fewer regulatory and legal barriers.

In recent years, economic turbulence has provided both opportunities and threats for small businesses. As large information technology companies such as Cisco, Oracle, and Sun Microsystems had to recover from an economic slowdown and an oversupply of Internet infrastructure products, some smaller firms found new niche markets. Smaller companies can react quickly to change and can stay close to their customers. While well-funded dot-coms were failing, many small businesses were learning how to use the Internet to promote themselves and sell products online. For example, arts and crafts dealers and makers of specialty products found they could sell their wares on existing websites, such as eBay. Service providers related to tourism, real estate, and construction also found they could reach customers through their own or existing websites.

TABLE 5.7

Top Cities to Launch a Small Business

1. Pittsburgh, PA

2. Miami, FL

3. Menlo Park, CA

4. Arlington, VA

5. Chattanooga, TN

6. Littleton, CO

7. Ventura, CA

8. Gahanna, OH

Source: "8 great cities to start a business," *CNNMoney*, http://money.cnn.com/smallbusiness/best_places_launch/2010/ (accessed March 21, 2011).

Deregulation of the energy market and interest in alternative fuels and in fuel conservation have spawned many small businesses. Southwest Windpower Inc. manufactures and markets small wind turbines for producing electric power for homes, sailboats, and telecommunications. Solar Attic Inc. has developed a process to recover heat from home attics to use in heating water or swimming pools. As entrepreneurs begin to realize that worldwide energy markets are valued in the hundreds of billions of dollars, the number of innovative companies entering this market will increase. In addition, many small businesses have the desire and employee commitment to purchase such environmentally friendly products. New Belgium Brewing Company received the U.S. Environmental Protection Agency and Department of Energy Award for leadership in conservation for making a 10-year commitment to purchase wind energy. The company's employees unanimously agreed to cover the increased costs of wind-generated electricity from the employee profit-sharing program.

The future for small business remains promising. The opportunities to apply creativity and entrepreneurship to serve customers are unlimited. While large organizations such as Walmart, which has more than 2.1 million employees, typically must adapt to change slowly, a small business can adapt immediately to customer and community needs and changing trends. This flexibility provides small businesses with a definite advantage over large companies.

Making Big Businesses Act "Small"

LO 5-7

The continuing success and competitiveness of small businesses through rapidly changing conditions in the business world have led many large corporations to take a closer look at what makes their smaller rivals tick. More and more firms are emulating small businesses in an effort to improve their own bottom line. Beginning in the 1980s and continuing through the present, the buzzword in business has been to *downsize* or *right-size* to reduce management layers, corporate staff, and work tasks in order to make the firm more flexible, resourceful, and innovative. Many well-known U.S. companies, including IBM, Ford, Apple Computer, General Electric, Xerox, and 3M, have downsized to improve their competitiveness, as have German, British, and Japanese firms. Other firms have sought to make their businesses "smaller" by making their operating units function more like independent small businesses, each responsible for its profits, losses, and resources. Of course, some large corporations, such as Southwest Airlines, have acted like small businesses from their inception, with great success.

Trying to capitalize on small-business success in introducing innovative new products, more and more companies are attempting to instill a spirit of entrepreneurship into even the largest firms. In major corporations, **intrapreneurs,** like entrepreneurs, take responsibility for, or "champion," the development of innovations of any kind *within* the larger organization.[34] Often, they use company resources and time to develop a new product for the company.

intrapreneurs
individuals in large firms who take responsibility for the development of innovations within the organizations

So You Want to Be an Entrepreneur or Small-Business Owner

In times when jobs are scarce, many people turn to entrepreneurship as a way to find employment. As long as there are unfulfilled needs from consumers, there will be a demand for entrepreneurs and small businesses. Entrepreneurs and small-business owners have been, and will continue to be, a vital part of the U.S. economy, whether in retailing, wholesaling, manufacturing, technology, or services. Creating a business around your idea has a lot of advantages. For many people, independence is the biggest advantage of forming their own small business, especially for those who do not work well in a corporate setting and like to call their own shots. Smaller businesses are also cheaper to start up than large ones in terms of salaries, infrastructure, and equipment. Smallness also provides a lot of flexibility to change with the times. If consumers suddenly start demanding new and different products or services, a small business is more likely to deliver quickly.

Starting your own business is not easy, especially in slow economic times. Even in a good economy, taking an idea and turning it into a business has a very high failure rate. The possibility of failure can increase even more when money is tight. Reduced revenues and expensive materials can hurt a small business more than a large one because small businesses have fewer resources. When people are feeling the pinch from rising food and fuel prices, they tend to cut back on other expenditures—which could potentially harm your small business. The increased cost of materials will also affect your bottom line. However, several techniques can help your company survive:

- Set clear payment schedules for all clients. Small businesses tend to be worse about collecting payments than large ones, especially if the clients are acquaintances. However, you need to keep cash flowing into the company in order to keep business going.

- Take the time to learn about tax breaks. A lot of people do not realize all of the deductions they can claim on items such as equipment and health insurance.

- Focus on your current customers, and don't spend a lot of time looking for new ones. It is far less expensive for a company to keep its existing customers happy.

- Although entrepreneurs and small-business owners are more likely to be friends with their customers, do not let this be a temptation to give things away for free. Make it clear to your customers what the basic price is for what you are selling and charge for extra features, extra services, etc.

- Make sure the office has the conveniences employees need—like a good coffee maker and other drinks and snacks. This will not only make your employees happy, but it will also help maintain productivity by keeping employees closer to their desks.

- Use your actions to set an example. If money is tight, show your commitment to cutting costs and making the business work by doing simple things like taking the bus to work or bringing a sack lunch every day.

- Don't forget to increase productivity in addition to cutting costs. Try not to focus so much attention on cost cutting that you don't try to increase sales.

In unsure economic times, these measures should help new entrepreneurs and small-business owners sustain their businesses. Learning how to run a business on a shoestring is a great opportunity to cut the fat and to establish lean, efficient operations.[35]

Review Your Understanding

Define entrepreneurship and small business.

An entrepreneur is a person who creates a business or product and manages his or her resources and takes risks to gain a profit; entrepreneurship is the process of creating and managing a business to achieve desired objectives. A small business is one that is not dominant in its competitive area and does not employ more than 500 people.

Investigate the importance of small business in the U.S. economy and why certain fields attract small business.

Small businesses are vital to the American economy because they provide products, jobs, innovation, and opportunities. Retailing, wholesaling, services, manufacturing, and high technology attract small businesses because these industries are relatively easy to enter, require relatively low initial financing, and may experience less heavy competition.

Specify the advantages of small-business ownership.

Small-business ownership offers some personal advantages, including independence, freedom of choice, and the option of working at home. Business advantages include flexibility, the ability to focus on a few key customers, and the chance to develop a reputation for quality and service.

Summarize the disadvantages of small-business ownership, and analyze why many small businesses fail.

Small businesses have many disadvantages for their owners such as expense, physical and psychological stress, and a high failure rate. Small businesses fail for many reasons: undercapitalization, management inexperience or incompetence, neglect, disproportionate burdens imposed by government regulation, and vulnerability to competition from larger companies.

Describe how you go about starting a small business and what resources are needed.

First, you must have an idea for developing a small business. Next, you need to devise a business plan to guide planning and development of the business. Then you must decide what form of business ownership to use: sole proprietorship, partnership, or corporation. Small-business owners are expected to provide some of the funds required to start their businesses, but funds also can be obtained from friends and family, financial institutions, other businesses in the form of trade credit, investors (venture capitalists), state and local organizations, and the Small Business Administration. In addition to loans, the Small Business Administration and other organizations offer counseling, consulting, and training services. Finally, you must decide whether to start a new business from scratch, buy an existing one, or buy a franchise operation.

Evaluate the demographic, technological, and economic trends that are affecting the future of small business.

Changing demographic trends that represent areas of opportunity for small businesses include more elderly people as baby boomers age, a large group in the 11 to 28 age range known as echo boomers, millennials, or Generation Y, and an increasing number of immigrants to the United States. Technological advances and an increase in service exports have created new opportunities for small companies to expand their operations abroad, while trade agreements and alliances have created an environment in which small business has fewer regulatory and legal barriers. Economic turbulence presents both opportunities and threats to the survival of small businesses.

Explain why many large businesses are trying to "think small."

More large companies are copying small businesses in an effort to make their firms more flexible, resourceful, and innovative, and generally to improve their bottom line. This effort often involves downsizing (reducing management layers, laying off employees, and reducing work tasks) and intrapreneurship, when an employee takes responsibility for (champions) developing innovations of any kind within the larger organization.

Assess two entrepreneurs' plans for starting a small business.

Based on the facts given in "Solve the Dilemma" on page 172 and the material presented in this chapter, you should be able to assess the feasibility and potential success of Gray and McVay's idea for starting a small business.

Revisit the World of Business

1. What were some of the risks involved with turning Five Guys into a franchise?

2. What differentiates Five Guys products from other fast-food burger franchises?

3. Describe some of the ways in which Murrell and his family retain control over the Five Guys franchise.

Learn the Terms

Check Your Progress

1. Why are small businesses so important to the U.S. economy?

2. Which fields tend to attract entrepreneurs the most? Why?

3. What are the advantages of starting a small business? The disadvantages?

4. What are the principal reasons for the high failure rate among small businesses?

5. What decisions must an entrepreneur make when starting a small business?

6. What types of financing do small entrepreneurs typically use? What are some of the pros and cons of each?

7. List the types of management and financial assistance that the Small Business Administration offers.

8. Describe the franchising relationship.

9. What demographic, technological, and economic trends are influencing the future of small business?

10. Why do large corporations want to become more like small businesses?

Get Involved

1. Interview a local small-business owner. Why did he or she start the business? What factors have led to the business's success? What problems has the owner experienced? What advice would he or she offer a potential entrepreneur?

2. Using business journals, find an example of a company that is trying to emulate the factors that make small businesses flexible and more responsive. Describe and evaluate the company's activities. Have they been successful? Why or why not?

3. Using the business plan outline in Appendix A, create a business plan for a business idea that you have. (A man named Fred Smith once did a similar project for a business class at Yale. His paper became the basis for the business he later founded: Federal Express!)

Build Your Skills

CREATIVITY

Background

The entrepreneurial success stories in this chapter are about people who used their creative abilities to develop innovative products or ways of doing something that became the basis of a new business. Of course, being creative is not just for entrepreneurs or inventors; creativity is an important tool to help you find the optimal solutions to the problems you face on a daily basis. Employees rely heavily on their creativity skills to help them solve daily workplace problems.

According to brain experts, the right-brain hemisphere is the source of creative thinking; and the creative part of the brain can "atrophy" from lack of use. Let's see how much "exercise" you're giving your right-brain hemisphere.

Task

1. Take the following self-test to check your Creativity Quotient.[36]

2. Write the appropriate number in the box next to each statement according to whether the statement describes your behavior always (3), sometimes (2), once in a while (1), or never (0).

	Always 3	Sometimes 2	Once in a While 1	Never 0
1. I am a curious person who is interested in other people's opinions.				
2. I look for opportunities to solve problems.				
3. I respond to changes in my life creatively by using them to redefine my goals and revising plans to reach them.				
4. I am willing to develop and experiment with ideas of my own.				
5. I rely on my hunches and insights.				
6. I can reduce complex decisions to a few simple questions by seeing the "big picture."				
7. I am good at promoting and gathering support for my ideas.				
8. I think further ahead than most people I associate with by thinking long term and sharing my vision with others.				
9. I dig out research and information to support my ideas.				
10. I am supportive of the creative ideas from my peers and subordinates and welcome "better ideas" from others.				
11. I read books and magazine articles to stay on the "cutting edge" in my areas of interest. I am fascinated by the future.				
12. I believe I am creative and have faith in my good ideas.				
Subtotal for each column				
Grand Total				

3. Check your score using the following scale:

   30–36   High creativity. You are giving your right-brain hemisphere a regular workout.

   20–29   Average creativity. You could use your creativity capacity more regularly to ensure against "creativity atrophy."

   10–19   Low creativity. You could benefit by reviewing the questions you answered "never" in the above assessment and selecting one or two of the behaviors that you could start practicing.

   0–9   Undiscovered creativity. You have yet to uncover your creative potential.

Solve the Dilemma   LO 5-8

THE SMALL-BUSINESS CHALLENGE

Jack Gray and his best friend, Bruce McVay, decided to start their own small business. Jack had developed recipes for fat-free and low-fat cookies and muffins in an effort to satisfy his personal health needs. Bruce had extensive experience in managing food-service establishments. They knew that a startup company needs a quality product, adequate funds, a written business plan, some outside financial support, and a good promotion program. Jack and Bruce felt they had all of this and more and were ready to embark on their new low-fat cookie/muffin store. Each had $35,000 to invest and with their homes and other resources, they had borrowing power of an additional $125,000.

However, they still have many decisions to make, including what form or organization to use, how to market their product, and how to determine exactly what products to sell—whether just cookies and muffins or additional products.

Discussion Questions

1. Evaluate the idea of a low-fat cookie and muffin retail store.

2. Are there any concerns in connection with starting a small business that Jack and Bruce have not considered?

3. What advice would you give Jack and Bruce as they start up their business?

Build Your Business Plan

SMALL BUSINESS, ENTREPRENEURSHIP, AND FRANCHISING

Now you can get started writing your business plan! Refer to Guidelines for the Development of the Business Plan following Chapter 1, which provides you with an outline for your business plan. As you are developing your business plan, keep in mind that potential investors might be reviewing it. Or you might have plans to go to your local Small Business Development Center for an SBA loan.

At this point in the process, you should think about collecting information from a variety of (free) resources. For example, if you are developing a business plan for a local business, product, or service, you might want to check out any of the following sources for demographic information: your local Chamber of Commerce, Economic Development office, census bureau, or City Planning office.

Go on the Internet and see if there have been any recent studies done or articles on your specific type of business, especially in your area. Remember, you always want to explore any secondary data before trying to conduct your own research.

See for Yourself Videocase

SONIC IS A SUCCESSFUL FRANCHISE THAT OFFERS AN OLD-FASHIONED DRIVE-IN EXPERIENCE

For those who are nostalgic for the classic drive-in diner experience, the Sonic fast-food chain helps fill that need. Sonic offers customers a dose of nostalgia with its 1950s-style curbside speakers and carhop service. As the United States' largest drive-in fast food chain, Sonic offers a unique and diverse menu selection that helps set it apart from a highly competitive fast-food franchise market. Founder Troy Smith launched the first Sonic Drive-In (known then as Top Hat Drive-In) in Shawnee, Oklahoma, in 1953 as a sole proprietorship. He later added a partner, Charlie Pappe, and eventually turned the business into a franchise.

Despite its old-fashioned feel, the company has seized upon new trends and is even testing different types of restaurants. In 2011, it opened up two locations in Florida called Sonic Beach, which were built to complement Florida's unique culture. Unlike other locations, Sonic Beach customers can sit on a patio, and its Fort Lauderdale location provides guests with an oceanfront view. However, even these newer restaurants maintain the Sonic theme of the "good old days," with sound systems playing popular music from the 1960s and 1970s.

Today, Sonic is a publicly traded company and ranks as the 10th largest fast-food franchise in terms of sales revenue. Franchising is an appealing option for entrepreneurs looking to begin businesses without creating them from scratch. In the case of Sonic, when a franchisee purchases a franchise, he or she is getting a business that already has a national reputation and a national advertising campaign. The company also offers its franchisees tremendous support and training. As a pioneer, Troy Smith was required to innovate; as a Sonic franchisee, one steps into an already proven system.

That being said, successfully running a franchise is not easy. Cody Barnett, owner of 22 Sonic franchises, says the franchisee's job is to ensure that each customer has the best experience possible, thereby making repeat visits more likely. To accomplish this, a franchisee must build his or her locations; purchase equipment; hire excellent employees; make certain the products live up to Sonic's reputation; maintain a clean, inviting facility; and much more. In order to run 22 franchises, Barnett runs his locations as limited partnerships, ensuring that a managing partner is on site at each location to keep day-to-day operations running smoothly.

Some of Sonic's success may be attributed to its stringent requirements for selecting franchisees. Although franchisees must have excellent financial credentials and prior restaurant/entrepreneurial experience, the most important factor is that each franchisee fit into the Sonic culture. Sonic offers two types of franchises. The traditional franchise, which includes the full restaurant setup, requires an initial investment of between $710,000 and $3 million. Franchisees are required to pay 4 to 5 percent in royalty fees and just under 6 percent in advertising fees. Sonic also offers the nontraditional franchise. A Sonic in a travel plaza, a mall food court, or a college campus are all examples of the nontraditional model. Because these setups do not include the drive-in and carhop features, initial investment is less—somewhere between $107,000 and more than half a million. Royalty and advertising fees still apply.

For entrepreneurs looking for limited risk, franchises like Sonic are great options. The advantages are abundant, as discussed earlier. There is a high failure rate among small businesses. Entering into a successful franchise significantly cuts down on the risk of failure, although a franchisee does have to watch for market saturation, poor location choice, and other determining factors. However, there are also disadvantages; chiefly, franchisees are often required to follow a strict model set by the franchiser. For instance, in addition to prior restaurant experience, Sonic requires its franchisees to be financially and operationally able to open two or more drive-ins. These types of requirements may make it difficult for entrepreneurs who want to set their own terms. However, with Sonic's successful business model and brand equity, there is no shortage of individuals who would like to operate a Sonic franchise.[37]

DISCUSSION QUESTIONS

1. What is Sonic's competitive advantage over other fast-food franchises?

2. What are the advantages of becoming a Sonic franchisee?

3. What are the disadvantages of buying into the Sonic franchise?

Remember to check out our Online Learning Center at www.mhhe.com/ferrell9e.

Team Exercise

Explore successful global franchises. Go to the companies' websites and find the requirements for applying for three franchises. The chapter provides examples of successful franchises. What do the companies provide, and what is expected to be provided by the franchiser? Compare and contrast each group's findings for the franchises researched. For example, at Subway, the franchisee is responsible for the initial franchise fee, finding locations, leasehold improvements and equipment, hiring employees and operating restaurants, and paying an 8 percent royalty to the company and a fee into the advertising fund. The company provides access to formulas and operational systems, store design and equipment ordering guidance, a training program, an operations manual, a representative on-site during opening, periodic evaluations and ongoing support, and informative publications.

part 3

Managing for Quality and Competitiveness

The Nature of Management

Learning Objectives

After reading this chapter, you will be able to:

LO 6-1 Define *management,* and explain its role in the achievement of organizational objectives.

LO 6-2 Describe the major functions of management.

LO 6-3 Distinguish among three levels of management and the concerns of managers at each level.

LO 6-4 Specify the skills managers need in order to be successful.

LO 6-5 Summarize the systematic approach to decision making used by many business managers.

LO 6-6 Recommend a new strategy to revive a struggling business.

Facebook Chief Operating Officer: Sheryl Sandberg

As chief operating officer of social networking phenomenon Facebook, Sheryl Sandberg is a powerful woman—so much so that she was listed in *Fortune* as being among the 50 most powerful women in business. She is in charge of controlling Facebook's massive user growth and increasing the site's earning capacity. Thus, the management of Facebook is no easy task. As second in command to CEO Mark Zuckerberg, Sandberg must deal with lawsuits, privacy issues, potential legislation to regulate the collection of user information, the decision over whether to enter China, and more. Sandberg handles all these

decisions while maintaining positive relationships with important stakeholders. This makes her the perfect foil for Zuckerberg, who is reputed to lack people skills.

Sandburg's pedigree is impressive—a Harvard graduate with time spent at the World Bank, in Washington, and at Google. At Harvard, she honed her leadership skills by co-founding and leading the group Women in Economics and Government as a way to encourage more women to tackle these male-dominated fields. Sandberg caught the attention of Google, becoming the company's vice president of global online sales and operations. She was hired away by Facebook in 2008. Sandberg is still passionate about supporting women in business, giving speeches and regularly holding Women in Silicon Valley events at her home.

Sandberg announced her next big task: attract more small businesses to Facebook. Under Sandberg's leadership, Facebook unveiled a strategy in which it will offer small companies $50 in advertising credits before starting to charge for ads. She hopes that

continued

small businesses will become hooked when they find that marketing through Facebook will help grow their customer base. Known for her down-to-earth, intelligent, and compassionate nature, it may well be Sandberg's passion and openness that have led to her success.[1]

---

management
a process designed to achieve an organization's objectives by using its resources effectively and efficiently in a changing environment

managers
those individuals in organizations who make decisions about the use of resources and who are concerned with planning, organizing, staffing, directing, and controlling the organization's activities to reach its objectives

LO 6-1

Introduction

For any organization—small or large, for profit or nonprofit—to achieve its objectives, it must have equipment and raw materials to turn into products to market, employees to make and sell the products, and financial resources to purchase additional goods and services, pay employees, and generally operate the business. To accomplish this, it must also have one or more managers to plan, organize, staff, direct, and control the work that goes on.

This chapter introduces the field of management. It examines and surveys the various functions, levels, and areas of management in business. The skills that managers need for success and the steps that lead to effective decision making are also discussed.

The Importance of Management

Management is a process designed to achieve an organization's objectives by using its resources effectively and efficiently in a changing environment. *Effectively* means having the intended result; *efficiently* means accomplishing the objectives with a minimum of resources. **Managers** make decisions about the use of the organization's resources and are concerned with planning, organizing, staffing, directing, and controlling the organization's activities so as to reach its objectives. The decision to introduce new products in order to reach objectives is often a key management duty. After several years of decline in the automobile industry, Ford management introduced the Ford Fiesta from Europe into the United States. The car provides good driving dynamics, European styling, a starting price of $16,000, and up to 40 mpg. The car fits well with Ford's existing product mix in the United States.[2] Management is universal. It takes place not only in business, but also in government, the military, labor unions, hospitals, schools, and religious groups—any organization requiring the coordination of resources.

Every organization must acquire resources (people, raw materials and equipment, money, and information) to

Sergio Marchionne, the CEO of Fiat, saved the company from near bankruptcy and put it on the road to multimillion dollar profits and the purchase of Chrysler. Since then, Chrylser has returned to profitability.

effectively pursue its objectives and coordinate their use to turn out a final good or service. Employees are one of the most important resources in helping a business attain its objectives. Successful companies recruit, train, compensate, and provide benefits (such as shares of stock and health insurance) to foster employee loyalty. Acquiring suppliers is another important part of managing resources and in ensuring that products are made available to customers. As firms reach global markets, companies such as Walmart, Corning, and Charles Schwab enlist hundreds of diverse suppliers that provide goods and services to support operations. A good supplier maximizes efficiencies and provides creative solutions to help the company reduce expenses and reach its objectives. Finally, the manager needs adequate financial resources to pay for essential activities. Primary funding comes from owners and shareholders, as well as banks and other financial institutions. All these resources and activities must be coordinated and controlled if the company is to earn a profit. Organizations must also have adequate supplies of resources of all types, and managers must carefully coordinate their use if they are to achieve the organization's objectives.

Management Functions

To harmonize the use of resources so that the business can develop, produce, and sell products, managers engage in a series of activities: planning, organizing, staffing, directing, and controlling (Figure 6.1). Although this book discusses each of the five functions separately, they are interrelated; managers may perform two or more of them at the same time.

Planning

Planning, the process of determining the organization's objectives and deciding how to accomplish them, is the first function of management. Planning is a crucial activity, for it designs the map that lays the groundwork for the other functions. It involves forecasting events and determining the best course of action from a set of options or choices. The plan itself specifies what should be done, by whom, where, when, and how. For example, General Electric implemented a plan to improve its reputation for sustainability and to reduce costs resulting from inefficiencies. Its planning resulted in a program called "Ecomagination," which addresses sustainability through calling attention to GE's solar energy programs, hybrid locomotives,

planning
the process of determining the organization's objectives and deciding how to accomplish them; the first function of management

FIGURE 6.1

The Functions of Management

Entrepreneurship in Action
Australis Aquaculture Discovers Sustainable Fish

Josh Goldman
Business: Australis Aquaculture
Founded: 2004, in Turners Falls, Massachusetts
Success: Australis Aquaculture's barramundi fish are sold in 3,000 supermarkets and have been promoted by celebrities such as television show host Dr. Oz and actress Nicole Kidman.

Josh Goldman's goal was to find the perfect fish for aquaculture. Because 32 percent of the world's fish stock is overexploited, aquaculture—or fish farming—may be the key to feeding our growing population. However, aquaculture presents many issues, including water contamination and using wild fish stock to feed farmed fish (many farmed fish are carnivores). Therefore, Goldman developed strict criteria that would ensure sustainable fish of high quality.

He soon found that implementing his criteria would not be easy. For 20 years, Goldman explored fish options with little success. Then in 2000 an entrepreneur introduced him to the Australian fish barramundi. Not only does barramundi thrive in aquaculture, its omnivorous nature allows Goldman to use less than 20 percent of fish meal and oil as feed. Goldman opened Australis Aquaculture in 2004 by creating a vertically integrated fish facility that uses a closed system to reduce waste. As a manager, Goldman has the responsibility of convincing Americans to eat an unfamiliar fish. Yet, so far, demand for barramundi has risen, enabling Australis to expand into Indonesia and Vietnam.[3]

fuel cell development, lower-emissions aircraft, and development of lighter and stronger materials, among many other projects. Ecomagination is part of GE's specific plans to produce products with an emphasis on clean technology and renewable energy.[4] The program has a presence on Facebook, Twitter, and other websites to create conversations to assist in planning. All businesses—from the smallest restaurant to the largest multinational corporation—need to develop plans for achieving success. But before an organization can plan a course of action, it must first determine what it wants to achieve.

mission
the statement of an organization's fundamental purpose and basic philosophy

Mission. A **mission,** or mission statement, is a declaration of an organization's fundamental purpose and basic philosophy. It seeks to answer the question: "What business are we in?" Good mission statements are clear and concise statements that explain the organization's reason for existence. A well-developed mission statement, no matter what the industry or size of business, will answer five basic questions:

1. Who are we?
2. Who are our customers?
3. What is our operating philosophy (basic beliefs, values, ethics, etc.)?
4. What are our core competencies and competitive advantages?
5. What are our responsibilities with respect to being a good steward of environmental, financial, and human resources?

A mission statement that delivers a clear answer to these questions provides the foundation for the development of a strong organizational culture, a good marketing plan, and a coherent business strategy. Sustainable cleaning products company Seventh Generation states that its mission is to "inspire a revolution that nurtures the health of the next seven generations."[5]

Goals. A goal is the result that a firm wishes to achieve. A company almost always has multiple goals, which illustrates the complex nature of business. A goal has three key components: an attribute sought, such as profits, customer satisfaction, or product quality; a target to be achieved, such as the volume of sales or extent of management training to be achieved; and a time frame, which is the time period in which the goal is to be achieved. Walmart, for example, under its former CEO Lee Scott, set goals of improving its reputation as an environmentally friendly company. Some of its goals involve reducing greenhouse gas emissions, increasing the fuel efficiency of its fleet, and requiring its suppliers to use less packaging. To be successful, company goals should be specific. Walmart planned to improve the fuel efficiency of its truck fleet by 25 percent within a specified time frame. It also implemented systems to measure its progress toward these goals. To be successful at achieving goals, it is necessary to know what is to be achieved, how much, when, and how succeeding at a goal is to be determined.

Southwest Airlines acquired AirTran as a part of its strategic plan to expand operations.

Objectives.   Objectives, the ends or results desired by an organization, derive from the organization's mission. A business's objectives may be elaborate or simple. Common objectives relate to profit, competitive advantage, efficiency, and growth. The principal difference between goals and objectives is that objectives are generally stated in such a way that they are measurable. Organizations with profit as an objective want to have money and assets left over after paying off business expenses. Objectives regarding competitive advantage are generally stated in terms of percentage of sales increase and market share, with the goal of increasing those figures. Efficiency objectives involve making the best use of the organization's resources. Dalhousie University has developed energy calculators for small and medium-sized businesses to help them become more aware of their energy usage and to reduce their energy expenditure. Growth objectives relate to an organization's ability to adapt and to get new products to the marketplace in a timely fashion. One of the most important objectives for businesses is sales. For example, when the Fiat 500 was introduced in the United States, the first year's sales objectives were 50,000 units. Sales slightly below 20,000 units prompted Fiat to replace its U.S. sales chief and hire Jennifer Lopez to be spokeswoman in its new advertisements.[6] Objectives provide direction for all managerial decisions; additionally, they establish criteria by which performance can be evaluated.

Plans.   There are three general types of plans for meeting objectives—strategic, tactical, and operational. A firm's highest managers develop its **strategic plans,** which establish the long-range objectives and overall strategy or course of action by which the firm fulfills its mission. Strategic plans generally cover periods ranging from one year or longer. They include plans to add products, purchase companies, sell unprofitable segments of the business, issue stock, and move into international markets. For example, Ford sold its Volvo division to China's Geely automotive group to acquire new resources and increase profits. Faced with stiff competition, rising costs, and slowing sales, some companies are closing U.S. plants and moving production to factories abroad. For example, Converse Inc. (tennis shoes), Lionel LLC (model trains), and Zebco (fishing reels) all stopped U.S. production in favor of Asian factories. Strategic plans must take into account the organization's capabilities

strategic plans
those plans that establish the long-range objectives and overall strategy or course of action by which a firm fulfills its mission

Firms need to develop contingency plans—sometimes quickly. To prevent folding, the investment banking firm Merrill Lynch hastily arranged to sell itself to Bank of America in 2008. The move saved Merrill, but Bank of America's stock price plummeted because investors feared it had paid too much for Merrill.

and resources, the changing business environment, and organizational objectives. Plans should be market-driven, matching customers' desire for value with operational capabilities, processes, and human resources.[7]

tactical plans
short-range plans designed to implement the activities and objectives specified in the strategic plan

Tactical plans are short range and designed to implement the activities and objectives specified in the strategic plan. These plans, which usually cover a period of one year or less, help keep the organization on the course established in the strategic plan. Because tactical plans allow the organization to react to changes in the environment while continuing to focus on the company's overall strategy, management must periodically review and update them. Declining performance or failure to meet objectives set out in tactical plans may be one reason for revising them. As part of changes to its tactical planning, Cisco made the decision to "slim down" different areas of the company. This included reducing its number of councils (internal committees) to three main ones whose focus will be setting direction for projects rather than engaging in tactical planning. Tactical planning will be more decentralized.[8] The differences between the two types of planning result in different activities in the short-term versus the long-term. For instance, a strategic plan might include the use of social media to reach consumers. A tactical plan could involve finding ways to increase traffic to the site or promoting premium content to those who visit the site. A fast-paced and ever-changing market requires companies to develop short-run or tactical plans to deal with the changing environment.

A retailing organization with a five-year strategic plan to invest $5 billion in 500 new retail stores may develop five tactical plans (each covering one year) specifying how much to spend to set up each new store, where to locate, and when to open each new store. Tactical plans are designed to execute the overall strategic plan. Because of their short-term nature, they are easier to adjust or abandon if changes in the environment or the company's performance so warrant.

Operational plans are very short term and specify what actions specific individuals, work groups, or departments need to accomplish in order to achieve the tactical plan and ultimately the strategic plan. They apply to details in executing activities in one month, week, or even day. For example, a work group may be assigned a weekly production quota to ensure there are sufficient products available to elevate market share (tactical goal) and ultimately help the firm be number one in its product category (strategic goal). Returning to our retail store example, operational plans may specify the schedule for opening one new store, hiring and training new employees, obtaining merchandise, and opening for actual business.

Another element of planning is **crisis management** or **contingency planning,** which deals with potential disasters such as product tampering, oil spills, fire, earthquake, computer viruses, or even a reputation crisis due to unethical or illegal conduct by one or more employees. Unfortunately, many businesses do not have updated contingency plans to handle the types of crises that their companies might encounter. A recent study reveals that more than 85 percent of small or mid-sized businesses have ineffective or outdated emergency recovery plans.[9] Businesses that have correct and well-thought-out contingency plans tend to respond more effectively when problems occur than do businesses who lack such planning.

Many companies, including Ashland Oil, H. J. Heinz, and Johnson & Johnson, have crisis management teams to deal specifically with problems, permitting other managers to continue to focus on their regular duties. Some companies even hold periodic disaster drills to ensure that their employees know how to respond when a crisis does occur. After the horrific earthquake in Japan, many companies in U.S. earthquake zones reevaluated their crisis management plans. Crisis management plans generally cover maintaining business operations throughout a crisis and communicating with the public, employees, and officials about the nature of and the company's response to the problem. Communication is especially important to minimize panic and damaging rumors; it also demonstrates that the company is aware of the problem and plans to respond.

Sometimes disasters occur that no one can anticipate, but companies can still plan for how to react to the disaster. The investment company Fred Alger Management Inc. was one company that displayed exemplary disaster recovery planning. When the company's core investment team—including its president—was killed during the September 11 attacks (the office was located in the World Trade Center), the firm relied upon its employee assistance programs and a recovery office located in New Jersey to help weather the emergency. Ten years later, the successful company continues to maintain disaster recovery plans, such as an unoccupied office for emergencies and the use of vendors to back up essential data in case the company's own data are destroyed.[10] Incidents such as this highlight the importance of planning for crises and the need to respond publicly and quickly when a disaster occurs.

operational plans
very short-term plans that specify what actions individuals, work groups, or departments need to accomplish in order to achieve the tactical plan and ultimately the strategic plan

crisis management (contingency planning)
an element in planning that deals with potential disasters such as product tampering, oil spills, fire, earthquake, computer virus, or airplane crash

Organizing

organizing
the structuring of resources and activities to accomplish objectives in an efficient and effective manner

Rarely are individuals in an organization able to achieve common goals without some form of structure. **Organizing** is the structuring of resources and activities to accomplish objectives in an efficient and effective manner. Managers organize by reviewing plans and determining what activities are necessary to implement them; then, they divide the work into small units and assign it to specific individuals, groups, or departments. As companies reorganize for greater efficiency, more often than not, they are organizing work into teams to handle core processes such as new product development instead of organizing around traditional departments such as marketing and production. Organizing occurs continuously because change is inevitable.

Organizing is important for several reasons. It helps create synergy, whereby the effect of a whole system equals more than that of its parts. It also establishes lines of authority, improves communication, helps avoid duplication of resources, and can improve competitiveness by speeding up decision making. When Japanese consumer electronics firm Panasonic decided to reorganize its business, it reduced its workforce, formed overseas alliances to expand into new product areas such as industrial-use solar systems, and stopped investing in less profitable areas. Although eliminating jobs was a difficult move, Panasonic believed that it must reduce redundancies and streamline operations to create a more efficient business.[11] Because organizing is so important, we'll take a closer look at it in Chapter 7.

Staffing

staffing
the hiring of people to carry out the work of the organization

Once managers have determined what work is to be done and how it is to be organized, they must ensure that the organization has enough employees with appropriate skills to do the work. Hiring people to carry out the work of the organization is known as **staffing.** Beyond recruiting people for positions within the firm, managers must determine what skills are needed for specific jobs, how to motivate and train employees, how much to pay, what benefits to provide, and how to prepare employees for higher-level jobs in the firm at a later date. These elements of staffing will be explored in detail in Chapters 9 and 10.

downsizing
the elimination of a significant number of employees from an organization

Another aspect of staffing is **downsizing,** the elimination of significant numbers of employees from an organization, which has been a pervasive and much-talked-about trend. Staffing can be outsourced to companies that focus on hiring and managing employees. For instance, the Bartech Group provides search and staffing services, workforce solutions, business processes outsourcing, and consulting services. The Bartech Group bills and manages $1 billion for customers such as General Motors and Eaton.[12] Many firms downsize by outsourcing production, sales, and technical positions to companies in other countries with lower labor costs. Downsizing has helped numerous firms reduce costs quickly and become more profitable (or become profitable after lengthy losses) in a short period of time. Whether it is called downsizing, rightsizing, trimming the fat, or the new reality in business, the implications of downsizing have been dramatic. During the recent economic recession, many companies laid off workers to cut costs. The nationwide unemployment rate climbed above 10 percent, but after the recovery, unemployment dropped significantly.[13]

Downsizing and outsourcing, however, have painful consequences. Obviously, the biggest casualty is those who lose their jobs, along with their incomes, insurance, and pensions. Some find new jobs quickly; others do not. Another victim is the morale of the remaining employees at downsized firms. Those left behind often feel insecure, angry, and sad, and their productivity may decline as a result, the opposite of the effect sought. Studies have found that firms that lay off more than 10 percent of their surviving workforce can expect to see turnover increase to 15.5 percent versus 10.4 percent at firms that do not have layoffs.[14]

After a downsizing situation, an effective manager will promote optimism and positive thinking and minimize criticism and fault-finding. Management should also build teamwork and encourage positive group discussions. Honest communication is important during a time of change and will lead to trust. In reality, when departments are downsized, the remaining employees end up working harder to fill the gaps left by layoffs. Truthfulness about what has happened and about future expectations is essential.

Some companies choose to recruit people to hire through online job websites such as Monster.com. Monster.com is one of the world's largest employment websites. Using websites like Monster.com would fall under the staffing function of management.

Directing

Once the organization has been staffed, management must direct the employees. **Directing** is motivating and leading employees to achieve organizational objectives. Good directing involves telling employees what to do and when to do it through the implementation of deadlines, and then encouraging them to do their work. For example, as a sales manager, you would need to learn how to motivate salespersons; provide leadership; teach sales teams to be responsive to customer needs; and manage organizational issues as well as evaluate sales results. Finally, directing also involves determining and administering appropriate rewards and recognition. All managers are involved in directing, but it is especially important for lower-level managers who interact daily with the employees operating the organization. For example, an assembly-line supervisor for Frito-Lay must ensure that her workers know how to use their equipment properly and have the resources needed to carry out their jobs safely and efficiently, and she must motivate her workers to achieve their expected output of packaged snacks.

directing
motivating and leading employees to achieve organizational objectives

Managers may motivate employees by providing incentives—such as the promise of a raise or promotion—for them to do a good job. But most workers want more than money from their jobs: They need to know that their employer values their ideas and input. Managers should give younger employees some decision-making authority as soon as possible. Smart managers, therefore, ask workers to contribute ideas for reducing costs, making equipment more efficient, improving customer service, or even developing new products. For example, Travelocity has made employee engagement a top priority to bring customer service to the highest level. This participation makes workers feel important, and the company benefits. Recognition and appreciation are often the best motivators. Employees who understand more about their effect on the financial success of the company may be induced to work harder for that success, and managers who understand the needs and desires of workers can encourage their employees to work harder and more productively. The motivation of employees is discussed in detail in Chapter 9.

Controlling

controlling
the process of evaluating and correcting activities to keep the organization on course

Planning, organizing, staffing, and directing are all important to the success of an organization, whether its objective is earning a profit or something else. But what happens when a firm fails to reach its goals despite a strong planning effort? **Controlling** is the process of evaluating and correcting activities to keep the organization on course. Control involves five activities: (1) measuring performance, (2) comparing present performance with standards or objectives, (3) identifying deviations from the standards, (4) investigating the causes of deviations, and (5) taking corrective action when necessary.

Controlling and planning are closely linked. Planning establishes goals and standards. By monitoring performance and comparing it with standards, managers can determine whether performance is on target. When performance is substandard, management must determine why and take appropriate actions to get the firm back on course. In short, the control function helps managers assess the success of their plans. You might relate this to your performance in this class. If you did not perform as well on early projects or exams, you must take corrective action such as increasing studying or using website resources to achieve your overall objective of getting an A or B in the course. When the outcomes of plans do not meet expectations, the control process facilitates revision of the plans. Control can take many forms such as visual inspections, testing, and statistical modeling processes. The basic idea is to ensure that operations meet requirements and are satisfactory to reach objectives.

The control process also helps managers deal with problems arising outside the firm. For example, if a firm is the subject of negative publicity, management should use the control process to determine why and to guide the firm's response.

Types of Management

LO 6-3

All managers—whether the sole proprietor of a jewelry store or the hundreds of managers of a large company such as Paramount Pictures—perform the five functions just discussed. In the case of the jewelry store, the owner handles all the functions, but in a large company with more than one manager, responsibilities must be divided and delegated. This division of responsibility is generally achieved by establishing levels of management and areas of specialization—finance, marketing, and so on.

Levels of Management

As we have hinted, many organizations have multiple levels of management—top management, middle management, and first-line, or supervisory management. These levels form a pyramid, as shown in Figure 6.2. As the pyramid shape implies, there are generally more middle managers than top managers, and still more first-line managers. Very small organizations may have only one manager (typically, the owner), who assumes the responsibilities of all three levels. Large businesses have many managers at each

Interestingly, Mark Zuckerberg is an example of a CEO who does not receive high annual compensation. In 2012, it was announced that Zuckerberg would go from a base salary of $600,000 to an annual pay of just $1 per year.

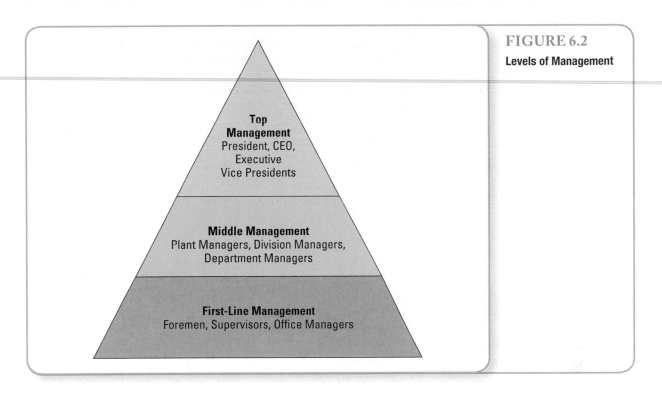

FIGURE 6.2
Levels of Management

level to coordinate the use of the organization's resources. Managers at all three levels perform all five management functions, but the amount of time they spend on each function varies, as we shall see (Figure 6.3).

Top Management.   In businesses, **top managers** include the president and other top executives, such as the chief executive officer (CEO), chief financial officer (CFO), and chief operations officer (COO), who have overall responsibility for the organization. For example, Mark Zuckerberg, CEO and founder of Facebook, manages the overall strategic direction of the company and plays a key role in representing the company to stakeholders. Sheryl Sandberg, Facebook's chief operating officer, is responsible for the daily operation of the company. The COO reports to the CEO and is often considered to be number two in command. In public corporations, even chief executive officers have a boss—the firm's board of directors. With technological advances accelerating and privacy concerns increasing, some companies are adding a new top management position—chief privacy officer (CPO). The position of privacy officer has grown so widespread that the International Association of Privacy Professionals boasts 7,700 members in 52 countries. In government, top management refers to the president, a governor, or a mayor or city manager; in education, a chancellor of a university or a superintendent of education.

Top-level managers spend most of their time planning. They make the organization's strategic decisions, decisions that focus on an overall scheme or key idea for using resources to take advantage of opportunities. They decide whether to add products, acquire companies, sell unprofitable business segments, and

top managers
the president and other top executives of a business, such as the chief executive officer (CEO), chief financial officer (CFO), and chief operations officer (COO), who have overall responsibility for the organization

DID YOU KNOW?   Only 3 percent of *Fortune* 500 CEOs are women.[15]

FIGURE 6.3

Importance of Management Functions to Managers in Each Level

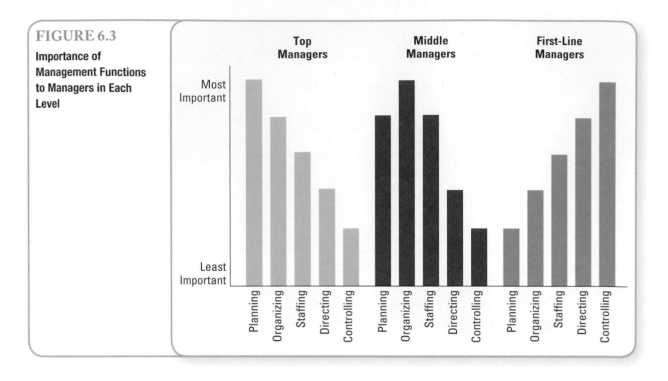

move into foreign markets. Top managers also represent their company to the public and to government regulators.

Given the importance and range of top managements' decisions, top managers generally have many years of varied experience and command top salaries. In addition to salaries, top managers' compensation packages typically include bonuses, long-term incentive awards, stock, and stock options. Table 6.1 lists the 10 highest paid CEOs, including bonuses, stock options, and other compensation. Top management may also get perks and special treatment that is criticized by stakeholders.

Compensation committees are increasingly working with boards of directors and CEOs to attempt to keep pay in line with performance in order to benefit stockholders and key stakeholders. The majority of major companies cite their concern about attracting capable leadership for the CEO and other top executive positions in their organizations. However, many firms are trying to curb criticism of excessive executive compensation by trying to align CEO compensation with performance. In other words, if the company performs poorly, the CEO will not be paid as well. Executive compensation has become such an issue that even the government has gotten involved. It capped the CEO salaries at Fannie Mae and Freddie Mac at less than $220,000. Pay at these two companies has been especially controversial because they are government conservatorships.[16] Successful management translates into happy stockholders who are willing to compensate their top executives fairly and in line with performance.

Workforce diversity is an important issue in today's corporations. Effective managers at enlightened corporations have found that diversity is good for workers and for the bottom line. Putting together different kinds of people to solve problems often results in better solutions. Irene Rosenfeld, CEO of Kraft Foods, said that "fostering a workplace that welcomes diversity of all kinds—perspectives, experiences,

Rank	CEO	Company	Compensation (millions)	TABLE 6.1
				The Highest Paid CEOs
1.	John Hammergren	McKesson	$131.2	
2.	Ralph Lauren	Polo Ralph Lauren	66.7	
3.	Michael Fascitelli	Vornado Realty	64.4	
4.	Robert Iger	Walt Disney	53.3	
5.	George Paz	Express Scripts	51.5	
6.	Jeffrey Boyd	Priceline.com	50.2	
7.	Lew Frankfort	Coach	49.5	
8.	Stephen Hemsley	UnitedHealth Group	48.8	
9.	John D. Wren	Omnicom Group	45.6	
10.	Michael Watford	Ultra Petroleum	43.7	

Source: Christopher Helman, "America's 25 Highest-Paid CEOs," *Forbes,* October 12, 2011, www.forbes.com/sites/christopherhelman/2011/10/12/americas-25-highest-paid-ceos/ (accessed March 6, 2012).

backgrounds and cultures—is a proven way to attract and keep talented people and inspire them to do great things."[17] A diverse workforce is better at making decisions regarding issues related to consumer diversity. W. Garrison Jackson runs a multicultural public relations and advertising agency that helps corporate America reach black, Hispanic, Asian, and other minority consumers. These fast growing demographic groups are key target markets for many companies, including Colgate-Palmolive, General Mills, and IBM.[18] Managers from companies devoted to workforce diversity devised five rules that make diversity recruiting work (see Table 6.2). Diversity is explored in greater detail in Chapter 10.

Middle Management.   Rather than making strategic decisions about the whole organization, **middle managers** are responsible for tactical planning that will implement the general guidelines established by top management. Thus, their responsibility is more narrowly focused than that of top managers. Middle managers are involved in the specific operations of the organization and spend more time organizing than other managers. In business, plant managers, division managers, and department managers make up middle management. The product manager for laundry detergent at a consumer products manufacturer, the department chairperson in a university, and the head of a state public health department are all middle managers. The ranks of middle managers have been shrinking as more and more companies downsize to be more productive.

middle managers those members of an organization responsible for the tactical planning that implements the general guidelines established by top management

First-Line Management.   Most people get their first managerial experience as **first-line managers,** those who supervise workers and the daily operations of the organization. They are responsible for implementing the plans established by middle management and directing workers' daily performance on the job. They spend most of their time directing and controlling. Common titles for first-line managers are foreman, supervisor, and office service manager.

first-line managers those who supervise both workers and the daily operations of an organization

TABLE 6.2	Rule	Action
Five Rules of Successful Diversity Recruiting	1. Get everyone involved.	Educate all employees on the tangible benefits of diversity recruiting to garner support and enthusiasm for those initiatives.
	2. Showcase your diversity.	Prospective employees are not likely to become excited about joining your company just because you say that your company is diversity-friendly; they need to see it.
	3. Work with diversity groups within your community.	By supporting community-based diversity organizations, your company will generate the priceless word-of-mouth publicity that will lead qualified diversity candidates to your company.
	4. Spend money.	If you are serious about diversity recruiting, you will need to spend some money getting your message out to the right places.
	5. Sell, sell, sell—and measure your return on investment.	Employers need to sell their company to prospective diversity employees and present them with a convincing case as to why their company is a good fit for the diversity candidate.

Source: Adapted from Juan Rodriguez, "The Five Rules of Successful Diversity Recruiting," *Diversityjobs.com*, www.diversityjobs.com/Rules-of-Successful-Diversity-Recruiting (accessed February 25, 2010).

financial managers
those who focus on obtaining needed funds for the successful operation of an organization and using those funds to further organizational goals

Areas of Management

At each level, there are managers who specialize in the basic functional areas of business: finance, production and operations, human resources (personnel), marketing, and administration.

Financial Management. **Financial managers** focus on obtaining the financial resources needed for the successful operation of the organization. Among the responsibilities of financial managers are projecting income and expenses over a specified period, determining short- and long-term financing needs and finding sources of financing to fill those needs, identifying and selecting appropriate ways to invest extra funds, monitoring the flow of financial resources, and protecting the financial resources of the organization. A financial manager at Ford, for example, may be asked to analyze the costs and revenues of a car model to determine its contribution to Ford's profitability. All organizations must have adequate financial resources to acquire the physical and human resources that are necessary to create goods and services. Consequently, financial resource management is of the utmost importance.

This financial manager of a city hedge fund analyzes data from financial charts. Financial managers are responsible for obtaining the necessary funding for organizations to succeed, both in the short term and in the long term.

Production and Operations Management. **Production and operations managers** develop and administer the activities involved in transforming resources into goods, services, and ideas ready for the marketplace. Production and operations managers are typically involved in planning and designing production facilities, purchasing raw materials and supplies, managing inventory, scheduling processes to meet demand, and ensuring that products meet quality standards. Because no business can exist without the production of goods and services, production and operations managers are vital to an organization's success. Production can be a complicated process because companies, no matter what the size, must balance different considerations such as cost, performance, extra features, and styling. For example, the Ford Mustang is faster than the Chevrolet Camaro, but it does not handle as well. Both Ford and General Motors face the challenges inherent in producing products that balance high performance and maintaining quality standards in order to gain competitive advantage from their designs, production, and operations excellence. An additional challenge to small companies is to do all these things while remaining profitable.

> **production and operations managers** those who develop and administer the activities involved in transforming resources into goods, services, and ideas ready for the marketplace

Human Resources Management. **Human resources managers** handle the staffing function and deal with employees in a formalized manner. Once known as personnel managers, they determine an organization's human resource needs; recruit and hire new employees; develop and administer employee benefits, training, and performance appraisal programs; and deal with government regulations concerning employment practices. For example, some companies recognize that their employees' health affects their costs. Therefore, more progressive companies provide health care facilities and outside health club memberships, encourage proper nutrition, and discourage smoking in an effort to improve employee health and lower the costs of providing health care benefits.

> **human resources managers** those who handle the staffing function and deal with employees in a formalized manner

Marketing Management. **Marketing managers** are responsible for planning, pricing, and promoting products and making them available to customers through distribution. The marketing manager who oversees Samsung televisions, for example, must make decisions regarding a new television's size, features, name, price, and packaging, as well as plan what type of stores to distribute the television through and the advertising campaign that will introduce the new television to consumers. The chief marketing officer for Gap Inc. is repositioning the company's clothing lines in the United States by focusing on denim as the core product. Its line of 1969 jeans has been positioned as a product that represents Gap's strong heritage in the American fashion industry.[19] Within the realm of marketing, there are several areas of specialization: product development and management, pricing, promotion, and distribution. Specific jobs are found in areas such as marketing research, advertising, personal selling, retailing, and digital marketing.

> **marketing managers** those who are responsible for planning, pricing, and promoting products and making them available to customers

Information Technology (IT) Management. **Information technology (IT) managers** are responsible for implementing, maintaining, and controlling technology applications in business, such as computer networks. Google, the world's largest online search engine, employs more than 30,000 employees, many of whom are IT managers. Google searches for IT managers and employees who are enthusiastic about their field and Google's products. To keep their engineers motivated, Google allows them to spend up to 20 percent of their time working on personal projects.[20] One major task in IT management is securing computer systems from unauthorized users while making the system easy to use for employees, suppliers, and others who have legitimate reasons to access the system. Another crucial task is protecting the systems' data, even during a disaster such as a fire. IT managers are

> **information technology (IT) managers** those who are responsible for implementing, maintaining, and controlling technology applications in business, such as computer networks

also responsible for teaching and helping employees use technology resources efficiently through training and support. At many companies, some aspects of IT management are outsourced to third-party firms that can perform this function expertly and efficiently.

administrative managers
those who manage an entire business or a major segment of a business; they are not specialists but coordinate the activities of specialized managers

Administrative Management. **Administrative managers** are not specialists; rather they manage an entire business or a major segment of a business. Such managers coordinate the activities of specialized managers, which would include marketing managers, production managers, and financial managers. Because of the broad nature of their responsibilities, administrative managers are often called general managers. However, this does not mean that administrative managers lack expertise in any particular area. Many top executives have risen through the ranks of financial management, production and operations management, or marketing management; but most top managers are actually administrative managers, employing skills in all areas of management.

Skills Needed by Managers

LO 6-4

Managers are typically evaluated using the metrics of how effective and efficient they are. Managing effectively and efficiently requires certain skills—leadership, technical expertise, conceptual skills, analytical skills, and human relations skills. Table 6.3 describes some of the roles managers may fulfill.

Leadership

leadership
the ability to influence employees to work toward organizational goals

Leadership is the ability to influence employees to work toward organizational goals. Strong leaders manage and pay attention to the culture of their organizations and the needs of their customers. Table 6.4 offers some tips for successful leadership

TABLE 6.3	**Managerial Roles**	
Type of Role	**Specific Role**	**Examples of Role Activities**
Decisional	Entrepreneur	Commit organizational resources to develop innovative goods and services; decide to expand internationally to obtain new customers for the organization's products.
	Disturbance handler	Move quickly to take corrective action to deal with unexpected problems facing the organization from the external environment, such as a crisis like an oil spill, or from the internal environment, such as producing faulty goods or services.
	Resource allocator	Allocate organizational resources among different functions and departments of the organization; set budgets and salaries of middle and first-level managers.
	Negotiator	Work with suppliers, distributors, and labor unions to reach agreements about the quality and price of input, technical, and human resources; work with other organizations to establish agreements to pool resources to work on joint projects.
Informational	Monitor	Evaluate the performance of managers in different functions and take corrective action to improve their performance; watch for changes occurring in the external and internal environment that may affect the organization in the future.
	Disseminator	Inform employees about changes taking place in the external and internal environment that will affect them and the organization; communicate to employees the organization's vision and purpose.
	Spokesperson	Launch a national advertising campaign to promote new goods and services; give a speech to inform the local community about the organization's future intentions.
Interpersonal	Figurehead	Outline future organizational goals to employees at company meetings; open a new corporate headquarters building; state the organization's ethical guidelines and the principles of behavior employees are to follow in their dealings with customers and suppliers.
	Leader	Provide an example for employees to follow; give direct commands and orders to subordinates; make decisions concerning the use of human and technical resources; mobilize employee support for specific organizational goals.
	Liaison	Coordinate the work of managers in different departments; establish alliances between different organizations to share resources to produce new goods and services.

Source: Gareth R. Jones and Jennifer M. George, *Essentials of Contemporary Management* (Burr Ridge, IL: McGraw-Hill/Irwin, 2007, 3rd edition), p. 14.

while Table 6.5 lists the world's 10 most admired companies and their CEOs. The list is compiled annually for *Fortune* magazine by executives and analysts who grade companies according to nine attributes, including quality of management.

Managers often can be classified into three types based on their leadership style. *Autocratic leaders* make all the decisions and then tell employees what must be done and how to do it. They generally use their authority and economic rewards to get employees to comply with their directions. Martha Stewart is an example of an autocratic leader. She built up her media empire by paying close attention to every detail.[22] *Democratic leaders* involve their employees in decisions. The manager presents a situation and encourages his or her subordinates to express opinions and contribute ideas. The manager then considers the employees' points of view and makes the decision. Herb Kelleher, co-founder of Southwest Airlines, had a democratic leadership style. Under his leadership, employees were encouraged to discuss

Need help understanding Management and Leadership Styles?

http://bit.ly/FerrellQR6_1

Flight attendant David Holmes became a YouTube sensation by rapping passenger instructions on Southwest Airlines flights. Southwest Airlines' managers and employees are well-known for their excellent human relations skills and making the workplace fun.

that require analytical skills are often a part of job interviews. Questions such as "Tell me how you would resolve a problem at work if you had access to a large amount of data?" may be part of the interview process. The answer would require the interviewee to try to explain how to sort data to find relevant facts that could resolve the issue. Analytical thinking is required in complex or difficult situations where the solution is often not clear. Resolving ethical issues often requires analytical skills.

Human Relations Skills

human relations skills
the ability to deal with people, both inside and outside the organization

People skills, or **human relations skills,** are the ability to deal with people, both inside and outside the organization. Those who can relate to others, communicate well with others, understand the needs of others, and show a true appreciation for others are generally more successful than managers who lack such skills. People skills are especially important in hospitals, airline companies, banks, and other organizations that provide services. For example, at Southwest Airlines, every new employee attends "You, Southwest and Success," a day-long class designed to teach employees about the airline and its reputation for impeccable customer service. All employees in management positions at Southwest take mandatory leadership classes that address skills related to listening, staying in touch with employees, and handling change without compromising values.

Where Do Managers Come From?

Good managers are not born; they are made. An organization acquires managers in three ways: promoting employees from within, hiring managers from other organizations, and hiring managers straight out of universities.

Responding to Business Challenges
Managers and Employees See Different Corporate Cultures

Many top managers believe that their organizations have values-based cultures in which employees can grow and make ethical decisions. However, employees disagree. In a recent study of the American workplace, 43 percent of employee respondents described the workplace as "command-and-control" or "top-down management." This indicates a management style in which the top managers make the rules and employees follow them. However, employers were eight times more likely to respond that their organizations allow employees to make decisions based upon organizational values, thus contributing to a values-based organizational culture.

In a traditional top-down chain of command, managers perform most of the planning, organizing, and directing functions of the firm. However, as views toward management change and employees are expected to take on greater roles, stakeholders are advocating for a self-governance approach. Such an approach calls for employee engagement, a greater emphasis on employee well-being, and the adoption of a culture that inspires through values rather than strictly rules. Additionally, managers must look beyond the bottom line when providing rewards.

The good news is that managers are recognizing the benefits of this system. The bad news is that according to employees, managers are not successfully implementing this new management style. Better communication is needed to understand employee concerns, disseminate corporate values throughout the company, and create an incentives system that rewards the successful practice of these values in the workplace.[26]

Discussion Questions

1. How does a values-based culture differ from a top-down chain of command?
2. Why do you think more managers want to adopt a values-based corporate culture?
3. How can managers make sure that they are successfully implementing a values-based managerial approach?

Promoting people within the organization into management positions tends to increase motivation by showing employees that those who work hard and are competent can advance in the company. Internal promotion also provides managers who are already familiar with the company's goals and problems. Procter & Gamble prefers to promote managers from within, which creates managers who are familiar with the company's products, policies, and culture and builds company loyalty. Promoting from within, however, can lead to problems: It may limit innovation. The new manager may continue the practices and policies of previous managers. Thus it is vital for companies—even companies committed to promotion from within—to hire outside people from time to time to bring fresh ideas to the table.

General Electric's excellent managerial training programs are renowned around the world. The company knows good managers aren't born. They are made.

Finding managers with the skills, knowledge, and experience required to run an organization or department can be difficult. Specialized executive employment agencies—sometimes called headhunters, recruiting managers, or executive search firms—can help locate candidates from other companies. The downside is that even though outside people can bring fresh ideas to a company, hiring them may cause resentment among existing employees as well as involve greater expense in relocating an individual to another city or state.

Schools and universities provide a large pool of potential managers, and entry-level applicants can be screened for their developmental potential. People with specialized management skills such as those with an MBA (master's of business administration) degree may be good candidates. Business students in the 21st century must remain flexible during their job searches. Before applying for a job, graduates should understand the company, the people, and the company's core values to ascertain whether they would be a good fit. Students may not have the exact skills for which the company is searching, but if they fit well with the culture, they can be trained. On-the-job training and socialization can help new recruits achieve success in their position and can help them reach their objectives. Finding employees who are trainable and a good fit with corporate culture means that organizations have a workforce staffed with potential future managers. Businesses that are recovering from the most recent economic recession should be willing to embrace new ideas and new employees willing to undergo change.

Decision Making

LO 6-5

Managers make many different kinds of decisions, such as the hours in a workday, which employees to hire, what products to introduce, and what price to charge for a product. Decision making is important in all management functions and at all levels, whether the decisions are on a strategic, tactical, or operational level. A systematic approach using the following six steps usually leads to more effective decision making: (1) recognizing and defining the decision situation, (2) developing options to resolve the situation, (3) analyzing the options, (4) selecting the best option, (5) implementing the decision, and (6) monitoring the consequences of the decision (Figure 6.4).

Recognizing and Defining the Decision Situation

The first step in decision making is recognizing and defining the situation. The situation may be negative—for example, huge losses on a particular product—or positive—for example, an opportunity to increase sales.

Situations calling for small-scale decisions often occur without warning. Situations requiring large-scale decisions, however, generally occur after some warning signs. Effective managers pay attention to such signals. Declining profits, small-scale losses in previous years, inventory buildup, and retailers' unwillingness to stock a product are signals that may foreshadow huge losses to come. If managers pay attention to such signals, problems can be contained.

Once a situation has been recognized, management must define it. Losses reveal a problem—for example, a failing product. One manager may define the situation as a product quality problem; another may define it as a change in consumer preference. These two viewpoints may lead to vastly different solutions. The first manager, for example, may seek new sources of raw materials of better quality. The second

FIGURE 6.4

Steps in the Decision-Making Process

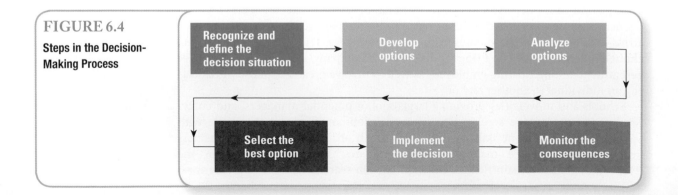

manager may believe that the product has reached the end of its lifespan and decide to discontinue it. This example emphasizes the importance of carefully defining the problem rather than jumping to conclusions.

Developing Options

Once the decision situation has been recognized and defined, the next step is to develop a list of possible courses of action. The best lists include both standard and creative plans. As a general rule, more time and expertise are devoted to the development stage of decision making when the decision is of major importance. When the decision is of less importance, less time and expertise will be spent on this stage. Options may be developed individually, by teams, or through analysis of similar situations in comparable organizations. Creativity is a very important part of selecting the most viable option. Creativity depends on new and useful ideas, regardless of where they originate or the method used to create them. The best option can range from a required solution to an identified problem or a volunteered solution, to an observed problem by an outside work group member.[27]

Analyzing Options

After developing a list of possible courses of action, management should analyze the practicality and appropriateness of each option. An option may be deemed impractical because of a lack of financial resources, legal restrictions, ethical and social responsibility considerations, authority constraints, technological constraints, economic limitations, or simply a lack of information and expertise. For example, a small computer manufacturer may recognize an opportunity to introduce a new type of computer but lack the financial resources to do so. Other options may be more practical for the computer company: It may consider selling its technology to another computer company that has adequate resources, or it may allow itself to be purchased by a larger company that can introduce the new technology.

Technology such as the RIM Blackberry Smart Phone can help managers maintain an agenda, analyze options, and aid in decision making.

When assessing appropriateness, the decision maker should consider whether the proposed option adequately addresses the situation. When analyzing the consequences of an option, managers should consider its impact on the situation and on the organization as a whole. For example, when considering a price cut to boost sales, management must think about the consequences of the action on the organization's cash flow and consumers' reaction to the price change.

Selecting the Best Option

When all courses of action have been analyzed, management must select the best one. Selection is often a subjective procedure because many situations do not lend themselves to quantitative analysis. Of course, it is not always necessary to select only one option and reject all others; it may be possible to select and use a combination of several options. William Wrigley Jr. made a decision to sell his firm to Mars for $23 billion. The firm was founded by his great-grandfather in 1891, but hard times forced Wrigley to take what was considered to be the best option. This option was to create the Mars-Wrigley firm, currently the world's largest confectionary company with a distribution network in 180 countries.[28] A different set of choices would have been available to the company had it been able to purchase Hershey for $12 billion a few years earlier.

Implementing the Decision

To deal with the situation at hand, the selected option or options must be put into action. Implementation can be fairly simple or very complex, depending on the nature of the decision. Effective implementation of a decision to abandon a product, close a plant, purchase a new business, or something similar requires planning. For example, when a product is dropped, managers must decide how to handle distributors and customers and what to do with the idle production facility. Additionally, they should anticipate resistance from people within the organization. (People tend to resist change because they fear the unknown.) Finally, management should be ready to deal with the unexpected consequences. No matter how well planned implementation is, unforseen problems will arise. Management must be ready to address these situations when they occur.

Monitoring the Consequences

After managers have implemented the decision, they must determine whether it has accomplished the desired result. Without proper monitoring, the consequences of decisions may not be known quickly enough to make efficient changes. If the desired result is achieved, management can reasonably conclude that it made a good choice. If the desired result is not achieved, further analysis is warranted. Was the decision simply wrong, or did the situation change? Should some other option have been implemented?

If the desired result is not achieved, management may discover that the situation was incorrectly defined from the beginning. That may require starting the decision-making process all over again. Finally, management may determine that the decision was good even though the desired results have not yet shown up, or it may determine a flaw in the decision's implementation. In the latter case, management would not change the decision but would change the way in which it is implemented.

The Reality of Management

Management is not a cut-and-dried process. There is no mathematical formula for managing an organization and achieving organizational goals, although many managers passionately wish for one! Managers plan, organize, staff, direct, and control, but management expert John P. Kotter says even these functions can be boiled down to two basic activities:

1. Figuring out what to do despite uncertainty, great diversity, and an enormous amount of potentially relevant information, and
2. Getting things done through a large and diverse set of people despite having little direct control over most of them.[29]

Managers spend as much as 75 percent of their time working with others—not only with subordinates but with bosses, people outside their hierarchy at work, and people outside the organization itself. In these interactions, they discuss anything and everything remotely connected with their business.

agenda
a calender, containing both specific and vague items, that covers short-term goals and long-term objectives

Managers spend a lot of time establishing and updating an agenda of goals and plans for carrying out their responsibilities. An **agenda** contains both specific and vague items, covering short-term goals and long-term objectives. Like a calendar, an agenda helps the manager figure out what must be done and how to get it done to meet the objectives set by the organization. Technology tools such as smart phones can help managers manage their agendas, contacts, communications, and time.

Managers also spend a lot of time **networking**—building relationships and sharing information with colleagues who can help them achieve the items on their agendas. Managers spend much of their time communicating with a variety of people and participating in activities that on the surface do not seem to have much to do with the goals of their organization. Nevertheless, these activities are crucial to getting the job done. Networks are not limited to immediate subordinates and bosses; they include other people in the company as well as customers, suppliers, and friends. These contacts provide managers with information and advice on diverse topics. Managers ask, persuade, and even intimidate members of their network in order to get information and to get things done. Networking helps managers carry out their responsibilities. Social media sites have increased the ability of both managers and subordinates to network. Internal social networks such as Yammer allow employees to connect with one another, while social networks such as Facebook or Twitter enable managers to connect with customers. Sales managers are even using social networks to communicate with their distributors. LinkedIn has been used for job networking and is gaining in popularity among the younger generation as an alternative to traditional job hunting. Some speculate that social networks might eventually replace traditional résumés and job boards.[30]

networking
the building of relationships and sharing of information with colleagues who can help managers achieve the items on their agendas

Websites like LinkedIn are helping managers and employees network with one another to achieve their professional goals.

Finally, managers spend a great deal of time confronting the complex and difficult challenges of the business world today. Some of these challenges relate to rapidly changing technology (especially in production and information processing), increased scrutiny of individual and corporate ethics and social responsibility, the impact of social media, the changing nature of the workforce, new laws and regulations, increased global competition and more challenging foreign markets, declining educational standards (which may limit the skills and knowledge of the future labor and customer pool), and time itself—that is, making the best use of it. But such diverse issues cannot simply be plugged into a computer program that supplies correct, easy-to-apply solutions. It is only through creativity and imagination that managers can make effective decisions that benefit their organizations.

So You Want to Be a Manager

What Kind of Manager Do You Want to Be?

Managers are needed in a wide variety of organizations. Experts suggest that employment will increase by millions of jobs by 2016. But the requirements for the jobs become more demanding with every passing year—with the speed of technology and communication increasing by the day, and the stress of global commerce increasing pressures to perform. However, if you like a challenge and if you have the right kind of personality, management remains a viable field. Even as companies are forced to restructure, management remains a vital role in business. In fact, the Bureau of Labor Statistics predicts that management positions in public relations, marketing, and advertising are set to increase around 12 percent overall between 2006 and 2016. Financial managers will be in even more demand, with jobs increasing 13 percent in the same time period. Computer and IT managers will continue to be in strong demand, with the number of jobs increasing 16 percent between 2006 and 2016.[31]

Salaries for managerial positions remain strong overall. While pay can vary significantly depending on your level of experience, the firm where you work, and the region of the country where you live, below is a list of the nationwide average incomes for a variety of different managers:

Chief executive officers: $173,350
Computer and IT manager: $123,280
Marketing manager: $122,720
Financial manager: $116,970
General and operations manager: $113,100
Medical/health services manager: $93,670
Administrative services manager: $84,390
Human resources manager: $108,600
Sales manager: $114,110[32]

In short, if you want to be a manager, there are opportunities in almost every field. There may be fewer middle management positions available in firms, but managers remain a vital part of most industries and will continue to be long into the future—especially as navigating global business becomes ever more complex.

Review Your Understanding

Define management, and explain its role in the achievement of organizational objectives.

Management is a process designed to achieve an organization's objectives by using its resources effectively and efficiently in a changing environment. Managers make decisions about the use of the organization's resources and are concerned with planning, organizing, staffing, directing, and controlling the organization's activities so as to reach its objectives.

Describe the major functions of management.

Planning is the process of determining the organization's objectives and deciding how to accomplish them. Organizing is the structuring of resources and activities to accomplish those objectives efficiently and effectively. Staffing obtains people with the necessary skills to carry out the work of the company. Directing is motivating and leading employees to achieve organizational objectives. Controlling is the process of evaluating and correcting activities to keep the organization on course.

Distinguish among three levels of management and the concerns of managers at each level.

Top management is responsible for the whole organization and focuses primarily on strategic planning. Middle management develops plans for specific operating areas and carries out the general guidelines set by top management. First-line, or supervisory, management supervises the workers and day-to-day operations. Managers can also be categorized as to their area of responsibility: finance, production and operations, human resources, marketing, or administration.

Specify the skills managers need in order to be successful.

To be successful, managers need leadership skills (the ability to influence employees to work toward organizational goals), technical expertise (the specialized knowledge and training needed to perform a job), conceptual skills (the ability to think in abstract terms and see how parts fit together to form the whole), analytical skills (the ability to identify relevant issues and recognize their importance, understand the relationships between issues, and perceive the underlying causes of a situation), and human relations (people) skills.

Summarize the systematic approach to decision making used by many business managers.

A systematic approach to decision making follows these steps: recognizing and defining the situation, developing options, analyzing options, selecting the best option, implementing the decision, and monitoring the consequences.

Recommend a new strategy to revive a struggling business.

Using the decision-making process described in this chapter, analyze the struggling company's problems described in "Solve the Dilemma" on page 205 and formulate a strategy to turn the company around and aim it toward future success.

Revisit the World of Business

1. Why is Sheryl Sandberg's job as chief operating officer so important?
2. How do you think that Sandberg's job as a Google executive prepared her to help run Facebook?
3. Why do you think Facebook is trying to attract small businesses?

Learn the Terms

administrative managers 192
agenda 200
analytical skills 195
conceptual skills 195
controlling 186
crisis management or contingency planning 183
directing 185
downsizing 184
financial managers 190
first-line managers 189

human relations skills 196
human resources managers 191
information technology (IT) managers 191
leadership 192
management 178
managers 178
marketing managers 191
middle managers 189
mission 180
networking 201

operational plans 183
organizing 184
planning 179
production and operations managers 191
staffing 184
strategic plans 181
tactical plans 182
technical expertise 195
top managers 187

Check Your Progress

1. Why is management so important, and what is its purpose?
2. Explain why the American Heart Association would need management, even though its goal is not profit related.
3. Why must a company have financial resources before it can use human and physical resources?
4. Name the five functions of management, and briefly describe each function.
5. Identify the three levels of management. What is the focus of managers at each level?
6. In what areas can managers specialize? From what area do top managers typically come?
7. What skills do managers need? Give examples of how managers use these skills to do their jobs.
8. What are three styles of leadership? Describe situations in which each style would be appropriate.
9. Explain the steps in the decision-making process.
10. What is the mathematical formula for perfect management? What do managers spend most of their time doing?

Get Involved

1. Give examples of the activities that each of the following managers might be involved in if he or she worked for the Coca-Cola Company:

Financial manager
Production and operations manager
Personnel manager
Marketing manager
Administrative manager
Information technology manager
Foreman

2. Interview a small sample of managers, attempting to include representatives from all three levels and all areas of management. Discuss their daily activities and relate these activities to the management functions of planning, organizing, staffing, directing, and controlling. What skills do the managers say they need to carry out their tasks?

3. You are a manager of a firm that manufactures conventional ovens. Over the past several years, sales of many of your products have declined; this year, your losses may be quite large. Using the steps of the decision-making process, briefly describe how you arrive at a strategy for correcting the situation.

Build Your Skills

FUNCTIONS OF MANAGEMENT

Background:

Although the text describes each of the five management functions separately, you learned that these five functions are interrelated, and managers sometimes perform two or more of them at the same time. Here you will broaden your perspective of how these functions occur simultaneously in management activities.

Task:

1. Imagine that you are the manager in each scenario described in the following table and you have to decide which management function(s) to use in each.

2. Mark your answers using the following codes:

Codes	Management Functions
P	Planning
O	Organizing
S	Staffing
D	Directing
C	Controlling

No.	Scenario	Answer(s)
1	Your group's work is centered on a project that is due in two months. Although everyone is working on the project, you have observed your employees involved in what you believe is excessive socializing and other time-filling behaviors. You decide to meet with the group to have them help you break down the project into smaller subprojects with mini-deadlines. You believe this will help keep the group members focused on the project and that the quality of the finished project will then reflect the true capabilities of your group.	
2	Your first impression of the new group you'll be managing is not too great. You tell your friend at dinner after your first day on the job: "Looks like I got a baby sitting job instead of a management job."	
3	You call a meeting of your work group and begin it by letting them know that a major procedure used by the work group for the past two years is being significantly revamped, and your department will have to phase in the change during the next six weeks. You proceed by explaining to them the reasoning your boss gave you for this change. You then say, "Let's take the next 5 to 10 minutes to let you voice your reactions to this change." After 10 minutes elapse with the majority of comments being critical of the change, you say: "I appreciate each of you sharing your reactions; and I, too, recognize that *all* change creates problems. The way I see it, however, is that we can spend the remaining 45 minutes of our meeting focusing on why we don't want the change and why we don't think it's necessary; or we can work together to come up with viable solutions to solve the problems that implementing this change will most likely create." After about five more minutes of comments being exchanged, the consensus of the group is that the remainder of the meeting needs to be focused on how to deal with the potential problems the group anticipates having to deal with as the new procedure is implemented.	
4	You are preparing for the annual budget allocation meetings to be held in the plant manager's office next week. You are determined to present a strong case to support your department getting money for some high-tech equipment that will help your employees do their jobs better. You will stand firm against any suggestions of budget cuts in your area.	

| 5 | Early in your career, you learned an important lesson about employee selection. One of the nurses on your floor unexpectedly quit. The other nurses were putting pressure on you to fill the position quickly because they were overworked even before the nurse left, and then things were really bad. After a hasty recruitment effort, you made a decision based on insufficient information. You ended up regretting your quick decision during the three months of problems that followed until you finally had to discharge the new hire. Since then, you have never let anybody pressure you into making a quick hiring decision. | |

Solve the Dilemma   LO 6-6

MAKING INFINITY COMPUTERS COMPETITIVE

Infinity Computers Inc. produces notebook computers, which it sells through direct mail catalog companies under the Infinity name and in some retail computer stores under their private brand names. Infinity's products are not significantly different from competitors', nor do they have extra product-enhancing features, although they are very price competitive. The strength of the company has been its CEO and president, George Anderson, and a highly motivated, loyal workforce. The firm's weakness is having too many employees and too great a reliance on one product. The firm switched to computers with the Intel Core i5 processors after it saw a decline in its netbook computer sales.

Recognizing that the strategies that initially made the firm successful are no longer working effectively, Anderson wants to reorganize the company to make it more responsive and competitive and to cut costs. The threat of new technological developments and current competitive conditions could eliminate Infinity.

Discussion Questions

1. Evaluate Infinity's current situation and analyze its strengths and weaknesses.

2. Evaluate the opportunities for Infinity, including using its current strategy, and propose alternative strategies.

3. Suggest a plan for Infinity to compete successfully over the next 10 years.

Build Your Business Plan

THE NATURE OF MANAGEMENT

The first thing you need to be thinking about is "What is the mission of your business? What is the shared vision your team members have for this business? How do you know if there is demand for this particular business? Remember, you need to think about the customer's *ability and willingness* to try this particular product.

Think about the various processes or stages of your business in the creation and selling of your product, or service. What functions need to be performed for these processes to be completed? These functions might include buying, receiving, selling, customer service, and/or merchandising.

Operationally, if you are opening up a retail establishment, how do you plan to provide your customers with superior customer service? What hours will your customers expect you to be open? At this point in time, how many employees are you thinking you will need to run your business? Do you (or one of your partners) need to be there all the time to supervise?

The organizational structure at TOMS Shoes consists of two parts. The for-profit component of the company manages overall operations. Its nonprofit component, Friends of TOMS, is responsible for volunteer activities and shoe donations.

are mostly cutthroat in collecting intelligence about competition, creating a corporate culture in which unethical acts might be tolerated if it means beating the competition.[7]

Organizational culture helps ensure that all members of a company share values and suggests rules for how to behave and deal with problems within the organization. Table 7.1 confirms that executives in this study believe that corporate culture has a significant impact on organizational performance and the ability to retain good employees. The key to success in any organization is satisfying stakeholders, especially customers. Establishing a positive organizational culture sets the tone for all other decisions, including building an efficient organizational structure.

Developing Organizational Structure

LO 7-1

structure
the arrangement or relationship of positions within an organization

Structure is the arrangement or relationship of positions within an organization. Rarely is an organization, or any group of individuals working together, able to achieve common objectives without some form of structure, whether that structure is explicitly defined or only implied. A professional baseball team such as the Colorado Rockies is a business organization with an explicit formal structure that guides the team's activities so that it can increase game attendance, win games, and sell souvenirs such as T-shirts. But even an informal group playing softball for fun has an organization that specifies who will pitch, catch, bat, coach, and so on. Governments and nonprofit organizations also have formal organizational structures to facilitate the achievement of their objectives. Getting people to work together efficiently and coordinating the skills of diverse individuals require careful planning. Developing appropriate organizational structures is therefore a major challenge for managers in both large and small organizations.

TABLE 7.1

Impact of Corporate Culture on Business Performance

Culture has a strong or very strong impact on an organization's performance	82%
My corporate culture has a strong impact on the ability to retain top talent	68
My organization's culture drives sales and increases revenue	61
My organization's culture creates a sense of belonging	57
My organization's culture lowers turnover	53

Source: "Ten Most Admired Corporate Cultures," February 10, 2010, http://cthrc.ca/en/member_area/member_news/ten_most_admired_corporate_cultures.aspx (accessed March 1, 2010).

An organization's structure develops when managers assign work tasks and activities to specific individuals or work groups and coordinate the diverse activities required to reach the firm's objectives. When Macy's, for example, has a sale, the store manager must work with the advertising department to make the public aware of the sale, with department managers to ensure that extra salespeople are scheduled to handle the increased customer traffic, and with merchandise buyers to ensure that enough sale merchandise is available to meet expected consumer demand. All the people occupying these positions must work together to achieve the store's objectives.

The best way to begin to understand how organizational structure develops is to consider the evolution of a new business such as a clothing store. At first, the business is a sole proprietorship in which the owner does everything—buys, prices, and displays the merchandise; does the accounting and tax records; and assists customers. As the business grows, the owner hires a salesperson and perhaps a merchandise buyer to help run the store. As the business continues to grow, the owner hires more salespeople. The growth and success of the business now require the owner to be away from the store frequently, meeting with suppliers, engaging in public relations, and attending trade shows. Thus, the owner must designate someone to manage the salespeople and maintain the accounting, payroll, and tax functions. If the owner decides to expand by opening more stores, still more managers will be needed. Figure 7.1 shows these stages of growth with three **organizational charts** (visual displays of organizational structure, chain of command, and other relationships).

Growth requires organizing—the structuring of human, physical, and financial resources to achieve objectives in an effective and efficient manner. Growth necessitates hiring people who have specialized skills. With more people and greater specialization, the organization needs to develop a formal structure to function efficiently. Imagine the organizational changes that Nathan's Famous hot dogs underwent from 1916 when they operated a single Coney Island hot dog shop to a company that now operates an international chain of fast-food restaurants as well as selling food products through supermarkets. The company sells more than 425 million hot dogs a year and generates nearly $51 million in revenue.[8] As we shall

organizational chart
a visual display of the organizational structure, lines of authority (chain of command), staff relationships, permanent committee arrangements, and lines of communication

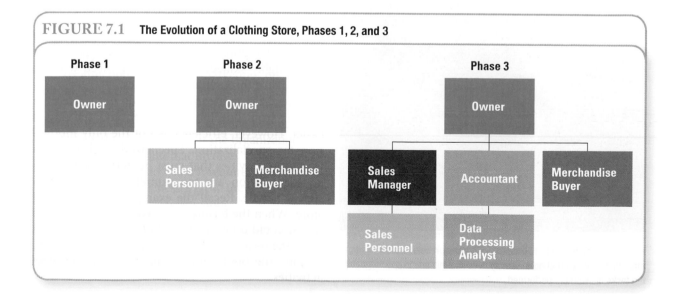

FIGURE 7.1   **The Evolution of a Clothing Store, Phases 1, 2, and 3**

Entrepreneurship in Action

Family Team Makes Johnny Cupcakes a Business Success

John Earle
Business: Johnny Cupcakes
Founded: 2001, in Hull, Massachusetts
Success: Johnny Cupcakes has achieved a cult-like following with stores in Massachusetts, California, and the United Kingdom.

It might sound like a bakery, but Johnny Cupcakes is actually the name of a successful apparel retailer. Founded in 2001 by John Earle, Johnny Cupcakes sells limited edition clothing and accessories—all featuring cupcake designs. John began selling his first T-shirts out of the trunk of his car and the suitcase he used while touring with his band. As business accelerated, John's mother and sister began helping him fill orders.

His parent's house became his warehouse. Along the road to success, John turned down distribution offers from Nordstrom, Urban Outfitters, and more. Instead, he opened up his own stores in Hull, Massachusetts (his hometown), Los Angeles, Boston, and London. Customers often camp outside to score new designs and attend special events. Through it all, John has been supported by his family and friends, who are also his co-workers. His mother serves as his chief financial officer, his sister runs human resources and customer service, his sister's best friend is training as bookkeeper, and his father assists with various aspects of the business. Although the creative inspiration rests with John, Johnny Cupcakes is truly a family affair.[12]

including GE, IBM, Google, and Nike have decentralized decision-making authority. McDonald's, realizing most of its growth outside the United States, is becoming increasingly decentralized and "glo-cal," varying products in specific markets to better meet consumer demands. This change in organizational structure for McDonald's is fostering greater innovation and local market success. McDonald's, which was long known for the homogeneity of its products, has embraced local cuisine on a limited scale. For instance, because cows are sacred in India, McDonald's has introduced the McVeggie and the Veg McMuffin. It also sells the Spicy Paneer wrap, made with chicken, paneer cheese, and spicy batter, to appeal to Indians' preferences for spicy food.[13] Diversity and decentralization seem to be McDonald's keys to being better, not just bigger. Nonprofit organizations benefit from decentralization as well.

Span of Management

How many subordinates should a manager manage? There is no simple answer. Experts generally agree, however, that top managers should not directly supervise more than four to eight people, while lower-level managers who supervise routine tasks are capable of managing a much larger number of subordinates. For example, the manager of the finance department may supervise 25 employees, whereas the vice president of finance may supervise only five managers. **Span of management** refers to the number of subordinates who report to a particular manager. A *wide span of management* exists when a manager directly supervises a very large number of employees. A *narrow span of management* exists when a manager directly supervises only a few subordinates (Figure 7.4). At Whole Foods, the best employees are recruited and placed in small teams. Employees are empowered to discount, give away, and sample products, as well as to assist in creating a respectful workplace where goals are achieved, individual employees succeed, and customers are core in business decisions. Whole Foods teams get to vote on new employee hires as well. This approach allows Whole Foods to offer unique and "local market" experiences in each of its stores. This level of customization is in contrast to more centralized national supermarket chains such as Kroger, Safeway, and Publix.[14]

span of management
the number of subordinates who report to a particular manager

Should the span of management be wide or narrow? To answer this question, several factors need to be considered. A narrow span of management is appropriate when superiors and subordinates are not in close proximity, the manager has many responsibilities in addition to the supervision, the interaction between superiors and subordinates is frequent, and problems are common. However, when superiors and subordinates are located close to one another, the manager has few responsibilities other than supervision, the level of interaction between superiors and subordinates is low, few problems arise, subordinates are highly competent, and a set of specific operating procedures governs the activities of managers and their subordinates, a wide span of management will be more appropriate. Narrow spans of management are typical in centralized organizations, while wide spans of management are more common in decentralized firms.

Organizational Layers

Complementing the concept of span of management is **organizational layers,** the levels of management in an organization. A company with many layers of managers is considered tall; in a tall organization, the span of management is narrow (see Figure 7.4). Because each manager supervises only a few subordinates, many layers of management are necessary to carry out the operations of the business. McDonald's, for example, has a tall organization with many layers, including store managers, district managers, regional managers, and functional managers (finance, marketing, and so on), as well as a chief executive officer and many vice presidents. Because there are more managers in tall organizations than in flat organizations, administrative costs are usually higher. Communication is slower because information must pass through many layers.

organizational layers
the levels of management
in an organization

Organizations with few layers are flat and have wide spans of management. When managers supervise a large number of employees, fewer management layers are needed to conduct the organization's activities. Managers in flat organizations typically perform more administrative duties than managers in tall organizations because there are fewer of them. They also spend more time supervising and working with subordinates.

Many of the companies that have decentralized also flattened their structures and widened their spans of management, often by eliminating layers of middle management. As mentioned earlier in this chapter, Green Mountain Coffee has both a decentralized and flat organizational structure. Other corporations, including Avon, AT&T, and Ford Motor Company, embraced a more decentralized structure to reduce costs, speed up decision making, and boost overall productivity.

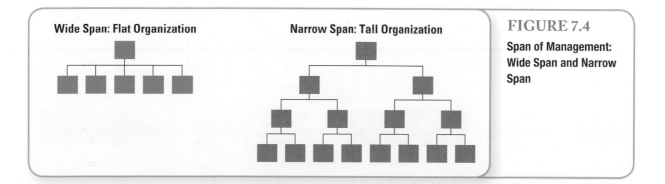

Wide Span: Flat Organization   **Narrow Span: Tall Organization**

FIGURE 7.4

Span of Management: Wide Span and Narrow Span

LO 7-4

Forms of Organizational Structure

Along with assigning tasks and the responsibility for carrying them out, managers must consider how to structure their authority relationships—that is, what structure the organization itself will have and how it will appear on the organizational chart. Common forms of organization include line structure, line-and-staff structure, multidivisional structure, and matrix structure.

Line Structure

line structure
the simplest organizational structure, in which direct lines of authority extend from the top manager to the lowest level of the organization

The simplest organizational structure, **line structure,** has direct lines of authority that extend from the top manager to employees at the lowest level of the organization. For example, a convenience store employee at 7-Eleven may report to an assistant manager, who reports to the store manager, who reports to a regional manager, or, in an independent store, directly to the owner (Figure 7.5). This structure has a clear chain of command, which enables managers to make decisions quickly. A mid-level manager facing a decision must consult only one person, his or her immediate supervisor. However, this structure requires that managers possess a wide range of knowledge and skills. They are responsible for a variety of activities and must be knowledgeable about them all. Line structures are most common in small businesses.

Line-and-Staff Structure

line-and-staff structure
a structure having a traditional line relationship between superiors and subordinates and also specialized managers—called staff managers—who are available to assist line managers

The **line-and-staff structure** has a traditional line relationship between superiors and subordinates, and specialized managers—called staff managers—are available to assist line managers (Figure 7.6). Line managers can focus on their area of expertise in the operation of the business, while staff managers provide advice and support to line departments on specialized matters such as finance, engineering, human resources, and the law. In the city of Corpus Christi (refer back for Figure 7.3), for example, assistant city managers are line managers who oversee groups of related departments. However, the city attorney, police chief, and fire chief are effectively staff managers who report directly to the city manager (the city equivalent of a business chief executive officer). Staff managers do not have direct authority over line managers or over the line manager's subordinates, but they do have direct authority over subordinates in their own departments. However, line-and-staff organizations may experience problems with overstaffing and ambiguous lines of communication. Additionally, employees may become frustrated because they lack the authority to carry out certain decisions.

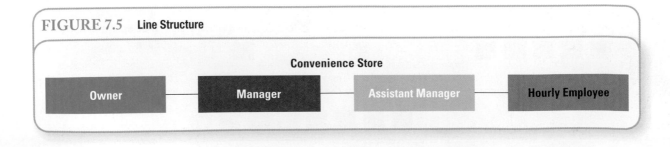

FIGURE 7.5   **Line Structure**

Convenience Store

Owner — Manager — Assistant Manager — Hourly Employee

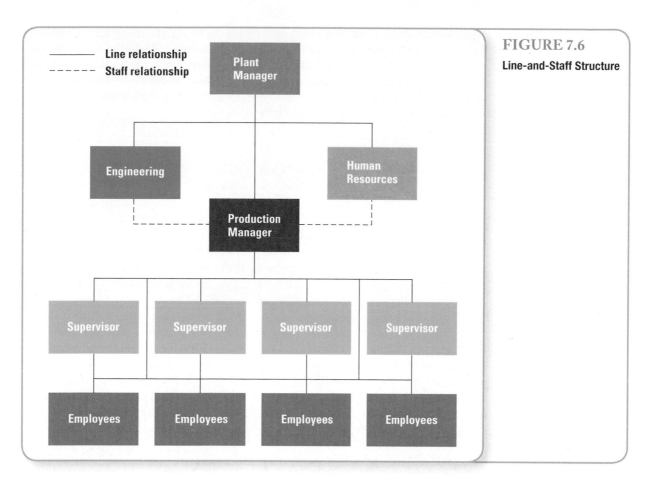

Line relationship
- - - - - **Staff relationship**

Plant Manager

Engineering

Human Resources

Production Manager

Supervisor   Supervisor   Supervisor   Supervisor

Employees   Employees   Employees   Employees

FIGURE 7.6

Line-and-Staff Structure

Multidivisional Structure

As companies grow and diversify, traditional line structures become difficult to coordinate, making communication difficult and decision making slow. When the weaknesses of the structure—the "turf wars," miscommunication, and working at cross-purposes—exceed the benefits, growing firms tend to restructure, often into the divisionalized form. A **multidivisional structure** organizes departments into larger groups called divisions. Just as departments might be formed on the basis of geography, customer, product, or a combination of these, so too divisions can be formed based on any of these methods of organizing. Within each of these divisions, departments may be organized by product, geographic region, function, or some combination of all three. Indra Nooyi, CEO of PepsiCo, rearranged the company's organizational structure. Prior to her tenure, PepsiCo was organized geographically. She created new units—PepsiCo Americas Foods (PAF), PepsiCo Americas Beverages (PAB), PepsiCo Europe, and PepsiCo Asia, Middle East & Africa—that span international boundaries and make it easier for employees in different geographic regions to share business practices.[15]

Multidivisional structures permit delegation of decision-making authority, allowing divisional and department managers to specialize. They allow those closest to the action to make the decisions that will affect them. Delegation of authority

Need help understanding the Differences between Line and Staff Employees?

http://bit.ly/FerrellQR7-1

multidivisional structure
a structure that organizes departments into larger groups called divisions

and divisionalized work also mean that better decisions are made faster, and they tend to be more innovative. Most importantly, by focusing each division on a common region, product, or customer, each is more likely to provide products that meet the needs of its particular customers. However, the divisional structure inevitably creates work duplication, which makes it more difficult to realize the economies of scale that result from grouping functions together.

Matrix Structure

matrix structure
a structure that sets up teams from different departments, thereby creating two or more intersecting lines of authority; also called a project-management structure

Another structure that attempts to address issues that arise with growth, diversification, productivity, and competitiveness, is the matrix. A **matrix structure,** also called a project management structure, sets up teams from different departments, thereby creating two or more intersecting lines of authority (Figure 7.7). One of the first organizations to design and implement a matrix structure was the National Aeronautics and Space Administration (NASA) for the space program because it needed to coordinate different projects at the same time. The matrix structure superimposes project-based departments on the more traditional, function-based departments. Project teams bring together specialists from a variety of areas to work together on a single project, such as developing a new fighter jet. In this arrangement, employees are responsible to two managers—functional managers and project managers. Matrix structures are usually temporary: Team members typically go back to their functional or line department after a project is finished. However, more firms are becoming permanent matrix structures, creating and dissolving project teams as needed to meet customer needs. The aerospace industry was one of the first to apply the matrix structure, but today it is used by universities and schools, accounting firms, banks, and organizations in other industries.

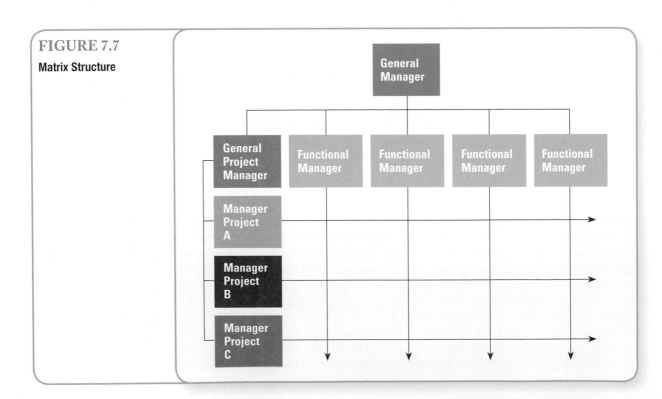

FIGURE 7.7
Matrix Structure

Matrix structures provide flexibility, enhanced cooperation, and creativity, and they enable the company to respond quickly to changes in the environment by giving special attention to specific projects or problems. However, they are generally expensive and quite complex, and employees may be confused as to whose authority has priority—the project manager's or the immediate supervisor's.

The Role of Groups and Teams in Organizations

LO 7-5

Regardless of how they are organized, most of the essential work of business occurs in individual work groups and teams, so we'll take a closer look at them now. Although some experts do not make a distinction between groups and teams, in recent years there has been a gradual shift toward an emphasis on teams and managing them to enhance individual and organizational success. Some experts now believe that highest productivity results only when groups become teams.[16]

Traditionally, a **group** has been defined as two or more individuals who communicate with one another, share a common identity, and have a common goal. A **team** is a small group whose members have complementary skills; have a common purpose, goals, and approach; and hold themselves mutually accountable.[17] All teams are groups, but not all groups are teams. Table 7.2 points out some important differences between them. Work groups emphasize individual work products, individual accountability, and even individual leadership. Salespeople working independently for the same company could be a work group. In contrast, work teams share leadership roles, have both individual and mutual accountability, and create collective work products. In other words, a work group's performance depends on what its members do as individuals, while a team's performance is based on creating a knowledge center and a competency to work together to accomplish a goal.

group
two or more individuals who communicate with one another, share a common identity, and have a common goal

team
a small group whose members have complementary skills; have a common purpose, goals, and approach; and hold themselves mutually accountable

TABLE 7.2

Differences between Groups and Teams

Working Group	Team
Has strong, clearly focused leader	Has shared leadership roles
Has individual accountability	Has individual and group accountability
Has the same purpose as the broader organizational mission	Has a specific purpose that the team itself delivers
Creates individual work products	Creates collective work products
Runs efficient meetings	Encourages open-ended discussion and active problem-solving meetings
Measures its effectiveness indirectly by its effects on others (e.g., financial performance of the business)	Measures performance directly by assessing collective work products
Discusses, decides, and delegates	Discusses, decides, and does real work together

Source: Robert Gatewood, Robert Taylor, and O. C. Ferrell, *Management: Comprehension Analysis and Application*, 1995, p. 427. Copyright © 1995 Richard D. Irwin, a Times Mirror Higher Education Group, Inc., company. Reproduced with permission of the McGraw-Hill Companies.

On the other hand, it is also important for team members to retain their individuality and avoid becoming just "another face in the crowd." According to former corporate lawyer and negotiations consultant Susan Cain, the purpose of teams should be toward collaboration versus collectivism. Although the team is working toward a common goal, it is important that all team members actively contribute their ideas and work together to achieve this common goal.[18]

The type of groups an organization establishes depends on the tasks it needs to accomplish and the situation it faces. Some specific kinds of groups and teams include committees, task forces, project teams, product-development teams, quality-assurance teams, and self-directed work teams. All of these can be *virtual teams*—employees in different locations who rely on e-mail, audio conferencing, fax, Internet, videoconferencing, or other technological tools to accomplish their goals. With more than 84 percent of American employees working in a different location than their supervisors, virtual teams are becoming a part of everyday business.[19] Virtual teams have also opened up opportunities for different companies. Not only does Cisco Systems Inc. work in virtual teams, but the company makes networking technology to support video conferencing. At Cisco Europe, 10,000 employees across 21 countries developed a set of team operating principles to aid team collaboration.[20]

Committees

committee
a permanent, formal group that performs a specific task

A **committee** is usually a permanent, formal group that does some specific task. For example, many firms have a compensation or finance committee to examine the effectiveness of these areas of operation as well as the need for possible changes. Ethics committees are formed to develop and revise codes of ethics, suggest methods for implementing ethical standards, and review specific issues and concerns.

Task Forces

task force
a temporary group of employees responsible for bringing about a particular change

A **task force** is a temporary group of employees responsible for bringing about a particular change. They typically come from across all departments and levels of an organization. Task force membership is usually based on expertise rather than organizational position. Occasionally, a task force may be formed from individuals outside a company. When Toyota experienced a major product recall, the president, Akio Toyoda, formed and led a Global Quality Task Force to conduct quality improvements throughout the worldwide operations of the company. With massive recalls looming, the company focused on (1) improving the quality inspection process, (2) enhancing customer research, (3) establishing an automotive center of quality excellence, (4) utilizing external industry experts, (5) increasing the frequency of communication with regional authorities, and (6) improving regional autonomy.[21]

Teams

Teams are becoming far more common in the U.S. workplace as businesses strive to enhance productivity and global competitiveness. In general, teams have the benefit of being able to pool members' knowledge and skills and make greater use of them than can individuals working alone. Team building is becoming increasingly popular in organizations, with around half of executives indicating their companies had team-building training. Teams require harmony, cooperation, synchronized effort, and flexibility to maximize their contribution.[22] Teams can also create more solutions to problems than can individuals. Furthermore, team participation enhances employee acceptance of, understanding of, and commitment to team goals. Teams motivate workers by providing internal rewards in the form of an enhanced sense of accomplishment for employees as they achieve more, and external rewards in the form of praise and certain perks. Consequently, they can help get workers more involved. They can help companies be more innovative, and they can boost productivity and cut costs.

According to psychologist Ivan Steiner, team productivity peaks at about five team members. People become less motivated and group coordination becomes more difficult after this size. Jeff Bezos, Amazon.com CEO, says that he has a "two-pizza rule": If a team cannot be fed by two pizzas, it is too large. Keep teams small enough where everyone gets a piece of the action.[23]

Project Teams.   **Project teams** are similar to task forces, but normally they run their operation and have total control of a specific work project. Like task forces, their membership is likely to cut across the firm's hierarchy and be composed of people from different functional areas. They are almost always temporary, although a large project, such as designing and building a new airplane at Boeing Corporation, may last for years.

Product-development teams are a special type of project team formed to devise, design, and implement a new product. Sometimes product-development teams exist within a functional area—research and development—but now they more frequently include people from numerous functional areas and may even include customers to help ensure that the end product meets the customers' needs. Washington State University's School of Food Science has several student product development teams. Students develop innovative new food products and present them annually at the Institute of Food Technologists Student Association competition. WSU student projects include Tu Mazi, a mango-flavored probiotic milk powder created for consumers in developing nations, and Erupt-a-Cake, a ready-to-bake dessert featuring gummy dinosaurs.[24]

Quality-Assurance Teams.   **Quality-assurance teams,** sometimes called **quality circles,** are fairly small groups of workers brought together from throughout the organization to solve specific quality, productivity, or service problems. Although the *quality circle* term is not as popular as it once was, the concern about quality is stronger than ever. Companies such as IBM and Xerox as well as companies in the automobile industry have used quality circles to shift the organization to a more participative culture. The use of teams to address quality issues will no doubt continue to increase throughout the business world.

Self-directed Work Teams.   A **self-directed work team (SDWT)** is a group of employees responsible for an entire work process or segment that delivers a product to an internal or external customer.[25] SDWTs permit the flexibility to change rapidly to meet the competition or respond to customer needs. The defining characteristic of an SDWT is the extent to which it is empowered or given authority to make and implement work decisions. Thus, SDWTs are designed to give employees a feeling of "ownership" of a whole job. Employees at 3M as well as an increasing number of companies encourage employees to be active to perform a function or operational task. With shared team responsibility for work outcomes, team members often have broader job assignments and cross-train to master other jobs, thus permitting greater team flexibility.

project teams
groups similar to task forces that normally run their operation and have total control of a specific work project

product-development teams
a specific type of project team formed to devise, design, and implement a new product

quality-assurance teams (or quality circles)
small groups of workers brought together from throughout the organization to solve specific quality, productivity, or service problems

self-directed work team (SDWT)
a group of employees responsible for an entire work process or segment that delivers a product to an internal or external customer

Responding to Business Challenges
Creating a Corporate Culture . . . Virtually

It seems unlikely that businesses would encourage employees to engage in social networking, but clients of Yammer do just that. Yammer supplies internal social networking for organizations. These internal networks provide many benefits. For example, Yammer enables global employees to communicate easily in real time, cutting down significantly on e-mail. Yammer CEO David Sacks says employees using his service more easily develop relationships and a commitment to their companies—a claim bolstered by research. Although the networks are designed for conducting business, employees often share jokes, light banter, and personal information. Many companies also use Yammer and the equivalent to track ideas from conception through production and beyond in a streamlined fashion.

Despite advantages, internal social networking has pitfalls. Disadvantages primarily affect employees, who may be too free with their comments. Anything posted on an internal social network is potentially admissible during performance reviews, promotion decisions, and legal proceedings.

More than 100,000 companies currently use Yammer, and most love it. They do agree, however, that it's important to implement user guidelines to avoid trouble. For instance, the technology company Xerox states that employees should use discretion, professionalism, and common sense in the tone an aunt might use with a favorite nephew. With gentle guidance, Yammer and others can enhance company culture and the workplace experience. As social networking continues to grow, it's likely the internal version will thrive as well.[26]

Discussion Questions

1. How does Yammer contribute to a firm's corporate culture?
2. How can Yammer be used as a way to improve productivity?
3. What are some potential pitfalls of Yammer, and how can these pitfalls be avoided?

LO 7-6

Communicating in Organizations

Communication within an organization can flow in a variety of directions and from a number of sources, each using both oral and written forms of communication. The success of communication systems within the organization has a tremendous effect on the overall success of the firm. Communication mistakes can lower productivity and morale.

DID YOU KNOW? A survey of managers and executives found that they feel 28 percent of meetings are a waste of time and that information could be communicated more effectively using other methods.[27]

Alternatives to face-to-face communications—such as meetings—are growing, thanks to technology such as voice-mail, e-mail, social media, and online newsletters. Many companies use internal networks called intranets to share information with employees. Intranets increase communication across different departments and levels of management and help with the flow of everyday business activities. Another innovative approach is cloud computing. Rather than using physical products, companies using cloud computing technology can access computing resources and information over a network. Cloud computing allows companies to have more control over computing resources and can be less expensive than hardware or software. Salesforce.com uses cloud computing in its customer relationship management solutions.[28] Companies can even integrate aspects of social media into their intranets, allowing employees to post comments and pictures, participate in polls, and create group calendars. However, increased access to the Internet at work has also created many problems, including employee abuse of company mail and Internet access.[29]

Formal Communication

Formal channels of communication are intentionally defined and designed by the organization. They represent the flow of communication within the formal organizational structure, as shown on organizational charts. Traditionally, formal communication patterns were classified as vertical and horizontal, but with the increased use of teams and matrix structures, formal communication may occur in a number of patterns (Figure 7.8).

Upward communication flows from lower to higher levels of the organization and includes information such as progress reports, suggestions for improvement, inquiries, and grievances. *Downward communication* refers to the traditional flow of information from upper organizational levels to lower levels. This type of communication typically involves directions, the assignment of tasks and responsibilities, performance feedback, and certain details about the organization's strategies and goals. Speeches, policy and procedures manuals, employee handbooks, company leaflets, telecommunications, and job descriptions are examples of downward communication.

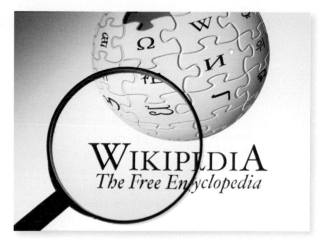

Online sites such as wikis are allowing employee teams to share information and work collaboratively on documents. The most well-known wiki is the online encyclopedia Wikipedia.

Horizontal communication involves the exchange of information among colleagues and peers on the same organizational level, such as across or within departments. Horizontal information informs, supports, and coordinates activities both within the department and with other departments. At times, the business will formally require horizontal communication among particular organizational members, as is the case with task forces or project teams.

With more and more companies downsizing and increasing the use of self-managed work teams, many workers are being required to communicate with others in different departments and on different levels to solve problems and coordinate work. When these individuals from different units and organizational levels communicate, it is *diagonal communication*. One benefit of companies doing more with fewer employees is that productivity (output per work hour) increased by 9.5 percent in one year. Increased productivity allows companies to increase wages and leads to increased standards of living.[30]

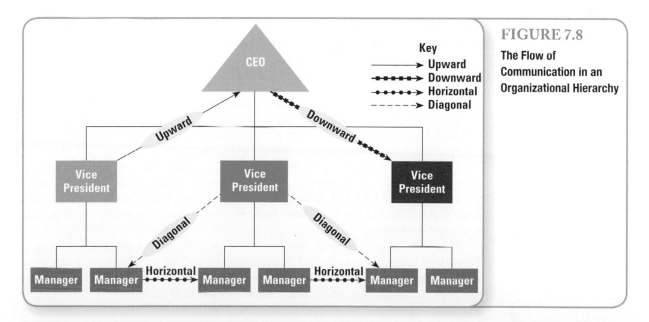

FIGURE 7.8

The Flow of Communication in an Organizational Hierarchy

Informal Communication Channels

Along with the formal channels of communication shown on an organizational chart, all firms communicate informally as well. Communication between friends, for instance, cuts across department, division, and even management–subordinate boundaries. Such friendships and other nonwork social relationships comprise the *informal organization* of a firm, and their impact can be great.

The most significant informal communication occurs through the **grapevine,** an informal channel of communication, separate from management's formal, official communication channels. Grapevines exist in all organizations. Information passed along the grapevine may relate to the job or organization, or it may be gossip and rumors unrelated to either. The accuracy of grapevine information has been of great concern to managers.

Additionally, managers can turn the grapevine to their advantage. Using it as a "sounding device" for possible new policies is one example. Managers can obtain valuable information from the grapevine that could improve decision making. Some organizations use the grapevine to their advantage by floating ideas, soliciting feedback, and reacting accordingly. People love to gossip, and managers need to be aware that grapevines exist in every organization. Managers who understand how the grapevine works also can use it to their advantage by feeding it facts to squelch rumors and incorrect information.

grapevine
an informal channel of communication, separate from management's formal, official communication channels

Monitoring Communications

Technological advances and the increased use of electronic communication in the workplace have made monitoring its use necessary for most companies. Failing to monitor employees' use of e-mail, social media, and the Internet can be costly. Many companies require that employees sign and follow a policy on appropriate Internet use. These agreements often require that employees will use corporate computers only for work-related activities. Additionally, several companies use software programs to monitor employee computer usage.[31] Instituting practices that show respect for employee privacy but do not abdicate employer responsibility are increasingly necessary in today's workplace. Several websites provide model policies and detailed guidelines for conducting electronic monitoring, including the Model Electronic Privacy Act on the American Civil Liberties Union site.

Improving Communication Effectiveness

Without effective communication, the activities and overall productivity of projects, groups, teams, and individuals will be diminished. Communication is an important area for a firm to address at all levels of management. Apple supplier Foxconn is one example of how essential communication is to a firm. Despite criticisms of unfair labor conditions, the Fair Labor Association determined that Foxconn had formal procedures in place at its factories to prevent many major accidents. However, it concluded that the firm had a communication problem. These procedures were not being communicated to the factory workers, contributing to unsafe practices and two tragic explosions.[32]

One of the major issues of effective communication is in obtaining feedback. If feedback is not provided, then communication will be ineffective and can drag down overall performance. Managers should always encourage feedback, including concerns and challenges about issues. Listening is a skill that involves hearing, and most employees listen much more than they actively communicate to others. Therefore, managers should encourage employees to provide feedback—even if it is negative. This will allow the organization to identify strengths and weaknesses and make adjustments when needed. At the same time, strong feedback mechanisms help to empower employees as they feel that their voices are being heard.

Interruptions can be a serious threat to effective communication. Various activities can interrupt the message. For example, interjecting a remark can create discontinuance in the communication process or disrupt the uniformity of the message. Even small interruptions can be a problem if the messenger cannot adequately understand or interpret the communicator's message. One suggestion is to give the communicator space or time to make another statement rather than quickly responding or making your own comment.

Strong and effective communication channels are a requirement for companies to distribute information to different levels of the company. Businesses have several channels for communication, including face-to-face, e-mail, phone, and written communication (for example, memos). Each channel has advantages and disadvantages, and some are more appropriate to use than others. For instance, a small task requiring little instruction might be communicated through a short memo or e-mail. An in-depth task would most likely require a phone conversation or face-to-face contact. E-mail has become especially helpful for businesses, and both employees and managers are increasingly using e-mail rather than memos or phone conversations. However, it is important that employees use e-mail correctly. It is quite easy to send the wrong e-mail to the wrong person, and messages sent over e-mail can be misinterpreted. Inappropriate e-mails can be forwarded without a second thought, and employees have gotten in trouble for sending personal e-mails in the workplace. It is therefore important for companies to communicate their e-mail policies throughout the organization. Communicators using e-mail, whether managers or employees, must exert caution before pushing that "Send" button.

Communication is necessary in helping every organizational member understand what is expected of him or her. Many business problems can be avoided if clear communication exists within the company. Even the best business strategies are of little use if those who will oversee them cannot understand what is intended. Communication might not seem to be as big of a concern to management as finances, human resources, and marketing, but in reality it can make the difference between successful implementation of business activities or failure.

So You Want a Job in Managing Organizational Culture, Teamwork, and Communication

Jobs dealing with organizational culture and structure are usually at the top of the organization. If you want to be a CEO or high-level manager, you will help shape these areas of business. On the other hand, if you are an entrepreneur or small-business person, you will need to make decisions about assigning tasks, departmentalization, and assigning responsibility. Even managers in small organizations have to make decisions about decentralization, span of management, and forms of organizational structure. While these decisions may be part of your job, there are usually no job titles dealing with these specific areas. Specific jobs that attempt to improve organizational culture could include ethics and compliance positions as well as those who are in charge of communicating memos, manuals, and policies that help establish the culture. These positions will be in communications, human resources, and positions that assist top organizational managers.

Teams are becoming more common in the workplace, and it is possible to become a member of a product development group or quality assurance team. There are also human resource positions that encourage teamwork through training activities. The area of corporate communications provides lots of opportunities for specific jobs that facilitate communication systems. Thanks to technology, there are job positions to help disseminate information through online newsletters, intranets, or internal computer networks to share information to increase collaboration. In addition to the many advances using electronic communications, there are technology concerns that create new job opportunities. Monitoring workplace communications such as the use of e-mail and the Internet have created new industries. There have to be internal controls in the organization to make sure that the organization does not engage in any copyright infringement. If this is an area of interest, there are specific jobs that provide an opportunity to use your technological skills to assist in maintaining appropriate standards in communicating and using technology.

If you go to work for a large company with many divisions, you can expect a number of positions dealing with the tasks discussed here. If you go to work for a small company, you will probably engage in most of these tasks as a part of your position. Organizational flexibility requires individual flexibility, and those employees willing to take on new domains and challenges will be the employees who survive and prosper in the future.

Review Your Understanding

Define organizational structure, and relate how organizational structures develop.

Structure is the arrangement or relationship of positions within an organization; it develops when managers assign work activities to work groups and specific individuals and coordinate the diverse activities required to attain organizational objectives. Organizational structure evolves to accommodate growth, which requires people with specialized skills.

Describe how specialization and departmentalization help an organization achieve its goals.

Structuring an organization requires that management assign work tasks to specific individuals and groups. Under specialization, managers break labor into small, specialized tasks and assign employees to do a single task, fostering efficiency. Departmentalization is the grouping of jobs into working units (departments, units, groups, or divisions). Businesses may departmentalize by function, product, geographic region, or customer, or they may combine two or more of these.

Distinguish between groups and teams, and identify the types of groups that exist in organizations.

A group is two or more persons who communicate, share a common identity, and have a common goal. A team is a small group whose members have complementary skills, a common purpose, goals, and approach and who hold themselves mutually accountable. The major distinction is that individual performance is most important in groups, while collective work group performance counts most in teams. Special kinds of groups include task forces, committees, project teams, product-development teams, quality-assurance teams, and self-directed work teams.

Determine how organizations assign responsibility for tasks and delegate authority.

Delegation of authority means assigning tasks to employees and giving them the power to make commitments, use resources, and take whatever actions are necessary to accomplish the tasks. It lays responsibility on employees to carry out assigned tasks satisfactorily and holds them accountable to a superior for the proper execution of their assigned work. The extent to which authority is delegated throughout an organization determines its degree of centralization. Span of management refers to the number of subordinates who report to a particular manager. A wide span of management occurs in flat organizations; a narrow one exists in tall organizations.

Compare and contrast some common forms of organizational structure.

Line structures have direct lines of authority that extend from the top manager to employees at the lowest level of the organization. The line-and-staff structure has a traditional line relationship between superiors and subordinates, and specialized staff managers are available to assist line managers. A multidivisional structure gathers departments into larger groups called divisions. A matrix, or project-management, structure sets up teams from different departments, thereby creating two or more intersecting lines of authority.

Describe how communication occurs in organizations.

Communication occurs both formally and informally in organizations. Formal communication may be downward, upward,

horizontal, and even diagonal. Informal communication takes place through friendships and the grapevine.

Analyze a business's use of teams.

"Solve the Dilemma" on page 235 introduces a firm attempting to restructure to a team environment. Based on the material presented in this chapter, you should be able to evaluate the firm's efforts and make recommendations for resolving the problems that have developed.

Revisit the World of Business

1. Describe how Green Mountain Coffee Roasters (GMCR) uses a decentralized and flat organizational structure.

2. How does empowerment work at GMCR?

3. What are some of the challenges GMCR must overcome as it continues to expand?

Learn the Terms

accountability 218
centralized organization 219
committee 226
customer departmentalization 218
decentralized organization 219
delegation of authority 218
departmentalization 215
functional departmentalization 215
geographical departmentalization 218
grapevine 230

group 225
line-and-staff structure 222
line structure 222
matrix structure 224
multidivisional structure 223
organizational chart 213
organizational culture 210
organizational layers 221
product departmentalization 215
product-development teams 227

project teams 227
quality-assurance teams (or quality circles) 227
responsibility 218
self-directed work team (SDWT) 227
span of management 220
specialization 214
structure 212
task force 226
team 225

Check Your Progress

1. Identify four types of departmentalization and give an example of each type.

2. Explain the difference between groups and teams.

3. What are self-managed work teams and what tasks might they perform that traditionally are performed by managers?

4. Explain how delegating authority, responsibility, and accountability are related.

5. Distinguish between centralization and decentralization. Under what circumstances is each appropriate?

6. Define span of management. Why do some organizations have narrow spans and others wide spans?

7. Discuss the different forms of organizational structure. What are the primary advantages and disadvantages of each form?

8. Discuss the role of the grapevine within organizations. How can managers use it to further the goals of the firm?

9. How have technological advances made electronic oversight a necessity in many companies?

10. Discuss how an organization's culture might influence its ability to achieve its objectives. Do you think that managers can "manage" the organization's culture?

Introduction

All organizations create products—goods, services, or ideas—for customers. Thus, organizations as diverse as Toyota, Campbell Soup, UPS, and a public hospital share a number of similarities relating to how they transform resources into the products we consume. Most hospitals use similar admission procedures, while online social media companies, like Facebook and Twitter, use their technology and operating systems to create social networking opportunities and sell advertising. Such similarities are to be expected. But even organizations in unrelated industries take similar steps in creating goods or services. The check-in procedures of hotels and commercial airlines are comparable, for example. The way Subway assembles a sandwich and the way GMC assembles a truck are similar (both use automation and an assembly line). These similarities are the result of operations management, the focus of this chapter.

Here, we discuss the role of production or operations management in acquiring and managing the resources necessary to create goods and services. Production and operations management involves planning and designing the processes that will transform those resources into finished products, managing the movement of those resources through the transformation process, and ensuring that the products are of the quality expected by customers.

The Nature of Operations Management

Operations management (OM), the development and administration of the activities involved in transforming resources into goods and services, is of critical importance. Operations managers oversee the transformation process and the planning and designing of operations systems, managing logistics, quality, and productivity. Quality and productivity have become fundamental aspects of operations management because a company that cannot make products of the quality desired by consumers, using resources efficiently and effectively, will not be able to remain in business. OM is the "core" of most organizations because it is responsible for the creation of the organization's goods and services. Some organizations like General Motors produce tangible products, but service is an important part of the total product for the customer.

Historically, operations management has been called "production" or "manufacturing" primarily because of the view that it was limited to the manufacture of physical goods. Its focus was on methods and techniques required to operate a factory efficiently. The change from "production" to "operations" recognizes the increasing importance of organizations that provide services and ideas. Additionally, the term *operations* represents an interest in viewing the operations function as a whole rather than simply as an analysis of inputs and outputs.

Today, OM includes a wide range of organizational activities and situations outside of manufacturing, such as health care, food service, banking, entertainment, education, transportation, and charity. Thus, we use the terms **manufacturing** and **production** interchangeably to represent the activities and processes used in making *tangible* products, whereas we use the broader term **operations** to describe those processes used in the making of *both tangible and intangible products*. Manufacturing provides tangible products such as Hewlett-Packard's latest printer, and operations provides intangibles such as a stay at Wyndham Hotels and Resorts.

LO 8-1

operations management (OM)
the development and administration of the activities involved in transforming resources into goods and services

manufacturing
the activities and processes used in making tangible products; also called production

production
the activities and processes used in making tangible products; also called manufacturing

operations
the activities and processes used in making both tangible and intangible products

The Transformation Process

At the heart of operations management is the transformation process through which **inputs** (resources such as labor, money, materials, and energy) are converted into **outputs** (goods, services, and ideas). The transformation process combines inputs in predetermined ways using different equipment, administrative procedures, and technology to create a product (Figure 8.1). To ensure that this process generates quality products efficiently, operations managers control the process by taking measurements (feedback) at various points in the transformation process and comparing them to previously established standards. If there is any deviation between the actual and desired outputs, the manager may take some sort of corrective action. All adjustments made to create a satisfying product are a part of the transformation process.

Transformation may take place through one or more processes. In a business that manufactures oak furniture, for example, inputs pass through several processes before being turned into the final outputs—furniture that has been designed to meet the desires of customers (Figure 8.2). The furniture maker must first strip the oak trees of their bark and saw them into appropriate sizes—one step in the transformation process. Next, the firm dries the strips of oak lumber, a second form of transformation. Third, the dried wood is routed into its appropriate shape and made smooth. Fourth, workers assemble and treat the wood pieces, then stain or varnish the piece of assembled furniture. Finally, the completed piece of furniture is stored until it can be shipped to customers at the appropriate time. Of course, many businesses choose to eliminate some of these stages by purchasing already processed materials—lumber, for example—or outsourcing some tasks to third-party firms with greater expertise.

inputs
the resources—such as labor, money, materials, and energy—that are converted into outputs

outputs
the goods, services, and ideas that result from the conversion of inputs

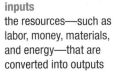

Need help understanding the Transformation Process for Goods and Services?

http://bit.ly/FerrellIQR8-1

Operations Management in Service Businesses

Different types of transformation processes take place in organizations that provide services, such as airlines, colleges, and most nonprofit organizations. An airline transforms inputs such as employees, time, money, and equipment through

LO 8-2

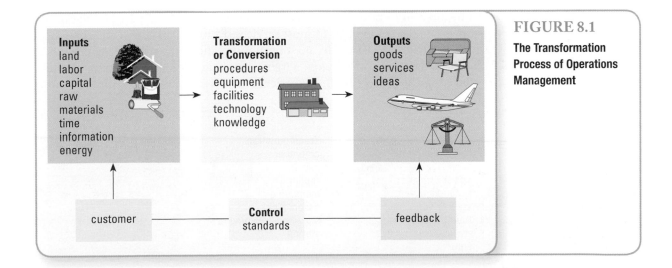

Inputs	Transformation or Conversion	Outputs
land	procedures	goods
labor	equipment	services
capital	facilities	ideas
raw materials	technology	
time	knowledge	
information		
energy		

customer ——— **Control** standards ——— feedback

FIGURE 8.1

The Transformation Process of Operations Management

processes such as booking flights, flying airplanes, maintaining equipment, and training crews. The output of these processes is flying passengers and/or packages to their destinations. In a nonprofit organization like Habitat for Humanity, inputs such as money, materials, information, and volunteer time and labor are used to transform raw materials into homes for needy families. In this setting, transformation processes include fund-raising and promoting the cause in order to gain new volunteers and donations of supplies, as well as pouring concrete, raising walls, and setting roofs. Transformation processes occur in all organizations, regardless of what they produce or their objectives. For most organizations, the ultimate objective is for the produced outputs to be worth more than the combined costs of the inputs.

Unlike tangible goods, services are effectively actions or performances that must be directed toward the consumers who use them. Thus, there is a significant customer-contact component to most services. Examples of high-contact services include health care, real estate, tax preparation, and food service. At the Inn at Little Washington in Washington, Virginia, for example, food servers are critical to delivering the perfect dining experience expected by the most discriminating

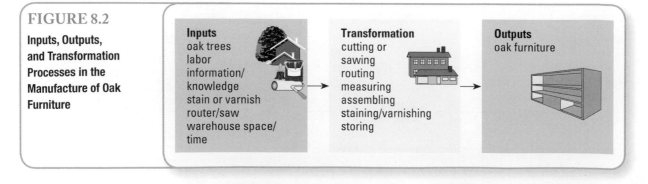

FIGURE 8.2

Inputs, Outputs, and Transformation Processes in the Manufacture of Oak Furniture

Inputs
oak trees
labor
information/
knowledge
stain or varnish
router/saw
warehouse space/
time

Transformation
cutting or
sawing
routing
measuring
assembling
staining/varnishing
storing

Outputs
oak furniture

diners. Wait staff are expected not only to be courteous, but also to demonstrate a detailed knowledge of the restaurant's offerings, and even to assess the mood of guests in order to respond to diners appropriately.[3] Low-contact services, such as online auction services like eBay, often have a strong high-tech component.

Regardless of the level of customer contact, service businesses strive to provide a standardized process, and technology offers an interface that creates an automatic and structured response. The ideal service provider will be high-tech and high-touch. JetBlue, for example, strives to maintain an excellent website; friendly, helpful customer contact; and satellite TV service at every seat on each plane. Thus, service organizations must build their operations around good execution, which comes from hiring and training excellent employees, developing flexible systems, customizing services, and maintaining adjustable capacity to deal with fluctuating demand.[4]

Another challenge related to service operations is that the output is generally intangible and even perishable. Few services can be saved, stored, resold, or returned.[5] A seat on an airline or a table in a restaurant, for example, cannot be sold or used at a later date. Because of the perishability of services, it can be extremely difficult for service providers to accurately estimate the demand in order to match the right supply of a service. If an airline overestimates demand, for example, it will still have to fly each plane even with empty seats. The flight costs the same regardless of whether it is 50 percent full

Although service organizations tend to vary depending on the service provider, businesses strive to standardize operations to ensure a high level of quality. The Ritz-Carlton has become famous for its high level of customer service.

or 100 percent full, but the former will result in much higher costs per passenger. If the airline underestimates demand, the result can be long lines of annoyed customers or even the necessity of bumping some customers off of an overbooked flight.

Businesses that manufacture tangible goods and those that provide services or ideas are similar yet different. For example, both types of organizations must make design and operating decisions. Most goods are manufactured prior to purchase, but most services are performed after purchase. Flight attendants at Southwest Airlines, hotel service personnel, and even the New York Giants football team engage in performances that are a part of the total product. Though manufacturers and service providers often perform similar activities, they also differ in several respects. We can classify these differences in five basic ways.

Nature and Consumption of Output.   First, manufacturers and service providers differ in the nature and consumption of their output. For example, the term *manufacturer* implies a firm that makes tangible products. A service provider, on the other hand, produces more intangible outputs such as U.S. Postal Service delivery of priority mail or a business stay in a Hyatt hotel. As mentioned earlier, the very nature of the service provider's product requires a higher degree of customer contact. Moreover, the actual performance of the service typically occurs at the point of consumption. At the Hyatt, the business traveler may evaluate in-room communications and the restaurant. Automakers, on the other hand, can separate the production of a car from its actual use, but the service dimension requires closer contact with the consumer. Manufacturing, then, can occur in an isolated environment, away from the customer. However, service providers, because of their need for customer contact, are often more limited than manufacturers in selecting work methods, assigning jobs, scheduling work, and exercising control over operations. At FedEx, the Quality Improvement Process (QIP) includes sayings such as "Do it right the first time," and "Make the first time you do it the only time anyone has to do it." The quality of the service experience is often controlled by a service contact employee. However, some hospitals are studying the manufacturing processes and quality control mechanisms applied in the automotive industry in an effort to improve their service quality. By analyzing work processes to find unnecessary steps to eliminate and using teams to identify and address problems as soon as they occur, these hospitals are slashing patient waiting times, decreasing inventories of wheelchairs, readying operating rooms sooner, and generally moving patients through their hospital visit more quickly, with fewer errors, and at a lower cost.[6]

Uniformity of Inputs.   A second way to classify differences between manufacturers and service providers has to do with the uniformity of inputs. Manufacturers typically have more control over the amount of variability of the resources they use than do service providers. For example, each customer calling Fidelity Investments is likely to require different services due to differing needs, whereas many of the tasks required to manufacture a Ford Focus are the same across each unit of output. Consequently, the products of service organizations tend to be more "customized" than those of their manufacturing counterparts. Consider, for example, a haircut versus a bottle of shampoo. The haircut is much more likely to incorporate your specific desires (customization) than is the bottle of shampoo.

Subway's inputs are sandwich components such as bread, tomatoes, and lettuce, while its outputs are customized sandwiches.

Uniformity of Output.   Manufacturers and service providers also differ in the uniformity of their output, the final product. Because of the human element inherent in providing services, each service tends to be performed differently. Not all grocery checkers, for example, wait on customers in the same way. If a barber or stylist performs 15 haircuts in a day, it is unlikely that any two of them will be exactly the same. Consequently, human and technological elements associated with a service can result in a different day-to-day or even hour-to-hour performance of that service. The service experience can even vary at McDonald's or Burger King despite the fact that the two chains employ very similar procedures and processes. Moreover, no two customers are exactly alike in their perception of the service experience. Health care offers another excellent example of this challenge. Every diagnosis, treatment, and surgery varies because every individual is different. In manufacturing, the high degree of automation available allows manufacturers to generate uniform outputs and, thus, the operations are more effective and efficient. For example, we would expect every TAG Heuer or Rolex watch to maintain very high standards of quality and performance.

Labor Required.   A fourth point of difference is the amount of labor required to produce an output. Service providers are generally more labor-intensive (require more labor) because of the high level of customer contact, perishability of the output (must be consumed immediately), and high degree of variation of inputs and outputs (customization). For example, Adecco provides temporary support personnel. Each temporary worker's performance determines Adecco's product quality. A manufacturer, on the other hand, is likely to be more capital-intensive because of the machinery and technology used in the mass production of highly similar goods. For instance, it would take a considerable investment for Ford to make an electric car that has batteries with a longer life.

Measurement of Productivity.   The final distinction between service providers and manufacturers involves the measurement of productivity for each output produced. For manufacturers, measuring productivity is fairly straightforward because of the tangibility of the output and its high degree of uniformity. For the service provider, variations in demand (for example, higher demand for air travel in some seasons than in others), variations in service requirements from job to job, and the intangibility of the product make productivity measurement more difficult. Consider, for example, how much easier it is to measure the productivity of employees involved in the production of Intel computer processors as opposed to serving the needs of Prudential Securities' clients.

It is convenient and simple to think of organizations as being either manufacturers or service providers as in the preceding discussion. In reality, however, most organizations are a combination of the two, with both tangible and intangible qualities embodied in what they produce. For example, Porsche provides customer services such as toll-free hotlines and warranty protection, while banks may sell checks and other tangible products that complement their primarily intangible product offering. Thus, we consider "products" to include both tangible physical goods as well as intangible service offerings. It is the level of tangibility of its principal product that tends to classify a company as either a manufacturer or a service provider. From an OM standpoint, this level of tangibility greatly influences the nature of the company's operational processes and procedures.

Planning and Designing Operations Systems

Before a company can produce any product, it must first decide what it will produce and for what group of customers. It must then determine what processes it will use to make these products as well as the facilities it needs to produce them. These decisions comprise operations planning. Although planning was once the sole realm of the production and operations department, today's successful companies involve all departments within an organization, particularly marketing and research and development, in these decisions.

LO 8-3

Planning the Product

Before making any product, a company first must determine what consumers want and then design a product to satisfy that want. Most companies use marketing research (discussed in Chapter 11) to determine the kinds of goods and services to provide and the features they must possess. Twitter and Facebook provide new opportunities for businesses to discover what consumers want, then design the product accordingly. For instance, mineral-based makeup company Bare Escentuals Cosmetics uses Facebook to interact with its customers and generate feedback. From Facebook, Bare Escentuals learned that customers preferred makeup packaging that was more portable so it would be easier to take the makeup with them. This feedback led the company to redesign its packaging by adopting the more portable "Click, Lock, Go" container. By listening to its customers, Bare Escentuals was able to meet their needs more effectively, leading to greater customer satisfaction.[7] Marketing research can also help gauge the demand for a product and how much consumers are willing to pay for it. But when a market's environment changes, firms have to be flexible.

Developing a product can be a lengthy, expensive process. For example, in the automobile industry, developing the new technology for night vision, parking assist systems, and a satellite service that locates and analyzes car problems has been a lengthy, expensive process. Most companies work to reduce development time and costs. For example, through Web collaboration, faucet manufacturer Moen reduced the time required to take an idea to a finished product in stores to just 16 months, a drop of 33 percent.[8] Once management has developed an idea for a product that customers will buy, it must then plan how to produce the product.

Within a company, the engineering or research and development department is charged with turning a product idea into a workable design that can be produced economically. In smaller companies, a single individual (perhaps the owner) may be solely responsible for this crucial activity. Regardless of who is responsible for product design, planning does not stop with a blueprint for a product or a description of a service; it must also work out efficient production of the product to ensure that enough is available to satisfy consumer demand. How does a lawn mower company transform steel, aluminum, and other materials into a mower design that satisfies consumer and environmental requirements? Operations managers must plan for the types and quantities of materials needed to produce the product, the skills and quantity of people needed to make the product, and the actual processes through which the inputs must pass in their transformation to outputs.

Designing the Operations Processes

Before a firm can begin production, it must first determine the appropriate method of transforming resources into the desired product. Often, consumers' specific needs and desires dictate a process. Customer needs, for example, require that all 3/4-inch bolts have the same basic thread size, function, and quality; if they did not, engineers and builders could not rely on 3/4-inch bolts in their construction projects. A bolt manufacturer, then, will likely use a standardized process so that every 3/4-inch bolt produced is like every other one. On the other hand, a bridge often must be customized so that it is appropriate for the site and expected load; furthermore, the bridge must be constructed on site rather than in a factory. Typically, products are designed to be manufactured by one of three processes: standardization, modular design, or customization.

Standardization.   Most firms that manufacture products in large quantities for many customers have found that they can make them cheaper and faster by standardizing designs. **Standardization** is making identical, interchangeable

standardization
the making of identical interchangeable components or products

components or even complete products. With standardization, a customer may not get exactly what he or she wants, but the product generally costs less than a custom-designed product. Television sets, ballpoint pens, and tortilla chips are standardized products; most are manufactured on an assembly line. Standardization speeds up production and quality control and reduces production costs. And, as in the example of the 3/4-inch bolts, standardization provides consistency so that customers who need certain products to function uniformly all the time will get a product that meets their expectations. Standardization becomes more complex on a global scale because different countries have different standards for quality. To help solve this problem, the International Organization for Standardization (ISO) has developed a list of global standards that companies can adopt to assure stakeholders that they are complying with the highest quality, environmental, and managerial guidelines.

Modular Design.   **Modular design** involves building an item in self-contained units, or modules, that can be combined or interchanged to create different products. Dell laptops, for example, are composed of a number of components—LCD screen, AC adapter, keyboard, motherboard, etc.—that can be installed in different configurations to meet customers' needs.[9] Because many modular components are produced as integrated units, the failure of any portion of a modular component usually means replacing the entire component. Modular design allows products to be repaired quickly, thus reducing the cost of labor, but the component itself is expensive, raising the cost of repair materials. Many automobile manufacturers use modular design in the production process. Manufactured homes are built on a modular design and often cost about one-fourth the cost of a conventionally built house.

modular design
the creation of an item in self-contained units, or modules, that can be combined or interchanged to create different products

Customization.   **Customization** is making products to meet a particular customer's needs or wants. Products produced in this way are generally unique. Such products include repair services, photocopy services, custom artwork, jewelry, and furniture, as well as large-scale products such as bridges, ships, and computer software. Custom designs are used in communications and service products. A Web-based design service, myemma.com, creates a custom template using a company's logo and colors to create a unique page for a website. It also provides tools for interacting with customers and tracking deliveries.[10] Ship design is another industry that uses customization. Builders generally design and build each ship to meet the needs of the customer who will use it. Delta Marine Industries, for example, custom-builds each luxury yacht to the customer's exact specifications and preferences for things like helicopter garages, golf courses, and swimming pools. Mass customization relates to making products that meet the needs or wants of a large number of individual customers. The customer can select the model, size, color, style, or design of the product. Dell can customize a computer with the exact configuration that fits a customer's needs. Services such as fitness programs and travel packages can also be custom designed for a large number of individual customers. For both goods and services, customers get to make choices and have options to determine the final product.

customization
making products to meet a particular customer's needs or wants

Planning Capacity

Planning the operational processes for the organization involves two important areas: capacity planning and facilities planning. The term **capacity** basically refers to the maximum load that an organizational unit can carry or operate. The unit

capacity
the maximum load that an organizational unit can carry or operate

of measurement may be a worker or machine, a department, a branch, or even an entire plant. Maximum capacity can be stated in terms of the inputs or outputs provided. For example, an electric plant might state plant capacity in terms of the maximum number of kilowatt-hours that can be produced without causing a power outage, while a restaurant might state capacity in terms of the maximum number of customers who can be effectively—comfortably and courteously—served at any one particular time.

Efficiently planning the organization's capacity needs is an important process for the operations manager. Capacity levels that fall short can result in unmet demand, and consequently, lost customers. On the other hand, when there is more capacity available than needed, operating costs are driven up needlessly due to unused and often expensive resources. To avoid such situations, organizations must accurately forecast demand and then plan capacity based on these forecasts. Another reason for the importance of efficient capacity planning has to do with long-term commitment of resources. Often, once a capacity decision—such as factory size—has been implemented, it is very difficult to change the decision without incurring substantial costs. Large companies have come to realize that although change can be expensive, not adjusting to future demand and stakeholder desires will be more expensive in the long run. For this reason, Honda has begun to adopt ISO 14001 guidelines for environmental management systems in its factories. These systems help firms monitor their impact on the environment. Thirteen of Honda's 14 North American factories have received certification.[12]

DID YOU KNOW? Hershey's has the production capacity to make more than 80 million chocolate kisses per day.[11]

Planning Facilities

Once a company knows what process it will use to create its products, it then can design and build an appropriate facility in which to make them. Many products are manufactured in factories, but others are produced in stores, at home, or where the product ultimately will be used. Companies must decide where to locate their operations facilities, what layout is best for producing their particular product, and even what technology to apply to the transformation process.

Many firms are developing both a traditional organization for customer contact as well as a virtual organization. Charles Schwab Corporation, a securities brokerage and investment company, maintains traditional offices and has developed complete telephone and Internet services for customers. Through its website, investors can obtain personal investment information and trade securities over the Internet without leaving their home or office.

Facility Location.   Where to locate a firm's facilities is a significant question because, once the decision has been made and implemented, the firm must live with it due to the high costs involved. When a company decides to relocate or open a facility at a new location, it must pay careful attention to factors such as proximity to market, availability of raw materials, availability of transportation, availability of power, climatic influences, availability of labor, community characteristics (quality of life), and taxes and inducements. Inducements and tax reductions have become an increasingly important criterion in recent years. To increase production and to provide incentives for small startups, many states are offering tax inducements for solar companies. State governments are willing to forgo some tax revenue in exchange for job growth, getting in on a burgeoning industry as well as the good publicity generated by the company. In a very solar-friendly state like Colorado, companies may get tax reductions for starting production, and consumers receive additional rebates for installing solar systems in their homes and businesses.[13] Apple has followed the lead of other major companies by locating its manufacturing facilities in China to take advantage of lower labor and production costs. The facility-location decision is complex because it involves the evaluation of many factors, some of which cannot be measured with precision. Because of the long-term impact of the decision, however, it is one that cannot be taken lightly.

Apple stores are designed to make the most efficient use of space. The layout of the stores allows customers to test its products before purchasing.

Facility Layout.   Arranging the physical layout of a facility is a complex, highly technical task. Some industrial architects specialize in the design and layout of certain types of businesses. There are three basic layouts: fixed-position, process, and product.

A company using a **fixed-position layout** brings all resources required to create the product to a central location. The product—perhaps an office building, house, hydroelectric plant, or bridge—does not move. A company using a fixed-position layout may be called a **project organization** because it is typically involved in large, complex projects such as construction or exploration. Project organizations generally make a unique product, rely on highly skilled labor, produce very few units, and have high production costs per unit.

Firms that use a **process layout** organize the transformation process into departments that group related processes. A metal fabrication plant, for example, may have a cutting department, a drilling department, and a polishing department. A hospital may have an X-ray unit, an obstetrics unit, and so on. These types of organizations are sometimes called **intermittent organizations,** which deal with products of a lesser magnitude than do project organizations, and their products are not necessarily unique but possess a significant number of differences. Doctors, makers of custom-made cabinets, commercial printers, and advertising agencies are intermittent organizations because they tend to create products to customers' specifications and produce relatively few units of each product. Because of the low level of output, the cost per unit of product is generally high.

The **product layout** requires that production be broken down into relatively simple tasks assigned to workers, who are usually positioned along an assembly line. Workers remain in one location, and the product moves from one worker to another. Each person in turn performs his or her required tasks or activities. Companies that use assembly lines are usually known as **continuous manufacturing organizations,** so named because once they are set up, they run continuously, creating products with many similar characteristics. Examples of products produced on assembly lines are automobiles, television sets, vacuum cleaners, toothpaste, and meals from a cafeteria. Continuous manufacturing organizations using a product layout are characterized by the standardized product they produce, the large number of units produced, and the relatively low unit cost of production.

fixed-position layout
a layout that brings all resources required to create the product to a central location

project organization
a company using a fixed-position layout because it is typically involved in large, complex projects such as construction or exploration

process layout
a layout that organizes the transformation process into departments that group related processes

intermittent organizations
organizations that deal with products of a lesser magnitude than do project organizations; their products are not necessarily unique but possess a significant number of differences

product layout
a layout requiring that production be broken down into relatively simple tasks assigned to workers, who are usually positioned along an assembly line

continuous manufacturing organizations
companies that use continuously running assembly lines, creating products with many similar characteristics

Many companies actually use a combination of layout designs. For example, an automobile manufacturer may rely on an assembly line (product layout) but may also use a process layout to manufacture parts.

Technology.   Every industry has a basic, underlying technology that dictates the nature of its transformation process. The steel industry continually tries to improve steelmaking techniques. The health care industry performs research into medical technologies and pharmaceuticals to improve the quality of health care service. Two developments that have strongly influenced the operations of many businesses are computers and robotics.

computer-assisted design (CAD)
the design of components, products, and processes on computers instead of on paper

computer-assisted manufacturing (CAM)
manufacturing that employs specialized computer systems to actually guide and control the transformation processes

Computers have been used for decades and on a relatively large scale since IBM introduced its 650 series in the late 1950s. The operations function makes great use of computers in all phases of the transformation process. **Computer-assisted design (CAD),** for example, helps engineers design components, products, and processes on the computer instead of on paper. **Computer-assisted manufacturing (CAM)** goes a step further, employing specialized computer systems to actually guide and control the transformation processes. Such systems can monitor the transformation process, gathering information about the equipment used to produce the products and about the product itself as it goes from one stage of the transformation process to the next. The computer provides information to an operator who may, if necessary, take corrective action. In some highly automated systems, the computer itself can take corrective action. At Dell's OptiPlex Plant, electronic instructions are sent to double-decker conveyor belts that speed computer components to assembly stations. Two-member teams are told by computers which PC or server to build, with initial assembly taking only three to four minutes. Then more electronic commands move the products (more than 20,000 machines on a typical day) to a finishing area to be customized, boxed, and sent to waiting delivery trucks.

flexible manufacturing
the direction of machinery by computers to adapt to different versions of similar operations

Using **flexible manufacturing,** computers can direct machinery to adapt to different versions of similar operations. For example, with instructions from a computer, one machine can be programmed to carry out its function for several different versions of an engine without shutting down the production line for refitting.

Robots are also becoming increasingly useful in the transformation process. These "steel-collar" workers have become particularly important in industries such as nuclear power, hazardous-waste disposal, ocean research, and space construction and maintenance, in which human lives would otherwise be at risk. Robots are used in numerous applications by companies around the world. Many assembly operations—cars, television sets, telephones, stereo equipment, and numerous other products—depend on industrial robots. The Robotic Industries Association estimates that about 213,000 robots are now at work in U.S. factories, making the United States one of the two largest users of robotics, second only to Japan.[14] Researchers continue to make more sophisticated robots, and some speculate that in the future, robots will not be limited to space programs and production and operations, but will also be able to engage in farming, laboratory research, and even household activities. Moreover, robotics are increasingly being used in the medical field. There are more than 1 million robots being used in manufacturing around the world, most of them in high-tech industries. They now help doctors perform more than 85 percent of prostate cancer surgeries in the United States.[15]

computer-integrated manufacturing (CIM)
a complete system that designs products, manages machines and materials, and controls the operations function

When all these technologies—CAD/CAM, flexible manufacturing, robotics, computer systems, and more—are integrated, the result is **computer-integrated manufacturing (CIM),** a complete system that designs products, manages machines

Entrepreneurship in Action

Stella & Chewy's: The Food Dogs Love

Marie Moody
Business: Stella & Chewy's
Founded: 2003, in Muskego, Wisconsin
Success: Marie Moody created an $8 million organic pet food company that broke even after one year of operations.

After being told that her dog Chewy was deathly ill, Marie Moody's only chance of saving him was to change his diet. She began purchasing organic meat and vegetables to create her own dog food. Almost immediately, Chewy's health improved. Moody began feeding her other dog, Stella, the same mixture and noticed positive results in her as well. Stella & Chewy's dog food, consisting of fresh meats and organic produce, was born.

Moody began in her apartment kitchen and later moved to Wisconsin to expand manufacturing. She developed partnerships with organic and antibiotic-free meat producers and hired animal scientists to help create technology to keep the food pathogen-free. Today, Stella & Chewy's uses hydrostatic high pressure to pasteurize without removing nutrients and taste. The company has a third party test each batch of food. Maintaining quality is critical to a raw food diet and for building a product that consumers trust. Stella and Chewy's has flourished, becoming the dog food of choice for many pet lovers.[16]

and materials, and controls the operations function. Companies adopt CIM to boost productivity and quality and reduce costs. Such technology, and computers in particular, will continue to make strong inroads into operations on two fronts—one dealing with the technology involved in manufacturing and one dealing with the administrative functions and processes used by operations managers. The operations manager must be willing to work with computers and other forms of technology and to develop a high degree of computer literacy.

Sustainability and Manufacturing

Manufacturing and operations systems are moving quickly to establish environmental sustainability and minimize negative impact on the natural environment. Sustainability deals with conducting activities in such as way as to provide for the long-term well-being of the natural environment, including all biological entities. Sustainability issues are becoming increasingly important to stakeholders and consumers, as they pertain to the future health of the planet. Some sustainability issues include pollution of the land, air, and water, climate change, waste management, deforestation, urban sprawl, protection of biodiversity, and genetically modified foods.

For example, Johnson Controls has incorporated sustainability into many different facets of its operations. The company purchases green energy, works with suppliers to "green" its supply chain, and designs more eco-friendly products. Overseeing these activities is Johnson Control's Global Environmental Sustainability Council, which measures the company's progress toward its sustainability goals. In 2011, Johnson Controls opened up a battery recycling facility to encourage stakeholders to recycle their lead-acid batteries rather than disposing of them improperly.[17]

New Belgium Brewing is another company that illustrates green initiatives in operations and manufacturing. New Belgium was the first brewery to adopt 100 percent wind-powered electricity, reducing carbon emissions by 1,800 metric tons a year. It uses a steam condenser to capture hot water to be reused for boiling the next batch of barley and hops. Then the steam is redirected to heat the floor tiles and de-ice the loading docks in cold Colorado weather. Used barley and hops are given to local farmers to feed cattle. The company is moving to aluminum

what is recyclable?

find out how to recycle more than you might expect:
patagonia.com/recycle

patagonia

800 638 6464 © 2007 Patagonia, Inc.

The outdoor clothing company Patagonia is always looking for a greener way to design, produce, and recycle its products. The company's mission statement: *Build the best product, cause no unnecessary harm, and use business to inspire and implement solutions to the environmental crisis.*

cans because they can be recycled an infinite number of times, and recycling one can save enough electricity to run a television for three hours or save a half gallon of gasoline.

Johnson Controls and New Belgium Brewing demonstrate that reducing waste, recycling, conserving, and using renewable energy not only protect the environment, but can also gain the support of stakeholders. Green operations and manufacturing can improve a firm's reputation along with customer and employee loyalty, leading to improved profits.

Much of the movement to green manufacturing and operations is the belief that global warming and climate change must decline. The McKinsey Global Institute (MGI) says that just by investing in existing technologies, the world's energy use could be reduced by 50 percent by the year 2020. Creating green buildings and higher mileage cars could yield $900 billion in savings per year by 2020.[18] Companies like General Motors and Ford are adapting to stakeholder demands for greater sustainability by producing smaller and more fuel-efficient cars. For example, the Chevy Volt can run for up to 35 miles on one overnight charge before switching to a gas-powered generator. The Volt is also a FlexFuel vehicle, which means that it can use either traditional gasoline or E85 ethanol, which some people believe is better for the environment.[19] Green products produced through green operations and manufacturing are our future. A report authored by the Center for American Progress cites ways that cities and local governments can play a role. For example, Los Angeles plans to save the city utility costs by retrofitting hundreds of city buildings while creating a green careers training program for low-income residents. Newark, New Jersey, and Richmond, California, also have green jobs training programs. Albuquerque, New Mexico, was the first city to sign on to a pledge to build a green economy as part of its efforts to create green jobs to stimulate the city's economy.[20] Government initiatives provide space for businesses to innovate their green operations and manufacturing.

Managing the Supply Chain

LO 8-4

supply chain management connecting and integrating all parties or members of the distribution system in order to satisfy customers

A major function of operations is **supply chain management,** which refers to connecting and integrating all parties or members of the distribution system in order to satisfy customers.[21] Also called logistics, supply chain management includes all the activities involved in obtaining and managing raw materials and component parts, managing finished products, packaging them, and getting them to customers. Sunny Delight had to quickly re-create its supply chain after spinning off from Procter & Gamble. This means it had to develop ordering, shipping, and billing, as well as warehouse management systems and transportation, so it could focus on growing and managing the Sunny Delight brand.[22] The supply chain integrates firms such as raw material suppliers, manufacturers, retailers, and ultimate consumers into a seamless flow of information and products.[23] Some aspects of logistics (warehousing, packaging, distributing) are so closely linked with marketing that we will discuss them in Chapter 12. In this section, we look at purchasing, managing inventory, outsourcing, and scheduling, which are vital tasks in the transformation of raw materials into finished goods. To illustrate logistics, consider a hypothetical small business—we'll call it Rushing Water Canoes Inc.—that manufactures aluminum canoes, which it sells primarily to sporting goods stores and river-rafting expeditions. Our company also makes paddles and helmets, but the focus of the following discussion is the manufacture of the company's quality canoes as they proceed through the logistics process.

purchasing
the buying of all the materials needed by the organization; also called procurement

Purchasing

Purchasing, also known as procurement, is the buying of all the materials needed by the organization. The purchasing department aims to obtain items of the desired quality in the right quantities at the lowest possible cost. Rushing Water Canoes, for example, must procure not only aluminum and other raw materials, and various canoe parts and components, but also machines and equipment, manufacturing supplies (oil, electricity, and so on), and office supplies in order to make its canoes. People in the purchasing department locate and evaluate suppliers of these items. They must constantly be on the lookout for new materials or parts that will do a better job or cost less than those currently being used. The purchasing function can be quite complex and is one area made much easier and more efficient by technological advances.

Not all companies purchase all of the materials needed to create their products. Oftentimes, they can make some components more economically and efficiently than can an outside supplier. Coors, for example, manufactures its own

We make **logistics** child's play.

Managed Logistics. Truck, Rail, Ocean, Air, and Intermodal – We manage it all.
Managed Logistics means owning the whole process. Whether it involves over the road, LTL, intermodal, air or ocean, we'll manage all or select modes for you. Our flexible solutions give you tracking information so you can proactively plan internally and ensure on-time delivery. We have the multi-modal contracts, the assets and a global network of agents to effectively manage your ocean shipments. From door-to-door or port-to-port, we will help you find, choose and execute your optimal solution. So no matter what your logistics challenge, it's child's play to us.

Full service. Full solutions. Flexible logistics.
1.800.787.2334 | www.corporate-traffic.com

CORPORATE TRAFFIC
L O G I S T I C S
NEVER SETTLE.

| Truckload | Intermodal | LTL | Ocean | Air | Retail Logistics | TMS |

Corporate Traffic Logistics helps manage the supply and transportation of products, whether it be via truck, rail, air, or ocean transport.

cans at a subsidiary plant. On the other hand, firms sometimes find that it is uneconomical to make or purchase an item, and instead arrange to lease it from another organization. Some airlines, for example, lease airplanes rather than buy them. Whether to purchase, make, or lease a needed item generally depends on cost, as well as on product availability and supplier reliability.

Managing Inventory

inventory
all raw materials, components, completed or partially completed products, and pieces of equipment a firm uses

Once the items needed to create a product have been procured, some provision has to be made for storing them until they are needed. Every raw material, component, completed or partially completed product, and piece of equipment a firm uses—its **inventory**—must be accounted for, or controlled. There are three basic types of inventory. *Finished-goods inventory* includes those products that are ready for sale, such as a fully assembled automobile ready to ship to a dealer. *Work-in-process inventory* consists of those products that are partly completed or are in some stage of the transformation process. At McDonald's, a cooking hamburger represents work-in-process inventory because it must go through several more stages before it can be sold to a customer. *Raw materials inventory* includes all the materials that have been purchased to be used as inputs for making other products. Nuts and bolts are raw materials for an automobile manufacturer, while hamburger patties, vegetables, and buns are raw materials for the fast-food restaurant. Our fictional Rushing Water Canoes has an inventory of materials for making canoes, paddles, and helmets, as well as its inventory of finished products for sale to consumers. **Inventory control** is the process of determining how many supplies and goods are needed and keeping track of quantities on hand, where each item is, and who is responsible for it.

inventory control
the process of determining how many supplies and goods are needed and keeping track of quantities on hand, where each item is, and who is responsible for it

Operations management must be closely coordinated with inventory control. The production of televisions, for example, cannot be planned without some knowledge of the availability of all the necessary materials—the chassis, picture tubes, color guns, and so forth. Also, each item held in inventory—any type of inventory—carries with it a cost. For example, storing fully assembled televisions in a warehouse to sell to a dealer at a future date requires not only the use of space, but also the purchase of insurance to cover any losses that might occur due to fire or other unforeseen events.

At Walmart, managing inventory involves finding the right balance between excess inventory and not enough inventory. Walmart uses just-in-time inventory management to minimize inventory costs and become more efficient.

Inventory managers spend a great deal of time trying to determine the proper inventory level for each item. The answer to the question of how many units to hold in inventory depends on variables such as the usage rate of the item, the cost of maintaining the item in inventory, future costs of inventory and other procedures associated with ordering or making the item, and the cost of the item itself. For example, the price of copper has fluctuated between $1.50 and $4 a pound over the last five years. Firms using copper wiring for construction, copper pipes for plumbing, and other industries requiring copper have to analyze the trade-offs between inventory costs and expected changes in the price of copper. Several approaches may be used to determine how many units of a given item should be procured at one time and when that procurement should take place.

The Economic Order Quantity Model.   To control the number of items maintained in inventory, managers need to determine how much of any given item they should order. One popular approach is the **economic order quantity (EOQ) model,** which identifies the optimum number of items to order to minimize the costs of managing (ordering, storing, and using) them.

Just-in-Time Inventory Management.   An increasingly popular technique is **just-in-time (JIT) inventory management,** which eliminates waste by using smaller quantities of materials that arrive "just in time" for use in the transformation process and therefore require less storage space and other inventory management expense. JIT minimizes inventory by providing an almost continuous flow of items from suppliers to the production facility. Many U.S. companies, including Hewlett-Packard, IBM, and Harley Davidson, have adopted JIT to reduce costs and boost efficiency.

Let's say that Rushing Water Canoes uses 20 units of aluminum from a supplier per day. Traditionally, its inventory manager might order enough for one month at a time: 440 units per order (20 units per day times 22 workdays per month). The expense of such a large inventory could be considerable because of the cost of insurance coverage, recordkeeping, rented storage space, and so on. The just-in-time approach would reduce these costs because aluminum would be purchased in smaller quantities, perhaps in lot sizes of 20, which the supplier would deliver once a day. Of course, for such an approach to be effective, the supplier must be extremely reliable and relatively close to the production facility.

On the other hand, there are some downsides to just-in-time inventory management that marketers must take into account. When the earthquake and tsunami hit Japan, resulting in a nuclear reactor crisis, several Japanese companies halted their operations. Some multinationals relied so much upon their Japanese suppliers that their supply chains were also affected. In the case of natural disasters, having only enough inventory to meet current needs could create delays in production and hurt the company's bottom line. For this reason, many economists suggest that businesses store components that are essential for production and diversify their supply chains. That way, if a natural disaster knocks out a major supplier, the company can continue to operate.[24]

Material-requirements Planning.   Another inventory management technique is **material-requirements planning (MRP),** a planning system that schedules the precise quantity of materials needed to make the product. The basic components of MRP are a master production schedule, a bill of materials, and an inventory status file. At Rushing Water Canoes, for example, the inventory-control manager will look at the production schedule to determine how many canoes the company plans to make. He or she will then prepare a bill of materials—a list of all the materials needed to make that quantity of canoes. Next, the manager will determine the quantity of these items that RWC already holds in inventory (to avoid ordering excess materials) and then develop a schedule for ordering and accepting delivery of the right quantity of materials to satisfy the firm's needs. Because of the large number of parts and materials that go into a typical production process, MRP must be done on a computer. It can be, and often is, used in conjunction with just-in-time inventory management.

economic order quantity (EOQ) model
a model that identifies the optimum number of items to order to minimize the costs of managing (ordering, storing, and using) them

just-in-time (JIT) inventory management
a technique using smaller quantities of materials that arrive "just in time" for use in the transformation process and therefore require less storage space and other inventory management expense

material-requirements planning (MRP)
a planning system that schedules the precise quantity of materials needed to make the product

Many athletic shoe manufacturers such as Nike outsource production to China and Vietnam to take advantage of lower labor costs.

Outsourcing

Increasingly, outsourcing has become a component of supply chain management in operations. As we mentioned in Chapter 3, outsourcing refers to the contracting of manufacturing or other tasks to independent companies, often overseas. Many companies elect to outsource some aspects of their operations to companies that can provide these products more efficiently, at a lower cost, and with greater customer satisfaction. Globalization has put pressure on supply chain managers to improve speed and balance resources against competitive pressures. Companies outsourcing to China, in particular, face heavy regulation, high transportation costs, inadequate facilities, and unpredictable supply chain execution. Therefore, suppliers need to provide useful, timely, and accurate information about every aspect of the quality requirements, schedules, and solutions to dealing with problems. Companies that hire suppliers must also make certain that their suppliers are following company standards; failure to do so could lead to criticism of the parent company. For example, Hershey was criticized for sourcing from suppliers that used child labor on chocolate plantations. Although suppliers are responsible for hiring underage workers, it is ultimately the responsibility of Hershey to ensure the compliance of suppliers in its supply chain.[25]

Many high-tech firms have outsourced the production of chips, computers, and telecom equipment to Asian companies. The hourly labor costs in countries such as China, India, and Vietnam are far less than in the United States, Europe, or even Mexico. These developing countries have improved their manufacturing capabilities, infrastructure, and technical and business skills, making them more attractive regions for global sourcing. For instance, Nike outsources almost all of its production to Asian countries such as China and Vietnam. On the other hand, the cost of outsourcing halfway around the world must be considered in decisions. While information technology is often outsourced today, transportation, human resources, services, and even marketing functions can be outsourced. Our hypothetical Rushing Water Canoes might contract with a local janitorial service to clean its offices and with a local accountant to handle routine bookkeeping and tax-preparation functions.

Outsourcing, once used primarily as a cost-cutting tactic, has increasingly been linked with the development of competitive advantage through improved product quality, speeding up the time it takes products to get to the customer, and overall supply-chain efficiencies. Table 8.1 provides the world's top five outsourcing providers that assist mainly in information technology. Outsourcing allows companies to free up time and resources to focus on what they do best and to create better opportunities to focus on customer satisfaction. Many executives view outsourcing as an innovative way to boost productivity and remain competitive against low-wage offshore factories. However, outsourcing may create conflict with labor and negative public opinion when it results in U.S. workers being replaced by lower-cost workers in other countries.

Routing and Scheduling

After all materials have been procured and their use determined, managers must then consider the **routing,** or sequence of operations through which the product must pass. For example, before employees at Rushing Water Canoes can form aluminum sheets into a canoe, the aluminum must be cut to size. Likewise, the canoe's flotation material must be installed before workers can secure the wood seats. The sequence depends on the product specifications developed by the engineering department of the company.

routing
the sequence of operations through which the product must pass

Once management knows the routing, the actual work can be scheduled. **Scheduling** assigns the tasks to be done to departments or even specific machines, workers, or teams. At Rushing Water, cutting aluminum for the company's canoes might be scheduled to be done by the "cutting and finishing" department on machines designed especially for that purpose.

scheduling
the assignment of required tasks to departments or even specific machines, workers, or teams

Company	Services
Alsbridge	Global advisory services
KPMG	Audit, tax, and advisory services
TPI	Information services and market intelligence
Kirkland & Ellis	Law services
EquaTerra (since acquired by KPMG)	Information technology and business process transformation advisory services

TABLE 8.1

The World's Top Five Outsourcing Providers

Source: "IAOP Announces 2010 Rankings for the World's Best Outsourcing Providers and Advisors," International Association of Outsourcing Professionals, www.iaop.org/content/23/152/2042/ (accessed February 22, 2012).

FIGURE 8.3   **A Hypothetical PERT Diagram for a McDonald's Big Mac**

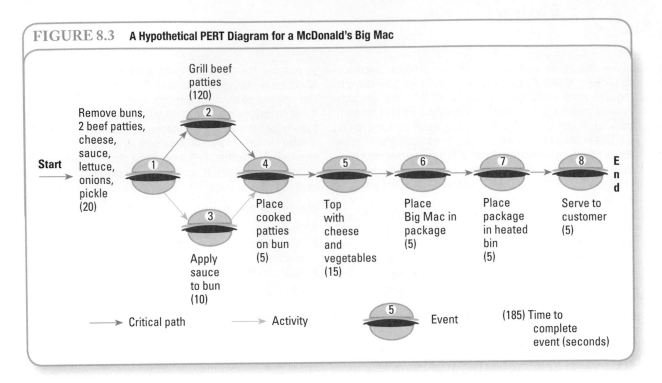

Many approaches to scheduling have been developed, ranging from simple trial and error to highly sophisticated computer programs. One popular method is the *Program Evaluation and Review Technique (PERT),* which identifies all the major activities or events required to complete a project, arranges them in a sequence or path, determines the critical path, and estimates the time required for each event. Producing a McDonald's Big Mac, for example, involves removing meat, cheese, sauce, and vegetables from the refrigerator; grilling the hamburger patties; assembling the ingredients; placing the completed Big Mac in its package; and serving it to the customer (Figure 8.3). The cheese, pickles, onions, and sauce cannot be put on before the hamburger patty is completely grilled and placed on the bun. The path that requires the longest time from start to finish is called the *critical path* because it determines the minimum amount of time in which the process can be completed. If any of the activities on the critical path for production of the Big Mac fall behind schedule, the sandwich will not be completed on time, causing customers to wait longer than they usually would.

Managing Quality

LO 8-5

Quality, like cost and efficiency, is a critical element of operations management, for defective products can quickly ruin a firm. Quality reflects the degree to which a good or service meets the demands and requirements of customers. Customers are increasingly dissatisfied with the quality of service provided by many airlines. Table 8.2 gives the rankings of U.S. airlines in certain operational areas. Determining quality can be difficult because it depends on customers' perceptions of how well the product meets or exceeds their expectations. For example, customer satisfaction on airlines can vary wildly depending on individual customers' perspectives.

Rank	Overall Rank	On-Time Arrival	Cancelled Flights	Baggage Handling	Bumping Passengers	Customer Complaints
1	Alaska	Alaska	Alaska	JetBlue	JetBlue	Southwest
2	Delta	Delta	Southwest	Delta	Delta	Alaska
3	Southwest	US Airways	Delta	US Airways	Southwest	JetBlue
4	US Airways	Southwest	United	Alaska	Alaska	Delta
5	JetBlue	American	US Airways	United	US Airways	American
6	United	United	JetBlue	Southwest	American	US Airways
7	American	JetBlue	American	American	United	United

TABLE 8.2

2011 Airline Scorecard (Best to Worst)

Sources: FlightStats.com; U.S. Department of Transportation.

However, the airline industry is notorious for its dissatisfied customers. Flight delays are a common complaint from airline passengers; 20 percent of all flights arrive more than 15 minutes late. However, most passengers do not select an airline based on how often flights arrive on time.[27]

The fuel economy of an automobile or its reliability (defined in terms of frequency of repairs) can be measured with some degree of precision. Although automakers rely on their own measures of vehicle quality, they also look to independent sources such as the J. D. Power & Associates annual initial quality survey for confirmation of their quality assessment as well as consumer perceptions of quality for the industry, as indicated in Figure 8.4.

It is especially difficult to measure quality characteristics when the product is a service. A company has to decide exactly which quality characteristics it considers important and then define those characteristics in terms that can be measured. The inseparability of production and consumption and the level of customer contact influence the selection of characteristics of the service that are most important. Employees in high-contact services such as hairstyling, education, legal services, and even the barista at Starbucks are an important part of the product.

The Malcolm Baldrige National Quality Award is given each year to companies that meet rigorous standards of quality. The Baldrige criteria are (1) leadership, (2) information and analysis, (3) strategic planning, (4) human resource development and management, (5) process management, (6) business results, and (7) customer focus and satisfaction. The criteria have become a worldwide framework for driving business improvement. Four companies won the award in 2011, representing two different categories: Concordia Publishing House (nonprofit), Henry Ford Health System (health care), Schneck Medical Center (health care), and Southcentral Foundation in Anchorage, Alaska (health care).[28]

Quality is so important that we need to examine it in the context of operations management. **Quality control** refers to the processes an organization uses to maintain its established quality standards. Kia recognized the importance of quality control when it sought to revamp its image. For years, Kia vehicles were seen as low quality. To change consumer perceptions of the Kia brand, the company had its quality-control managers provide final approval for its products instead of sales executives,

quality control the processes an organization uses to maintain its established quality standards

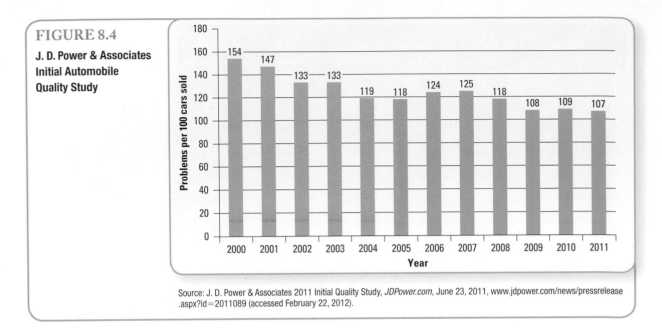

FIGURE 8.4

J. D. Power & Associates Initial Automobile Quality Study

Source: J. D. Power & Associates 2011 Initial Quality Study, *JDPower.com,* June 23, 2011, www.jdpower.com/news/pressrelease .aspx?id=2011089 (accessed February 22, 2012).

implemented benchmarks for improving product quality, developed strong marketing campaigns promoting the brand, and cut dealers that they did not feel were supporting the Kia franchise. Kia's quality efforts were largely successful; its overall sales grew 27 percent in a one-year period.[29] Quality has become a major concern in many organizations, particularly in light of intense foreign competition and increasingly demanding customers. To regain a competitive edge, a number of firms have adopted a total quality management approach. **Total quality management (TQM)** is a philosophy that uniform commitment to quality in all areas of the organization will promote a culture that meets customers' perceptions of quality. It involves coordinating efforts to improve customer satisfaction, increasing employee participation, forming and strengthening supplier partnerships, and facilitating an organizational culture of continuous quality improvement. TQM requires constant improvements in all areas of the company as well as employee empowerment.

Continuous improvement of an organization's goods and services is built around the notion that quality is free; by contrast, *not* having high-quality goods and services can be very expensive, especially in terms of dissatisfied customers.[30] A primary tool of the continuous improvement process is *benchmarking,* the measuring and evaluating of the quality of the organization's goods, services, or processes as compared with the quality produced by the best-performing companies in the industry.[31] Benchmarking lets the organization know where it stands competitively in its industry, thus giving it a goal to aim for over time. Now that online digital media are becoming more important in businesses, companies such as Compuware Gomez offer benchmarking tools so companies can monitor and compare the success of their websites. Such tools allow companies to track traffic to the site versus competitors' sites. Studies have shown a direct link between website performance and online sales, meaning this type of benchmarking is important.[32]

Companies employing total quality management (TQM) programs know that quality control should be incorporated throughout the transformation process, from the initial plans to the development of a specific product through the product and production-facility design processes to the actual manufacture of the product.

total quality management (TQM)
a philosophy that uniform commitment to quality in all areas of an organization will promote a culture that meets customers' perceptions of quality

In other words, they view quality control as an element of the product itself, rather than as simply a function of the operations process. When a company makes the product correctly from the outset, it eliminates the need to rework defective products, expedites the transformation process itself, and allows employees to make better use of their time and materials. One method through which many companies have tried to improve quality is **statistical process control,** a system in which management collects and analyzes information about the production process to pinpoint quality problems in the production system.

statistical process control
a system in which management collects and analyzes information about the production process to pinpoint quality problems in the production system

International Organization for Standardization (ISO)

Regardless of whether a company has a TQM program for quality control, it must first determine what standard of quality it desires and then assess whether its products meet that standard. Product specifications and quality standards must be set so the company can create a product that will compete in the marketplace. Rushing Water Canoes, for example, may specify that each of its canoes has aluminum walls of a specified uniform thickness, that the front and back be reinforced with a specified level of steel, and that each contain a specified amount of flotation material for safety. Production facilities must be designed that can produce products with the desired specifications.

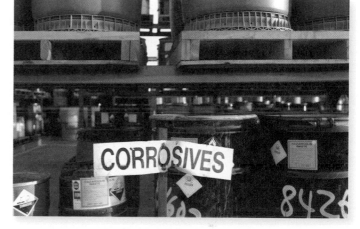

The ISO 9000 standards are international standards that relate to quality management. ISO14000 standards relate to environmental management—managing businesses to minimize harmful effects to the environment.

Quality standards can be incorporated into service businesses as well. A hamburger chain, for example, may establish standards relating to how long it takes to cook an order and serve it to customers, how many fries are in each order, how thick the burgers are, or how many customer complaints might be acceptable. Once the desired quality characteristics, specifications, and standards have been stated in measurable terms, the next step is inspection.

The International Organization for Standardization (ISO) has created a series of quality management standards—**ISO 9000**—designed to ensure the customer's quality standards are met. The standards provide a framework for documenting how a certified business keeps records, trains employees, tests products, and fixes defects. To obtain ISO 9000 certification, an independent auditor must verify that a business's factory, laboratory, or office meets the quality standards spelled out by the International Organization for Standardization. The certification process can require significant investment, but for many companies, the process is essential to being able to compete. Thousands of companies have been certified, including General Electric Analytical Instruments, which has applied ISO standards to everything from the design to the manufacturing practices of its global facilities.[33] Certification has become a virtual necessity for doing business in Europe in some high-technology businesses. ISO 9002 certification was established for service providers. **ISO 14000** is a comprehensive set of environmental standards that encourages a cleaner and safer world. ISO 14000 is a valuable standard because currently considerable variation exists between the regulations in different nations, and even regions within a nation. These variations make it difficult for organizations

ISO 9000
a series of quality assurance standards designed by the International Organization for Standardization (ISO) to ensure consistent product quality under many conditions

ISO 14000
a comprehensive set of environmental standards that encourages companies to conduct business in a cleaner, safer, and less wasteful way. ISO 14000 provides a uniform set of standards globally.

committed to sustainability to find acceptable global solutions to problems. The goal of the ISO 14000 standards is to promote a more uniform approach to environmental management and to help companies attain and measure improvements in their environmental performance.

Inspection

Inspection reveals whether a product meets quality standards. Some product characteristics may be discerned by fairly simple inspection techniques—weighing the contents of cereal boxes or measuring the time it takes for a customer to receive his or her hamburger. As part of the ongoing quality assurance program at Hershey Foods, all wrapped Hershey Kisses are checked, and all imperfectly wrapped kisses are rejected. Other inspection techniques are more elaborate. Automobile manufacturers use automated machines to open and close car doors to test the durability of latches and hinges. The food-processing and pharmaceutical industries use various chemical tests to determine the quality of their output. Rushing Water Canoes might use a special device that can precisely measure the thickness of each canoe wall to ensure that it meets the company's specifications.

Organizations normally inspect purchased items, work-in-process, and finished items. The inspection of purchased items and finished items takes place after the fact; the inspection of work-in-process is preventive. In other words, the purpose of inspection of purchased items and finished items is to determine what the quality level is. For items that are being worked on—an automobile moving down the assembly line or a canoe being assembled—the purpose of the inspection is to find defects before the product is completed so that necessary corrections can be made.

Sampling

An important question relating to inspection is how many items should be inspected. Should all canoes produced by Rushing Water be inspected or just some of them? Whether to inspect 100 percent of the output or only part of it is related to the cost of the inspection process, the destructiveness of the inspection process (some tests last until the product fails), and the potential cost of product flaws in terms of human lives and safety.

Some inspection procedures are quite expensive, use elaborate testing equipment, destroy products, and/or require a significant number of hours to complete. In such cases, it is usually desirable to test only a sample of the output. If the sample passes inspection, the inspector may assume that all the items in the lot from which the sample was drawn would also pass inspection. By using principles of statistical inference, management can employ sampling techniques that ensure a relatively high probability of reaching the right conclusion—that is, rejecting a lot that does not meet standards and accepting a lot that does. Nevertheless, there will always be a risk of making an incorrect conclusion—accepting a population that *does not* meet standards (because the sample was satisfactory) or rejecting a population that *does* meet standards (because the sample contained too many defective items).

Sampling is likely to be used when inspection tests are destructive. Determining the life expectancy of lightbulbs by turning them on and recording how long they last would be foolish: There is no market for burned-out lightbulbs. Instead, a generalization based on the quality of a sample would be applied to the entire population of lightbulbs from which the sample was drawn. However, human life and safety often depend on the proper functioning of specific items, such as the navigational systems installed in commercial airliners. For such items, even though the inspection process is costly, the potential cost of flawed systems—in human lives and safety—is too great not to inspect 100 percent of the output.

Integrating Operations and Supply Chain Management

Managing operations and supply chains can be complex and challenging due to the number of independent organizations that must perform their responsibilities in creating product quality. Managing supply chains requires constant vigilance and the ability to make quick tactical changes. For example, an Australian firm experienced severe supply chain problems when it sent 50 goldfish to media companies as part of a public relations campaign. The fish died in transit, requiring the company to issue an apology and donate money to animal protection organizations.[34] Even Apple Inc., the most admired company in the world, has had supply chain problems. Reports of forced overtime, underage workers, and dangerous conditions at its Chinese supplier factories have resulted in negative publicity for the company.[35] Therefore, managing the various partners involved in supply chains and operations is important because many stakeholders hold the firm responsible for appropriate conduct related to product quality. This requires that the company exercise oversight over all suppliers involved in producing a product. Encouraging suppliers to report problems, issues, or concerns requires excellent communication systems to obtain feedback. Ideally, suppliers will report potential problems before they reach the next level of the supply chain, which reduces damage.

Despite the challenges of monitoring global operations and supply chains, there are steps businesses can take to manage these risks. All companies who work with global suppliers should adopt a Global Supplier Code of Conduct and ensure that it is effectively communicated. Additionally, companies should encourage compliance and procurement employees to work together to find ethical suppliers at reasonable costs. Those in procurement are concerned with the costs of obtaining materials for the company. As a result, supply chain and procurement managers must work together to make operational decisions to ensure the selection of the best suppliers from an ethical and cost-effective standpoint. Businesses must also work to make certain that their supply chains are diverse. Having only a few suppliers in one area can disrupt operations should a disaster strike. Finally, companies must perform regular audits on its suppliers and take action against those found to be in violation of company standards.[36]

So You Want a Job in Operations Management

While you might not have been familiar with terms such as *supply chain* or *logistics* or *total quality management* before taking this course, careers abound in the operations management field. You will find these careers in a wide variety of organizations—manufacturers, retailers, transportation companies, third-party logistics firms, government agencies, and service firms. Approximately $1.3 trillion is spent on transportation, inventory, and related logistics activities, and logistics alone accounts for more than 9.5 percent of U.S. gross domestic product.[37] Closely managing how a company's inputs and outputs flow from raw materials to the end consumer is vital to a firm's success. Successful companies also need to ensure that quality is measured and actively managed at each step.

Supply chain managers have a tremendous impact on the success of an organization. These managers are engaged in every facet of the business process, including planning, purchasing, production, transportation, storage and distribution, customer service, and more. Their performance helps organizations control expenses, boost sales, and maximize profits.

Warehouse managers are a vital part of manufacturing operations. A typical warehouse manager's duties include overseeing and recording deliveries and pickups, maintaining inventory records and the product tracking system, and adjusting inventory levels to reflect receipts and disbursements.

Warehouse managers also have to keep in mind customer service and employee issues. Warehouse managers can earn up to $60,000 in some cases.

Operations management is also required in service businesses. With more than 80 percent of the U.S. economy in services, jobs exist for services operations. Many service contact operations require standardized processes that often use technology to provide an interface that provides an automatic quality performance. Consider jobs in health care, the travel industry, fast food, and entertainment. Think of any job or task that is a part of the final product in these industries. Even an online retailer such as Amazon.com has a transformation process that includes information technology and human activities that facilitate a transaction. These services have a standardized process and can be evaluated based on their level of achieved service quality.

Total quality management is becoming a key attribute for companies to ensure that quality pervades all aspects of the organization. Quality assurance managers may make salaries in the $55,000 to $65,000 range. These managers monitor and advise on how a company's quality management system is performing and publish data and reports regarding company performance in both manufacturing and service industries.

Review Your Understanding

Define operations management, and differentiate between operations and manufacturing.

Operations management (OM) is the development and administration of the activities involved in transforming resources into goods and services. Operations managers oversee the transformation process and the planning and designing of operations systems, managing logistics, quality, and productivity. The terms *manufacturing* and *production* are used interchangeably to describe the activities and processes used in making tangible products, whereas *operations* is a broader term used to describe the process of making both tangible and intangible products.

Explain how operations management differs in manufacturing and service firms.

Manufacturers and service firms both transform inputs into outputs, but service providers differ from manufacturers in several ways: They have greater customer contact because the service typically occurs at the point of consumption; their inputs and outputs are more variable than manufacturers', largely because of the human element; service providers are generally more labor intensive; and their productivity measurement is more complex.

Describe the elements involved in planning and designing an operations system.

Operations planning relates to decisions about what product(s) to make, for whom, and what processes and facilities are needed to produce them. OM is often joined by marketing and research and development in these decisions. Common facility layouts include fixed-position layouts, process layouts, or product layouts. Where to locate operations facilities is a crucial decision that depends on proximity to the market, availability of raw materials, availability of transportation, availability of power, climatic influences, availability of labor, and community characteristics. Technology is also vital to operations, particularly computer-assisted design, computer-assisted manufacturing, flexible manufacturing, robotics, and computer-integrated manufacturing.

Specify some techniques managers may use to manage the logistics of transforming inputs into finished products.

Logistics, or supply chain management, includes all the activities involved in obtaining and managing raw materials and component parts, managing finished products, packaging them, and getting them to customers. The organization must first make or purchase (procure) all the materials it needs. Next, it must control its inventory by determining how many supplies and goods it needs and keeping track of every raw material, component, completed or partially completed product, and piece of equipment, how many of each are on hand, where they are, and who has responsibility for them. Common approaches to inventory control include the economic order quantity (EOQ) model, the just-in-time (JIT) inventory concept, and material-requirements planning (MRP). Logistics also includes routing and scheduling processes and activities to complete products.

Assess the importance of quality in operations management.

Quality is a critical element of OM because low-quality products can hurt people and harm the business. Quality control

refers to the processes an organization uses to maintain its established quality standards. To control quality, a company must establish what standard of quality it desires and then determine whether its products meet that standard through inspection.

Evaluate a business's dilemma and propose a solution.

Based on this chapter and the facts presented in "Solve the Dilemma" on page 267, you should be able to evaluate the business's problem and propose one or more solutions for resolving it.

Revisit the World of Business

1. Why was it so important for Taco Bell to create a seamless drive-thru process?

2. How does the Taco Bell drive-thru process manage for quality?

3. Why is speed and accuracy of service just as important as the quality of finished food for Taco Bell?

Learn the Terms

capacity 247
computer-assisted design (CAD) 250
computer-assisted manufacturing (CAM) 250
computer-integrated manufacturing (CIM) 250
continuous manufacturing organizations 250
customization 247
economic order quantity (EOQ) model 255
fixed-position layout 249
flexible manufacturing 250
inputs 241

intermittent organizations 249
inventory 254
inventory control 254
ISO 9000 261
ISO 14000 261
just-in-time (JIT) inventory management 255
manufacturing 240
material-requirements planning (MRP) 255
modular design 247
operations 240
operations management (OM) 240

outputs 241
process layout 249
product layout 249
production 240
project organization 249
purchasing 253
quality control 259
routing 257
scheduling 257
standardization 246
statistical process control 261
supply chain management 252
total quality management (TQM) 260

Check Your Progress

1. What is operations management?

2. Differentiate among the terms *operations, production,* and *manufacturing.*

3. Compare and contrast a manufacturer versus a service provider in terms of operations management.

4. Who is involved in planning products?

5. In what industry would the fixed-position layout be most efficient? The process layout? The product layout? Use real examples.

6. What criteria do businesses use when deciding where to locate a plant?

7. What is flexible manufacturing? How can it help firms improve quality?

See for Yourself Videocase

TOYOTA EXCELS AT CONTINUOUS IMPROVEMENT

The original Toyota organization was a far cry from the company of today. Its products in the 1920s were not cars, but looms. Yet even then, the firm was committed to quality. Founder Sakichi Toyoda built a special mechanism into his looms that would shut the machine off if no more than a single thread broke. This dedication to quality and the elimination of defects would become embedded in the company's culture.

In 1937, Toyoda's son spun off from his father's company to create Toyota Motor Company. Although it sold different products, the new spin-off would maintain the principle of quality that was so important to its parent. Knowing that it would have to be more efficient than competitors, Toyota implemented a number of innovative operational concepts over its long history. For instance, the company became famous for its just-in-time management (JIT) systems. This involves ordering materials when they are needed rather than storing large amounts as inventory. These materials would arrive just in time to be transformed into outputs. This concept enabled Toyota to eliminate waste, inventory costs, and storage costs.

The other part of the Toyota Production System (TPS) is known as *jidoka,* or "automation with a human touch." *Jidoka* states that any employee, no matter his or her status in the factory, is empowered to stop the production line if he or she detects a problem. This is similar to the founder's loom mechanism that shut down the machine if a problem was detected. The purpose of *jidoka* is to eliminate all defects in the production line before they are turned into the finished product. This quality control mechanism secured the company's reputation as a company where defects were not allowed.

Finally, Toyota also implemented the use of *kaizen,* or continuous improvement. One of Toyota's founding principles is that "good enough is never enough." The firm must constantly seek to improve operations, cut costs, and create better products. The concept of *kaizen* reduces complacency. One of its major principles is that all employees have the opportunity—and even the responsibility—to look for ways to improve the company. While *kaizen* can be used to fix problems, it also can lead to new opportunities. For instance, when certain employees began

experimenting with cast molds, they discovered a new process to make engines at half the cost. These innovations have propelled Toyota into being one of the world's top automakers. They also profoundly affected the business world, as companies worldwide try to emulate the Toyota Way.

However, even companies founded on strong principles can falter when they begin pursuing growth or profits over quality. In 2009 and 2010, Toyota issued massive recalls due to safety problems in some of its vehicles. The vehicles' accelerators would sometimes get stuck on floor mats, which led to crashes and sometimes deaths. Toyota was accused of acting too slowly to address the defects and was fined $16.4 million for allegedly trying to cover them up. Toyota experienced decreased sales and a tarnished reputation as a result.

Toyota was exonerated somewhat when a National Highway Traffic Safety Administration report ruled that most of the accidents were a result of driver error. This helped to begin restoring trust in Toyota products. Sales have rebounded since then. The Toyota Camry and Toyota Corolla are two of the best sold cars in the United States, its Lexus is considered to be the top luxury car brand, and its Prius is one of the most popular hybrid brands. Toyota also appears to be the car brand of choice for many minority car buyers. Although the recalls caused Honda to overtake Toyota in terms of quality perceptions, recent trends show that American perceptions of Toyota's quality are climbing once more. The company's re-commitment to operational excellence is once again cementing its reputation for quality and continuous improvement.[40]

DISCUSSION QUESTIONS

1. Describe how Toyota's just-in-time management principles contribute to quality.
2. Why is empowering employees to look for ways to continuously improve operations so effective for Toyota?
3. Why do you think Toyota's reputation is recovering so quickly after the recalls?

Remember to check out our Online Learning Center at www.mhhe.com/ferrell9e.

Team Exercise

Form groups and assign the responsibility of finding companies that outsource their production to other countries. What are the key advantages of this outsourcing decision? Do you see any drawbacks or weaknesses in this approach? Why would a company not outsource when such a tactic can be undertaken to cut manufacturing costs? Report your findings to the class.

part 4

Creating the Human Resource Advantage

Introduction

Because employees do the actual work of the business and influence whether the firm achieves its objectives, most top managers agree that employees are an organization's most valuable resource. To achieve organizational objectives, employees must have the motivation, ability (appropriate knowledge and skills), and tools (proper training and equipment) to perform their jobs. Chapter 10 covers topics related to managing human resources, such as those listed earlier. This chapter focuses on how to motivate employees.

We examine employees' needs and motivation, managers' views of workers, and several strategies for motivating employees. Managers who understand the needs of their employees can help them reach higher levels of productivity and thus contribute to the achievement of organizational goals.

LO 9-1

human relations
the study of the behavior of individuals and groups in organizational settings

motivation
an inner drive that directs a person's behavior toward goals

Nature of Human Relations

What motivates employees to perform on the job is the focus of **human relations,** the study of the behavior of individuals and groups in organizational settings. In business, human relations involves motivating employees to achieve organizational objectives efficiently and effectively. The field of human relations has become increasingly important over the years as businesses strive to understand how to boost workplace morale, maximize employees' productivity and creativity, and motivate their ever more diverse employees to be more effective.

Motivation is an inner drive that directs a person's behavior toward goals. A goal is the satisfaction of some need, and a need is the difference between a desired state and an actual state. Both needs and goals can be motivating. Motivation explains why people behave as they do; similarly, a lack of motivation explains, at times, why people avoid doing what they should do. Motivating employees to do the wrong things or for the wrong reasons can be problematic, however. Encouraging employees to take excessive risks through high compensation, for example, led to the downfall of AIG and most major U.S. banks. Also, encouraging employees to lie to customers or to create false documentation is unethical and could even have legal ramifications. A person who recognizes or feels a need is motivated to take action to satisfy the need and achieve a goal (Figure 9.1). Consider a person who takes a job as a salesperson. If his or her performance is far below other salespeople's, he or she will likely recognize a need to increase sales. To satisfy that need and achieve success, the person may try to acquire new insights from successful salespeople or obtain additional training to improve sales skills. In addition, a sales manager might try different means to motivate the salesperson

Many companies offer onsite day care as a benefit for employees who have children. Company benefits such as these tend to increase employee satisfaction and motivation.

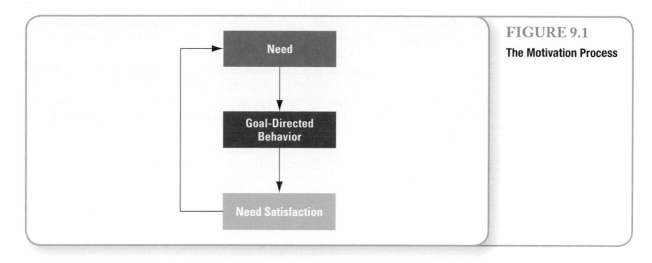

FIGURE 9.1

The Motivation Process

to work harder and to improve his or her skills. Human relations is concerned with the needs of employees, their goals and how they try to achieve them, and the impact of those needs and goals on job performance.

Effectively motivating employees helps keep them engaged in their work. Engagement involves emotional involvement and commitment. Being engaged results in carrying out the expectations and obligations of employment. Many employees are actively engaged in their jobs, while others are not. Some employees do the minimum amount of work required to get by, and some employees are completely disengaged. Motivating employees to stay engaged is a key responsibility of management. For example, to test if his onsite production managers were fully engaged in their jobs, former Van Halen frontman David Lee Roth placed a line in the band's rider asking for a bowl of M&Ms with the brown ones removed. It was a means for the band to test local stage production crews' attention to detail. Because their shows were highly technical, David Lee Roth would demand a complete recheck of everything if he found brown M&Ms in the bowl.[2]

One prominent aspect of human relations is **morale**—an employee's attitude toward his or her job, employer, and colleagues. High morale contributes to high levels of productivity, high returns to stakeholders, and employee loyalty. Conversely, low morale may cause high rates of absenteeism and turnover (when employees quit or are fired and must be replaced by new employees). Google recognizes the value of happy, committed employees and strives to engage in practices that will minimize turnover. Employees have the opportunity to have a massage every other week; onsite laundry service; free all-you-can-eat gourmet meals and snacks; and the "20% a week" rule, which allows engineers to work on whatever project they want for one day each week.[3]

Employees are motivated by their perceptions of extrinsic and intrinsic rewards. An **intrinsic reward** is the personal satisfaction and enjoyment that you feel from attaining a goal. For example, in this class you may feel personal enjoyment in learning how business works and aspire to have a

morale
an employee's attitude toward his or her job, employer, and colleagues

intrinsic rewards
the personal satisfaction and enjoyment felt after attaining a goal

Even small symbols of recognition, such as an "Employee of the Month" parking space, can serve as strong motivators for employees.

extrinsic rewards
benefits and/or recognition
received from someone else

career in business or to operate your own business one day. **Extrinsic rewards** are benefits and/or recognition that you receive from someone else. In this class, your grade is extrinsic recognition of your efforts and success in the class. In business, praise and recognition, pay increases, and bonuses are extrinsic rewards. If you believe that your job provides an opportunity to contribute to society or the environment, then that aspect would represent an intrinsic reward. Both intrinsic and extrinsic rewards contribute to motivation that stimulates employees to do their best in contributing to business goals.

Respect, involvement, appreciation, adequate compensation, promotions, a pleasant work environment, and a positive organizational culture are all morale boosters. Table 9.1 lists some ways to retain good employees. Nike seeks to provide a comprehensive compensation and benefits package, which includes traditional elements such as medical, dental, vision, life and disability insurance, paid holidays and time off, sabbaticals, and team as well as individual compensation plans. More comprehensive benefits include employee discounts on Nike products, scholarships for children of employees, employee assistance plans, tuition assistance, group legal plans, and matching gift programs. At the Beaverton, Oregon, world headquarters, Nike employees may take advantage of onsite day care and fitness centers, onsite cafés and restaurants, an onsite hair and nail salon, discounted annual TriMet transit passes ($25 annual fee versus $600), and several other work/life resources.[5] Many companies offer a diverse array of benefits designed to improve the quality of employees' lives and increase their morale and satisfaction. Some of the "best companies to work for"

DID YOU KNOW? Absenteeism can cost a company as much as 36 percent of payroll.[4]

TABLE 9.1

Top 10 Ways to Retain Great Employees

1. Satisfied employees know clearly what is expected from them every day at work.

2. The quality of the supervision an employee receives is critical to employee retention.

3. The ability of the employee to speak his or her mind freely within the organization is another key factor in employee retention.

4. Talent and skill utilization is another environmental factor your key employees seek in your workplace.

5. The perception of fairness and equitable treatment is important in employee retention.

6. Employees must have the tools, time, and training necessary to do their jobs well—or they will move to an employer who provides them.

7. The best employees, those employees you want to retain, seek frequent opportunities to learn and grow in their careers, knowledge, and skill.

8. Take time to meet with new employees to learn about their talents, abilities, and skills. Meet with each employee periodically.

9. No matter the circumstances, never, never, ever threaten an employee's job or income.

10. Staff members must feel rewarded, recognized, and appreciated.

Source: Susan M. Heathfield, "Top Ten Ways to Retain Your Great Employees," About.com, http://humanresources.about.com/od/retention/a/more_retention.htm (accessed February 18, 2010).

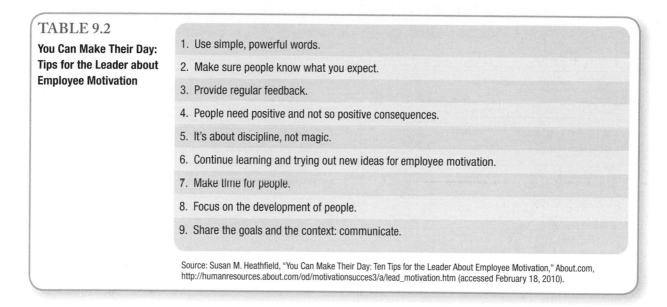

TABLE 9.2

You Can Make Their Day: Tips for the Leader about Employee Motivation

1. Use simple, powerful words.

2. Make sure people know what you expect.

3. Provide regular feedback.

4. People need positive and not so positive consequences.

5. It's about discipline, not magic.

6. Continue learning and trying out new ideas for employee motivation.

7. Make time for people.

8. Focus on the development of people.

9. Share the goals and the context: communicate.

Source: Susan M. Heathfield, "You Can Make Their Day: Ten Tips for the Leader About Employee Motivation," About.com, http://humanresources.about.com/od/motivationsucces3/a/lead_motivation.htm (accessed February 18, 2010).

offer onsite day care, concierge services (e.g., dry cleaning, shoe repair, prescription renewal), domestic partner benefits to same-sex couples, and fully paid sabbaticals. Table 9.2 offers suggestions as to how leaders can motivate employees on a daily basis.

Historical Perspectives on Employee Motivation

Throughout the 20th century, researchers have conducted numerous studies to try to identify ways to motivate workers and increase productivity. From these studies have come theories that have been applied to workers with varying degrees of success. A brief discussion of two of these theories—the classical theory of motivation and the Hawthorne studies—provides a background for understanding the present state of human relations.

LO 9-2

Classical Theory of Motivation

The birth of the study of human relations can be traced to time and motion studies conducted at the turn of the century by Frederick W. Taylor and Frank and Lillian Gilbreth. Their studies analyzed how workers perform specific work tasks in an effort to improve the employees' productivity. These efforts led to the application of scientific principles to management.

According to the **classical theory of motivation,** money is the sole motivator for workers. Taylor suggested that workers who were paid more would produce more, an idea that would benefit both companies and workers. To improve productivity, Taylor thought that managers should break down each job into its component tasks (specialization), determine the best way to perform each task, and specify the output to be achieved by a worker performing the task. Taylor also believed that incentives would motivate employees to be more productive. Thus, he suggested that managers link workers' pay directly to their output. He developed the piece-rate

classical theory of motivation
theory suggesting that money is the sole motivator for workers

system, under which employees were paid a certain amount for each unit they produced; those who exceeded their quota were paid a higher rate per unit for all the units they produced.

We can still see Taylor's ideas in practice today in the use of financial incentives for productivity. Moreover, companies are increasingly striving to relate pay to performance at both the hourly and managerial level. Incentive planners choose an individual incentive to motivate and reward their employees. In contrast, team incentives are used to generate partnership and collaboration to accomplish organizational goals. Boeing develops sales teams for most of its products, including commercial airplanes. The team dedicated to each product shares in the sales incentive program.

More and more corporations are tying pay to performance in order to motivate—even up to the CEO level. The topic of executive pay has become controversial in recent years, and many corporate boards of directors have taken steps to link executive compensation more closely to corporate performance. Despite these changes, many top executives still receive large compensation packages. John Hammergren, CEO of McKesson, is the highest paid executive, with $131.2 million in annual compensation.[7]

Like most managers of the early 20th century, Taylor believed that satisfactory pay and job security would motivate employees to work hard. However, later studies showed that other factors are also important in motivating workers.

The Hawthorne Studies

Elton Mayo and a team of researchers from Harvard University wanted to determine what physical conditions in the workplace—such as light and noise levels—would stimulate employees to be most productive. From 1924 to 1932, they studied a group of workers at the Hawthorne Works Plant of the Western Electric Company and measured their productivity under various physical conditions.

What the researchers discovered was quite unexpected and very puzzling: Productivity increased regardless of the physical conditions. This phenomenon has been labeled the Hawthorne effect. When questioned about their behavior, the employees expressed satisfaction because their co-workers in the experiments were friendly and, more importantly, because their supervisors had asked for their help and cooperation in the study. In other words, they were responding to the attention they received, not the changing physical work conditions. The researchers concluded that social and psychological factors could significantly affect productivity and morale. Medtronic, often called the "Microsoft of the medical-device industry," has a built-in psychological factor that influences employee morale. The company makes life-saving medical devices, such as pacemakers, neurostimulators, and stents. New hires at Medtronic receive medallions inscribed with a portion of the firm's mission statement, "alleviate pain, restore health, and extend life." There is an annual party where people whose bodies function thanks to Medtronic devices give testimonials. Obviously, Medtronic employees feel a sense of satisfaction in their jobs. Figure 9.2 indicates how employees value a healthy work/life balance.

Working conditions are important. However, the Hawthorne studies, which were carried out at the electric company shown here beginning in the 1920s, found that the workers became more productive because of the attention they received—regardless of their working conditions.

The Hawthorne experiments marked the beginning of a concern for human relations in the workplace. They revealed that human factors do influence workers' behavior and that managers who understand the needs, beliefs, and expectations of people have the greatest success in motivating their workers.

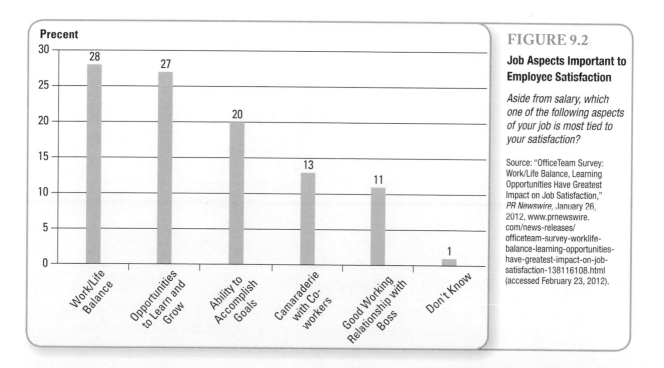

FIGURE 9.2

Job Aspects Important to Employee Satisfaction

Aside from salary, which one of the following aspects of your job is most tied to your satisfaction?

Source: "OfficeTeam Survey: Work/Life Balance, Learning Opportunities Have Greatest Impact on Job Satisfaction," *PR Newswire*, January 26, 2012, www.prnewswire.com/news-releases/officeteam-survey-worklife-balance-learning-opportunities-have-greatest-impact-on-job-satisfaction-138116108.html (accessed February 23, 2012).

Precent

Job Aspect	Percent
Work/Life Balance	28
Opportunities to Learn and Grow	27
Ability to Accomplish Goals	20
Camaraderie with Co-workers	13
Good Working Relationship with Boss	11
Don't Know	1

Theories of Employee Motivation

The research of Taylor, Mayo, and many others has led to the development of a number of theories that attempt to describe what motivates employees to perform. In this section, we will discuss some of the most important of these theories. The successful implementation of ideas based on these theories will vary, of course, depending on the company, its management, and its employees. It should be noted, too, that what worked in the past may no longer work today. Good managers must have the ability to adapt their ideas to an ever-changing, diverse group of employees.

Maslow's Hierarchy of Needs

Psychologist Abraham Maslow theorized that people have five basic needs: physiological, security, social, esteem, and self-actualization. **Maslow's hierarchy** arranges these needs into the order in which people strive to satisfy them (Figure 9.3).

   Physiological needs, the most basic and first needs to be satisfied, are the essentials for living—water, food, shelter, and clothing. According to Maslow, humans devote all their efforts to satisfying physiological needs until they are met.

Maslow's hierarchy
a theory that arranges the five basic needs of people—physiological, security, social, esteem, and self-actualization—into the order in which people strive to satisfy them

LO 9-3

physiological needs
the most basic human needs to be satisfied— water, food, shelter, and clothing

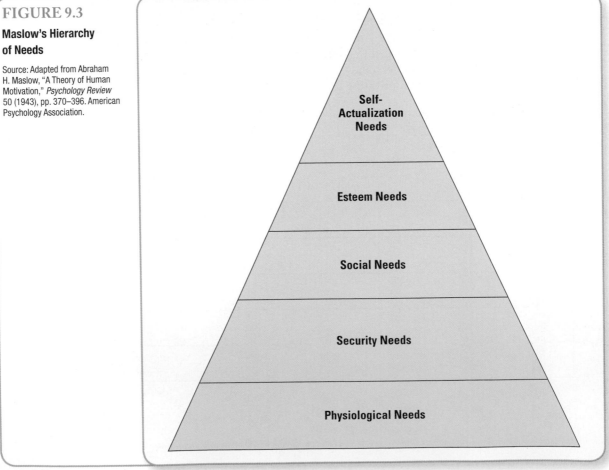

FIGURE 9.3

Maslow's Hierarchy of Needs

Source: Adapted from Abraham H. Maslow, "A Theory of Human Motivation," *Psychology Review* 50 (1943), pp. 370–396. American Psychology Association.

Self-Actualization Needs

Esteem Needs

Social Needs

Security Needs

Physiological Needs

Only when these needs are met can people focus their attention on satisfying the next level of needs—security.

Security needs relate to protecting yourself from physical and economic harm. Actions that may be taken to achieve security include reporting a dangerous workplace condition to management, maintaining safety equipment, and purchasing insurance with income protection in the event you become unable to work. Once security needs have been satisfied, people may strive for social goals.

Social needs are the need for love, companionship, and friendship—the desire for acceptance by others. To fulfill social needs, a person may try many things: making friends with a co-worker, joining a group, volunteering at a hospital, throwing a party. Once their social needs have been satisfied, people attempt to satisfy their need for esteem.

Esteem needs relate to respect—both self-respect and respect from others. One aspect of esteem needs is competition—the need to feel that you can do something better than anyone else. Competition often motivates people to increase their productivity. Esteem needs are not as easily satisfied as the needs at lower levels in Maslow's hierarchy because they do not always provide tangible evidence of success. However, these needs can be realized through rewards and increased involvement in organizational activities. Until esteem needs are met, people focus their attention on achieving respect. When they feel they have achieved some measure of respect, self-actualization becomes the major goal of life.

Self-actualization needs, at the top of Maslow's hierarchy, mean being the best you can be. Self-actualization involves maximizing your potential. A self-actualized person feels that she or he is living life to its fullest in every way. For Stephen King, self-actualization might mean being praised as the best fiction writer in the world; for actress Halle Berry, it might mean winning an Oscar.

Maslow's theory maintains that the more basic needs at the bottom of the hierarchy must be satisfied before higher-level goals can be pursued. Thus, people who are hungry and homeless are not concerned with obtaining respect from their colleagues. Only when physiological, security, and social needs have been more or less satisfied do people seek esteem. Maslow's theory also suggests that if a low-level need is suddenly reactivated, the individual will try to satisfy that need rather than higher-level needs. Many laid off workers probably shift their focus from high-level esteem needs to the need for security. When U.S. unemployment reached 10 percent during the last recession and the job market appeared increasingly insecure, many employees, particularly those in manufacturing, banking, and finance, felt they had to shift their focus back to security needs. Managers should learn from Maslow's hierarchy that employees will be motivated to contribute to organizational goals only if they are able to first satisfy their physiological, security, and social needs through their work.

Herzberg's Two-Factor Theory

In the 1950s, psychologist Frederick Herzberg proposed a theory of motivation that focuses on the job and on the environment where work is done. Herzberg studied various factors relating to the job and their relation to employee motivation and concluded that they can be divided into hygiene factors and motivational factors (Table 9.3).

Hygiene factors, which relate to the work setting and not to the content of the work, include adequate wages, comfortable and safe working conditions, fair

security needs
the need to protect oneself from physical and economic harm

social needs
the need for love, companionship, and friendship—the desire for acceptance by others

esteem needs
the need for respect—both self-respect and respect from others

self-actualization needs
the need to be the best one can be; at the top of Maslow's hierarchy

Need help understanding Maslow's Hierachy?
http://bit.ly/FerrellQR9-1

hygiene factors
aspects of Herzberg's theory of motivation that focus on the work setting and not the content of the work; these aspects include adequate wages, comfortable and safe working conditions, fair company policies, and job security

TABLE 9.3	Hygiene Factors	Motivational Factors
Herzberg's Hygiene and Motivational Factors	Company policies	Achievement
	Supervision	Recognition
	Working conditions	Work itself
	Relationships with peers, supervisors, and subordinates	Responsibility
	Salary	Advancement
	Security	Personal growth

company policies, and job security. These factors do not necessarily motivate employees to excel, but their absence may be a potential source of dissatisfaction and high turnover. Employee safety and comfort are clearly hygiene factors.

Many people feel that a good salary is one of the most important job factors, even more important than job security and the chance to use one's mind and abilities. Salary and security, two of the hygiene factors identified by Herzberg, make it possible for employees to satisfy the physiological and security needs identified by Maslow. However, the presence of hygiene factors is unlikely to motivate employees to work harder. For example, many people do not feel motivated to pursue a career as a gastroenterologist (doctors who specialize in the digestive system). Although the job is important and pays more than $250,000 on average, the tasks are routine and most patients are not looking forward to their appointments.[8]

motivational factors
aspects of Herzberg's theory of motivation that focus on the content of the work itself; these aspects include achievement, recognition, involvement, responsibility, and advancement

Motivational factors, which relate to the content of the work itself, include achievement, recognition, involvement, responsibility, and advancement. The absence of motivational factors may not result in dissatisfaction, but their presence is likely to motivate employees to excel. Many companies are beginning to employ methods to give employees more responsibility and control and to involve them more in their work, which serves to motivate them to higher levels of productivity and quality. L.L. Bean employees have tremendous latitude to satisfy customer's needs. One employee drove 500 miles from Maine to New York to deliver a canoe to a customer who was leaving on a trip. L.L. Bean is one of the top 25 companies on *BusinessWeek*'s list of "Customer Service Champs." L.L. Bean also ranks high in employee satisfaction. When the company decided to close down a call center, L.L. Bean allowed the call-center employees to act as home-based agents rather than laying them off and outsourcing the work. Besides empowering employees, the company has strict service training, answering every call within 20 seconds.[9]

The *Dirty Jobs* television series recognizes individuals who take on society's undesirable, but essential, jobs.

Herzberg's motivational factors and Maslow's esteem and self-actualization needs are similar. Workers' low-level needs (physiological and security) have largely been satisfied by minimum-wage laws and occupational-safety standards set by various government agencies and are therefore not motivators. Consequently, to improve productivity, management should focus on satisfying workers' higher-level needs (motivational factors) by providing opportunities for achievement, involvement, and advancement and by recognizing good performance.

McGregor's Theory X and Theory Y

In *The Human Side of Enterprise,* Douglas McGregor related Maslow's ideas about personal needs to management. McGregor contrasted two views of management—the traditional view, which he called Theory X, and a humanistic view, which he called Theory Y.

LO 9-4

According to McGregor, managers adopting **Theory X** assume that workers generally dislike work and must be forced to do their jobs. They believe that the following statements are true of workers:

Theory X
McGregor's traditional view of management whereby it is assumed that workers generally dislike work and must be forced to do their jobs

1. The average person naturally dislikes work and will avoid it when possible.
2. Most workers must be coerced, controlled, directed, or threatened with punishment to get them to work toward the achievement of organizational objectives.
3. The average worker prefers to be directed and to avoid responsibility, has relatively little ambition, and wants security.[10]

Managers who subscribe to the Theory X view maintain tight control over workers, provide almost constant supervision, try to motivate through fear, and make decisions in an autocratic fashion, eliciting little or no input from their subordinates. The Theory X style of management focuses on physiological and security needs and virtually ignores the higher needs discussed by Maslow. Foxconn, a manufacturing company that creates components for tech products such as the Apple iPad, is a company that had adopted the Theory X perspective. In China, Foxconn workers live in crowded dorms and often work more than 60 hours per week.

The Theory X view of management does not take into account people's needs for companionship, esteem, and personal growth, whereas Theory Y, the contrasting view of management, does. Managers subscribing to the **Theory Y** view assume that workers like to work and that under proper conditions employees will seek out responsibility in an attempt to satisfy their social, esteem, and self-actualization needs. McGregor describes the assumptions behind Theory Y in the following way:

Theory Y
McGregor's humanistic view of management whereby it is assumed that workers like to work and that under proper conditions employees will seek out responsibility in an attempt to satisfy their social, esteem, and self-actualization needs

1. The expenditure of physical and mental effort in work is as natural as play or rest.
2. People will exercise self-direction and self-control to achieve objectives to which they are committed.
3. People will commit to objectives when they realize that the achievement of those goals will bring them personal reward.
4. The average person will accept and seek responsibility.
5. Imagination, ingenuity, and creativity can help solve organizational problems, but most organizations do not make adequate use of these characteristics in their employees.
6. Organizations today do not make full use of workers' intellectual potential.[11]

Entrepreneurship in Action

Namasté Solar Embraces Employee Democracy Model of Management

Blake Jones, Wes Kennedy, and Ray Tuomey
Business: Namasté Solar
Founded: 2005, in Boulder, Colorado
Success: Namasté Solar has motivated employees to help the company achieve $20 million in annual revenues.

At Namasté Solar, CEO Blake Jones's ideas can easily be shot down by employees. And this is the way he designed it. Jones became disillusioned with power inequality in business. So when he got together with his co-founders to construct a solar energy technology firm, Jones wanted to adopt a model in which employees and managers were equal. To make this into a reality, Namasté Solar gives employees the right to purchase stock in the company, has an equal pay scale for all employees, allows six-week paid vacations, and embraces what it calls FOH—frank, open, honest communication—to encourage collaboration and discourage gossip. Each employee who owns stock (priced at about $5,000 a share) gets one vote in the company decision-making process, with about 70 percent of employees owning stock. This flat structure means that decisions are usually arrived at through employee consensus. Although board members tackle some major decisions, employees elect the board members for one- to two-year terms. At Namasté Solar, employees truly have a voice in all business operations.[12]

Obviously, managers subscribing to the Theory Y philosophy have a management style very different from managers subscribing to the Theory X philosophy. Theory Y managers maintain less control and supervision, do not use fear as the primary motivator, and are more democratic in decision making, allowing subordinates to participate in the process. Theory Y managers address the high-level needs in Maslow's hierarchy as well as physiological and security needs. For instance, Google is one well-known example of a company that has adopted the Theory Y philosophy. From its famous employee perks to the 20 percent time it gives its employees to pursue company projects they find interesting, Google believes that its employees are motivated and creative enough to significantly profit the company.[13] Today, Theory Y enjoys widespread support and may have displaced Theory X.

Theory Z

Theory Z
a management philosophy that stresses employee participation in all aspects of company decision making

Theory Z is a management philosophy that stresses employee participation in all aspects of company decision making. It was first described by William Ouchi in his book *Theory Z—How American Business Can Meet the Japanese Challenge.* Theory Z incorporates many elements associated with the Japanese approach to management, such as trust and intimacy, but Japanese ideas have been adapted for use in the United States. In a Theory Z organization, managers and workers share responsibilities; the management style is participative; and employment is long term and often lifelong. Japan has faced a significant period of slowing economic progress and competition from China and other Asian nations. This has led to experts questioning Theory Z, particularly at firms such as Sony and Toyota. Theory Z results in employees feeling organizational ownership. Research has found that such feelings of ownership may produce positive attitudinal and behavioral effects for employees.[14] In a Theory Y organization, managers focus on assumptions about the nature of the worker. The two theories can be seen as complementary. Table 9.4 compares the traditional American management style, the Japanese management style, and Theory Z (the modified Japanese management style).

Variations on Theory Z

Theory Z has been adapted and modified for use in a number of U.S. companies. One adaptation involves workers in decisions through quality circles. Quality circles

TABLE 9.4   Comparison of American, Japanese, and Theory Z Management Styles

	American	Japanese	Theory Z
Duration of employment	Relatively short term; workers subject to layoffs when business slows	Lifelong; no layoffs	Long term; layoffs rare
Rate of promotion	Rapid	Slow	Slow
Amount of specialization	Considerable; worker develops expertise in one area only	Minimal; worker develops expertise in all aspects of the organization	Moderate; worker learns all aspects of the organization
Decision making	Individual	Consensual; input from all concerned parties is considered	Consensual; emphasis on quality
Responsibility	Assigned to the individual	Shared by the group	Assigned to the individual
Control	Explicit and formal	Less explicit and less formal	Informal but with explicit performance measures
Concern for workers	Focus is on work only	Focus extends to worker's whole life	Focus includes worker's life and family

Source: Adapted from William Ouchi, *Theory Z—How American Business Can Meet the Japanese Challenge*, p. 58. © 1981 by Addison-Wesley Publishing Company, Inc. Reprinted by permission of Perseus Books Publishers, a member of Perseus Books, LLC.

(also called quality-assurance teams) are small, usually having five to eight members who discuss ways to reduce waste, eliminate problems, and improve quality, communication, and work satisfaction. Such quality teams are a common technique for harnessing the knowledge and creativity of hourly employees to solve problems in companies. As Theory Z has questioned the use of quality circles, their prevalence has declined. Quality circles have been replaced with quality methods.

Quality circles are often modified and operate under names such as *participative management, employee involvement,* or *self-directed work teams.* Regardless of the term used to describe such programs, they strive to give employees more control over their jobs while making them more responsible for the outcome of their efforts. Such programs often organize employees into work teams of 5 to 15 members who are responsible for producing an entire product item. Team members are cross-trained and can therefore move from job to job within the team. Each team essentially manages itself and is responsible for its quality, scheduling, ordering and use of materials, and problem solving. Many firms have successfully employed work teams to boost morale, productivity, quality, and competitiveness.

Equity Theory

According to **equity theory,** how much people are willing to contribute to an organization depends on their assessment of the fairness, or equity, of the rewards they will receive in exchange. In a fair situation, a person receives rewards proportional to the contribution he or she makes to the organization. However, in practice, equity is a subjective notion. Each worker regularly develops a personal input-output ratio by taking stock of his or her contribution (inputs) to the organization in time, effort,

equity theory
an assumption that how much people are willing to contribute to an organization depends on their assessment of the fairness, or equity, of the rewards they will receive in exchange

skills, and experience and assessing the rewards (outputs) offered by the organization in pay, benefits, recognition, and promotions. The worker compares his or her ratio to the input-output ratio of some other person—a "comparison other," who may be a co-worker, a friend working in another organization, or an "average" of several people working in the organization. If the two ratios are close, the individual will feel that he or she is being treated equitably.

Let's say you have a high-school education and earn $25,000 a year. When you compare your input-output ratio with that of a co-worker who has a college degree and makes $35,000 a year, you will probably feel that you are being paid fairly. However, if you perceive that your personal input-output ratio is lower than that of your college-educated co-worker, you may feel that you are being treated unfairly and be motivated to seek change. Or if you learn that your co-worker who makes $35,000 has only a high-school diploma, you may feel cheated by your employer. To achieve equity, you could try to increase your outputs by asking for a raise or promotion. You could also try to have your co-worker's inputs increased or his or her outputs decreased. Failing to achieve equity, you may be motivated to look for a job at a different company.

Equity theory might explain why many consumers are upset about CEO compensation. Although the job of the CEO can be incredibly stressful, the fact that they take home millions in compensation, bonuses, and stock options has been questioned. The high unemployment rate coupled with the misconduct that occurred at some large corporations prior to the recession contributed largely to the Occupy Wall Street protests. To counter this perception of pay inequality, several corporations have now begun to tie CEO compensation with company performance. If the company performs poorly for the year, then firms such as Goldman Sachs will cut bonuses and other compensation.[15] While lower compensation rates might appease the general public, some companies are worried that lower pay might deter talented individuals from wanting to assume the position of CEO at their firms.

Because almost all the issues involved in equity theory are subjective, they can be problematic. Author David Callahan has argued that feelings of inequity may underlie some unethical or illegal behavior in business. For example, due to employee theft and shoplifting, Walmart experiences billions in inventory losses every year. Some employees may take company resources to restore what they perceive to be equity. Theft of company resources is a major ethical issue, based on a survey by the Ethics Resource Center.[16] Callahan believes that employees who do not feel they are being treated equitably may be motivated to equalize the situation by lying, cheating, or otherwise "improving" their pay, perhaps by stealing.[17] Managers should try to avoid equity problems by ensuring that rewards are distributed on the basis of performance and that all employees clearly understand the basis for their pay and benefits.

Expectancy Theory

expectancy theory
the assumption that motivation depends not only on how much a person wants something but also on how likely he or she is to get it

Psychologist Victor Vroom described **expectancy theory,** which states that motivation depends not only on how much a person wants something but also on the person's perception of how likely he or she is to get it. A person who wants something and has reason to be optimistic will be strongly motivated. For example, say you really want a promotion. And let's say because you have taken some night classes to improve your skills, and moreover, have just made a large, significant sale, you feel confident that you are qualified and able to handle the new position. Therefore, you are motivated to try to get the promotion. In contrast, if you do not believe you are likely to get what you want, you may not be motivated to try to get it, even though you really want it.

Strategies for Motivating Employees

Based on the various theories that attempt to explain what motivates employees, businesses have developed several strategies for motivating their employees and boosting morale and productivity. Some of these techniques include behavior modification and job design, as well as the already described employee involvement programs and work teams.

Your motivation depends not only on how much you want something, but how likely you believe you are to get it.

Behavior Modification

Behavior modification involves changing behavior and encouraging appropriate actions by relating the consequences of behavior to the behavior itself. The concept of behavior modification was developed by psychologist B. F. Skinner, who showed that there are two types of consequences that can modify behavior—reward and punishment. Skinner found that behavior that is rewarded will tend to be repeated, while behavior that is punished will tend to be eliminated. For example, employees who know that they will receive a bonus such as an expensive restaurant meal for making a sale over $2,000 may be more motivated to make sales. Workers who know they will be punished for being tardy are likely to make a greater effort to get to work on time.

However, the two strategies may not be equally effective. Punishing unacceptable behavior may provide quick results but may lead to undesirable long-term side effects, such as employee dissatisfaction and increased turnover. In general, rewarding appropriate behavior is a more effective way to modify behavior.

LO 9-5

behavior modification
changing behavior and encouraging appropriate actions by relating the consequences of behavior to the behavior itself

Job Design

Herzberg identified the job itself as a motivational factor. Managers have several strategies that they can use to design jobs to help improve employee motivation. These include job rotation, job enlargement, job enrichment, and flexible scheduling strategies.

Job Rotation.   **Job rotation** allows employees to move from one job to another in an effort to relieve the boredom that is often associated with job specialization. Businesses often turn to specialization in hopes of increasing productivity, but there is a negative side effect to this type of job design: Employees become bored and dissatisfied, and productivity declines. Job rotation reduces this boredom by allowing workers to undertake a greater variety of tasks and by giving them the opportunity to learn new skills. With job rotation, an employee spends a specified amount of time performing one job and then moves on to another, different job. The worker eventually returns to the initial job and begins the cycle again.

Job rotation is a good idea, but it has one major drawback. Because employees may eventually become bored with all the jobs in the cycle, job rotation does not

job rotation
movement of employees from one job to another in an effort to relieve the boredom often associated with job specialization

totally eliminate the problem of boredom. Job rotation is extremely useful, however, in situations where a person is being trained for a position that requires an understanding of various units in an organization. Eli Lilly is a strong believer in the benefits of job rotation. The company leaves employees in their current jobs and asks them to take on short-term assignments outside their field of expertise or interest. The results of the process have been positive, and Nokia is trying the same process with similar outcomes.[18] Many executive training programs require trainees to spend time learning a variety of specialized jobs. Job rotation is also used to cross-train today's self-directed work teams.

job enlargement
the addition of more tasks to a job instead of treating each task as separate

Job Enlargement.   **Job enlargement** adds more tasks to a job instead of treating each task as separate. Like job rotation, job enlargement was developed to overcome the boredom associated with specialization. The rationale behind this strategy is that jobs are more satisfying as the number of tasks performed by an individual increases. Employees sometimes enlarge, or craft, their jobs by noticing what needs to be done and then changing tasks and relationship boundaries to adjust. Individual orientation and motivation shape opportunities to craft new jobs and job relationships. Job enlargement strategies have been more successful in increasing job satisfaction than have job rotation strategies. IBM, AT&T, and Maytag are among the many companies that have used job enlargement to motivate employees.

job enrichment
the incorporation of motivational factors, such as opportunity for achievement, recognition, responsibility, and advancement, into a job

Job Enrichment.   **Job enrichment** incorporates motivational factors such as opportunity for achievement, recognition, responsibility, and advancement into a job. It gives workers not only more tasks within the job, but more control and authority over the job. Job enrichment programs enhance a worker's feeling of responsibility and provide opportunities for growth and advancement when the worker is able to take on the more challenging tasks. Hyatt Hotels Corporation and General Foods use job enrichment to improve the quality of work life for their employees. The potential benefits of job enrichment are great, but it requires careful planning and execution.

Flexible Scheduling Strategies.   Many U.S. workers work a traditional 40-hour workweek consisting of five 8-hour days with fixed starting and ending times. Facing problems of poor morale and high absenteeism as well as a diverse workforce with changing needs, many managers have turned to flexible scheduling strategies such as flextime, compressed workweeks, job sharing, part-time work, and telecommuting. A survey by CareerBuilder.com showed that 40 percent of working fathers were offered flexible work schedules versus 53 percent of working mothers.[19]

flextime
a program that allows employees to choose their starting and ending times, provided that they are at work during a specified core period

Flextime is a program that allows employees to choose their starting and ending times, as long as they are at work during a specified core period (Figure 9.4). It does not reduce the total number of hours that employees work; instead, it gives employees more flexibility in choosing which hours they work. A firm may specify that employees must be present from 10:00 a.m. to 3:00 p.m. One employee may choose to come in at 7:00 a.m. and leave at the end of the core time, perhaps to attend classes at a nearby college after work. Another employee, a mother who lives in the suburbs, may come in at 9:00 a.m. in order to have time to drop off her children at a day-care center and commute by public transportation to her job. Flextime provides many benefits, including improved ability to recruit and retain workers who wish to balance work and home life. Customers can be better served by allowing more coverage of customers over longer hours, workstations and facilities can be better utilized by staggering employee use, and rush hour traffic may be reduced. In addition,

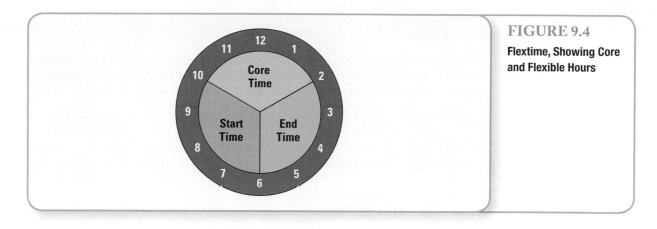

FIGURE 9.4

Flextime, Showing Core and Flexible Hours

flexible schedules have been associated with an increase in healthy behaviors on the part of employees. More flexible schedules are associated with healthier lifestyle choices such as increased physical activity and healthier sleep habits.[20]

Related to flextime are the scheduling strategies of the compressed workweek and job sharing. The **compressed workweek** is a four-day (or shorter) period in which an employee works 40 hours. Under such a plan, employees typically work 10 hours per day for four days and have a three-day weekend. The compressed workweek reduces the company's operating expenses because its actual hours of operation are reduced. It is also sometimes used by parents who want to have more days off to spend with their families. The U.S. Bureau of Labor Statistics notes that the following career options provide greater flexibility in scheduling: medical transcriptionist, financial manager, nurse, database administrator, accountant, software developer, physical therapist assistant, paralegal, graphic designer, and private investigator.[21]

Job sharing occurs when two people do one job. One person may work from 8:00 a.m. to 12:30 p.m.; the second person comes in at 12:30 p.m. and works until 5:00 p.m. Job sharing gives both people the opportunity to work as well as time to fulfill other obligations, such as parenting or school. With job sharing, the company has the benefit of the skills of two people for one job, often at a lower total cost for salaries and benefits than one person working eight hours a day would be paid.

Two other flexible scheduling strategies attaining wider use include allowing full-time workers to work part time for a certain period and allowing workers to work at home either full or part time. Employees at some firms may be permitted to work part time for several months in order to care for a new baby or an elderly parent or just to slow down for a little while to "recharge their batteries." When the employees return to full-time work, they are usually given a position comparable to their original full-time position. Other firms are allowing employees to telecommute or telework (work at home a few days of the week), staying connected via computers, modems, and telephones. Most

compressed workweek
a four-day (or shorter) period during which an employee works 40 hours

job sharing
performance of one full-time job by two people on part-time hours

REI, the outdoor-sporting company, encourages its workers to have a healthy work/life balance. Among other benefits, employees get paid to take a sabbatical after a number of years of service.

Responding to Business Challenges
Bad Moods Contribute to Decreased Productivity

There is no getting around it: Bad moods produce bad results. Employees who come to work unhappy tend to carry that unhappiness throughout the day. Until recently, just how much bad moods affect the work environment was not clear. However, a study by business professor Steffanie Wilk found that employees who start the day in a bad mood can see their productivity levels reduced more than 10 percent. Additionally, bad moods tend to be contagious, affecting other employees and customers and reducing the bottom line.

This does not bode well for companies in the current work climate. The Gallup-Healthways Well-Being Index reveals that American employees are becoming unhappier with their jobs. Much of this can be attributed to economic uncertainty. With businesses cutting back, employees are often expected to take on greater roles with fewer benefits. As a result, employees experience more dissatisfaction with their jobs and a less positive relationship with their employers.

The upshot is that managers can take steps to improve employees' moods in simple ways. Some companies offer very small incentives that make employees feel appreciated. CHG Healthcare Services, for instance, provides baskets of fruit for its employees every morning. 3M gives its employees time to pursue their own projects, an act that not only increases employee morale but has also yielded some of 3M's greatest product ideas. Employers might also encourage short periods of socialization among employees, which can improve moods and build cohesiveness. It seems like carrots, not sticks, are the key to creating a more productive work environment.[22]

Discussion Questions

1. Why might an uncertain economic climate contribute to decreased productivity?
2. Why do employee bad moods have such a negative effect on an organization?
3. What can employers do to improve the moods of its employees?

telecommuters tend to combine going into the office with working from home. Only about 2.8 million employees (not including entrepreneurs) cite the home as their primary workplace.[23]

Although many employees ask for the option of working at home to ease the responsibilities of caring for family members, some have discovered that they are more productive at home without the distractions of the workplace. An assessment of 12 company telecommuting programs, including Apple, AT&T, and the state of California, found that positive productivity changes occurred. Perhaps due to the positive morale that telecommuting can create, 82 percent of *Fortune*'s "100 Best Companies to Work For" allow their employees to telecommute at least part of the time.[24] Other employees, however, have discovered that they are not suited for working at home. For telecommuting to work, it must be a feasible alternative and must not create significant costs for the company.[25] Still, work-at-home programs do help reduce overhead costs for businesses. For example, some companies used to maintain a surplus of office space but have reduced the surplus through employee telecommuting, "hoteling" (being assigned to a desk through a reservation system), and "hot-desking" (several people using the same desk but at different times).

Companies are turning to flexible work schedules to provide more options to employees who are trying to juggle their work duties with other responsibilities and needs. Preliminary results indicate that flexible scheduling plans increase job satisfaction, which, in turn, leads to increases in productivity. Some recent research, however, has indicated there are potential problems with telecommuting. Some managers are reluctant to adopt the practice because the pace of change in today's workplace is faster than ever, and telecommuters may be left behind or actually cause managers more work in helping them stay abreast of changes. Some employers also worry that telecommuting workers create a security risk by creating more opportunities for computer hackers or equipment thieves. Some employees have found that working outside the office may hurt career advancement opportunities, and some report that instead of helping them balance work and family responsibilities, telecommuting increases the strain by blurring the barriers between the office and home. Co-workers call at all hours, and telecommuters are apt to continue to work when they are not supposed to (after regular business hours or during vacation time).

Importance of Motivational Strategies

Motivation is more than a tool that managers can use to foster employee loyalty and boost productivity. It is a process that affects all the relationships within an organization and influences many areas such as pay, promotion, job design, training opportunities, and reporting relationships. Employees are motivated by the nature of the

Businesses have come up with different ways to motivate employees, including rewards such as trophies and plaques to show the company's appreciation.

relationships they have with their supervisors, by the nature of their jobs, and by characteristics of the organization. Table 9.5 shows the top 10 companies in the *Fortune* 100 Best Companies to Work For, along with the types of strategies they use to motivate employees. Even the economic environment can change an employee's motivation. In a slow growth or recession economy, sales can flatten or decrease

Rank	Company	Motivational Strategies
1	Google	Employee perks such as bocce courts, free meals, and a bowling alley
2	Boston Consulting Group	Good pay, dedication toward recruitment
3	SAS Institute	Subsidized child care, sports leagues, free health care center
4	Wegmans Food Markets	Emphasis on employee well-being, successful smoking-cessation clinic
5	Edward Jones	No layoffs during the recession
6	Netapp	Generous pay and large bonuses
7	Camden Property Trust	Surprise bonuses
8	Recreational Equipment (REI)	Free equipment rentals and large merchandise discounts
9	CHG Healthcare Services	Employee suggestions incorporated into the firm, such as building a gym at the Fort Lauderdale office
10	Quicken Loans	Employee pride in company's efforts to revitalize downtown Detroit

TABLE 9.5

Best Companies to Work For

Source: "The 100 Best Companies to Work For," *Fortune*, February 6, 2012, pp. 117–27.

Learn the Terms

Check Your Progress

1. Why do managers need to understand the needs of their employees?

2. Describe the motivation process.

3. What was the goal of the Hawthorne studies? What was the outcome of those studies?

4. Explain Maslow's hierarchy of needs. What does it tell us about employee motivation?

5. What are Herzberg's hygiene and motivational factors? How can managers use them to motivate workers?

6. Contrast the assumptions of theory X and theory Y. Why has theory Y replaced theory X in management today?

7. What is theory Z? How can businesses apply theory Z to the workplace?

8. Identify and describe four job-design strategies.

9. Name and describe some flexible scheduling strategies. How can flexible schedules help motivate workers?

10. Why are motivational strategies important to both employees and employers?

Get Involved

1. Consider a person who is homeless: How would he or she be motivated and what actions would that person take? Use the motivation process to explain. Which of the needs in Maslow's hierarchy are likely to be most important? Least important?

2. View the video *Cheaper by the Dozen* (1950) and report on how the Gilbreths tried to incorporate their passion for efficiency into their family life.

3. What events and trends in society, technology, and economics do you think will shape human relations management theory in the future?

Build Your Skills

MOTIVATING

Background

Do you think that, if employers could make work more like play, employees would be as enthusiastic about their jobs as they are about what they do in their leisure time? Let's see where this idea might take us.

Task

After reading the "Characteristics of PLAY," place a √ in column one for those characteristics you have experienced in your leisure time activities. Likewise, check column three for those "Characteristics of WORK" you have experienced in any of the jobs you've held.

All That Apply	Characteristics of PLAY	All That Apply	Characteristics of WORK
	1. New games can be played on different days.		1. Job enrichment, job enlargement, or job rotation.
	2. Flexible duration of play.		2. Job sharing.
	3. Flexible time of when to play.		3. Flextime, telecommuting.
	4. Opportunity to express oneself.		4. Encourage and implement employee suggestions.
	5. Opportunity to use one's talents.		5. Assignment of challenging projects.
	6. Skillful play brings applause, praise, and recognition from spectators.		6. Employee-of-the-month awards, press releases, employee newsletter announcements.
	7. Healthy competition, rivalry, and challenge exist.		7. Production goals with competition to see which team does best.
	8. Opportunity for social interaction.		8. Employee softball or bowling teams.
	9. Mechanisms for scoring one's performance are available (feedback).		9. Profit sharing; peer performance appraisals.
	10. Rules ensure basic fairness and justice.		10. Use tactful and consistent discipline.

Discussion Questions

1. What prevents managers from making work more like play?

2. Are these forces real or imagined?

3. What would be the likely (positive and negative) results of making work more like play?

4. Could others in the organization accept such creative behaviors?

Solve the Dilemma   LO 9-6

MOTIVATING TO WIN

Eagle Pharmaceutical has long been recognized for its innovative techniques for motivating its salesforce. It features the salesperson who has been the most successful during the previous quarter in the company newsletter, "Touchdown." The salesperson also receives a football jersey, a plaque, and $1,000 worth of Eagle stock. Eagle's "Superbowl Club" is for employees who reach or exceed their sales goal, and a "Heisman Award," which includes a trip to the Caribbean, is given annually to the top 20 salespeople in terms of goal achievement.

Eagle employs a video conference hookup between the honored salesperson and four regional sales managers to capture some of the successful tactics and strategies the winning salesperson uses to succeed. The managers summarize these ideas and pass them along to the salespeople they manage. Sales managers feel strongly that programs such as this are important and that, by sharing strategies and tactics with one another, they can be a successful team.

Discussion Questions

1. Which motivational theories are in use at Eagle?

2. What is the value of getting employees to compete against a goal instead of against one another?

3. Put yourself in the shoes of one of the four regional sales managers and argue against potential cutbacks to the motivational program.

Theladders.com is a website that targets job seekers looking for jobs with an annual pay of $100,000 or more.

Internal sources of applicants include the organization's current employees. Many firms have a policy of giving first consideration to their own employees—or promoting from within. The cost of hiring current employees to fill job openings is inexpensive when compared with the cost of hiring from external sources, and it is good for employee morale. However, hiring from within creates another job vacancy to be filled.

External sources of applicants consist of advertisements in newspapers and professional journals, employment agencies, colleges, vocational schools, recommendations from current employees, competing firms, unsolicited applications, online websites, and social networking sites such as LinkedIn. Internships are also a good way to solicit for potential employees. Many companies hire college students or recent graduates to low-paying internships that give them the opportunity to get hands-on experience on the job. If the intern proves to be a good fit, an organization may then hire the intern as a full-time worker. There are also hundreds of websites where employers can post job openings and job seekers can post their résumés, including Monster.com, USAJobs, Simply Hired, SnagaJob, and CareerBuilder.com. Theladders.com is a website that focuses on jobs starting at $100,000 a year. It seeks higher educated and more experienced individuals for high-paying positions. Employers looking for employees for specialized jobs can use more focused sites such as computerwork.com. Increasingly, companies can turn to their own websites for potential candidates: Nearly all of the *Fortune* 500 firms provide career websites where they recruit, provide employment information, and take applications. Using these sources of applicants is generally more expensive than hiring from within, but it may be necessary if there are no current employees who meet the job specifications or there are better-qualified people outside of the organization. Recruiting for entry-level managerial and professional positions is often carried out on college and university campuses. For managerial or professional positions above the entry level, companies sometimes depend on employment agencies or executive search firms, sometimes called *headhunters,* which specialize in luring qualified people away from other companies. Employers are also increasingly using professional social networking sites such as LinkedIn and Viadeo as recruitment tools.

Selection

selection
the process of collecting information about applicants and using that information to make hiring decisions

Selection is the process of collecting information about applicants and using that information to decide which ones to hire. It includes the application itself, as well as interviewing, testing, and reference checking. This process can be quite lengthy and expensive. Procter & Gamble, for example, offers online applications for jobs in 80 countries. The first round of evaluation involves assessment, and if this stage goes well, the candidate interviews in the region or country to which the applicant applied.[3] Such rigorous scrutiny is necessary to find those applicants who can do the work expected and fit into the firm's structure and culture. If an organization finds the "right" employees through its recruiting and selection process, it will not have to spend as much money later in recruiting, selecting, and training replacement employees.

The Application.   In the first stage of the selection process, the individual fills out an application form and perhaps has a brief interview. The application form asks for the applicant's name, address, telephone number, education, and previous work experience. The goal of this stage of the selection process is to get acquainted with the applicants and to weed out those who are obviously not qualified for the

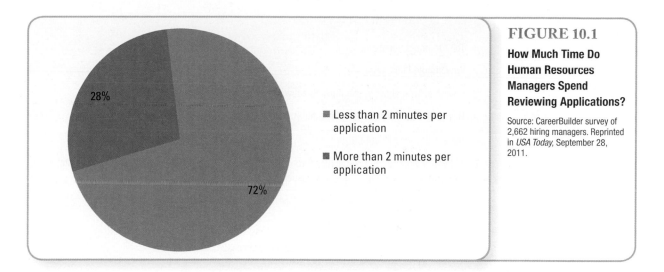

FIGURE 10.1

How Much Time Do Human Resources Managers Spend Reviewing Applications?

Source: CareerBuilder survey of 2,662 hiring managers. Reprinted in *USA Today,* September 28, 2011.

28%

72%

■ Less than 2 minutes per application

■ More than 2 minutes per application

job. Figure 10.1 indicates how much time human resources managers spend reviewing applications. For employees with work experience, most companies ask for the following information before contacting a potential candidate: current salary, reason for seeking a new job, years of experience, availability, and level of interest in the position. In addition to identifying obvious qualifications, the application can provide subtle clues about whether a person is appropriate for a particular job. For instance, an applicant who gives unusually creative answers may be perfect for a position at an advertising agency; a person who turns in a sloppy, hurriedly scrawled application probably would not be appropriate for a technical job requiring precise adjustments. Many companies now accept online applications. The online application for Target is designed not only to collect biographical data on the applicant, but also to create a picture of the applicant and how that person might contribute to the company. The completion of the survey takes about 15–45 minutes, depending on the position. To get a better view of the fit between the applicant and the company, the online application contains a questionnaire that asks applicants more specific questions, from how they might react in a certain situation to personality attributes like self-esteem or ability to interact with people.[4]

The Interview.   The next phase of the selection process involves interviewing applicants. Table 10.1 provides some insights on finding the right work environment. Interviews allow management to obtain detailed information about the applicant's

TABLE 10.1
Interviewing Tips

1. Evaluate the work environment. Do employees seem to get along and work well in teams?

2. Evaluate the attitude of employees. Are employees happy, tense, or overworked?

3. Are employees enthusiastic and excited about their work?

4. What is the organizational culture, and would you feel comfortable working there?

Source: Adapted from "What to Look for During Office Visits," http://careercenter.tamu.edu/guides/interviews/lookforinoffice.cfm?sn=parents (accessed April 23, 2012).

TABLE 10.2

Most Common Questions Asked during the Interview

1. Tell me about yourself.
2. Why should I hire you?
3. Please tell me about your future objectives.
4. Has your education prepared you for your career?
5. Have you been a team player?
6. Did you encounter any conflict with your previous professors or employer? What are the steps that you have taken to resolve this issue?
7. What is your biggest weakness?
8. How would your professors describe you?
9. What are the qualities that a manager should possess?
10. If you could turn back time, what would you change?

Source: "Job Interview Skills Training: Top Ten Interview Questions for College Graduates," February 17, 2010, www.articlesbase.com/business-articles/job-interview-skills-training-top-ten-interview-questions-for-college-graduates-1871741.html (accessed April 13, 2011).

TABLE 10.3

Mistakes Made in Interviewing

1. Not taking the interview seriously.
2. Not dressing appropriately (dressing down).
3. Not appropriately discussing experience, abilities, and education.
4. Being too modest about your accomplishments.
5. Talking too much.
6. Too much concern about compensation.
7. Speaking negatively of a former employer.
8. Not asking enough or appropriate questions.
9. Not showing the proper enthusiasm level.
10. Not engaging in appropriate follow-up to the interview.

Source: "Avoid the Top 10 Job Interview Mistakes," All Business, www.allbusiness.com/human-resources/careers-job-interview/1611-1.html (April 23, 2012).

experience and skills, reasons for changing jobs, attitudes toward the job, and an idea of whether the person would fit in with the company. Table 10.2 lists some of the most common questions asked by interviewers while Table 10.3 reveals some common mistakes candidates make in interviewing. Furthermore, the interviewer can answer the applicant's questions about the requirements for the job, compensation, working conditions, company policies, organizational culture, and so on. A potential employee's questions may be just as revealing as his or her answers. Today's students might be surprised to have an interviewer ask them, "What's on your Facebook account?" or have them show the interviewer their Facebook accounts. Currently, these are legal questions for an interviewer to ask.

Testing. Another step in the selection process is testing. Ability and performance tests are used to determine whether an applicant has the skills necessary for the job. Aptitude, IQ, or personality tests may be used to assess an applicant's potential for a certain kind of work and his or her ability to fit into the organization's culture. One of the most commonly used tests is the Myers-Briggs Type Indicator. Myers-Briggs Type Indicator Test is used worldwide by millions of people each year. Although polygraph ("lie detector") tests were once a common technique for evaluating the honesty of applicants, in 1988 their use was restricted to specific government jobs and those involving security or access to drugs. Applicants may also undergo physical examinations to determine their suitability for some jobs, and many companies require applicants to be screened for illegal drug use. Illegal drug use and alcoholism can be particularly damaging to businesses. It has been estimated that 8.4 percent of full-time employees engage in illicit drug use, while 29.7 percent engage in binge drinking and 8.5 percent are considered to be heavy drinkers.[5] Small businesses may have a higher percentage of these employees because they do not engage in systematic drug testing. If you employ a drug or alcohol abuser, you can expect a 33 percent loss in productivity from this employee. Loss in productivity from alcohol abuse alone costs companies $134 billion each year. Health care costs are also more expensive for those who abuse alcohol—twice as more than those for employees who do not abuse alcohol.[6]

Personality tests such as Myers-Brigg are used to assess an applicant's potential for a certain kind of job. For instance, extroversion and a love of people would be good qualities for a sales or retail job. Interestingly, there does not seem to be any difference between introversion and extroversion in making a good manager.

Because computer knowledge is a requirement for many jobs today, certain companies also require an applicant to take a typing test or tests to determine their knowledge of MS Word, Excel, PowerPoint, and/or other necessary programs. Like the application form and the interview, testing serves to eliminate those who do not meet the job specifications.

Reference Checking. Before making a job offer, the company should always check an applicant's references. Reference checking usually involves verifying educational background and previous work experience. An Internet search is often done to determine social media activities or other public activities. Until recently, the city of Bozeman, Montana, asked potential applicants for their passwords to their e-mail addresses and social networking sites. While public Internet searches are usually deemed acceptable, asking for private information—while legal—is deemed to be intrusive by many job seekers.[7] Public companies are likely to do more extensive background searches to make sure applicants are not misrepresenting themselves.

Accurate Background Inc. specializes in background checks. Background checks are important for detecting past misconduct or criminal activities committed by job applicants.

Background checking is important because applicants may misrepresent themselves on their applications or résumés. The star of *Dinner: Impossible* on the Food Network fabricated portions of his résumé, including the claim that he cooked for Britain's Royal Family. The Food Network, upon learning of these errors, did not renew Robert Irvine's contract, indicating that viewers place trust in the network and the accuracy of information that it provides and that Irvine "challenged that trust."[8] Irvine had to work for months to apologize and set the record straight about his chef credentials. Food Network ultimately did rehire him. As Table 10.4 illustrates, some of the most common types of résumé lies include the faking of credentials, overstatements of skills or accomplishments, lies concerning education/degrees, omissions of past employment, and the falsification of references.[9]

Reference checking is a vital, albeit often overlooked, stage in the selection process. Managers charged with hiring should be aware, however, that many organizations will confirm only that an applicant is a former employee, perhaps with beginning and ending work dates, and will not release details about the quality of the employee's work.

Legal Issues in Recruiting and Selecting

Legal constraints and regulations are present in almost every phase of the recruitment and selection process, and a violation of these regulations can result in lawsuits and fines. Therefore, managers should be aware of these restrictions to avoid legal problems. Some of the laws affecting human resources management are discussed here.

Title VII of the Civil Rights Act prohibits discrimination in employment and created the Equal Employment Opportunity Commission

Because one law pervades all areas of human resources management, we'll take a quick look at it now. **Title VII of the Civil Rights Act** of 1964 prohibits discrimination in employment. It also created the Equal Employment Opportunity Commission (EEOC), a federal agency dedicated to increasing job opportunities for women and minorities and eliminating job discrimination based on race, religion,

TABLE 10.4
Top 10 Résumé Lies

1. Stretching dates of employment
2. Inflating past accomplishments and skills
3. Enhancing job titles and responsibilities
4. Education exaggeration and fabricating degrees
5. Unexplained gaps and periods of "self employment"
6. Omitting past employment
7. Faking credentials
8. Fabricating reasons for leaving previous job
9. Providing fraudulent references
10. Misrepresenting military record

Source: Christopher T. Marquet and Lisa J. B. Peterson, "Résumé Fraud: The Top 10 Lies," www.marquetinternational.com/pdf/Resume%20Fraud-Top%20Ten%20Lies.pdf (accessed April 13, 2011).

color, sex, national origin, or handicap. As a result of Title VII, employers must not impose sex distinctions in job specifications, job descriptions, or newspaper advertisements. In 2011, workplace discrimination charges filed with the Equal Employment Opportunity Commission were 99,947—a record number. The EEOC received more than 11,000 charges of sexual harassment. Sexual harassment often makes up the largest number of claims the EEOC encounters each day.[10] The Civil Rights Act of 1964 also outlaws the use of discriminatory tests for applicants. Aptitude tests and other indirect tests must be validated; in other words, employers must be able to demonstrate that scores on such tests are related to job performance, so that no one race has an advantage in taking the tests or is alternatively discriminated against. Although many hope for improvements in organizational diversity, only 3.8 percent of *Fortune* 500 companies are run by people of color. Despite the low number, this is an improvement from the mid-1990s when no *Fortune* 500 company had a person of color as CEO. Additionally, 9.8 percent of board seats are now held by racial minorities.[11]

Other laws affecting HRM include the Americans with Disabilities Act (ADA), which prevents discrimination against disabled persons. It also classifies people with AIDS as handicapped and, consequently, prohibits using a positive AIDS test as reason to deny an applicant employment. The Age Discrimination in Employment Act specifically outlaws discrimination based on age. Its focus is banning hiring practices that discriminate against people 40 years and older. Generally, when companies need employees, recruiters head to college campuses, and when downsizing is necessary, many older workers are offered early retirement. Forced retirement based on age, however, is generally considered to be illegal in the United States, although claims of forced retirement still abound. Until recently, employees in the United Kingdom could be forced to retire at age 65. However, a new law abolished the default retirement age.[12] Indeed there are many benefits that companies are realizing in hiring older workers. Some of these benefits include the fact that they are more dedicated, punctual, honest, and detail-oriented; are good listeners; take pride in their work; exhibit good organizational skills; are efficient and confident; are mature; can be seen as role models; have good communication skills; and offer an opportunity for a reduced labor cost because of already having insurance plans.[13] Figure 10.2 shows that while the hiring of older workers has increased in the past few years, the hiring of younger workers has decreased.

The Equal Pay Act mandates that men and women who do equal work must receive the same wage. Wage differences are acceptable only if they are attributed to seniority, performance, or qualifications. In the United States, the typical full-time female employee earns 19 percent less than the average full-time male employee. In a study by PayScale, some of the biggest gender pay gaps can be found in positions such as chief executive (women earn 71 percent of what men earn), hospital administrator (women earn 77 percent of what men earn), and chief operating officer (women earn 80 percent of what men earn). Performance quality in these jobs is relatively subjective. Jobs like engineers, actuaries, or electricians, where the performance evaluation is more objective, result in greater salary parity between men and women.[14] However, despite the wage inequalities that still exist, women in the workplace are becoming increasingly accepted among both genders. The working mother is no longer a novelty; in fact, many working mothers seek the same amount of achievement as working men and women who are not mothers. Figure 10.3 shows the percentage of women who hold some of the country's top leadership positions.

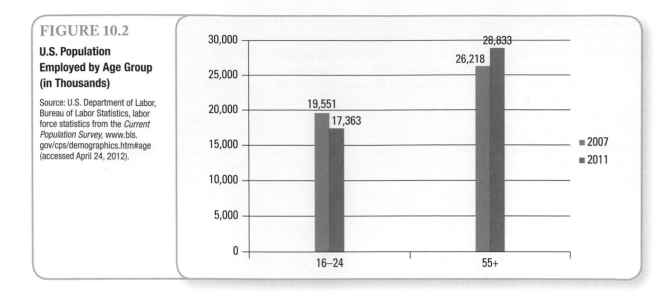

FIGURE 10.2

U.S. Population Employed by Age Group (in Thousands)

Source: U.S. Department of Labor, Bureau of Labor Statistics, labor force statistics from the *Current Population Survey,* www.bls.gov/cps/demographics.htm#age (accessed April 24, 2012).

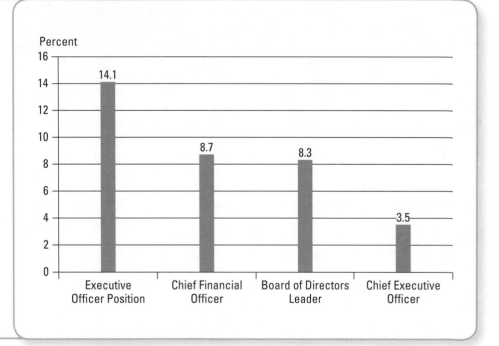

FIGURE 10.3

Women Leaders at *Furtune* 500 Companies

Sources: Catalyst®, *Women on Boards,* 2012, www.catalyst.org/file/589/qt_women_on_boards.pdf (accessed April 4, 2012); Catalyst®, *Women on Financial Services,* 2012, www.catalyst.org/file/577/qt_women_in_financial_services.pdf (accessed April 4, 2012); Catalyst®, "Women CEOs of the Fortune 1000," March 2012, www.catalyst.org/publication/271/women-ceos-of-the-fortune-1000 (accessed April 4, 2012); Rachel Soares, Baye Cobb, Ellen Lebow, Allyson Regis, Hannah Winsten, and Veronica Wojnas, "2011 Catalyst Census: Fortune 500 Women Executive Officers and Top Earners," Catalyst®, December 2011, www.catalyst.org/publication/516/2011-catalyst-census-fortune-500-women-executive-officers-and-top-earners (accessed April 4, 2012).

Developing the Workforce

Once the most qualified applicants have been selected, have been offered positions, and have accepted their offers, they must be formally introduced to the organization and trained so they can begin to be productive members of the workforce. **Orientation** familiarizes the newly hired employees with fellow workers, company procedures, and the physical properties of the company. It generally includes a tour of the building; introductions to supervisors, co-workers, and subordinates; and

orientation
familiarizing newly hired employees with fellow workers, company procedures, and the physical properties of the company

the distribution of organizational manuals describing the organization's policy on vacations, absenteeism, lunch breaks, company benefits, and so on. Orientation also involves socializing the new employee into the ethics and culture of the new company. Many larger companies now show videotapes of procedures, facilities, and key personnel in the organization to help speed the adjustment process.

Training and Development

Although recruiting and selection are designed to find employees who have the knowledge, skills, and abilities the company needs, new employees still must undergo **training** to learn how to do their specific job tasks. *On-the-job training* allows workers to learn by actually performing the tasks of the job, while *classroom training* teaches employees with lectures, conferences, videotapes, case studies, and web-based training. For instance, McDonald's trains those interested in company operations and leadership development at the Fred L. Turner Training Center, otherwise known as Hamburger University. Hamburger University employs full-time professors to train students in a variety of topics, including crew development, restaurant management, middle management, and executive development. Training includes classroom instruction, hands-on instruction, and computer e-learning.[15]

Development is training that augments the skills and knowledge of managers and professionals. Training and development are also used to improve the skills of employees in their present positions and to prepare them for increased responsibility and job promotions. Training is therefore a vital function of human resources management. At the Container Store, for example, first-year sales personnel receive 263 hours of training about the company's products.[16] Companies are engaging in more experiential and involvement-oriented training exercises for employees. Use of role-plays, simulations, and online training methods are becoming increasingly popular in employee training.

Assessing Performance

Assessing an employee's performance—his or her strengths and weaknesses on the job—is one of the most difficult tasks for managers. However, performance appraisal is crucial because it gives employees feedback on how they are doing and what they need to do to improve. It also provides a basis for determining how to compensate and reward employees, and it generates information about the quality of the firm's selection, training, and development activities. Table 10.5 identifies 16 characteristics that may be assessed in a performance review.

Performance appraisals may be objective or subjective. An objective assessment is quantifiable. For example, a Westinghouse employee might be judged by how many circuit boards he typically

LO 10-3

training
teaching employees to do specific job tasks through either classroom development or on-the-job experience

development
training that augments the skills and knowledge of managers and professionals

McDonald's has expanded its famous Hamburger University into China. This branch of Hamburger University will train a new generation of Chinese students in such areas as restaurant management, leadership development, and other skills.

TABLE 10.5

Performance Characteristics

- **Productivity**—rate at which work is regularly produced
- **Quality**—accuracy, professionalism, and deliverability of produced work
- **Job knowledge**—understanding of the objectives, practices, and standards of work
- **Problem solving**—ability to identify and correct problems effectively
- **Communication**—effectiveness in written and verbal exchanges
- **Initiative**—willingness to identify and address opportunities for improvement
- **Adaptability**—ability to become comfortable with change
- **Planning and organization skills**—reflected through the ability to schedule projects, set goals, and maintain organizational systems
- **Teamwork and cooperation**—effectiveness of collaborations with co-workers
- **Judgment**—ability to determine appropriate actions in a timely manner
- **Dependability**—responsiveness, reliability, and conscientiousness demonstrated on the job
- **Creativity**—extent to which resourceful ideas, solutions, and methods for task completion are proposed
- **Sales**—demonstrated through success in selling products, services, yourself, and your company
- **Customer service**—ability to communicate effectively with customers, address problems, and offer solutions that meet or exceed their expectations
- **Leadership**—tendency and ability to serve as a doer, guide, decision maker, and role model
- **Financial management**—appropriateness of cost controls and financial planning within the scope defined by the position

Source: "Performance Characteristics," Performance Review from www.salary.com/Careerresources/docs/related_performance_review_part2_popup.html (accessed June 12, 2001). Used with permission.

produces in one day or by how many of his boards have defects. A Century 21 real estate agent might be judged by the number of houses she has shown or the number of sales she has closed. A company can also use tests as an objective method of assessment. Whatever method they use, managers must take into account the work environment when they appraise performance objectively.

When jobs do not lend themselves to objective appraisal, the manager must relate the employee's performance to some other standard. One popular tool used in subjective assessment is the ranking system, which lists various performance factors on which the manager ranks employees against each other. Although used by many large companies, ranking systems are unpopular with many employees. Qualitative criteria, such as teamwork and communication skills, used to evaluate employees are generally hard to gauge. Such grading systems have triggered employee lawsuits that allege discrimination in grade/ranking assignments. For example, one manager may grade a company's employees one way, while another manager grades a group more harshly depending on the managers' grading style. If layoffs occur, then employees graded by the second manager may be more likely to lose their jobs. Other criticisms of grading systems include unclear wording or inappropriate words that a manager may unintentionally write in a performance evaluation, like *young* or *pretty* to describe an employee's appearance. These liabilities can all be fodder for lawsuits should employees allege that they were treated unfairly. It is therefore crucial that managers use clear language in performance evaluations and be consistent with all employees. Several employee grading computer packages have been developed to make performance evaluations easier for managers and clearer for employees.[17]

Another performance appraisal method used by many companies is the 360-degree feedback system, which provides feedback from a panel that typically includes superiors, peers, and subordinates. Because of the tensions it may cause, peer appraisal appears to be difficult for many. However, companies that have success with 360-degree feedback tend to be open to learning and willing to experiment and are

Amazon holds a job fair in the virtual world Second Life. Companies have started using digital media for posting job applications, holding job fairs, and even training employees.

led by executives who are direct about the expected benefits as well as the challenges.[18] Managers and leaders with a high emotional intelligence (sensitivity to their own as well as others' emotions) assess and reflect upon their interactions with colleagues on a daily basis. In addition, they conduct follow-up analysis on their projects, asking the right questions and listening carefully to responses without getting defensive of their actions.[19]

Whether the assessment is objective or subjective, it is vital that the manager discuss the results with the employee, so that the employee knows how well he or she is doing the job. The results of a performance appraisal become useful only when they are communicated, tactfully, to the employee and presented as a tool to allow the employee to grow and improve in his or her position and beyond. Performance appraisals are also used to determine whether an employee should be promoted, transferred, or terminated from the organization.

Turnover

Turnover, which occurs when employees quit or are fired and must be replaced by new employees, results in lost productivity from the vacancy, costs to recruit replacement employees, management time devoted to interviewing, training, and socialization expenses for new employees. However, some companies have created innovative solutions for reducing turnover. After learning that its employees felt micromanaged, Best Buy implemented a system for some of its employees called Results Only Work Environment (ROWE) to reduce turnover and increase employee morale. Under this program, employees who were able to do their work away from the workplace could choose to do so. The initiative offered flexibility and a better work/life balance for employees. A study that analyzed the impact that ROWE had upon employee turnover found that turnover had decreased by 45 percent.[20] Part of the reason for turnover may be overworked employees as a result of downsizing and a lack of training and advancement opportunities.[21] Figure 10.4 provides some of the top reasons employees give for leaving the company. Of course, turnover is not always an unhappy occasion when its takes the form of a promotion or transfer.

LO 10-4

turnover
occurs when employees quit or are fired and must be replaced by new employees

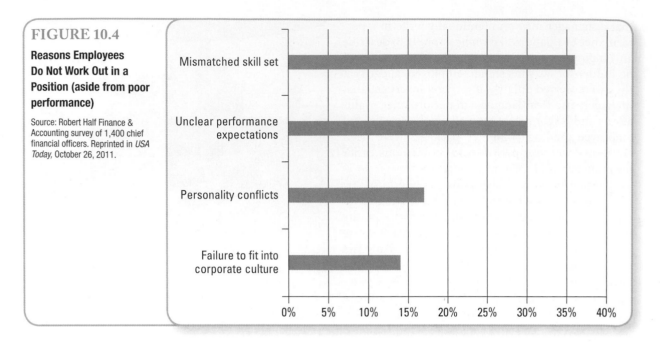

FIGURE 10.4

Reasons Employees Do Not Work Out in a Position (aside from poor performance)

Source: Robert Half Finance & Accounting survey of 1,400 chief financial officers. Reprinted in *USA Today,* October 26, 2011.

promotion
an advancement to a higher-level job with increased authority, responsibility, and pay

transfer
a move to another job within the company at essentially the same level and wage

A **promotion** is an advancement to a higher-level job with increased authority, responsibility, and pay. In some companies and most labor unions, seniority—the length of time a person has been with the company or at a particular job classification—is the key issue in determining who should be promoted. Most managers base promotions on seniority only when they have candidates with equal qualifications: Managers prefer to base promotions on merit.

A **transfer** is a move to another job within the company at essentially the same level and wage. Transfers allow workers to obtain new skills or to find a new position within an organization when their old position has been eliminated because of automation or downsizing.

Separations occur when employees resign, retire, are terminated, or are laid off. Employees may be terminated, or fired, for poor performance, violation of work rules, absenteeism, and so on. Businesses have traditionally been able to fire employees *at will,* that is, for any reason other than for race, religion, sex, or age, or because an employee is a union organizer. However, recent legislation and court decisions now require that companies fire employees fairly, for just cause only. Managers must take care, then, to warn employees when their performance is unacceptable and may lead to dismissal, elevating the importance of performance evaluations. They should also document all problems and warnings in employees' work records. To avoid the possibility of lawsuits from individuals who may feel they have been fired unfairly, employers should provide clear, business-related reasons for any firing, supported by written documentation if possible. Employee disciplinary procedures should be carefully explained to all employees and should be

Many companies in recent years are choosing to downsize by eliminating jobs. Reasons for downsizing might be due to financial constraints or the need to become more productive and competitive.

TABLE 10.6

What You Should Not Do When You Are Terminated

1. Do not tell off your boss and co-workers, even if you think they deserve it.

2. Do not damage company property or steal something.

3. Do not forget to ask for a reference.

4. Do not badmouth your employer or any of your co-workers to your replacement.

5. Do not badmouth your employer to a prospective employer when you go on a job interview.

Source: Dawn Rosenberg McKay, "Five Things Not to Do When You Leave Your Job," http://careerplanning.about.com/od/jobseparation/a/leave_mistakes.htm (accessed April 13, 2011).

set forth in employee handbooks. Table 10.6 illustrates what *not* to do when you are terminated.

Many companies have downsized in recent years, laying off tens of thousands of employees in their effort to become more productive and competitive. For example, Gap had to lay off workers after it decided to close 200 stores in the United States. Declining sales convinced Gap to adapt its marketing strategy and focus more on the overseas market.[22] Layoffs are sometimes temporary; employees may be brought back when business conditions improve. When layoffs are to be permanent, employers often help employees find other jobs and may extend benefits while the employees search for new employment. Such actions help lessen the trauma of the layoffs. Fortunately, there are several business areas that are choosing not to downsize. Table 10.7 shows some industries that are planning to hire in the near future.

A well-organized human resources department strives to minimize losses due to separations and transfers because recruiting and training new employees is very expensive. Note that a high turnover rate in a company may signal problems with the selection and training process, the compensation program, or even the type of company. To help reduce turnover, companies have tried a number of strategies, including giving employees more interesting job responsibilities (job enrichment), allowing for increased job flexibility, and providing more employee benefits.

separations
employment changes involving resignation, retirement, termination, or layoff

Compensating the Workforce

People generally don't work for free, and how much they are paid for their work is a complicated issue. Also, designing a fair compensation plan is an important task because pay and benefits represent a substantial portion of an organization's expenses. Wages that are too high may result in the company's products being priced too high, making them uncompetitive in the market. Wages that are too low may damage employee morale and result in costly turnover. Remember that compensation is one of the hygiene factors identified by Herzberg.

Designing a fair compensation plan is a difficult task because it involves evaluating the relative worth of all jobs within the business while allowing for individual efforts. Compensation for a specific job is typically determined through a **wage/salary survey**, which tells the company how much compensation comparable firms are paying for specific jobs that the firms have in common. Compensation for individuals within a specific job category depends on both the compensation for that job and the individual's productivity. Therefore, two employees with identical jobs may not receive exactly the same pay because of individual differences in performance.

LO 10-5

wage/salary survey
a study that tells a company how much compensation comparable firms are paying for specific jobs that the firms have in common

| TABLE 10.7 | Job Areas for Which Employers Are Hiring Recent Graduates | | | | | |

Industry	Hiring %	Recent MBA Graduates		Recent Bachelor's Degree Hires		Experienced Direct Industry Hires	
		2010	2011	2010	2011	2010	2011
Consulting	% hiring	69%	72%	49%	54%	66%	68%
	Mean	14	12	22	26	12	11
	Maximum	353	135	200	250	100	80
Energy/Utilities	% hiring	63%	64%	57%	53%	59%	62%
	Mean	3	6	43	10	67	81
	Maximum	6	25	350	38	300	400
Finance/Accounting	% hiring	67%	71%	59%	58%	58%	59%
	Mean	14	19	75	82	236	65
	Maximum	269	402	1,586	1,837	5,880	1,300
Health care/ Pharmaceutical	% hiring	67%	68%	42%	43%	59%	63%
	Mean	24	11	93	69	28	26
	Maximum	451	150	675	700	250	275
High technology	% hiring	57%	62%	61%	59%	62%	67%
	Mean	16	18	50	65	76	71
	Maximum	175	100	550	600	1,000	900
Manufacturing	% hiring	68%	76%	66%	68%	69%	73%
	Mean	6	7	12	18	56	43
	Maximum	35	40	60	80	350	350
Nonprofit or government	% hiring	31%	36%	49%	44%	36%	36%
	Mean	8	6	10	26	44	73
	Maximum	36	10	60	90	255	350
Products and services	% hiring	57%	61%	53%	56%	50%	55%
	Mean	8	10	27	45	117	139
	Maximum	46	50	500	900	2,000	3,000

Source: GMAC®, *Corporate Recruiters Survey,* 2011, www.gmac.com/~/media/Files/gmac/Research/Employment%20Outlook/2011GMAC_CorporateRecruiters_SR.pdf (accessed April 4, 2012).

Financial Compensation

wages

financial rewards based on the number of hours the employee works or the level of output achieved

Financial compensation falls into two general categories—wages and salaries. **Wages** are financial rewards based on the number of hours the employee works or the level of output achieved. Wages based on the number of hours worked are called time wages. The federal minimum wage increased to $7.25 per hour in 2009 for covered nonexempt workers.[23] Tipped wages must be $2.13 per hour as long as tips plus the wage of $2.13 per hour equal the minimum wage of $7.25 per hour.[24] Many

Going Green
Google Rewards Employees for Being Sustainable

For employees at Google, it pays to be green. Google employees can save money, donate to charities, and receive discounts on eco-friendly technology by taking advantage of the company's green incentives. For instance, employees can save fuel costs by riding to work on Google's biodiesel shuttles. They can also use Google's GFleet car-sharing program, GBikes, or taxi service GRide for traveling across the company campus or attending meetings offsite. For employees who choose to bike, walk, or pogo to work, the company provides them with digital stamps, which can be redeemed for company donations to the employee's favorite charity.

Many of Google's green initiatives help both employees and society. In 2011, Google announced that it was creating a $280 million fund for SolarCity in a partnership to support the installation of solar panels on residential homes. While it may be difficult to convince the average consumer to adopt solar technology, Google offers its employees discounts. The company also created the largest corporate electronic-vehicle charging station in the country, not only to support the electric vehicles in its GFleet but also to inspire employees to purchase their own. Google seeks to make a difference in the field of sustainability—starting with its employees.[25]

Discussion Questions

1. Describe some of Google's green initiatives.
2. How is Google rewarding employees for adopting greener behaviors?
3. Why do you think it might be beneficial for Google to pay for solar panels on employee houses, even if it costs the company money?

states also mandate minimum wages; in the case where the two wages are in conflict, the higher of the two wages prevails. There may even be differences between city and state minimum wages. In New Mexico, the minimum wage is $7.50, whereas in the state capital of Santa Fe, the minimum wage is $10.29, due to a higher cost of living.[26] When Santa Fe went to $10.29 per hour on May 1, 2012, this became the highest minimum wage in the United States.[27] Table 10.8 compares wage and other information for Costco and Walmart, two well-known discount chains. Time wages are appropriate when employees are continually interrupted and when quality is more important than quantity. Assembly-line workers, clerks, and maintenance personnel are commonly paid on a time-wage basis. The advantage of time wages is the ease of computation. The disadvantage is that time wages provide no incentive to increase productivity. In fact, time wages may encourage employees to be less productive.

TABLE 10.8   Costco versus Walmart

	Costco	Walmart
Number of employees	160,000+	2,100,000+
Revenues	$78 billion	$422 billion
Average pay per hour	$17	$11.75
World's most admired ranking	20	24
Strengths	Management quality; financial soundness; people management	Management quality; financial soundness; global competitiveness

Sources: "Fortune Global 500," *CNNMoney.com,* http://money.cnn.com/magazines/fortune/global500/2011/snapshots/2255.html; "World's Most Admired Companies," *CNNMoney.com,* http://money.cnn.com/magazines/fortune/most-admired/2012/full_list/; Lora Keleher, ""Average Salaries at Costco," *Money & Business,* June 22, 2011, www.moneyandbusiness.com/careers/compensation/salary/average-salaries-costco; "Walmart," October 25, 2011, http://nyjobsource.com/walmart.html; "Investor Relations," Costco Wholesale, http://phx.corporate-ir.net/phoenix.zhtml?c583830&p5irol-homeprofile (accessed April 5, 2012).

To overcome these disadvantages, many companies pay on an incentive system, using piece wages or commissions. Piece wages are based on the level of output achieved. A major advantage of piece wages is that they motivate employees to supervise their own activities and to increase output. Skilled craftworkers are often paid on a piece-wage basis.

commission
an incentive system that pays a fixed amount or a percentage of the employee's sales

The other incentive system, **commission,** pays a fixed amount or a percentage of the employee's sales. Kele & Co Jewelers in Plainfield, Illinois, make sterling silver jewelry and offer semi-precious and gemstones at affordable prices. Their handcrafted jewelry is sold through the Internet (www.keleonline.com) and through independent sales representatives (ISRs) all over the country. The unique aspect of Kele's sales process is their innovative sales and commission structure. ISRs have no minimum sales quotas, sales are shared among team members during training and after being promoted, and there is no requirement to purchase inventory as jewelry is shipped from Kele headquarters. ISRs receive a 30 to 50 percent commission on sales. The goal is to increase the profit margin and earning potential of the salespeople. The company's goal is to become the largest direct sales company in the industry.[28] This method motivates employees to sell as much as they can. Some companies also combine payment based on commission with time wages or salaries.

salary
a financial reward calculated on a weekly, monthly, or annual basis

A **salary** is a financial reward calculated on a weekly, monthly, or annual basis. Salaries are associated with white-collar workers such as office personnel, executives, and professional employees. Although a salary provides a stable stream of income, salaried workers may be required to work beyond usual hours without additional financial compensation.

bonuses
monetary rewards offered by companies for exceptional performance as incentives to further increase productivity

In addition to the basic wages or salaries paid to employees, a company may offer **bonuses** for exceptional performance as an incentive to increase productivity further. Many workers receive a bonus as a "thank you" for good work and an incentive to continue working hard. Many owners and managers are recognizing that simple bonuses and perks foster happier employees and reduce turnover. Bonuses are especially popular among Wall Street firms. Employees at JP Morgan Chase received bonuses of as much as $125,000 in 2011. These bonuses were actually less than what employees at the banking firm might have otherwise received due to the difficult economic environment.[29]

profit sharing
a form of compensation whereby a percentage of company profits is distributed to the employees whose work helped to generate them

Another form of compensation is **profit sharing,** which distributes a percentage of company profits to the employees whose work helped to generate those profits. Some profit-sharing plans involve distributing shares of company stock to employees. Usually referred to as *ESOPs*—employee stock ownership plans—they have been gaining popularity in recent years. One reason for the popularity of ESOPs is the sense of partnership that they create between the organization and employees. Profit sharing can also motivate employees to work hard, because increased productivity and sales mean that the profits or the stock dividends will increase. Many organizations offer employees a stake in the company through stock purchase plans, ESOPs, or stock investments through 401(k) plans. Employees below senior management levels rarely received stock options until recently. Companies are adopting broad-based stock option plans to build a stronger link between employees' interests and the organization's interests. ESOPs have met with enormous success over the years, and employee-owned stock has even outperformed the stock market during certain periods. Many businesses have found employee stock options a great way to boost productivity and increase morale. As of 2011, there were an estimated 10,900 ESOPs in the United States.[30]

Benefits

Benefits are nonfinancial forms of compensation provided to employees, such as pension plans for retirement; health, disability, and life insurance; holidays and paid days off for vacation or illness; credit union membership; health programs; child care; elder care; assistance with adoption; and more. According to the Bureau of Labor Statistics, employer costs for employee compensation for civilian workers in the United States average $27.42 per hour worked. Wages and salaries account for approximately 70.8 percent of those costs, while benefits account for 29.2 percent of the cost. Legally required benefits (Social Security, Medicare, federal and state employment insurance, and workers' compensation) account for 7.7 percent of total compensation.[31] Such benefits increase employee security and, to a certain extent, their morale and motivation.

An on-site fitness center is just one of the benefits that large companies have begun to offer employees. Such on-site benefits like fitness centers and child-care are particulary important for employees who work long hours or who struggle to maintain a healthy work–life balance.

Table 10.9 lists some of the benefits Internet search engine Google offers its employees. Although health insurance is a common benefit for full-time employees, rising health care costs have forced a growing number of employers to trim this benefit. Even government workers, whose wages and benefits used to be virtually guaranteed safe, have seen reductions in health care and other benefits. Surveys have revealed that with the decrease in benefits comes a decrease in employee loyalty. Only 42 percent of employees say they feel a strong sense of loyalty to their employers. However, more than half of respondents indicated that employee benefits were important in decisions to stay with the company. Benefits are particularly important to younger generations of employees.[32] Starbucks recognizes the importance of how benefits can significantly impact an employee's health and well-being. As a result, it is the only fast-food company to offer its part-time employees health insurance.

A benefit increasingly offered is the employee assistance program (EAP). Each company's EAP is different, but most offer counseling for and assistance with those employees' personal problems that might hurt their job performance if not addressed. The most common counseling services offered include drug- and alcohol-abuse treatment programs, fitness programs, smoking cessation clinics, stress-management clinics, financial counseling, family counseling, and career counseling. Lowe's, for example, offers work/life seminars, smoking cessation clinics, and other assistance programs for its employees.[33] EAPs help reduce costs associated with poor productivity, absenteeism, and other workplace issues by helping employees deal with personal problems that contribute to these issues. For example, exercise and fitness programs reduce health insurance costs by helping employees stay healthy. Family counseling may help workers trying to cope with a divorce or other personal problems to better focus on their jobs.

Companies try to provide the benefits they believe their employees want, but diverse people may want different things. In recent years, some single workers have felt that co-workers with spouses and children seem to get "special breaks" and extra time off to deal with family issues. Some companies use flexible benefit programs to allow employees to choose the benefits they would like, up to a specified amount.

benefits
nonfinancial forms of compensation provided to employees, such as pension plans, health insurance, paid vacation and holidays, and the like

TABLE 10.9	
Google's Employees' Benefits	• Health insurance:
	– Employee medical insurance
	– Dental insurance
	– Vision insurance
	• Vacation (15 days per year for one–three years' employment; 20 days off for four–five years' employment; 25 days for more than six years' employment)
	• Twelve paid holidays/year
	• Savings plans
	– 401(k) retirement plan, matched by Google
	– Flexible spending accounts
	• Disability and life insurance
	• Employee Assistance Program
	• Free lunches and snacks
	• Massages, gym membership, hair stylist, fitness class, and bike repair
	• Weekly activities
	• Maternity leave
	• Adoption assistance
	• Tuition reimbursement
	• Employee referral plan
	• On-site doctor
	• Backup child care
	• Holiday parties, health fair, credit union, roller hockey, outdoor volleyball court, discounts for local attractions

Source: "Google Benefits," www.google.com/intl/en/jobs/lifeatgoogle/benefits (accessed April 13, 2012).

Fringe benefits include sick leave, vacation pay, pension plans, health plans, and any other extra compensation. Soft benefits include perks that help balance life and work. They include onsite child care, spas, food service, and even laundry services and hair salons. These soft benefits motivate employees and give them more time to focus on their job.

Cafeteria benefit plans provide a financial amount to employees so that they can select the specific benefits that fit their needs. The key is making benefits flexible, rather than giving employees identical benefits. As firms go global, the need for cafeteria or flexible benefit plans becomes even more important. For some employees, benefits are a greater motivator and differentiator in jobs than wages. For many Starbucks employees who receive health insurance when working part time, this benefit could be the most important compensation.

Entrepreneurship in Action
Employees Feel at Home at SAS

Charles Goodnight, Anthony Barr, John Sall, and Jane Helwig

Business: Statistical Analysis Software (SAS)

Founded: 1976, in Cary, North Carolina

Success: As the largest privately held software company, SAS has seen revenues grow for 35 consecutive years.

According to founder Charles Goodnight, "95 percent of [his] assets drive out the gate every evening." When Goodnight and his partners founded SAS in 1976, they knew they wanted to create a desirable workplace for employees. Shortly after the firm was founded, SAS began to offer health care, profit sharing, and child care. Today, the perks at SAS facilities also include recreation and fitness centers, aquatic centers, racquetball courts, and more.

Although the recession caused problems for SAS, Goodnight didn't lay off employees. Rather, he encouraged them to develop ideas to help SAS reduce costs. The resulting solutions enabled SAS to cut expenses by 6 to 7 percent. As a result of its employee-friendly atmosphere, SAS has been number one on *Fortune*'s "100 Best Places to Work For" list for two consecutive years. And these employee benefits not only contribute to a happy workplace; its low turnover rate of 4 percent versus the industry average of 20 percent also saves the company between $60 and $80 million in annual costs.[34]

Over the past two decades, the list of fringe benefits has grown dramatically, and new benefits are being added every year.

Managing Unionized Employees

Employees who are dissatisfied with their working conditions or compensation have to negotiate with management to bring about change. Dealing with management on an individual basis is not always effective, however, so employees may organize themselves into **labor unions** to deal with employers and to achieve better pay, hours, and working conditions. Organized employees are backed by the power of a large group that can hire specialists to represent the entire union in its dealings with management. Union workers make significantly more than nonunion employees. The United States has a roughly 11.8 percent unionization rate. Figure 10.5 displays unionization rates by state. On average, the median usual weekly earnings of unionized full-time and salary workers are about $200 more than their non-union counterparts.[35]

However, union growth has slowed in recent years, and prospects for growth do not look good. One reason is that most blue-collar workers, the traditional members of unions, have already been organized. Factories have become more automated and need fewer blue-collar workers. The United States has shifted from a manufacturing to a service economy, further reducing the demand for blue-collar workers. Moreover, in response to foreign competition, U.S. companies are scrambling to find ways to become more productive and cost efficient. Job enrichment programs and participative management have blurred the line between management and workers. Because workers' say in the way plants are run is increasing, their need for union protection is decreasing.

Nonetheless, labor unions have been successful in organizing blue-collar manufacturing, government, and health care workers, as well as smaller percentages of employees in other industries. Consequently, significant aspects of HRM, particularly compensation, are dictated to a large degree by union contracts at many companies. Therefore, we'll take a brief look at collective bargaining and dispute resolution in this section.

LO 10-6

labor unions
employee organizations formed to deal with employers for achieving better pay, hours, and working conditions

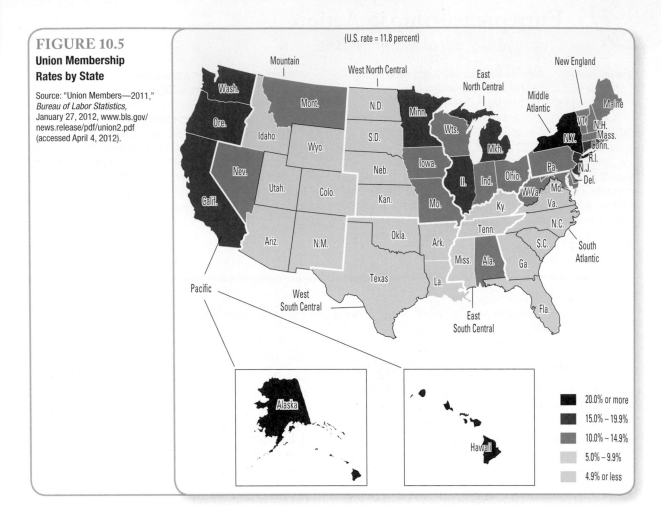

FIGURE 10.5
Union Membership Rates by State

Source: "Union Members—2011," *Bureau of Labor Statistics,* January 27, 2012, www.bls.gov/news.release/pdf/union2.pdf (accessed April 4, 2012).

(U.S. rate = 11.8 percent)

Legend:
- 20.0% or more
- 15.0% – 19.9%
- 10.0% – 14.9%
- 5.0% – 9.9%
- 4.9% or less

Collective Bargaining

collective bargaining
the negotiation process through which management and unions reach an agreement about compensation, working hours, and working conditions for the bargaining unit

labor contract
the formal, written document that spells out the relationship between the union and management for a specified period of time— usually two or three years

Collective bargaining is the negotiation process through which management and unions reach an agreement about compensation, working hours, and working conditions for the bargaining unit (Figure 10.6). The objective of negotiations is to reach agreement about a **labor contract,** the formal, written document that spells out the relationship between the union and management for a specified period of time, usually two or three years.

In collective bargaining, each side tries to negotiate an agreement that meets its demands; compromise is frequently necessary. Management tries to negotiate a labor contract that permits the company to retain control over things like work schedules; the hiring and firing of workers; production standards; promotions, transfers, and separations; the span of management in each department; and discipline. Unions tend to focus on contract issues such as magnitude of wages; better pay rates for overtime, holidays, and undesirable shifts; scheduling of pay increases; and benefits. These issues will be spelled out in the labor contract, which union members will vote to either accept (and abide by) or reject.

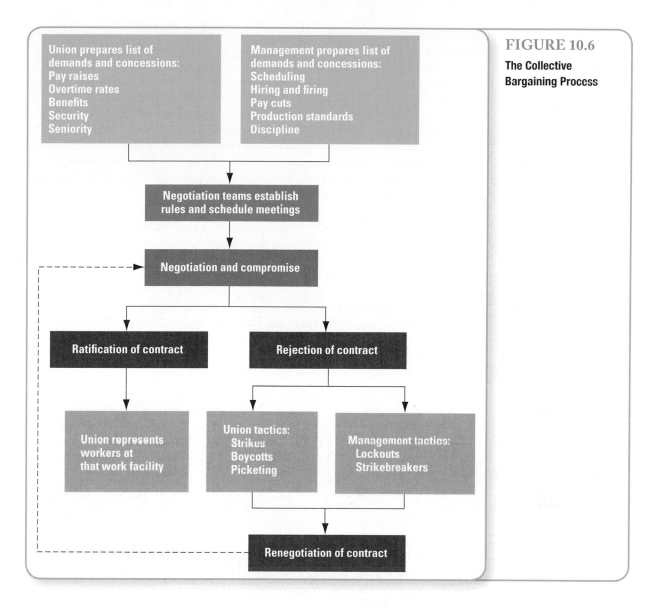

FIGURE 10.6

The Collective Bargaining Process

Many labor contracts contain a *cost-of-living escalator* (or *adjustment*) *(COLA) clause,* which calls for automatic wage increases during periods of inflation to protect the "real" income of the employees. During tough economic times, unions may be forced to accept *givebacks*—wage and benefit concessions made to employers to allow them to remain competitive or, in some cases, to survive and continue to provide jobs for union workers.

Resolving Disputes

Sometimes, management and labor simply cannot agree on a contract. Most labor disputes are handled through collective bargaining or through grievance procedures. When these processes break down, however, either side may resort to more drastic measures to achieve its objectives.

picketing
a public protest against management practices that involves union members marching and carrying antimanagement signs at the employer's plant or work site

strikes
employee walkouts; one of the most effective weapons of labor unions

boycott
an attempt to keep people from purchasing the products of a company

lockout
management's version of a strike, wherein a work site is closed so that employees cannot go to work

strikebreakers
people hired by management to replace striking employees; called "scabs" by striking union members

Labor Tactics.   **Picketing** is a public protest against management practices and involves union members marching (often waving antimanagement signs and placards) at the employer's plant or work site. Picketing workers hope that their signs will arouse sympathy for their demands from the public and from other unions. Picketing may occur as a protest or in conjunction with a strike.

Strikes (employee walkouts) are one of the most effective weapons labor has. By striking, a union makes carrying out the normal operations of a business difficult at best and impossible at worst. Strikes receive widespread publicity, but they remain a weapon of last resort. For example, the United Kingdom experienced significant disruption with closed schools, refusals to collect refuse, and the suspension of nonemergency hospital services after 2 million public-sector workers staged a strike. The workers were protesting against government announcements to change public-sector worker pension plans. Such disruption in daily operations is one reason both unions and companies try to avoid strikes.[36] The threat of a strike is often enough to get management to back down. In fact, the number of worker-days actually lost to strikes is less than the amount lost to the common cold.

A **boycott** is an attempt to keep people from purchasing the products of a company. In a boycott, union members are asked not to do business with the boycotted organization. Some unions may even impose fines on members who ignore the boycott. To gain further support for their objectives, a union involved in a boycott may also ask the public—through picketing and advertising—not to purchase the products of the picketed firm.

Management Tactics.   Management's version of a strike is the **lockout;** management actually closes a work site so that employees cannot go to work. Lockouts are used, as a general rule, only when a union strike has partially shut down a plant and it seems less expensive for the plant to close completely. Caterpillar locked out workers from its 62-year-old plant in Ontario, Canada, after failure to reach an agreement with unionized employees over wages. In a controversial move, Caterpillar then announced it would close the plant entirely and relocate to Muncie, Indiana. The wages of factory workers in Muncie would not be as high as those paid to the company's Canadian workers.[37]

Strikebreakers, called "scabs" by striking union members, are people hired by management to replace striking employees. Managers hire strikebreakers to continue operations and reduce the losses associated with strikes—and to show the unions that they will not bow to their demands. Strikebreaking is generally a last-resort measure for management because it does great damage to the relationship between management and labor.

Outside Resolution. Management and union members normally reach mutually agreeable decisions without outside assistance. Sometimes though, even after lengthy negotiations, strikes, lockouts, and other tactics, management and labor still cannot resolve a contract dispute. In such cases, they have three choices: conciliation, mediation, and arbitration. **Conciliation** brings in a neutral third party to keep labor and management talking. The conciliator

Unions urged people to boycott the Hyatt hotel chain to protest allegedly abusive working conditions for Hyatt employees.

has no formal power over union representatives or over management. The conciliator's goal is to get both parties to focus on the issues and to prevent negotiations from breaking down. Like conciliation, **mediation** involves bringing in a neutral third party, but the mediator's role is to suggest or propose a solution to the problem. After employees from the American Licorice Co. went on strike, for instance, company officials met with union leaders at a federal mediator's office to work on the dispute.[38] Mediators have no formal power over either labor or management. With **arbitration,** a neutral third party is brought in to settle the dispute, but the arbitrator's solution is legally binding and enforceable. JP Morgan lost an arbitration case against American Century Investment Management and paid the firm $384 million in a settlement. The investment company maintained that JP Morgan had allegedly breached an agreement concerning the purchase of a retirement services business. JP Morgan continued to deny wrongdoing but complied with the arbitration decision.[39] Generally, arbitration takes place on a voluntary basis— management and labor must agree to it, and they usually split the cost (the arbitrator's fee and expenses) between them. Occasionally, management and labor submit to *compulsory arbitration,* in which an outside party (usually the federal government) requests arbitration as a means of eliminating a prolonged strike that threatens to disrupt the economy.

conciliation
a method of outside resolution of labor and management differences in which a third party is brought in to keep the two sides talking

mediation
a method of outside resolution of labor and management differences in which the third party's role is to suggest or propose a solution to the problem

arbitration
settlement of a labor/management dispute by a third party whose solution is legally binding and enforceable

The Importance of Workforce Diversity

Customers, employees, suppliers—all the participants in the world of business—come in different ages, genders, races, ethnicities, nationalities, and abilities, a truth that business has come to label **diversity.** Understanding this diversity means recognizing and accepting differences as well as valuing the unique perspectives such differences can bring to the workplace.

LO 10-7

diversity
the participation of different ages, genders, races, ethnicities, nationalities, and abilities in the workplace

The Characteristics of Diversity

When managers speak of diverse workforces, they typically mean differences in gender and race. While gender and race are important characteristics of diversity, others are also important. We can divide these differences into primary and secondary characteristics of diversity. In the lower segment of Figure 10.7, age, gender, race, ethnicity, abilities, and sexual orientation represent *primary characteristics* of diversity that are inborn and cannot be changed. In the upper section of Figure 10.7 are eight *secondary characteristics* of diversity—work background, income, marital status, military experience, religious beliefs, geographic location, parental status, and education—which *can* be changed. We acquire, change, and discard them as we progress through our lives.

Defining characteristics of diversity as either primary or secondary enhances our understanding, but we must remember that each person is defined by the interrelation of all characteristics. In dealing with diversity in the workforce, managers must consider the complete person—not one or a few of a person's differences.

Need help understanding Mediation vs Arbitration?

http://bit.ly/FerrellQR10-2

Why Is Diversity Important?

The U.S. workforce is becoming increasingly diverse. Once dominated by white men, today's workforce includes significantly more women, African Americans, Hispanics, and other minorities, as well as disabled and older workers. Table 10.10 presents

FIGURE 10.7

Characteristics of Diversity

Source: Marilyn Loden and Judy B. Rosener, *Workforce America! Managing Employee Diversity as a Vital Resource,* 1991, p. 20. Used with permission. Copyright © 1991 The McGraw-Hill Companies.

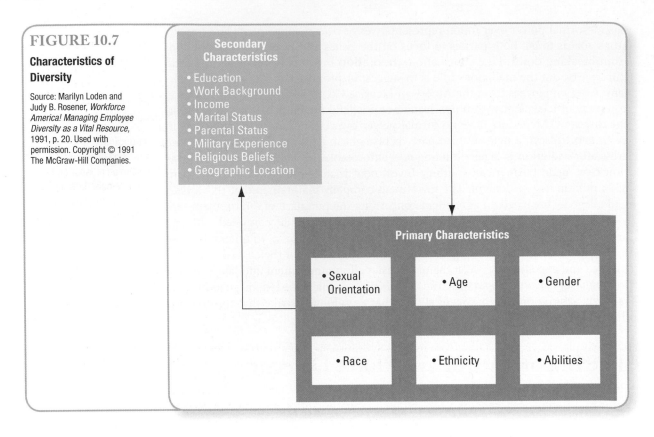

Secondary Characteristics

- Education
- Work Background
- Income
- Marital Status
- Parental Status
- Military Experience
- Religious Beliefs
- Geographic Location

Primary Characteristics

- Sexual Orientation
- Age
- Gender
- Race
- Ethnicity
- Abilities

some of the population data from the census bureau. The census bureau has predicted that by 2042, minorities will make up more than 50 percent of the U.S. population.[40] These groups have traditionally faced discrimination and higher unemployment rates and have been denied opportunities to assume leadership roles in corporate America. Consequently, more and more companies are trying to improve HRM programs to recruit, develop, and retain more diverse employees to better serve their diverse customers. Some firms are providing special programs such as sponsored affinity groups, mentoring programs, and special career development opportunities. Kaiser Permanente has incorporated diversity into its goals and corporate strategies. Half of the company's board of directors consists of minorities, while 36 percent are women. Similar trends are seen with Kaiser Permanente's top management, with one-fourth consisting of women and more than one-third minorities. Diversity and equal rights is so important to Kaiser

Some of the major benefits of diversity include a wider range of employee perspectives, greater innovation and creativity, and the ability to target a diverse customer base more effectively.

Permanente that it has established the Institute for Culturally Competent Care and the nine Centers of Excellence to pave the way for equal health care for all, including minorities, immigrants, and those with disabilities.[42] Table 10.11 shows the top 20 companies for minorities according to a study by DiversityInc. Effectively managing diversity in the workforce involves cultivating and valuing its benefits and minimizing its problems.

TABLE 10.10
Population by Race

Ethnic Group	Percentages	Total
Total population	100	308.7 million
White	72	223.6 million
Hispanic*	16	50.5 million
Black	13	38.9 million
Asian	5	14.7 million
American Indian or Alaskan Native	0.9	2.9 million
Hawaiian or Pacific Islander	0.2	0.5 million
Other race	6	19.1 million
Two or more races	3	9 million

* The U.S. Bureau of the Census does not include a separate listing for Hispanic origin. The 16 percent who are classified as Hispanic are included in the given segments (they may be classified as white, black, etc., depending on origins). This is why the percentages will come out greater than 100 percent.

Source: "2010 Census Shows America's Diversity," U.S. Bureau of the Census, March 24, 2011, www.census.gov/newsroom/releases/archives/2010_census/cb11-cn125.html (accessed April 13, 2011).

TABLE 10.11		
The DiversityInc Top 50 Companies for Diversity	1. Kaiser Permanente	26. Health Care Service Corp.
	2. Sodexo	27. General Mills
	3. PriceWaterHouseCoopers	28. Time Warner
	4. AT&T	29. KPMG
	5. Ernst & Young	30. Dell
	6. Johnson & Johnson	31. MasterCard Worldwide
	7. IBM Corp.	32. Booz Hamilton Allen
	8. Deloitte	33. SC Johnson
	9. Kraft Foods	34. Starwood Hotels & Resorts Worldwide
	10. Colgate-Palmolive	35. JCPenney
	11. Bank of America	36. WellPoint
	12. The Coca-Cola Company	37. Northrop Grumman Corp.
	13. American Express Co.	38. Automatic Data Processing
	14. Marriot International	39. Eli Lilly
	15. Merck & Co.	40. Wells Fargo & Co.
	16. Prudential	41. Monsanto Co.
	17. CSX Corporation	42. Rockwell Collins
	18. Cummins	43. Allstate Insurance Co.
	19. Aetna	44. Target Corp.
	20. Cox Communications	45. Time Warner Cable
	21. Novartis Pharmaceuticals Corp	46. Toyota Motor North America
	22. Verizon Communications	47. Ford Motor Co.
	23. Accenture	48. AXA Equitable Life Insurance Co.
	24. Abbott	49. Whirlpool Corp.
	25. Procter & Gamble	50. Chrysler Group

Source: "The 2011 DiversityInc Top 50 List," DiversityInc, 2012, http://diversityinc.com/the-diversityinc-top-50-companies-for-diversity-2011/ (accessed April 4, 2012).

The Benefits of Workforce Diversity

There are a number of benefits to fostering and valuing workforce diversity, including the following:

1. More productive use of a company's human resources.
2. Reduced conflict among employees of different ethnicities, races, religions, and sexual orientations as they learn to respect each other's differences.
3. More productive working relationships among diverse employees as they learn more about and accept each other.
4. Increased commitment to and sharing of organizational goals among diverse employees at all organizational levels.

5. Increased innovation and creativity as diverse employees bring new, unique perspectives to decision-making and problem-solving tasks.
6. Increased ability to serve the needs of an increasingly diverse customer base.[43]

Companies that do not value their diverse employees are likely to experience greater conflict, as well as prejudice and discrimination. Among individual employees, for example, racial slurs and gestures, sexist comments, and other behaviors by co-workers harm the individuals at whom such behavior is directed. The victims of such behavior may feel hurt, depressed, or even threatened and suffer from lowered self-esteem, all of which harm their productivity and morale. In such cases, women and minority employees may simply leave the firm, wasting the time, money, and other resources spent on hiring and training them. When discrimination comes from a supervisor, employees may also fear for their jobs. A discriminatory atmosphere not only can harm productivity and increase turnover, but it may also subject a firm to costly lawsuits and negative publicity.

Astute businesses recognize that they need to modify their human resources management programs to target the needs of *all* their diverse employees as well as the needs of the firm itself. They realize that the benefits of diversity are long term in nature and come only to those organizations willing to make the commitment. Most importantly, as workforce diversity becomes a valued organizational asset, companies spend less time managing conflict and more time accomplishing tasks and satisfying customers, which is, after all, the purpose of business.

Affirmative Action

Many companies strive to improve their working environment through **affirmative action programs,** legally mandated plans that try to increase job opportunities for minority groups by analyzing the current pool of workers, identifying areas where women and minorities are underrepresented, and establishing specific hiring and promotion goals along with target dates for meeting those goals to resolve the discrepancy. Affirmative action began in 1965 as Lyndon B. Johnson issued the first of a series of presidential directives. It was designed to make up for past hiring and promotion prejudices, to overcome workplace discrimination, and to provide equal employment opportunities for blacks and whites. Since then, minorities have made solid gains.

Legislation passed in 1991 reinforces affirmative action but prohibits organizations from setting hiring quotas that might result in reverse discrimination. Reverse discrimination occurs when a company's policies force it to consider only minorities or women instead of concentrating on hiring the person who is best qualified. More companies are arguing that affirmative action stifles their ability to hire the best employees, regardless of their minority status. Because of these problems, affirmative action became politically questionable.

affirmative action programs
legally mandated plans that try to increase job opportunities for minority groups by analyzing the current pool of workers, identifying areas where women and minorities are underrepresented, and establishing specific hiring and promotion goals, with target dates, for addressing the discrepancy

Trends in Management of the Workforce

As unemployment reached 10 percent during the last recession, businesses laid off almost 9 million employees. Even after the recession and financial crisis, many firms reduced hiring and pushed workers to spend more time on the job for the same or less pay. Because of the economic uncertainty, this post-recession austerity

these strengths give you an advantage relative to your peers/competitors?

B. Personal Weaknesses
1. Three key weaknesses
   a) Weakness 1:
   b) Weakness 2:
   c) Weakness 3:
2. How do these weaknesses cause you to fall short of meeting the needs of your potential employers?
3. How do these weaknesses compare to those of your peers/competitors? Do these weaknesses put you at a disadvantage relative to your peers/competitors?

C. Career Opportunities
1. Three key career opportunities
   a) Opportunity 1:
   b) Opportunity 2:
   c) Opportunity 3:
2. How are these opportunities related to serving the needs of your potential employers?
3. What actions must be taken to capitalize on these opportunities in the short term? In the long term?

D. Career Threats
1. Three key career threats
   a) Threat 1:
   b) Threat 2:
   c) Threat 3:
2. How are these threats related to serving the needs of your potential employers?
3. What actions must be taken to prevent these threats from limiting your capabilities in the short-term? In the long-term?

E. The SWOT Matrix

F. Matching, Converting, Minimizing, and Avoiding Strategies
1. How can you match your strengths to your opportunities to better serve the needs of your potential employers?
2. How can you convert your weaknesses into strengths?
3. How can you convert your threats into opportunities?
4. How can you minimize or avoid those weaknesses and threats that cannot be converted successfully?

IV. Resources

A. Financial
1. Do you have the financial resources necessary to undertake and successfully complete this plan (that is, preparation/ duplication/mailing of a résumé; interviewing costs, including proper attire; etc.)?

B. Human
1. Is the industry in which you are interested currently hiring? Are companies in your area currently hiring?

C. Experience and Expertise
1. Do you have experience from either part-time or summer employment that could prove useful in your current plan?
2. Do you have the required expertise or skills to qualify for a job in your desired field? If not, do you have the resources to obtain them?

V. Strategies

A. Objective(s)
1. Potential employer A:
   a) Descriptive characteristics:
   b) Geographic locations:
   c) Culture/values/mission:
   d) Basic employee needs:
   e) Recruiting/hiring practices:
   f) Employee training/compensation practices:
   g) Justification for selection:
2. Potential employer B:
   a) Descriptive characteristics:
   b) Geographic locations:
   c) Culture/values/mission:
   d) Basic employee needs:
   e) Recruiting/hiring practices:
   f) Employee training/compensation practices:
   g) Justification for selection:

B. Strategy(ies) for Using Capabilities and Resources
1. Strategy A (to meet the needs of potential employer A)
   a) Personal skills, abilities, and resources
      (1) Description of your skills and abilities:

(2) Specific employer needs that your skills/abilities can fulfill:

(3) Differentiation relative to peers/competitors (why should *you* be hired?):

(4) Additional resources that you have to offer:

(5) Needed or expected starting salary:

(6) Expected employee benefits:

(7) Additional employer-paid training that you require:

(8) Willingness to relocate:

(9) Geographic areas to target:

(10) Corporate divisions or offices to target:

(11) Summary of overall strategy:

(12) Tactics for standing out among the crowd of potential employees:

(13) Point of contact with potential employer:

(14) Specific elements
  (a) Résumé:
  (b) Internships:
  (c) Placement offices:
  (d) Job fairs:
  (e) Personal contacts:
  (f) Unsolicited:

(15) Specific objectives and budget:

2. Strategy B (to meet the needs of potential employer B)
  a) Personal skills, abilities, and resources

(1) Description of your skills and abilities:

(2) Specific employer needs that your skills/abilities can fulfill:

(3) Differentiation relative to peers/competitors (why should *you* be hired?):

(4) Additional resources that you have to offer:

(5) Needed or expected starting salary:

(6) Expected employee benefits:

(7) Additional employer-paid training that you require:

(8) Willingness to relocate:

(9) Geographic areas to target:

(10) Corporate divisions or offices to target:

(11) Summary of overall strategy:

(12) Tactics for standing out among the crowd of potential employees:

(13) Point of contact with potential employer:

(14) Specific elements
  (a) Résumé:
  (b) Internships:
  (c) Placement offices:
  (d) Job fairs:
  (e) Personal contacts:
  (f) Unsolicited:

(15) Specific objectives and budget:

C. **Strategy Summary**
  1. How does strategy A (B) give you a competitive advantage in serving the needs of potential employer A (B)?
  2. Is this competitive advantage sustainable? Why or why not?

VI. **Financial Projections and Budgets**
  A. Do you have a clear idea of your budgetary requirements (for example, housing, furnishings, clothing, transportation, food, other living expenses)?
  B. Will the expected salaries/benefits from potential employers meet these requirements? If not, do you have an alternative plan (that is, a different job choice, a second job, requesting a higher salary)?

VII. **Controls and Evaluation**
  A. **Performance Standards**
    1. What do you have to offer? Corrective actions that can be taken if your skills, abilities, and resources do not match the needs of potential employers:
    2. Are you worth it? Corrective actions that can be taken if potential employers do not think your skills/abilities are worth your asking price:
    3. Where do you want to go? Corrective actions that can be taken if potential employers do not offer you

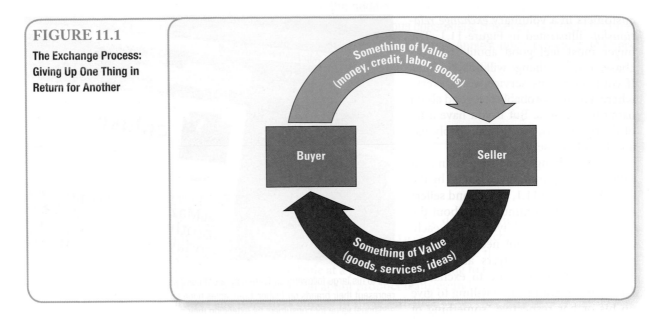

FIGURE 11.1

The Exchange Process: Giving Up One Thing in Return for Another

Transporting. Transporting is the process of moving products from the seller to the buyer. Marketers focus on transportation costs and services.

Storing. Like transporting, storing is part of the physical distribution of products and includes warehousing goods. Warehouses hold some products for lengthy periods in order to create time utility. Time utility has to do with being able to satisfy demand in a timely manner. This especially pertains to a seasonal good such as orange juice. Fresh oranges are only available for a few months annually, but consumers demand juice throughout the entire year. Sellers must arrange for cold storage of orange juice concentrate so that they can maintain a steady supply all of the time.

Grading. Grading refers to standardizing products by dividing them into subgroups and displaying and labeling them so that consumers clearly understand their nature and quality. Many products, such as meat, steel, and fruit, are graded according to a set of standards that often are established by the state or federal government.

Financing. For many products, especially large items such as automobiles, refrigerators, and new homes, the marketer arranges credit to expedite the purchase.

Marketing Research. Through research, marketers ascertain the need for new goods and services. By gathering information regularly, marketers can detect new trends and changes in consumer tastes.

Risk Taking. Risk is the chance of loss associated with marketing decisions. Developing a new product creates a chance of loss if consumers do not like it enough to buy it. Spending money to hire a sales force or to conduct marketing research also involves risk. The implication of risk is that most marketing decisions result in either success or failure.

Creating Value with Marketing[2]

Value is an important element of managing long-term customer relationships and implementing the marking concept. We view **value** as a customer's subjective assessment of benefits relative to costs in determining the worth of a product (customer value = customer benefits − customer costs).

Customer benefits include anything a buyer receives in an exchange. Hotels and motels, for example, basically provide a room with a bed and bathroom, but each firm provides a different level of service, amenities, and atmosphere to satisfy its guests. Hampton Inn offers the minimum services necessary to maintain a quality, efficient, low-price overnight accommodation. In contrast, the Ritz-Carlton provides every imaginable service a guest might desire and strives to ensure that all service is of the highest quality. Customers judge which type of accommodation offers them the best value according to the benefits they desire and their willingness and ability to pay for the costs associated with the benefits.

Customer costs include anything a buyer must give up to obtain the benefits the product provides. The most obvious cost is the monetary price of the product, but nonmonetary costs can be equally important in a customer's determination of value. Two nonmonetary costs are the time and effort customers expend to find and purchase desired products. To reduce time and effort, a company can increase product availability, thereby making it more convenient for buyers to purchase the firm's products. Another nonmonetary cost is risk, which can be reduced by offering good basic warranties for an additional charge. Another risk-reduction strategy is increasingly popular in today's catalog/telephone/Internet shopping environment. L.L. Bean, for example, uses a guarantee to reduce the risk involved in ordering merchandise from its catalogs.

In developing marketing activities, it is important to recognize that customers receive benefits based on their experiences. For example, many computer buyers consider services such as fast delivery, ease of installation, technical advice, and training assistance to be important elements of the product. Customers also derive benefits from the act of shopping and selecting products. These benefits can be affected by the atmosphere or environment of a store, such as Red Lobster's nautical/seafood theme.

value
A customer's subjective assessment of benefits relative to costs in determining the worth of a product

The Marketing Concept

A basic philosophy that guides all marketing activities is the **marketing concept,** the idea that an organization should try to satisfy customers' needs through coordinated activities that also allow it to achieve its own goals. According to the marketing concept, a business must find out what consumers desire and then develop the good, service, or idea that fulfills their needs or wants. The business must then get the product to the customer. In addition, the business must continually alter, adapt, and develop products to keep pace with changing consumer needs and wants. For instance, Domino's has announced that it will begin to offer pizza with a gluten-free crust. With 6 to 8 percent of consumers on a gluten-free diet, many restaurants and fast-food companies are developing new food products to meet the needs of this growing segment.[3] To remain competitive, companies must be prepared to add to or adapt their product lines to satisfy customers' desires for new fads or changes in eating habits. Each business must determine how best to implement the marketing concept, given its own goals and resources.

LO 11-3

marketing concept
the idea that an organization should try to satisfy customers' needs through coordinated activities that also allow it to achieve its own goals

Entrepreneurship in Action
Chinese Bottled Water Brand Challenges Foreign Brands

Yu Yiping Wallace and Wang Jian
Business: Tibet 5100 Water Resources
Founded: 2006, in Wanchai, Hong Kong
Success: While many Chinese bottled water companies have trouble competing against foreign brands, Tibet 5100 Water Resources achieved profitability in two years.

Bottled water is taking off in China. For a long time, foreign bottled water brands such as Evian dominated the market, but domestic bottled water manufacturers are ready to challenge them. One such Chinese company is Tibet 5100 Water Resources. The water that Tibet 5100 sells is high-quality mineral water from a glacial water source in Tibet. Due to the prestige associated with its water, Tibet 5100 prices its water at a 500 percent premium over other domestic water brands. The price may be high, but the increase in consumers' disposable income and the demand for quality water (most water sources in China are polluted) enabled Tibet 5100 to become profitable in two years. Due to its success, Tibet 5100 went public and plans to use the money to try and gain market share from competitors. Its high-end, "pristine" water as well as its relationships with large customers such as China Railway Express and Air China may make Tibet 5100's lofty goals possible.[4]

Trader Joe's, which sells many different lines of organic and natural food products, is often thought to have better deals than some of its competitiors. The grocery chain attempts to meet consumer demands for high-quality food at reasonable prices.

Trying to determine customers' true needs is increasingly difficult because no one fully understands what motivates people to buy things. However, Estée Lauder, founder of her namesake cosmetics company, had a pretty good idea. When a prestigious store in Paris rejected her perfume in the 1960s, she "accidentally" dropped a bottle on the floor where nearby customers could get a whiff of it. So many asked about the scent that Galeries Lafayette was obliged to place an order. Lauder ultimately built an empire using then-unheard-of tactics like free samples and gifts with purchases to market her "jars of hope."[5]

Although customer satisfaction is the goal of the marketing concept, a business must also achieve its own objectives, such as boosting productivity, reducing costs, or achieving a percentage of a specific market. If it does not, it will not survive. For example, Dell could sell computers for $50 and give customers a lifetime guarantee, which would be great for customers but not so great for Dell. Obviously, the company must strike a balance between achieving organizational objectives and satisfying customers.

To implement the marketing concept, a firm must have good information about what consumers want, adopt a consumer orientation, and coordinate its efforts throughout the entire organization; otherwise, it may be awash with goods, services, and ideas that consumers do not want or need. Successfully implementing the marketing concept requires that a business view the customer's perception of value as the ultimate measure of work performance and improving value, and the rate at which this is done, as the measure of success.[6] Everyone in the organization who interacts with customers—*all* customer-contact employees—must know what customers want. They are selling ideas, benefits, philosophies, and experiences—not just goods and services.

Someone once said that if you build a better mousetrap, the world will beat a path to your door. Suppose you do build a better mousetrap. What will happen? Actually, consumers are not likely to beat a path to your door because the market is so competitive. A coordinated effort by everyone involved with the mousetrap is needed to sell the product. Your company must reach out to customers and tell them about your mousetrap, especially how your mousetrap works better than those offered by competitors. If you do not make the benefits of your product widely known, in most cases, it will not be successful. One reason that Apple is so successful is because of its stores. Apple's more than 300 national and international retail stores market computers and electronics in a way unlike any other computer manufacturer or retail establishment. The upscale stores, located in high-rent shopping districts, show off Apple's products in modern, spacious settings to encourage consumers to try new things—like making a movie on a computer. The stores also incorporate its products into the selling process. Not only are consumers allowed to try out or "test drive" Apple's tech products, but the company has also begun to install iPad stations in its stores equipped with a customer service app to answer customer questions.[7] So for some companies, like Apple Inc., you need to create stores to sell your product to consumers. You could also find stores that are willing to sell your product to consumers for you. In either situation, you must implement the marketing concept by making a product with satisfying benefits and making it available and visible.

Orville Wright said that an airplane is "a group of separate parts flying in close formation." This is what most companies are trying to accomplish: They are striving for a team effort to deliver the right good or service to customers. A breakdown at any point in the organization—whether it be in production, purchasing, sales, distribution, or advertising—can result in lost sales, lost revenue, and dissatisfied customers.

Evolution of the Marketing Concept

The marketing concept may seem like the obvious approach to running a business and building relationships with customers. However, businesspeople are not always focused on customers when they create and operate businesses. Many companies fail to grasp the importance of customer relationships and fail to implement customer strategies. A firm's marketing department needs to share information about customers and their desires with the entire organization. Our society and economic system have changed over time, and marketing has become more important as markets have become more competitive.

The Production Orientation.   During the second half of the 19th century, the Industrial Revolution was well under way in the United States. New technologies, such as electricity, railroads, internal combustion engines, and mass-production techniques, made it possible to manufacture goods with ever increasing efficiency. Together with new management ideas and ways of using labor, products poured into the marketplace, where demand for manufactured goods was strong.

The Sales Orientation.   By the early part of the 20th century, supply caught up with and then exceeded demand, and businesspeople began to realize they would have to "sell" products to buyers. During the first half of the 20th century, businesspeople viewed sales as the primary means of increasing profits in what has become known as a sales orientation. Those who adopted the sales orientation perspective believed the most important marketing activities were personal selling and advertising. Today some people still inaccurately equate marketing with a sales orientation.

The Market Orientation.   By the 1950s, some businesspeople began to recognize that even efficient production and extensive promotion did not guarantee sales. These businesses, and many others since, found that they must first determine what customers want and then produce it, rather than making the products first and then trying to persuade customers that they need them. Managers at General Electric first suggested that the marketing concept was a companywide philosophy of doing business. As more organizations realized the importance of satisfying customers' needs, U.S. businesses entered the marketing era, one of market orientation.

A **market orientation** requires organizations to gather information about customer needs, share that information throughout the entire firm, and use it to help build long-term relationships with customers. Top executives, marketing managers, nonmarketing managers (those in production, finance, human resources, and so on), and customers all become mutually dependent and cooperate in developing and carrying out a market orientation. Nonmarketing managers must communicate with marketing managers to share information important to understanding the customer. Consider the 121-year history of Wrigley's gum. In 1891, the gum was given away to promote sales of baking powder (the company's original product). The gum was launched as its own product in 1893, and after four generations of Wrigley family CEOs, the company continues to reinvent itself and focus on consumers. Eventually, the family made the decision to sell the company to Mars. Wrigley now functions as a stand-alone subsidiary of Mars. The deal combined such popular brands as Wrigley's gums and Life Savers with Mars' M&M's, Snickers, and Skittles to form the world's largest confectionary company.

Trying to assess what customers want, which is difficult to begin with, is further complicated by the rate at which trends, fashions, and tastes can change. Businesses today want to satisfy customers and build meaningful long-term relationships with them. It is more efficient and less expensive for the company to retain existing customers and even increase the amount of business each customer provides the organization than to find new customers. Most companies' success depends on increasing the amount of repeat business; therefore, relationship building between

market orientation
an approach requiring organizations to gather information about customer needs, share that information throughout the firm, and use that information to help build long-term relationships with customers

The Nissan Leaf meets the needs of consumers who care about the environment and wish to improve their environmental footprint by driving an electric vehicle.

The Marquis Jet Card allows business travelers to have more flexible location-specific travel options at a much lower cost on NetJets operated planes than that of operating a corporate jet or chartering a small plane.

Responding to Business Challenges
Campgrounds Reach Out to a New Breed of Camper

In response to the recent recession, campgrounds around the United States and Europe are reaching out to a new breed of camper—the glamper. Simply put, this is someone who shuns roughing it, loves to vacation, and enjoys some exposure to nature. Prior to the recession, the glamper likely vacationed in a hotel, perhaps spending on airfare and expensive accommodations. Today, this traveler is sticking close to home and saving money. Fortunately, campsites can help the newly anointed glamper meet his or her goals.

This new target market includes busy families, couples, individuals, or groups of friends. To target those with kids, many campsites offer magic shows, arts and crafts, themed hikes, heated pools, water parks, and more. Draws for adults include Wi-Fi, onsite laundry, deluxe bathrooms, and even dinner shows. Those who prefer to avoid tents can reserve yurts, tee-pees, cottages, and cabins. Although some options are costly, staying closer to home makes it more likely that consumers will save money than if they traveled farther away. The trick for the owners of these facilities is to provide comfortable accommodations with the look and feel of the camping experience.

Overall, revenue for campgrounds and RV parks has risen 3 percent in a one-year period and is expected to continue this growth. The challenge for marketers will be to maintain this popularity as the economy provides more opportunities. To keep demand high, the National Association of RV Parks and Campgrounds is undertaking a marketing campaign that includes more informational websites and partnerships with packaged-goods firms to sell branded products in campsite stores.[8]

Discussion Questions

1. What is a glamper?
2. How has the uncertain economic climate affected glampers?
3. How are campgrounds accommodating glampers?

company and customer is key. Many companies are turning to technologies associated with customer relationship management to help build relationships and boost business with existing customers.

Although it might be easy to dismiss customer relationship management as time-consuming and expensive, this mistake could destroy a company. Customer relationship management (CRM) is important in a market orientation because it can result in loyal and profitable customers. Without loyal customers, businesses would not survive; therefore, achieving the full profit potential of each customer relationship should be the goal of every marketing strategy. At the most basic level, profits can be obtained through relationships by acquiring new customers, enhancing the profitability of existing customers, and extending the duration of customer relationships. The profitability of loyal customers throughout their relationship with the company (their lifetime customer value) should not be underestimated. For instance, Pizza Hut has a lifetime customer value of approximately $8,000, whereas Cadillac's lifetime customer value is approximately $332,000.[9]

Communication remains a major element of any strategy to develop and manage long-term customer relationships. By providing multiple points of interactions with customers—that is, websites, telephone, fax, e-mail, and personal contact—companies can personalize customer relationships.[10] Like many online retailers, Amazon.com stores analyzes purchase data in an attempt to understand each customer's interests. This information helps the online retailer improve its ability to satisfy individual customers and thereby increase sales of books, music, movies, and other products to each customer. The ability to identify individual customers allows marketers to shift their focus from targeting groups of similar customers to increasing their share of an individual customer's purchases. Regardless of the medium through which communication occurs, customers should ultimately be the drivers of marketing strategy because they understand what they want. Customer relationship management systems should ensure that marketers listen to customers in order to respond to their needs and concerns and build long-term relationships.

marketing strategy
a plan of action for developing, pricing, distributing, and promoting products that meet the needs of specific customers

market
a group of people who have a need, purchasing power, and the desire and authority to spend money on goods, services, and ideas

target market
a specific group of consumers on whose needs and wants a company focuses its marketing efforts

total-market approach
an approach whereby a firm tries to appeal to everyone and assumes that all buyers have similar needs

market segmentation
a strategy whereby a firm divides the total market into groups of people who have relatively similar product needs

market segment
a collection of individuals, groups, or organizations who share one or more characteristics and thus have relatively similar product needs and desires

Developing a Marketing Strategy

To implement the marketing concept and customer relationship management, a business needs to develop and maintain a **marketing strategy,** a plan of action for developing, pricing, distributing, and promoting products that meet the needs of specific customers. This definition has two major components: selecting a target market and developing an appropriate marketing mix to satisfy that target market.

Selecting a Target Market

A **market** is a group of people who have a need, purchasing power, and the desire and authority to spend money on goods, services, and ideas. A **target market** is a more specific group of consumers on whose needs and wants a company focuses its marketing efforts. For instance, Lego focused on young boys as the target market for its products. This narrower strategic focus allowed the company to tailor products to attract this demographic with much success: revenues increased 105 percent since 2006. In the past few years, the company has performed market studies on girls to reposition its brand to attract both genders.[11]

Marketing managers may define a target market as a relatively small number of people within a larger market, or they may define it as the total market (Figure 11.2). Rolls Royce, for example, targets its products at a very exclusive, high-income market—people who want the ultimate in prestige in an automobile. On the other hand, Ford Motor Company manufactures a variety of vehicles including Lincolns, Mercurys, and Ford Trucks in order to appeal to varied tastes, needs, and desires.

Some firms use a **total-market approach,** in which they try to appeal to everyone and assume that all buyers have similar needs and wants. Sellers of salt, sugar, and many agricultural products use a total-market approach because everyone is a potential consumer of these products. Most firms, though, use **market segmentation** and divide the total market into groups of people. A **market segment** is a collection of individuals, groups, or organizations who share one or more characteristics and thus have relatively similar product needs and desires. Women are the largest market segment, with 51 percent of the U.S. population. At the household level, segmentation can identify each woman's social attributes, culture, and stages in life to determine preferences and needs.

Another market segment on which many marketers are focusing is the growing Hispanic population. MillerCoors sponsored a Mexican soccer league and placed more Spanish on its cartons and labels. Its rival Anheuser-Busch InBev developed Spanish advertisements and sponsored Cuban-American rapper Pitbull. The companies hope to create relationships with Hispanic consumers in order to gain their loyalty.[12] One of the challenges for marketers in the future will be to effectively address an increasingly racially diverse United States. The minority population of the United States is about 112 million (36 percent of the total population).[13] In future decades, the purchasing power of minority market segments is set to grow by leaps and bounds. Table 11.1 shows the buying power and market share percentages of different market segments. Companies will have to learn how to most effectively reach these growing segments. Companies use market segmentation to focus their efforts and resources on specific target markets so that they can develop a productive marketing strategy. Two common approaches to segmenting markets are the concentration approach and the multisegment approach.

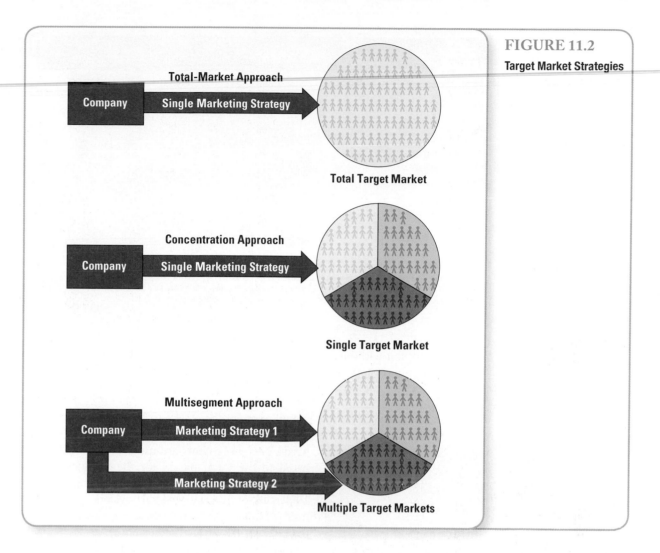

FIGURE 11.2
Target Market Strategies

Market Segmentation Approaches.   In the **concentration approach,** a company develops one marketing strategy for a single market segment. The concentration approach allows a firm to specialize, focusing all its efforts on the one market segment. Porsche, for example, directs all its marketing efforts toward high-income individuals who want to own high-performance vehicles. A firm can generate a large sales volume by penetrating a single market segment deeply. The concentration approach may be especially effective when a firm can identify and develop products for a segment ignored by other companies in the industry.

In the **multisegment approach,** the marketer aims its marketing efforts at two or more segments, developing a marketing strategy for each. Many firms use a multisegment approach that includes different advertising messages for different segments. Companies also develop product variations to appeal to different market segments. The U.S. Post Office, for example, offers personalized stamps, while Mars Inc. sells personalized M&M's through mymms.com. For the "glamper" market segment mentioned earlier in the boxed feature, companies like GlampingHub. com provide luxury camping options for consumers who want to experience the

concentration approach
a market segmentation approach whereby a company develops one marketing strategy for a single market segment

multisegment approach
a market segmentation approach whereby the marketer aims its efforts at two or more segments, developing a marketing strategy for each

TABLE 11.1

U.S. Buying Power Statistics by Race (billions)

	1990	2000	2010	2015
Total	4,200	7,300	11,100	14,100
White	3,800	6,350	9,400	11,800
Black	316	600	957	1,200
American Indian	19.6	40	67.7	90.4
Asian	117	274	544	775
Multiracial	N/A	58.4	115.5	164.6
Hispanic*	210	499	1,000	1,500

*Because Hispanic is an ethnic group, they may belong to any of the other races.

Source: Jeffrey M. Humphreys, "The Multicultural Economy 2009," *GBEC* 69 (3rd Quarter, 2009), p. 3, www.terry.uga.edu/selig/docs/GBEC0903q.pdf (accessed March 30, 2010); Jeffrey M. Humphreys, *The Multicultural Economy 2010*, www.diversityresources.com/att/pdfs/Multicultural%20Economy%202010.pdf (accessed April 6, 2012).

"feel" of camping without having to rough it.[14] Many other firms also attempt to use a multisegment approach to market segmentation, such as the manufacturer of Raleigh bicycles, which has designed separate marketing strategies for racers, tourers, commuters, and children.

Niche marketing is a narrow market segment focus when efforts are on one small, well-defined group that has a unique, specific set of needs. Niche segments are usually very small compared to the total market for the products. Many airlines cater to first-class flyers, who comprise only 10 percent of international air travelers. To meet the needs of these elite customers, airlines include special perks along with the spacious seats. To take advantage of the growing market niche for gluten-free products, Anheuser-Busch launched Michelob Ultra Light Cider, a gluten-free beer.[15]

For a firm to successfully use a concentration or multisegment approach to market segmentation, several requirements must be met:

1. Consumers' needs for the product must be heterogeneous.
2. The segments must be identifiable and divisible.
3. The total market must be divided in a way that allows estimated sales potential, cost, and profits of the segments to be compared.
4. At least one segment must have enough profit potential to justify developing and maintaining a special marketing strategy.
5. The firm must be able to reach the chosen market segment with a particular market strategy.

Procter & Gamble uses a multisegment marketing strategy around the globe. In India, it offers laundry detergents at three distinct performance and pricing levels to account for the fact that many Indian consumers operate on a limited income.

Bases for Segmenting Markets.   Companies segment markets on the basis of several variables:

1. *Demographic*—age, sex, race, ethnicity, income, education, occupation, family size, religion, social class. These characteristics are often closely related to customers' product needs and purchasing behavior, and they can be readily measured. For example, deodorants are often segmented by sex: Secret and Soft n' Dri for women; Old Spice and Mennen for men.

2. *Geographic*—climate, terrain, natural resources, population density, subcultural values. These influence consumers' needs and product usage. Climate, for example, influences consumers' purchases of clothing, automobiles, heating and air conditioning equipment, and leisure activity equipment.

3. *Psychographic*—personality characteristics, motives, lifestyles. Soft-drink marketers provide their products in several types of packaging, including two-liter bottles and cases of cans, to satisfy different lifestyles and motives.

4. *Behavioristic*—some characteristic of the consumer's behavior toward the product. These characteristics commonly involve some aspect of product use.

Developing a Marketing Mix

The second step in developing a marketing strategy is to create and maintain a satisfying marketing mix. The **marketing mix** refers to four marketing activities—product, price, distribution, and promotion—that the firm can control to achieve specific goals within a dynamic marketing environment (Figure 11.3). The buyer or the target market is the central focus of all marketing activities.

marketing mix
the four marketing activites—product, price, promotion, and distribution—that the firm can control to achieve specific goals within a dynamic marketing environment

Product.   A product—whether a good, a service, an idea, or some combination—is a complex mix of tangible and intangible attributes that provide satisfaction and benefits. A *good* is a physical entity you can touch. A Porsche Cayenne, a Hewlett-Packard printer, and a kitten available for adoption at an animal shelter are examples of goods. A *service* is the application of human and mechanical efforts to people or objects to provide intangible benefits to customers. Air travel, dry cleaning, haircuts, banking, insurance, medical care, and day care are examples of services. *Ideas*

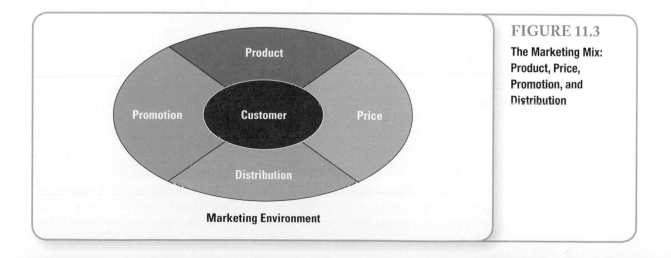

FIGURE 11.3

The Marketing Mix: Product, Price, Promotion, and Distribution

include concepts, philosophies, images, and issues. For instance, an attorney, for a fee, may advise you about what rights you have in the event that the IRS decides to audit your tax return. Other marketers of ideas include political parties, churches, and schools.

A product has emotional and psychological, as well as physical characteristics, that include everything that the buyer receives from an exchange. This definition includes supporting services such as installation, guarantees, product information, and promises of repair. Products usually have both favorable and unfavorable attributes; therefore, almost every purchase or exchange involves trade-offs as consumers try to maximize their benefits and satisfaction and minimize unfavorable attributes.

Products are among a firm's most visible contacts with consumers. If they do not meet consumer needs and expectations, sales will be difficult, and product life spans will be brief. The product is an important variable—often the central focus—of the marketing mix; the other variables (price, promotion, and distribution) must be coordinated with product decisions.

price
a value placed on an object exchanged between a buyer and a seller

Price.   Almost anything can be assessed by a **price,** a value placed on an object exchanged between a buyer and a seller. Although the seller usually establishes the price, it may be negotiated between buyer and seller. The buyer usually exchanges purchasing power—income, credit, wealth—for the satisfaction or utility associated with a product. Because financial price is the measure of value commonly used in an exchange, it quantifies value and is the basis of most market exchanges.

DID YOU KNOW? During its first year of operation, sales of Coca-Cola averaged just nine drinks per day for total first-year sales of $50. Today, Coca-Cola products are consumed at the rate of 1.8 billion drinks per day.[16]

Marketers view price as much more than a way of assessing value, however. It is a key element of the marketing mix because it relates directly to the generation of revenue and profits. Prices can also be changed quickly to stimulate demand or respond to competitors' actions. The sudden increase in the cost of commodities such as oil can create price increases or a drop in consumer demand for a product. When gas prices rise, consumers purchase more fuel-efficient cars; when prices fall, consumers return to larger vehicles.[17]

distribution
making products available to customers in the quantities desired

Distribution.   **Distribution** (sometimes referred to as "place" because it helps to remember the marketing mix as the "4 Ps") is making products available to customers in the quantities desired. For example, consumers can rent DVDs and videogames from a physical store, a vending machine, or an online service. Intermediaries, usually wholesalers and retailers, perform many of the activities required to move products efficiently from producers to consumers or industrial buyers. These activities involve transporting, warehousing, materials handling, and inventory control, as well as packaging and communication.

Critics who suggest that eliminating wholesalers and other middlemen would result in lower prices for consumers do not recognize that eliminating intermediaries would not do away with the need for their services. Other institutions would have to perform those services, and consumers would still have to pay for them. In addition, in the absence of wholesalers, all producers would have to deal directly with retailers or customers, keeping voluminous records and hiring extra people to deal with customers.

promotion
a persuasive form of communication that attempts to expedite a marketing exchange by influencing individuals, groups, and organizations to accept goods, services, and ideas

Promotion.   **Promotion** is a persuasive form of communication that attempts to expedite a marketing exchange by influencing individuals, groups, and organizations to accept goods, services, and ideas. Promotion includes advertising, personal selling, publicity, and sales promotion, all of which we will look at more closely in Chapter 12.

The aim of promotion is to communicate directly or indirectly with individuals, groups, and organizations to facilitate exchanges. When marketers use advertising and other forms of promotion, they must effectively manage their promotional resources and understand product and target-market characteristics to ensure that these promotional activities contribute to the firm's objectives.

Redbox departed from the more traditional brick-and-mortar rental stores by choosing to distribute its DVD rentals through vending machines.

Most major companies have set up websites on the Internet to promote themselves and their products. While traditional advertising media such as television, radio, newspapers, and magazines remain important, digital advertising on websites and social media sites is growing. Not only can digital advertising be less expensive, but advertising offerings such as Google AdWords allow companies to only pay when users click on the link or advertisement.[18] Additionally, social media sites offer advertising opportunities for both large and small companies. Firms can create a Facebook page and post corporate updates for free. To appeal to smaller businesses, Facebook has begun offering deals such as a certain amount in free advertising credits.[19] However, many companies—particularly big-name brands—continue to use Facebook's free features rather than pay much for advertising.[20]

Need help understanding the Marketing Mix?

http://bit.ly/FerrellQR11-2

Marketing Research and Information Systems

Before marketers can develop a marketing mix, they must collect in-depth, up-to-date information about customer needs. **Marketing research** is a systematic, objective process of getting information about potential customers to guide marketing decisions. Such information might include data about the age, income, ethnicity, gender, and educational level of people in the target market, their preferences for product features, their attitudes toward competitors' products, and the frequency with which they use the product. For instance, marketing research has revealed that consumers often make in-store purchase decisions in three seconds or less.[21] Marketing research is vital because the marketing concept cannot be implemented without information about customers.

A marketing information system is a framework for accessing information about customers from sources both inside and outside the organization. Inside the organization, there is a continuous flow of information about prices, sales, and expenses. Outside the organization, data are readily available through private or public reports and census statistics, as well as from many other sources. Computer networking technology provides a framework for companies to connect to useful databases and customers with instantaneous information about product acceptance, sales performance, and buying behavior. This information is important to planning and marketing strategy development.

Two types of data are usually available to decision makers. **Primary data** are observed, recorded, or collected directly from respondents. If you've ever participated in a telephone survey about a product, recorded your TV viewing habits for

LO 11-5

marketing research
a systematic, objective process of getting information about potential customers to guide marketing decisions

primary data
marketing information that is observed, recorded, or collected directly from respondents

Marketing News is a good source for secondary marketing research. The publication contains up-to-date information on market trends and data.

secondary data
information that is compiled inside or outside an organization for some purpose other than changing the current situation

A. C. Nielsen or Arbitron, or even responded to a political opinion poll, you provided the researcher with primary data. Primary data must be gathered by researchers who develop a method to observe phenomena or research respondents. Many companies use "mystery shoppers" to visit their retail establishments and report on whether the stores were adhering to the companies' standards of service. These undercover customers document their observations of store appearance, employee effectiveness, and customer treatment. Mystery shoppers provide valuable information that helps companies improve their organizations and refine their marketing strategies.[22] Companies also use surveys and focus groups to gauge customer opinion. Table 11.2 provides the results of a survey conducted by MSN Money-Zogby on organizations with the best customer service. A weakness of surveys is that respondents are sometimes untruthful in order to avoid seeming foolish or ignorant. Although focus groups can be more expensive than surveys, they allow marketers to understand how consumers express themselves as well as observe their behavior patterns.[23]

Some methods for marketing research use passive observation of consumer behavior and open-ended questioning techniques. Called ethnographic or observational research, the approach can help marketers determine what consumers really think about their products and how different ethnic or demographic groups react to them.

Secondary data are compiled inside or outside the organization for some purpose other than changing the current situation. Marketers typically use information compiled by the U.S. census bureau and other government agencies, databases created by marketing research firms, as well as sales and other internal reports, to gain information about customers.

Online Marketing Research

The marketing of products and collecting of data about buying behavior—information on what people actually buy and how they buy it—represents marketing research of the future. New information technologies are changing the way businesses learn about their customers and market their products. Interactive multimedia research, or *virtual testing*, combines sight, sound, and animation to facilitate the testing of concepts as well as packaging and design features for consumer products. The evolving development of telecommunications and computer technologies is allowing marketing researchers quick and easy access to a growing number of online services and a vast database of potential respondents.

Marketing research can use digital media and social networking sites to gather useful information for marketing decisions. Sites such as Twitter, Facebook, Myspace,

Rank	Companies	Excellence Rating (%)
1	Amazon.com	50.4
2	Trader Joe's	48.9
3	Netflix	48
4	Nordstrom	45.2
5	Publix Super Markets	45
6	Southwest Airlines	45
7	Apple	40.8
8	FedEx	40.2
9	Costco	37.2
10	UPS	35.9

TABLE 11.2

Companies with the Best Customer Service

Source: Karen Aho, "The 2011 Customer Service Hall of Fame," *MSN Money*, http://money.msn.com/investing/the-2011-customer-service-hall-of-fame.aspx?cp-documentid=6820771 (accessed April 10, 2012).

and LinkedIn can be good substitutes for focus groups. Online surveys can serve as an alternative to mail, telephone, or personal interviews.

Social networks are a great way to obtain information from consumers who are willing to share their experiences about products and companies. In a way, this process identifies those consumers who develop an identity or passion for certain products, as well as those consumers who have concerns about quality or performance. It is possible for firms to tap into existing online social networks and simply "listen" to what consumers have on their mind. Firms can also encourage consumers to join a community or group so that they can share their opinions with the business.

A good outcome from using social networks is the opportunity to reach new voices and gain varied perspectives on the creative process of developing new products and promotions. For instance, Kickstarter gives aspiring entrepreneurs the ability to market their ideas online. Funders can then choose whether to fund those ideas in return for a finished product or a steep discount.[24] To some extent, social networking is democratizing design by welcoming consumers to join in the development process for new products.[25]

Online surveys are becoming an important part of marketing research. Traditionally, the process of conducting surveys online involved sending questionnaires to respondents either through email or through a website. However, digital communication has increased the ability of marketers to conduct polls on blogs and social networking sites. The amount

Starbucks hopes to influence consumers' buying behavior by offering them incentives, such as free coffee or tea if you bring your own cup on Earth Day.

that marketers spend on Internet surveys has increased 33 percent from 2005.[26] The benefits of online market research include lower costs and quicker feedback. For instance, when GNC launched its coconut-water beverage, it monitored online feedback to determine how customers viewed the product. The company found that feedback was negative, which convinced them to make product adjustments.[27] By monitoring consumers' feedback, companies can understand customer needs and adapt their products or services.

Buying Behavior

buying behavior
the decision processes and actions of people who purchase and use products

Carrying out the marketing concept is impossible unless marketers know what, where, when, and how consumers buy; conducting marketing research into the factors that influence buying behavior helps marketers develop effective marketing strategies. **Buying behavior** refers to the decision processes and actions of people who purchase and use products. It includes the behavior of both consumers purchasing products for personal or household use as well as organizations buying products for business use. Marketers analyze buying behavior because a firm's marketing strategy should be guided by an understanding of buyers. People view pets as part of their families, and they want their pets to have the best of everything. Iams, which markets the Iams and Eukanuba pet food brands, recognized this trend and shifted its focus. Today, it markets high-quality pet food, fancy pet treats, sauces, and other items. Both psychological and social variables are important to an understanding of buying behavior.

Psychological Variables of Buying Behavior

perception
the process by which a person selects, organizes, and interprets information received from his or her senses

motivation
inner drive that directs a person's behavior toward goals

learning
changes in a person's behavior based on information and experience

attitude
knowledge and positive or negative feelings about something

personality
the organization of an individual's distinguishing character traits, attitudes, or habits

Psychological factors include the following:

- **Perception** is the process by which a person selects, organizes, and interprets information received from his or her senses, as when experiencing an advertisement or touching a product to better understand it.

- **Motivation,** as we said in Chapter 9, is an inner drive that directs a person's behavior toward goals. A customer's behavior is influenced by a set of motives rather than by a single motive. A buyer of a tablet computer, for example, may be motivated by ease of use, ability to communicate with the office, and price.

- **Learning** brings about changes in a person's behavior based on information and experience. For instance, a smart phone app that provides digital news or magazine content could eliminate the need for print copies. If a person's actions result in a reward, he or she is likely to behave the same way in similar situations. If a person's actions bring about a negative result, however—such as feeling ill after eating at a certain restaurant—he or she will probably not repeat that action.

- **Attitude** is knowledge and positive or negative feelings about something. For example, a person who feels strongly about protecting the environment may refuse to buy products that harm the earth and its inhabitants.

- **Personality** refers to the organization of an individual's distinguishing character traits, attitudes, or habits. Although market research on the

Going Green
Monsanto Faces Threats from New Superweeds

Superweeds are bad news for Monsanto, one of the world's leading agricultural products companies. Monsanto's Roundup is the best-selling herbicide in the nation. However, because of the wide-scale use of Roundup, superweeds—weeds that are resistant to herbicides and are therefore harder to control—are becoming a major challenge for farmers. When first introduced, Roundup was heralded for its remarkable ability to ward off weeds. Even when Roundup resistance first became a problem less than a decade ago, Monsanto officials claimed that resistance was rare and "manageable." Today, despite continued reassurance from Monsanto, this is no longer the case. Superweeds are increasing, with 11 species now resistant to the herbicide in more than 25 states.

Competitors such as Dow Chemical and Syngenta are jumping at the chance to grab market share from Monsanto. They have begun promoting older herbicides and herbicide mixtures to combat superweeds. However, scientists caution that even mixing herbicides can eventually lead to resistance.

The problem is not the herbicides themselves, but the way they are used. For many years, farmers and scientists have known that crop rotation prevents pests from developing resistance to certain chemicals. However, because Roundup was so effective, many farmers would rotate one Roundup Ready (seeds that are genetically engineered to resist the herbicide) crop with another. Therefore, in order to prevent future resistance, many farmers and companies will have to change their tactics. To help in this endeavor, Monsanto has the responsibility to promote and design its products in a way that will better consider their long-term impact on the environment.[28]

Discussion Questions

1. Why are superweeds becoming a problem for Monsanto?
2. How are competitors capitalizing on Roundup-resistant superweeds?
3. What are some of the reasons weeds have become resistant to Roundup herbicide?

relationship between personality and buying behavior has been inconclusive, some marketers believe that the type of car or clothing a person buys reflects his or her personality.

Social Variables of Buying Behavior

Social factors include **social roles,** which are a set of expectations for individuals based on some position they occupy. A person may have many roles: mother, wife, student, executive. Each of these roles can influence buying behavior. Consider a woman choosing an automobile. Her father advises her to buy a safe, gasoline-efficient car, such as a Volvo. Her teenaged daughter wants her to buy a cool car, such as a Ford Mustang; her young son wants her to buy a Ford Explorer to take on camping trips. Some of her colleagues at work say she should buy a hybrid Prius to help the environment. Thus, in choosing which car to buy, the woman's buying behavior may be affected by the opinions and experiences of her family and friends and by her roles as mother, daughter, and employee.

Other social factors include reference groups, social classes, and culture.

- **Reference groups** include families, professional groups, civic organizations, and other groups with whom buyers identify and whose values or attitudes they adopt. A person may use a reference group as a point of comparison or a source of information. A person new to a community may ask other group members to recommend a family doctor, for example.

- **Social classes** are determined by ranking people into higher or lower positions of respect. Criteria vary from one society to another. People within a particular social class may develop common patterns of behavior. People in the upper-middle class, for example, might buy a Lexus or a BMW as a symbol of their social class.

social roles
a set of expectations for individuals based on some position they occupy

reference groups
groups with whom buyers identify and whose values or attitudes they adopt

social classes
a ranking of people into higher or lower positions of respect

culture
the integrated, accepted pattern of human behavior, including thought, speech, beliefs, actions, and artifacts

People's cultures have a big impact on what they buy. The food-seller Goya Foods sells more than three dozen types of beans to U.S. supermarkets because people with different cultural roots demand different types of beans. Which products are delivered to which stores depends on the heritage of those living in each area.

LO 11-6

- **Culture** is the integrated, accepted pattern of human behavior, including thought, speech, beliefs, actions, and artifacts. Culture determines what people wear and eat and where they live and travel. Many Hispanic Texans and New Mexicans, for example, buy *masa trigo,* the dough used to prepare flour tortillas, which are basic to Southwestern and Mexican cuisine.

Understanding Buying Behavior

Although marketers try to understand buying behavior, it is extremely difficult to explain exactly why a buyer purchases a particular product. The tools and techniques for analyzing consumers are not exact. Marketers may not be able to determine accurately what is highly satisfying to buyers, but they know that trying to understand consumer wants and needs is the best way to satisfy them. To combat declining gum sales, companies have begun to turn gum into a "fashion statement." For instance, Kraft is engaging young artists to create designs for its gum packaging, while Rockstar Iced Mint Energy is touting its energy-boosting caffeine and taurine content. These overhauls are an attempt to reconnect with the teen market, which is the largest purchaser of gum products.[29]

The Marketing Environment

A number of external forces directly or indirectly influence the development of marketing strategies; the following political, legal, regulatory, social, competitive, economic, and technological forces comprise the marketing environment.

- *Political, legal, and regulatory forces*—laws and regulators' interpretation of laws, law enforcement and regulatory activities, regulatory bodies, legislators and legislation, and political actions of interest groups. Specific laws, for example, require that advertisements be truthful and that all health claims be documented.
- *Social forces*—the public's opinions and attitudes toward issues such as living standards, ethics, the environment, lifestyles, and quality of life. For example, social concerns have led marketers to design and market safer toys for children.
- *Competitive and economic forces*—competitive relationships such as those in the technology industry, unemployment, purchasing power, and general economic conditions (prosperity, recession, depression, recovery, product shortages, and inflation).
- *Technological forces*—computers and other technological advances that improve distribution, promotion, and new-product development.

Marketing requires creativity and consumer focus because environmental forces can change quickly and dramatically. Changes can arise from social concerns and economic forces such as price increases, product shortages, and altering levels of demand for commodities. Recently, climate change, global warming, and the impact of carbon emissions on our environment have become social concerns and are causing businesses to rethink marketing strategies. These environmental issues have persuaded governments to institute stricter limits on greenhouse gas emissions. For instance, in the United States the government has mandated that by 2025 vehicles must be able to reach 54.5 miles per gallon.[30] This is causing automobile companies like General Motors to investigate ways to make their cars more fuel-efficient without significantly raising the price. At the same time, these laws are also introducing opportunities for new products. Concerns over the environment are encouraging automobile companies to begin releasing electric vehicles, such as the Chevrolet Volt and the Nissan Leaf.

Because such environmental forces are interconnected, changes in one may cause changes in others. Consider that because of evidence linking children's consumption of soft drinks and fast foods to health issues such as obesity, diabetes, and osteoporosis, marketers of such products have experienced negative publicity and calls for legislation regulating the sale of soft drinks in public schools.

Although the forces in the marketing environment are sometimes called uncontrollables, they are not totally so. A marketing manager can influence some environmental variables. For example, businesses can lobby legislators to dissuade them from passing unfavorable legislation. Figure 11.4 shows the variables in the marketing environment that affect the marketing mix and the buyer.

Importance of Marketing to Business and Society

As this chapter has shown, marketing is a necessary function to reaching consumers, establishing relationships, and driving sales. While some critics might view marketing as a way to change what consumers want, marketing is essential in communicating the value of products and services. For consumers, marketing is necessary to ensure that they get the products they desire at the right places in the right quantities at a reasonable price. From the perspective of businesses, marketing is necessary in order to form valuable relationships with customers to increase profitability and customer support.

It is not just for-profit businesses that engage in marketing activities. Nonprofits, government institutions, and even people must market themselves to spread awareness and achieve desired outcomes. All organizations must reach their target markets, communicate their offerings, and establish

Benetton appeals to environmentally responsible and fashion conscious individuals.

$84 billion firm. After failing to convince his boss of the idea, Bezos left to start Amazon.com.[6]

New Idea Screening.   The next step in developing a new product is idea screening. In this phase, a marketing manager should look at the organization's resources and objectives and assess the firm's ability to produce and market the product. Important aspects to be considered at this stage are consumer desires, the competition, technological changes, social trends, and political, economic, and environmental considerations. Basically, there are two reasons new products succeed: They are able to meet a need or solve a problem better than products already available or they add variety to the product selection currently on the market. Bringing together a team of knowledgeable people including designers, engineers, marketers, and customers is a great way to screen ideas. Using the Internet to encourage collaboration represents a rich opportunity for marketers to screen ideas. Most new product ideas are rejected during screening because they seem inappropriate or impractical for the organization.

Business Analysis.   Business analysis is a basic assessment of a product's compatibility in the marketplace and its potential profitability. Both the size of the market and competing products are often studied at this point. The most important question relates to market demand: How will the product affect the firm's sales, costs, and profits?

Product Development.   If a product survives the first three steps, it is developed into a prototype that should reveal the intangible attributes it possesses as perceived by the consumer. Product development is often expensive, and few product ideas make it to this stage. New product research and development costs vary. Adding a new color to an existing item may cost $100,000 to $200,000, but launching a completely new product can cost millions of dollars. During product development, various elements of the marketing mix must be developed for testing. Copyrights, tentative advertising copy, packaging, labeling, and descriptions of a target market are integrated to develop an overall marketing strategy.

test marketing
a trial minilaunch of a product in limited areas that represent the potential market

Test Marketing.   **Test marketing** is a trial minilaunch of a product in limited areas that represent the potential market. It allows a complete test of the marketing strategy in a natural environment, giving the organization an opportunity to discover weaknesses and eliminate them before the product is fully launched. Caterpillar Inc. often engages in test marketing before launching into full-scale production of its machinery and equipment. It introduced its Cat® CT660 Vocational Truck in limited markets to test the product as well as to ensure that it met quality standards. After successful test marketing, the Cat CT660 Vocational Truck was made ready for commercialization.[7] Because test marketing requires significant resources and expertise, market research companies like ACNielson can assist firms in test marketing their products. Figure 12.2 shows the permanent sites as well as custom locations for test marketing.

commercialization
the full introduction of a complete marketing strategy and the launch of the product for commercial success

Commercialization.   **Commercialization** is the full introduction of a complete marketing strategy and the launch of the product for commercial success. During commercialization, the firm gears up for full-scale production, distribution, and promotion. After achieving success with its McCafé line, McDonald's expanded into the smoothie market. When the company entered the commercialization stage, it

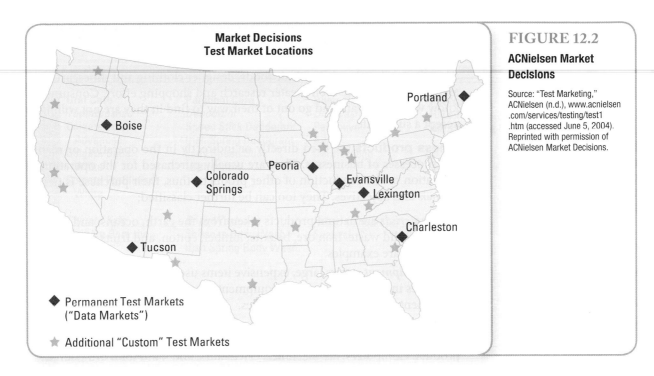

**Market Decisions
Test Market Locations**

Portland

Boise

Peoria

Colorado
Springs

Evansville

Lexington

Charleston

Tucson

◆ Permanent Test Markets
("Data Markets")

★ Additional "Custom" Test Markets

FIGURE 12.2

ACNielsen Market Decisions

Source: "Test Marketing,"
ACNielsen (n.d.), www.acnielsen
.com/services/testing/test1
.htm (accessed June 5, 2004).
Reprinted with permission of
ACNielsen Market Decisions.

released coupons and free smoothie promotions to spread awareness about its newest product, Real Fruit Smoothies. During this stage, competitors often take the opportunity to emphasize their own product offerings and discredit their rival's new product. Jamba Juice, a competitor in the smoothie market, countered the launch of Real Fruit Smoothies by releasing a spoof commercial of a hamburger-flavored smoothie and vowed to redeem McDonald's smoothie coupons at Jamba locations in select cities.[8]

consumer products
products intended for
household or family use

Classifying Products

Products are usually classified as either consumer products or industrial products. **Consumer products** are for household or family use; they are not intended for any purpose other than daily living. They can be further classified as convenience products, shopping products, and specialty products on the basis of consumers' buying behavior and intentions.

- *Convenience products,* such as eggs, milk, bread, and newspapers, are bought frequently, without a lengthy search, and often for immediate consumption. Consumers spend virtually no time planning where to purchase these products and usually accept whatever brand is available.

- *Shopping products,* such as furniture, audio equipment, clothing, and sporting goods,

The DeLorean automobile from the 1980s is an example of a product that did not survive. However, it is still popular among car collectors. Because there are so few of these cars left, DeLoreans would be classified as specialty products requiring greater shopping effort.

Comcast is attempting to increase market share by using a penetration pricing strategy of $29.99 per month for 12 months.

and Petco—which can charge premium prices for high-quality, prestige products—as well as Sam's Clubs and Costco—which offer basic household products at everyday low prices.

Price is a key element in the marketing mix because it relates directly to the generation of revenue and profits. In large part, the ability to set a price depends on the supply of and demand for a product. For most products, the quantity demanded goes up as the price goes down, and as the price goes up, the quantity demanded goes down. Changes in buyers' needs, variations in the effectiveness of other marketing mix variables, the presence of substitutes, and dynamic environmental factors can influence demand. Taiwanese company AU Optronics Corp. experienced a lack of demand for its liquid-crystal displays because of many different factors, including a weak global economy and decreasing demand for computers and televisions. Prices were therefore reduced to try and boost demand and get rid of an oversupply of products.[24]

Price is probably the most flexible variable in the marketing mix. Although it may take years to develop a product, establish channels of distribution, and design and implement promotion, a product's price may be set and changed in a few minutes. Under certain circumstances, of course, the price may not be so flexible, especially if government regulations prevent dealers from controlling prices. Of course, price also depends on the cost to manufacture a good or provide a service or idea. A firm may temporarily sell products below cost to match competition, to generate cash flow, or even to increase market share, but in the long run, it cannot survive by selling its products below cost.

Pricing Objectives

Pricing objectives specify the role of price in an organization's marketing mix and strategy. They usually are influenced not only by marketing mix decisions but also by finance, accounting, and production factors. Maximizing profits and sales, boosting market share, maintaining the status quo, and survival are four common pricing objectives.

Specific Pricing Strategies

Pricing strategies provide guidelines for achieving the company's pricing objectives and overall marketing strategy. They specify how price will be used as a variable in the marketing mix. Significant pricing strategies relate to the pricing of new products, psychological pricing, and price discounting.

The pricing strategy of an independently owned ice cream business can use a premium price objective because of the quality of the product and the unique atmosphere.

Pricing New Products.   Setting the price for a new product is critical: The right price leads to profitability; the wrong price may kill the product. In general, there are two basic strategies to setting the base price for a new product. **Price skimming** is charging the highest possible price that buyers who want the product will pay. Price skimming is used with luxury goods items. Gucci bags, for example, often run into the thousands of dollars. Price skimming is often used to allow the company to generate much-needed revenue to help offset the costs of research and development. Conversely, a **penetration price** is a low price designed to help a product enter the market and gain market share rapidly. When Netflix entered the market, it offered its rentals at prices much lower than the average rental stores and did not charge late fees. Netflix quickly gained market share and eventually drove many rental stores out of business. Penetration pricing is less flexible than price skimming; it is more difficult to raise a penetration price than to lower a skimming price. Netflix found this out the hard way when it faced consumer backlash for raising the fees on one of its most popular rental packages. Penetration pricing is used most often when marketers suspect that competitors will enter the market shortly after the product has been introduced.

price skimming
charging the highest possible price that buyers who want the product will pay

penetration price
a low price designed to help a product enter the market and gain market share rapidly

Psychological Pricing.   **Psychological pricing** encourages purchases based on emotional rather than rational responses to the price. For example, the assumption behind *even/odd pricing* is that people will buy more of a product for $9.99 than $10 because it seems to be a bargain at the odd price. The assumption behind *symbolic/ prestige pricing* is that high prices connote high quality. Thus the prices of certain fragrances and cosmetics are set artificially high to give the impression of superior quality. Some over-the-counter drugs are priced high because consumers associate a drug's price with potency.

psychological pricing
encouraging purchases based on emotional rather than rational responses to the price

discounts
temporary price reductions, often employed to boost sales

Price Discounting.   Temporary price reductions, or **discounts,** are often employed to boost sales. Although there are many types, quantity, seasonal, and promotional discounts are among the most widely used. Quantity discounts reflect the economies of purchasing in large volumes. Seasonal discounts to buyers who purchase goods or services out of season help even out production capacity. Promotional discounts attempt to improve sales by advertising price reductions on selected products to increase customer interest. Often promotional pricing is geared toward increased profits. Taco Bell, with its reputation for value, has been labeled the "best-positioned U.S. brand" to do well in a recession economy as consumers look for cheaper fast-food options. Taco Bell offers a Why Pay More? menu with selections priced at 89¢ and 99¢. KFC, Wendy's, and McDonald's all offer Value Menus as well, with items priced around $1.

Distribution Strategy

LO 12-3

The best products in the world will not be successful unless companies make them available where and when customers want to buy them. In this section, we will explore dimensions of distribution strategy, including the channels through which products are distributed, the intensity of market coverage, and the physical handling of products during distribution.

Marketing Channels

marketing channel
a group of organizations that moves products from their producer to customers; also called a channel of distribution

retailers
intermediaries who buy products from manufacturers (or other intermediaries) and sell them to consumers for home and household use rather than for resale or for use in producing other products

A **marketing channel,** or channel of distribution, is a group of organizations that moves products from their producer to customers. Marketing channels make products available to buyers when and where they desire to purchase them. Organizations that bridge the gap between a product's manufacturer and the ultimate consumer are called *middlemen,* or intermediaries. They create time, place, and ownership utility. Two intermediary organizations are retailers and wholesalers.

Retailers buy products from manufacturers (or other intermediaries) and sell them to consumers for home and household use rather than for resale or for use in producing other products. Toys 'Я' Us, for example, buys products from Mattel and other manufacturers and resells them to consumers. By bringing together an assortment of products from competing producers, retailers create utility. Retailers arrange for products to be moved from producers to a convenient retail establishment (place utility). They maintain hours of operation for their retail stores to make merchandise available when consumers want it (time utility). They also assume the risk of ownership of inventories (ownership utility). Table 12.4 describes various types of general merchandise retailers.

Today, there are too many stores competing for too few customers, and, as a result, competition between similar retailers has never been more intense. In addition, retailers face challenges such as shoplifting, as indicated in Table 12.5. Further, competition between different types of stores is changing the nature of retailing. Supermarkets compete with specialty food stores, wholesale clubs, and discount stores. Department stores compete with nearly every other type of store, including specialty stores, off-price chains, category killers, discount stores, and online retailers. For this reason, many businesses have turned to nonstore retailing to sell their products. Some nonstore retailing is performed by traditional retailers to complement their in-store offerings. For instance, Walmart and Macy's have created online shopping sites to retain customers and compete against other businesses.

TABLE 12.4   **General Merchandise Retailers**

Type of Retailer	Description	Examples
Department store	Large organization offering wide product mix and organized into separate departments	Macy's, JCPenney, Sears
Discount store	Self-service, general merchandise store offering brand name and private brand products at low prices	Walmart, Target, Kmart
Convenience store	Small self-service store offering narrow product assortment in convenient locations	7-Eleven
Supermarket	Self-service store offering complete line of food products and some nonfood products	Kroger, Safeway, Publix
Superstore	Giant outlet offering all food and nonfood products found in supermarkets, as well as most routinely purchased products	Walmart Supercenters, SuperTarget
Hypermarket	Combination supermarket and discount store, larger than a superstore	Carrefour
Warehouse club	Large-scale, members-only establishments combining cash-and-carry wholesaling with discount retailing	Sam's Club, Costco
Warehouse showroom	Facility in a large, low-cost building with large on-premises inventories and minimum service	Ikea

Source: William M. Pride and O. C. Ferrell, *Marketing Foundations,* 2013, p. 431. Copyright South-Western, a part of Cengage Learning. Reprinted with permission.

TABLE 12.5

Profile of Shoplifting in the United States

Shoplifters in the United States	28 million (1 in 11 people)
Amount retailers lose from shoplifting	$119 billion
Percent of shoplifters considered professional	3%
Percent of shoplifters who are adults	75%
Percent of shoplifting aided by a corrupt employee	35%

Source: Robert Klara, "Steal This: 'Tis the Season, Ye Merry Retailers, for Shoplifting," *Adweek,* November 29, 2011, www.adweek.com/news/advertising-branding/steal-136712 (accessed April 12, 2012).

Other companies retail outside of physical stores entirely. The Internet, vending machines, mail-order catalogs, and entertainment such as going to a Chicago Bulls basketball game all provide opportunities for retailing outside of a store environment. For instance, although traditional vending machines are decreasing, some businesses are finding success by using vending machines in unusual ways. PA Live Bait Vending Machines use a refrigeration system and rotation process to sell minnows, mealworms, and nightcrawlers for fishing. PA Live Bait Vending now has 400 machines in operation.[26]

wholesalers
intermediaries who buy from producers or from other wholesalers and sell to retailers

Wholesalers are intermediaries who buy from producers or from other wholesalers and sell to retailers. They usually do not sell in significant quantities to ultimate consumers. Wholesalers perform the functions listed in Table 12.6.

Wholesalers are extremely important because of the marketing activities they perform, particularly for consumer products. Although it is true that wholesalers can be eliminated, their functions must be passed on to some other entity, such as the producer, another intermediary, or even the customer. Wholesalers help consumers and retailers by buying in large quantities, then selling to retailers in smaller quantities. By stocking an assortment of products, wholesalers match products to demand. Sysco is a food wholesaler for the food services industry. The company provides food, preparation, and serving products to restaurants, hospitals, and other institutions that provide meals outside of the home.[27]

Supply Chain Management.   In an effort to improve distribution channel relationships among manufacturers and other channel intermediaries, supply chain management creates alliances between channel members. In Chapter 8, we defined supply chain management as connecting and integrating all parties or members of the distribution system in order to satisfy customers. It involves long-term partnerships among marketing channel members working together to reduce costs, waste, and unnecessary movement in the entire marketing channel in order to satisfy customers. It goes beyond traditional channel members (producers, wholesalers, retailers, customers) to include *all* organizations involved in moving products from the producer to the ultimate customer. In a survey of business managers, a disruption in the supply chain was viewed as the number-one crisis that could decrease revenue.[28]

TABLE 12.6   **Major Wholesaling Functions**

Supply chain management	Creating long-term partnerships among channel members
Promotion	Providing a sales force, advertising, sales promotion, and publicity
Warehousing, shipping, and product handling	Receiving, storing, and stockkeeping Packaging Shipping outgoing orders Materials handling Arranging and making local and long-distance shipments
Inventory control and data processing	Processing orders Controlling physical inventory Recording transactions Tracking sales data for financial analysis
Risk taking	Assuming responsibility for theft, product obsolescence, and excess inventories
Financing and budgeting	Extending credit Making capital investments Forecasting cash flow
Marketing research and information systems	Providing information about market Conducting research studies Managing computer networks to facilitate exchanges and relationships

Source: William M. Pride and O. C. Ferrell, *Marketing: Concepts and Strategies,* 2008, p. 389. Copyright 2008 by Houghton Mifflin Company. Reprinted with permission.

The focus shifts from one of selling to the next level in the channel to one of selling products *through* the channel to a satisfied ultimate customer. Information, once provided on a guarded, "as needed" basis, is now open, honest, and ongoing. Perhaps most importantly, the points of contact in the relationship expand from one-on-one at the salesperson–buyer level to multiple interfaces at all levels and in all functional areas of the various organizations.

Channels for Consumer Products.   Typical marketing channels for consumer products are shown in Figure 12.7. In Channel A, the product moves from the producer directly to the consumer. Farmers who sell their fruit and vegetables to consumers at roadside stands or farmer's markets use a direct-from-producer-to-consumer marketing channel.

In Channel B, the product goes from producer to retailer to consumer. This type of channel is used for products such as college textbooks, automobiles, and appliances. In Channel C, the product is handled by a wholesaler and a retailer before it reaches the consumer. Producer-to-wholesaler-to-retailer-to-consumer marketing channels distribute a wide range of products including refrigerators, televisions, soft drinks, cigarettes, clocks, watches, and office products. In Channel D, the product goes to an agent, a wholesaler, and a retailer before going to the consumer. This long channel of distribution is especially useful for convenience products. Candy and some produce are often sold by agents who bring buyers and sellers together.

Services are usually distributed through direct marketing channels because they are generally produced *and* consumed simultaneously. For example, you cannot take a haircut home for later use. Many services require the customer's presence

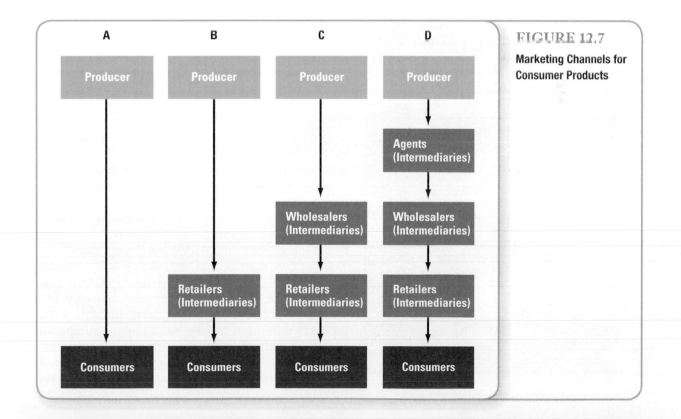

FIGURE 12.7

Marketing Channels for Consumer Products

intensive distribution
a form of market coverage whereby a product is made available in as many outlets as possible

selective distribution
a form of market coverage whereby only a small number of all available outlets are used to expose products

and participation: The sick patient must visit the physician to receive treatment; the child must be at the day care center to receive care; the tourist must be present to sightsee and consume tourism services.

Channels for Business Products.   In contrast to consumer goods, more than half of all business products, especially expensive equipment or technically complex products, are sold through direct marketing channels. Business customers like to communicate directly with producers of such products to gain the technical assistance and personal assurances that only the producer can offer. For this reason, business buyers prefer to purchase expensive and highly complex mainframe computers directly from IBM, Unisys, and other mainframe producers. Other business products may be distributed through channels employing wholesaling intermediaries such as industrial distributors and/or manufacturer's agents.

Intensity of Market Coverage

A major distribution decision is how widely to distribute a product—that is, how many and what type of outlets should carry it. The intensity of market coverage depends on buyer behavior, as well as the nature of the target market and the competition. Wholesalers and retailers provide various intensities of market coverage and must be selected carefully to ensure success. Market coverage may be intensive, selective, or exclusive.

Intensive distribution makes a product available in as many outlets as possible. Because availability is important to purchasers of convenience products such as bread, milk, gasoline, soft drinks, and chewing gum, a nearby location with a minimum of time spent searching and waiting in line is most important to the consumer. To saturate markets intensively, wholesalers and many varied retailers try to make the product available at every location where a consumer might desire to purchase it. Zoom Systems provides robotic vending machines for products beyond candy and drinks. Zoom has more than a thousand machines in airports and hotels across the United States, some selling items such as Apple iPods, Neutrogena hair and skin products, and Sony products. The vending machines accept credit cards and allow sales to occur in places where storefronts would be impossible.[29] Through partnering with different companies, today's ZoomShops sell a variety of brands, including products from Sephora, Best Buy, Macy's, and Rosetta Stone.[30]

Selective distribution uses only a small number of all available outlets to expose products. It is used most often for products that consumers buy only after shopping and comparing price, quality, and style. Many products sold on a selective basis require salesperson assistance, technical advice, warranties, or repair service to maintain consumer satisfaction. Typical products include automobiles, major appliances, clothes, and furniture. Ralph Lauren is a brand that uses selective distribution.

Sears has exclusive distribution of the Kardashian Kollection line of clothing.

Exclusive distribution exists when a manufacturer gives an intermediary the sole right to sell a product in a defined geographic territory. Such exclusivity provides an incentive for a dealer to handle a product that has a limited market. Exclusive distribution is the opposite of intensive distribution in that products are purchased and consumed over a long period of time, and service or information is required to develop a satisfactory sales relationship. Products distributed on an exclusive basis include high-quality musical instruments, yachts, airplanes, and high-fashion leather goods. Aircraft manufacturer Piper Aircraft uses exclusive distribution by choosing only a few dealers in each region. The company has only six dealers throughout the Americas.[31]

Physical Distribution

Physical distribution includes all the activities necessary to move products from producers to customers—inventory control, transportation, warehousing, and materials handling. Physical distribution creates time and place utility by making products available when they are wanted, with adequate service and at minimum cost. Both goods and services require physical distribution. Many physical distribution activities are part of supply chain management, which we discussed in Chapter 8; we'll take a brief look at a few more now.

Transportation.   **Transportation,** the shipment of products to buyers, creates time and place utility for products, and thus is a key element in the flow of goods and services from producer to consumer. The five major modes of transportation used to move products between cities in the United States are railways, motor vehicles, inland waterways, pipelines, and airways.

Railroads offer the least expensive transportation for many products. Heavy commodities, foodstuffs, raw materials, and coal are examples of products carried by railroads. Trucks have greater flexibility than railroads because they can reach more locations. Trucks handle freight quickly and economically, offer door-to-door service, and are more flexible in their packaging requirements than are ships or airplanes. Air transport offers speed and a high degree of dependability but is the most expensive means of transportation; shipping is the least expensive and slowest form. Pipelines are used to transport petroleum, natural gas, semiliquid coal, wood chips, and certain chemicals. Pipelines have the lowest costs for products that can be transported via this method. Many products can be moved most efficiently by using more than one mode of transportation.

Factors affecting the selection of a mode of transportation include cost, capability to handle the product, reliability, and availability, and, as suggested, selecting transportation modes requires trade-offs. Unique characteristics of the product and consumer desires often determine the mode selected.

exclusive distribution
the awarding by a manufacturer to an intermediary of the sole right to sell a product in a defined geographic territory

physical distribution
all the activities necessary to move products from producers to customers— inventory control, transportation, warehousing, and materials handling

transportation
the shipment of products to buyers

The Burlington/Northern/Santa Fe Railroad is the second-largest freight railroad in North America. Although passenger trains have dwindled in favor of other forms of transport, the railroad continues to be important for carrying freight to other parts of the country.

warehousing
the design and operation
of facilities to receive, store,
and ship products

Warehousing.   **Warehousing** is the design and operation of facilities to receive, store, and ship products. A warehouse facility receives, identifies, sorts, and dispatches goods to storage; stores them; recalls, selects, or picks goods; assembles the shipment; and finally, dispatches the shipment.

Companies often own and operate their own private warehouses that store, handle, and move their own products. Firms might want to own or lease a private warehouse when their goods require special handling and storage or when it has large warehousing needs in a specific geographic area. Private warehouses are beneficial because they provide customers with more control over their goods. However, fixed costs for maintaining these warehouses can be quite high.[32] They can also rent storage and related physical distribution services from public warehouses. While public warehouses store goods for more than one company, providing firms with less control over distribution, they are often less expensive than private warehouses and are useful for seasonal production or low-volume storage.[33] Regardless of whether a private or a public warehouse is used, warehousing is important because it makes products available for shipment to match demand at different geographic locations.

materials handling
the physical handling and
movement of products
in warehousing and
transportation

Materials Handling.   **Materials handling** is the physical handling and movement of products in warehousing and transportation. Handling processes may vary significantly due to product characteristics. Efficient materials-handling procedures increase a warehouse's useful capacity and improve customer service. Well-coordinated loading and movement systems increase efficiency and reduce costs.

Importance of Distribution in a Marketing Strategy

Distribution decisions are among the least flexible marketing mix decisions. Products can be changed over time; prices can be changed quickly; and promotion is usually changed regularly. But distribution decisions often commit resources and establish contractual relationships that are difficult if not impossible to change. As a company attempts to expand into new markets, it may require a complete change in distribution. Moreover, if a firm does not manage its marketing channel in the most efficient manner and provide the best service, then a new competitor will evolve to create a more effective distribution system.

LO 12-4

Promotion Strategy

The role of promotion is to communicate with individuals, groups, and organizations to facilitate an exchange directly or indirectly. It encourages marketing exchanges by attempting to persuade individuals, groups, and organizations to accept goods, services, and ideas. Promotion is used not only to sell products but also to influence opinions and attitudes toward an organization, person, or cause. The state of Texas, for example, has successfully used promotion to educate people about the costs of highway litter and thereby reduce littering. Most people probably equate promotion with advertising, but it also includes personal selling, publicity, and sales promotion. The role that these elements play in a marketing strategy is extremely important.

The Promotion Mix

Advertising, personal selling, publicity, and sales promotion are collectively known as the promotion mix because a strong promotion program results from the careful selection and blending of these elements. The process of coordinating the promotion mix elements and synchronizing promotion as a unified effort is called

Entrepreneurship in Action
Lululemon Popularizes Yoga Fashions

Chip Wilson
Business: Lululemon
Founded: 1998, in Vancouver, British Columbia
Success: Lululemon has achieved $1 billion in revenues after popularizing the yoga apparel movement.

Behind the rise of fashionable yoga gear stands Lululemon Athletica, an athletic apparel retailer with $1 billion in annual sales. Sports enthusiast Chip Wilson founded Lululemon in 1998 after recognizing the need for better yoga clothing. After consulting with yoga instructors, Wilson created a fashionable line of yoga and sports apparel. Unlike competitors, Lululemon offers specific numbered sizes instead of small, medium, and large. The line's stretching and wicking fabrics keep athletes warm and dry while allowing for better movement. Other products include bags, yoga mats, and athletic equipment.

Lululemon's stores appeal to women who want premium customer service in a comfortable environment. Retail locations offer free yoga classes, workshops, and community events in their showrooms. This customer experience is the key to Lululemon's grassroots marketing strategy, which emphasizes quality, product, integrity, balance, entrepreneurship, and fun.

With its popularity, Lululemon faces challenges from competitors. Nike and Gap have created their own yoga lines and sell their apparel lines at lower prices than Lululemon's. Despite this added competition, Lululemon remains committed to its mission of creating "components for people to live a longer, healthier, more fun life."[34]

integrated marketing communications. When planning promotional activities, an integrated marketing communications approach results in the desired message for customers. Different elements of the promotion mix are coordinated to play their appropriate roles in delivery of the message on a consistent basis.

Advertising. Perhaps the best-known form of promotion, **advertising** is a paid form of nonpersonal communication transmitted through a mass medium, such as television commercials, magazine advertisements, or online ads. Even Google, one of the most powerful brands in the world, advertises. Google has turned to outdoor advertising on buses, trains, and ballparks in San Francisco and Chicago to promote

integrated marketing communications
coordinating the promotion mix elements and synchronizing promotion as a unified effort

advertising
a paid form of nonpersonal communication transmitted through a mass medium, such as television commercials or magazine advertisements

This ad for Hot Wheels conveys the fun and thrilling "ride" children can experience with this toy—so much so that it almost becomes a crime.

Need help understanding Integrated Marketing Communications?

http://blt.ly/FerrellQR12-1

TABLE 12.7

The 10 Leading National Advertisers

Rank	Company	Advertising Expenditures (in Millions)	Sales (in Millions)	Advertising Expenditures as a Percentage of Sales
1	Procter & Gamble	$4,615	$ 78,938	5.8
2	AT&T	2,989	124,280	2.4
3	General Motors Co.	2,869	135,592	2.1
4	Verizon Communications	2,451	106,565	2.3
5	American Express Co.	2,223	30,242	7.4
6	Pfizer	2,124	67,809	3.1
7	Wal-Mart Stores	2,055	408,214	0.5
8	Time Warner	2,044	18,868	10.8
9	Johnson & Johnson	2,027	61,587	3.3
10	L'Oreal	1,979	19,495	10.2

Source: Reprinted with permission from the June 20, 2011, issue of *Advertising Age*. Copyright Crain Communications Inc, 2011; hoovers.com (accessed March 21, 2012).

its Google Maps feature.[35] Commercials featuring celebrities, customers, or unique creations (Doug, Ford's "spokespuppet" for example) serve to grab viewers' attention and pique their interest in a product. Table 12.7 shows companies that spent more than $1 billion on ads in the United States in one year.

advertising campaign designing a series of advertisements and placing them in various media to reach a particular target market

An **advertising campaign** involves designing a series of advertisements and placing them in various media to reach a particular target audience. The basic content and form of an advertising campaign are a function of several factors. A product's features, uses, and benefits affect the content of the campaign message and individual ads. Characteristics of the people in the target audience—gender, age, education, race, income, occupation, lifestyle, and other attributes—influence both content and form. When Procter & Gamble promotes Crest toothpaste to children, the company emphasizes daily brushing and cavity control, whereas it promotes tartar control and whiter teeth when marketing to adults. To communicate effectively, advertisers use words, symbols, and illustrations that are meaningful, familiar, and attractive to people in the target audience.

An advertising campaign's objectives and platform also affect the content and form of its messages. If a firm's advertising objectives involve large sales increases, the message may include hard-hitting, high-impact language and symbols. When campaign objectives aim at increasing brand awareness, the message may use much repetition of the brand name and words and illustrations associated with it. Thus, the advertising platform is the foundation on which campaign messages are built.

Advertising media are the vehicles or forms of communication used to reach a desired audience. Print media include newspapers, magazines, direct mail, and billboards, while electronic media include television, radio, and Internet advertising.

Responding to Business Challenges
Disney English: A New Market Niche for Disney

Although Disney had high hopes for developing a theme park in Hong Kong, it was soon disappointed. Attendance at Hong Kong Disneyland was below expectations, costing Disney millions of dollars. Although attendance has risen in recent years, Hong Kong Disney still faced 2011 losses of more than $30 million. The company plans to open a bigger $4.4 billion resort on the Chinese mainland in Shanghai. Although this new venture might be successful, it could also further cannibalize Hong Kong Disneyland sales. Disney theme parks face many challenges as the company tries to adapt to different cultures.

Ironically, there is one business niche in China where Disney appears to be thriving: English education. In 2008, the Walt Disney Company launched Disney English in China. Learning English early in China is big business, and the growing private education sector is a $3.7 billion market. Chinese parents are determined that their children learn English early as a component of future academic and job success. Disney English caters to children ages 2 through 6 and to grade-school children. Its locations have tripled to 22 in a one-year period. Lessons, books, songs, exercises, and more are based on Disney stories and characters, fully immersing children in all things Disney. The program is expensive for the average Chinese citizen, but many parents are willing to pay.

Disney claims its schools in China were created solely to teach English, saying that it saw an opportunity to use its characters to motivate learning. However, it also has the unique marketing opportunity to make both parents and children aware of Disney offerings. Many parents and children appear happy with the program, which could cause them to view Disney favorably in the future. One has to wonder whether these favorable relationships with Disney English participants will help to increase demand for its Hong Kong and Shanghai theme parks.[36]

Discussion Questions

1. Why do you think Disney has decided to open up a larger park in Shanghai?
2. Why has Disney English been such a successful program?
3. How might the Disney English program indirectly market the theme parks?

Choice of media obviously influences the content and form of the message. Effective outdoor displays and short broadcast spot announcements require concise, simple messages. Magazine and newspaper advertisements can include considerable detail and long explanations. Because several kinds of media offer geographic selectivity, a precise message can be tailored to a particular geographic section of the target audience. For example, a company advertising in *Time* might decide to use one message in the New England region and another in the rest of the nation. A company may also choose to advertise in only one region. Such geographic selectivity lets a firm use the same message in different regions at different times. On the other hand, some companies are willing to pay extensive amounts of money to reach national audiences. Marketers spent approximately $3.5 million for one 30-second advertising slot during the 2012 Super Bowl due to its national reach and popularity.[37]

The use of online advertising is increasing. However, advertisers are demanding more for their ad dollars and proof that they are working, which is why Google AdWords only charges companies when users click on the ad. Certain types of ads are more popular than pop-up ads and banner ads that consumers find annoying. One technique is to blur the lines between television and online advertising. TV commercials may point viewers to a website for more information, where short "advertainment" films continue the marketing message. Marketers might also use the Internet to show advertisements or videos that were not accepted by mainstream television. When CBS rejected an ad from the National Football League Players Association involving the lockout of players during a collective bargaining dispute, the ad was played on the association's YouTube channel and other social media outlets.[38]

Infomercials—typically 30-minute blocks of radio or television air time featuring a celebrity or upbeat host talking about and demonstrating a product—have evolved as an advertising method. Toll-free numbers and website addresses are usually provided so consumers can conveniently purchase the product or obtain additional information. Although many consumers and companies have negative feelings about infomercials, apparently they get results.

personal selling
direct, two-way communication with buyers and potential buyers

Personal Selling. **Personal selling** is direct, two-way communication with buyers and potential buyers. For many products—especially large, expensive ones with specialized uses, such as cars, appliances, and houses—interaction between a salesperson and the customer is probably the most important promotional tool.

Personal selling is the most flexible of the promotional methods because it gives marketers the greatest opportunity to communicate specific information that might trigger a purchase. Only personal selling can zero in on a prospect and attempt to persuade that person to make a purchase. Although personal selling has a lot of advantages, it is one of the most costly forms of promotion. A sales call on an industrial customer can cost more than $400.

There are three distinct categories of salespersons: order takers (for example, retail sales clerks and route salespeople), creative salespersons (for example, automobile, furniture, and insurance salespeople), and support salespersons (for example, customer educators and goodwill builders who usually do not take orders). For most of these salespeople, personal selling is a six-step process:

Many Internet companies such as Google offer advertising services to companies who want to target consumers through digital media.

1. *Prospecting:* Identifying potential buyers of the product.
2. *Approaching:* Using a referral or calling on a customer without prior notice to determine interest in the product.
3. *Presenting:* Getting the prospect's attention with a product demonstration.
4. *Handling objections:* Countering reasons for not buying the product.
5. *Closing:* Asking the prospect to buy the product.
6. *Following up:* Checking customer satisfaction with the purchased product.

publicity
nonpersonal communication transmitted through the mass media but not paid for directly by the firm

Publicity. **Publicity** is nonpersonal communication transmitted through the mass media but not paid for directly by the firm. A firm does not pay the media cost for publicity and is not identified as the originator of the message; instead, the message is presented in news story form. Obviously, a company can benefit from publicity by releasing to news sources newsworthy messages about the firm and its involvement with the public. Many companies have *public relations* departments to try to gain favorable publicity and minimize negative publicity for the firm.

Although advertising and publicity are both carried by the mass media, they differ in several major ways. Advertising messages tend to be informative, persuasive, or both; publicity is mainly informative. Advertising is often designed to have an immediate impact or to provide specific information to persuade a person to act; publicity describes what a firm is doing, what products it is launching, or other newsworthy information, but seldom calls for action. When advertising is used, the organization must pay for media time and select the media that will best reach target audiences. The mass media willingly carry publicity because they believe it has general public interest. Advertising can be repeated a number of times; most publicity appears in the mass media once and is not repeated.

Advertising, personal selling, and sales promotion are especially useful for influencing an exchange directly. Publicity is extremely important when communication focuses on a company's activities and products and is directed at interest groups, current and potential investors, regulatory agencies, and society in general.

A variation of traditional advertising is buzz marketing, in which marketers attempt to create a trend or acceptance of a product. Companies seek out trendsetters in communities and get them to "talk up" a brand to their friends, family, co-workers, and others. Dell spread awareness of its brand by creating buzz among high school and college communities. It sent 170 brand ambassadors to campuses and communicated with students through social media. The company also held a contest to award one high school with the "prom of a lifetime." Because most young consumers purchase their first computers around this time in their lives, Dell believes that its buzz marketing campaign will positively affect the students' purchasing decisions.[39] Other marketers using the buzz technique include Hebrew National ("mom squads" grilled the company's hot dogs), and Chrysler (its retro PT Cruiser was planted in rental fleets). The idea behind buzz marketing is that an accepted member of a particular social group will be more credible than any form of paid communication.[40] The concept works best as part of an integrated marketing communication program that also includes traditional advertising, personal selling, sales promotion, and publicity.

A related concept is viral marketing, which describes the concept of getting Internet users to pass on ads and promotions to others. For example, the restaurant Kogi, which operates Korean taco trucks that traverse the Los Angeles area, was dubbed by *Newsweek* as "America's First Viral Restaurant" after it began using Twitter and the web to announce the whereabouts of its taco trucks.[41]

Sales Promotion.   **Sales promotion** involves direct inducements offering added value or some other incentive for buyers to enter into an exchange. Sales promotions are generally easier to measure and less expensive than advertising. The major tools of sales promotion are store displays, premiums, samples and demonstrations, coupons, contests and sweepstakes, refunds, and trade shows. Coupon-clipping in particular has become more common during the recent recession. While coupons in the past decade traditionally had a fairly low redemption rate, with about 2 percent being redeemed, the recent recession caused an upsurge in coupon usage. There has also been a major upsurge in the use of mobile coupons, or coupons sent to consumers over mobile devices. It is estimated that the redemption rates for mobile coupons will reach 8 percent of total coupon redemption rates by 2016.[42] While coupons can be a valuable tool in sales promotion, they cannot be relied upon to stand by themselves, but should be part of an overall promotion mix. Sales promotion stimulates customer purchasing and increases dealer effectiveness in selling products. It is used to enhance and supplement other forms of promotion. Sampling a product may also encourage consumers to buy. This is why many grocery stores provide free samples in the hopes of influencing consumers' purchasing decisions. In a given year, almost three-fourths of consumer product companies may use sampling.

sales promotion direct inducements offering added value or some other incentive for buyers to enter into an exchange

Companies use a pull strategy by offering coupons through the RetailMeNot website in the hopes of convincing customers to visit their stores.

Promotion Strategies: To Push or to Pull

push strategy
an attempt to motivate intermediaries to push the product down to their customers

In developing a promotion mix, organizations must decide whether to fashion a mix that pushes or pulls the product (Figure 12.8). A **push strategy** attempts to motivate intermediaries to push the product down to their customers. When a push strategy is used, the company attempts to motivate wholesalers and retailers to make the product available to their customers. Sales personnel may be used to persuade intermediaries to offer the product, distribute promotional materials, and offer special promotional incentives for those who agree to carry the product. For example, Kimberly Clark has begun partnering with its retailers to create a "win–win situation" for both types of companies. By sharing point-of-sales data with retailers and running more effective promotions, Kimberly Clark hopes to create favorable relationships with its intermediaries to push its products through the system.[43] A **pull strategy** uses promotion to create consumer demand for a product so that consumers exert pressure on marketing channel members to make it available. For example, the Travel Channel holds an annual sweepstakes contest awarding the grand prize winner with a trip for two to a foreign country. In order to win, participants must take a multiple-choice quiz with questions relating to what is on the Travel Channel. By holding this sweepstakes contest, the Travel Channel is encouraging more consumers to watch its television show, a type of pull marketing tactic.[44] Additionally, offering free samples prior to a product rollout encourages consumers to request the product from their favorite retailer.

pull strategy
the use of promotion to create consumer demand for a product so that consumers exert pressure on marketing channel members to make it available

A company can use either strategy, or it can use a variation or combination of the two. The exclusive use of advertising indicates a pull strategy. Personal selling to marketing channel members indicates a push strategy. The allocation of promotional resources to various marketing mix elements probably determines which strategy a marketer uses.

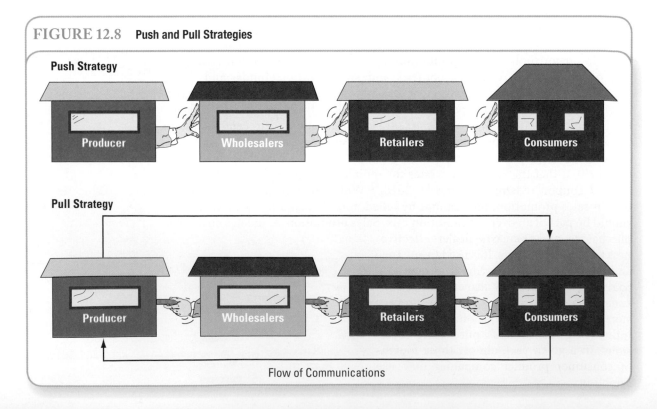

FIGURE 12.8   Push and Pull Strategies

Push Strategy

Producer — Wholesalers — Retailers — Consumers

Pull Strategy

Producer — Wholesalers — Retailers — Consumers

Flow of Communications

Objectives of Promotion

The marketing mix a company uses depends on its objectives. It is important to recognize that promotion is only one element of the marketing strategy and must be tied carefully to the goals of the firm, its overall marketing objectives, and the other elements of the marketing strategy. Firms use promotion for many reasons, but typical objectives are to stimulate demand, to stabilize sales, and to inform, remind, and reinforce customers.

Increasing demand for a product is probably the most typical promotional objective. Stimulating demand, often through advertising and sales promotion, is particularly important when a firm is using a pull strategy.

Another goal of promotion is to stabilize sales by maintaining the status quo—that is, the current sales level of the product. During periods of slack or decreasing sales, contests, prizes, vacations, and other sales promotions are sometimes offered to customers to maintain sales goals. Advertising is often used to stabilize sales by making customers aware of slack use periods. For example, auto manufacturers often provide rebates, free options, or lower-than-market interest rates to stabilize sales and thereby keep production lines moving during temporary slowdowns. A stable sales pattern allows the firm to run efficiently by maintaining a consistent level of production and storage and utilizing all its functions so that it is ready when sales increase.

An important role of any promotional program is to inform potential buyers about the organization and its products. A major portion of advertising in the United States, particularly in daily newspapers, is informational. Providing information about the availability, price, technology, and features of a product is very important in encouraging a buyer to move toward a purchase decision. Nearly all forms of promotion involve an attempt to help consumers learn more about a product and a company.

Promotion is also used to remind consumers that an established organization is still around and sells certain products that have uses and benefits. Often advertising reminds customers that they may need to use a product more frequently or in certain situations. Pennzoil, for example, has run television commercials reminding car owners that they need to change their oil every 3,000 miles to ensure proper performance of their cars.

Reinforcement promotion attempts to assure current users of the product that they have made the right choice and tells them how to get the most satisfaction from the product. Also, a company could release publicity statements through the news media about a new use for a product. Additionally, firms can have salespeople communicate with current and potential customers about the proper use and maintenance of a product—all in the hope of developing a repeat customer.

Promotional Positioning

Promotional positioning uses promotion to create and maintain an image of a product in buyers' minds. It is a natural result of market segmentation. In both promotional positioning and market segmentation, the firm targets a given product or brand at a portion of the total market. A promotional strategy helps differentiate the product and makes it appeal to a particular market segment. For example, to appeal to safety-conscious consumers, Volvo heavily promotes the safety and crashworthiness of Volvo automobiles in its advertising. Volkswagen has done the same thing with its edgy ads showing car crashes. Promotion can be used to change or reinforce an image. Effective promotion influences customers and persuades them to buy.

promotional positioning the use of promotion to create and maintain an image of a product in buyers' minds

Importance of Marketing Strategy

Marketing creates value through the marketing mix. For customers, value means receiving a product in which the benefit of the product outweighs the cost, or price paid for it. For marketers, value means that the benefits (usually monetary) received from selling the product outweigh the costs it takes to develop and sell it. This requires carefully integrating the marketing mix into an effective marketing strategy. One misstep could mean a loss in profits, whether it be from a failed product idea, shortages or oversupply of a product, a failure to effectively promote the product, or prices that are too high or too low. And while some of these marketing mix elements can be easily fixed, other marketing mix elements such as distribution can be harder to adapt.

On the other hand, firms that develop an effective marketing mix to meet customer needs will gain competitive advantages over those that do not. Often, these advantages occur when the firm excels at one or more elements of the marketing mix. Walmart has a reputation for its everyday low prices, while Tiffany's is known for its high-quality jewelry. However, excelling at one element of the marketing mix does not mean that a company can neglect the others. The best product cannot succeed if consumers do not know about it or if they cannot find it in stores. Additionally, firms must constantly monitor the market environment to understand how demand is changing and whether adaptations in the marketing mix are needed. It is therefore essential that every element of the marketing mix be carefully evaluated and synchronized with the marketing strategy. Only then will firms be able to achieve the marketing concept of providing products that satisfy customers' needs while allowing the organization to achieve its goals.

So You Want to Be a Marketing Manager

Many jobs in marketing are closely tied to the marketing mix functions: distribution, product, promotion, and price. Often the job titles could be sales manager, distribution or supply chain manager, advertising account executive, or store manager.

A distribution manager arranges for transportation of goods within firms and through marketing channels. Transportation can be costly, and time is always an important factor, so minimizing their effects is vital to the success of a firm. Distribution managers must choose one or a combination of transportation modes from a vast array of options, taking into account local, federal, and international regulations for different freight classifications; the weight, size, and fragility of products to be shipped; time schedules; and loss and damage ratios. Manufacturing firms are the largest employers of distribution managers.

A product manager is responsible for the success or failure of a product line. This requires a general knowledge of advertising, transportation modes, inventory control, selling and sales management, promotion, marketing research, packaging, and pricing. Frequently, several years of selling and sales management experience are prerequisites for such a position as well as college training in business administration. Being a product manager can be rewarding both financially and psychologically.

Some of the most creative roles in the business world are in the area of advertising. Advertising pervades our daily lives, as businesses and other organizations try to grab our attention and tell us about what they have to offer. Copywriters, artists, and account executives in advertising must have creativity, imagination, artistic talent, and expertise in expression and persuasion. Advertising is an area of business in which a wide variety of educational backgrounds may be useful, from degrees in advertising itself, to journalism or liberal arts degrees. Common entry-level positions in an advertising agency are found in the traffic department, account service (account coordinator), or the media department (media assistant). Advertising jobs are also available in many manufacturing or retail firms, nonprofit organizations, banks, professional associations, utility companies, and other arenas outside of an advertising agency.

Although a career in retailing may begin in sales, there is much more to retailing than simply selling. Many retail personnel occupy management positions, focusing on selecting and ordering merchandise, promotional activities, inventory control, customer credit operations, accounting, personnel, and store security. Many specific examples of retailing jobs can be found in large department stores. A section manager coordinates inventory and promotions and interacts with buyers, salespeople, and consumers. The buyer's job is fast-paced, often involving much travel and pressure. Buyers must be open-minded and foresighted in their hunt for new, potentially successful items. Regional managers coordinate the activities of several retail stores within a specific geographic area, usually monitoring and supporting sales, promotions, and general procedures. Retail management can be exciting and challenging. Growth in retailing is expected to accompany the growth in population and is likely to create substantial opportunities in the coming years.

While a career in marketing can be very rewarding, marketers today agree that the job is getting tougher. Many advertising and marketing executives say the job has gotten much more demanding in the past 10 years, viewing their number-one challenge as balancing work and personal obligations. Other challenges include staying current on industry trends or technologies, keeping motivated/inspired on the job, and measuring success. If you are up to the challenge, you may find that a career in marketing is just right for you to utilize your business knowledge while exercising your creative side as well.

Review Your Understanding

Describe the role of product in the marketing mix, including how products are developed, classified, and identified.

Products (goods, services, ideas) are among a firm's most visible contacts with consumers and must meet consumers' needs and expectations to ensure success. New-product development is a multistep process: idea development, the screening of new ideas, business analysis, product development, test marketing, and commercialization. Products are usually classified as either consumer or business products. Consumer products can be further classified as convenience, shopping, or specialty products. The business product classifications are raw materials, major equipment, accessory equipment, component parts, processed materials, supplies, and industrial services. Products also can be classified by the stage of the product life cycle (introduction, growth, maturity, and decline). Identifying products includes branding (the process of naming and identifying products); packaging (the product's container); and labeling (information, such as content and warnings, on the package).

Define price, and discuss its importance in the marketing mix, including various pricing strategies a firm might employ.

Price is the value placed on an object exchanged between a buyer and a seller. It is probably the most flexible variable of the marketing mix. Pricing objectives include survival, maximization of profits and sales volume, and maintaining the status quo. When a firm introduces a new product, it may use price skimming or penetration pricing. Psychological pricing and price discounting are other strategies.

Identify factors affecting distribution decisions, such as marketing channels and intensity of market coverage.

Making products available to customers is facilitated by middlemen, or intermediaries, who bridge the gap between the producer of the product and its ultimate user. A marketing channel is a group of marketing organizations that directs the flow of products from producers to consumers. Market coverage relates to the number and variety of outlets that make products available to customers; it may be intensive, selective, or exclusive. Physical distribution is all the activities necessary to move products from producers to consumers, including inventory planning and control, transportation, warehousing, and materials handling.

Specify the activities involved in promotion, as well as promotional strategies and promotional positioning.

Promotion encourages marketing exchanges by persuading individuals, groups, and organizations to accept goods,

services, and ideas. The promotion mix includes advertising (a paid form of nonpersonal communication transmitted through a mass medium), personal selling (direct, two-way communication with buyers and potential buyers), publicity (nonpersonal communication transmitted through the mass media but not paid for directly by the firm), and sales promotion (direct inducements offering added value or some other incentive for buyers to enter into an exchange). A push strategy attempts to motivate intermediaries to push the product down to their customers, whereas a pull strategy tries to create consumer demand for a product so that consumers exert pressure on marketing channel members to make the product available. Typical promotion objectives are to stimulate demand; stabilize sales; and inform, remind, and reinforce customers. Promotional positioning is the use of promotion to create and maintain in the buyer's mind an image of a product.

Evaluate an organization's marketing strategy plans.

Based on the material in this chapter, you should be able to answer the questions posed in "Solve the Dilemma" on page 402 and evaluate the company's marketing strategy plans, including its target market and marketing mix.

Revisit the World of Business

1. Describe the Red Bull product and how it is used to target athletes.
2. Describe Red Bull's promotional strategy.
3. Why do you think Red Bull is expanding into other forms of media such as magazines and television?

Learn the Terms

advertising 391
advertising campaign 392
branding 377
business products 374
commercialization 372
consumer products 373
discounts 384
exclusive distribution 389
generic products 378
integrated marketing
  communications 391
intensive distribution 388
labeling 379

manufacturer brands 377
marketing channel 384
materials handling 390
packaging 379
penetration price 383
personal selling 394
physical distribution 389
price skimming 383
private distributor brands 377
product line 374
product mix 374
promotional positioning 397
psychological pricing 383

publicity 394
pull strategy 396
push strategy 396
quality 380
retailers 384
sales promotion 395
selective distribution 388
test marketing 372
trademark 377
transportation 389
warehousing 390
wholesalers 386

Check Your Progress

1. What steps do companies generally take to develop and introduce a new product?

2. What is the product life cycle? How does a product's life cycle stage affect its marketing strategy?

3. Which marketing mix variable is probably the most flexible? Why?

4. Distinguish between the two ways to set the base price for a new product.

5. What is probably the least flexible marketing mix variable? Why?

6. Describe the typical marketing channels for consumer products.

7. What activities are involved in physical distribution? What functions does a warehouse perform?

8. How do publicity and advertising differ? How are they related?

9. What does the personal selling process involve? Briefly discuss the process.

10. List the circumstances in which the push and pull promotional strategies are used.

Get Involved

1. Pick three products you use every day (in school, at work, or for pleasure—perhaps one of each). Determine what phase of the product life cycle each is in. Evaluate the marketer's strategy (product, price, promotion, and distribution) for the product and whether it is appropriate for the life-cycle stage.

2. Design a distribution channel for a manufacturer of stuffed toys.

3. Pick a nearby store, and briefly describe the kinds of sales promotion used and their effectiveness

Build Your Skills

ANALYZING MOTEL 6'S MARKETING STRATEGY

Background

Made famous through the well-known radio and TV commercials spoken in the distinctive "down-home" voice of Tom Bodett, the Dallas-based Motel 6 chain of budget motels is probably familiar to you. Based on the information provided here and any personal knowledge you may have about the company, you will analyze the marketing strategy of Motel 6.

Task

Read the following paragraphs; then complete the questions that follow.

Motel 6 was established in 1962 with the original name emphasizing its low-cost, no-frills approach. Rooms at that time were $6 per night. Today, Motel 6 has more than 760 units, and the average nightly cost is $49.99. Motel 6 is the largest company-owned and operated lodging chain in the United States. Customers receive HBO, ESPN, free morning coffee, and free local phone calls, and most units have pools and some business services. Motel 6 has made a name for itself by offering clean, comfortable rooms at the lowest prices of any national motel chain and by standardizing both its product offering and its operating policies and procedures. The company's national spokesperson, Tom Bodett, is featured in radio and television commercials that use humorous stories to show why it makes sense to stay at Motel 6 rather than a pricey hotel.

In appealing to pleasure travelers on a budget as well as business travelers looking to get the most for their dollar, one commercial makes the point that all hotel and motel rooms look the same at night when the lights are out—when customers are getting what they came for, a good night's sleep. Motel 6 location sites are selected based on whether they provide convenient access to the highway system and whether they are close to areas such as shopping centers, tourist attractions, or business districts.

1. In SELECTING A TARGET MARKET, which approach is Motel 6 using to segment markets?
   a. concentration approach
   b. multisegment approach

2. In DEVELOPING A MARKETING MIX, identify in the second column of the table what the current strategy is and then identify any changes you think Motel 6 should consider for carrying it successfully through the next five years.

Marketing Mix Variable	Current Strategy	5-Year Strategy
a. Product		
b. Price		
c. Distribution		
d. Promotion		

Solve the Dilemma   LO 12-5

BETTER HEALTH WITH SNACKS

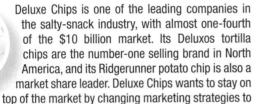

Deluxe Chips is one of the leading companies in the salty-snack industry, with almost one-fourth of the $10 billion market. Its Deluxos tortilla chips are the number-one selling brand in North America, and its Ridgerunner potato chip is also a market share leader. Deluxe Chips wants to stay on top of the market by changing marketing strategies to match changing consumer needs and preferences. Promoting specific brands to market segments with the appropriate price and distribution channel is helping Deluxe Chips succeed.

As many middle-aged consumers modify their snacking habits, Deluxe Chips is considering a new product line of light snack foods with less fat and cholesterol and targeted at the 35- to 50-year-old consumer who enjoys snacking but wants to be more health conscious. Marketing research suggests that the product will succeed as long as it tastes good and that consumers may be willing to pay more for it. Large expenditures on advertising may be necessary to overcome the competition. However, it may be possible to analyze customer profiles and retail store characteristics and then match the right product with the right neighborhood. Store-specific micromarketing would allow Deluxe Chips to spend its promotional dollars more efficiently.

Discussion Questions

1. Design a marketing strategy for the new product line.
2. Critique your marketing strategy in terms of its strengths and weaknesses.
3. What are your suggestions for implementation of the marketing strategy?

Build Your Business Plan

DIMENSIONS OF MARKETING STRATEGY

If you think your product/business is truly new to or unique to the market, you need to substantiate your claim. After a thorough exploration on the web, you want to make sure there has not been a similar business/service recently launched in your community. Check with your Chamber of Commerce or Economic Development Office that might be able to provide you with a history of recent business failures. If you are not confident about the ability or willingness of customers to try your new product or service, collecting your own primary data to ascertain demand is highly advisable.

The decision of where to initially set your prices is a critical one. If there are currently similar products in the market, you need to be aware of the competitors' prices before you determine yours. If your product/service is new to the market, you can price it high (market skimming strategy) as long as you realize that the high price will probably attract competitors to the market more quickly (they will think they can make the same product for less), which will force you to drop your prices sooner than you would like. Another strategy to consider is market penetration pricing, a strategy that sets price lower and discourages competition from entering the market as quickly. Whatever strategy you decide to use, don't forget to examine your product/service's elasticity.

At this time, you need to start thinking about how to promote your product. Why do you feel your product/service is different or new to the market? How do you want to position your product/service so customers view it favorably? Remember this is all occurring *within the consumer's mind*.

See for Yourself Videocase

GROUPON MASTERS PROMOTION TO BECOME A POPULAR DAILY DEAL SITE

In 2008, a start-up company called Groupon launched an innovative business model. The model works in the following way: Groupon partners with businesses to offer subscribers daily deals. These deals are provided through the Groupon website, e-mail, and mobile devices. Groupon deals are similar to coupons, but with one major catch. A certain number of people (a group) must agree to purchase the deal. If enough people purchase, then the deal becomes available to everyone. If not enough people purchase, then no one receives that particular deal. In this way, Groupon has made the idea of coupons or deals into a social process.

The model quickly caught on with consumers. In many ways, Groupon lowers the risk for consumers when purchasing a new product because the product or activity costs less than its regular price. This encourages consumers to try out new activities such as skydiving or dining at a certain restaurant. Groupon also alerts consumers about deals that they were not aware of beforehand. Making consumers aware of products is one of the major purposes of promotion.

When it first started promoting Groupon deals, the company used social media sites such as Twitter and Facebook. One of the advantages of this type of advertising is the chance for an Internet ad or posting to go viral. With just a simple click of a button, an Internet user can inform his or her friends about the deal, spreading awareness of the company or product. This word-of-mouth marketing has been proven to be one of the most effective and trusted forms of promotion.

The benefit for businesses is the possibility of attracting repeat customers. By offering deals through the Groupon site, businesses are able to get consumers into the store. If consumers have a good experience, then they might return or tell their friends about the business. Groupon therefore acts as a type of conduit that brings consumers and businesses together. Bo Hurd, national sales manager/business development, describes how this works for businesses. "We're going get the word out there, and then we're actually going to have these people decide that they want to come in and try your services. And then it's up to you to actually convert them into long-term, full-paying customers."

Because Groupon depends on businesses as much as consumers, they must get businesses to agree to offer deals through its site. Groupon engages heavily in public relations to make its name known among companies. Personal selling is also very important to Groupon's promotion mix. Groupon's sales force uses phone calls and e-mails to contact businesses in the major cities in which it does business. Because it wants to offer the best deals, Groupon will generate leads by looking at review websites such as Yelp and Citysearch. By looking at how consumers rate certain businesses, Groupon can get a better idea of which businesses to target.

The introduction of rival deal sites such as Google Offers and Living Social is requiring Groupon to continue innovating. The firm has begun to invest in new product offerings, such as Groupon Now!, which is a mobile app that provides time-specific deals to consumers based on their location at a particular moment. Each new product that Groupon introduces requires adaptations to the promotion mix. For instance, promoting Groupon Now! to businesses resulted in some challenges. At first, there were two separate sales teams: one for Groupon's daily deal service and another for Groupon Now! The problem was that both sales teams would call up the same business, essentially duplicating the sales calls and making the business feel overwhelmed. As a result, Groupon changed its structure so that now one sales representative will offer both products during the sales call. Because promotion is an easier variable to modify than distribution or product, Groupon was able to adapt part of its promotion mix to increase its effectiveness.

Groupon's ability to master different forms of promotion has contributed to its success as a company. Going forward, it will need to continue to communicate its value, particularly of its new products, to both businesses and consumers.[45]

DISCUSSION QUESTIONS

1. How has Groupon effectively used personal selling, advertising, and public relations to market its products and services?

2. Is there a difference in how Groupon markets itself to consumers versus how it markets itself to businesses? If so, describe these differences.

3. Groupon had to adapt the personal selling component of the promotion mix. Why is it sometimes necessary for businesses to adapt the promotion mix?

Remember to check out our Online Learning Center at www.mhhe.com/ferrell9e.

Team Exercise

Form groups and search for examples of convenience products, shopping products, specialty products, and business products. How are these products marketed? Provide examples of any ads that you can find to show examples of the promotional strategies for these products. Report your findings to the class.

13

Chapter Outline

Digital Marketing and Social Networking

Learning Objectives

After reading this chapter, you will be able to:

LO 13-1 Define *digital media* and *digital marketing* and recognize their increasing value in strategic planning.

LO 13-2 Demonstrate the role of digital marketing and social networking in today's business environment.

LO 13-3 Show how digital media affect the marketing mix.

LO 13-4 Define social networking and illustrate how businesses can use different types of social networking media.

LO 13-5 Identify legal and ethical considerations in digital media.

LO 13-6 Evaluate a marketer's dilemma and propose recommendations.

Weibo: Micro-Blogging for the Chinese Population

Micro-blogging isn't just for Americans. In China, micro-blogging is revolutionizing the way consumers network and access news. Chinese micro-blogs, or *weibos,* are growing at an enormous rate. The *weibo* platform provided by the Chinese Internet company Sina has 140 million registered users compared to Twitter's 17 million.

Weibos share many similarities with Twitter. The limit for most *weibo* posts is 140 words. Just as Twitter has been utilized to organize events such as protests, Chinese Internet users have also utilized *weibo* to encourage political

新浪微博
weibo.com
测试版

加入微博，分享単！
随时随地发布你身边的新鲜事，
一亿人已经加入，再不来

activism. On the other hand, *weibo* has incorporated more social networking elements than has Twitter. For instance, *weibo* enables users to post short messages, videos, and audio content. While Twitter makes money from sponsored tweets, *weibo* sites allow for advertising, e-commerce, and group purchasing deals. It also offers social games like Farmville, and Sina *weibo* has given users the ability to purchase virtual currency. In these respects, *weibo* incorporates elements of micro-blogging, social networking, and virtual realities.

The popularity of *weibo* is providing a number of opportunities for marketers. *Weibo* has become a major source of information, and one study estimates that *weibo* is the third most popular online resource for public opinions in China. More than 450 media companies have registered on Sina's *weibo* platform. Other types of organizations are following suit. For instance, the U.S. Embassy in China has created a *weibo* account and is using it to post news on American culture, colleges, and visas.

continued

Weibo has one other advantage over major social networking sites—it is supported by the government. *Weibo* companies censor some of their more sensitive postings to satisfy the Chinese government. Twitter and Facebook are currently banned in China, giving *weibo* companies first-mover advantages. Sina's *weibo* is thus becoming a formidable competitor to the more established Facebook and Twitter.[1]

Introduction[2]

The Internet and information technology have dramatically changed the environment for business. Marketers' new ability to convert all types of communications into digital media has created efficient, inexpensive ways of connecting businesses and consumers and has improved the flow and the usefulness of information. Businesses have the information they need to make more informed decisions, and consumers have access to a greater variety of products and more information about choices and quality.

The defining characteristic of information technology in the 21st century is accelerating change. New systems and applications advance so rapidly that it is almost impossible to keep up with the latest developments. Startup companies emerge that quickly overtake existing approaches to digital media. When Google first arrived on the scene, a number of search engines were fighting for dominance. With its fast, easy-to-use search engine, Google became number one and is now challenging many industries, including advertising, newspapers, mobile phones, and book publishing. Despite its victory, Google is constantly being challenged itself by competitors like Yahoo! and Baidu. Baidu is gaining ground with 75 percent of the Chinese search engine market. Baidu has also announced it will create its own mobile technology to challenge Google's more than 40 percent market share in mobile operating systems in China.[3] Social networking continues to advance as the channel most observers believe will dominate digital communication in the near future. Today, people spend more time on social networking sites, such as Facebook, than they spend on e-mail.

In this chapter, we first provide some key definitions related to digital marketing and social networking. Next, we discuss using digital media in business and digital marketing. We look at marketing mix considerations when using digital media and pay special attention to social networking. Then we focus on digital marketing strategies—particularly new communication channels like social networks—and consider how consumers are changing their information searches and consumption behavior to fit emerging technologies and trends. Finally, we examine the legal and social issues associated with information technology, digital media, and e-business.

LO 13-1

e-business
carrying out the goals of business through utilization of the Internet

digital media
electronic media that function using digital codes via computers, cellular phones, smart phones, and other digital devices that have been released in recent years

Growth and Benefits of Digital Communication

Let's start with a clear understanding of our focus in this chapter. First, we can distinguish **e-business** from traditional business by noting that conducting e-business means carrying out the goals of business through the use of the Internet. **Digital media** are electronic media that function using digital codes—when we refer to digital media, we mean media available via computers and other digital devices, including mobile and wireless ones like cell phones and smart phones.

Digital marketing uses all digital media, including the Internet and mobile and interactive channels, to develop communication and exchanges with customers. Digital marketing is a term we will use often, because we are interested in all types of digital communications, regardless of the electronic channel that transmits the data. Digital marketing goes beyond the Internet and includes mobile phones, banner ads, digital outdoor marketing, and social networks.

The Internet has created tremendous opportunities for businesses to forge relationships with consumers and business customers, target markets more precisely, and even reach previously inaccessible markets at home and around the world. The Internet also facilitates business transactions, allowing companies to network with manufacturers, wholesalers, retailers, suppliers, and outsource firms to serve customers more quickly and more efficiently. The telecommunication opportunities created by the Internet have set the stage for digital marketing's development and growth.

Digital communication offers a completely new dimension in connecting with others. Some of the characteristics that distinguish digital from traditional communication are addressability, interactivity, accessibility, connectivity, and control. These terms are discussed in Table 13.1.

The website Nextag puts power in the hands of consumers by allowing them to compare prices of products at different stores before buying.

digital marketing uses all digital media, including the Internet and mobile and interactive channels, to develop communication and exchanges with customers

TABLE 13.1

Characteristics of Digital Marketing

Characteristic	Definition	Example
Addressability	The ability of the marketer to identify customers before they make a purchase	Amazon installs cookies on a user's computer that allows it to identify the owner when he or she returns to the website.
Interactivity	The ability of customers to express their needs and wants directly to the firm in response to its marketing communications	Texas Instruments interacts with its customers on its Facebook page by answering concerns and posting updates.
Accessibility	The ability for marketers to obtain digital information	Google can use web searches done through its search engine to learn about customer interests.
Connectivity	The ability for consumers to be connected with marketers along with other consumers	The Avon Voices website encouraged singers to upload their singing videos, which can then be voted on by other users for the chance to be discovered.
Control	The customer's ability to regulate the information they view as well as the rate and exposure to that information	Consumers use Kayak to discover the best travel deals.

LO 13-2

Using Digital Media in Business

The phenomenal growth of digital media has provided new ways of conducting business. Given almost instant communication with precisely defined consumer groups, firms can use real-time exchanges to create and stimulate interactive communication, forge closer relationships, and learn more accurately about consumer and supplier needs. Consider that Amazon.com, one of the most successful electronic businesses, ranked number 78 on the *Fortune* 500 list of America's largest corporations.[4] Amazon is a true digital marketer and was one of the early success stories in the industry, getting 50 percent of its revenue from international sales.[5] Many of you may not remember a world before Amazon because it has completely transformed how many people shop.

Because it is fast and inexpensive, digital communication is making it easier for businesses to conduct marketing research, provide and obtain price and product information, and advertise, as well as to fulfill their business goals by selling goods and services online. Even the U.S. government engages in digital marketing activities—marketing everything from Treasury bonds and other financial instruments to oil-drilling leases and wild horses. Procter & Gamble uses the Internet as a fast, cost-effective means for marketing research, judging consumer demand for potential new products by inviting online consumers to sample new-product prototypes and provide feedback. If a product gets rave reviews from the samplers, the company might decide to introduce it. By testing concepts online, companies can save significant time and money in getting new products to market.

New businesses and even industries are evolving that would not exist without digital media. Hulu is a video website that lets consumers watch a broad collection of premium videos from more than 350 content companies, any time and from anywhere. The company has partnered with several companies to advertise on their sites, including Johnson & Johnson and Best Buy. In fact, Hulu's growing popularity is allowing it to compete with YouTube.[6]

The reality, however, is that Internet markets are more similar to traditional markets than they are different. Thus, successful digital marketing strategies, like traditional business strategies, focus on creating products that customers need or want, not merely developing a brand name or reducing the costs associated with online transactions. Instead of changing all industries, digital technology has had much more impact in certain industries where the cost of business and customer transactions has been very high. For example, investment trading is less expensive online because customers can buy and sell investments, such as stocks and mutual funds, on their own. Firms such as Charles Schwab Corp., the biggest online brokerage firm, have been innovators in promoting online trading. Traditional brokers such as Merrill Lynch have had to follow with online trading for their customers.

Because the Internet lowers the cost of communication, it can contribute significantly to any industry or activity that depends on the flow of digital

Need paint? Benjamin Moore & Co. has an app that can help you pick out the perfect color on your iPhone.

information such as entertainment, health care, government services, education, and computer services like software development. The publishing industry is transitioning away from print newspapers, magazines, and books as more consumers purchase e-readers, like the Kindle Fire or the new iPad, or read the news online. Even your textbook is available electronically. Because publishers save money on paper, ink, and shipping, many times electronic versions of books are cheaper than their paper counterparts.

Digital media can also improve communication within and between businesses. In the future, most significant gains will come from productivity improvements within businesses. Communication is a key business function, and improving the speed and clarity of communication can help businesses save time and improve employee problem-solving abilities. Digital media can be a communications backbone that helps to store knowledge, information, and records in management information systems so co-workers can access it when faced with a problem to solve. A well-designed management information system that utilizes digital technology can, therefore, help reduce confusion, improve organization and efficiency, and facilitate clear communications. Given the crucial role of communication and information in business, the long-term impact of digital media on economic growth is substantial, and it will inevitably grow over time.

Firms also need to control access to their digital communication systems to ensure worker productivity. This can be a challenge. For example, in companies across the United States, employees are surfing the Internet for as much as an hour during each workday. Many firms are trying to curb this practice by limiting employees' access to instant messaging services, streaming music, and websites with adult content.[7]

Digital Media and the Marketing Mix   LO 13-3

While digital marketing shares some similarities with conventional marketing techniques, a few valuable differences stand out. First, digital media make customer communications faster and interactive. Second, digital media help companies reach new target markets more easily, affordably, and quickly than ever before. Finally, digital media help marketers utilize new resources in seeking out and communicating with customers. One of the most important benefits of digital marketing is the ability of marketers and customers to easily share information. Through websites, social networks, and other digital media, consumers can learn about everything they consume and use in their lives, ask questions, voice complaints, indicate preferences, and otherwise communicate about their needs and desires. Many marketers use e-mail, mobile phones, social networking, wikis, media sharing, blogs, video-conferencing, and other technologies to coordinate activities and communicate with employees, customers, and suppliers. Twitter, considered both a social network and a micro-blog, illustrates how these digital technologies can combine to create new communication opportunities.

Nielsen Marketing Research revealed that consumers now spend more time on social networking sites than they do on e-mail, and social network use is still growing. The most avid online social networkers are users from Israel, followed by the United States (see Figure 13.1). With digital media, even small businesses can reach new markets through these inexpensive communication channels. Brick-and-mortar companies like Walmart utilize online catalogs and company websites and blogs to supplement their retail stores. Internet companies like Amazon.com and Zappos.com

- *Location-based networks:* Location-based networks are built for mobile devices. One of the most popular location-based networks is Foursquare, which lets users check in and share their location with others. Businesses such as Walgreen's and Chili's Grill & Bar have partnered with Foursquare to offer incentives to consumers who check in at their venues.[60]
- *Mobile applications:* Mobile applications (known as *apps*) are software programs that run on mobile devices and give users access to certain content.[61] Businesses release apps to help consumers access more information about their company or to provide incentives. Apps are discussed in further detail in the next section.

Applications and Widgets

Applications are adding an entirely new layer to the marketing environment, as approximately half of all American adult cell phone users have applications on their mobile devices.[62] The most important feature of apps is the convenience and cost savings they offer to the consumer. Certain apps allow consumers to scan a product's barcode and then compare it with the prices of identical products in other stores. Mobile apps also enable customers to download in-store discounts. Shoppers using the Shopkick application can download rewards at Best Buy, Macy's, Target, and other retailers.[63]

To remain competitive, companies are beginning to use mobile marketing to offer additional incentives to consumers. International Hotel Group, for instance, has both a mobile website and a Priority Club Reward app. As a result of its mobile marketing strategy, the company experienced a 20 percent boost in mobile site jumps per month.[64] Another application that marketers are finding useful is the QR scanning app. QR codes are black-and-white squares that sometimes appear in magazines, posters, and storefront displays. Smart phone users who have downloaded the QR scanning application can open their smart phones and scan the code, which contains a hidden message accessible with the app. The QR scanning app recognizes the code and opens the link, video, or image on the phone's screen. Marketers are using QR codes to promote their companies and offer consumer discounts.[65]

Mobile payments are also gaining traction, and companies like Google are working to capitalize on this opportunity.[66] Google Wallet is a mobile app that stores credit card information on the smart phone. When the shopper is ready to check out, he or she can tap the phone at the point of sale for the transaction to be registered.[67] The success of mobile payments in revolutionizing the shopping experience will largely depend upon retailers to adopt this payment system, but companies such as Starbucks are already jumping at the opportunity. An estimated 70 percent of U.S. consumers will own smart phones by 2014, so businesses cannot afford to miss out on the chance to profit from these new trends.[68]

Widgets are small bits of software on a website, desktop, or mobile device that enables users "to interface with the application and operating system." Marketers might use widgets to display news headlines, clocks, or games on their web pages.[69] Widgets have been used by companies such as A&E Television Network as a form of viral marketing—users can download the widget and send it to their friends with a click of a button.[70] Widgets downloaded to a user's desktop can update the user on the latest company or product information, enhancing relationship marketing between companies and their fans. For instance, Krispy Kreme® Doughnuts developed a widget that will alert users when their Original Glazed® doughnuts are hot off the oven at their favorite Krispy Kreme shop.[71] Widgets are an innovative digital marketing tool to personalize web pages, alert users to the latest company information, and spread awareness of the company's products.

Using Digital Media to Reach Consumers

We've seen that customer-generated communications and digital media connect consumers as never before. These connections let consumers share information and experiences without company interference so they get more of the "real story" on a product or company feature. In many ways, these media take some of the professional marketer's power to control and dispense information and place it in the hands of the consumer.

However, this shift does not have to spell doom for marketers, who can choose to utilize the power of the consumer and Internet technology to their advantage. While consumers use digital media to access more product information, marketers can use the same sites to get better and more targeted information about the consumer— often more than they could gather through traditional marketing venues. Marketers increasingly use consumer-generated content to aid their own marketing efforts, even going so far as to incorporate Internet bloggers in their publicity campaigns. Finally, marketers are also beginning to use the Internet to track the success of their online marketing campaigns, creating an entirely new way of gathering marketing research.

The challenge for digital media marketers is to constantly adapt to new technologies and changing consumer patterns. Unfortunately, the attrition rate for digital media channels is very high, with some dying off each year as new ones emerge. Social networks are no exception: the earliest ones, like Six Degrees, disappeared when it failed to catch on with the general public, and Friendster, though still active, has been far surpassed by newer networks. As time passes, digital media are becoming more sophisticated so as to reach consumers in more effective ways. Those that are not able to adapt and change eventually fail.

Mastering digital media presents a daunting task for businesses, particularly those used to more traditional means of marketing. For this reason, it is essential that marketers focus on the changing social behaviors of consumers, the ways in which they gather and use information, and the way the Internet is enabling them to get involved in the marketing process.

Charlene Li and Josh Bernoff of Forrester Research, a technology and market research company, emphasize the need for marketers to understand these changing relationships in the online media world. By grouping consumers into different segments based on how they utilize digital media, marketers can gain a better understanding of the online market and how best to proceed.[72]

Table 13.2 shows seven ways that Forrester Research groups consumers based on their Internet activity (or lack thereof). The categories are not mutually exclusive; online consumers can participate in more than one at a time.

Yowza!!, a mobile phone app, uses the GPS devices in cell phones to locate consumers and send them coupons from retailers in that area.

TABLE 13.2

Social Technographics

Creators	Publish a blog
	Publish personal web pages
	Upload original video
	Upload original audio/music
	Write articles or stories and post them
Conversationalists	Update status on social networking sites
	Post updates on Twitter
Critics	Post ratings/reviews of products or services
	Comment on someone else's blog
	Contribute to online forums
	Contribute to/edit articles in a wiki
Collectors	Use RSS feeds
	Add tags to web pages or photos
	"Vote" for websites online
Joiners	Maintain profile on a social networking site
	Visit social networking sites
Spectators	Read blogs
	Watch video from other users
	Listen to podcasts
	Read online forums
	Read customer ratings/reviews
Inactives	None of the activities

Source: Charlene Li and Josh Bernoff, *Groundswell* (Boston: Harvard Business Press, 2008), p. 43. "Forrester Unveils New Segment of Social Technographics – The Conversationalists," *360 Digital Connections,* January 21, 2010, http://blog.360i.com/social-media/forrester-new-segment-social-technographics-conversationalists (accessed April 17, 2012).

Creators are consumers who create their own media outlets, such as blogs, podcasts, consumer-generated videos, and wikis.[73] Consumer-generated media are increasingly important to online marketers as a conduit for addressing consumers directly. The second group of Internet users is *conversationalists.* Conversationalists regularly update their Twitter feeds or status updates on social networking sites. Although they are less involved than creators, conversationalists spend time at least once a week (and often more) on digital media sites posting updates.[74] The third category, *critics,* consists of people who comment on blogs or post ratings and reviews on review websites such as Yelp. Because many online shoppers read ratings and reviews to aid their purchasing decisions, critics should be a primary component in a company's digital marketing strategy. The next category is *collectors*. They collect information and organize content generated by critics and creators.[75] Because

Responding to Business Challenges
Should Facebook Expand into China?

Facebook is in a quandary. For years, the social network has toed the line between promoting open communication and protecting user privacy. Yet as Facebook seeks to grow internationally, Chinese expansion might require the company to compromise its openness.

In China, Facebook is blocked. The Chinese government views Facebook as a threat because of its open nature, particularly after social networks were used in the 2011 Middle Eastern protests to coordinate and assemble protestors. It is therefore unlikely that the country will accept Facebook without some censorship.

Facebook CEO Mark Zuckerberg has expressed his goal to "connect the world," which will be difficult if 1.3 billion Chinese consumers cannot access the site. He feels that Facebook could help promote change in China, even if some of its use is restricted. But will allowing government censorship conflict with its core values? Additionally, while 70 percent of Facebook's users are non-U.S. residents, much of the company's advertising revenue comes from the United States.

Compromising its transparency could alienate Facebook's domestic consumers.

There is also great concern over how the Chinese government might use Facebook. China has expressed an interest in purchasing shares in Facebook, leading some to fear that China might be trying to gain more control in the social media industry. Consumers also worry that if Facebook is allowed in China, the government might use it to track dissidents, especially considering that Facebook makes people register under their real names. Finally, because Yahoo! and Google were unsuccessful in China, some analysts predict that Facebook will fail as well. If this occurs, then Facebook might damage its reputation of open communication for nothing.[76]

Discussion Questions

1. Why has Facebook been blocked in China?
2. Why does Facebook want to enter China?
3. What are the ethical issues of Facebook's proposed expansion into China?

collectors are active members of the online community, a company story or site that catches the eye of a collector is likely to be posted, discussed on collector sites, and made available to other online users looking for information.

Joiners include all who become users of Twitter, Facebook, or other social networking sites. It is not unusual for consumers to be members of several social networking sites at once. Joiners use these sites to connect and network with other users, but as we've seen, marketers too can take significant advantage of these sites to connect with consumers and form customer relationships.[77] The last two segments are Spectators and Inactives. *Spectators,* who read online information but do not join groups or post anywhere, are the largest group in most countries. *Inactives* are online users who do not participate in any digital online media, but their numbers are dwindling.

Marketers who want to capitalize on social and digital media marketing need to consider what proportion of online consumers are creating, conversing, rating, collecting, joining, or simply reading online materials. As in traditional marketing efforts, they need to know their target market. For instance, where spectators make up the majority of the online population, companies should post their own corporate messages through blogs and websites promoting their organizations.

Using Digital Media to Learn about Consumers

Marketing research and information systems can use digital media and social networking sites to gather useful information about consumers and their preferences. Sites such as Twitter, Facebook, and Myspace can be good substitutes for focus groups. Online surveys can serve as an alternative to mail, telephone, or personal interviews.

About three-quarters of online shoppers read ratings and reviews before making a decision.

Crowdsourcing describes how marketers use digital media to find out the opinions or needs of the crowd (or potential markets). Communities of interested consumers join sites like threadless.com, which designs T-shirts, or crowdspring.com, which creates logos and print and web designs. These companies give interested consumers opportunities to contribute and give feedback on product ideas. Crowdsourcing lets companies gather and utilize consumers' ideas in an interactive way when creating new products.

Consumer feedback is an important part of the digital media equation. Ratings and reviews have become exceptionally popular; 25 percent of the U.S. online population reads this type of consumer-generated feedback.[78] Retailers such as Amazon, Netflix, and Priceline allow consumers to post comments on their sites about the books, movies, and travel arrangements they sell. Today, most online shoppers search the Internet for ratings and reviews before making major purchase decisions.

While consumer-generated content about a firm can be either positive or negative, digital media forums do allow businesses to closely monitor what their customers are saying. In the case of negative feedback, businesses can communicate with consumers to address problems or complaints much more easily than through traditional communication channels. Yet despite the ease and obvious importance of online feedback, many companies do not yet take full advantage of the digital tools at their disposal.

Legal and Social Issues in Internet Marketing

LO 13-5

The extraordinary growth of information technology, the Internet, and social networks has generated many legal and social issues for consumers and businesses. These issues include privacy concerns, the risk of identity theft and online fraud, and the need to protect intellectual property. The U.S. Federal Trade Commission (FTC) compiles an annual list of consumer complaints related to the Internet and digital media. We discuss these in this section, as well as steps that individuals, companies, and the government have taken to address them.

Privacy

Businesses have long tracked consumers' shopping habits with little controversy. However, observing the contents of a consumer's shopping cart or the process a consumer goes through when choosing a box of cereal generally does not result in the collection of specific, personally identifying data. Although using credit cards, shopping cards, and coupons forces consumers to give up a certain degree of anonymity in the traditional shopping process, they can still choose to remain anonymous by paying cash. Shopping on the Internet, however, allows businesses to track them on a far more personal level, from the contents of their online purchases to the websites they favor. Current technology has made it possible for marketers to amass vast quantities of personal information, often without consumers' knowledge, and to share and sell this information to interested third parties.

How is personal information collected on the web? Many sites follow users online by storing a "cookie," or an identifying string of text, on users' computers. Cookies permit website operators to track how often a user visits the site, what he or she looks at while there, and in what sequence. They also allow website visitors to customize services, such as virtual shopping carts, as well as the particular content they see when they log onto a web page. Users have the option of turning off cookies on their machines, but nevertheless the potential for misuse has left many consumers uncomfortable with this technology.

Facebook and other social networking sites have also come under fire for privacy issues. Facebook and Google both agreed to undergo independent privacy audits for 20 years due to alleged privacy transgressions. The Federal Trade Commission determined that Facebook's 2009 changes to its privacy policies were done without warning users. It charged Google with using the personal information from its Gmail users for its Google Buzz service, despite telling users otherwise. Such changes were deemed to have violated users' rights to know how their information was being utilized.[79] Another Internet privacy issue occurring more frequently is "scraping," an activity where companies offer to collect personal information from social networking sites and other forums. Such events have prompted both consumers and the federal government alike to consider an online privacy "Bill of Rights" to protect consumers from having their information tracked without permission. Such a bill might also require more companies to submit to privacy audits.[80]

Due to consumer concerns over privacy, the Federal Trade Commission (FTC) is considering developing regulations that would better protect consumer privacy by limiting the amount of consumer information that businesses can gather online. Other countries are pursuing similar actions. The European Union passed a law requiring companies to get users' consent before using cookies to track their information. In the United States, one proposed solution for consumer Internet privacy is a "do not track" bill, similar to the "do not call" bill for telephones, to allow users to opt out of having their information tracked.[81] While consumers may welcome such added protections, web advertisers, who use consumer information to better target advertisements to online consumers, see it as a threat. In response to impending legislation, many web advertisers are attempting self-regulation in order to stay ahead of the game. For instance, the Interactive Advertising Board is encouraging its members to adopt a do-not-track icon that users can click on to avoid having their online activity tracked. However, it is debatable whether members will choose to participate or honor users' do-not-track requests.[82]

Identity Theft

Identity theft occurs when criminals obtain personal information that allows them to impersonate someone else in order to use the person's credit to access financial accounts and make purchases. Many of these breaches occur at banks, universities, and other businesses that contain sensitive consumer information.[83] This requires organizations to implement increased security measures to prevent database theft. As you can see in Figure 13.3, the most common complaints relate to government

identity theft
when criminals obtain personal information that allows them to impersonate someone else in order to use their credit to access financial accounts and make purchases

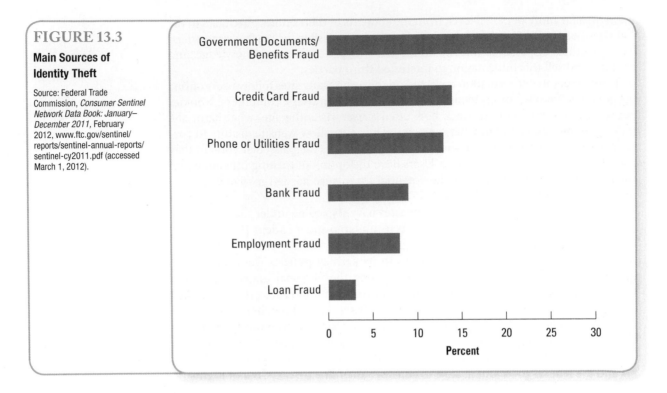

FIGURE 13.3

Main Sources of Identity Theft

Source: Federal Trade Commission, *Consumer Sentinel Network Data Book: January–December 2011,* February 2012, www.ftc.gov/sentinel/reports/sentinel-annual-reports/sentinel-cy2011.pdf (accessed March 1, 2012).

documents/benefits fraud, followed by credit card fraud, utility fraud, bank fraud, employment fraud, and loan fraud.

The Internet's relative anonymity and speed make possible both legal and illegal access to databases storing Social Security numbers, drivers' license numbers, dates of birth, mothers' maiden names, and other information that can be used to establish a credit card or bank account in another person's name in order to make fraudulent transactions. One growing scam used to initiate identity theft fraud is the practice of *phishing,* whereby con artists counterfeit a well-known website and send out e-mails directing victims to it. There visitors find instructions to reveal sensitive information such as their credit card numbers. Phishing scams have faked websites for PayPal, AOL, and the Federal Deposit Insurance Corporation.

Some identity theft problems are resolved quickly, while other cases take weeks and hundreds of dollars before a victim's bank balances and credit standings are restored. To deter identity theft, the National Fraud Center wants financial institutions to implement new technologies such as digital certificates, digital signatures, and biometrics—the use of fingerprinting or retina scanning.

Online Fraud

online fraud
any attempt to conduct fraudulent activities online

Online fraud includes any attempt to conduct fraudulent activities online, such as by deceiving consumers into releasing personal information. It is becoming a major source of frustration among users of social networking sites, because cybercriminals are finding new ways to use sites like Facebook and Twitter to commit fraudulent activities. For instance, they will create profiles under a company's name to either damage the company's reputation (particularly larger, more controversial companies) or lure that company's customers into releasing personal information the perpetrators can use for monetary gain.

Another tactic some fraudsters have used is to create typosquatting sites based on common misspellings of search engines or social networks (e.g., faecbook vs. facebook). Fraudsters then trick visitors into releasing their information.[84] Cybercriminals also create fake social network profiles to con people during times of natural disasters. Some criminals have posed as charitable institutions to solicit donations, while others have used fraudulent tactics to convince users to release their personal information. For instance, in the aftermath of the 2011 Japanese earthquake and tsunami disaster, a fraudster posted fake video footage to try to get users to go to a malicious site and then convince them to release personal information.[85]

Despite any number of safeguards, the best protection for consumers is to be careful when they divulge information online. The surest way to stay out of trouble is never to give out personal information, like a Social Security or credit card number, unless it is a site you trust and that you know is legitimate.

Intellectual Property

In addition to protecting personal privacy, Internet users and others want to protect their rights to property they may create, including songs, movies, books, and software. Such intellectual property consists of the ideas and creative materials developed to solve problems, carry out applications, and educate and entertain others.

Although intellectual property is generally protected by patents and copyrights, each year losses from the illegal copying of computer programs, music, movies, compact discs, and books reaches billions of dollars in the United States alone. This has become a particular problem with digital media sites. YouTube has often faced lawsuits on intellectual property infringement. With millions of users uploading content to YouTube, it can be hard for Google to monitor and remove all the videos that may contain copyrighted materials. The file hosting service Magaupload was shut down and owner Kim Dotcom arrested after prosecutors accused the site of being a front for massive Internet piracy. Legitimate users of the site were cut off from their files as well.[86]

Online piracy has become such an issue that the U.S. government proposed two bills, the Stop Online Piracy Act and the Protect Intellectual Property Act, that would enable the government to shut down sites that appeared to violate another stakeholder's intellectual property. Although studios and record labels supported the bills, online Internet companies and many consumers were against them. They feared that giving Congress more authority to regulate the Internet would infringe on freedom of speech. To protest the proposed bills, Wikipedia went offline for a day and Google blackened out its "Google" lettering on its main page. The pressure caused the government to drop the bills. The fine line between protecting intellectual property and maintaining freedom of speech makes this a difficult problem to address.[87]

Illegal sharing of content is another major intellectual property problem. Consumers rationalize the pirating of software, videogames, movies, and music for a number of reasons. First, many feel they just don't have the money to pay for what they want. Second, because their friends engage in piracy and swap digital content, some users feel influenced to engage in this activity. Others enjoy the thrill of getting away with something with a low risk of consequences. And finally, some people feel being tech savvy allows them to take advantage of the opportunity to pirate content.[88]

The software industry loses more than $50 billion globally each year due to theft and illegal use of software products, according to the Business Software Alliance.[89]

The file-sharing protocol BitTorrent allows users to share and download files. The U.S. Copyright Group recently obtained the IP addresses of users who downloaded specific movies using BitTorrent technology and are taking action against thousands of BitTorrent users for illegally downloading protected content.

About 90 percent of illegal software copying is actually done by businesses. For example, a firm may obtain a license to install a specific application on 100 of its computers but actually installs it on 300. In some cases, software is illegally made available through the Internet by companies that have taken the software from the producer and set up their own distribution system.

Digital Media's Impact on Marketing

To be successful in business, you need to know much more than how to use a social networking site to communicate with friends. Developing a strategic understanding of how digital marketing can make business more efficient and productive is increasingly necessary. If you are thinking of becoming an entrepreneur, then the digital world can open doors to new resources and customers. Smart phones, mobile broadband, and webcams are among the tools that can make the most of an online business world, creating greater efficiency at less cost. For example, rather than using traditional phone lines, Skype helps people make and receive calls via the Internet and provides free video calling and text messaging for about 10 percent of the cost of a land line.[90] It is up to businesses and entrepreneurs to develop strategies that achieve business success using existing and future technology, software, and networking opportunities.

Traditional businesses accustomed to using print media can find the transition to digital challenging. New media may require employees with new skills or additional training for current employees. There is often a gap between technical knowledge of how to develop sites and how to develop effective digital marketing strategies to enhance business success. Determining the correct blend of traditional and new media requires careful consideration; the mix will vary depending on the business, its size, and its target market. Future career opportunities will require skills in both traditional and digital media areas so that marketers properly understand and implement marketing strategies that help businesses achieve a competitive advantage.

So You Want to Be a Digital Marketer

The business world has grown increasingly dependent on digital marketing to maintain communication with stakeholders. Reaching customers is often a major concern, but digital marketing can also be used to communicate with suppliers, concerned community members, and special interest groups about issues related to sustainability, safety practices, and philanthropic activities. Many types of jobs exist: account executive directors of social media and director of marketing for digital products, as well as digital advertisers, online marketers, global digital marketers, and brand managers are prominently listed on career opportunity websites.

Entrepreneurs are taking advantage of the low cost of digital marketing, building social networking sites to help market their products. In fact, some small businesses such as specialty publishing, personal health and beauty, and other specialty products can use digital marketing as the primary channel for reaching consumers. Many small businesses are posting signs outside their stores with statements such as "Follow us on Twitter" or "Check out our Facebook page."

To utilize digital marketing, especially social networking, requires more than information technology skills related to constructing websites, graphics, videos, podcasts, etc. Most importantly, one must be able to determine how digital media can be used in implementing a marketing strategy. All marketing starts with identifying a target market and developing a marketing mix to satisfy customers. Digital marketing is just another way to reach customers, provide information, and develop relationships. Therefore, your opportunity for a career in this field is greatly based on understanding the messages, desired level of interactivity, and connectivity that helps achieve marketing objectives.

As social media use skyrockets, digital marketing professionals will be in demand. The experience of many businesses and research indicate digital marketing is a powerful way to increase brand exposure and generate traffic. In fact, a study conducted on Social Media Examiner found that 85 percent of marketers surveyed believe generating exposure for their business is their number-one advantage in Internet marketing. As consumers use social networking for their personal communication, they will be more open to obtaining information about products through this channel. Digital marketing could be the fastest-growing opportunity in business.

To prepare yourself for a digital marketing career, learn not only the technical aspects, but also how social media can be used to maximize marketing performance. A glance at careerbuilder.com indicates that management positions such as account manager, digital marketing manager, and digital product manager can pay from $60,000 to $170,000 or more per year.

Review Your Understanding

Define *digital media* and *digital marketing* and recognize their increasing value in strategic planning.

Digital media are electronic media that function using digital codes and are available via computers, cellular phones, smart phones, and other digital devices. Digital marketing refers to the strategic process of distributing, promoting, pricing products, and discovering the desires of customers in the virtual environment of the Internet. Because they can enhance the exchange of information between the marketer and the customer, digital media have become an important component of firms' marketing strategies.

Demonstrate the role of digital marketing and social networking in today's business environment.

Digital communication facilitates marketing research and lowers the cost of communication and consumer service and support. Through websites, social networks, and other digital media, consumers can learn about everything they purchase and use in life and businesses can reach new markets through inexpensive and interactive communication channels. Social networking is expanding so fast that no business can ignore its impact on customer relationships.

Show how digital media affect the marketing mix.

The ability to process orders electronically and increase the speed of communications via the Internet has reduced many distribution inefficiencies, costs, and redundancies while increasing speed throughout the marketing channel. Digital media help firms increase brand awareness, connect with consumers, form relationships, and spread positive publicity about their products. Because consumers are more informed than ever and consumer consumption patterns are changing, marketers must adapt their promotional efforts. The Internet gives consumers access to more information about costs and prices.

Define social networking and illustrate how businesses can use different types of social networking media.

Social networking occurs when online consumers interact with other users on a web-based platform to discuss or view topics of interest. Types of social networking media include social networking sites, blogs, wikis, media sharing sites, virtual reality sites, mobile marketing, mobile applications, and widgets.

Blogs give consumers power but also allow companies to answer consumer concerns and obtain free publicity. Wikis give marketers a better understanding of how consumers feel about their companies. Photo sharing sites enable companies to share images of their businesses or products with consumers and often have links that connect users to company-sponsored blogs. Video sharing is allowing many businesses to engage in viral marketing. Amateur filmmakers are also becoming a potential low-cost, effective marketing venue for companies. Podcasts are audio or video files that can be downloaded from the Internet with a subscription that automatically delivers new content to listening devices or personal computers.

Marketers have begun joining and advertising on social networking sites like Facebook and Twitter due to their global reach. Virtual realities can be fun and creative ways to reach consumers, create brand loyalty, and use consumer knowledge to benefit companies. Mobile marketing includes advertising, text messages, and other types of digital marketing through mobile devices. Mobile apps can be anything from games, to news updates, to shopping assistance. They provide a way for marketers to reach consumers via their cell phones. Apps can help consumers to perform services and make purchases more easily, such as checking in at a hotel or comparing and contrasting the price of appliances or a new dress. Widgets are

small bits of software on a website, desktop, or mobile device. They can be used to inform consumers about company updates and can easily go viral.

Identify legal and ethical considerations in digital media.

Increasing consumer concerns about privacy are prompting the FTC to look into regulating the types of information marketers can gather from Internet users, while many web advertisers and trade groups try to engage in self-regulation to prevent the passage of new Internet privacy laws. Online fraud includes any attempt to conduct fraudulent activities online. Intellectual property losses cost the U.S. billions of dollars and have become a particular problem for sites such as YouTube, which often finds it hard to monitor the millions of videos uploaded to its site for copyright infringement.

Based on the material in this chapter, you should be able to answer the questions posed in "Solve the Dilemma" on page 431 and evaluate where the company's marketing strategy has failed. How could Paul utilize new digital media to help promote his product and gather data on how to improve it?

Revisit the World of Business

1. Compare and contrast China's *weibo* platforms and Twitter.
2. Why have some foreign companies been eager to register on Sina's *weibo* platform?
3. What are some of the barriers preventing Twitter from competing against *weibo* sites?

Learn the Terms

blog 415
digital marketing 407
digital media 406
e-business 406

identity theft 425
online fraud 426
podcast 417
social network 412

viral marketing 416
wiki 415

Check Your Progress

1. What is digital marketing?
2. How can marketers utilize digital media to improve business?
3. Define *accessibility, addressability, connectivity, interactivity,* and *control.* What do these terms have to do with digital marketing?
4. What is e-business?
5. How is the Internet changing the practice of marketing?
6. What impact do digital media have on the marketing mix?
7. How can businesses utilize new digital and social networking channels in their marketing campaigns?

8. What are some of the privacy concerns associated with the Internet and e-business? How are these concerns being addressed in the United States?
9. What is identity theft? How can consumers protect themselves from this crime?
10. Why do creators want to protect their intellectual property? Provide an example on the Internet where intellectual property may not be protected or where a copyright has been infringed.

Get Involved

1. Amazon.com is one of the most recognized e-businesses. Visit the site (**www.amazon.com**) and identify the types of products the company sells. Explain its privacy policy.

2. Visit some of the social networking sites identified in this chapter. How do they differ in design, audience, and features? Why do you think some social networking sites like Facebook are more popular than others?

3. It has been stated that digital technology and the Internet are to business today what manufacturing was to business during the Industrial Revolution. The technology revolution requires a strategic understanding greater than learning the latest software and programs or determining which computer is the fastest. Leaders in business can no longer delegate digital media to specialists and must be the connectors and the strategists of how digital media will be used in the company. Outline a plan for how you will prepare yourself to function in a business world where digital marketing knowledge will be important to your success.

Build Your Skills

PLANNING A DIGITAL MARKETING AND SOCIAL NETWORKING SITE

Background

Many companies today utilize new digital media in a way that reflects their images and goals. They can also help to improve customer service, loyalty, and satisfaction while reaching out to new target markets. Companies use these sites in a variety of ways, sometimes setting up Facebook pages or Twitter accounts to gather customer feedback, to promote new products, or even to hold competitions.

The U.S. economy has experienced many ups and downs in recent decades, but e-commerce has been an area that has continued to grow throughout economic ups and downs. Many dot-com companies and social networking sites have risen and collapsed. Others, such as Amazon.com, eBay, Facebook, and Twitter have not only survived, but thrived. Many that succeed are "niche players"; that is, they cater to a very specific market that a brick-and-mortar business (existing only in a physical marketplace) would find hard to reach. Others are able to compete with brick-and-mortar stores because they offer a wider variety of products, lower prices, or better customer service. Many new digital media outlets help companies compete on these fronts.

As a manager of Biodegradable Packaging Products Inc., a small business that produces packaging foam from recycled agricultural waste (mostly corn), you want to expand into e-business by using digital media to help market your product. Your major customers are other businesses and could include environmentally friendly companies like Tom's of Maine (natural toothpaste) and Celestial Seasonings (herbal tea). Your first need is to develop a social networking site or blog that will help you reach your potential customers. You must decide who your target market is and which medium will attract it the best.

Task

Plan a digital media marketing campaign using online social networking sites, blogs, or another digital media outlet using the template below.

Social networking/blog/other site: _____

Overall image and design of your site: _____

Strategy for attracting followers to your site: _____

Potential advertising partners to draw in more customers: _____

Solve the Dilemma   LO 13-6

DEVELOPING SUCCESSFUL FREEWARE

Paul Easterwood, a recent graduate of Colorado State University with a degree in computer science, entered the job market during a slow point in the economy. Tech sector positions were hard to come by, and Paul felt he wouldn't be making anywhere near what he was worth. The only offer he received was from an entrepreneurial firm, Pentaverate Inc., that produced freeware. Freeware, or public domain software, is offered to consumers free of charge in exchange for revenues generated later. Makers of freeware (such as Adobe and Netscape)

can earn high profits through advertisements their sites carry, from purchases made on the freeware site, or, for more specialized software, through fee-based tutorials and workshops offered to help end users. Paul did some research and found an article in *Worth* magazine documenting the enormous success of freeware.

Pentaverate Inc. offered compensation mainly in the form of stock options, which had the potential to be highly profitable if the company did well. Paul's job would be to develop freeware that people could download from the Internet and that would generate significant income for Pentaverate. With this in mind, he decided to accept the position, but he quickly realized he knew very little about business. With no real experience in marketing, Paul was at a loss to know what software he should produce that would make the company money. His first project, IOWatch, was designed to take users on virtual tours of outer space, especially the moons of Jupiter (Paul's favorite subject), by continually searching the Internet for images and video clips associated with the cosmos and downloading them directly to a PC. The images would then appear as soon as the person

logged on. Advertisements would accompany each download, generating income for Pentaverate.

However, IOWatch experienced low end-user interest and drew little advertising income as a result. Historically at Pentaverate, employees were fired after two failed projects. Desperate to save his job, Paul decided to hire a consultant. He needed to figure out what customers might want so he could design some useful freeware for his second project. He also needed to know what went wrong with IOWatch, because he loved the software and couldn't figure out why it had failed to find an audience. The job market has not improved, so Paul realizes how important it is for his second project to succeed.

Discussion Questions

1. As a consultant, what would you do to help Paul figure out what went wrong with IOWatch?

2. What ideas for new freeware can you give Paul? What potential uses will the new software have?

3. How will it make money?

Build Your Business Plan

DIGITAL MARKETING AND SOCIAL NETWORKING

If you are considering developing a business plan for an established product or service, find out whether it is currently marketed digitally. If it is not, think about why that is the case. Can you think of how you might overcome any obstacles and engage in digital marketing on the Internet?

If you are thinking about introducing a new product or service, now is the time to think about whether you might want to market this product on the Internet. Remember, you do not have to have a brick-and-mortar store to open your own business anymore. Perhaps you might want to consider click instead of brick!

See for Yourself Videocase

SHOULD EMPLOYEES USE SOCIAL MEDIA SITES AT WORK?

As Facebook and other social media sites have gained popularity and expanded, managing their use at work has become an increasingly hot topic. Studies on the use of social media in the workplace conflict over how much it inhibits productivity. Should employees be allowed to access social media at work? Many offices have banned access to the site. The results are as mixed as the research. The 2011 National Business Ethics Survey® revealed that 11 percent of employees who engage in social networking are "active" social networkers who spend 30 percent or more of the work day on social networking sites. Many managers are conflicted as to whether this constitutes enough of a problem to be banned outright.

Another study conducted by Nucleus Research (an IT research company) revealed a 1.5 percent loss of productivity for businesses allowing social media access. It found that 77 percent of Facebook users used the site during work for as much as two hours a day; 87 percent of those surveyed admitted they were using social media sites to waste time. NBES also found that active social networkers were more likely to find certain questionable behaviors to be acceptable, such as criticizing the company or its managers on social networking sites. Procter & Gamble realized that many of its employees were using social networking sites for nonwork purposes. Its investigations revealed that employees across the company were watching an average of 50,000 five-minute YouTube videos and listening to 4,000 hours of music on Pandora daily.

However, an outright ban could cause problems. Some younger employees have expressed that they do not want to work for companies without social media access; they view restricting or eliminating access like removing a benefit. Employees at companies with an outright ban often resent the lack of trust associated with such a move and feel that management is censuring their activities. Additionally, Procter & Gamble uses YouTube and Facebook extensively for marketing purposes. Banning these sites would disrupt the firm's marketing efforts.

An Australian study indicates that employees taking time out to pursue Facebook and other social media were actually 9 percent more productive than those who did not. Brent Coker, the study's author and University of Melbourne faculty member, says people are more productive when they take time to "zone out" throughout the work day. Doing so can improve concentration. Coker's study focused on those using less than 20 percent of the workday on such breaks, which is less than the amount of time "active" social networkers spend on these sites.

Some companies actually encourage employees to use social networking as part of their integrated marketing strategy. For example, Patrick Hoover Law Offices charges employees with the responsibility to use social media in ways that the employees believe can benefit the company. Although this does potentially allow employees to use social media for personal purposes rather than for work, this tactic has been effective in getting new clients and publicizing the organization. By trusting its employees and giving them leeway to use social media

in ways they see fit, Patrick Hoover Law Offices has taken a potential problem and reworked it to its own advantage.

Despite the benefits that companies like Patrick Hoover Law Offices have received from allowing their employees to use social media, many companies have gone ahead with social media bans. Procter & Gamble has restricted the use of Netflix and Pandora, but not Facebook or YouTube. Companies all need to ask, "Can management use social media to benefit the company?" If so, it may be more advantageous to take the risks of employees using social media for personal use if they can also be encouraged to use social networks to publicize their organizations, connect with customers, and view consumer comments or complaints. By restricting social media use, companies may be forfeiting an effective marketing tool.[91]

DISCUSSION QUESTIONS

1. Why do you think results are so mixed on the use of social networking in the workplace?
2. What are some possible upsides to utilizing social media as part of an integrated marketing strategy, especially in digital marketing?
3. What are the downsides to restricting employee access to social networking sites?

Remember to check out our Online Learning Center at www.mhhe.com/ferrell9e.

Team Exercise

Develop a digital marketing promotion for a local sports team. Use Twitter, Facebook, and other social networking media to promote ticket sales for next season's schedule. In your plan, provide specific details and ideas for the content you would

use on the sites. Also, describe how you would encourage fans and potential fans to go to your site. How would you use digital media to motivate sports fans to purchase tickets and merchandise and attend games?

part 6

Financing the Enterprise

14

Accounting and Financial Statements

Learning Objectives

After reading this chapter, you will be able to:

LO 14-1   Define accounting, and describe the different uses of accounting information.

LO 14-2   Demonstrate the accounting process.

LO 14-3   Examine the various components of an income statement in order to evaluate a firm's "bottom line."

LO 14-4   Interpret a company's balance sheet to determine its current financial position.

LO 14-5   Analyze the statement of cash flows to evaluate the increase and decrease in a company's cash balance.

LO 14-6   Assess a company's financial position using its accounting statements and ratio analysis.

Web Retailers Fight against State Sales Tax

Accountants play a key role in helping individuals and organizations manage their responsibilities to pay taxes. However, for years web retailers such as Amazon.com and eBay have avoided paying states sales tax. Citing a 1992 U.S. Supreme Court case, they argued that because they do not have a physical presence in most states, they are not required to pay those states' sales taxes.

ENTER THE WORLD OF BUSINESS

However, in 2011 California passed a law requiring online retailers to collect sales taxes from their customers. Web retailers already pay sales taxes in New York thanks to a similar law. Since it enacted the sales tax law, New York has collected $250 million from Internet retailers. Amazon deferred paying sales taxes in California until September 2012.

At first, Amazon claimed the laws violated the 1992 Supreme Court decision. However, in a stunning reversal, Amazon has expressed its support for a federal law that would make it easier for online retailers to charge a uniform sales tax. eBay, on the other hand, continues to oppose the ability of states to collect sales taxes on online purchases. It claims that such a tax would harm smaller online retailers. However, online retailers making less than $500,000 in annual sales would be exempted from collecting state sales taxes.

continued

Much of the controversy depends on how one defines "physical presence." Online Internet companies operate warehouses through subsidiaries in different states. In the past, Amazon has argued that because the warehouses are used for shipping, not selling, they do not qualify for sales taxation. States, on the other hand, accuse large online retailers of using a narrow definition to define their physical presence. Whatever the outcome, accountants will be involved in assisting in firms' tax decisions.

If the new laws are successful, states and local governments could collect more than $10 billion in additional annual revenue from web-based retailers. On the other hand, eBay maintains that this revenue will not come from the company's pockets, but from those of sellers and consumers.[1]

Introduction

Accounting, the financial "language" that organizations use to record, measure, and interpret all of their financial transactions and records, is very important in business. All businesses—from a small family farm to a giant corporation—use the language of accounting to make sure they use their money wisely and to plan for the future. Nonbusiness organizations such as charities and governments also use accounting to demonstrate to donors and taxpayers how well they are using their funds and meeting their stated objectives.

This chapter explores the role of accounting in business and its importance in making business decisions. First, we discuss the uses of accounting information and the accounting process. Then, we briefly look at some simple financial statements and accounting tools that are useful in analyzing organizations worldwide.

The Nature of Accounting

LO 14-1

accounting
the recording, measurement, and interpretation of financial information

Simply stated, **accounting** is the recording, measurement, and interpretation of financial information. Large numbers of people and institutions, both within and outside businesses, use accounting tools to evaluate organizational operations. The Financial Accounting Standards Board has been setting the principles standards of financial accounting and reporting in the private sector since 1973. Its mission is to establish and improve standards of financial accounting and reporting for the guidance and education of the public, including issuers, auditors, and users of financial information. However, the accounting scandals at the turn of the last century resulted when many accounting firms and businesses failed to abide by generally accepted accounting principles, or GAAP. Consequently, the federal government has taken a greater role in making rules, requirements, and policies for accounting firms and businesses through the Securities and Exchange Commission's (SEC) Public Company Accounting Oversight Board. For example, the Public Company Accounting Oversight Board charged the Chinese branch of Deloitte Touche Tohmatsu CPA Ltd. with not providing audit information related to a Chinese-based firm—a violation of U.S. securities law. The China-based audit firm was under investigation for possible accounting fraud. Chinese-based audit firms have been reluctant to allow U.S. authorities to investigate their activities.[2]

To better understand the importance of accounting, we must first understand who prepares accounting information and how it is used.

Accountants

Many of the functions of accounting are carried out by public or private accountants.

Public Accountants.   Individuals and businesses can hire a **certified public accountant (CPA),** an individual who has been certified by the state in which he or she practices to provide accounting services ranging from the preparation of financial records and the filing of tax returns to complex audits of corporate financial records. Certification gives a public accountant the right to express, officially, an unbiased opinion regarding the accuracy of the client's financial statements. Most public accountants are either self-employed or members of large public accounting firms such as Ernst & Young, KPMG, Deloitte, and PricewaterhouseCoopers, together referred to as "the Big Four." In addition, many CPAs work for one of the second-tier accounting firms that are much smaller than the Big Four firms, as illustrated in Table 14.1.

While there will always be companies and individual money managers who can successfully hide illegal or misleading accounting practices for a while, eventually they are exposed. After the accounting scandals of Enron and Worldcom in the early 2000s, Congress passed the Sarbanes-Oxley Act, which required firms to be more rigorous in their accounting and reporting practices. Sarbanes-Oxley made accounting firms separate their consulting and auditing businesses and punished corporate executives with potential jail sentences for inaccurate, misleading, or illegal accounting statements. This seemed to reduce the accounting errors among nonfinancial companies, but declining housing prices exposed some of the questionable practices by banks and mortgage companies. Only five years after the passage of

certified public accountant (CPA)
an individual who has been state certified to provide accounting services ranging from the preparation of financial records and the filing of tax returns to complex audits of corporate financial records

Rank 2013	Rank 2012	Firm	Revenues (millions of $) 2011	Score	Location
1	22	Ernst & Young LLP	$22,000	7.941	New York, NY
2	1	Grant Thornton LLP	3,000	7.818	Chicago, IL
3	3	Deloitte LLP	28,000	7.615	New York, NY
4	2	PricewaterhouseCoopers LLP	29,200	7.612	New York, NY
5	23	KPMG LLP	22,700	7.452	New York, NY
6	27	Plante Moran	303	7.314	Southfield, MI
7	6	Moss Adams LLP	323	6.926	Seattle, WA
8	16	Baker Tilly Virchow Krause, LLP	242	6.833	Chicago, IL

TABLE 14.1

Prestige Ranking of Accounting Firms

* Rankings are based on issues that accounting professionals care most about.

Source: "Accounting Firms Rankings 2013: Vault Accounting 50," *Vault,* www.vault.com/wps/portal/usa/rankings/individual?rankingId1=252&rankingId2=252&rankings=1&rankingYear=2013 (accessed May 18, 2012).

KPMG is part of the "Big Four," or the four largest international accounting firms. The other three are PricewaterhouseCoopers, Ernst & Young, and Deloitte Touche Tohmatsu.

the Sarbanes-Oxley Act, the world experienced a financial crisis starting in 2008—part of which was due to excessive risk taking and inappropriate accounting practices. Many banks failed to understand the true state of their financial health. Banks also developed questionable lending practices and investments based on subprime mortgages made to individuals who had poor credit. When housing prices declined and people suddenly found that they owed more on their mortgages than their homes were worth, they began to default. To prevent a depression, the government intervened and bailed out some of the United States' largest banks. Congress passed the Dodd-Frank Act in 2010 to strengthen the oversight of financial institutions. This act gave the Federal Reserve Board the task of implementing the legislation. It is expected that financial institutions will have at least one year to implement the requirements. This legislation will limit the types of assets commercial banks can buy; the amount of capital they must maintain; and the use of derivative instruments such as options, futures, and structured investment products.

A growing area for public accountants is *forensic accounting*, which is accounting that is fit for legal review. It involves analyzing financial documents in search of fraudulent entries or financial misconduct. Functioning as much like detectives as accountants, forensic accountants have been used since the 1930s. In the wake of the accounting scandals of the early 2000s, many auditing firms are rapidly adding or expanding forensic or fraud-detection services. Additionally, many forensic accountants root out evidence of "cooked books" for federal agencies like the Federal Bureau of Investigation or the Internal Revenue Service. The

DID YOU KNOW? Corporate fraud costs are estimated at $2.9 trillion annually.[3]

Association of Certified Fraud Examiners, which certifies accounting professionals as *certified fraud examiners (CFEs)*, has grown to more than 60,000 members.[4]

Private Accountants.   Large corporations, government agencies, and other organizations may employ their own **private accountants** to prepare and analyze their financial statements. With titles such as controller, tax accountant, or internal auditor, private accountants are deeply involved in many of the most important financial decisions of the organizations for which they work. Private accountants can be CPAs and may become **certified management accountants (CMAs)** by passing a rigorous examination by the Institute of Management Accountants.

Accounting or Bookkeeping?

The terms *accounting* and *bookkeeping* are often mistakenly used interchangeably. Much narrower and far more mechanical than accounting, bookkeeping is typically limited to the routine, day-to-day recording of business transactions. Bookkeepers are responsible for obtaining and recording the information that accountants require to analyze a firm's financial position. They generally require less training than accountants. Accountants, on the other hand, usually complete course work beyond their basic four- or five-year college accounting degrees. This additional training allows accountants not only to record financial information, but to understand, interpret, and even develop the sophisticated accounting systems necessary to classify and analyze complex financial information.

The Uses of Accounting Information

Accountants summarize the information from a firm's business transactions in various financial statements (which we'll look at in a later section of this chapter) for a variety of stakeholders, including managers, investors, creditors, and government agencies. Many business failures may be directly linked to ignorance of the information "hidden" inside these financial statements. Likewise, most business successes can be traced to informed managers who understand the consequences of their decisions. While maintaining and even increasing short-run profits is desirable, the failure to plan sufficiently for the future can easily lead an otherwise successful company to insolvency and bankruptcy court.

Basically, managers and owners use financial statements (1) to aid in internal planning and control and (2) for external purposes such as reporting to the Internal Revenue Service, stockholders, creditors, customers, employees, and other interested parties. Figure 14.1 shows some of the users of the accounting information generated by a typical corporation.

Internal Uses.   **Managerial accounting** refers to the internal use of accounting statements by managers in planning and directing the organization's activities. Perhaps management's greatest single concern is **cash flow,** the movement of money through an organization over a daily, weekly, monthly, or yearly basis. Obviously, for any business to succeed, it needs to generate enough cash to pay its bills as they fall due. However, it is not at all unusual for highly successful and rapidly growing companies to struggle to make payments to employees, suppliers, and lenders because of an inadequate cash flow. One common reason for a so-called cash crunch, or shortfall, is poor managerial planning.

private accountants accountants employed by large corporations, government agencies, and other organizations to prepare and analyze their financial statements

certified management accountants (CMAs) private accountants who, after rigorous examination, are certified by the National Association of Accountants and who have some managerial responsibility

managerial accounting the internal use of accounting statements by managers in planning and directing the organization's activities

cash flow the movement of money through an organization over a daily, weekly, monthly, or yearly basis

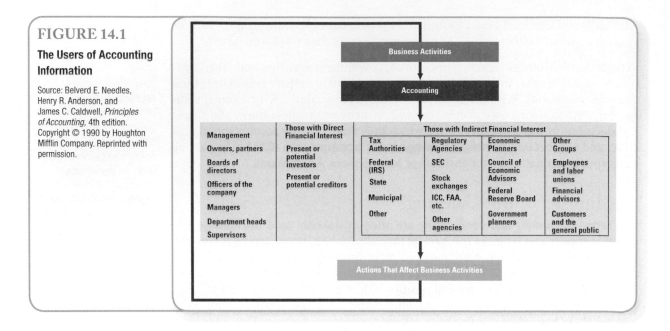

FIGURE 14.1

The Users of Accounting Information

Source: Belverd E. Needles, Henry R. Anderson, and James C. Caldwell, *Principles of Accounting,* 4th edition. Copyright © 1990 by Houghton Mifflin Company. Reprinted with permission.

budget
an internal financial plan that forecasts expenses and income over a set period of time

Managerial accountants also help prepare an organization's **budget,** an internal financial plan that forecasts expenses and income over a set period of time. It is not unusual for an organization to prepare separate daily, weekly, monthly, and yearly budgets. Think of a budget as a financial map, showing how the company expects to move from Point A to Point B over a specific period of time. While most companies prepare *master budgets* for the entire firm, many also prepare budgets for smaller segments of the organization such as divisions, departments, product lines, or projects. "Top-down" master budgets begin at the upper management level and filter down to the individual department level, while "bottom-up" budgets start at the department or project level and are combined at the chief executive's office. Generally, the larger and more rapidly growing an organization, the greater will be the likelihood that it will build its master budget from the ground up.

Regardless of focus, the principal value of a budget lies in its breakdown of cash inflows and outflows. Expected operating expenses (cash outflows such as wages, materials costs, and taxes) and operating revenues (cash inflows in the form of payments from customers) over a set period of time are carefully forecast and subsequently compared with actual results. Deviations between the two serve as a "trip wire" or "feedback loop" to launch more detailed financial analyses in an effort to pinpoint trouble spots and opportunities.

External Uses.   Managers also use accounting statements to report the business's financial performance to outsiders. Such statements are used for filing income taxes, obtaining credit from lenders, and reporting results to the firm's stockholders. They become the basis for the information provided in the official corporate **annual report,** a summary of the firm's financial information, products, and growth plans for owners and potential investors. While frequently presented between slick, glossy covers prepared by major advertising firms, the single most important component of an annual report is the signature of a certified public accountant attesting that the

annual report
summary of a firm's financial information, products, and growth plans for owners and potential investors

Going Green
Accounting Goes Green

Accounting and sustainability may seem like an unusual combination. After all, the purpose of the accounting profession is handling and reporting financial information, not adopting green practices. However, an increasing emphasis on sustainability has prompted the American Institute of CPAs (AICPA), the Chartered Institute of Management Accountants, the Canadian Institute of Chartered Accountants, and other global organizations to rethink the importance of sustainability to the financial profession.

Studies by these organizations have determined that at least one-third of smaller companies are incorporating sustainability strategies into their businesses, with another quarter indicating that they intend to do the same in the next few years. For instance, organizations such as French firm Esker have begun adopting cloud-based hiring tools to replace traditional paper résumés. For such practices to succeed, managers from all levels of the organization must support these initiatives, particularly company accountants and finance executives. These finance professionals are essential to the process because they are the ones who are in the best position to understand the "big picture." Although sustainability is important, businesses

must still succeed financially if they want to survive. Therefore, it is up to financial professionals—who have in-depth knowledge of the company's financial information—to find ways to use sustainability initiatives to improve operations.

Accounting organizations have created recommendations for finance professionals to determine which sustainable strategies to adopt. For instance, finance professionals must link sustainability to profit and find out which initiatives would cut costs and increase efficiency. They must create metrics to measure the success of these initiatives and determine whether changes are needed. Additionally, these organizations recommend that accountants incorporate the company's sustainability efforts into "mainstream reporting" for stakeholders.[5]

Discussion Questions

1. Why should accountants be involved in a company's decision to incorporate greener business practices?
2. Describe some of the recommendations that accounting organizations have developed regarding sustainability strategies.
3. What could happen if companies arbitrarily adopt sustainability strategies without assessing their impact?

required financial statements are an accurate reflection of the underlying financial condition of the firm. Financial statements meeting these conditions are termed *audited*. The primary external users of audited accounting information are government agencies, stockholders and potential investors, and lenders, suppliers, and employees.

During the global financial crisis, it turns out that Greece had been engaging in deceptive accounting practices, with the help of U.S. investment banks. Greece was using financial techniques that hid massive amounts of debt from its public balance sheets. Eventually, the markets figured out the country might not be able to pay off its creditors. The European Union and the International Monetary Fund came up with a plan to give Greece some credit relief, but tied to this was the message to "get your financial house in order." By the middle of 2012, the European problem was often referred to as the PIGS. This referred to Portugal, Italy, Ireland, Greece and Spain—all of which were having debt problems. The PIGS have caused cracks in the European Monetary Union. While Germany demanded austerity, others wanted more growth-oriented strategies.

The annual report is a summary of the firm's financial information, products, and growth plans for owners and potential investors. Many investors look at a firm's annual report to determine how well the company is doing financially.

As one of the biggest banks in the United States, Wells Fargo specializes in banking, mortgage, and financial services. The data it provides can be used in financial statements.

To top this off, *The New York Times* reported that many states, such as Illinois and California, seem to have the same problems as many EU countries—debt overload. These states have "budgets that will not balance, accounting that masks debt, the use of derivatives to plug holes, and armies of retired public workers who are counting on pension benefits that are proving harder and harder to pay." Clearly, the financial crisis will have some lasting effects that need clear accounting solutions.[6]

Financial statements evaluate the return on stockholders' investment and the overall quality of the firm's management team. As a result, poor performance, as documented in the financial statements, often results in changes in top management. Potential investors study the financial statements in a firm's annual report to determine whether the company meets their investment requirements and whether the returns from a given firm are likely to compare favorably with other similar companies.

Banks and other lenders look at financial statements to determine a company's ability to meet current and future debt obligations if a loan or credit is granted. To determine this ability, a short-term lender examines a firm's cash flow to assess its ability to repay a loan quickly with cash generated from sales. A long-term lender is more interested in the company's profitability and indebtedness to other lenders.

Labor unions and employees use financial statements to establish reasonable expectations for salary and other benefit requests. Just as firms experiencing record profits are likely to face added pressure to increase employee wages, so too are employees unlikely to grant employers wage and benefit concessions without considerable evidence of financial distress.

The Accounting Process

LO 14-2

Many view accounting as a primary business language. It is of little use, however, unless you know how to "speak" it. Fortunately, the fundamentals—the accounting equation and the double-entry bookkeeping system—are not difficult to learn. These two concepts serve as the starting point for all currently accepted accounting principles.

The Accounting Equation

assets
a firm's economic resources, or items of value that it owns, such as cash, inventory, land, equipment, buildings, and other tangible and intangible things

Accountants are concerned with reporting an organization's assets, liabilities, and owners' equity. To help illustrate these concepts, consider a hypothetical floral shop called Anna's Flowers, owned by Anna Rodriguez. A firm's economic resources, or items of value that it owns, represent its **assets**—cash, inventory, land, equipment, buildings, and other tangible and intangible things. The assets of Anna's Flowers include counters, refrigerated display cases, flowers, decorations, vases, cards, and other gifts, as well as something known as "goodwill," which in this case is Anna's reputation for preparing and delivering beautiful floral arrangements on a timely basis. **Liabilities,** on the other hand, are debts the firm owes to others. Among the liabilities of Anna's Flowers are a loan from the Small Business Administration and money owed to flower suppliers and other creditors for items purchased. The **owners' equity** category contains all of the money that has ever been contributed to the company that never has to be paid back. The funds can come from investors who have given money or assets to the company, or it can come from past profitable operations. In the case of Anna's Flowers, if Anna were to sell off, or liquidate, her business, any money left over after selling all the shop's assets and paying off its liabilities would comprise her owner's equity. The relationship among assets, liabilities, and owners' equity is a fundamental concept in accounting and is known as the **accounting equation:**

The owner's equity portion of a company's balance sheet, such as that of Rendezvous Barbecue in Memphis, Tennessee, includes the money the company's owners have put into the firm.

$$\text{Assets} = \text{Liabilities} + \text{Owner's equity}$$

Double-Entry Bookkeeping

Double-entry bookkeeping is a system of recording and classifying business transactions in separate accounts in order to maintain the balance of the accounting equation. Returning to Anna's Flowers, suppose Anna buys $325 worth of roses on credit from the Antique Rose Emporium to fill a wedding order. When she records this transaction, she will list the $325 as a liability or a debt to a supplier. At the same time, however, she will also record $325 worth of roses as an asset in an account known as "inventory." Because the assets and liabilities are on different sides of the accounting equation, Anna's accounts increase in total size (by $325) but remain in balance:

$$\text{Assets} = \text{Liabilities} + \text{Owner's equity}$$
$$\$325 = \$325$$

Thus, to keep the accounting equation in balance, each business transaction must be recorded in two separate accounts.

In the final analysis, all business transactions are classified as assets, liabilities, or owners' equity. However, most organizations further break down these three accounts to provide more specific information about a transaction. For example, assets may be broken down into specific categories such as cash, inventory, and equipment, while liabilities may include bank loans, supplier credit, and other debts.

Figure 14.2 shows how Anna used the double-entry bookkeeping system to account for all of the transactions that took place in her first month of business. These transactions include her initial investment of $2,500, the loan from the Small Business Administration, purchases of equipment and inventory, and the purchase of roses on credit. In her first month of business, Anna generated revenues of $2,000 by selling $1,500 worth of inventory. Thus, she deducts, or (in accounting notation that is appropriate for assets) *credits,* $1,500 from inventory and adds, or *debits,*

liabilities
debts that a firm owes to others

owners' equity
equals assets minus liabilities and reflects historical values

accounting equation
assets equal liabilities plus owners' equity

double-entry bookkeeping
a system of recording and classifying business transactions that maintains the balance of the accounting equation

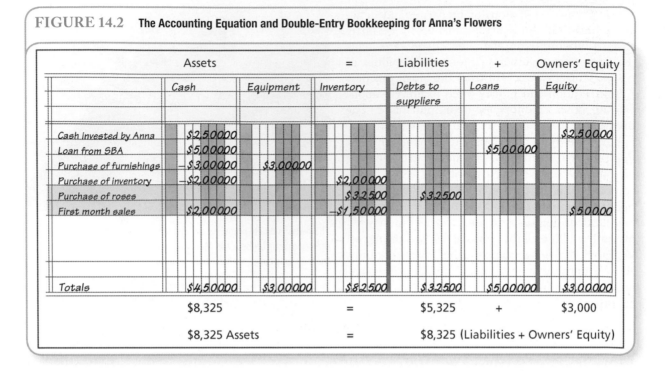

FIGURE 14.2   **The Accounting Equation and Double-Entry Bookkeeping for Anna's Flowers**

	Assets			=	Liabilities	+	Owners' Equity
	Cash	Equipment	Inventory		Debts to suppliers	Loans	Equity
Cash invested by Anna	$2,500.00						$2,500.00
Loan from SBA	$5,000.00					$5,000.00	
Purchase of furnishings	−$3,000.00	$3,000.00					
Purchase of inventory	−$2,000.00		$2,000.00				
Purchase of roses			$325.00		$325.00		
First month sales	$2,000.00		−$1,500.00				$500.00
Totals	$4,500.00	$3,000.00	$825.00		$325.00	$5,000.00	$3,000.00

$8,325   = $5,325   + $3,000

$8,325 Assets   = $8,325 (Liabilities + Owners' Equity)

$2,000 to the cash account. The difference between Anna's $2,000 cash inflow and her $1,500 outflow is represented by a credit to owners' equity, because it is money that belongs to her as the owner of the flower shop.

The Accounting Cycle

accounting cycle
the four-step procedure of an accounting system: examining source documents, recording transactions in an accounting journal, posting recorded transactions, and preparing financial statements

In any accounting system, financial data typically pass through a four-step procedure sometimes called the **accounting cycle.** The steps include examining source documents, recording transactions in an accounting journal, posting recorded transactions, and preparing financial statements. Figure 14.3 shows how Anna works through them. Traditionally, all of these steps were performed using paper, pencils, and erasers (lots of erasers!), but today the process is often fully computerized.

Step One: Examine Source Documents.   Like all good managers, Anna Rodriguez begins the accounting cycle by gathering and examining source documents—checks, credit card receipts, sales slips, and other related evidence concerning specific transactions.

journal
a time-ordered list of account transactions

Step Two: Record Transactions.   Next, Anna records each financial transaction in a **journal,** which is basically just a time-ordered list of account transactions. While most businesses keep a general journal in which all transactions are recorded, some classify transactions into specialized journals for specific types of transaction accounts.

ledger
a book or computer file with separate sections for each account

Step Three: Post Transactions.   Anna next transfers the information from her journal into a **ledger,** a book or computer program with separate files for each account. This process is known as *posting.* At the end of the accounting period (usually yearly, but occasionally quarterly or monthly), Anna prepares a *trial balance,* a summary of the balances of all the accounts in the general ledger. If, upon

FIGURE 14.3 The Accounting Process for Anna's Flowers

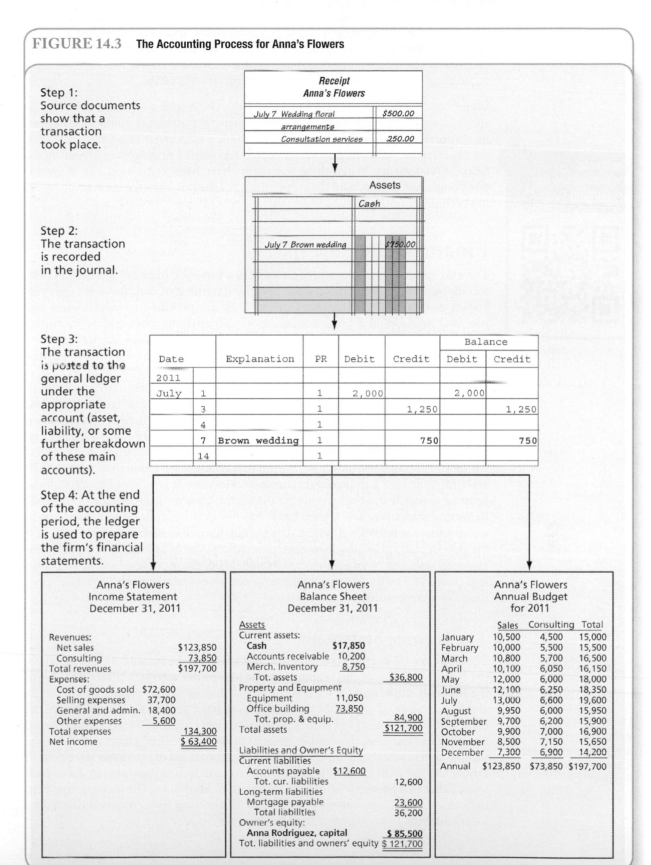

totalling, the trial balance doesn't balance (that is, the accounting equation is not in balance), Anna or her accountant must look for mistakes (typically an error in one or more of the ledger entries) and correct them. If the trial balance is correct, the accountant can then begin to prepare the financial statements.

Step Four: Prepare Financial Statements.   The information from the trial balance is also used to prepare the company's financial statements. In the case of public corporations and certain other organizations, a CPA must *attest,* or certify, that the organization followed generally accepted accounting principles in preparing the financial statements. When these statements have been completed, the organization's books are "closed," and the accounting cycle begins anew for the next accounting period.

Financial Statements

The end result of the accounting process is a series of financial statements. The income statement, the balance sheet, and the statement of cash flows are the best-known examples of financial statements. They are provided to stockholders and potential investors in a firm's annual report as well as to other relevant outsiders such as creditors, government agencies, and the Internal Revenue Service.

It is important to recognize that not all financial statements follow precisely the same format. The fact that different organizations generate income in different ways suggests that when it comes to financial statements, one size definitely does not fit all. Manufacturing firms, service providers, and nonprofit organizations each use a different set of accounting principles or rules upon which the public accounting profession has agreed. As we have already mentioned, these are sometimes referred to as *generally accepted accounting principles (GAAP).* Each country has a different set of rules that the businesses within that country are required to use for their accounting process and financial statements. However, a number of countries have adopted a standard set of accounting principles known as International Financial Reporting Standards. The United States has discussed adopting these standards to create a more standardized system of reporting for global investors. Moreover, as is the case in many other disciplines, certain concepts have more than one name. For example, *sales* and *revenues* are often interchanged, as are *profits, income,* and *earnings.* Table 14.2 lists a few common equivalent terms that should help you decipher their meaning in accounting statements.

The Income Statement

The question, "What's the bottom line?" derives from the income statement, where the bottom line shows the overall profit or loss of the company after taxes. Thus, the **income statement** is a financial report that shows an organization's profitability over a period of time, be that a month, quarter, or year. By its very design, the income statement offers one of the clearest possible pictures of the company's overall revenues and the costs incurred in generating those revenues. Other names for the income statement include profit and loss (P&L) statement or operating statement. A sample income statement with line-by-line explanations is presented in Table 14.3, while Table 14.4 presents the income statement of Starbucks. The income statement indicates the firm's profitability or income (the bottom line), which is derived by subtracting the firm's expenses from its revenues.

Need help understanding the Accounting Cycle?

http://bit.ly/FerrellQR14-1

LO 14-3

income statement
a financial report that shows an organization's profitability over a period of time—month, quarter, or year

TABLE 14.2

**Equivalent Terms
in Accounting**

Term	Equivalent Term
Revenues	Sales
	Goods or services sold
Gross profit	Gross income
	Gross earnings
Operating income	Operating profit
	Earnings before interest and taxes (EBIT)
	Income before interest and taxes (IBIT)
Income before taxes (IBT)	Earnings before taxes (EBT)
	Profit before taxes (PBT)
Net income (NI)	Earnings after taxes (EAT)
	Profit after taxes (PAT)
Income available to common stockholders	Earnings available to common stockholders

Revenue.   **Revenue** is the total amount of money received (or promised) from the sale of goods or services, as well as from other business activities such as the rental of property and investments. Nonbusiness entities typically obtain revenues through donations from individuals and/or grants from governments and private foundations. One of the controversies in accounting has been when a business should recognize revenue. For instance, should an organization book revenue during a project or after the project is completed? Differences in revenue recognition have caused similar organizations to book different accounting results. A proposed rule states that firms should book revenue when "it satisfie[s] a performance obligation by transferring a promised good or service to a customer."[7] Starbucks' income statement (see Table 14.4) shows three sources of revenue: retail sales; licensing; and consumer processed goods, food service, and other.

For most manufacturing and retail concerns, the next major item included in the income statement is the **cost of goods sold,** the amount of money the firm spent (or promised to spend) to buy and/or produce the products it sold during the accounting period. This figure may be calculated as follows:

Cost of goods sold = Beginning inventory + Interim purchases − Ending inventory

Let's say that Anna's Flowers began an accounting period with an inventory of goods for which it paid $5,000. During the period, Anna bought another $4,000 worth of goods, giving the shop a total inventory available for sale of $9,000. If, at the end of the accounting period, Anna's inventory was worth $5,500, the cost of goods sold during the period would have been $3,500 ($5,000 + $4,000 − $5,500 = $3,500). If Anna had total revenues of $10,000 over the same period of time, subtracting the cost of goods sold ($3,500) from the total revenues of $10,000 yields the store's **gross income** or **profit** (revenues minus the cost of goods sold required to generate the revenues): $6,500. The same process occurs at Starbucks. As indicated in Table 14.4,

revenue
the total amount of money received from the sale of goods or services, as well as from related business activities

cost of goods sold
the amount of money a firm spent to buy or produce the products it sold during the period to which the income statement applies

gross income (profit)
revenues minus the cost of goods sold required to generate the revenues

TABLE 14.3   Sample Income Statement

The following exhibit presents a sample income statement with all the terms defined and explained.

Company Name for the Year Ended December 31	
Revenues (sales)	Total dollar amount of products sold (includes income from other business services such as rental-lease income and interest income).
Less: Cost of goods sold	The cost of producing the goods and services, including the cost of labor and raw materials as well as other expenses associated with production.
Gross profit	The income available after paying all expenses of production.
Less: Selling and administrative expense	The cost of promoting, advertising, and selling products as well as the overhead costs of managing the company. This includes the cost of management and corporate staff. One non-cash expense included in this category is depreciation, which approximates the decline in the value of plant and equipment assets due to use over time. In most accounting statements, depreciation is not separated from selling and administrative expenses. However, financial analysts usually create statements that include this expense.
Income before interest and taxes (operating income or EBIT)	This line represents all income left over after operating expenses have been deducted. This is sometimes referred to as operating income since it represents all income after the expenses of operations have been accounted for. Occasionally, this is referred to as EBIT, or earnings before interest and taxes.
Less: Interest expense	Interest expense arises as a cost of borrowing money. This is a financial expense rather than an operating expense and is listed separately. As the amount of debt and the cost of debt increase, so will the interest expense. This covers the cost of both short-term and long-term borrowing.
Income before taxes (earnings before taxes—EBT)	The firm will pay a tax on this amount. This is what is left of revenues after subtracting all operating costs, depreciation costs, and interest costs.
Less: Taxes	The tax rate is specified in the federal tax code.
Net income	This is the amount of income left after taxes. The firm may decide to retain all or a portion of the income for reinvestment in new assets. Whatever it decides not to keep it will usually pay out in dividends to its stockholders.
Less: Preferred dividends	If the company has preferred stockholders, they are first in line for dividends. That is one reason why their stock is called "preferred."
Income to common stockholders	This is the income left for the common stockholders. If the company has a good year, there may be a lot of income available for dividends. If the company has a bad year, income could be negative. The common stockholders are the ultimate owners and risk takers. They have the potential for very high or very poor returns since they get whatever is left after all other expenses.
Earnings per share	Earnings per share is found by taking the income available to the common stockholders and dividing by the number of shares of common stock outstanding. This is income generated by the company for each share of common stock.

Fiscal Year Ended	Oct 2, 2011	Oct 3, 2010	Sep 27, 2009
Net revenues:			
Company-operated stores	$ 9,632.4	$ 8,963.5	$8,180.1
Licensed stores	1,007.5	875.2	795.0
CPG, foodservice and other	1,060.5	868.7	799.5
Total net revenues	11,700.4	10,707.4	9,774.6
Cost of sales including occupancy costs	4,949.3	4,458.6	4,324.9
Store operating expenses	3,665.1	3,551.4	3,425.1
Other operating expenses	402.0	293.2	264.4
Depreciation and amortization expenses	523.3	510.4	534.7
General and administrative expenses	636.1	569.5	453.0
Restructuring charges	0.0	53.0	332.4
Total operating expenses	10,175.8	9,436.1	9,334.5
Gain on sale of properties	30.2	0.0	0.0
Income from equity investees	173.7	148.1	121.9
Operating income	1,728.5	1,419.4	562.0
Interest income and other, net	115.9	50.3	37.0
Interest expense	(33.3)	(32.7)	(39.1)
Earnings before income taxes	1,811.1	1,437.0	559.9
Income taxes	563.1	488.7	168.4
Net earnings including noncontrolling interests	1,248.0	948.3	391.5
Net earnings (loss) attributable to noncontrolling interests	2.3	2.7	0.7
Net earnings attributable to Starbucks	$ 1,245.7	$ 945.6	$ 390.8
Earnings per share—basic	$ 1.66	$ 1.27	$ 0.53
Earnings per share—diluted	$ 1.62	$ 1.24	$ 0.52
Weighted average shares outstanding:			
Basic	748.3	744.4	738.7
Diluted	769.7	764.2	745.9
Cash dividends declared per share	$ 0.56	$ 0.36	$ 0.00

TABLE 14.4

Starbucks Corporation Consolidated Statements of Earnings (in millions, except per share data)

Source: Starbucks 2011 Annual Report, p. 43.

the cost of goods sold was more than $4.9 million in 2011. Notice that Starbucks calls it cost of sales, rather than cost of goods sold. This is because Starbucks buys raw materials and supplies and produces drinks.

Expenses. **Expenses** are the costs incurred in the day-to-day operations of an organization. Three common expense accounts shown on income statements are (1) selling, general, and administrative expenses; (2) research, development, and engineering expenses; and (3) interest expenses (remember that the costs directly attributable to selling goods or services are included in the cost of goods sold). Selling expenses include advertising and sales salaries. General and administrative expenses include salaries of executives and their staff and the costs of owning and maintaining the general office. Research and development costs include scientific, engineering, and marketing personnel and the equipment and information used to design and build prototypes and samples. Interest expenses include the direct costs of borrowing money.

The number and type of expense accounts vary from organization to organization. Included in the general and administrative category is a special type of expense known as **depreciation,** the process of spreading the costs of long-lived assets such as buildings and equipment over the total number of accounting periods in which they are expected to be used. Consider a manufacturer that purchases a $100,000 machine expected to last about 10 years. Rather than showing an expense of $100,000 in the first year and no expense for that equipment over the next nine years, the manufacturer is allowed to report depreciation expenses of $10,000 per year in each of the next 10 years because that better matches the cost of the machine to the years the machine is used. Each time this depreciation is "written off" as an expense, the book value of the machine is also reduced by $10,000. The fact that the equipment has a zero value on the firm's balance sheet when it is fully depreciated (in this case, after 10 years) does not necessarily mean that it can no longer be used or is economically worthless. Indeed, in some industries, machines used every day have been reported as having no book value whatsoever for more than 30 years.

Net Income. **Net income** (or net earnings) is the total profit (or loss) after all expenses including taxes have been deducted from revenue. Generally, accountants divide profits into individual sections such as operating income and earnings before interest and taxes. Starbucks, for example, lists earnings before income taxes, net earnings, and earnings per share of outstanding stock (see Table 14.4). Like most companies, Starbucks presents not only the current year's results but also the previous two years' income statements to permit comparison of performance from one period to another.

Temporary Nature of the Income Statement Accounts. Companies record their operational activities in the revenue and expense accounts during an accounting period. Gross profit, earnings before interest and taxes, and net income are the results of calculations made from the revenues and expenses accounts; they are not actual accounts. At the end of each accounting period, the dollar amounts in all the revenue and expense accounts are moved into an account called "Retained Earnings," one of the owners' equity accounts. Revenues increase owners' equity, while expenses decrease it. The resulting change in the owners' equity account is exactly equal to the net income. This shifting of dollar values from the revenue and expense

expenses
the costs incurred in the day-to-day operations of an organization

depreciation
the process of spreading the costs of long-lived assets such as buildings and equipment over the total number of accounting periods in which they are expected to be used

net income
the total profit (or loss) after all expenses, including taxes, have been deducted from revenue; also called net earnings

accounts allows the firm to begin the next accounting period with zero balances in those accounts. Zeroing out the balances enables a company to count how much it has sold and how many expenses have been incurred during a period of time. The basic accounting equation (Assets = Liabilities + Owners' equity) will not balance until the revenue and expense account balances have been moved or "closed out" to the owners' equity account.

One final note about income statements: You may remember that corporations may choose to make cash payments called dividends to shareholders out of their net earnings. When a corporation elects to pay dividends, it decreases the cash account (in the assets category of the balance sheet) as well as a capital account (in the owners' equity category of the balance sheet). During any period of time, the owners' equity account may change because of the sale of stock (or contributions/withdrawals by owners), the net income or loss, or the dividends paid.

The Balance Sheet

The second basic financial statement is the **balance sheet,** which presents a "snapshot" of an organization's financial position at a given moment. As such, the balance sheet indicates what the organization owns or controls and the various sources of the funds used to pay for these assets, such as bank debt or owners' equity.

The balance sheet takes its name from its reliance on the accounting equation: Assets *must* equal liabilities plus owners' equity. Table 14.5 provides a sample balance sheet with line-by-line explanations. Unlike the income statement, the balance sheet does not represent the result of transactions completed over a specified accounting period. Instead, the balance sheet is, by definition, an accumulation of all financial transactions conducted by an organization since its founding. Following long-established traditions, items on the balance sheet are listed on the basis of their original cost less accumulated depreciation, rather than their present values.

LO 14-4

balance sheet
a "snapshot" of an organization's financial position at a given moment

TABLE 14.7   **Consolidated Statements of Cash Flows (in millions)** *(continued)*

CASH AND CASH EQUIVALENTS:			
Beginning of period	1,164.0	599.8	269.8
End of period	$1,148.1	$1,164.0	$ 599.8
SUPPLEMENTAL DISCLOSURE OF CASH FLOW INFORMATION:			
Cash paid during the period for:			
Interest, net of capitalized interest	$ 34.4	$ 32.0	$ 39.8
Income taxes	$ 350.1	$ 527.0	$ 162.0

Source: Starbucks 2011 Annual Report, p. 45.

The change in cash is explained through details in three categories: cash from (used for) operating activities, cash from (used for) investing activities, and cash from (used for) financing activities. *Cash from operating activities* is calculated by combining the changes in the revenue accounts, expense accounts, current asset accounts, and current liability accounts. This category of cash flows includes all the accounts on the balance sheet that relate to computing revenues and expenses for the accounting period. If this amount is a positive number, as it is for Starbucks, then the business is making extra cash that it can use to invest in increased long-term capacity or to pay off debts such as loans or bonds. A negative number may indicate a business that is in a declining position with regards to operations. Negative cash flow is not always a bad thing, however. It may indicate that a business is growing, with a very negative cash flow indicating rapid growth.

Cash from investing activities is calculated from changes in the long-term or fixed asset accounts. If this amount is negative, as is the case with Starbucks, the company is purchasing long-term assets for future growth. A positive figure indicates a business that is selling off existing long-term assets and reducing its capacity for the future.

Finally, *cash from financing activities* is calculated from changes in the long-term liability accounts and the contributed capital accounts in owners' equity. If this amount is negative, the company is likely paying off long-term debt or returning contributed capital to investors. As in the case of Starbucks, if this amount is positive, the company is either borrowing more money or raising money from investors by selling more shares of stock.

Ratio Analysis: Analyzing Financial Statements

ratio analysis
calculations that measure an organization's financial health

The income statement shows a company's profit or loss, while the balance sheet itemizes the value of its assets, liabilities, and owners' equity. Together, the two statements provide the means to answer two critical questions: (1) How much did the firm make or lose? and (2) How much is the firm presently worth based on historical values found on the balance sheet? **Ratio analysis,** calculations that measure an organization's financial health, brings the complex information from the income statement and balance sheet into sharper focus so that managers, lenders, owners, and other interested parties can measure and compare the organization's productivity, profitability, and financing mix with other similar entities.

As you know, a ratio is simply one number divided by another, with the result showing the relationship between the two numbers. For example, we measure fuel efficiency with miles per gallon. This is how we know that 55 mpg in a Toyota Prius is much better than the average car. Financial ratios are used to weigh and evaluate a firm's performance. An absolute value such as earnings of $70,000 or accounts receivable of $200,000 almost never provides as much useful information as a well-constructed ratio. Whether those numbers are good or bad depends on their relation to other numbers. If a company earned $70,000 on $700,000 in sales (a 10 percent return), such an earnings level might be quite satisfactory. The president of a company earning this same $70,000 on sales of $7 million (a 1 percent return), however, should probably start looking for another job!

Ratios by themselves are not very useful. It is the relationship of the calculated ratios to both prior organizational performance and the performance of the organization's "peers," as well as its stated goals, that really matters. Remember, while the profitability, asset utilization, liquidity, debt ratios, and per share data we'll look at here can be very useful, you will never see the forest by looking only at the trees.

Profitability Ratios

Profitability ratios measure how much operating income or net income an organization is able to generate relative to its assets, owners' equity, and sales. The numerator (top number) used in these examples is always the net income after taxes. Common profitability ratios include profit margin, return on assets, and return on equity. The following examples are based on the 2011 income statement and balance sheet for Starbucks, as shown in Tables 14.4 and 14.6. Except where specified, all data are expressed in millions of dollars.

The **profit margin,** computed by dividing net income by sales, shows the overall percentage of profits earned by the company. It is based solely upon data obtained from the income statement. The higher the profit margin, the better the cost controls within the company and the higher the return on every dollar of revenue. Starbucks' profit margin is calculated as follows:

$$\text{Profit margin} = \frac{\text{Net income (Net earnings)}}{\text{Sales (Total net revenues)}} = \frac{\$1,245.7}{\$11,700.4} = 10.65\%$$

Thus, for every $1 in sales, Starbucks generated profits after taxes of almost 11 cents.

Return on assets, net income divided by assets, shows how much income the firm produces for every dollar invested in assets. A company with a low return on assets is probably not using its assets very productively—a key managerial failing. For its construction, the return on assets calculation requires data from both the income statement and the balance sheet.

$$\text{Return on assets} = \frac{\text{Net income (Net earnings)}}{\text{Total assets}} = \frac{\$1,245.7}{\$7,360.4} = 16.92\%$$

In the case of Starbucks, every $1 of assets generated a return of close to 17 percent, or profits of 16.92 cents per dollar.

profitability ratios ratios that measure the amount of operating income or net income an organization is able to generate relative to its assets, owners' equity, and sales

profit margin net income divided by sales

return on assets net income divided by assets

Responding to Business Challenges
Should the United States Adopt International Financial Accounting Standards?

If you've ever taken an accounting class, then you've probably heard of GAAP, or generally accepted accounting principles. GAAP are standardized rules used to ensure the clarity, consistency, and accuracy of financial statements for U.S. firms.

However, there is one problem with GAAP. As the world becomes increasingly globalized, multinational companies find it difficult to adhere to the different accounting standards of the countries in which they operate. Many countries have their own sets of generally accepted accounting principles that differ from U.S. GAAP. This situation also creates difficulty for investors. How can an investor compare a French company with a U.S. company when their accounting statements each use a different set of rules?

To eliminate this problem, about 120 countries have fully or partially adopted the International Financial Reporting Standards (IFRS). Support for IFRS adoption in the United States is strong. Ford, for instance, supports the move to IFRS because it would streamline and standardize Ford's accounting processes in the 138 nations in which the company operates. Another widely supported process is known as *condorsement,* which advocates assimilation of IFRS rules into GAAP over time.

Despite the widespread support for IFRS adoption, the standards have many critics. One criticism relates to the costs involved. Accountants would have to be retrained, and some of the rules allowed under GAAP will have to be dropped altogether. Analysts predict that switching costs could be 1 percent of annual company revenues. Small companies that do not conduct business overseas argue that IFRS adoption would be too costly. Another argument is that IFRS is based more on guidelines than actual rules, which could result in less accurate financial statements and the potential for more lawsuits. Finally, opponents argue that there is no definitive proof that IFRS is any more beneficial than GAAP.[9]

Discussion Questions

1. Why has it been difficult to compare financial statements of companies in different countries?
2. What would be some of the benefits of adopting International Financial Reporting Standards (IFRS) in the United States?
3. What would be some potential disadvantages of adopting IFRS in the United States?

---

return on equity
net income divided by owners' equity; also called return on investment (ROI)

Stockholders are always concerned with how much money they will make on their investment, and they frequently use the return on equity ratio as one of their key performance yardsticks. **Return on equity** (also called return on investment [ROI]), calculated by dividing net income by owners' equity, shows how much income is generated by each $1 the owners have invested in the firm. Obviously, a low return on equity means low stockholder returns and may indicate a need for immediate managerial attention. Because some assets may have been financed with debt not contributed by the owners, the value of the owners' equity is usually considerably lower than the total value of the firm's assets. Starbucks' return on equity is calculated as follows:

$$\text{Return on equity} = \frac{\text{Net income}}{\text{Stockholders' equity}} = \frac{\$1,245.7}{\$4,387.3} = 28.39\%$$

For every dollar invested by Starbucks stockholders, the company earned a 28.39 percent return, or 28.39 cents per dollar invested.

Asset Utilization Ratios

asset utilization ratios
ratios that measure how well a firm uses its assets to generate each $1 of sales

Asset utilization ratios measure how well a firm uses its assets to generate each $1 of sales. Obviously, companies using their assets more productively will have higher returns on assets than their less efficient competitors. Similarly, managers can use asset utilization ratios to pinpoint areas of inefficiency in their operations. These ratios (receivables turnover, inventory turnover, and total asset turnover) relate balance sheet assets to sales, which are found on the income statement.

The **receivables turnover,** sales divided by accounts receivable, indicates how many times a firm collects its accounts receivable in one year. It also demonstrates how quickly a firm is able to collect payments on its credit sales. Obviously, no payments means no profits. Starbucks collected its receivables a little more than 30 times per year. The reason the number is so high is that most of Starbucks' sales are for cash and not credit.

receivables turnover
sales divided by accounts receivable

$$\text{Receivables turnover} = \frac{\text{Sales (Total net revenues)}}{\text{Receivables}} = \frac{\$11,700.4}{\$386.5} = 30.27 \times$$

Inventory turnover, sales divided by total inventory, indicates how many times a firm sells and replaces its inventory over the course of a year. A high inventory turnover ratio may indicate great efficiency but may also suggest the possibility of lost sales due to insufficient stock levels. Starbucks' inventory turnover indicates that it replaced its inventory 12.11 times last year, or slightly more than once a month.

inventory turnover
sales divided by total inventory

$$\text{Inventory turnover} = \frac{\text{Sales (Total net revenues)}}{\text{Inventory}} = \frac{\$11,700.4}{\$965.8} = 12.11 \times$$

Total asset turnover, sales divided by total assets, measures how well an organization uses all of its assets in creating sales. It indicates whether a company is using its assets productively. Starbucks generated $1.59 in sales for every $1 in total corporate assets.

total asset turnover
sales divided by total assets

$$\text{Total asset turnover} = \frac{\text{Sales (Total net revenues)}}{\text{Total assets}} = \frac{\$11,700.4}{\$7,360.4} = 1.59 \times$$

Liquidity Ratios

Liquidity ratios compare current (short-term) assets to current liabilities to indicate the speed with which a company can turn its assets into cash to meet debts as they fall due. High liquidity ratios may satisfy a creditor's need for safety, but ratios that are too high may indicate that the organization is not using its current assets efficiently. Liquidity ratios are generally best examined in conjunction with asset utilization ratios because high turnover ratios imply that cash is flowing through an organization very quickly—a situation that dramatically reduces the need for the type of reserves measured by liquidity ratios.

liquidity ratios
ratios that measure the speed with which a company can turn its assets into cash to meet short-term debt

The **current ratio** is calculated by dividing current assets by current liabilities. Starbucks's current ratio indicates that for every $1 of current liabilities, the firm had $1.83 of current assets on hand. This number improved from previous years, and indicates that Starbucks has increased its liquidity as it restructures its business. Current assets increased faster than current liabilities between 2010 and 2011 making for a much improved current ratio. Additionally, accounts receivable has increased over the same time period.

current ratio
current assets divided by current liabilities

$$\text{Current ratio} = \frac{\text{Current assets}}{\text{Current liabilities}} = \frac{\$3,794.9}{\$2,075.8} = 1.83 \times$$

quick ratio (acid test)
a stringent measure of liquidity that eliminates inventory

The **quick ratio** (also known as the **acid test**) is a far more stringent measure of liquidity because it eliminates inventory, the least liquid current asset. It measures how well an organization can meet its current obligations without resorting to the sale of its inventory. In 2011, Starbucks had $1.36 cents invested in current assets (after subtracting inventory) for every $1 of current liabilities, an increase over previous years.

$$\text{Quick ratio} = \frac{\text{Current assets} - \text{Inventory}}{\text{Current liabilities}} = \frac{\$2,829.1}{\$2,075.8} = 1.36 \times$$

Debt Utilization Ratios

debt utilization ratios
ratios that measure how much debt an organization is using relative to other sources of capital, such as owners' equity

Debt utilization ratios provide information about how much debt an organization is using relative to other sources of capital, such as owners' equity. Because the use of debt carries an interest charge that must be paid regularly regardless of profitability, debt financing is much riskier than equity. Unforeseen negative events such as recessions affect heavily indebted firms to a far greater extent than those financed exclusively with owners' equity. Because of this and other factors, the managers of most firms tend to keep debt-to-asset levels below 50 percent. However, firms in very stable and/or regulated industries, such as electric utilities, often are able to carry debt ratios well in excess of 50 percent with no ill effects.

debt to total assets ratio
a ratio indicating how much of the firm is financed by debt and how much by owners' equity

The **debt to total assets ratio** indicates how much of the firm is financed by debt and how much by owners' equity. To find the value of Starbucks' total debt, you must add current liabilities to long-term debt and other liabilities.

$$\text{Debt to total assets} = \frac{\text{Debt (Total liabilities)}}{\text{Total assets}} = \frac{\$2,973.1}{\$7,360.4} = 40\%$$

Thus, for every $1 of Starbucks' total assets, 40 percent is financed with debt. The remaining 60 percent is provided by owners' equity.

times interest earned ratio
operating income divided by interest expense

The **times interest earned ratio,** operating income divided by interest expense, is a measure of the safety margin a company has with respect to the interest payments it must make to its creditors. A low times interest earned ratio indicates that even a small decrease in earnings may lead the company into financial straits. Because Starbucks has more interest income than interest expense, it would appear that their times interest earned ratio is not able to be calculated by using the income statement. However, in the statement of cash flows in Table 14.7 on the second line from the bottom, we can see that Starbucks paid $33.3 million in interest expense, an amount that was covered nearly 51.91 times by income before interest and taxes. A lender would not have to worry about receiving interest payments.

$$\text{Times interest earned} = \frac{\text{EBIT (Operating income)}}{\text{Interest}} = \frac{\$1,728.5}{\$33.3} = 51.91 \times$$

Per Share Data

per share data
data used by investors to compare the performance of one company with another on an equal, per share basis

Investors may use **per share data** to compare the performance of one company with another on an equal, or per share, basis. Generally, the more shares of stock a company issues, the less income is available for each share.

earnings per share
net income or profit divided by the number of stock shares outstanding

Earnings per share is calculated by dividing net income or profit by the number of shares of stock outstanding. This ratio is important because yearly changes in earnings per share, in combination with other economywide factors, determine a company's overall stock price. When earnings go up, so does a company's stock price—and so does the wealth of its stockholders.

$$\text{Diluted earnings per share} = \frac{\text{Net income}}{\text{Number of shares outstanding (diluted)}}$$

$$= \frac{\$1,245.7}{769.7} = \$1.62$$

We can see from the income statement that Starbucks' basic earnings per share more than tripled between 2009 and 2011 as Starbucks staged a dramatic turnaround. Notice that Starbucks lists diluted earnings per share, calculated here, of $0.52 per share in 2009 and $1.62 per share in 2011. You can see from the income statement that diluted earnings per share include more shares than the basic calculation; this is because diluted shares include potential shares that could be issued due to the exercise of stock options or the conversion of certain types of debt into common stock. Investors generally pay more attention to diluted earnings per share than basic earnings per share.

Dividends per share are paid by the corporation to the stockholders for each share owned. The payment is made from earnings after taxes by the corporation but is taxable income to the stockholder. Thus, dividends result in double taxation: The corporation pays tax once on its earnings, and the stockholder pays tax a second time on his or her dividend income. Starbucks began paying dividends in 2010 and increased them in 2011. The dividend declared on the income statement is 0 per share but the actual dividends paid were $0.52. There is a difference between dividends paid and declared. Dividends are paid quarterly and Starbucks declared a higher dividend in its fourth quarter, but it won't be paid until the next year.

dividends per share the actual cash received for each share owned

$$\text{Dividends per share} = \frac{\text{Dividends paid}}{\text{Number of shares outstanding}} = \frac{\$389.5}{748.3} = \$0.52$$

Industry Analysis

We have used McDonald's as a comparison to Starbucks because there are no real national and international coffee houses that compete with Starbucks on the same scale. While McDonald's is almost two and one-half times larger than Starbucks in terms of sales, they both have a national and international presence and, to some extent, compete for the consumer's dollars. In recent years, McDonald's has moved into Starbucks' market by putting McCafé coffee shops in many of its locations. Table 14.8 indicates that McDonald's dominates Starbucks in two out of three profitability categories.

Since 2009, McDonald's has increased its after-tax profits by 21 percent while Starbucks profits increased by more than 300 percent. Starbucks stumbled in 2007 and 2008 as it overexpanded and lost focus. Howard Schultz, the founder, returned as CEO and successfully restructured the company. Investors rewarded the company's turnaround by pushing the stock price from a low of $8.12 in early 2009

Many of Netflix's financial ratios were higher than the industry average. However, after the company raised the price on one of its most popular rental plans, the value of its stock price fell significantly. This could impact Netflix's future financial ratios.

TABLE 14.8

Industry Analysis, Year Ending 2011

	Starbucks	McDonald's
Profit margin	10.65%	20.38%
Return on assets	16.92%	16.68%
Return on equity	28.39%	38.24%
Receivables turnover	30.27×	20.23×
Inventory turnover	12.11×	231.22×
Total asset turnover	1.59×	0.82×
Current ratio	1.83×	1.25×
Quick ratio	1.36×	1.22×
Debt to total assets	40.00%	56%
Times interest earned	51.91×	17.43×
Diluted earnings per share	$1.62	$5.27
Dividends per share	$0.52	$2.53

Source: Data calculated from 2011 annual reports.

to a high of $62.00 in early 2012. Both companies have very little accounts receivables relative to the size of their sales, so the ratios are very high, indicating a lot of cash and credit card sales. McDonald's pushes off much of its inventory holding costs onto its suppliers, so it has much higher inventory turnover ratios. Both have current ratios that are reasonably solid given their level of profitability. The difference in the current ratios and the quick ratio is of little consequence to the financial analyst or lender because both companies have high times interest earned ratios. Starbucks has a much lower debt to asset ratio and therefore less financial risk than McDonald's, and this also is emphasized by Starbucks' much higher times interest earned ratio.

While McDonald's net income has grown more slowly in the past three years, its earnings per share grew from $1.93 in 2007 to $5.27 in 2011. On the other hand, Starbucks' earnings per share in 2007 were $0.87. It dropped to $0.43 in 2008, recovered slightly to $0.52 in 2009, finally took off again in 2010, and reached $1.62 in 2011. Starbucks instituted its first dividend in 2010 and raised it from $0.10 per quarter to $0.13 per quarter to $0.17 per quarter for a projected annual rate of $0.68. Both companies are in good financial health, and Starbucks has regained its past glow. One thing is for sure: If Starbucks could earn the same profit margin as McDonald's, it would improve its other profitability ratios and its stock price.

Importance of Integrity in Accounting

The financial crisis and the recession that followed provided another example of a failure in accounting reporting. Many firms attempted to exploit loopholes and manipulate accounting processes and statements. Banks and other financial institutions often held assets off their books by manipulating their accounts. In 2010, the examiner for the Lehman Brothers' bankruptcy found that the most common example of removing assets or liabilities from the books was entering into what is called a "repurchase agreement." In a repurchase agreement, assets are transferred to another entity with the contractual promise of buying them back at a set price. In the case of Lehman Brothers and other companies, repurchase agreements were used as a method of "cooking the books" that allowed them to manipulate accounting statements so that their ratios looked better than they actually were. If the accountants, the SEC, and the bank regulators had been more careful, these types of transactions would have been discovered and corrected.

On the other hand, strong compliance to accounting principles creates trust among stakeholders. The city of El Dorado, Kansas, makes transparency, accuracy, and disclosure of financial information top priorities. The city government wants to inform constituents about the amount of funds it receives as well as where that money is being spent. The government spends a significant amount of time in the audit process and creates an annual financial report that breaks down its financial information. Because of its diligence, the city has won the Certificate of Achievement for Financial Accounting from the Government Finance Officers Association every year since 1977.[10]

It is most important to remember that integrity in accounting processes requires ethical principles and compliance with both the spirit of the law and professional standards in the accounting profession. Most states require accountants preparing to take the CPA exam to take accounting ethics courses. Transparency and accuracy in reporting revenue, income, and assets develops trust from investors and other stakeholders.

So You Want to Be an Accountant

Do you like numbers and finances? Are you detail oriented, a perfectionist, and highly accountable for your decisions? If so, accounting may be a good field for you. If you are interested in accounting, there are always job opportunities available no matter the state of the economy. Accounting is one of the most secure job options in business. Of course, becoming an accountant is not easy. You will need at least a bachelor's degree in accounting to get a job, and many positions require additional training. Many states demand coursework beyond the 120 to 150 credit hours collegiate programs require for an accounting degree. If you are really serious about getting into the accounting field, you will probably want to consider getting your master's in accounting and taking the CPA exam. The field of accounting can be complicated, and the extra training provided through a master's in accounting program will prove invaluable when you go out looking for a good job. Accounting is a volatile discipline affected by changes in legislative initiatives.

With corporate accounting policies changing constantly and becoming more complex, accountants are needed to help keep a business running smoothly and within the bounds of the law. In fact, the number of jobs in the accounting and auditing field are expected to increase 16 percent between 2010 and 2020, with more than 1.4 million jobs in the United States alone by 2020. Jobs in accounting tend to pay quite well, with the median salary standing at $61,690. If you go on to get your master's degree in accounting, expect to see an even higher starting wage. Of course, your earnings could be higher or lower than these averages, depending on where you work, your level of experience, the firm, and your particular position.

Accountants are needed in the public and the private sectors, in large and small firms, in for-profit and not-for-profit organizations. Accountants in firms are generally in charge of preparing and filing tax forms and financial reports. Public-sector accountants are responsible for checking the veracity of corporate and personal records in order to prepare tax filings. Basically, any organization that has to deal with money and/or taxes in some way or another will be in need of an accountant, either for in-house service or occasional contract work. Requirements for audits under the Sarbanes-Oxley Act and rules from the Public Company Accounting Oversight Board are creating more jobs and increased responsibility to maintain internal controls and accounting ethics. The fact that accounting rules and tax filings tend to be complex virtually ensures that the demand for accountants will never decrease.[11]

Review Your Understanding

Define accounting, and describe the different uses of accounting information.

Accounting is the language businesses and other organizations use to record, measure, and interpret financial transactions. Financial statements are used internally to judge and control an organization's performance and to plan and direct its future activities and measure goal attainment. External organizations such as lenders, governments, customers, suppliers, and the Internal Revenue Service are major consumers of the information generated by the accounting process.

Demonstrate the accounting process.

Assets are an organization's economic resources; liabilities, debts the organization owes to others; and owners' equity, the difference between the value of an organization's assets and liabilities. This principle can be expressed as the accounting equation: Assets = Liabilities + Owners' equity. The double-entry bookkeeping system is a system of recording and classifying business transactions in accounts that maintain the balance of the accounting equation. The accounting cycle involves examining source documents, recording transactions in a journal, posting transactions, and preparing financial statements on a continuous basis throughout the life of the organization.

Decipher the various components of an income statement in order to evaluate a firm's "bottom line."

The income statement indicates a company's profitability over a specific period of time. It shows the "bottom line," the total profit (or loss) after all expenses (the costs incurred in the day-to-day operations of the organization) have been deducted from revenue (the total amount of money received from the sale of goods or services and other business activities). The cash flow statement details how much cash is moving through the firm and thus adds insight to a firm's "bottom line."

Interpret a company's balance sheet to determine its current financial position.

The balance sheet, which summarizes the firm's assets, liabilities, and owners' equity since its inception, portrays its financial position as of a particular point in time. Major classifications included in the balance sheet are current assets (assets that can be converted to cash within one calendar year), fixed assets

(assets of greater than one year's duration), current liabilities (bills owed by the organization within one calendar year), long-term liabilities (bills due more than one year hence), and owners' equity (the net value of the owners' investment).

Analyze financial statements, using ratio analysis, to evaluate a company's performance.

Ratio analysis is a series of calculations that brings the complex information from the income statement and balance sheet into sharper focus so that managers, lenders, owners, and other interested parties can measure and compare the organization's productivity, profitability, and financing mix with similar entities. Ratios may be classified in terms of profitability (measure dollars of return for each dollar of employed assets),

asset utilization (measure how well the organization uses its assets to generate $1 in sales), liquidity (assess organizational risk by comparing current assets to current liabilities), debt utilization (measure how much debt the organization is using relative to other sources of capital), and per share data (compare the performance of one company with another on an equal basis).

Assess a company's financial position using its accounting statements and ratio analysis.

Based on the information presented in the chapter, you should be able to answer the questions posed in "Solve the Dilemma" on page 471. Formulate a plan for determining BrainDrain's bottom line, current worth, and productivity.

Revisit the World of Business

1. Why have Internet retailers such as Amazon and eBay been able to avoid collecting state sales taxes?

2. What reasons does eBay provide for opposing the collection of state sales taxes by web retailers?

3. Do you think it is fair that web retailers do not have to collect state sales taxes?

Learn the Terms

accounting   438
accounting cycle   446
accounting equation   445
accounts payable   457
accounts receivable   455
accrued expenses   458
annual report   442
asset utilization ratios   462
assets   444
balance sheet   453
budget   442
cash flow   441
certified management accountants (CMAs)   441
certified public accountant (CPA)   439
cost of goods sold   449
current assets   455

current liabilities   457
current ratio   463
debt to total assets ratio   464
debt utilization ratios   464
depreciation   452
dividends per share   465
double-entry bookkeeping   445
earnings per share   464
expenses   452
gross income (profit)   449
income statement   448
inventory turnover   463
journal   446
ledger   446
liabilities   445
liquidity ratios   463
managerial accounting   441

net income   452
owners' equity   445
per share data   464
private accountants   441
profit margin   461
profitability ratios   461
quick ratio (acid test)   464
ratio analysis   460
receivables turnover   463
return on assets   461
return on equity   462
revenue   449
statement of cash flows   458
times interest earned ratio   464
total asset turnover   463

Check Your Progress

1. Why are accountants so important to a corporation? What function do they perform?

2. Discuss the internal uses of accounting statements.

3. What is a budget?

4. Discuss the external uses of financial statements.

5. Describe the accounting process and cycle.

6. The income statements of all corporations are in the same format. True or false? Discuss.

7. Which accounts appear under "current liabilities"?

8. Together, the income statement and the balance sheet answer two basic questions. What are they?

9. What are the five basic ratio classifications? What ratios are found in each category?

10. Why are debt ratios important in assessing the risk of a firm?

Get Involved

1. Go to the library or the Internet and get the annual report of a company with which you are familiar. Read through the financial statements, then write up an analysis of the firm's performance using ratio analysis. Look at data over several years and analyze whether the firm's performance is changing through time.

2. Form a group of three or four students to perform an industry analysis. Each student should analyze a company in the same industry, and then all of you should compare your results. The following companies would make good group projects:

Automobiles: DaimlerChrysler, Ford, General Motors

Computers: Apple, IBM, Dell

Brewing: MillerCoors, Molson Coors, G. Heileman

Chemicals: Du Pont, Dow Chemical, Monsanto

Petroleum: Chevron, ExxonMobil, BP

Pharmaceuticals: Merck, Lilly, UpJohn

Retail: Sears, JCPenney, Macy's, The Limited

Build Your Skills

FINANCIAL ANALYSIS

Background

The income statement for Western Grain Company, a producer of agricultural products for industrial as well as consumer markets, is shown below. Western Grain's total assets are $4,237.1 million, and its equity is $1,713.4 million.

Consolidated Earnings and Retained Earnings Year Ended December 31

(Millions)	2010
Net sales	$6,295.4
Cost of goods sold	2,989.0
Selling and administrative expense	2,237.5
Operating profit	1,068.9
Interest expense	33.3
Other income (expense), net	(1.5)
Earnings before income taxes	1,034.1
Income taxes	353.4
Net earnings	680.7
(Net earnings per share)	$2.94
Retained earnings, beginning of year	3,033.9
Dividends paid	(305.2)
Retained earnings, end of year	$3,409.4

Task

Calculate the following profitability ratios: profit margin, return on assets, and return on equity. Assume that the industry averages for these ratios are as follows: profit margin, 12 percent; return on assets, 18 percent; and return on equity, 25 percent. Evaluate Western Grain's profitability relative to the industry averages. Why is this information useful?

Solve the Dilemma   LO 14-6

EXPLORING THE SECRETS OF ACCOUNTING

You have just been promoted from vice president of marketing of BrainDrain Corporation to president and CEO! That's the good news. Unfortunately, while you know marketing like the back of your hand, you know next to nothing about finance. Worse still, the "word on the street" is that BrainDrain is in danger of failure if steps to correct large and continuing financial losses are not taken immediately. Accordingly, you have asked the vice president of finance and accounting for a complete set of accounting statements detailing the financial operations of the company over the past several years.

Recovering from the dual shocks of your promotion and feeling the weight of the firm's complete accounting report for the very first time, you decide to attack the problem systematically and learn the "hidden secrets" of the company, statement by statement. With Mary Pruitt, the firm's trusted senior financial analyst, by your side, you delve into the accounting statements as never before. You resolve to "get to the bottom" of the firm's financial problems and set a new course for the future—a course that will take the firm from insolvency and failure to financial recovery and perpetual prosperity.

Discussion Questions

1. Describe the three basic accounting statements. What types of information does each provide that can help you evaluate the situation?
2. Which of the financial ratios are likely to prove to be of greatest value in identifying problem areas in the company? Why? Which of your company's financial ratios might you expect to be especially poor?
3. Discuss the limitations of ratio analysis.

Build Your Business Plan

ACCOUNTING AND FINANCIAL STATEMENTS

After you determine your initial *reasonable selling price,* you need to estimate your sales forecasts (in terms of units and dollars of sales) for the first year of operation. Remember to be conservative and set forecasts that are more modest.

While customers may initially try your business, many businesses have seasonal patterns. A good budgeting/planning system allows managers to anticipate problems, coordinate activities of the business (so that subunits within the organization are all working toward the common goal of the organization), and control operations (how do we know whether spending is "in line").

The first financial statement you need to prepare is the income statement. Beginning with your estimated sales revenue,

determine what expenses will be necessary to generate that level of sales revenue.

The second financial statement you need to create is your balance sheet. Your balance sheet is a snapshot of your financial position in a moment in time. Refer to Table 14.6 to assist you in listing your assets, liabilities, and owner's equity.

The last financial statement, the cash flow statement, is the most important one to a bank. It is a measure of your ability to get and repay the loan from the bank. Referring to Table 14.7, be as realistic as possible as you are completing it. Allow yourself enough cash on hand until the point in which the business starts to support itself.

See for Yourself Videocase

THE ACCOUNTING FUNCTION AT GOODWILL INDUSTRIES INTERNATIONAL INC.

Goodwill Industries International Inc. consists of a network of 165 independent, community-based organizations located throughout the United States and Canada. The mission of this nonprofit is to enhance the lives of individuals, families, and communities "through

learning and the power of work." Local Goodwills sell donated goods and then donate the proceeds to fund job training programs, placement services, education, and more. Despite its nonprofit status, Goodwill establishments are, in many ways, run similar to for-profit businesses. One of these similarities involves the accounting function.

Like for-profit firms, nonprofit organizations like Goodwill must provide detailed information about how they are using the donations that are provided to them. Indeed, fraud can occur just as easily at a nonprofit organization as for a for-profit company, making it necessary for nonprofits to reassure stakeholders that they are using their funds legitimately. Additionally, donors want to know how much of their donations is going toward activities such as job creation and how much is going toward operational and administrative expenses. It sometimes surprises people that nonprofits use part of the funds they receive for operational costs. Yet such a perspective fails to see that nonprofits must also pay for electricity, rent, wages, and other services.

"We have revenue and support for the revenue pieces, and then we have direct and indirect expenses for our program services, and then we have G and A, general administrative services. And we have what's called the bottom line, or other people call net profit. We have what's called net change in assets. The concept is pretty much the same as far as accounting," says Jeff McGraw, CFO of Goodwill.

Goodwill creates the equivalent of a balance sheet and income statement. Yet because Goodwill is a nonprofit entity, its financials are known by the names "statement of financial position" and "statement of activities." These financials have some differences compared to financial statements of for-profit companies. For instance, Goodwill's statement of financial position does not have shareholder's equity but instead has net assets. The organization's financials are audited, and stakeholders can find the firm's information in Form 990 through Goodwill's public website (Form 990 is the IRS form for nonprofits).

Because Goodwill sells goods at its store, the company must also figure in costs of goods sold. In fact, most of the organization's revenue comes from its store activities. According to Rosa Proctor, CFO of Goodwill of Greater Washington, about "55 percent comes from the retail division or sale of donated goods and contributed goods, 37 percent comes from the contracts division, which provides custodial, janitorial, lawn maintenance service contracts to the government agencies. Eight percent comes from grants, from foundations, corporations, individuals." The fact that Goodwill is able to generate

much of its own funding through store activities and contracts is important. Many nonprofits that rely solely on donated funds find it hard to be sustainable in the long run, particularly during economic downturns.

Remember that even though nonprofits are different from for-profit companies, they must still make certain that their financial information is accurate. This requires nonprofit accountants to be meticulous and thorough in gathering and analyzing information. Like all accountants, accountants at Goodwill record transactions in journals and then carefully review the information before it is recorded in the general ledger. The organization uses trial balances to ensure that everything balances out, as well as advanced software to record transactions, reconcile any discrepancies, and provide an idea of how much cash the organization has on hand.

Finally, Goodwill uses ratio analysis to determine the financial health of the company. For instance, the common ratio allows Goodwill to determine how much revenue it brings in for every dollar it spends on costs. The organization also uses ratio analysis to compare its results to similar organizations. It is important for Goodwill to identify the best performers in its field so that it can generate ideas and even form partnerships with other organizations. By using accounting to identify how best to use its resources, Goodwill is advancing its mission of helping others.[12]

DISCUSSION QUESTIONS

1. What are some similarities between the type of accounting performed at Goodwill and accounting at for-profit companies?

2. What are some differences between the type of accounting performed at Goodwill and accounting at for-profit companies?

3. How can Goodwill use ratio analysis to improve its operations?

Remember to check out our Online Learning Center at www.mhhe.com/ferrell9e.

Team Exercise

You can look at websites such as Yahoo! Finance (http://finance.yahoo.com/), under the company's "key statistics" link, to find many of its financial ratios, such as return on assets and return on equity. Have each member of your team look up a different company, and explain why you think there are differences in the ratio analysis for these two ratios among the selected companies.

Money and the Financial System

Learning Objectives

After reading this chapter, you will be able to:

LO 15-1   Define money, its functions, and its characteristics.

LO 15-2   Describe various types of money.

LO 15-3   Specify how the Federal Reserve Board manages the money supply and regulates the American banking system.

LO 15-4   Compare and contrast commercial banks, savings and loan associations, credit unions, and mutual savings banks.

LO 15-5   Distinguish among nonbanking institutions such as insurance companies, pension funds, mutual funds, and finance companies.

LO 15-6   Investigate the challenges ahead for the banking industry.

LO 15-7   Recommend the most appropriate financial institution for a hypothetical small business.

Will the Yuan Become the Next Global Currency?

As the world's second-largest economy, China is increasing efforts to make the yuan a global currency. China hopes that the yuan will achieve the status of the dollar, euro, and yen as an international currency for trade and investment. In order to encourage the yuan's internationalization, China has begun to allow other countries, including the United States, to trade in the yuan (previously such trade was restricted to the Chinese mainland). An increase in yuan trading and investment would help to buffer China against the dollar's decrease in value. Currently, 60 percent of the world's foreign reserves consist of the

ENTER THE WORLD OF BUSINESS

U.S. dollar and are used to help stabilize the global economy during economic unrest. A massive decrease in the dollar's value could, therefore, disrupt the world economy.

Making the yuan a global currency could be beneficial for businesses as well. For example, Caterpillar and McDonald's are financing China-based projects using the yuan. According to Caterpillar, this is more efficient and less expensive than having to convert U.S. dollars to yuan first. Despite these possibilities, China has many obstacles to overcome before the yuan can achieve status as a global currency. Demand among foreign businesses for trading and investing in the yuan is not high, and the yuan must be convertible to be used as a major currency in the foreign reserves. Convertibility means that currency must be easily converted into other currencies, which requires the currency to be valued at the current market rate. China was reluctant to do this in the past, keeping its currency rates lower than market value in a highly criticized move. Although China has expressed its intention to make its currency fully convertible, this will create many challenges for China in maintaining its competitive advantage in international trade.[1]

Introduction

finance
the study of money; how it's made, how it's lost, and how it's managed

From Wall Street to Main Street, both overseas and at home, money is the one tool used to measure personal and business income and wealth. **Finance** is the study of money: how it's made, how it's lost, and how it's managed. This chapter introduces you to the role of money and the financial system in the economy. Of course, if you have a checking account, automobile insurance, a college loan, or a credit card, you already have personal experience with some key players in the financial world.

We begin our discussion with a definition of money and then explore some of the many forms money may take. Next, we examine the roles of the Federal Reserve Board and other major institutions in the financial system. Finally, we explore the future of the finance industry and some of the changes likely to occur over the course of the next several years.

Money in the Financial System

LO 15-1

money
anything generally accepted in exchange for goods and services

Strictly defined, **money,** or *currency,* is anything generally accepted in exchange for goods and services. Materials as diverse as salt, cattle, fish, rocks, shells, cloth, as well as precious metals such as gold, silver, and copper have long been used by various cultures as money. Most of these materials were limited-supply commodities that had their own value to society (for example, salt can be used as a preservative and shells and metals as jewelry). The supply of these commodities therefore determined the supply of "money" in that society. The next step was the development of "IOUs," or slips of paper that could be exchanged for a specified supply of the underlying commodity. "Gold" notes, for instance, could be exchanged for gold, and the money supply was tied to the amount of gold available. While paper money was first used in North America in 1685 (and even earlier in Europe), the concept of *fiat money*—a paper money not readily convertible to a precious metal such as gold—did not gain full acceptance until the Great Depression in the 1930s. The U.S. abandoned its gold-backed currency standard largely in response to the Great Depression and converted to a fiduciary, or fiat, monetary system. In the United States, paper money is really a government "note" or promise, worth the value specified on the note.

Functions of Money

No matter what a particular society uses for money, its primary purpose is to enable a person or organization to transform a desire into an action. These desires may be for entertainment actions, such as party expenses; operating actions, such as paying for rent, utilities, or employees; investing actions, such as buying property or equipment; or financing actions, such as for starting or growing a business. Money serves three important functions: as a medium of exchange, a measure of value, and a store of value.

Medium of Exchange.   Before fiat money, the trade of goods and services was accomplished through *bartering*—trading one good or service for another of similar value. As any school-age child knows, bartering can become quite inefficient—particularly in the case of complex, three-party transactions involving peanut butter sandwiches, baseball cards, and hair barrettes. There had to be a simpler way, and that was to decide on a single item—money—that can be freely converted to any other good upon agreement between parties.

Measure of Value.   As a measure of value, money serves as a common standard or yardstick of the value of goods and services. For example, $2 will buy a dozen large eggs and $25,000 will buy a nice car in the United States. In Japan, where the currency is known as the yen, these same transactions would cost about 185 yen and 2.3 million yen, respectively. Money, then, is a common denominator that allows people to compare the different goods and services that can be consumed on a particular income level. While a star athlete and a "burger-flipper" are paid vastly different wages, each uses money as a measure of the value of their yearly earnings and purchases.

For centuries people on the Micronesian island of Yap have used giant round stones, like the ones shown here, for money. The stones aren't moved, but their ownership can change.

Store of Value.   As a store of value, money serves as a way to accumulate wealth (buying power) until it is needed. For example, a person making $1,000 per week who wants to buy a $500 computer could save $50 per week for each of the next 10 weeks. Unfortunately, the value of stored money is directly dependent on the health of the economy. If, due to rapid inflation, all prices double in one year, then the purchasing power value of the money "stuffed in the mattress" would fall by half. On the other hand, deflation occurs when prices of goods fall. Deflation might seem like a good thing for consumers, but in many ways it can be just as problematic as inflation. Periods of major deflation often lead to decreases in wages and increases in debt burdens.[2] Deflation also tends to be an indicator of problems in the economy. When Ireland experienced deflation in 2009—the first time it had experienced deflation in 49 years—the country blamed it on decreasing mortgage interest rate costs.[3] Ireland was undergoing a serious deficit and required a bailout from the European commission, the International Monetary Fund, and the European Central Bank.[4]

Characteristics of Money

To be used as a medium of exchange, money must be acceptable, divisible, portable, stable in value, durable, and difficult to counterfeit.

Acceptability.   To be effective, money must be readily acceptable for the purchase of goods and services and for the settlement of debts. Acceptability is probably the most important characteristic of money: If people do not trust the value of money, businesses will not accept it as a payment for goods and services, and consumers will have to find some other means of paying for their purchases.

Divisibility.   Given the widespread use of quarters, dimes, nickels, and pennies in the United States, it is no surprise that the principle of divisibility is an important one. With barter, the lack of divisibility often makes otherwise preferable trades impossible, as would be an attempt to trade a steer for a loaf of bread. For money to serve effectively as a measure of value, all items must be valued in terms of comparable units—dimes for a piece of bubble gum, quarters for laundry machines, and dollars (or dollars and coins) for everything else.

Portability.   Clearly, for money to function as a medium of exchange, it must be easily moved from one location to the next. Large colored rocks could be used as money, but you couldn't carry them around in your wallet. Paper currency and metal coins, on the other hand, are capable of transferring vast purchasing power into small, easily carried (and hidden!) bundles. Few Americans realize it, but more U.S. currency is in circulation outside the United States than within. Currently, about $1.102 trillion of U.S. currency is in circulation, and the majority is held outside the United States.[5] Some countries, such as Panama, even use the U.S. dollar as their currency. Retailers in other countries often state prices in dollars and in their local currency.

Stability.   Money must be stable and maintain its declared face value. A $10 bill should purchase the same amount of goods or services from one day to the next. The principle of stability allows people who wish to postpone purchases and save their money to do so without fear that it will decline in value. As mentioned earlier, money declines in value during periods of inflation, when economic conditions cause prices to rise. Thus, the same amount of money buys fewer and fewer goods and services. In some countries, people spend their money as fast as they can in order to keep it from losing any more of its value. Instability destroys confidence in a nation's money and its ability to store value and serve as an effective medium of exchange. Ultimately, people faced with spiraling price increases avoid the increasingly worthless paper money at all costs, storing all of their savings in the form of real assets such as gold and land.

Durability.   Money must be durable. The crisp new dollar bills you trade at the music store for the hottest new CD will make their way all around town for about 20 months before being replaced (see Table 15.1). Were the value of an old, faded bill to fall in line with the deterioration of its appearance, the principles of stability and universal acceptability would fail (but, no doubt, fewer bills would pass through the washer!). Although metal coins, due to their much longer useful life, would appear to be an ideal form of money, paper currency is far more portable than metal because of its light weight. Today, coins are used primarily to provide divisibility.

TABLE 15.1
The Life Expectancy of Paper Currency

Denomination of Bill	Life Expectancy (Years)
$1	1.8
$5	1.3
$10	1.5
$20	2.0
$50	4.6
$100	7.4

Source: "How Currency Gets into Circulation", Federal Reserve Bank of Bank of New York, www.newyorkfed.org/aboutthefed/fedpoint/fed01.html (accessed May 15, 2012).

banking institutions, nonbanking financial institutions such as finance companies, and systems that provide for the electronic transfer of funds throughout the world. Over the past 20 years, the rate at which money turns over, or changes hands, has increased exponentially. Different cultures place unique values on saving, spending, borrowing, and investing. The combination of this increased turnover rate and increasing interactions with people and organizations from other countries has created a complex money system. First, we need to meet the guardian of this complex system.

The Federal Reserve System

LO 15-3

The guardian of the American financial system is the **Federal Reserve Board**, or "the Fed," as it is commonly called, an independent agency of the federal government established in 1913 to regulate the nation's banking and financial industry. The Federal Reserve System is organized into 12 regions, each with a Federal Reserve Bank that serves its defined area (Figure 15.2). All the Federal Reserve banks except those in Boston and Philadelphia have regional branches. The Cleveland Federal Reserve Bank, for example, is responsible for branch offices in Pittsburgh and Cincinnati.

Federal Reserve Board an independent agency of the federal government established in 1913 to regulate the nation's banking and financial industry

FIGURE 15.2   Federal Reserve System

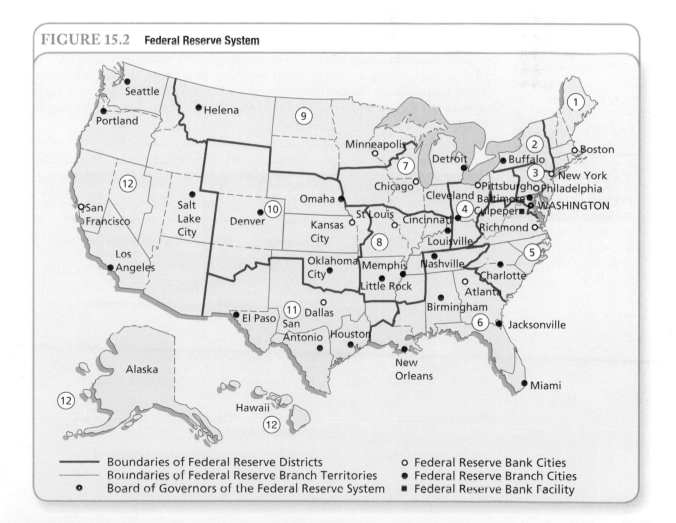

Boundaries of Federal Reserve Districts
Boundaries of Federal Reserve Branch Territories
● Board of Governors of the Federal Reserve System
○ Federal Reserve Bank Cities
● Federal Reserve Branch Cities
■ Federal Reserve Bank Facility

The U.S. government redesigns currency in order to stay ahead of counterfeiters and protect the public.

Difficulty to Counterfeit. Finally, to remain stable and enjoy universal acceptance, it almost goes without saying that money must be very difficult to counterfeit—that is, to duplicate illegally. Every country takes steps to make counterfeiting difficult. Most use multicolored money, and many use specially watermarked papers that are virtually impossible to duplicate. Counterfeit bills represent less than 0.03 percent of the currency in circulation in the United States,[7] but it is becoming increasingly easy for counterfeiters to print money with just a modest inkjet printer. This illegal printing of money is fueled by hundreds of people who often circulate only small amounts of counterfeit bills. To thwart the problem of counterfeiting, the U.S. Treasury Department redesigned the U.S. currency, starting with the $20 bill in 2003, the $50 bill in 2004, the $10 bill in 2006, the $5 bill in 2008, and the $100 bill in 2010. For the first time, U.S. money includes subtle colors in addition to the traditional green, as well as enhanced security features, such as a watermark, security thread, and color-shifting ink.[8] Although counterfeiting is not as much of an issue with coins, U.S. metal coins are usually worth more for the metal than their face value. It has begun to cost more to manufacture coins than what they are worth monetarily.

In 2006 the new Jefferson nickel was introduced, showing a profile of the nation's third president. Due to the increased price of metals, it costs 11.2 cents to make the 5 cent piece.[9] As Table 15.2 indicates, it costs more than a penny to manufacture a penny, resulting in a call to discontinue it. Because it costs more to produce pennies and nickels than what they are worth, these coins have generated losses of $359.80 million in a five-year period.[10]

DID YOU KNOW? Around 75 percent of counterfeit currency is found and destroyed before it ever reaches the public.[6]

Types of Money

LO 15-2

While paper money and coins are the most visible types of money, the combined value of all of the printed bills and all of the minted coins is actually rather insignificant when compared with the value of money kept in checking accounts, savings accounts, and other monetary forms.

TABLE 15.

Costs to Produ
Pennies and Ni

checking accou
money stored in
at a bank or othe
institution that ca
withdrawn withou
notice; also calle
deposit

savings account
accounts with fu
usually cannot be
without advance
known as time de

money market a
accounts that off
interest rates tha
bank rates but w
restrictions

certificates of
deposit (CDs)
savings accounts
guarantee a depo
interest rate over
interval as long a
are not withdraw
the end of the pe
months or one ye
example

There is a minimum monthly payment with interest charged on the remaining balance. Some people pay off their credit cards monthly, while other make monthly payments. Charges for unpaid balances can run 18 percent or higher at an annual rate, making credit card debt one of the most expensive ways to borrow money.

Besides the major credit card companies, many stores—Target, Saks Fifth Avenue, Macy's, Bloomingdales, Sears, and others—have their own branded credit cards. They use credit rating agencies to check the credit of the cardholders and they generally make money on the finance charges.

The Credit CARD (Card Accountability Responsibility and Disclosure) Act of 2009 was passed to regulate the practices of credit card companies that were coming under attack by consumers during the most recent recession. Without going into the details, the law limited the ability of card issuers to raise interest rates, limited credit to young adults, gave people more time to pay bills, required that if there were various levels of interest rates that the balances with the highest rate would be paid off first, and made clearer due dates on billing cycles, along with several other provisions. For college students, the most important part of the law is that young adults under the age of 21 will have to have an adult co-signer or show proof that they have enough income to handle the debt limit on the card.

This act is important to all companies and cardholders. Research indicates that approximately 40 percent of lower- and middle-income households use credit cards to pay for basic necessities. Yet there is also good news. The average credit card debt for lower- and middle-income households has decreased in recent years to about $7,145. On the other hand, studies also show that college students tend to lack the financial literacy needed to understand credit cards and their requirements. Approximately 90 percent of college students with credit cards have credit card debt. Therefore, vulnerable segments of the population such as college students should be careful about which credit cards to choose and how often they use them.[11]

debit card
a card that looks like a
credit card but works like
a check; using it results
in a direct, immediate,
electronic payment from
the cardholder's checking
account to a merchant or
third party

A **debit card** looks like a credit card but works like a check. The use of a debit card results in a direct, immediate, electronic payment from the cardholder's checking account to a merchant or other party. While they are convenient to carry and profitable for banks, they lack credit features, offer no purchase "grace period," and provide no hard "paper trail." Debit cards are gaining more acceptance with merchants, and consumers like debit cards because of the ease of getting cash from an increasing number of ATM machines. Financial institutions also want consumers to use debit cards because they reduce the number of teller transactions and check processing costs. Some cash management accounts at retail brokers like Merrill Lynch offer deferred debit cards. These act like a credit card but debit to the cash management account once a month. During that time, the cash earns a money market return.

Traveler's checks, money orders, and cashier's checks are other common forms of "near money." Although each is slightly different from the others, they all share a common characteristic: A financial institution, bank, credit company, or neighborhood currency exchange issues them in exchange for cash and guarantees that the purchased note will be honored and exchanged for cash when it is presented to the institution making the guarantee.

The American Financial System

The U.S. financial system fuels our economy by storing money, fostering investment opportunities, and making loans for new businesses and business expansion as well as for homes, cars, and college educations. This amazingly complex system includes

The Federal Reserve Board is the chief economic policy arm of the United States. Working with Congress and the president, the Fed tries to create a positive economic environment capable of sustaining low inflation, high levels of employment, a balance in international payments, and long-term economic growth. To this end, the Federal Reserve Board has four major responsibilities: (1) to control the supply of money, or monetary policy; (2) to regulate banks and other financial institutions; (3) to manage regional and national checking account procedures, or check clearing; and (4) to supervise the federal deposit insurance programs of banks belonging to the Federal Reserve System.

monetary policy
means by which the Fed
controls the amount of
money available in the
economy

Monetary Policy. The Fed controls the amount of money available in the economy through **monetary policy.** Without this intervention, the supply of and demand for money might not balance. This could result in either rapid price increases (inflation) because of too little money or economic recession and a slowdown of price increases (disinflation) because of too little growth in the money supply. In very rare cases (the depression of the 1930s) the United States has suffered from deflation, when the actual purchasing power of the dollar has increased as prices declined. To effectively control the supply of money in the economy, the Fed must have a good idea of how much money is in circulation at any given time. This has become increasingly challenging because the global nature of our economy means that more and more U.S. dollars are circulating overseas. Using several different measures of the money supply, the Fed establishes specific growth targets which, presumably, ensure a close balance between money supply and money demand. The Fed fine-tunes money growth by using four basic tools: open market operations, reserve requirements, the discount rate, and credit controls (see Table 15.3). There is generally a lag of 6 to 18 months before the effect of these charges shows up in economic activity.

TABLE 15.3

Fed Tools for Regulating the Money Supply

Activity	Effect on the Money Supply and the Economy
Buy government securities	The money supply increases; economic activity increases.
Sell government securities	The money supply decreases; economic activity slows down.
Raise discount rate	Interest rates increase; the money supply decreases; economic activity slows down.
Lower discount rate	Interest rates decrease; the money supply increases; economic activity increases.
Increase reserve requirements	Banks make fewer loans; the money supply declines; economic activity slows down.
Decrease reserve requirements	Banks make more loans; the money supply increases; economic activity increases.
Relax credit controls	More people are encouraged to make major purchases, increasing economic activity.
Restrict credit controls	People are discouraged from making major purchases, decreasing economic activity.

Open market operations refer to decisions to buy or sell U.S. Treasury bills (short-term debt issued by the U.S. government; also called T-bills) and other investments in the open market. The actual purchase or sale of the investments is performed by the New York Federal Reserve Bank. This monetary tool, the most commonly employed of all Fed operations, is performed almost daily in an effort to control the money supply.

When the Fed buys securities, it writes a check on its own account to the seller of the investments. When the seller of the investments (usually a large bank) deposits the check, the Fed transfers the balance from the Federal Reserve account into the seller's account, thus increasing the supply of money in the economy and, hopefully, fueling economic growth. The opposite occurs when the Fed sells investments. The buyer writes a check to the Federal Reserve, and when the funds are transferred out of the purchaser's account, the amount of money in circulation falls, slowing economic growth to a desired level.

One of the roles of the Federal Reserve is to use its policies to keep money flowing. Money is the lifeblood of the economy. If banks become too protective of their funds and stop lending money, the economy can grind to a halt.

The second major monetary policy tool is the **reserve requirement,** the percentage of deposits that banking institutions must hold in reserve ("in the vault," as it were). Funds so held are not available for lending to businesses and consumers. For example, a bank holding $10 million in deposits, with a 10 percent reserve requirement, must have reserves of $1 million. If the Fed were to reduce the reserve requirement to, say, 5 percent, the bank would need to keep only $500,000 in reserves. The bank could then lend to customers the $500,000 difference between the old reserve level and the new lower reserve level, thus increasing the supply of money. Because the reserve requirement has such a powerful effect on the money supply, the Fed does not change it very often, relying instead on open market operations most of the time.

The third monetary policy tool, the **discount rate,** is the rate of interest the Fed charges to loan money to any banking institution to meet reserve requirements. The Fed is the lender of last resort for these banks. When a bank borrows from the Fed, it is said to have borrowed at the "discount window," and the interest rates charged there are often higher than those charged on loans of comparable risk elsewhere in the economy. This added interest expense, when it exists, serves to discourage banks from borrowing from the Fed.

When the Fed wants to expand the money supply, it lowers the discount rate to encourage borrowing. Conversely, when the Fed wants to decrease the money supply, it raises the discount rate. The increases in interest rates that occurred in the United States from 2003 through 2006 were the result of more than 16 quarter-point (0.25 percent) increases in the Fed discount rate. The purpose was to keep inflation under control and to raise rates to a more normal level as the economy recovered from the recession of 2001. During the most recent recession, which started in 2007, the Fed lowered interest rates to nearly zero in order to encourage borrowing. In an environment where credit markets were nearly frozen, the Fed utilized monetary policy to stimulate spending. Not surprisingly, economists watch changes in this sensitive interest rate as an indicator of the Fed's monetary policy.

open market operations decisions to buy or sell U.S. Treasury bills (short-term debt issued by the U.S. government) and other investments in the open market

reserve requirement the percentage of deposits that banking institutions must hold in reserve

discount rate the rate of interest the Fed charges to loan money to any banking institution to meet reserve requirements

Need help understanding How the Fed Tries to Stabalize the Economy?

http://bit.ly/FerrellQR15-1

credit controls
the authority to establish and enforce credit rules for financial institutions and some private investors

The final tool in the Fed's arsenal of weapons is **credit controls**—the authority to establish and enforce credit rules for financial institutions and some private investors. For example, the Fed can determine how large a down payment individuals and businesses must make on credit purchases of expensive items such as automobiles, and how much time they have to finish paying for the purchases. By raising and lowering minimum down payment amounts and payment periods, the Fed can stimulate or discourage credit purchases of "big ticket" items. The Fed also has the authority to set the minimum down payment investors must use for the credit purchases of stock. Buying stock with credit—"buying on margin"—is a popular investment strategy among individual speculators. By altering the margin requirement (currently set at 50 percent of the price of the purchased stocks), the Fed can effectively control the total amount of credit borrowing in the stock market.

Regulatory Functions.   The second major responsibility of the Fed is to regulate banking institutions that are members of the Federal Reserve System. Accordingly, the Fed establishes and enforces banking rules that affect monetary policy and the overall level of the competition between different banks. It determines which nonbanking activities, such as brokerage services, leasing, and insurance, are appropriate for banks and which should be prohibited. The Fed also has the authority to approve or disapprove mergers between banks and the formation of bank holding companies. In an effort to ensure that all rules are enforced and that correct accounting procedures are being followed at member banks, surprise bank examinations are conducted by bank examiners each year.

Check Clearing.   The Federal Reserve provides national check processing on a huge scale. Divisions of the Fed known as check clearinghouses handle almost all the checks written against a bank in one city and presented for deposit to a bank in a second city. Any banking institution can present the checks it has received from others around the country to its regional Federal Reserve Bank. The Fed passes the checks to the appropriate regional Federal Reserve Bank, which then sends the checks to the issuing bank for payment. With the advance of electronic payment systems and the passage of the Check Clearing for the 21st Century Act (Check 21 Act), checks can now be processed in a day. The Check 21 Act allows banks to clear checks electronically by presenting an electronic image of the check. This eliminates mail delays and time-consuming paper processing.

Depository Insurance.   The Fed is also responsible for supervising the federal insurance funds that protect the deposits of member institutions. These insurance funds will be discussed in greater detail in the following section.

LO 15-4

Banking Institutions

Banking institutions accept money deposits from and make loans to individual consumers and businesses. Some of the most important banking institutions include commercial banks, savings and loan associations, credit unions, and mutual savings banks. Historically, these have all been separate institutions. However, new hybrid forms of banking institutions that perform two or more of these functions have emerged over the past two decades. The following all have one thing in common: They are businesses whose objective is to earn money by managing, safeguarding, and lending money to others. Their sales revenues come from the fees and interest that they charge for providing these financial services.

Commercial Banks.   The largest and oldest of all financial institutions are **commercial banks,** which perform a variety of financial services. They rely mainly on checking and savings accounts as their major source of funds and use only a portion of these deposits to make loans to businesses and individuals. Because it is unlikely that all the depositors of any one bank will want to withdraw all of their funds at the same time, a bank can safely loan out a large percentage of its deposits.

Today, banks are quite diversified and offer a number of services. Commercial banks make loans for virtually any conceivable legal purpose, from vacations to cars, from homes to college educations. Banks in many states offer *home equity loans,* by which home owners can borrow against the appraised value of their already purchased homes. Banks also issue Visa and Master-Card credit cards and offer CDs and trusts (legal entities set up to hold and manage assets for a beneficiary). Many banks rent safe deposit boxes in bank vaults to

JP Morgan Chase is the second largest commercial bank in the United States behind Bank of America.

customers who want to store jewelry, legal documents, artwork, and other valuables. In 1999, Congress passed the Financial Services Modernization Act, also known as the Gramm-Leach-Bliley Bill. This act repealed the Glass Steagall Act, which was enacted in 1929 after the stock market crash and prohibited commercial banks from being in the insurance and investment banking business. This puts U.S. commercial banks on the same competitive footing as European banks and provides a more level playing field for global banking competition. As commercial banks and investment banks have merged, the financial landscape has changed. Consolidation remains the norm in the U.S. banking industry. The financial crisis and the economic recession only accelerated the consolidation as large, healthy banks ended up buying weak banks that were in trouble. JP Morgan Chase bought Wachovia and the investment bank Bear Stearns; Wells Fargo bought Washington Mutual; PNC bought National City Bank; and Bank of America bought Countrywide Credit and Merrill Lynch. Most of these purchases were made with financial help from the U.S. Treasury and Federal Reserve. By 2012, the banks had paid back their loans, but the financial meltdown exposed some high-risk activities in the banking industry that Congress wanted to curtail. The result was the passage of the Dodd-Frank Act. This act added many new regulations, but the two most important changes raised the required capital banks had to hold on their balance sheet and limited certain types of high-risk trading activities. Despite these new regulations, in 2012 JP Morgan Chase lost billions of dollars in trading activities from taking excessive risks.[12]

commercial banks
the largest and oldest of all financial institutions, relying mainly on checking and savings accounts as sources of funds for loans to businesses and individuals

Savings and Loan Associations.   **Savings and loan associations (S&Ls),** often called "thrifts," are financial institutions that primarily offer savings accounts and make long-term loans for residential mortgages. A mortgage is a loan made so that a business or individual can purchase real estate, typically a home; the real estate itself is pledged as a guarantee (called *collateral*) that the buyer will repay the loan. If the loan is not repaid, the savings and loan has the right to repossess the property. Prior to the 1970s, S&Ls focused almost exclusively on real estate lending and accepted only savings accounts. Today, following years of regulatory changes, S&Ls compete directly with commercial banks by offering many types of services.

savings and loan associations (S&Ls)
financial institutions that primarily offer savings accounts and make long-term loans for residential mortgages; also called "thrifts"

Savings and loans have gone through a metamorphosis since the early 1990s, after having almost collapsed in the 1980s. Today, many of the largest savings and loans have merged with commercial banks. This segment of the financial services industry plays a diminished role in the mortgage lending market.

credit union
a financial institution owned and controlled by its depositors, who usually have a common employer, profession, trade group, or religion

Credit Unions.   A **credit union** is a financial institution owned and controlled by its depositors, who usually have a common employer, profession, trade group, or religion. The Aggieland Credit Union in College Station, Texas, for example, provides banking services for faculty, employees, and current and former students of Texas A&M University. A savings account at a credit union is commonly referred to as a share account, while a checking account is termed a share draft account. Because the credit union is tied to a common organization, the members (depositors) are allowed to vote for directors and share in the credit union's profits in the form of higher interest rates on accounts and/or lower loan rates.

While credit unions were originally created to provide depositors with a short-term source of funds for low-interest consumer loans for items such as cars, home appliances, vacations, and college, today they offer a wide range of financial services. Generally, the larger the credit union, the more sophisticated its financial service offerings will be.

mutual savings banks
financial institutions that are similar to savings and loan associations but, like credit unions, are owned by their depositors

Mutual Savings Banks.   **Mutual savings banks** are similar to savings and loan associations, but, like credit unions, they are owned by their depositors. Among the oldest financial institutions in the United States, they were originally established to provide a safe place for savings of particular groups of people, such as fishermen. Found mostly in New England, they are becoming more popular in the rest of the country as some S&Ls have converted to mutual savings banks to escape the stigma created by the widespread S&L failures in the 1980s.

Federal Deposit Insurance Corporation (FDIC)
an insurance fund established in 1933 that insures individual bank accounts

Insurance for Banking Institutions.   The **Federal Deposit Insurance Corporation (FDIC)**, which insures individual bank accounts, was established in

1933 to help stop bank failures throughout the country during the Great Depression. Today, the FDIC insures personal accounts up to a maximum of $250,000 at nearly 8,000 FDIC member institutions.[14] While most major banks are insured by the FDIC, small institutions in some states may be insured by state insurance funds or private insurance companies. Should a member bank fail, its depositors can recover all of their funds, up to $250,000. Amounts over $250,000, while not legally covered by the insurance, are in fact usually covered because the Fed understands very well the enormous damage that would result to the financial system should these large depositors withdraw their money. When the financial crisis occurred, the FDIC was worried about people taking their money out of banks, so they increased the deposit insurance amount from $100,000 to $250,000. The amount is scheduled to revert back to $100,000 on December 31, 2013. The *Federal Savings and Loan Insurance Corporation (FSLIC)* insured thrift deposits prior to its insolvency and failure during the S&L crisis of the 1980s. Now, the insurance functions once overseen by the FSLIC are handled directly by the FDIC through its Savings Association Insurance Fund. The **National Credit Union Administration (NCUA)** regulates and charters credit unions and insures their deposits through its National Credit Union Insurance Fund.

When they were originally established, Congress hoped that these insurance funds would make people feel secure about their savings so that they would not panic and withdraw their money when news of a bank failure was announced. The "bank run" scene in the perennial Christmas movie *It's a Wonderful Life*, when dozens of Bailey Building and Loan depositors attempted to withdraw their money (only to have the reassuring figure of Jimmy Stewart calm their fears), was not based on mere fiction. During the Great Depression, hundreds of banks failed and their depositors lost everything. The fact that large numbers of major financial institutions failed in the 1980s and 1990s—without a single major banking panic—underscores the effectiveness of the current insurance system. Large bank failures occurred once again during the most recent recession. More than 380 banks have failed between 2009 and 2011.[15] While the future may yet bring unfortunate surprises, most depositors go to sleep every night without worrying about the safety of their savings.

National Credit Union Administration (NCUA) an agency that regulates and charters credit unions and insures their deposits through its National Credit Union Insurance Fund

Nonbanking Institutions

LO 15-5

Nonbank financial institutions offer some financial services, such as short-term loans or investment products, but do not accept deposits. These include insurance companies, pension funds, mutual funds, brokerage firms, nonfinancial firms, and finance companies. Table 15.4 lists some other diversified financial services firms.

Diversified Firms.   Recently, a growing number of traditionally nonfinancial firms have moved onto the financial field. These firms include manufacturing organizations, such as General Motors and General Electric, that traditionally confined their financial activities to financing their customers' purchases. GE was once so successful in the financial arena that its credit subsidiary accounted for more than 40 percent of the company's revenues and earnings. Unfortunately, GE Capital became a liability to GE during the financial crisis, and is in the process of recovery as GE cuts the size of its finance unit and writes off billions of dollars in bad loans.

Insurance Companies.   **Insurance companies** are businesses that protect their clients against financial losses from certain specified risks (death, injury, disability,

insurance companies businesses that protect their clients against financial losses from certain specified risks (death, accident, and theft, for example)

Most brokerage firms are really part financial conglomerates that provide many different kinds of services besides buying and selling securities for clients. For example, Merrill Lynch also is an investment banker, as is Morgan Stanley, Smith Barney, and Goldman Sachs. The **investment banker** underwrites new issues of securities for corporations, states, and municipalities needed to raise money in the capital markets. The new issue market is called a *primary market* because the sale of the securities is for the first time. After the first sale, the securities trade in the *secondary markets* by brokers. The investment banker advises on the price of the new securities and generally guarantees the sale while overseeing the distribution of the securities through the selling brokerage houses. Investment bankers also act as dealers who make markets in securities. They do this by offering to sell the securities at an asked price (which is a higher rate) and buy the securities at a bid price (which is a lower rate)—the difference in the two prices represents the profit for the dealer.

investment banker
underwrites new issues of securities for corporations, states, and municipalities

Finance Companies. **Finance companies** are businesses that offer short-term loans at substantially higher rates of interest than banks. Commercial finance companies make loans to businesses, requiring their borrowers to pledge assets such as equipment, inventories, or unpaid accounts as collateral for the loans. Consumer finance companies make loans to individuals. Like commercial finance companies, these firms require some sort of personal collateral as security against the borrower's possible inability to repay their loans. Because of the high interest rates they charge and other factors, finance companies typically are the lender of last resort for individuals and businesses whose credit limits have been exhausted and/or those with poor credit ratings.

finance companies
businesses that offer short-term loans at substantially higher rates of interest than banks

Electronic Banking

Since the advent of the computer age, a wide range of technological innovations has made it possible to move money all across the world electronically. Such "paperless" transactions have allowed financial institutions to reduce costs in what has been, and continues to be, a virtual competitive battlefield. **Electronic funds transfer (EFT)** is any movement of funds by means of an electronic terminal, telephone, computer, or magnetic tape. Such transactions order a particular financial institution to subtract money from one account and add it to another. The most commonly used forms of EFT are automated teller machines, automated clearinghouses, and home banking systems.

Automated Teller Machines.   Probably the most familiar form of electronic banking is the **automated teller machine (ATM),** which dispenses cash, accepts deposits, and allows balance inquiries and cash transfers from one account to another. ATMs provide 24-hour banking services—both at home (through a local bank) and far away (via worldwide ATM networks such as Cirrus and Plus). Rapid growth, driven by both strong consumer acceptance and lower transaction costs for banks (about half the cost of teller transactions), has led to the installation of hundreds of thousands of ATMs worldwide. Table 15.5 presents some interesting statistics about ATMs.

Automated Clearinghouses.   **Automated clearinghouses (ACHs)** permit payments such as deposits or withdrawals to be made to and from a bank account by magnetic computer tape. Most large U.S. employers, and many others worldwide, use ACHs to deposit their employees' paychecks directly to the employees' bank accounts. While direct deposit is used by only 50 percent of U.S. workers, nearly 100 percent of Japanese workers and more than 90 percent of European workers utilize it. The largest user of automated clearinghouses in the United States is the federal government, with 99 percent of federal government employees and 65 percent of the private workforce receiving their pay via direct deposit. More than 82 percent of all Social Security payments are made through an ACH system. The Social Security Administration is trying to reduce costs and reduce theft and fraud, so if you apply for Social Security benefits on or after May 1, 2011, you must receive your payments electronically.

The advantages of direct deposits to consumers include convenience, safety, and potential interest earnings. It is estimated that more than 4 million paychecks are lost or stolen annually, and FBI studies show that 2,000 fraudulent checks are cashed every day in the United States. Checks can never be lost or stolen with direct

electronic funds transfer (EFT)
any movement of funds by means of an electronic terminal, telephone, computer, or magnetic tape

automated teller machine (ATM)
the most familiar form of electronic banking, which dispenses cash, accepts deposits, and allows balance inquiries and cash transfers from one account to another

automated clearinghouses (ACHs)
a system that permits payments such as deposits or withdrawals to be made to and from a bank account by magnetic computer tape

TABLE 15.5

Facts about ATM Use

There are 2.2 million ATM machines currently in use.

The average cash withdrawal from ATMs is $60.

The typical ATM consumer will visit an ATM 7.4 times per month.

The total ratio of people per ATM machine is 3,000:1.

ATM users spend approximately 23 percent more than non-ATM users.

The top ATM owners are Cardtronics, Payment Alliance, Bank of America, JP Morgan Chase, and Wells Fargo.

Source: Lenpenzo, Trends Today, "ATM Machines Statistics," March 2, 2012, www.statisticbrain.com/atm-machine-statistics/ (accessed May 24, 2012).

deposit. The benefits to businesses include decreased check-processing expenses and increased employee productivity. Research shows that businesses that use direct deposit can save more than $1.25 on each payroll check processed. Productivity could increase by $3 to $5 billion annually if all employees were to use direct deposit rather than taking time away from work to deposit their payroll checks.

Some companies also use ACHs for dividend and interest payments. Consumers can also use ACHs to make periodic (usually monthly) fixed payments to specific creditors without ever having to write a check or buy stamps. The estimated number of bills paid annually by consumers is 20 billion, and the total number paid through ACHs is estimated at only 8.5 billion. The average consumer who writes 10 to 15 checks each month would save $41 to $62 annually in postage alone.[17]

Online Banking.   Many banking activities are now conducted on a computer at home or at work, or through wireless devices such as cell phones and PDAs anywhere there is a wireless "hot point." Consumers and small businesses can now make a bewildering array of financial transactions at home or on the go 24 hours a day. Functioning much like a vast network of personal ATMs, companies like Google and Apple provide online banking services through mobile phones, allowing subscribers

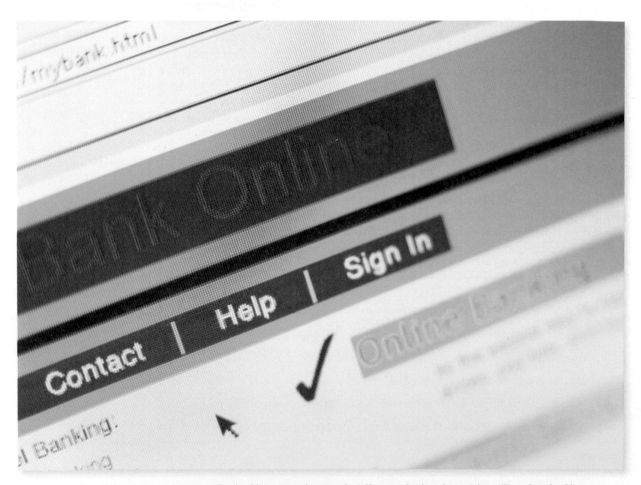

Computers and handheld devices have made online banking extremely convenient. However, hackers have stolen millions from banking customers by tricking them into visiting websites and downloading malicious software that gives the hackers access to their passwords.

to make sophisticated banking transactions, buy and sell stocks and bonds, and purchase products and airline tickets without ever leaving home or speaking to another human being. Many banks allow customers to log directly into their accounts to check balances, transfer money between accounts, view their account statements, and pay bills via home computer or other Internet-enabled devices. Computer and advanced telecommunications technology have revolutionized world commerce; 62 percent of adults list Internet banking as their preferred banking method, making it the most popular banking method in the United States.[18]

Future of Banking

LO 15-6

Rapid advances and innovations in technology are challenging the banking industry and requiring it to change. As we said earlier, more and more banks, both large and small, are offering electronic access to their financial services. ATM technology is rapidly changing, with machines now dispensing more than just cash. Online financial services, ATM technology, and bill presentation are just a few of the areas where rapidly changing technology is causing the banking industry to change as well.

The premise that banks will get bigger over the next 10 years is uncertain. During 2007–2008, the financial markets collapsed under the weight of declining housing prices, subprime mortgages (mortgages with low-qualifying borrowers), and risky securities backed by these subprime mortgages. Because the value of bank assets declined dramatically, most large banks like CitiBank, Bank of America and Wachovia had a shrinking capital base. That is, the amount of debt in relation to their equity was so high that they were below the minimum required capital requirements. This was a financial environment where banks did not trust the counterparties to their loans and asset-backed securities. In this environment, the markets ceased to function in an orderly fashion. To keep the banking system from total collapse, the U.S. Treasury and the Federal Reserve created the TARP program, an acronym for Troubled Asset Relief Program. This program allowed the Treasury to purchase up to $250 billion of senior preferred shares of bank securities.[19]

Most of the big banks either needed to take the cash infusion from the U.S. Treasury or were forced to sell preferred stock to the Treasury. The rationale from the government's point of view was that it didn't want to signal to the financial community which banks were strong and which ones were weak for fear that depositors would move massive amounts of money from weak banks to strong banks. This phenomenon actually occurred several times and forced banks like Wachovia to be merged with Wells Fargo.

The total amount of preferred stock bought amounted to $204 billion. In the case of Citibank (Citigroup), its Tier 1 capital ratio fell under the minimum because it had to write off billions of dollars in bad loans, which reduced its asset base. This forced Citibank to give the Treasury common stock in exchange for the preferred stock, and so, as of spring 2010, the U.S. government was the largest stockholder in Citigroup. By December of that year, the U.S. government sold its last remaining shares of Citigroup. Not only did the government get a return of its $45 billion investment, but it reaped a profit of $12 billion. By spring 2012, all the banks had repaid their loans. However, most were not able to generate such hefty profits as Citigroup.[20]

During this period, the Federal Reserve took unprecedented actions that included buying up troubled assets from the banks and lending money at the discount window to nonbanks such as investment banks and brokers. The Fed also entered into

Build Your Business Plan

MONEY AND THE FINANCIAL SYSTEM

This chapter provides you with the opportunity to think about money and the financial system and just how many new businesses fail every year. In some industries, the failure rate is as high as 80 percent. One reason for such a high failure rate is the inability to manage the finances of the organization. From the start of the business, financial planning plays a key role. Try getting a loan without an accompanying budget/forecast of earnings and cash flow.

While obtaining a loan from a family member may be the easiest way to fund your business, it may cause more problems for you later on if you are unable to pay the money back as scheduled. Before heading to a lending officer at a bank, contact your local SBA center to see what assistance it might provide.

See for Yourself Videocase

BANKS CONTINUE TO EXTEND LESS CREDIT FOLLOWING RECESSION

The recent global recession affected people and businesses in different ways, including the temporary restriction of credit both for businesses and individuals. As the recession worsened, banks turned inward and significantly reduced or stopped lending money, and businesses began having difficulty accessing credit. Bank credit usually falls under a business's notes payable or long-term debt. This increases liabilities on the balance sheet because businesses must pay off this debt over a certain time period. A company that depends too much on credit might incur long-term debt that it will be unable to pay off, resulting in bankruptcy. However, during the recession, the opposite problem occurred: a severe reduction in credit and loans.

While credit does result in debt, it is usually necessary in order for small-business owners to have the necessary funds available to start a business. Indeed, small-business owners were among those most affected by the loss of credit, which in turn harmed the economy. It is estimated that the United States alone supports 27 million small businesses, making up roughly 50 percent of the economy. Many small businesses that rely on credit to survive were forced to lay off employees or shut down altogether, resulting in the loss of hundreds of thousands of jobs.

The main roadblock that faced people seeking these types of loans was their credit score. Banks hesitated to lend to anyone with a credit score of less than 700 out of 850, while the average credit score hovers around 680. Financial experts advise individuals to focus on improving their credit scores as a critical component of financial security. Additionally, a healthy amount of current assets that are liquid—easily converted to cash—is advisable for businesses, which can then use this cash to pay for inventory, equipment, or debt in case credit becomes unavailable.

Now that the United States appears to be in a recovery, one would think that bank lending would increase. However, this is not necessarily the case. Bank loans and leases are 3 percent lower than they were in 2008. This decrease in lending is occurring for a few different reasons. At the four largest banks—Wells Fargo, Bank of America, JP Morgan Chase, and Citigroup—lending has fallen significantly. Interestingly, regulation might be one of the reasons for the decrease. Due to increased regulation, large banks feel pressured to get rid of their risky loans. This bodes ill for large banks but is good for smaller regional banks that are not subject to these regulatory requirements. The extension of credit at smaller banks has gone up. However, are these smaller banks equipped to deal with riskier loans? Indeed, because they are smaller, these banks might be even less likely to loan to individuals perceived to be of higher risk.

Another potential theory for why banks are not lending is that they are provided with an incentive not to lend. Some economists believe that because the Fed is paying banks interest on their reserves, these interest payments are convincing banks to hold more money in reserve. Every bank is required to hold a certain amount of money in reserve as a form of protection. Traditionally, banks want to hold as little in reserve as necessary because money that is in reserve cannot earn income. However, in 2008 the Fed began to pay interest on reserves. Could this be one reason banks are not extending as much credit?

Banks themselves claim otherwise. They state that the reason that they are not extending as much credit is due to lack of demand. Demand does fluctuate, and if this is the reason, then in the near future, banks will be lending more if demand increases. Banks claim that they would be happy to loan more as the interest they can earn from extending credit would be greater than the interest income the Fed provides on excess reserves. It is true that during the recession businesses tended to "sit on" their extra cash—namely, avoid taking the risk of investing in new products or expanding. There are many signs that this is still occurring. Therefore, perhaps businesses themselves should share some of the blame. Of course, as recovery gains strength, it is possible that by the time you read this, banks will be lending more.[23]

DISCUSSION QUESTIONS

1. While it does involve taking on debt, why is credit so important for businesses to function?

2. How do you think people can improve their credit scores in order to look more attractive for loans?

3. How might a lack of demand for business credit affect the economy?

Remember to check out our Online Learning Center at www.mhhe.com/ferrell9e.

Team Exercise

Mutual funds pool individual investor dollars and invest them in a number of different securities. Go to **http://finance.yahoo.com/** and select some top-performing funds using criteria such as sector, style, or strategy. Assume that your group has $100,000 to invest in mutual funds. Select five funds in which to invest, representing a balanced (varied industries, risk, etc.) portfolio, and defend your selections.

16

Chapter Outline

Financial Management and Securities Markets

Learning Objectives

After reading this chapter, you will be able to:

LO 16-1 Describe some common methods of managing current assets.

LO 16-2 Identify some sources of short-term financing (current liabilities).

LO 16-3 Summarize the importance of long-term assets and capital budgeting.

LO 16-4 Specify how companies finance their operations and manage fixed assets with long-term liabilities, particularly bonds.

LO 16-5 Discuss how corporations can use equity financing by issuing stock through an investment banker.

LO 16-6 Describe the various securities markets in the United States.

LO 16-7 Critique the short-term asset and liabilities position of a small manufacturer, and recommend corrective action.

Is Bank of America Too Big to Fail?

One purpose of the 2010 Dodd-Frank Act was to eliminate firms that are "too-big-to-fail." Too-big-to-fail firms are linked to so many organizations that if they fail, the repercussions would be disastrous for the economy. Despite these new regulations, Bank of America (BofA), the largest bank in the United States, epitomizes the too-big-to-fail concept.

With $400 billion in cash and liquid investments, $2.3 trillion in assets, and as the owner or servicer of one-fifth of the country's homes, BofA's downfall would have a negative impact across the United States. CEO Brian Moynihan

has struggled to reassure investors, cut costs, and raise capital to meet new regulatory requirements.

BofA's precarious situation resulted from a series of high-risk decisions. Its investment in mortgage-related securities made it vulnerable to the housing crisis. Additionally, BofA's purchase of failed mortgage lender Countrywide Financial has been deemed one of the worst acquisitions in history. Although BofA gained control over the mortgage market, it also acquired Countrywide's debts and lawsuits. For instance, BofA was forced to pay $108 million on allegations that Countrywide had overcharged its customers. In 2011 BofA's stock decreased by almost 50 percent, although its stock price seemed to recover in the first half of 2012.

Moynihan believes cost-cutting will help increase BofA's profits. However, these costs will come at a price. His cost-cutting measures will eliminate approximately 30,000 jobs. Additionally, new regulations have capped the fees banks can charge

continued

merchants for debit card use. BofA was initially going to charge $5 in consumer monthly fees for debit card use, but changed its mind after the ensuing consumer outrage.

It is unclear whether these measures will boost the bank's profits. One positive sign was the purchase of $5 billion in BofA's preferred stock by trusted financial company Berkshire Hathaway, which might serve to reassure investors. Time will tell whether BofA will rebound from its personal financial crisis.[1]

Introduction

While it's certainly true that money makes the world go around, financial management is the discipline that makes the world turn more smoothly. Indeed, without effective management of assets, liabilities, and owners' equity, all business organizations are doomed to fail—regardless of the quality and innovativeness of their products. Financial management is the field that addresses the issues of obtaining and managing the funds and resources necessary to run a business successfully. It is not limited to business organizations: All organizations, from the corner store to the local nonprofit art museum, from giant corporations to county governments, must manage their resources effectively and efficiently if they are to achieve their objectives.

In this chapter, we look at both short- and long-term financial management. First, we discuss the management of short-term assets, which companies use to generate sales and conduct ordinary day-to-day business operations. Next we turn our attention to the management of short-term liabilities, the sources of short-term funds used to finance the business. Then, we discuss the management of long-term assets such as plants, equipment, and the use of common stock (equity) and bonds (long-term liability) to finance these long-term corporate assets. Finally, we look at the securities markets, where stocks and bonds are traded.

Managing Current Assets and Liabilities

Managing short-term assets and liabilities involves managing the current assets and liabilities on the balance sheet (discussed in Chapter 14). Current assets are short-term resources such as cash, investments, accounts receivable, and inventory. Current liabilities are short-term debts such as accounts payable, accrued salaries, accrued taxes, and short-term bank loans. We use the terms *current* and *short term* interchangeably because short-term assets and liabilities are usually replaced by new assets and liabilities within three or four months, and always within a year. Managing short-term assets and liabilities is sometimes called **working capital management** because short-term assets and liabilities continually flow through an organization and are thus said to be "working."

working capital management
the managing of short-term assets and liabilities

Managing Current Assets

LO 16-1

The chief goal of financial managers who focus on current assets and liabilities is to maximize the return to the business on cash, temporary investments of idle cash, accounts receivable, and inventory.

Going Green

Finance Executives Recognize the Benefits of Method's Green Efficiencies

Method is a green company in more ways than one. Not only does it sell eco-friendly household supplies, but it also generates more than $100 million in annual revenues. Thanks to companies like Method, finance executives are beginning to realize the financial benefits of going green. At a time when the prices of commodities are rapidly fluctuating, finance executives are looking for ways to cut costs. Eco-friendly options such as decreasing energy use, using recycled materials, and reducing packaging are becoming viable methods for saving money and improving efficiency. A recent poll found that 40 percent of finance executives are increasing their facilities' efficiency through better energy management, while one-third are undertaking initiatives to increase the efficiency of their shipping, including the adoption of more fuel-efficient vehicles. Method, for instance, has significantly increased its use of biodiesel trucks, which get 13 percent more miles per gallon than traditional trucks.

Method aligns its environmental objectives with its cost-saving goals. The operations and finance departments routinely work together to look at what ingredients and processes would save money while also reducing Method's environmental impact. Sometimes, this requires the company to adopt additional costs in the short run in order to save money in the long term. Method's long-term perspective, efficient operations, and popularity with customers are catching on with competitors. It is estimated that eco-friendly household supplies will grow from 3 percent of the household cleaning market in 2008 to 30 percent by 2013. And as green products and operational processes increase, Method already has a head start.[2]

Discussion Questions

1. If greener operations cut company costs, how will this affect current assets and liabilities?
2. Why might Method decide to pursue greener business activities that are costly in the short run?
3. Do you think other household supply companies are beginning to realize how green products can improve their financial conditions?

Managing Cash. A crucial element facing any financial manager is effectively managing the firm's cash flow. Remember that cash flow is the movement of money through an organization on a daily, weekly, monthly, or yearly basis. Ensuring that sufficient (but not excessive) funds are on hand to meet the company's obligations is one of the single most important facets of financial management.

Idle cash does not make money, and corporate checking accounts typically do not earn interest. As a result, astute money managers try to keep just enough cash on hand, called **transaction balances,** to pay bills—such as employee wages, supplies, and utilities—as they fall due. To manage the firm's cash and ensure that enough cash flows through the organization quickly and efficiently, companies try to speed up cash collections from customers.

To facilitate collection, some companies have customers send their payments to a **lockbox,** which is simply an address for receiving payments, instead of directly to the company's main address. The manager of the lockbox, usually a commercial bank, collects payments directly from the lockbox several times a day and deposits them into the company's bank account. The bank can then start clearing the checks and get the money into the company's checking account much more quickly than if the payments had been submitted directly to the company. However, there is no free lunch: The costs associated with lockbox systems make them worthwhile only for those companies that receive thousands of checks from customers each business day.

Large firms with many stores or offices around the country, such as HSBC Finance Corporation, frequently use electronic funds transfer to speed up collections. HSBC Finance Corporation's local offices deposit checks received each business day into their local banks and, at the end of the day, HSBC Finance Corporation's corporate office initiates the transfer of all collected funds to its central bank for overnight

transaction balances
cash kept on hand by a firm to pay normal daily expenses, such as employee wages and bills for supplies and utilities

lockbox
an address, usually a commercial bank, at which a company receives payments in order to speed collections from customers

trade credit
credit extended by suppliers
for the purchase of their
goods and services

The most widely used source of short-term financing, and therefore the most important account payable, is **trade credit**—credit extended by suppliers for the purchase of their goods and services. While varying in formality, depending on both the organizations involved and the value of the items purchased, most trade credit agreements offer discounts to organizations that pay their bills early. A supplier, for example, may offer trade terms of "1/10 net 30," meaning that the purchasing organization may take a 1 percent discount from the invoice amount if it makes payment by the 10th day after receiving the bill. Otherwise, the entire amount is due within 30 days. For example, pretend that you are the financial manager in charge of payables. You owe Ajax Company $10,000, and it offers trade terms of 2/10 net 30. By paying the amount due within 10 days, you can save 2 percent of $10,000, or $200. Assume you place orders with Ajax once per month and have 12 bills of $10,000 each per year. By taking the discount every time, you will save 12 times $200, or $2,400, per year. Now assume you are the financial manager of Gigantic Corp., and it has monthly payables of $100 million per month. Two percent of $100 million is $2 million per month. Failure to take advantage of such trade discounts can add up to large opportunity losses over the span of a year.

Bank Loans. Virtually all organizations—large and small—obtain short-term funds for operations from banks. In most instances, the credit services granted these firms take the form of a line of credit or fixed dollar loan. A **line of credit** is an arrangement by which a bank agrees to lend a specified amount of money to the organization upon request—provided that the bank has the required funds to make the loan. In general, a business line of credit is very similar to a consumer credit card, with the exception that the preset credit limit can amount to millions of dollars.

line of credit
an arrangement by which
a bank agrees to lend a
specified amount of money
to an organization upon
request

secured loans
loans backed by collateral
that the bank can claim if
the borrowers do not repay
them

unsecured loans
loans backed only by the
borrowers' good reputation
and previous credit rating

In addition to credit lines, banks also make **secured loans**—loans backed by collateral that the bank can claim if the borrowers do not repay the loans—and **unsecured loans**—loans backed only by the borrowers' good reputation and previous credit rating. Both individuals and businesses build their credit rating from their history of borrowing and repaying borrowed funds on time and in full. The three national credit-rating services are Equifax, TransUnion, and Experian. A lack of credit history or a poor credit history can make it difficult to get loans from financial institutions. The *principal* is the amount of money borrowed; *interest* is a percentage of the principal that the bank charges for use of its money. As we mentioned in Chapter 15, banks also pay depositors interest on savings accounts and some checking accounts. Thus, banks charge borrowers interest for loans and pay interest to depositors for the use of their money. In addition, these loans may include origination fees.

One of the complaints from borrowers during the financial meltdown and recession was that banks weren't willing to lend. There were several causes. Banks were trying to rebuild their capital, and they didn't want to take the extra risk that lending offers in an economic recession. They were drowning in bad debts and were not sure how future loan losses would affect their capital. The banks' lack of lending caused problems for small businesses. Smaller regional banks did a better job of maintaining small business loans than the major money center banks who suffered most in the recession.

prime rate
the interest rate that
commercial banks charge
their best customers
(usually large corporations)
for short-term loans

The **prime rate** is the interest rate commercial banks charge their best customers (usually large corporations) for short-term loans. While for many years, loans at the prime rate represented funds at the lowest possible cost, the rapid development of the market for commercial paper has dramatically reduced the importance of commercial banks as a source of short-term loans. Today, most "prime" borrowers are actually small- and medium-sized businesses.

The interest rates on commercial loans may be either fixed or variable. A variable, or floating-rate loan offers an advantage when interest rates are falling but represents a distinct disadvantage when interest rates are rising. Between 1999 and 2004, interest rates plummeted, and borrowers refinanced their loans with low-cost fixed-rate loans. Nowhere was this more visible than in the U.S. mortgage markets, where homeowners lined up to refinance their high-percentage home mortgages with lower-cost loans, in some cases as low as 5 percent on a 30-year loan. These mortgage interest rates had returned to 6.5 percent by mid-2006, but by 2012 they had declined to less than 4.0 percent. Individuals and corporations have the same motivation: to minimize their borrowing costs.

Nonbank Liabilities.   Banks are not the only source of short-term funds for businesses. Indeed, virtually all financial institutions, from insurance companies to pension funds, from money market funds to finance companies, make short-term loans to many organizations. The largest U.S. companies also actively engage in borrowing money from the eurodollar and commercial paper markets. As noted earlier, both of these funds' sources are typically slightly less expensive than bank loans.

In some instances, businesses actually sell their accounts receivable to a finance company known as a **factor,** which gives the selling organizations cash and assumes responsibility for collecting the accounts. For example, a factor might pay $60,000 for receivables with a total face value of $100,000 (60 percent of the total). The factor profits if it can collect more than what it paid for the accounts. Because the selling organization's customers send their payments to a lockbox, they may have no idea that a factor has bought their receivables.

Additional nonbank liabilities that must be efficiently managed to ensure maximum profitability are taxes owed to the government and wages owed to employees. Clearly, businesses are responsible for many different types of taxes, including federal, state, and local income taxes, property taxes, mineral rights taxes, unemployment taxes, Social Security taxes, workers' compensation taxes, excise taxes, and more. While the public tends to think that the only relevant taxes are on income and sales, many industries must pay other taxes that far exceed those levied against their income. Taxes and employees' wages represent debt obligations of the firm, which the financial manager must plan to meet as they fall due.

factor
a finance company to which businesses sell their accounts receivable—usually for a percentage of the total face value

Managing Fixed Assets

Up to this point, we have focused on the short-term aspects of financial management. While most business failures are the result of poor short-term planning, successful ventures must also consider the long-term financial consequences of their actions. Managing the long-term assets and liabilities and the owners' equity portion of the balance sheet is important for the long-term health of the business.

Long-term (fixed) assets are expected to last for many years—production facilities (plants), offices, equipment, heavy machinery, furniture, automobiles, and so on. In today's fast-paced world, companies need the most technologically advanced, modern facilities and equipment they can afford. Automobile, oil refining, and transportation companies are dependent on fixed assets.

LO 16-3

long-term (fixed) assets
production facilities (plants), offices, and equipment—all of which are expected to last for many years

Modern and high-tech equipment carry high price tags, and the financial arrangements required to support these investments are by no means trivial. Leasing is just one approach to financing. Obtaining major long-term financing can be challenging for even the most profitable organizations. For less successful firms, such challenges can prove nearly impossible. One approach is leasing assets such as equipment, machines, and buildings. Leasing involves paying a fee for usage rather than owning the asset. There are two kinds of leases: capital leases and operating leases. A capital lease is a long-term contract and shows up on the balance sheet as an asset and liability. The operating lease is a short-term cancelable lease and does not show up on the balance sheet. We'll take a closer look at long-term financing in a moment, but first let's address some issues associated with fixed assets, including capital budgeting, risk assessment, and the costs of financing fixed assets.

Capital Budgeting and Project Selection

capital budgeting
the process of analyzing the needs of the business and selecting the assets that will maximize its value

One of the most important jobs performed by the financial manager is to decide what fixed assets, projects, and investments will earn profits for the firm beyond the costs necessary to fund them. The process of analyzing the needs of the business and selecting the assets that will maximize its value is called **capital budgeting,** and the capital budget is the amount of money budgeted for investment in such long-term assets. But capital budgeting does not end with the selection and purchase of a particular piece of land, equipment, or major investment. All assets and projects must be continually reevaluated to ensure their compatibility with the organization's needs. Financial executives believe most budgeting activities are occasionally or frequently unrealistic or irrelevant. If a particular asset does not live up to expectations, then management must determine why and take necessary corrective action. Budgeting is not an exact process, and managers must be flexible when new information is available.

Assessing Risk

Every investment carries some risk. Figure 16.1 ranks potential investment projects according to estimated risk. When considering investments overseas, risk assessments must include the political climate and economic stability of a region. The decision to introduce a product or build a manufacturing facility in England would be much less risky than a decision to build one in the Middle East, for example.

The longer a project or asset is expected to last, the greater its potential risk because it is hard to predict whether a piece of equipment will wear out or become obsolete in 5 or 10 years. Predicting cash flows one year down the road is difficult, but projecting them over the span of a 10-year project is a gamble.

The level of a project's risk is also affected by the stability and competitive nature of the marketplace and the world economy as a whole. IBM's latest high-technology computer product is far more likely to become obsolete overnight than is a similar $10 million investment in a manufacturing plant.

Pharmaceutical companies spend millions of dollars developing new drugs without knowing if the drug will pass FDA approval and have a significant margin.

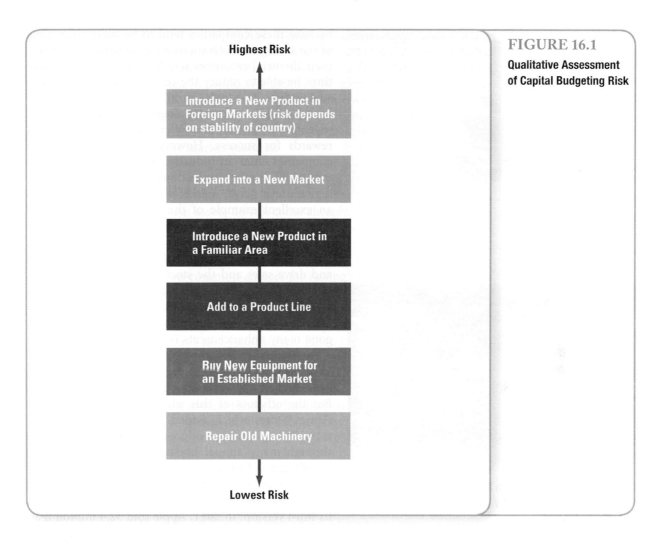

FIGURE 16.1

Qualitative Assessment of Capital Budgeting Risk

Dramatic changes in the marketplace are not uncommon. Indeed, uncertainty created by the rapid devaluation of Asian currencies in the late 1990s wrecked a host of assumptions in literally hundreds of projects worldwide. Financial managers must constantly consider such issues when making long-term decisions about the purchase of fixed assets.

Pricing Long-Term Money

The ultimate profitability of any project depends not only on accurate assumptions of how much cash it will generate, but also on its financing costs. Because a business must pay interest on money it borrows, the returns from any project must cover not only the costs of operating the project but also the interest expenses for the debt used to finance its construction. Unless an organization can effectively cover all of its costs—both financial and operating—it will eventually fail.

Clearly, only a limited supply of funds is available for investment in any given enterprise. The most efficient and profitable companies can attract the lowest-cost funds because they typically offer reasonable financial returns at very low relative risks. Newer and less prosperous firms must pay higher costs to attract capital

TABLE 16.2

Bonds—Global Investment Grade quoted in US $

30-Mar-10	Red Date[a]	Coupon[b]	S[c]	M[c]	F[c]	Bid Price[d]	Bid Yield[e]	Spread vs. Govts.[f]
GE Capital	01/16	5.00	AA+	Aa3	AA−	103.7	4.01	1.56
AT&T Wireless	03/31	8.75	A	A2	A	128.2	6.3	1.53
Goldman Sachs	02/33	6.13	A	A1	A+	98.29	6.27	1.49

[a]Red Date—the month and year that the bond matures and must pay back the borrowed amount.

[b]Coupon—the percentage in interest payment that the bond pays based on a $1,000 bond. For example, the GE Capital bond pays 5 percent on $1,000 or $50 per year while the AT&T bond pays $87.50.

[c]S-M-F—the ratings provided by the three major rating agenices: S (Standard and Poor's), M (Moody's), and F (Fitch). Using Standard and Poor's as an example, a rating of AAA would be the highest quality and lowest risk bond. Any bond in the A category is investment grade and considered high quality.

[d]Bid Price—the price as a percentage of par value ($1,000) that investors are willing to pay for a bond. For example, the GE capital bond has a bid price of 103.69, which would translate into 103% of $1,000 or a price of $1,036.90.

[e]Bid Yield—the annual rate of return the investor would receive if he or she held the bond to maturity. For example, with the GE bond you would get $50 per year until the bond matured in January 2016, and you would receive $1,000 par value at maturity. Because you paid $1,036.90, you would lose $36.90 on your investment. The 4.01 percent bid yield reflects both the income from the interest payment and the loss on the investment.

[f]Spread vs. Govts.—represents the premium yield the corporate bond pays over a U.S. government bond of equal maturity. Because corporate bonds are riskier than government bonds, an investor would expect the corporation to pay more than a risk-free government bond. In the case of GE Capital, the premium the company pays is an extra 1.56 percent.

Source: *The Financial Times,* March 31, 2010, p. 23.

and in the creditworthiness of the issuer. Bondholders receive the face value of the bond along with the final interest payment on the maturity date. The annual interest rate (often called the *coupon rate*) is the guaranteed percentage of face value that the company will pay to the bond owner every year. For example, a $1,000 bond with a coupon rate of 7 percent would pay $70 per year in interest. In most cases, bond indentures specify that interest payments be made every six months. In the example above, the $70 annual payment would be divided into two semiannual payments of $35.

In addition to the terms of interest payments and maturity date, the bond indenture typically covers other important topics, such as repayment methods, interest payment dates, procedures to be followed in case the organization fails to make the interest payments, conditions for the early repayment of the bonds, and any conditions requiring the pledging of assets as collateral.

Types of Bonds

unsecured bonds
debentures, or bonds that are not backed by specific collateral

secured bonds
bonds that are backed by specific collateral that must be forfeited in the event that the issuing firm defaults

serial bonds
a sequence of small bond issues of progressively longer maturity

floating-rate bonds
bonds with interest rates that change with current interest rates otherwise available in the economy

Not surprisingly, there are a great many different types of bonds. Most are **unsecured bonds,** meaning that they are not backed by collateral; such bonds are termed *debentures.* **Secured bonds,** on the other hand, are backed by specific collateral that must be forfeited in the event that the issuing firm defaults. Whether secured or unsecured, bonds may be repaid in one lump sum or with many payments spread out over a period of time. **Serial bonds,** which are different from secured bonds, are actually a sequence of small bond issues of progressively longer maturity. The firm pays off each of the serial bonds as they mature. **Floating-rate bonds** do not have fixed interest payments; instead, the interest rate changes with current interest rates otherwise available in the economy.

In recent years, a special type of high-interest-rate bond has attracted considerable attention (usually negative) in the financial press. High-interest bonds, or **junk bonds** as they are popularly known, offer relatively high rates of interest because they have higher inherent risks. Historically, junk bonds have been associated with companies in poor financial health and/or startup firms with limited track records. In the mid-1980s, however, junk bonds became a very attractive method of financing corporate mergers; they remain popular today with many investors as a result of their very high relative interest rates. But higher risks are associated with those higher returns (upward of 12 percent per year in some cases) and the average investor would be well-advised to heed those famous words: Look before you leap!

junk bonds
a special type of high interest-rate bond that carries higher inherent risks

Financing with Owners' Equity

A second means of long-term financing is through equity. Remember from Chapter 14 that owners' equity refers to the owners' investment in an organization. Sole proprietors and partners own all or a part of their businesses outright, and their equity includes the money and assets they have brought into their ventures. Corporate owners, on the other hand, own stock or shares of their companies, which they hope will provide them with a return on their investment. Stockholders' equity includes common stock, preferred stock, and retained earnings.

Common stock (introduced in Chapter 4) is the single most important source of capital for most new companies. On the balance sheet, the common stock account is separated into two basic parts—common stock at par and capital in excess of par. The *par value* of a stock is simply the dollar amount printed on the stock certificate and has no relation to actual *market value*—the price at which the common stock is currently trading. The difference between a stock's par value and its offering price is called *capital in excess of par*. Except in the case of some very low-priced stocks, the capital in excess of par account is significantly larger than the par value account. Table 16.3 briefly explains how to gather important information from a stock quote, as it might appear in *The Wall Street Journal* or on the NASDAQ website.

Preferred stock was defined in Chapter 14 as corporate ownership that gives the stockholder preference in the distribution of the company's profits but not the voting and control rights accorded to common stockholders. Thus, the primary advantage of owning preferred stock is that it is a safer investment than common stock.

All businesses exist to earn profits for their owners. Without the possibility of profit, there can be no incentive to risk investors' capital and succeed. When a corporation has profits left over after paying all of its expenses and taxes, it has the choice of retaining all or a portion of its earnings and/or paying them out to its shareholders in the form of dividends. **Retained earnings** are reinvested in the assets of the firm and belong to the owners in the form of equity. Retained earnings are an important source of funds and are, in fact, the only long-term funds that the company can generate internally.

Need help understanding Equity and Debt Financing?

http://bit.ly/FerrellQR16-1

retained earnings
earnings after expenses and taxes that are reinvested in the assets of the firm and belong to the owners in the form of equity

A McGraw-Hill stock certificate.

example, that the Dow Jones Industrial Average climbed from 860 in August 1982 to a high of 11,497 at the beginning of 2000, you can see clearly that the value of the Dow Jones Average increased more than 10 times in this 19-year period, making it one of the highest rate of return periods in the history of the stock market.

Unfortunately, prosperity did not last long once the Internet bubble burst. Technology stocks and new Internet companies were responsible for the huge increase in stock prices. Even companies with few sales and no earnings were selling at prices that were totally unreasonable. It is always easier to realize that a bubble existed after it has popped. By September 2002, the Dow Jones Industrial Average hit 7,461. The markets stabilized and the economy kept growing; investors were euphoric when the Dow Jones Industrial Average hit an all time high of 14,198 in October 2007. However, once the housing bubble burst, the economy and the stock market went into a free fall. The Dow Jones Industrial Average bottomed out at 6,470 in March 2009. The market entered a period of wild fluctuations, and by April 2010, it hit a new high for the year of 10,975. By the end of May 2012, it was at 12,454, but in retrospect, it was not much higher than the 11,497 at the beginning of 2000. The good news is that even though the market has been rather flat for the past 12 years, an investor would have collected dividends, which are not reflected in the index. Perhaps this roller coaster ride indicates why some people are afraid to enter the market and buy common stocks. If you look at the long-term trend and long-term returns in common stocks, they far outdistance bonds and government securities. When you are young, you should be playing the long-term trends, and as you get older your investments should become more conservative.

Recognizing financial bubbles can be difficult. It is too easy to get caught up in the enthusiasm that accompanies rising markets. Knowing what something is worth in economic terms is the test of true value. During the housing bubble, banks made loans to subprime borrowers to buy houses. (Remember that the prime rate is the rate for the highest quality borrowers and subprime loans are generally made to those who do not qualify for regular ones.) As more money poured into the housing market, the obvious supply and demand relationship from economics would indicate that housing prices would rise. As prices rose, speculators entered the real estate market trying to make a fast buck. States such as Florida, Arizona, Nevada, and California were the favorite speculative spots and the states with the largest decline in house prices. To make matters worse, banks had created the home equity loan years ago so that borrowers could take out a second mortgage against their house and deduct the interest payment for tax purposes. Many homeowners no longer thought about paying off their mortgages but instead used the increase in the price of their houses to borrow more money. This behavior was unsustainable.

The bankers engaged in risky financial behavior packaged up billions of dollars of mortgages into securitized assets. In other words, an investor could buy a pool of assets and collect the interest income and eventually get a payment at the end of the life of the product. This technique allowed banks to make a mortgage, collect a fee, package the mortgage, and collect another fee. These securitized mortgages were sold to the market as asset-backed securities with a AAA credit rating off their books and replaced with cash to make more loans. In this case, when the bubble burst, it had extremely severe consequences for the economy, workers, and investors.

People defaulted on loans when they could no longer afford to pay the mortgage. Many of these people shouldn't have been able to borrow in the first place. The defaults caused housing prices to fall, and some people who had home equity loans no longer had any equity left in their house. Some homeowners owed the bank more than the house was worth, and they started walking away from their mortgage. At the same time, investors realized that the mortgage-backed securities they owned were probably not worth what they thought they were worth, and prices of these assets plummeted. Banks and other financial service firms that had these assets on their books suffered a double whammy. They had loan losses and losses on mortgage-backed securities that another division of the bank had bought for investment purposes. Soon, many banks were close to violating their capital requirement, and the U.S. Treasury and Federal Reserve stepped in—with the help of funding from Congress—to make banks loans, buy securities that were illiquid, and invest in the capital of the banks by buying preferred stocks.

The consensus of most economists is that through the actions of the U.S. Treasury and the Federal Reserve, the U.S. economy escaped what might have been another depression equal to or worse than the depression of the 1930s. The recession of 2007–2009 lasted 18 months and was the longest recession since the 1930s. Hundreds of banks went bankrupt during 2008–2009, and the Federal Deposit Insurance Corporation closed these banks and reopened them as part of another healthy bank with no losses for the depositors. Given that the stock market is a leading indicator, it has been rising since the bottom in March 2009, and everyone—from investors to people relying on pensions tied to the market—hopes we can eventually get back to the 2007 high of more than 14,000 on the Dow Jones Industrial Average. Now you know why investing in the stock market takes discipline, knowledge, and the willingness to weather out economic storms.

For investors to make sound financial decisions, it is important that they stay in touch with business news, markets, and indexes. Of course, business and investment magazines, such as *Bloomberg Businessweek, Fortune,* and *Money,* offer this type of information. Many Internet sites, including the CNN/*Money, Business Wire, USA Today,* other online newspapers, and *PR Newswire,* offer this information, as well. Many sites offer searchable databases of information by topic, company, or keyword. However investors choose to receive and review business news, doing so is a necessity in today's market.

So You Want to Work in Financial Management or Securities

Taking classes in financial and securities management can provide many career options, from managing a small firm's accounts receivables to handling charitable giving for a multinational to investment banking to stock brokerage. We have entered into a less certain period for finance and securities jobs, however. In the world of investment banking, the past few years have been especially challenging. Tens of thousands of employees from Wall Street firms have lost their jobs. This phenomenon is not confined to New York City either, leaving the industry with a lot fewer jobs around the country. This type of phenomenon is not isolated to the finance sector. In the early 2000s, the tech sector experienced a similar downturn, from which it has subsequently largely recovered. Undoubtedly, markets will bounce back and job creation in finance and securities will increase again—but until that happens the atmosphere across finance and securities will be more competitive than it has been in the past. However, this does not mean that there are no jobs. All firms need financial analysts to determine whether a project should be implemented, when to issue stocks or bonds, or when to initiate loans. These and other forward-looking questions such as how to invest excess cash must be addressed by financial managers. Economic uncertainty in the financial and securities market has made for more difficulty in finding the most desirable jobs.

Why this sudden downturn in financial industry prospects? A lot of these job cuts came in response to the subprime lending fallout and subsequent bank failures such as Bear Stearns, which alone lost around 7,000 employees. All of these people had to look for new jobs in new organizations, increasing the competitive level in a lot of different employment areas. For young jobseekers with relatively little experience, this may result in a great deal of frustration. On the other hand, by the time you graduate, the job market for finance majors could be in recovery and rebuilding with new employees. Uncertainty results in hiring freezes and layoffs but leaves firms lean and ready to grow when the cycle turns around, resulting in hiring from the bottom up.

Many different industries require people with finance skills. So do not despair if you have a difficult time finding a job in exactly the right firm. Most students switch companies a number of times over the course of their careers. Many organizations require individuals trained in forecasting, statistics, economics, and finance. Even unlikely places like museums, aquariums, and zoos need people who are good at numbers. It may require some creativity, but if you are committed to a career in finance, look to less obvious sources—not just the large financial firms.[7]

Review Your Understanding

Describe some common methods of managing current assets.

Current assets are short-term resources such as cash, investments, accounts receivable, and inventory, which can be converted to cash within a year. Financial managers focus on minimizing the amount of cash kept on hand and increasing the speed of collections through lockboxes and electronic funds transfer and investing in marketable securities. Marketable securities include U.S. Treasury bills, certificates of deposit, commercial paper, and money market funds. Managing accounts receivable requires judging customer creditworthiness and creating credit terms that encourage prompt payment. Inventory management focuses on determining optimum inventory levels that minimize the cost of storing and ordering inventory without sacrificing too many lost sales due to stockouts.

Identify some sources of short-term financing (current liabilities).

Current liabilities are short-term debt obligations that must be repaid within one year, such as accounts payable, taxes payable, and notes (loans) payable. Trade credit is extended by suppliers for the purchase of their goods and services. A line of credit is an arrangement by which a bank agrees to lend a specified amount of money to a business whenever the business needs it. Secured loans are backed by collateral; unsecured loans are backed only by the borrower's good reputation.

Summarize the importance of long-term assets and capital budgeting.

Long-term, or fixed, assets are expected to last for many years, such as production facilities (plants), offices, and equipment. Businesses need modern, up-to-date equipment to succeed in today's competitive environment. Capital budgeting is the process of analyzing company needs and selecting the assets that will maximize its value; a capital budget is the amount of money budgeted for the purchase of fixed assets. Every investment in fixed assets carries some risk.

Specify how companies finance their operations and manage fixed assets with long-term liabilities, particularly bonds.

Two common choices for financing are equity financing (attracting new owners) and debt financing (taking on long-term liabilities). Long-term liabilities are debts that will be repaid over a number of years, such as long-term bank loans and bond issues. A bond is a long-term debt security that an organization sells to raise money. The bond indenture specifies the provisions of the bond contract—maturity date, coupon rate, repayment methods, and others.

Discuss how corporations can use equity financing by issuing stock through an investment banker.

Owners' equity represents what owners have contributed to the company and includes common stock, preferred stock, and retained earnings (profits that have been reinvested in the assets of the firm). To finance operations, companies can issue new common and preferred stock through an investment banker that sells stocks and bonds for corporations.

Describe the various securities markets in the United States.

Securities markets provide the mechanism for buying and selling stocks and bonds. Primary markets allow companies to raise capital by selling new stock directly to investors through investment bankers. Secondary markets allow the buyers of previously issued shares of stock to sell them to other owners. The major secondary markets are the New York Stock Exchange, the American Stock Exchange, and the over-the-counter market. Investors measure stock market performance by watching stock market averages and indexes such as the Dow Jones Industrial Average and the Standard and Poor's (S&P) Composite Index.

Critique the short-term asset and liabilities position of a small manufacturer, and recommend corrective action.

Using the information presented in this chapter, you should be able to "Solve the Dilemma" on page 529 presented by the current bleak working capital situation of Glasspray Corporation.

Revisit the World of Business

1. What are some of the economic repercussions that might occur if Bank of America fails?
2. Why has Bank of America's acquisition of Countrywide been criticized?
3. How might Berkshire Hathaway's preferred stock purchase help Bank of America?

Learn the Terms

bonds 515
capital budgeting 512
commercial certificates of deposit (CDs) 507
commercial paper 507
dividend yield 519
eurodollar market 507
factor 511
floating-rate bonds 516
investment banking 520
junk bonds 517

line of credit 510
lockbox 505
long-term (fixed) assets 511
long-term liabilities 515
marketable securities 506
over-the-counter (OTC) market 522
primary market 520
prime rate 510
retained earnings 517
secondary markets 520
secured bonds 516

secured loans 510
securities markets 520
serial bonds 516
trade credit 510
transaction balances 505
Treasury bills (T-bills) 506
unsecured bonds 516
unsecured loans 510
working capital management 504

Check Your Progress

1. Define working capital management.
2. How can a company speed up cash flow? Why should it?
3. Describe the various types of marketable securities.
4. What does it mean to have a line of credit at a bank?
5. What are fixed assets? Why is assessing risk important in capital budgeting?
6. How can a company finance fixed assets?
7. What are bonds and what do companies do with them?
8. How can companies use equity to finance their operations and long-term growth?
9. What are the functions of securities markets?
10. What were some of the principal causes of the most recent recession?

Get Involved

1. Using your local newspaper or *The Wall Street Journal,* find the current rates of interest on the following marketable securities. If you were a financial manager for a large corporation, which would you invest extra cash in? Which would you invest in if you worked for a small business?
   a. Three-month T-bills
   b. Six-month T-bills
   c. Commercial certificates of deposit
   d. Commercial paper
   e. Eurodollar deposits
   f. Money market deposits

2. Select five of the Dow Jones Industrials from Table 16.5. Look up their earnings, dividends, and prices for the past five years. What kind of picture is presented by this information? Which stocks would you like to have owned over this past period? Do you think the next five years will present a similar picture?

Build Your Skills

CHOOSING AMONG PROJECTS

Background

As the senior executive in charge of exploration for High Octane Oil Co., you are constantly looking for projects that will add to the company's profitability—without increasing the company's risk. High Octane Oil is an international oil company with operations in Latin America, the Middle East, Africa, the United States, and Mexico. The company is one of the world's leading experts in deep-water exploration and drilling. High Octane currently produces 50 percent of its oil in the United States, 25 percent in the Middle East, 5 percent in Africa, 10 percent in Latin America, and 10 percent in Mexico. You are considering six projects from around the world.

Project 1—Your deep-water drilling platform in the Gulf of Mexico is producing at maximum capacity from the Valdez oil field, and High Octane's geological engineers think there is a high probability that there is oil in the Sanchez field, which is adjacent to Valdez. They recommend drilling a new series of wells. Once commercial quantities of oil have been discovered, it will take two more years to build the collection platform and pipelines. It will be four years before the discovered oil gets to the refineries.

Project 2—The Brazilian government has invited you to drill on some unexplored tracts in the middle of the central jungle region. There are roads to within 50 miles of the tract and British Petroleum has found oil 500 miles away from this tract. It would take about three years to develop this property and several more years to build pipelines and pumping stations to carry the oil to the refineries. The Brazilian government wants 20 percent of all production as its fee for giving High Octane Oil Co. the drilling rights or a $500 million up-front fee and 5 percent of the output.

Project 3—Your fields in Saudi Arabia have been producing oil for 50 years. Several wells are old, and the pressure has diminished. Your engineers are sure that if you were to initiate high-pressure secondary recovery procedures, you would increase the output of these existing wells by 20 percent. High-pressure recovery methods pump water at high pressure into the underground limestone formations to enhance the movement of petroleum toward the surface.

Project 4—Your largest oil fields in Alaska have been producing from only 50 percent of the known deposits. Your geological engineers estimate that you could open up 10 percent of the remaining fields every two years and offset your current declining production from existing wells. The pipeline capacity is available and, while you can only drill during six months of the year, the fields could be producing oil in three years.

Project 5—Some of High Octane's west Texas oil fields produce in shallow stripper wells of 2,000- to 4,000-foot depths. Stripper wells produce anywhere from 10 to 2,000 barrels per day and can last for six months or 40 years. Generally, once you find a shallow deposit, there is an 80 percent chance that offset wells will find more oil. Because these wells are shallow, they can be drilled quickly at a low cost. High Octane's engineers estimate that in your largest tract, which is closest to the company's Houston refinery, you could increase production by 30 percent for the next 10 years by increasing the density of the wells per square mile.

Project 6—The government of a republic in Russia has invited you to drill for oil in Siberia. Russian geologists think that this oil field might be the largest in the world, but there have been no wells drilled and no infrastructure exists to carry oil if it should be found. The republic has no money to help you build the infrastructure but if you find oil, it will let you keep the first five years' production before taking its 25 percent share. Knowing that oil fields do not start producing at full capacity for many years after initial production, your engineers are not sure that your portion the first five years of production will pay for the

infrastructure they must build to get the oil to market. The republic also has been known to have a rather unstable government, and the last international oil company that began this project left the country when a new government demanded a higher than originally agreed-upon percentage of the expected output. If this field is in fact the largest in the world, High Octane's supply of oil would be ensured well into the 21st century.

Task

1. Working in groups, rank the six projects from lowest risk to highest risk.

2. Given the information provided, do the best you can to rank the projects from lowest cost to highest cost.

3. What political considerations might affect your project choice?

4. If you could choose one project, which would it be and why?

5. If you could choose three projects, which ones would you choose? In making this decision, consider which projects might be highly correlated to High Octane Oil's existing production and which ones might diversify the company's production on a geographical basis.

Solve the Dilemma   LO 16-7
SURVIVING RAPID GROWTH

Glasspray Corporation is a small firm that makes industrial fiberglass spray equipment. Despite its size, the company supplies a range of firms from small mom-and-pop boatmakers to major industrial giants, both overseas and here at home. Indeed, just about every molded fiberglass resin product, from bathroom sinks and counters to portable spas and racing yachts, is constructed with the help of one or more of the company's machines.

Despite global acceptance of its products, Glasspray has repeatedly run into trouble with regard to the management of its current assets and liabilities as a result of extremely rapid and consistent increases in year-to-year sales. The firm's president and founder, Stephen T. Rose, recently lamented the sad

state of his firm's working capital position: "Our current assets aren't, and our current liabilities are!" Rose shouted in a recent meeting of the firm's top officers. "We can't afford any more increases in sales! We're selling our way into bankruptcy! Frankly, our *working* capital doesn't!"

Discussion Questions

1. Normally, rapidly increasing sales are a good thing. What seems to be the problem here?

2. List the important components of a firm's working capital. Include both current assets and current liabilities.

3. What are some management techniques applied to current liabilities that Glasspray might use to improve its working capital position?

Build Your Business Plan
FINANCIAL MANAGEMENT AND SECURITIES MARKET

This chapter helps you realize that once you are making money, you need to be careful in determining how to invest it. Meanwhile, your team should consider the pros and cons of establishing a line of credit at the bank.

Remember the key to building your business plan is to be realistic!!

The Personal Balance Sheet

For businesses, net worth is usually defined as *assets minus liabilities,* and this is no different for individuals. **Personal net worth** is simply the total value of all personal assets less the total value of unpaid debts or liabilities. Although a business could not survive with a negative net worth since it would be technically insolvent, many students have negative net worth. As a student, you probably are not yet earning enough to have accumulated significant assets, such as a house or stock portfolio, but you are likely to have incurred various forms of debt, including student loans, car loans, and credit card debt.

At this stage in your life, negative net worth is not necessarily an indication of poor future financial prospects. Current investment in your "human capital" (education) is usually considered to have a resulting payoff in the form of better job opportunities and higher potential lifetime income, so this "upside-down" balance sheet should not stay that way forever. Unfortunately, there are many people in the United States who have negative net worth much later in their lives. This can result from unforeseen circumstances, like divorce, illness, or disability, but the easy availability of credit in the last couple of decades has also been blamed for the heavy debt loads of many American families. The most recent recession, caused partially by excessive risk-taking, has resulted in many bankruptcies and housing foreclosures. No matter the immediate trigger, it is usually poor financial planning—the failure to prepare in advance for those unforeseen

circumstances—that makes the difference between those who fail and those who survive. It is interesting to note that we could say the exact same thing about business failures. Most are attributable to poor financial planning. If your net worth is negative, you should definitely include debt reduction on your list of short and/or long-term goals.

You can use Table D.2 to estimate your net worth. On the left-hand side of the balance sheet, you should record the value of *assets,* all the things you own that have value. These include checking and savings account balances, investments, furniture, books, clothing, vehicles, houses, and the like. As with business balance sheets, assets are usually arranged from most liquid (easily convertible to cash) to least liquid. If you are a young student, it should not be surprising to find that you have little, if anything, to put on this side of your balance sheet. You should note that balance sheets are sensitive to the point in time chosen for evaluation. For example, if you always get paid on the first day of the month, your checking balance will be greatest at that point but will quickly be depleted as you pay for rent, food, and other needs. You may want to use your average daily balance in checking and savings accounts as a more accurate reflection of your financial condition. The right-hand side of the balance sheet is for recording *liabilities,* amounts of money that you owe to others. These include bank loans, mortgages, credit card debt, and other personal loans and are usually listed in order of how soon they must be paid back to the lender.

TABLE D.2   Personal Net Worth

Assets	$	Liabilities	$
Checking accounts	_____	Credit cards balances (list)	_____
Savings accounts	_____	1 _____	_____
Money market accounts	_____	2 _____	_____
Other short-term investment	_____	3 _____	_____
	_____	Personal Loans	_____
Market value of investments (stocks, bonds, mutual funds)	_____	Student loans	_____
	_____	Car Loans	_____

(continued)

TABLE D.2   Personal Net Worth *(continued)*

Value of retirement funds	_____	Home mortgage balance	_____
College savings plan	_____	Home equity loans	_____
Other savings plans	_____	Other real estate loans	_____
Market value of real estate	_____	Alimony/child support owed	_____
Cars	_____	Taxes owed (above withholding)	_____
Home furnishings	_____	Other investment loans	_____
Jewelry/art/collectibles	_____	Other liabilities/debts	_____
Clothing/personal assets	_____		_____
Other assets	_____		
TOTAL ASSETS	_____	TOTAL LIABILITIES	_____

PERSONAL NET WORTH = TOTAL ASSETS MINUS TOTAL LIABILITIES = $ _____

The Cash Flow Statement

Businesses forecast and track their regular inflows and outflows of cash with a cash budget and summarize annual cash flows on the statement of cash flows. Similarly, individuals should have a clear understanding of their flow of cash as they budget their expenditures and regularly check to be sure that they are sticking to their budget.

What is cash flow? Anytime you receive cash or pay cash (including payments with checks), the dollar amount that is moving from one person to another is a **cash flow.** For students, the most likely cash inflows will be student loans, grants, and income from part-time jobs. Cash outflows will include rent, food, gas, car payments, books, tuition, and personal care expenses. Although it may seem obvious that you need to have enough inflows to cover the outflows, it is very common for people to estimate incorrectly and overspend. This may result in hefty bank overdraft charges or increasing debt as credit lines are used to make up the difference. Accurate forecasting of cash inflows and outflows allows you to make arrangements to cover estimated shortfalls before they occur. For students, this can be particularly valuable when cash inflows primarily occur at the beginning of the semester (for example, student loans) but outflows are spread over the semester.

How should you treat credit card purchases on your cash flow worksheet? Because credit purchases do not require payment of cash *now,* your cash flow statement should not reflect the value of the purchase as an outflow until you pay the bill. Take for example the purchase of a television set on credit. The $500 purchase will increase your assets and your liabilities by $500 but will only result in a negative cash flow of a few dollars per month, since payments on credit cards are cash outflows when they are made. If you always pay your credit card balances in full each month, the purchases are really the same thing as cash, and your balance sheet will never reflect the debt. But if you purchase on credit and only pay minimum balances, you will be living beyond your means, and your balance sheet will get more and more "upside down." A further problem with using credit to purchase assets that decline in value is that the liability may still be there long after the asset you purchased has no value.

Table D.3 can be used to estimate your cash flow. The purpose of a cash flow worksheet for your financial plan is to heighten your awareness of where the cash is going. Many people are surprised to find that they are spending more than they make (by using too much credit) or that they have significant "cash leakage"—those little expenditures that add up to a lot without their even noticing. Examples include afternoon lattes or snacks, too many nights out at the local pub, eating lunch at the Student Center instead of packing a bag, and regularly paying for parking (or parking tickets) instead of biking or riding the bus to school. In many cases, plugging the little leaks can free up enough cash to make a significant contribution toward achieving long-term savings goals.

TABLE D.3   **Personal Cash Flow**

Cash Inflows	Monthly	Annual
Salary/wage income (gross)	$ _____	$ _____
Interest/dividend income	_____	_____
Other income (self-employment)	_____	_____
Rental income (after expenses)	_____	_____
Capital gains	_____	_____
Other income	_____	_____
Total income	_____	_____
Cash Outflows	**Monthly**	**Annual**
Groceries	$ _____	$ _____
Housing	_____	_____
Mortgage or rent	_____	_____
House repairs/expenses	_____	_____
Property taxes	_____	_____
Utilities	_____	_____
Heating	_____	_____
Electric	_____	_____
Water and sewer	_____	_____
Cable/phone/satellite/Internet	_____	_____
Car loan payments	_____	_____
Car maintenance/gas	_____	_____
Credit card payments	_____	_____
Other loan payments	_____	_____
Income and payroll taxes	_____	_____
Other taxes	_____	_____
Insurance	_____	_____
Life	_____	_____
Health	_____	_____

(continued)

TABLE D.3	**Personal Cash Flow** *(continued)*		
Auto		_____	_____
Disability		_____	_____
Other insurance		_____	_____
Clothing		_____	_____
Gifts		_____	_____
Other consumables (TVs, etc)		_____	_____
Child care expenses		_____	_____
Sports-related expenses		_____	_____
Health club dues		_____	_____
Uninsured medical expenses		_____	_____
Education		_____	_____
Vacations		_____	_____
Entertainment		_____	_____
Alimony/child support			_____
Charitable contributions		_____	_____
Required pension contributions		_____	_____
Magazine subscriptions/books		_____	_____
Other payments/expenses		_____	_____
Total Expenses		$ _____	$ _____

NET PERSONAL CASH FLOW = TOTAL INCOME − TOTAL EXPENSES = $ _____

Set Short-Term and Long-Term Financial Goals

Just as a business develops its vision and strategic plan, individuals should have a clear set of financial goals. This component of your financial plan is the road map that will lead you to achieving your short-term and long-term financial goals.

Short-term goals are those that can be achieved in two years or less. They may include saving for particular short-term objectives, such as a new car, a down payment for a home, a vacation, or other major consumer purchase. For many people, short-term financial goals should include tightening up on household spending patterns and reducing outstanding credit.

Long-term goals are those that require substantial time to achieve. Nearly everyone should include retirement planning as a long-term objective. Those who have or anticipate having children will probably consider college savings a priority. Protection of loved ones from the financial hazards of your unexpected death, illness, or disability is also a long-term objective for many individuals. If you have a spouse or other dependents, having adequate insurance and an estate plan in place should be part of your long-term goals.

Create and Adhere to a Budget

Whereas the cash flow table you completed in the previous section tells you what you are doing with your money currently, a **budget** shows what you plan to do with it in the future. A budget can be for any period of time, but it is common to budget in monthly and/or annual intervals.

Developing a Budget

You can use the cash flow worksheet completed earlier to create a budget. Begin with the amount of income you have for the month. Enter your nondiscretionary expenditures (that is, bills you *must* pay, such as tuition, rent, and utilities) on the worksheet and determine the leftover amount. Next list your discretionary expenditures, such as entertainment and cable TV, in order of importance. You can then work down your discretionary list until your remaining available cash flow is zero.

Do you know whether your expenses are going up or down? Use a budget to track them.

An important component of your budget is the amount that you allocate to savings. If you put a high priority on saving and you do not use credit to spend beyond your income each month, you will be able to accumulate wealth that can be used to meet your short-term and long-term financial goals. In the bestseller *The Millionaire Next Door,* authors Thomas J. Stanley and William D. Danko point out that most millionaires have achieved financial success through hard work and thriftiness as opposed to luck or inheritance. You cannot achieve your financial goals unless your budget process places a high priority on saving and investing.

Tracking Your Budgeting Success

Businesses regularly identify budget items and track their variance from budget forecasts. People who follow a similar strategy in their personal finances are better able to meet their financial goals as well. If certain budgeted expenses routinely turn out to be under or over your previous estimates, then it is important to either revise the budget estimate or develop a strategy for reducing that expense.

College students commonly have trouble adhering to their budget for food and entertainment expenses. A strategy that works fairly well is to limit yourself to cash payments. At the beginning of the week, withdraw an amount from checking that will cover your weekly budgeted expenses. For the rest of the week, leave your checkbook, ATM card, and debit and credit cards at home. When the cash is gone, don't spend any more. While this is easier said than done, after a couple of weeks, you will learn to cut down on the cash leakage that inevitably occurs without careful cash management.

A debit card looks like a credit card but works like a check. For example, in the Netherlands almost no one writes a check, and everything is paid by debit card, which drafts directly from a checking account. You do not build up your credit rating when using a debit card. Figure D.1 indicates that the use of debit cards is growing rapidly in the United States. On the other hand, credit cards allow you to promise to pay for something at a later date by using preapproved lines of credit granted by a bank or finance company. Credit cards are easy to use and are accepted by most retailers today.

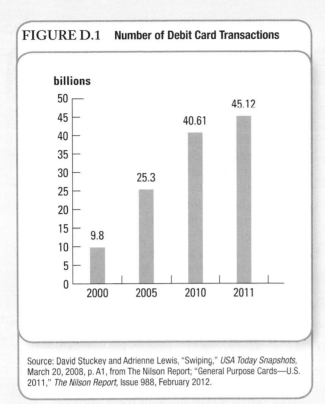

FIGURE D.1   Number of Debit Card Transactions

billions

45.12
40.61
25.3
9.8

2000   2005   2010   2011

Source: David Stuckey and Adrienne Lewis, "Swiping," *USA Today Snapshots,* March 20, 2008, p. A1, from The Nilson Report; "General Purpose Cards—U.S. 2011," *The Nilson Report,* Issue 988, February 2012.

Manage Credit Wisely

One of the cornerstones of your financial plan should be to keep credit usage to a minimum and to work at reducing outstanding debt. The use of credit for consumer and home purchases is well entrenched in our culture and has arguably fueled our economy and enabled Americans to better their standard of living as compared to earlier generations. Nevertheless, credit abuse is a serious problem in this country, and the most recent economic downturn undoubtedly pushed many households over the edge into bankruptcy as a result.

To consider the pros and cons of credit usage, compare the following two scenarios. In the first case, Joel takes an 8 percent fixed-rate mortgage to purchase a house to live in while he is a college student. The mortgage payment is comparable to alternative monthly rental costs, and his house appreciates 20 percent in value over the four years he is in college. At the end of college, Joel will be able to sell his house and reap the return, having invested only a small amount of his own cash. For example,

if he made an initial 5 percent down payment on a $100,000 home that is now worth $120,000 four years later, he has earned $12,800 (after a 6 percent commission to the real estate agent) on an investment of $5,000. This amounts to a sizable return on investment of more than 250 percent over four years. This example is oversimplified in that we did not take into account the principal that has been repaid over the four years, and we did not consider the mortgage payment costs or the tax deductibility of interest paid during that time. However, the point is still clear; borrowing money to buy an asset that appreciates in value by more than the cost of the debt is a terrific way to invest.

In the second case, Nicole uses her credit card to pay for some of her college expenses. Instead of paying off the balance each month, Nicole makes only the minimum payment and incurs 16 percent interest costs. Over the course of several years of college, Nicole's credit card debt is likely to amount to several thousand dollars, typical of college graduates in the United States. The beer and pizza Nicole purchased have long ago been digested, yet the debt remains, and the payments continue. If Nicole continues making minimum payments, it will take many years to pay back that original debt, and in the meantime the interest paid will far exceed the original amount borrowed. Credit card debt in the amount of $1,000 will usually require a minimum payment of at least $15 per month. At this payment level, it will take 166 months (almost 14 years) to pay the debt in full, and the total interest paid will be more than $1,400!

So when is borrowing a good financial strategy? A rule of thumb is that you should borrow only to buy assets that will appreciate in value or when your financing charges are less than what you are earning on the cash that you would otherwise use to make the purchase. This rule generally will limit your borrowing to home purchases and investments.

Use and Abuse of Credit Cards

Credit cards should be used only as a cash flow management tool. If you pay off your balance every month, you avoid financing charges (assuming no annual fee), you have proof of expenditures, which may be necessary for tax or business reasons, and you may be able to better match your cash inflows

Notes

Chapter 1

1. Scott Martin, "How Apple Rewrote the Rules of Retailing," *USA Today,* May 19, 2011, p. 1B; Steve Denning, "Apple's Retail Success Is More Than Magic," *Forbes,* June 17, 2011, **www.forbes.com/sites/stevedenning/2011/06/17/apples-retail-stores-more-than-magic/3/** (accessed August 22, 2011); Jefferson Graham, "At Apple Stores, iPads at Your Service," *USA Today,* May 23, 2011, p. 1B; "Apple Becomes World's Most Valuable Brand, Ending Google's Four-Year Term at the Top, says WPP'S BrandZ," Millward Brown, May 8, 2011, **www.millwardbrown.com/Global/News/PressReleases/PressReleaseDetails/11-05-08/Apple_Becomes_World_s_Most_Valuable_Brand_Ending_Google_s_Four-Year_Term_at_the_Top_says_WPP_S_BrandZ.aspx** (accessed September 20, 2011).

2. Lindsay Blakely, "Erasing the Line Between Marketing and Philanthropy," *CBS News,* April 21, 2011, **www.cbsnews.com/8301-505143_162-40244368/erasing-the-line-between-marketing-and-philanthropy/** (accessed January 17, 2012); "The Best of 2011," Charlotte Street Computers, **http://charlottestreetcomputers.com/the-best-of-2011/** (accessed January 17, 2012).

3. "GMAC® Diversity Initiatives," The Graduate Management Admissions Council, **www.gmac.com/gmac/SchoolServices/Diversity/GMACDiversityInitiatives.htm** (accessed February 22, 2010).

4. David A. Kaplan, "Chipotle's Growth Machine," *CNNMoney,* September 12, 2011, **http://features.blogs.fortune.cnn.com/2011/09/12/chipotles-growth-machine/** (accessed January 25, 2012).

5. Craig Torres and Anthony Field, "Campbell's Quest for Productivity," *Bloomberg Businessweek,* November 2–December 5, 2010, pp. 15–16.

6. Tahman Bradley, "Michelle Obama and Walmart Join Forces Promoting Healthy Food," *ABC News,* January 20, 2011, **http://abcnews.go.com/Politics/WorldNews/michelle-obama-walmart-join-forces-promote-healthy-eating/story?id=12723177** (accessed January 25, 2012).

7. Martinne Geller, "PepsiCo Lineup to Look Healthier in 10 Years: CEO," *Reuters,* October 17, 2011, **www.reuters.com/article/2011/10/17/us-pepsico-ceo-idUSTRE79G4ZO20111017** (accessed January 25, 2012).

8. "Got Milk?" **www.whymilk.com/celeb.php** (accessed February 25, 2010).

9. "About Bill Daniels," **www.danielsfund.org/BillDaniels/index.asp** (accessed February 23, 2010).

10. "Venecuba, A Single Nation," *Economist,* February 13–19, 2010, p. 40. Daniel Wallis and Mario Naranjo, "Obama: Iran and Cuba Ties Don't Benefit Venezuela," *Reuters,* December 19, 2011, **www.reuters.com/article/2011/12/20/us-venezuela-usa-obama-idUSTRE7BJ03J20111220** (accessed January 25, 2012).

11. "Reforms Please Cubans, But Is It Communism?" *Associated Press,* April 2, 2008, **www.msnbc.msn.com/id/23925259** (accessed April 18, 2008).

12. "Special Report: The Visible Hand," *The Economist,* January 21, 2012, pp. 3–5.

13. James T. Areddy and Craig Karmin, "China Stocks Once Frothy, Fall by Half in Six Months," *The Wall Street Journal,* April 16, 2008, pp. 1, 7.

14. "Special Report: The Visible Hand."

15. "Special Report: The World in Their Hands," *The Economist,* January 21, 2012, p. 15–17.

16. "The Shark Tank," *ABC,* **http://abc.go.com/shows/shark-tank/bios** (accessed February 20, 2012).

17. John D. Sutter and Doug Gross, "Apple Unveils the 'Magical' iPad," *CNN Tech,* January 28, 2010, **www.cnn.com/2010/TECH/01/27/apple.tablet/index.html?section=cnn_latest** (accessed February 3, 2010).

18. Felicity Barringer, "U.S. Declines to Protect the Overfished Bluefin Tuna," *The New York Times,* May 27, 2011, **www.nytimes.com/2011/05/28/science/earth/28tuna.html** (accessed June 15, 2011); David Helvarg, "Oil, Terror, Tuna and You," *The Huffington Post,* May 9, 2011, **www.huffingtonpost.com/david-helvarg/oil-terror-tuna-and-you_b_859106.html** (accessed June 15, 2011); "Endangered Species Listing for Atlantic Bluefin Tuna Not Warranted," NOAA, May 27, 2011, **www.noaanews.noaa.gov/stories2011/20110527_bluefintuna.html** (accessed June 18, 2011); David Jolly, "Many Mediterranean Fish Species Threatened With Extinction, Report Says," *The New York Times,* April 19, 2011, **http://green.blogs.nytimes.com/2011/04/19/mediterranean-fish-species-threatened-with-extinction/** (accessed June 18, 2011); "Giant Bluefin Tuna Sells for Record Breaking Price: Big Pic," *Discovery News,* January 5, 2011, **http://news.discovery.com/animals/bluefin-tuna-record-auction-110105.html** (accessed June 18, 2011); "The King of Sushi," *CBS—60 Minutes,* **www.youtube.com/watch?v=dsbx6dQuRhQ** (accessed June 18, 2011).

19. Solid State Technology, "China Patent Filings Could Overtake US, Japan in 2011," *ELECTROIQ,* October 11, 2010, **www.electroiq.com/index/display/semiconductors-article-display/1436725261/articles/solid-state-technology/semiconductors/industry-news/business-news/2010/october/china-patent_filings.html** (accessed January 3, 2011).

20. "Zimbabwe," *CIA—The World Factbook,* **https://www.cia.gov/library/publications/the-world-factbook/geos/zi.html#** (accessed February 3, 2010).

21. The Bureau of the Public Debt, "Monthly Statement of the Public Debt of the United States: December 31, 2011," **www.treasurydirect.gov/govt/reports/pd/mspd/2011/opds122011.pdf**.

22. "C40 Cities Climate Leadership Group," C40 Cities, **http://live.c40cities.org/cities/** (accessed October 17, 2011); "Greening the Concrete Jungle," *The Economist,* September 3, 2011, pp. 29–32; Wendy Koch, "Localities Push Own Bans on Plastic Bags," *USA Today,* October 6, 2010, p. 3A.

23. Haya El Nasser, Gregory Korte, and Paul Overberg, "308.7 million," *USA Today,* December 22, 2010, p. 1A.

24. "Facts about Working Women," *Women Employed,* **www.womenemployed.org/index.php?id=20** (accessed February 23, 2010).

25. Liz Welch, "Wolfgang Puck: From Potato Peeler to Gourmet-Pizza

Tycoon," *Inc.,* October 2009, pp. 87–88; "Restaurants," Wolfgang Puck, **www.wolfgangpuck.com/restaurants** (accessed March 17, 2011); "The Hershey Company," The United States Securities and Exchange Commission Form 10-K, February 18, 2011, **http://phx.corporate-ir.net/phoenix.zhtml?c=115590&p=irol-SECText&TEXT=aHR0cDovL2lyLmludC53ZXN0bGF3YnVzaW5lc3MuY29tL2RvY3V3TZW50L3YxLzAwMDExOTMxMjUtMTEtMDM5Nzg5L3htbtbA%3d%3d** (accessed March 17, 2011).

26. **www.warbyparker.com** (accessed July 31, 2011); Claire Cain Miller, "Defying Conventional Wisdom to Sell Glasses Online," *The New York Times,* January 16, 2011, **www.nytimes.com/2011/01/17/technology/17glasses.html?_r=2** (accessed July 31, 2011).

27. "About the Hershey Company," The Hershey Company, **www.thehersheycompany.com/** (accessed February 15, 2010).

28. "Fortune Global 500," *CNNMoney.com,* **http://money.cnn.com/magazines/fortune/global500/2009/snapshots/2255.html** (accessed February 19, 2010); Anthony Bianco and Wendy Zellner, "Is Wal-Mart Too Powerful?" *BusinessWeek,* October 6, 2003, pp. 100–10; "Wal Mart Stores, Inc. Business Information, Profile, and History," **http://companies.jrank.org/pages/4725/Wal-Mart-Stores-Inc.html** (accessed February 23, 2010); "Investors," Walmart Corporate, **http://investors.walmartstores.com/phoenix.zhtml?c=112761&p=irol-irhome** (accessed January 25, 2012).

29. "Samuel Robson Walton," *Bloomberg,* **http://topics.bloomberg.com/samuel-robson-walton/** (accessed July 19, 2012).

30. "Stopping SOPA," *The Economist,* January 21, 2012, p. 33.

31. "The 2011 World's Most Ethical Companies," *Ethisphere,* 2011, Q1, pp. 37–43.

32. Isabelle Maignon, Tracy L. Gonzalez-Padron, G. Tomas M. Hult, and O.C. Ferrell, "Stakeholder Orientation: Development and Testing of a Framework for Socially Responsible Marketing," *Journal of Strategic Marketing* 19, no. 4 (July 2011), pp. 313–338.

33. Joel Holland, "Save the World, Make a Million," *Entrepreneur,* April 2010, **www.entrepreneur.com/magazine/entrepreneur/2010/april/205556.html** (accessed April 20, 2010); iContact, **www.icontact.com** (accessed April 24, 2010).

34. Kevin Kelleher, "The Rise of Redbox Should Spook Netflix," *CNNMoney,* February 10, 2012, **http://tech.fortune.cnn.com/2012/02/10/the-rise-of-redbox-should-spook-netflix/** (accessed July 24, 2012).

Chapter 2

1. Russell Adams and Joann S. Lublin, "News Corp. Board Challenged," *The Wall Street Journal,* July 26, 2011, p. B4; James Poniewozik, "The Humbling of Rupert Murdoch," *Time,* August 8, 2011, p. 32; Catherine Mayer, "Tabloid Bites Man," *Time,* July 25, 2011, pp. 30–37; "Will the Scandal Tame Murdoch?" *Bloomberg Businessweek,* July 25 July 31, 2011, pp. 18–20; Bruce Orwall and Jeanne Whalen, "Murdoch Testimony Challenged," *The Wall Street Journal,* July 22, 2011, pp. A1, A12; Paul Sonne, Jeanne Whalen, and Bruce Orwall, "New Issues Emerge for News Corp. in Britain," *The Wall Street Journal,* August 17, 2011, pp. A1, A2; Dan Sabbagh and Mark Sweney, "James Murdoch: I didn't read crucial phone-hacking email," *The Guardian,* December 13, 2011, **www.guardian.co.uk/media/2011/dec/13/james-murdoch-phone-hacking-email** (accessed February 15, 2012); Robert Hutton, "News Corp. Hacking Report Delayed Amid Debate Over James Murdoch," *Bloomberg Businessweek,* February 15, 2012, **www.businessweek.com/news/2012-02-15/news-corp-hacking-report-delayed-amid-debate-over-james-murdoch.html** (accessed February 15, 2012); Andrew Edgecliffe, "News Corp Panel Suspects 'Serious Criminality,'" *Financial Times,* February 15, 2012, **www.ft.com/cms/s/0/4ff68b1e-57ee-11e1-ae89-00144feabdc0.html** (accessed February 15, 2012).

2. Gwen Moran, "Two-Wheeled Philanthropy," *Entrepreneur,* October 2010, p. 76; Angie Jackson, "Injury Puts the Brakes on Downtown Bike Clinic," *Colorado Springs Gazette,* June 5, 2011, **www.gazette.com/articles/mechanic-119291-clinic-peter.html** (accessed June 21, 2011); "Bike Clinic Too," Facebook, **www.facebook.com/bikeclinictoo?sk=info#!/bikeclinictoo?sk=wall** (accessed October 11, 2011).

3. Kimberly Blanton, "Creating a Culture of Compliance," *CFO,* July/August 2011, pp. 19–21.

4. Mandi Woodruff, "The DOJ Recovered a Record-Breaking $4 Billion in Medicare Fraud Last Year," *Business Insider,* February 15, 2012, **www.businessinsider.com/the-doj-just-recovered-a-record-shattering-41-billion-in-medicare-fraud-2012-2** (accessed February 15, 2012).

5. Ronald Alsop, "Corporate Scandals Hit Home," *The Wall Street Journal,* February 19, 2004, **www.driversofloyalty.com/services/pubs/The_Wall_Street_Journal_CorporateScandalsHitHome_2004.pdf** (accessed February 5, 2010).

6. Ruth Simon and Victoria McGrane, "Wells Penalty: $85 Million," *The Wall Street Journal,* July 21, 2011, p. C3.

7. Nick Timiraos and Ruth Simon, "Settlement Lifts Hopes for Housing Recovery," *The Wall Street Journal,* February 10, 2012, pp. A1–A2.

8. O. C. Ferrell, John Fraedrich, and Linda Ferrell, *Business Ethics: Ethical Decision Making and Cases,* 8th ed. (Mason, OH: South-Western Cengage Learning, 2011), p. 7.

9. David Callahan, as quoted in Archie Carroll, "Carroll: Do We Live in a Cheating Culture?" *Athens Banner-Herald,* February 21, 2004, **www.onlineathens.com/stores/022204/bus_20040222028.shtml** (accessed February 25, 2010).

10. Liz Rappaport, "Goldman Cuts Blankfein's Bonus," *The Wall Street Journal,* February 5, 2012, pp. B1–B2.

11. Joe Barrett, "Blagojevich Gets 14-Year Term," *The Wall Street Journal,* December 18, 2011, p. A5.

12. Hannah Karp, "Ohio State's No Win Season," *The Wall Street Journal,* July 9–July 10, 2011, p. A3.

13. Ferrell, Fraedrich, and Ferrell, *Business Ethics.*

14. Kimberley Blanton, "Creating a Culture of Compliance," *CFO,* July/August 2011, pp. 19–21.

15. Ethics Resource Center, *2011 National Business Ethics Survey®: Ethics in Transition* (Arlington, VA: Ethics Resource Center, 2012).

16. Bobby White, "The New Workplace Rules: No Video Watching," *The New York Times,* March 3, 2008, p. B1.

17. Laura Petrecca, "Bullying in Workplace Is Common, Hard to Fix," *USA Today,* December 28, 2010, pp. 1B–2B.

18. Peter Lattman, "Boeing's Top Lawyer Spotlights Company's Ethical Lapses," *The Wall Street Journal,* Law Blog, January 30, 2006, **http://blogs.wsj.com/law/2006/01/31/boeings-top-lawyer-rips-into-his-company/tab/article/** (accessed February 25, 2010).

19. Stephen J. Dunn, "Lawyer Charged with Tax Evasion for Paying Personal Expenses from Firm," *Forbes,* July 28, 2011, **www.forbes.com/sites/ stephendunn/2011/07/28/lawyer- charged-with-tax-evasion-for-paying- personal-expenses-from-firm/** (accessed February 15, 2012).

20. "Proper Use of Company, Customer, and Supplier Resources," Boeing, November 19, 2009, **www.boeing.com/ companyoffices/aboutus/ethics/pro10 .pdf** (accessed January 28, 2010).

21. Barbara Kiviat, "A Bolder Approach to Credit-Agency Rating Reform," *Time,* September 18, 2009, **http://curiouscapitalist.blogs.time. com/2009/09/18/a-bolder-approach-to- credit-rating-agency-reform/** (accessed January 28, 2010).

22. Reuters, "Rajat Gupta's Lawyer: Government 'Wildly Expanding' Case Against Ex-Goldman Director," *Huffington Post,* February 7, 2010, **www. huffingtonpost.com/2012/02/07/ rajat-gupta_n_1261313.html** (accessed February 15, 2012).

23. Robert Pear, "Senate Approves Ban on Insider Trading by Congress," *The New York Times,* February 2, 2012, **www.nytimes. com/2012/02/03/us/politics/senate- approves-ban-on-insider-trading-by- congress.html** (accessed February 15, 2012).

24. "Corruption Perceptions Index 2009," Transparency International, **www.transparency.org/policy_research/ surveys_indices/cpi/2009/cpi_2009_ table** (accessed January 22, 2010).

25. "Employee Theft: The Largest Source of Shrink in North America," *PI Newswire,* October 18, 2011, **www. pinewswire.net/article/employee- theftthe-largest-source-of-shrink-in- north-america/**.

26. Nathalie Tadena, "Pool Agrees to Settle FTC Charges of Anticompetitive Tactics," *The Wall Street Journal,* November 21, 2011, **http://online.wsj .com/article/BT-CO-20111121-709935 .html** (accessed January 26, 2012).

27. Ibid.

28. Abby Goodnough, "F.D.A. Issues Warning Over Alcoholic Energy Drinks," *The New York Times,* November 17, 2010, **www.nytimes.com/2010/11/18/ us/18drinks.html** (accessed January 26, 2012); "Setting the Record Straight About Four Loko," Phusion Projects, **www. phusionprojects.com/factvsfiction.html** (accessed January 26, 2012).

29. Josephson Institute Center for Youth Ethics, "The Ethics of American Youth: 2010," February 10, 2011, **http:// charactercounts.org/programs/ reportcard/2010/installment02_ report-card_honesty-integrity.html** (accessed January 17, 2012); Sophie Terbush, "Survey: Cheating, Lying Widespread among High School Students," **http://yourlife.usatoday. com/parenting-family/teen-ya/ story/2011/02/Survey-Cheating-lying- widespread-among-high-school- students/43627926/1** (accessed January 26, 2012).

30. Greg Toppo, "Atlanta Public School Exams Fudged," *USA Today,* July 7, 2011, p. 3A; Greg Toppo, "Feds Seek Help to Stop Teacher Cheats," *USA Today,* January 20, 2012, p. 3A.

31. David Voreacos, Alex Nussbaum and Greg Farrell, "Johnson & Johnson's Quality Catastrophe," *Bloomberg Businessweek,* March 31, 2011, **www.businessweek.com/magazine/ content/11_15/b4223064555570.htm** (accessed January 26, 2012).

32. "Campaign Warns about Drugs from Canada," *CNN,* February 5, 2004, **www. cnn.com;** Gardiner Harris and Monica Davey, "FDA Begins Push to End Drug Imports," *The New York Times,* January 23, 2004, p. C1.

33. Lara Salahi, "FDA Appeals Block on Cigarette Warning Label," *ABC News,* November 30, 2011, **http://abcnews .go.com/Health/Wellness/fda-appeals- block-cigarette-warning-labels/ story?id=15059707** (accessed January 26, 2012).

34. Ethics Resource Center, *2005 National Business Ethics Survey* (Washington, DC: Ethics Resource Center, 2005), p. 43.

35. Thomas M. Jones, "Ethical Decision Making by Individuals in Organizations: An Issue-Contingent Model," *Academy of Management Review* 2 (April 1991), pp. 371–73.

36. Sir Adrian Cadbury, "Ethical Managers Make Their Own Rules," *Harvard Business Review* 65 (September– October 1987), p. 72.

37. Robert Sutton, "How a Few Bad Apples Ruin Everything," *The Wall Street Journal,* October 24, 2011, p. R5; Isiah Carey, "Corporate Bullying Affects 1 in 3: Stats," Fox News Houston, November 18, 2010, **www. myfoxdetroit.com/dpp/news/national/ corporate-bullying-affects-1-in- 3-stats-20101118-wpms** (accessed February 11, 2011); Dale A. Reigle, "Workplace Bad Apples," American Academy of Orthopedic Surgeons, **www.aaos.org/news/aaosnow/nov10/ managing4.asp** (accessed October 26, 2011); University of Washington, "Rotten to the Core: How Workplace 'Bad Apples' Spoil Barrels of Good Employees," *ScienceDaily,* February 12, 2007, **www.sciencedaily.com/ releases/2007/02/070212113250.htm** (accessed October 26, 2011).

38. Ferrell, Fraedrich, and Ferrell, *Business Ethics,* pp. 174–75.

39. Ethics Resource Center, *2009 National Business Ethics Survey* (Washington, DC: Ethics Resource Center, 2009), p. 41.

40. "The 2010 World's Most Ethical Companies—Company Profile: Granite Construction," *Ethisphere,* Q1, p. 33.

41. Ethics Resource Center, *2011 National Business Ethics Survey*®, p. 23.

42. Skadden, Arps, Slate, Meagher & Flom LLP & Affiliates, *The Dodd Frank Act: Commentary and Insights,* July 12, 2010, **www.skadden.com/Cimages/siteFile/ Skadden_Insights_Special_Edition_ Dodd-Frank_Act1.pdf** (accessed January 7, 2011); Ethics Resource Center, *2011 National Business Ethics Survey*®, p. 43.

43. Ferrell, Fraedrich, and Ferrell, *Business Ethics,* p. 13.

44. "Trust in the Workplace: 2010 Ethics & Workplace Survey." Deloitte LLP (n.d.), **www.deloitte.com/assets/ Dcom-UnitedStates/Local%20Assets/ Documents/us_2010_Ethics_and_ Workplace_Survey_report_071910.pdf** (accessed July 19, 2012).

45. Archie B. Carroll, "The Pyramid of Corporate Social Responsibility: Toward the Moral Management of Organizational Stakeholders," *Business Horizons* 34 (July/ August 1991), p. 42.

46. Bryan Walsh, "Why Green Is the New Red, White and Blue," *Time,* April 28, 2008, p. 46.

47. Adam Shriver, "Not Grass-Fed, But at Least Pain-Free," *The New York Times,* February 18, 2010, **www.nytimes .com/2010/02/19/opinion/19shriver .html?scp=4&sq=animal%20rights&st = cse** (accessed February 25, 2010).

48. "ASES Green Collar Jobs Report Forecasts 37 Million Jobs from Renewable Energy and Energy Efficiency in U.S. by 2030," American Solar Energy Society, **www.ases.org/index. php?option=com_content&view=article**

&id=465&Itemid=58 (accessed January 26, 2012).

49. Alan Beattie, "Countries Rush to Restrict Trade in Basic Foods," *Financial Times,* April 2, 2008, p. 1.

50. Bill Roth, "Marketing Opportunity: Consumers Want Green and Health Explanations From Companies On Their Brand Claims," Earth 2017, **www.earth2017.com/best-practices/ marketing-opportunity-consumers-want-green-and-health-explanations-from-companies-on-their-brand-claims/** (accessed January 26, 2012).

51. "2010 World's Most Ethical Companies," *Ethisphere,* **http:// ethisphere.com/wme2010/** (accessed March 17, 2011).

52. Indra Nooyi, "The Responsible Company," *The Economist, The World in 2008 Special Edition,* March 2008, p. 132.

53. Ferrell, Fraedrich, and Ferrell, *Business Ethics,* pp. 13–19.

54. Matthew Dolan, "Ford to Begin Hiring at New Wages," *The New York Times,* January 26, 2010, **http://online .wsj.com/article/SB100014240527487 04762904575025420550494324.html** (accessed January 28, 2010).

55. Ann Zimmerman, "U.S. Charges Bass Pro Shops With Racial Bias," *The Wall Street Journal,* September 22, 2011, **http://online.wsj.com/article/SB100014 24053111904563904576585090889465 336.html** (accessed January 26, 2012).

56. Amy Schatz, "Phone-Bill 'Cramming' Takes a Toll, Study Finds," *The Wall Street Journal,* July 14, 2011, **http://online.wsj.com/article/SB100014 24052702304911104576443863004059 774.html** (accessed January 26, 2012).

57. Todd Littman, "Win-Win Emissions Reductions Strategies," Victoria Transport Policy Institute, **www.vtpi.org/wwclimate .pdf** (accessed February 25, 2010).

58. Lauren Etter, "Earth Day: 36 Years on, Plenty of Concerns Remain," *The Wall Street Journal,* April 22–23, 2006, p. A7.

59. Cornelia Dean, "Drugs Are in the Water, Does It Matter?" *The New York Times,* April 3, 2007, HEALTH, **www.nytimes.com/2007/04/03/ science/earth/03water.html?_r=1&sc p=55&sq=%22cornelia+dean%22&st =nyt&oref=slogin** (accessed February 25, 2010).

60. Bryan Walsh, "The Gas Dilemma," *Time,* April 11, 2011, pp. 40–48; Jim Efstathiou Jr. and Kim Chipman, "The Great Shale Gas Rush," *Bloomberg*

Businessweek, March 7–13, 2011, pp. 25–28; Tara Patel, "The French Say No to 'Le Fracking,'" *Bloomberg Businessweek,* April 4–10, 2011, pp. 60–62; "The Natural Gas and Fracking Controversy," *On Point Radio,* Host: Tom Ashbrook, June 10, 2011, **http://onpoint.wbur. org/2011/06/10/fracking** (accessed June 20, 2011).

61. "Amazon Rainforest Deforestation at Lowest in 23 Years, Brazil Government Says," *Reuters,* December 5, 2011, **www. huffingtonpost.com/2011/12/06/brazil-amazon-rainforest-deforestation-levels_n_1130554.html** (accessed January 26, 2012).

62. Kitt Doucette, "The Plastic Bag Wars," *Rolling Stone,* July 25, 2011, **www. rollingstone.com/politics/news/the-plastic-bag-wars-20110725** (accessed January 26, 2012).

63. "Whole Foods to Sack Disposable Plastic Grocery Bags," January 22, 2008, **www.wholefoodsmarket.com/cgi-bim/ print10pt.cgi?url=/pressroom/pr_01-22-08.html** (accessed February 25, 2010).

64. Josh Glasser, "T. Boone Pickens on Natural Gas: You Can't Beat it," *Fortune,* July 14, 2009, **http://bigtech.blogs .fortune.cnn.com/2009/07/14/news/ economy/pickens_natural_gas.fortun e/?postversion=2009071415** (accessed January 28, 2010). Brian Merchant, "The US Imports $1.5 Billion Barrels of Oil a Year from 'Dangerous or Unstable' Nations," Treehugger.com, January 14, 2010, **www.treehugger.com/ files/2010/01/us-imports-1-5-billion-barrels-oil-year-dangerous-unstable-nations.php** (accessed January 7, 2011); "US Spent Over $30 Billion for Foreign Oil in April," BusinessWire, May 17, 2010, **www.businesswire.com/news/ home/20100517006122/en/U.S.-Spent-30-Billion-Foreign-Oil-April** (accessed January 7, 2011).

65. "Energy Subsidies Stymie Wind, Solar Innovation," *Bloomberg,* November 27, 2011, **www.bloomberg.com/ news/2011-11-27/energy-subsidies-stymie-wind-solar-innovation-nathan-myhrvold.html** (accessed February 15, 2012); Michael Scherer, "The Solyndra Syndrome," *Time,* October 10, 2011, pp. 42–45.

66. "Wal-Mart's Motive Is No secret: Going Green Saves It Money," *Los Angeles Times,* June 4, 2011, **http://articles .latimes.com/2011/jun/04/business/ la-fi-walmart-green-20110604** (accessed January 26, 2012).

67. Jim Rogers, "Point of View: A New Model for Energy Efficiency," *The News & Observer,* February 19, 2008, **www. newsobserver.com/print/tuesday/ opinion/story/951188.html** (accessed February 25, 2010).

68. "GreenChoice: The #1 Green Power Program in America," Austin Energy (n.d.), **www.austinenergy.com/ Energy%20Efficiency/Programs/ Green%20Choice/index.htm** (accessed February 25, 2010).

69. "Certification," Home Depot, **www. homedepot.com/HDUS/EN_US/ corporate/corp_respon/certification. shtml** (accessed February 25, 2010).

70. Chiquita, Bananalink, **www.banana link.org.uk/content/view/62/22/lang,en/** (accessed February 25, 2010).

71. Mark Calvey, "Profile: Safeway's Grants Reflect Its People," *San Francisco Business Times,* July 14, 2003, **http://sanfrancisco.bizjournals.com/ sanfrancisco/stories/2003/07/14/focus9 .html** (accessed February 25, 2010).

72. "Environmentalism: What We Do," Patagonia, **www.patagonia.com/us/ patagonia.go?assetid=1960** (accessed January 17, 2012).

73. Mokoto Rich, "Job Gains Reflect Hope a Recovery Is Blooming," *The New York Times,* February 3, 2012, **www.nytimes. com/2012/02/04/business/economy/ us-economy-added-243000-jobs-in-january-unemployment-rate-is-8-3.html** (accessed February 15, 2012).

74. "Occupy Wall Street," Case written for the Daniels Fund Ethics Initiative, **http://danielsethics.mgt.unm.edu/pdf/ Occupy%20Wall%20Street%20DI.pdf** (accessed February 15, 2012).

75. James R. Hagerty, "Caterpillar Closes Plant In Canada After Lockout," *The Wall Street Journal,* February 4–5, 2012, p. B1.

76. Peter Cappelli, "Why Companies Aren't Getting the Employees They Need," *The Wall Street Journal,* October 24, 2011, pp. R1, R6.

77. Christie Garton, "Corporations Add Their Know-How to Charitable Efforts," *USA Today,* July 25, 2011, **https:// redcard.target.com/redcard/rc_main. jsp** (accessed January 17, 2012); REDcard, **https://redcard.target.com/redcard/ rc_main.jsp** (accessed January 17, 2012).

78. "100 Best Companies to Work For," *CNNMoney,* **http://money.cnn.com/ magazines/fortune/bestcompanies/ 2011/snapshots/2.html** (accessed February 15, 2012).

79. "Who Really Pays for CSR Initiatives," *Environmental Leader,* February 15, 2008, **www.environmentalleader.com/2008/02/15/who-really-pays-for-csr-initiatives/** (accessed February 25, 2010); "Global Fund," **www.joinred.com/globalfund** (accessed February 25, 2010); Reena Jana, "The Business of Going Green," *Business-Week Online,* June 22, 2007, **www.businessweek.com/innovate/content/jun2007/id20070622_491833.htm?chan=search** (accessed June 19, 2008).

80. Permission granted by the author of *Gray Matters,* George Sammet Jr., Vice President, Office of Corporate Ethics, Lockheed Martin Corporation, Orlando, Florida, to use these portions of *Gray Matters: The Ethics Game* © 1992. If you would like more information about the complete game, call 1-800-3ETHICS.

81. Edelman, *Edelman Trust Barometer,* 2012, **http://trust.edelman.com/trust-download/global-results/** (accessed July 26, 2012); "Occupying the Future: Benefit Corporations Now Opening Shop in NY, Six Other States," *Daily Kos,* December 14, 2011, **www.dailykos.com/story/2011/12/14/1043152/-Occupying-the-Future-Benefit-Corporations-now-opening-shop-in-NY-six-other-states** (accessed July 26, 2012); Jessica Silver-Greenberg, Tara Kalwarski, and Alexis Leondis, "CEO Pay Drops, But . . . Cash Is King," *Bloomberg Businessweek,* April 5, 2010, pp. 50–56; "The Dynamics of Public Trust in Business—Emerging Opportunities for Leaders," Business Roundtable Institute for Corporate Ethics, **www.corporate-ethics.org/pdf/public_trust_in_business.pdf/** (accessed July 26, 2012).

82. M. P. McQueen, "Agency Misses Chance to Curb Lead in Jewelry," *The Wall Street Journal,* February 12, 2008, p. D1.

83. "2ND UPDATE: AT&T Hit By IPhone Costs, T-Mobile Breakup Fee," *The Wall Street Journal,* January 26, 2012, **http://online.wsj.com/article/BT-CO-20120126-713581.html** (accessed January 26, 2012).

84. Drake Bennett and Carter Dougherty, "Elizabeth Warren's Dream Becomes a Real Agency She May Never Get to Lead," *Bloomberg Businessweek,* July 11–July 17, 2011, pp. 58–64.

85. Maureen Dorney, "Congress Passes Federal Anti-Spam Law: Preempts Most State Anti-Spam Laws," *DLA Piper,* December 3, 2003, **http://franchiseagreements.com/global/publications/detail.aspx?pub=622** (accessed February 25, 2010).

86. Elizabeth Alterman, "As Kids Go Online, Identity Theft Claims More Victims," *CNBC,* October 10, 2011, **www.cnbc.com/id/44583556/As_Kids_Go_Online_Identity_Theft_Claims_More_Victims** (accessed January 26, 2012).

87. Joelle Tessler, "Disney's Playdom to Pay $3M to Settle Kids Privacy Case," *The Wall Street Journal,* May 13, 2011, p. 3B.

88. Jean Eaglesham and Ashby Jones, "Whistle-blower Bounties Pose Challenges," *The Wall Street Journal,* December 13, 2010, pp. C1, C3.

89. "Durbin Statement on His Debit Card Swipe Fee Amendment," United States Senator Dick Durbin, May 13, 2010, **http://durbin.senate.gov/showRelease.cfm?releaseId=324958** (accessed February 22, 2011).

90. "Office of Financial Research," U.S. Department of Treasury, **www.treasury.gov/initiatives/Pages/ofr.aspx** (accessed February 22, 2011); "Initiatives: Financial Stability Oversight Council," U.S. Department of Treasury, **www.treasury.gov/initiatives/Pages/FSOC-index.aspx** (accessed February 22, 2011).

Chapter 3

1. Bruce Horovitz, "Consumer Products Giant Looks beyond U.S. Borders," *USA Today,* March 18, 2010, pp. B1–B2; Jon Newberry, "Aisles of Opportunity," *portfolio.com,* April 7, 2010, **www.portfolio.com/companies-executives/2010/04/07/proctor-and-gamble-is-aiming-to-expand-its-marketshare-in-india** (accessed June 12, 2010); Dyan Machan, "Q&A: Procter & Gamble CEO Bob McDonald," *SmartMoney,* May 26, 2010, **www.smartmoney.com/investing/stocks/interview-with-procter-gamble-ceo-bob-mcdonald** (accessed June 12, 2010); Anjali Cordeiro, "P&G Targets India for Expansion Push," *The Wall Street Journal,* June 23, 2010, **http://online.wsj.com/article/NA_WSJ_PUB:SB20001424052748704123604575322751934618996.html** (accessed August 16, 2010); Lauren Coleman-Lochner, "Why Procter & Gamble Needs to Shave More Indians," *Bloomberg Businessweek,* June 9, 2011, **www.businessweek.com/magazine/content/11_25/b4233021703857.htm** (accessed June 15, 2011).

2. Tim Kelly, "Squash the Caterpillar," *Forbes,* April 21, 2008, p. 136.

3. Julie Jargon, "Subway Runs Past McDonald's Chain," *The Wall Street Journal,* March 9, 2011, B4; Subway, **http://world.subway.com/Countries/frmMainPage.aspx?CC=CAN** (accessed January 25, 2012).

4. Starbucks Coffee International, **www.starbucks.com/business/international-stores** (accessed January 20, 2012).

5. Elisabeth Sullivan, "Choose Your Words Wisely," *Marketing News,* February 15, 2008, p. 22.

6. Ellen Byron, "P&G Turns Febreze Into a $1 Billion Brand," *The Wall Street Journal,* March 8, 2011, **http://online.wsj.com/article/SB10001424052748704076804576180683371307932.html** (accessed March 10, 2011).

7. Sullivan, "Choose Your Words Wisely."

8. Michelle Yun and Kathy Chu, "Philippines May Answer Call," *USA Today,* January 10, 2011, 1B–2B.

9. "Annual Trade Highlights," U.S. Bureau of the Census, **www.census.gov/foreigntrade/statistics/highlights/annual.html** (accessed July 19, 2012).

10. Roberts and Rocks, "China: Let a Thousand Brands Bloom."

11. Joseph O'Reilly, "Global Logistics: In China, Bigger Bull's-eye Better," *Inbound Logistics,* April 2008, p. 26.

12. "Annual Trade Highlights," U.S. Bureau of the Census, **www.census.gov/foreigntrade/statistics/highlights/annual.html** (accessed July 19, 2012).

13. U.S. Bureau of the Census, Foreign Trade Division, *U.S. Trade in Goods and Services—Balance of Payments (BOP) Basis,* February 10, 2012, **www.census.gov/foreign-trade/statistics/historical/gands.pdf** (accessed February 27, 2012).

14. U.S. Bureau of the Census, "Trade in Goods with China," **www.census.gov/foreign-trade/balance/c5700.html** (accessed February 27, 2012).

15. Keith Bradsher, "G.M. Plans to Develop Electric Cars With China," *The New York Times,* September 20, 2011, **www.nytimes.com/2011/09/21/business/global/gm-plans-to-develop-electric-cars-with-chinese-automaker.html** (accessed December 2, 2011).

16. Calum MacLeod, "Pollution Fogs China's Future," *USA Today,* September 13, 2011, 6A; Keith Bradsher, "China Fears Consumer Impact on Global Warming," July 4, 2010, **www.nytimes.com/2010/07/05/business/global/05warm.html?pagewanted=all** (accessed October 6, 2011); "China Leading Global Race to Make Clean Energy," *The New York Times,* January 30, 2010, **www.nytimes.com/2010/01/31/**

business/energy-environment/31renew.html (accessed October 6, 2011); Michael Scherer, "The Solyndra Syndrome," *Time,* October 10, 2011, 42–45; "Taxing Times Ahead," *The Economist,* October 29, 2011, 77.

17. Amol Sharma and Prasanta Sahu, *The Wall Street Journal,* January 11, 2012, **http://online.wsj.com/article/SB10001424052970204257504577152342214405180.html** (accessed January 27, 2012); Indranil Bose, Shilpi Banerjee, Edo de Vries Robbe, "Wal-Mart and Bharti: Transforming Retail in India," *Harvard Business Review,* August 27, 2009, **http://hbr.org/product/wal-mart-and-bharti-transforming-retail-in-india/an/HKU845-PDF-ENG** (accessed January 27, 2012).

18. O'Reilly, "Global Logistics: New Tax Treaty Raises U.S. Stakes in Belgium's Lowlands," p. 24.

19. "The Restricted Zone in Mexico," Penner & Associates— Mexico Law Firm and Business Consulting for Mexico, **www.mexicolaw.com/LawInfo17.htm** (accessed January 10, 2011).

20. "Sixth Annual BSA and IDC Global Software Piracy Study," Business Software Alliance, May 2009, **http://global.bsa.org/globalpiracy2008/index.html** (accessed February 20, 2010).

21. "USA: President Obama Should Take the Lead on Lifting Embargo against Cuba," Amnesty International, September 2, 2009, **www.amnesty.org/en/for-media/press-releases/usa-president-obama-should-take-lead-lifting-embargo-against-cuba-200909** (accessed March 15, 2010); Kitty Bean Yancey, "Back to Cuba: 'People-to-People Trips' Get the Green Light," *USA Today,* August 4, 2011, 4A.

22. Kitty Bean Yancey and Laura Bly, "Door May Be Inching Open for Tourism," *USA Today,* February 20, 2008, p. A5; Sue Kirchhoff and Chris Woodyard, "Cuba Trade Gets 'New Opportunity,'" *USA Today,* February 20, 2008, p. B1.

23. Aaron Back, "China, South Korea Comment on U.S. Anti-Dumping Probes," *The Wall Street Journal,* January 21, 2011, **http://online.wsj.com/article/SB10001424052970204301404577174501137863634.html**.

24. Julie Bennett, "Product Pitfalls Proliferate in Global Cultural Maze," *The Wall Street Journal,* May 14, 2001, p. B11.

25. Ann Blackman Moscow, Moscow's Big Mac Attack, *Time,* February 5, 1990, **www.time.com/time/magazine/article/0,9171,969321,00.html** (accessed March 8, 2010.

26. Slogans Gone Bad, Joe-ks, **www.joe-ks.com/archives_apr2004/slogans_gone_bad.htm** (accessed March 3, 2010).

27. David Ricks, *Blunders in International Business,* 4th ed. (Malden, MA: Blackwell Publishing, 2006), p. 70. Downloaded from Google Books, **http://books.google.com/books?id=S4L3ntwgs-8C&pg=PA68&lpg=PA68&dq=Mountain+Bell+company,+Saudi+advertisement&source=bl&ots=9apNX6s3hy&sig=Z5BEVaLe42p39kNYMlBd5sOX-GA&hl=en&ei= XJGFS6rfNpPKsAODk5zEDw&sa=X&oi=book_result&ct=result&resnum=5&ved=0CBcQ6AEwBA#v=onepage&q=airline&f=false** (accessed February 24, 2010).

28. J. Bonasia, "For Web, Global Reach Is Beauty—and Challenge," *Investor's Business Daily,* June 13, 2001, p. A6.

29. Matthew Wilkins, "Dell Retakes Second Rank in Global PC Market as Acer Stumbles," *iSuppli,* September 2, 2010, **www.isuppli.com/Home-and-Consumer-Electronics/News/Pages/Dell-Retakes-Second-Rank-in-Global-PC-Market-as-Acer-Stumbles.aspx** (accessed January 10, 2011).

30. "Our Approach, Sanergy, **http://saner.gy/ourapproach/** (accessed October 20, 2011); Patrick Clark, "Innovator: Cleaning Up," *Bloomberg Businessweek,* October 12, 2011, **www.businessweek.com/magazine/cleaning-up-david-auerbachs-sanergy-10132011.html** (accessed October 20, 2011); Jennifer Chu, "Waste-Conversion Startup Sanergy Bowls over Competition," *MIT News,* May 12, 2011, **http://web.mit.edu/newsoffice/2011/100k-competition-0512.html** (accessed October 20, 2011).

31. "What Is the WTO," World Trade Organization (n.d.), **www.wto.org/english/thewto_e/whatis_e/whatis_e.htm** (accessed March 3, 2010).

32. Matthew Dalton, "Beijing Sparks Ire of WTO over Curbs," *The Wall Street Journal,* July 6, 2011, A9.

33. The CIA, *The World Fact Book,* **www.cia.gov/library/publications/the-world-factbook/rankorder/rankorderguide.html** (accessed January 20, 2012).

34. "Trade in Goods (Imports, Exports and Trade Balance) with Canada," U.S. Bureau of the Census, **www.census.gov/foreign-trade/balance/c1220.html** (accessed February 24, 2010); "North America: Canada," *CIA—World Factbook,* **https://www.cia.gov/library/publications/the-world-factbook/geos/ca.html** (accessed February 24, 2010).

35. "America's Biggest Partners," *CNBC.com,* **www.cnbc.com/id/31064179?slide=11** (accessed February 24, 2010).

36. The CIA, *The World Fact Book,* **https://www.cia.gov/library/publications/the-world-factbook/rankorder/rankorderguide.html** (accessed January 20, 2012).

37. "Trade in Goods with Mexico," U.S. Bureau of the Census: Foreign Trade, **www.census.gov/foreign-trade/balance/c2010.html** (accessed January 23, 2012).

38. "Country Comparison: GDP (purchasing power parity)," *CIA—World Factbook,* **https://www.cia.gov/library/publications/the-world-factbook/rankorder/2001rank.html?countryName=United%20States&countryCode=us&regionCode=na&rank=2#us** (accessed February 3, 2010).

39. "A Tale of Two Mexicos: North and South," *The Economist,* April 26, 2008, pp. 53–54.

40. Josh Mitchell, "U.S. Jump-Starts Bid to End Truck Dispute with Mexico," *The Wall Street Journal,* January 7, 2011, **http://online.wsj.com/article/SB10001424052748704415104576065924125822128.html** (accessed January 10, 2011); Elizabeth Williamson, "U.S., Mexico Agree to Settle Truck Feud," *The Wall Street Journal,* March 4, 2011, **http://online.wsj.com/article/SB10001424052748703300904576178511087875924.html** (accessed March 18, 2011).

41. Geri Smith and Cristina Lindblad, "Mexico: Was NAFTA Worth It?" *BusinessWeek,* December 23, 2003, **www.businessweek.com/magazine/content/03_51/b3863008.htm** (accessed May 5, 2010).

42. Pete Engardio and Geri Smith, "Business Is Standing Its Ground," *BusinessWeek,* April 20, 2009, p. 34–39.

43. "Europe in 12 Lessons," **http://europa.eu/abc/12lessons/lesson_2/index_en.htm** (accessed March 3, 2010).

44. Herman Van Rompuy, "Europe in the New Global Game," *The Economist: The World in 2011 Special Edition,* 97; "European countries," *Europa,* **http://europa.eu/abc/european_countries/candidate_countries/index_en.htm** (accessed March 18, 2011).

45. Stanley Reed, with Ariane Sains, David Fairlamb, and Carol Matlack, "The Euro: How Damaging a Hit?" *BusinessWeek,* September 29, 2003, p. 63; "The Single Currency," *CNN* (n.d.), **www.cnn.com/SPECIALS/2000/ eurounion/story/currency/** (accessed July 3, 2001).

46. Stephen Fidler and Jacob Bunge, "NYSE Deal Nears Collapse," *The Wall Street Journal,* January 11, 2012, A1, A9.

47. Abigail Moses, "Greek Contagion Concern Spurs European Sovereign Default Risk to Record," *Bloomberg,* April 26, 2010, **www.bloomberg.com/ news/2010-04-26/greek-contagion- concern-spurs-european-sovereign- default-risk-to-record.html** (accessed March 18, 2011).

48. James G. Neuger and Joe Brennan, "Ireland Weighs Aid as EU Spars over Debt-Crisis Remedy," *Bloomberg,* **www. bloomberg.com/news/2010-11-16/ ireland-discusses-financial-bailout-as- eu-struggles-to-defuse-debt-crisis.html** (accessed March 18, 2011).

49. Charles Forelle and Marcus Walker, "Dithering at the Top Turned EU Crisis to Global Threat," *The Wall Street Journal,* December 29, 2011 A1; Jeff Cox, "US, Europe Face More Ratings Cuts in Coming Years," *CNBC,* January 20, 2012, **www. cnbc.com/id/46072354?__source=go ogle%7Ceditorspicks%7C&par=goo gle** (accessed January 20, 2012); Charles Forelle, "Greece Defaults and Tries to Move On," *The Wall Street Journal,* March 10, 2012, **http://online.wsj.com/article/ SB10 00142405297020460300457727054262 50 35960.html** (accessed July 19, 2012).

50. David Gauthier-Villars, "Europe Hit by Downgrades," *The Wall Street Journal,* January 14, 2012, **http://online.wsj.com/ article/SB10001424052970204542404 577158561838264378.html** (accessed February 1, 2012).

51. "Powerhouse Deutschland," *Bloomberg Businessweek,* January 3, 2011, 93; Alan S. Blinder, "The Euro Zone's German Crisis," *The Wall Street Journal,* **http://online.wsj.com/article/SB100014 24052970203430404577709431370719 07 08.html** (accessed January 20, 2012).

52. Gauthier-Villars, "Europe Hit by Downgrades."

53. "About APEC," Asia-Pacific Economic Cooperation, **www.apec.org/apec/about_ apec.html** (accessed February 25, 2010).

54. Lauren Pollock, "Starbucks Adds Division Focused on Asia," *The Wall Street Journal,* July 11, 2011, **http:// online.wsj.com/article/SB100014240 5270230367870457644029271248 16 .html** (accessed July 15, 2011); Matt Hodges, "Schultz Brews Up Major Push in China," *China Daily,* June 10–11, 2011, 5; "Starbucks Company Profile," **http://assets.starbucks.com/assets/ aboutuscompanyprofileq12011 final13111.pdf** (accessed July 15, 2011); Mariko Sanchanta, "Starbucks Plans Big Expansion in China," *The Wall Street Journal,* April 14, 2010, B10; "Asia Pacific," *Starbucks Newsroom,* **http:// news.starbucks.com/about+starbucks/ starbucks+coffee+international/ asia+pacific/** (accessed July 19, 2011); David Teather, "Starbucks Legend Delivers Recovery by Thinking Smaller," *The Guardian,* January 21, 2010, **www. guardian.co.uk/business/2010/jan/21/ starbucks-howard-schultz** (accessed July 19, 2011); "How Starbucks Colonised the World," *The Sunday Times,* February 17, 2008, **http://business.timesonline.co.uk/ tol/business/industry_sectors/leisure/ article3381092.ece** (accessed July 19, 2011); "Greater China," *Starbucks Newsroom,* **http://news.starbucks.com/ about+starbucks/starbucks+coffee+ international/greater+china** (accessed July 19, 2011).

55. Charles Sizemore, "China Won't Blow Up in 2012," *Forbes,* January 23, 2012, **www.forbes.com/sites/money builder/2012/01/23/china-wont-blow- up-in-2012/** (accessed January 23, 2012).

56. James T. Areddy, James Hookway, John Lyons, and Marcus Walker, "U.S. Slump Takes Toll Across Globe," *The Wall Street Journal,* April 3, 2008, p. A1; Pam Woodall, "The New Champions," *The Economist,* November 15, 2008, p. 55; Matt Jenkins, "A Really Inconvenient Truth," *Miller-McCune,* April/May 2008, p. 42.

57. "The Rise of Capitalism," *The Economist,* January 21, 2012, 11.

58. Elizabeth Holmes, "U.S. Apparel Retailers Turn Their Gaze Beyond China," *The Wall Street Journal,* June 16, 2010, B1.

59. "Overview," Association of Southeast Asian Nations, **www.aseansec.org/64 .htm** (accessed January 23, 2012).

60. Wang Yan, "ASEAN Works to 'Act as Unison' on Global Stage," *China Daily,* November 19, 2011, **www. chinadaily.com.cn/cndy/2011-11/19/ content_14122972.htm** (accessed January 27, 2012).

61. ASEAN website, **www.aseansec.org/** (accessed January 23, 2012).

62. "Common Effective Preferential Tariff (CEPT)," The Malaysia Government's Official Portal, **www. malaysia.gov.my/EN/Relevant%20 Topics/IndustryInMalaysia/ Business/BusinessAndEBusiness/ BusinessAndAgreement/CEPT/Pages/ CEPT.aspx** (accessed January 23, 2012).

63. R.C., "No Brussels Sprouts in Bali," *The Economist,* November 18, 2011, **www. economist.com/blogs/banyan/2011/11/ asean-summits** (accessed January 23, 2012).

64. Kathy Quiano, "ASEAN Summit Starts amid Cloud of Thai-Cambodia Border Row," *CNN,* May 7, 2011, **http:// articles.cnn.com/2011-05-07/world/ asia.asean.summit_1_asean-leaders- asean-summit-southeast-asian- nations?_s=PM:WORLD** (accessed January 23, 2012).

65. Eric Bellman, "Asia Seeks Integration Despite EU's Woes," *The Wall Street Journal,* July 22, 2011, A9.

66. David J. Lynch, "The IMF is . . . Tired Fund Struggles to Reinvent Itself," *USA Today,* April 19, 2006. p. B1.

67. Walter B. Wriston, "Ever Heard of Insourcing?" Commentary, *The Wall Street Journal,* March 24, 2004, p. A20.

68. Barclays Wealth, **www.census.gov/ hhes/w/cpstables/032009/hhinc/new01_ 009.htm** (accessed March 3, 2010); Nick Heath, "Banks: Offshoring, Not Outsourcing," *BusinessWeek,* March 10, 2009, **www.businessweek.com/globalbiz/ content/mar2009/gb20090310_619247 .htm** (accessed March 3, 2010).

69. Kejal Vyas, "Venezuela's PdVSA Forms Joint Venture With Brazil's Odebrecht," *The Wall Street Journal,* September 29, 2011, **http://online.wsj .com/article/BT-CO-20110929-710025 .html** (accessed January 24, 2012).

70. Matt O'Sullivan, "Virgin Blue Mines Fly-In, Fly-Out Boom," *The Sydney Morning Herald,* January 10, 2011, **www. smh.com.au/business/virgin-blue-mines- flyin-flyout-boom-20110110-19kb3. html** (accessed January 10, 2011); Matt O'Sullivan, "Virgin Blue Hooks Up with Regional Skywest," *The Sydney Morning Herald,* January 11, 2011, **www.smh.com. au/business/virgin-blue-hooks-up-with- regional-skywest-20110110-19l7d.html** (accessed January 11, 2011).

71. Sharon Silk Carty, "Ford Plans to Park Jaguar, Land Rover with Tata Motors," *USA Today,* March 26, 2008, p B1.

72. Guo Changdong and Ren Ruqin, "Nestle CEO visits Tianjin," *China Daily,* August 12, 2010, **www.chinadaily .com.cn/m/tianjin/e/2010-08/12/ content_11146560.htm** (accessed January 27, 2012); "Employee Profiles," Nestlé, **www.nestle-ea.com/en/jobssite/ beingatnestleear/Pages/Employess Profiles.aspx** (accessed February 2, 2012).

73. O.C. Ferrell, John Fraedrich, and Linda Ferrell, *Business Ethics,* 6th ed. (Boston: Houghton Mifflin, 2005), pp. 227–30.

74. Export.gov, **www.export.gov/about/ index.asp** (accessed March 3, 2010); CIBER Web, **http://CIBERWEB.msu .edu** (accessed March 3, 2010).

75. Zachary-Cy Vanasse, "Rendez Vous En France Brings the World Travel Industry to Paris," *Travel Hot News,* April 5, 2012, **www.travelhotnews .com/reportages.php?sequence_ no=38537** (accessed July 26, 2012); Malcolm Moore, "Disney Breaks Ground on Shanghai Theme Park," *The Telegraph,* April 8, 2011, **www.telegraph .co.uk/news/worldnews/asia/china /8437153/Disney-breaks-ground- on-Shanghai-theme-park.html** (accessed July 26, 2012); Jeff Chu, "Happily Ever After?" *Time,* March 18, 2002, **www.time.com/time/magazine/ article/0,9171,901020325-218398,00 .html** (accessed May 6, 2010); Wendy Leung, ""Disney Set to Miss Mark on Visitors," *The Standard,* September 5, 2006, **www.thestandard.com.hk/news_detail .asp?we_cat=4&art_id=26614&sid= 9732977&con_type=1&d_str=20060905** (accessed July 26, 2012); Robert Mendick, "Race Against Time to Make That Disney Magic Work," *The London Independent,* February 6, 2000, **www. independent.co.uk/news/uk/this- britain/race-againsttime-to-make-that- new-disney-magicwork-726623.html** (accessed May 6, 2010); "The Narrative of Numbers," Disneyland Paris, **http:// corporate.disneylandparis.com/about- ourcompany/the-narrative-of-numbers/ index.xhtml** (accessed April 20, 2010).

Chapter 4

1. REI, *2009 Stewardship Report,* **www. rei.com/aboutrei/csr/2009/2009- stewardship-report.html** (accessed November 2, 2011); "100 Best Companies to Work For," *CNNMoney,* **http:// money.cnn.com/magazines/fortune/ bestcompanies/2011/snapshots/9.html** (accessed May 31, 2011); "Overview,"

REI, **www.rei.com/aboutrei/business. html** (accessed May 31, 2011); "The REI Member Dividend," REI, **www.rei.com/ membership/dividend** (accessed May 31, 2011); "REI Outdoor School Classes and Outings," REI, **www.rei.com/ outdoorschool** (accessed November 2, 2011); Giselle Tsirulnik, "REI App Purpose Is Twofold: Sales and Service," *Mobile Commerce Daily,* March 25, 2011, **www.mobilecommercedaily. com/2011/03/25/rei-app-purpose-is- twofold-sales-and-service** (accessed June 1, 2011); "Workplace," REI, **www. rei.com/stewardship/rei_workplace** (accessed June 1, 2011).

2. The Entrepreneurs' Help Page, **www. tannedfeet.com/sole_proprietorship. htm** (accessed March 16, 2010); Kent Hoover, "Startups Down for Women Entrepreneurs, Up for Men," *SanFrancisco Business Times,* May 2, 2008, **http://san francisco.bizjournals.com/sanfrancisco/ stories/2008/05/05/smallb2.html** (accessed March 16, 2010).

3. Maggie Overfelt, "Start-Me-Up: How the Garage Became a Legendary Place to Rev Up Ideas," *Fortune Small Business,* September 1, 2003, **http:// money.cnn.com/magazines/fsb/fsb_ archive/2003/09/01/350784/index.htm** (accessed March 16, 2010).

4. Mark Henricks, B2B Service, Special Franchise Advertising Section, *Inc.,* February 2012; Stratus Building Solutions website, **www.stratusbuildingsolutions .com/** (accessed February 2, 2012).

5. Alyssa Giacobbe, "A Long and Bumpy Road," *Fast Company,* October 2011, 58–60; PlanetTran website, **www. planettran.com/Green-Transportation. php** (accessed September 22, 2011); Clifford Atiyeh, "Interview: Hybrid Livery CEO on Carbon Taxes and Why Hybrid Taxis Won't Matter," *Boston.com,* May 22, 2009, **www.boston.com/cars/ newsandreviews/overdrive/2009/05/ interview_seth_riney_planettran.html** (accessed September 22, 2011); Paul Sullivan, "The Goal Is to Do the Right Thing," *The New York Times,* May 21, 2008, **www.nytimes.com/2008/05/21/ business/smallbusiness/21image.html** (September 22, 2011).

6. Christian Sylt, "Cirque du Soleil May Leap for New Partner," *The Telegraph,* January 30, 2011, **www.telegraph.co.uk/ finance/newsbysector/banksandfinance/ privateequity/8290380/Cirque-du- Soleil-may-leap-for-new-partner.html#** (accessed March 18, 2011).

7. "The 2011 Global 100: Most Profits Per Partner," *The American Lawyer,* March 12, 2010, **www.law.com/jsp/tal/ PubArticleTAL.jsp?id=1202514395169** (accessed March 18, 2011).

8. Laura Petrecca, "A Partner Can Give Your Business Shelter or a Storm," *USA Today,* October 9, 2009, **www.usatoday .com/money/smallbusiness/startup/ week4-partnerships.htm** (accessed January 11, 2011).

9. Clarissa French, "Diversification Accounts for BKD Revenue Results," *sbj.net,* March 5, 2010, **http://sbj.net/ main.asp?SectionID=48&SubSectionID =108&ArticleID=86481** (accessed March 18, 2011); "About BKD," BKD website, **www.bkd.com/about/AtaGlance.htm** (accessed February 2, 2012).

10. Alexandra Berzon and Kate O'Keefe, "A Partners' Fight Erupts at Wynn," *The Wall Street Journal,* January 13, 2012, **http://online.wsj.com/article/SB100014 24052970204542404577156491314541590.html** (accessed February 2, 2012).

11. *Warren Buffett's Berkshire Hathaway Letter to Shareholders,* **www. berkshirehathaway.com/letters/2010ltr .pdf** (accessed March 14, 2011).

12. "America's Largest Private Companies," Forbes, November 16, 2011, **www.forbes.com/sites/ andreamurphy/2011/11/16/americas- largest-private-companies/** (accessed February 2, 2012).

13. "America's Largest Private Companies."

14. Deborah Orr, "The Secret World of Mars," *Forbes,* April 28, 2008, **www.forbes .com/2008/04/28/billionaires-mars-wrig ley-biz-billies-cz_do_0428marsfamily. html** (accessed March 16, 2010).

15. "Fortune 500," CNNMoney.com, **http://money.cnn.com/magazines/ fortune/fortune500/2012/full_list/** (accessed May 22, 2012).

16. Jay Hart, "Not His Father's CEO," *Yahoo! Sports,* January 22, 2010, **http://sports.yahoo.com/nascar/ news?slug=jh-france012209** (accessed March 2, 2010).

17. Scott DeCarlo, "The World's Leading Companies," *Forbes,* April 18, 2012 **www. forbes.com/sites/scottdecarlo/2012/ 04/18/the-worlds-biggest-companies/** (accessed May 22, 2012).

18. Ned Potter, "Facebook IPO: $5 Billion Filing to Sell Stock in May," February 1, 2011, **http://abcnews.go .com/Technology/facebook-ipo-billion- filing-sec-sell-stock/story?id=15483472**

what-has-triggered-the-suicide-cluster-at-foxconn/ (accessed April 9, 2012).

11. "2011 Update of the Corporate Social Responsibility Report," Campbell's, **www.campbellsoupcompany.com/csr/success_profile.asp** (accessed April 9, 2012).

12. Leigh Buchanan, "The Way I Work: 'I Have to Be the Worrywart So My Son Feels Free to Exercise his Imagination,' " *Inc.,* May 2010, pp. 125–28; **www.johnnycupcakes.com** (accessed October 11, 2011).

13. McDonald's India, **www.mcdonaldsindia.com/** (accessed February 17, 2012).

14. "Why Work Here?" **www.wholefoodsmarket.com/careers/workhere.php** (accessed March 3, 2010).

15. "PepsiCo Unveils New Organizational Structure, Names CEOs of Three Principle Operating Units," PepsiCo Media, November 5, 2007, **www.pepsico.com/PressRelease/PepsiCo-Unveils-New-Organizational-Structure-Names.html** (accessed May 19, 2010); "The PepsiCo Family," PepsiCo, **www.pepsico.com/Company/The-Pepsico-Family/PepsiCo-Americas-Beverages.html** (accessed January 12, 2010).

16. Jon R. Katzenbach and Douglas K. Smith, "The Discipline of Teams," *Harvard Business Review* 71 (March–April 1993), 19.

17. Ibid.

18. "The Secret to Team Collaboration: Individuality," *Inc.,* January 18, 2012, **www.inc.com/john-baldoni/the-secret-to-team-collaboration-is-individuality.html** (accessed February 17, 2012).

19. "How to Build a (Strong) Virtual Team," *CNNMoney.com,* **http://money.cnn.com/2009/11/19/news/companies/ibm_virtual_manager.fortune/index.htm** (accessed February 11, 2010).

20. Esther Shein, "Making the Virtual Team Real," *The Network,* April 2, 2008, **http://newsroom.cisco.com/dlls/2008/ts_040208.html** (accessed April 8, 2012).

21. "Toyota Motor Corporation President Akio Toyoda Announces Global Quality Task Force," February 5, **http://money.cnn.com/news/newsfeeds/articles/globenewswire/183685.htm** (accessed March 3, 2010).

22. Jerry Useem, "What's That Spell? TEAMWORK," *Fortune,* June 12, 2006, p. 66.

23. Jia Lynnyang, "The Power of Number 4.6," *Fortune,* June 12, 2006, p. 122.

24. "School of Food Science Student Groups," Washington State University, **www.sfs.wsu.edu/student_groups/FoodProdDevTeam.html** (accessed April 8, 2012).

25. Richard S. Wellins, William C. Byham, and Jeanne M. Wilson, *Empowered Teams: Creating Self-Directed Work Groups That Improve Quality, Productivity, and Participation* (San Francisco: Jossey-Bass Publishers, 1991), p. 5.

26. Ashlee Vance, "Trouble at the Virtual Water Cooler," *Bloomberg Businessweek,* May 2–8, 2011, pp. 31–32; Chris Brogan, "How to Foster Company Culture with Remote Employees," Entrepreneur, May 2011, **www.entrepreneur.com/article/219471** (accessed August 4, 2011); **www.yammer.com** (accessed August 4, 2011); "Yammer Guidelines," **http://blog.xero.com/2011/01/yammer-guidelines** (accessed August 5, 2011).

27. Matt Krumrie, "Are Meetings a Waste of Time? Survey Says Yes," *Minneapolis Workplace Examiner,* May 12, 2009, **www.examiner.com/x-2452-Minneapolis-Workplace-Examiner~y2009m5d12-Are-meetings-a-waste-of-time-Survey-says-yes** (accessed March 11, 2010).

28. Peter Mell and Timothy Grance, "The NIST Definition of Cloud Computing," National Institute of Standards and Technology, Special Publication 800-145, September 2011, **http://csrc.nist.gov/publications/nistpubs/800-145/SP800-145.pdf** (accessed April 9, 2012).

29. "Top 10 Ideas: Making the Most of Your Corporate Intranet," **www.claromentis.com/blog/2009/04/top-10-ideas-making-the-most-of-your-corporate-intranet** (accessed February 12, 2010).

30. "Corporate America vs. Workers: Companies Do More with Fewer Employees," *NY Daily News,* November 5, 2009, **www.nydailynews.com/money/2009/11/05/2009-11-05_corporate_america_vs_workers_companies_do_more_with_fewer_employees.html** (accessed March 4, 2010).

31. Kim Komando, "Why You Need a Company Policy on Internet Use," **www.microsoft.com/smallbusiness/resources/management/employee-relations/why-you-need-a-company-policy-on-internet-use.aspx#WhyyouneedacompanypolicyonInternetUse** (accessed February 12, 2010).

32. PBSNewsHour, "Apple Supplier Foxconn Pledges Better Working Conditions, but Will It Deliver?" *You Tube,* **www.youtube.com/watch?v=ZduorbCkSBQ** (accessed April 9, 2012).

33. Michael D. Maginn, *Effective Teamwork,* 1994, p. 10. © 1994 Richard D. Irwin, a Times Mirror Higher Education Group Inc. company.

34. Sue Shellenbarger, "Getting Results Without Face Time," *The Wall Street Journal,* May 3, 2011, **http://blogs.wsj.com/juggle/2011/05/03/getting-results-without-face-time/** (accessed July 27, 2012); "Our Clients," *Culture Rx,* **www.gorowe.com/about/clients/** (accessed July 27, 2012); Andrew Price, "Bosses, Stop Caring if Your Employees Are at Their Desks," *Fast Company,* **www.fastcoexist.com/1678950/bosses-stop-caring-if-your-employees-are-at-their-desks** (accessed July 27, 2012); Sasha Galbraith, "Counting Hours at Work Is So Yesterday," *Forbes,* May 10, 2012, **www.forbes.com/sites/sashagalbraith/2012/05/10/counting-hours-at-work-is-so-yesterday/** (accessed July 27, 2012); Jennifer Ludden, "The End of 9-to-5: When Work Time Is Anytime," *NPR,* March 16, 2010, **www.npr.org/templates/story/story.php?storyId=124705801** (accessed July 27, 2012); Patrick J. Kiger, "Throwing Out the Rules of Work," *Workforce Management,* **www.workforce.com/article/20061007/NEWS02/310079997** (accessed July 27, 2012); "Smashing the Clock," *BusinessWeek,* December 11, 2006, **www.businessweek.com/magazine/content/06_50/b4013001.htm** (accessed July 27, 2012).

Chapter 8

1. Karl Taro Greenfeld, "Fast and Furious," *Bloomberg Businessweek,* May 9-15, 2011, pp. 64–69; **www.yum.com/company/ourbrands.asp** (accessed August 5, 2011); **www.tacobell.com** (accessed August 5, 2011).

2. Andreas Cremer and Tim Higgins, "Volkswagen Rediscovers America," *Bloomberg Businessweek,* May 23–29, 2011, pp. 11–12; Paul A. Eisenstein, "VW Is Back in the USA and Aiming High with New Plant," *MSNBC,* May 26, 2011, **www.msnbc.msn.com/id/43159310/ns/business-autos/t/vw-back-usa-aiming-high-new-plant/** (accessed July 29, 2011); Deepa Seetharaman, "Volkswagen Sees U.S. Plant as Key to Topping Toyota," *Reuters,* May 24, 2011, **www.reuters**

.com/article/2011/05/24/us-volkswagen-idUSTRE74N6RA20110524 (accessed July 29, 2011); "Germany: VW PC Brand Sales Rise 17.2% in July," *Automotive World,* August 16, 2011, **www.automotiveworld.com/news/oems-and-markets/88694-germany-vw-pc-brand-sales-rise-17-2-in-july** (accessed August 16, 2011); Tom Mutchler, "First Look Video: 2012 Volkswagen Passat," *Consumer Reports,* August 5, 2011, **http://news.consumerreports.org/cars/2011/08/first-look-video-2012-volkswagen-passat.html** (accessed August 16, 2011).

3. Rina Rapuano, "Check Please!" *The Washingtonian Blog,* February 18, 2010, **www.washingtonian.com/blog articles/restaurants/bestbites/15008 .html** (accessed February 23, 2010).

4. Leonard L. Berry, *Discovering the Soul of Service* (New York: The Free Press, 1999), pp. 86–96.

5. Valerie A. Zeithaml and Mary Jo Bitner, *Services Marketing,* 3rd ed. (Boston: McGraw-Hill Irwin, 2003), pp. 3, 22.

6. Bernard Wysocki Jr., "To Fix Health Care, Hospitals Take Tips from the Factory Floor," *The Wall Street Journal,* April 9, 2004, via **www.chcanys.org/ clientuploads/downloads/Clinical_ resources/Leadership%20Articles/ LeanThinking_ACF28EB.pdf** (accessed March 5, 2010).

7. "20 Awesome Facebook Pages," *Inc.,* **www.inc.com/20-awesome-facebook-fan-pages-2011/index.html** (accessed February 22, 2012).

8. Faith Keenan, "Opening the Spigot," *BusinessWeek* e.biz, June 4, 2001, **www.businessweek.com/magazine/ content/01_23/b3735616.htm** (accessed March 5, 2010).

9. "Dell Laptop Parts," Partspeople, **www.parts-people.com/** (accessed March 23, 2012).

10. Ryan Underwood, "Dear Customer . . . Managing E-mail Campaigns," *Inc.,* March 2008, p. 59.

11. "Fun Facts," Hershey (n.d.), **www.hersheys.com/kisses/about/index.asp? contentid=3** (accessed February 16, 2010).

12. "Green Factories/Green Building," Honda, **www.honda.com/newsandviews/ report.aspx?id=4056-en** (accessed March 23, 2012); "ISO 14000 essentials," ISO, **www.iso.org/iso/iso_14000_ essentials** (accessed March 23, 2012).

13. "Top 10 Solar Friendly States," *Cooler Planet,* **http://solar.coolerplanet.com/ Articles/top-10-solar-friendly-states .aspx** (accessed February 23, 2010).

14. "North American Robot Orders Fall 25% in 2009 But Positive Signs Emerge in Fourth Quarter," *Robotics News,* February 8, 2010, **www.robotics.org/content-detail.cfm/Industrial-Robotics-News/ North-American-Robot-Orders-Fall-25-in-2009-But-Positive-Signs-Emerge-in-Fourth-Quarter/content_id/1990** (accessed February 23, 2010); Robotic Industries Association, "2011 Is Record-Breaking Year for North American Robotics Industry," *Robotics Online,* February 2, 2012, **www.robotics.org/ content-detail.cfm/Industrial-Robotics-News/2011-is-Record-Breaking-Year-for-North-American-Robotics-Industry/content_id/3240** (accessed February 22, 2012).

15. "Robotic Surgery Pioneer Reaches Historic Milestone with 5,000th Case," Florida Hospital Media Relations, October 26, 2011, **www. floridahospitalnews.com/robotic-surgery-pioneer-hits-historic-milestone-5000th-case** (accessed February 22, 2012); Keith Wagstaff, "How Foxconn's Million-Machine 'Robot Kingdom' Will Change the Face of Manufacturing," *Time,* November 9, 2011, **http://techland.time.com/2011/11/09/ how-foxconns-million-machine-robot-kingdom-will-change-the-face-of-manufacturing/** (accessed February 22, 2012).

16. K. W., "The Dog Lover," *Inc.,* October 2010, pp. 68–70; Rebecca Konya, "Marie Moody: Women of Influence 2010," *The Business Journal,* 2010, **www2.bizjournals.com/ milwaukee/events/2010/women_of_ influence/marie_moody_women_ of_influence_2010.html** (accessed October11, 2011); **www.stellaandchewys .com** (accessed October 11, 2011); "Stella & Chewy's," *Inc.,* **www.inc.com/inc5000/ profile/stella-chewys** (accessed February 24, 2012).

17. Johnson Controls, *2011 Business and Sustainability Report: Growth in Every Dimension* (Milwaukee, WI: Johnson Controls, Inc., 2011).

18. Bryan Walsh, "Why Green Is the New Red, White and Blue," *Time,* April 28, 2008, p. 53.

19. "2012 Chevrolet Volt," Chevrolet, **www.chevrolet.com/volt-electric-car/** (accessed February 22, 2012).

20. Megan Kamerick, "How To Go Green," *New Mexico Business Weekly,* May 23–29, 2008, p. 3.

21. O.C. Ferrell and Michael D. Hartline, *Marketing Strategy* (Mason, OH: South-Western, 2011), p. 215.

22. John Edwards, "Orange Seeks Agent," *Inbound Logistics,* January 2006, pp. 239–242.

23. Ferrell and Hartline, *Marketing Strategy,* p. 215.

24. "Broken Links," *The Economist,* March 31, 2011, **www.economist.com/ node/18486015** (accessed February 22, 2012).

25. Ari Lavaux, "Chocolate's Dark Side," *The Weekly Alibi,* February 9–15, 2012, p. 22.

26. John O'Mahony, "The Future Is Now," Special Advertising Section, *Bloomberg Businessweek,* pp. S1–S11; "Recycling & Conservation," UPS, **http:// responsibility.ups.com/Environment/ Recycling+and+Conservation** (accessed October 18, 2011); Rebecca Treacy-Lenda, "Sustainability Is. . ." UPS, July 28, 2011, **http://blog.ups .com/2011/07/28/sustainability-is/** (accessed October 18, 2011); Heather Clancy, "Sustainability Update: UPS Squeezes Out More Fuel Consumption," *SmartPlanet,* July 28, 2011, **www.smart planet.com/blog/business-brains/sus tainability-update-ups-squeezes-out-more-fuel-consumption/17597** (accessed October 18, 2011).

27. Susan Carey, "Airlines Play Up Improvements in On-Time Performance," *The Wall Street Journal,* February 10, 2010, p. B6.

28. "Four U.S. Organizations Honored with the 2011 Baldrige National Quality Award," Baldridge Performance Excellence Program, November 2, 2011, **www.nist.gov/baldrige/baldrige_recip ients2011.cfm** (accessed February 22, 2012).

29. Roger Yu, "Kia Looks to Buff Image with Value, New Designs," *USA Today,* June 29, 2011, **www.usatoday.com/ money/autos/2011-06-27-kia-rising_n .htm** (accessed February 22, 2012).

30. Philip B. Crosby, *Quality Is Free: The Art of Making Quality Certain* (New York: McGraw-Hill, 1979), pp. 9–10.

31. Nigel F. Piercy, *Market-Led Strategic Change* (Newton, MA: Butterworth-Heinemann, 1992), pp. 374–385.

32. "Compuware Gomez Introduces Free Web Performance Benchmarking

Tool," *CNN Money,* February 16, 2010, **http://money.cnn.com/news/newsfeeds/articles/globenewswire/184336.htm** (accessed February 23, 2010).

33. "ISO 9001 Certification," GE Power & Water, **www.geinstruments.com/company/iso-9001-certification.html** (accessed March 23, 2012).

34. "Mouthing Off By the Numbers," *Ethisphere,* 2011, Q3, p. 9.

35. Charles Duhigg and David Barboza, "Apple's iPad and the Human Costs for Workers in China," *The New York Times,* January 25, 2012, **www.nytimes.com/2012/01/26/business/ieconomy-apples-ipad-and-the-human-costs-for-workers-in-china.html?pagewanted=all** (accessed February 8, 2012).

36. "Monitoring and Auditing Global Supply Chains Is a Must," *Ethisphere,* 2011, Q3, pp. 38–45.

37. "Employment Opportunities," Careers in Supply Chain Management, **www.careersinsupplychain.org/career-outlook/empopp.asp** (accessed March 5, 2010).

38. James Wetherbe, "Principles of Cycle Time Reduction," *Cycle Time Research,* 1995, p. iv.

39. Stan Davis and Christopher Meyer, *Blur: The Speed of Change in the Connected Economy* (Reading, MA: Addison-Wesley, 1998), p. 5.

40. "Toyota Production System," Toyota, **www.toyota-global.com/company/vision_philosophy/toyota_production_system/** (accessed July 27, 2012); Craig Trudell, "Toyota Quality Perception Rebounds; GM's Chevy Declines," *Bloomberg,* May 31, 2012, **www.bloomberg.com/news/2012-05-31/toyota-quality-perception-rebounds-gm-s-chevy-declines.html** (accessed July 27, 2012); "History of Toyota," Toyota, **www.toyota-global.com/company/history_of_toyota/** (accessed July 27, 2012); Soyoung Kim and Bernie Woodall, "Toyota to Pay $16.4 Million Fine, Recall Lexus SUV," *Reuters,* April 19, 2010, **www.reuters.com/article/2010/04/19/us-toyota-fine-idUSTRE63G0AW20100419** (accessed July 27, 2012); Josh Mitchell, Mike Ramsey, and Chester Dawson, "U.S. Blames Drivers, Not Toyota," *The Wall Street Journal,* February 9, 2011, **http://online.WSJ.com/article/SB10001424052748704422204576131311592922574.html** (accessed March 23, 2012); Joann Muller, "The Best-Selling Cars of 2011," *Forbes,* November 2, 2011, **www.forbes.com/sites/joannmuller/2011/11/02/the-best-selling-cars-of-2011/** (accessed March 23, 2012); Sonari Glinton, "Toyota Steers Ads to Bring in More Minority Buyers," *NPR,* June 30, 2011, **www.npr.org/2011/06/30/137524757/toyota-steers-ads-to-bring-in-more-minority-buyers** (accessed March 23, 2012).

Chapter 9

1. Jill Rosen, "For Some Baltimore Employees, Every Day Is Take Your Dog to Work Day," *The Baltimore Sun,* June 23, 2011, **http://articles.baltimoresun.com/2011-06-23/features/bs-ae-pets-at-work-20110623_1_dog-owners-pet-owners-rescue-dog** (accessed October 17, 2011); "Man's Best Co-Worker," *Inc.,* 2011, **www.inc.com/winning-workplaces/articles/201105/mans-best-co-worker.html** (accessed October 17, 2011); Susan McCullough, "Pets Go to the Office," *HR Magazine* 43 June 1998), pp. 162–68; "Working Like a Dog," *CNNMoney,* January 24, 2006, **http://money.cnn.com/2006/01/24/news/funny/dog_work/index.htm** (accessed October 17, 2011).

2. Dan Heath and Chip Heath, "Business Advice from Van Halen," *Fast Company,* March 1, 2010, **www.fastcompany.com/magazine/143/made-to-stick-the-telltale-brown-mampm.html**, accessed March 11, 2010.

3. "100 Best Companies to Work For 2010," *Fortune,* **http://money.cnn.com/magazines/fortune/bestcompanies/2010/snapshots/4.html** (accessed February 18, 2010); "Benefits," Google Jobs, **www.google.com/support/jobs/bin/static.py?page=benefits.html** (accessed February 18, 2010).

4. "How Much Does Absenteeism Cost Your Business," Success Performance Solutions, December 10, 2008, **www.super-solutions.com/CostofAbsenteeism.asp**, accessed march 11, 2010.

5. "Careers," **Nikebiz.com, www.nikebiz.com/careers/benefits/other/whq_campus.html** (accessed February 9, 2010).

6. "Why Work Here," **www.wholefoodsmarket.com/careers/workhere.php** (accessed November 9, 2011); "Best Companies to Work For' Rankings," **www.wholefoodsmarket.com/careers/fortune100.php** (accessed November 9, 2011); "Whole Food Market's Core Values," **www.wholefoodsmarket.com/values/corevalues.php#supporting** (accessed November 9, 2011); "100 Best Companies to Work For: Whole Foods Market," *CNNMoney,* **http://money.cnn.com/magazines/fortune/bestcompanies/2011/snapshots/24.html** (accessed November); Kerry A. Dolan, "America's Greenest Companies 2011," *Forbes,* April 18, 2011, **www.forbes.com/2011/04/18/americas-greenest-companies.html** (accessed November 9, 2011); Joseph Brownstein, "Is Whole Foods' Get Healthy Plan Fair?" *ABC News,* January 29, 2010, **http://abcnews.go.com/Health/w_DietAndFitnessNews/foods-incentives-make-employees-healthier/story?id=9680047** (accessed November 9, 2011); Deborah Dunham, "At Whole Foods Thinner Employees Get Fatter Discounts," *That's Fit,* January 27, 2010, **www.thatsfit.com/2010/01/27/whole-foods-thin-employees-get-discounts/** (accessed November 9, 2011).

7. Christopher Helman, "America's 25 Highest-Paid CEOs," *Forbes,* October 12, 2011, **www.forbes.com/sites/christopherhelman/2011/10/12/americas-25-highest-paid-ceos/** (accessed March 6, 2012).

8. "25 Well-Paying Jobs that Most People Overlook (and Why)," *Business Pundit,* **www.businesspundit.com/25-well-paying-jobs-that-most-people-overlook-and-why/** (accessed April 16, 2012).

9. "L.L. Bean Named #1 in NRF Foundation Customer Service Survey," L.L. Bean News, February 21, 2008, **www.llbean.com/customerService/aboutLLBean/newsroom/stories/02212008_LLBean_News.html**, accessed March 12, 2010; Jena McGregor, "Customer Service Champs 2010," *Bloomberg Businessweek,* **http://images.businessweek.com/ss/10/02/0218_customer_service_champs/2.htm** (accessed January 13, 2011).

10. Douglas McGregor, *The Human Side of Enterprise* (New York: McGraw-Hill, 1960), pp. 33–34.

11. McGregor, *The Human Side of Enterprise.*

12. Leigh Buchanan, "Where the CEO Is Just Another Guy with a Vote," *Inc.,* June 2011, pp. 64–66; Namasté Solar website, **www.namastesolar.com/cmsPages/view/page:about_us/section:our_story/content:our_story** (accessed September 23, 2011); "Unique Business Aims to Spread Solar Power," *CNN,* July 17, 2008,

http://articles.cnn.com/2008-07-17/ tech/solar.office_1_solar-power-rene wable-energy-business-schools?_s=PM: TECH (accessed September 23, 2011); "Namasté Solar Electric, Inc.," *Bloomberg Businessweek,* http://investing.business week.com/research/stocks/private/ snapshot.asp?privcapId=39182908 (accessed October 11, 2011).

13. Bharat Mediratta, "The Google Way: Give Engineers Room," *The New York Times,* October 21, 2007, www.nytimes .com/2007/10/21/jobs/21pre.html (accessed April 16, 2012).

14. Jon L. Pierce, Tatiana Kostova, and Kurt T. Kirks, "Toward a Theory of Psychological Ownership in Organizations, *Academy of Management Review* 26, no. 2 (2001), p. 298.

15. Liz Rappaport, "Goldman Cuts Blankfein's Bonus," *The Wall Street Journal,* February 4, 2012, http://online. wsj.com/article/SB100014240529702 046622045772014833477787346.html (accessed April 17, 2012).

16. Ethics Resource Center, *2011 National Business Ethics Survey®: Ethics in Transition* (Arlington, VA: Ethics Resource Center, 2012), p. 16.

17. Archie Carroll, "Carroll: Do We Live in a Cheating Culture?" *Athens Banner-Herald,* February 21, 2004, www. onlineathens.com/stories/022204/ bus_20040222028.shtml, accessed March 12, 2010.

18. Geoff Colvin, "How Top Companies Breed Stars," September 20, 2007, http:// money.cnn.com/magazines/fortune/ fortune_archive/2007/10/01/100351829/ index.htm (accessed March 12, 2010).

19. My Guides USA.com, "Which Jobs Offer Flexible Work Schedules?" http:// jobs.myguidesusa.com/answers-to-my-questions/which-jobs-offer-flexible-work-schedules?/ (accessed March 12, 2010).

20. Robert Preidt, "Workplace Flexibility Can Boost Healthy Behaviors," Wake Forest University Baptist Medical Center, news release, December 10, 2007, http://yourtotalhealth.ivillage. com/workplace-flexibility-can-boost-healthy-behaviors.html (accessed March 12, 2010).

21. My Guides USA.com, "Which Jobs Offer Flexible Work Schedules?"

22. Nancy Rothbard, "Put on a Happy Face. Seriously." *The Wall Street Journal,* October 24, 2011, p. R2; "How 3M Gave Everyone Days Off and Created

an Innovation Dynamo," February 1, 2011, www.fastcodesign.com/1663137/ how-3m-gave-everyone-days-off-and-created-an-innovation-dynamo (accessed October 31, 2011); "Americans Increasingly Unhappy at Work," *BusinessNewsDaily* March 10, 2011, www. businessnewsdaily.com/work-wellness-index-1073/ (accessed October 31, 2011); "Employee Mood Impacts Bottom Line," *BusinessNewsDaily* April 5, 2011, www.businessnewsdaily.com/employee-mood-customer-service-1152/ (accessed October 31, 2011).

23. "The Latest Telecommuting Statistics," Telework Research Network, www.teleworkresearchnetwork.com/ telecommuting-statistics (accessed April 3, 2012).

24. Dori Meinert, "Make Telecommuting Pay Off," *Society for Human Resource Management,* June 1, 2011, www. shrm.org/Publications/hrmagazine/ EditorialContent/2011/0611/ Pages/0611meinert.aspx (accessed April 3, 2012).

25. Dori Meinert, "Make Telecommuting Pay Off," *Society for Human Resource Management,* June 1, 2011, www. shrm.org/Publications/hrmagazine/ EditorialContent/2011/0611/ Pages/0611meinert.aspx (accessed April 3, 2012).

26. "Best Places For Business and Careers," *Forbes,* March 25, 2009, www. forbes.com/lists/2009/1/bizplaces09_ Best-Places-For-Business-And-Careers_ Rank.html (accessed February 23, 2010).

27. Kurt Badenhausen, "The Best Places for Business and Careers," *Forbes,* June 29, 2011, www.forbes.com/best-places-for-business/ (accessed April 3, 2012).

28. "100 Best Companies to Work For 2009," *Fortune,* http://money. cnn.com/magazines/fortune/ bestcompanies/2009/snapshots/32.html (accessed March 7, 2011); "The Container Store: An Employee-Centric Retailer," UNM Daniels Fund Business Ethics Initiative, http://danielsethics.mgt.unm. edu/pdf/Container%20Store%20Case. pdf (accessed July 30, 2012).

Chapter 10

1. George Anders, "The Rare Find," *Bloomberg Businessweek,* October 17–October 23, 2011, pp. 106–12; Philip Delves Broughton, "Spotting the Exceptionally Talented," *Financial Times,*

October 13, 2011, www.ft.com/intl/ cms/s/0/25dc1872-f4ba-11e0-a286-00144feab49a.html#axzz1birOQlih (accessed October 24, 2011); Joe Light, "Recruiters Rethink Online Playbook," *The Wall Street Journal,* January 18, 2011, http://online.wsj.com/article/SB100 01424052748704307404576080492613858846.html (accessed October 24, 2011); Kris Maher, "A Tactical Recruiting Effort Pays Off," *The Wall Street Journal,* October 24, 2011, p. R6; Peter Cappelli, "Why Companies Aren't Getting the Employees They Need," *The Wall Street Journal,* October 24, 2011, pp. R1, R6.

2. "About O*NET," O*NET Resource Center, www.onetcenter.org/overview. html (accessed April 23, 2012).

3. Procter & Gamble Recruiting Process, www.pg.com/jobs/recruitblue/recprocess. shtml (accessed March 13, 2010).

4. "Job Opportunities," *Borders,* https:// wss6a.unicru.com/hirepro/C406/ applicant.jsp?Eurl=4%2Fhirepro%2 FC406%2Fapplicant.jsp%3FSite%3D-3%26C%3D406%26k%3Dno%26conten t%3Dsearch%26Lang%3Den&Site=10 0585&C=406&k=no&content=start& Lang=en (accessed March 9, 2010).

5. U.S. Department of Health and Human Services, "Results from the 2010 National Survey on Drug Use and Health: Summary of National Findings," September 2011, www.samhsa.gov/data/ NSDUH/2k10NSDUH/2k10Results. htm#3.1.7 (accessed April 5, 2012).

6. "Substance Abuse Costs Employers Billions," *The National Registry of Workers' Compensation Specialists,* www.nrwcs.com/substance-abuse-costs-billions (accessed April 5, 2012).

7. Manuel Valdes and Shannon McFarland, "Job Seekers' Facebook Password Asked for During U.S. Interviews," *Huffington Post,* March 20, 2012, www.huffingtonpost. com/2012/03/20/facebook-passwords-job-seekers_n_1366577.html (accessed April 23, 2012).

8. Associated Press, "Food Network Chef Fired After Resume Fraud," *USA Today,* March 3, 2008, www.usatoday .com/news/nation/2008-03-03-chef-fired_N.htm (accessed March 16, 2010).

9. Christopher T. Marquet and Lisa J.B. Peterson, "Résumé Fraud: The Top Ten Lies," Marquet International, Ltd., www.marquetinternational.com/pdf/ Resume%20Fraud-Top%20Ten%20Lies. pdf (accessed March 9, 2010).

10. "Private Sector Bias Charges Hit All-Time High," U.S. Equal Employment Opportunity Commission, January 15, 2012, **www.eeoc.gov/eeoc/newsroom/release/1-24-12a.cfm** (accessed April 5, 2012); "Sexual Harassment Charges: EEOC & FEPAs Combined: FY 1997–FY 2011," U.S. Equal Employment Opportunity Commission, **www.eeoc.gov/eeoc/statistics/enforcement/sexual_harassment.cfm** (accessed April 5, 2012).

11. "Fortune 500 Black, Latino, Asian CEOs," DiversityInc, February 19, 2012, **http://diversityinc.com/leadership/fortune-500-black-latino-asian-ceos/** (accessed April 5, 2012); Alliance for Board Diversity, "Missing Pieces: Women and Minorities on *Fortune* 500 Boards," *2010 Alliance for Board Diversity Census, 2011,* **http://theabd.org/Missing_Pieces_Women_and_Minorities_on_Fortune_500_Boards.pdf** (accessed April 5, 2012).

12. "Compulsory Retirement Age at 65 Fully Abolished," *BBC News,* October 1, 2011, **www.bbc.co.uk/news/business-15127835** (accessed April 4, 2012); "Can You Legally Force Someone to Retire or Is It Age Discrimination?" *LawInfo blog,* **http://blog.lawinfo.com/2011/04/10/can-you-legally-force-someone-to-retire-or-is-it-age-discrimination/** (accessed April 5, 2012).

13. Stephen Bastien, "12 Benefits of Hiring Older Workers," *Entrepreneur.com,* September 20, 2006, **www.entrepreneur.com/humanresources/hiring/article167500.html** (accessed March 17, 2010).

14. Catherine Rampell, "The Gender Wage Gap, Around the World," March 9, 2010, **http://economix.blogs.nytimes.com/2010/03/09/the-gender-wage-gap-around-the-world** (accessed March 13, 2010).

15. "Our Curriculum," Hamburger University, **www.aboutmcdonalds.com/mcd/careers/hamburger_university/our_curriculum.html** (accessed March 9, 2010).

16. "100 Best Companies to Work For 2011," *Fortune,* February 7, 2011, **http://money.cnn.com/magazines/fortune/bestcompanies/2011/snapshots/21.html** (accessed February 7, 2011).

17. Doug Stewart, "Employee-Appraisal Software," *Inc.,* **www.inc.com/magazine/19940615/3288_pagen_2.html** (accessed March 10, 2010).

18. Maury A. Peiperl, "Getting 360-Degree Feedback Right," *Harvard Business Review,* January 2001, pp. 142–48.

19. Chris Musselwhite, "Self Awareness and the Effective Leader," Inc.com, **www.inc.com/resources/leadership/articles/20071001/musselwhite.html** (accessed March 16, 2010).

20. Rick Nauert, "Flexible Work Place Improves Family Life, Reduces Turnover," PsychCentral, April 7, 2011, **http://psychcentral.com/news/2011/04/07/flexible-workplace-improves-family-life-reduces-turnover/25094.html** (accessed April 5, 2012).

21. Marcia Zidle, "Employee Turnover: Seven Reasons Why People Quit Their Jobs," **http://ezinearticles.com/?Employee-Turnover:-Seven-Reasons-Why-People-Quit-Their-Jobs&id=42531** (accessed March 16, 2010).

22. Andrea Chang, "Gap to Close about 200 Stores in N. America as It Expands Overseas," *The Los Angeles Times,* October 14, 2011, **http://articles.latimes.com/2011/oct/14/business/la-fi-gap-downsize-20111014** (accessed April 5, 2012).

23. "Wage and Hour Division (WHD)," U.S. Department of Labor, **www.dol.gov/whd/flsa/index.htm** (accessed March 10, 2010).

24. "Fair Labor Standards Act Advisor," U.S. Department of Labor, **www.dol.gov/elaws/faq/esa/flsa/002.htm** (accessed April 23, 2012).

25. Alison van Diggelen, "*Working@Google: Green Carrots & Pogo Sticks,*" *Fresh Dialogues,* **www.freshdialogues.com/** (accessed November 9, 2011); "Can We Commute Carbon-Free," *Google Green,* **www.google.com/green/operations/commuting-carbon-free.html** (accessed November 9, 2011); Tiffany Hsu, "Google Creates $280-Million Solar Power Fund," *Los Angeles Times,* June 14, 2011, **http://articles.latimes.com/2011/jun/14/business/la-fi-google-solar-20110614** (accessed November 9, 2011).

26. Associated Press, "Santa Fe Not Likely to Raise Minimum Wage," kvia.com, December 22, 2009, **www.kvia.com/global/story.asp?s=11716158** (accessed March 10, 2010).

27. Zelie Pollon, "Santa Fe, N.M., to Have Nation's Highest Minimum Wage." *Reuters,* January 27, 2012, **www.reuters.com/article/2012/01/27/us-minimum-wage-santa-fe-idUSTRE80Q24K20120127** (accessed April 23, 2012).

28. "Kele & Co: First Innovative Jewelry Company in Direct Sales," May 5, 2008, **www.pressreleasepoint.com/kele-amp-co-first-innovative-jewelry-company-direct-sales** (accessed March 16, 2010). Kele & Co., "About Kele & Co," 2010, **www.keleonline.com/pages/about.html** (accessed April 5, 2012).

29. Aaron Lucchetti and Alison Tudor, "Bonuses Are Sinking at Morgan Stanley," *The Wall Street Journal,* January 17, 2012, **http://online.wsj.com/article/SB10001424052970204555904577165322098252812.html** (accessed April 23, 2012).

30. "A Statistical Profile of Employee Ownership," *The National Center for Employee Ownership,* February 2012, **www.nceo.org/main/article.php/id/2/** (accessed April 5, 2012).

31. "Employer Costs for Employee Compensation," U.S. Bureau of Labor Statistics, March 10, 2010, **www.bls.gov/news.release/ecec.nr0.htm** (accessed March 16, 2010).

32. Stephan Miller, "Employee Loyalty Hits 7-Year Low; Benefits Promote Retention," *Society for Human Resource Management,* March 22, 2012, **www.shrm.org/hrdisciplines/benefits/Articles/Pages/LoyaltyLow.aspx** (accessed April 5, 2012).

33. "Work/Life," Lowe's, **https://careers.lowes.com/benefits_work.aspx** (accessed April 23, 2012).

34. "No Doubt About It," *Inc.,* September 2011, pp. 104–10; Michael Lee Stallard, "Has SAS Chairman Jim Goodnight Cracked the Code of Corporate Culture?" *The Economic Times,* June 18, 2010, **http://economictimes.indiatimes.com/features/corporate-dossier/has-sas-chairman-jim-goodnight-cracked-the-code-of-corporate-culture/articleshow/6060110.cms** (accessed February 15, 2011); "100 Best Companies to Work For: SAS," *CNNMoney,* **http://money.cnn.com/magazines/fortune/bestcompanies/2011/snapshots/1.html** (accessed February 15, 2011).

35. "Union Members—2011," *Bureau of Labor Statistics,* January 27, 2012, **www.bls.gov/news.release/pdf/union2.pdf** (accessed April 4, 2012).

36. Severin Carrell, Dan Milmo, Alan Travis and Nick Hopkins, "Day of Strikes as Millions Heed Unions' Call to Fight Pension Cuts," *The Guardian,* November 29, 2011, **www.guardian.co.uk/society/2011/nov/30/public-sector-workers-strike-uk** (accessed April 5, 2012).

37. James R. Hagerty, "Caterpillar Closes Plant in Canada after Lockout," *The Wall Street Journal*, February 3, 2012, **http://online.wsj.com/article/SB10001424052970203889904577200953014575964.html** (accessed April 5, 2012).

38. "Union City Licorice Company Strike Heads To Mediation," *CBS San Francisco*, January 9, 2012, **http://sanfrancisco.cbslocal.com/2012/01/09/union-city-licorice-company-strike-heads-to-mediation/** (accessed April 23, 2012).

39. Reuters, "JP Morgan Discloses It Lost in an Arbitration Last Year," *The New York Times*, March 22, 2012, **www.nytimes.com/2012/03/23/business/jpmorgan-discloses-it-lost-in-arbitration-to-american-century.html** (accessed August 5, 2012).

40. "US Will Have Minority Whites Sooner, Says Demographer," *NPR*, June 27, 2011, **www.npr.org/2011/06/27/137448906/us-will-have-minority-whites-sooner-says-demographer** (accessed April 5, 2012).

41. Pat Wechsler, "And You Thought Cigarettes Were Pricey," *Bloomberg BusinessWeek*, July 4–10, 2011, pp. 24–26; A.G. Sulzberger, "Hospitals Shift Smoking Ban to Smokers Ban," *The New York Times*, February 10, 2011, **www.nytimes.com/2011/02/11/us/11smoking.html?pagewanted=all** (accessed August 12, 2011); Ken Alltucker, "Humana Won't Hire Smokers in Arizona," *USA Today*, July 1, 2011, **www.usatoday.com/money/industries/health/2011-06-30-smokers-jobs-humana_n.htm** (accessed August 16, 2011)

42. "No. 1: Kaiser Permanente," **http://diversityinc.com/the-2011-diversityinctop-50/no-1-kaiser-permanente/** (accessed April 4, 2012).

43. Taylor H. Cox Jr., "The Multicultural Organization," *Academy of Management Executives* 5 (May 1991), pp. 34–47; Marilyn Loden and Judy B. Rosener, *Workforce America! Managing Employee Diversity as a Vital Resource* (Homewood, IL: Business One Irwin, 1991).

44. Paul Davidson, "Overworked and Underpaid?" *USA Today*, April 16, 2012, pp. 1A–2A.

45. Ibid.

46. Ethics Resource Center, *2011 National Business Ethics Survey®: Ethics in Transition* (Arlington, VA: Ethics Resource Center, 2012), pp. 39–40.

47. Davidson, "Overworked and Underpaid?"

48. Melanie Trottman, "For Angry Employees, Legal Cover for Rants," *The Wall Street Journal*, December 2, 2011, **http://online.wsj.com/article/SB10001424052970203710704577049822809710332.html** (accessed April 23, 2012).

49. Martin Crutsinger, "Hiring Grows as Companies Hit Limits with Workers," *MPR News*, March 7, 2012, **http://minnesota.publicradio.org/display/web/2012/03/07/hiring-grows-as-companies-hit-limit/** (accessed April 23, 2012).

50. Actors Equity Association, "Equity Timeline," *Actors Equity, 2006*, **www.actorsequity.org/aboutequity/timeline/timeline_1919.html** (accessed July 30, 2012); Writers Guild of America, West, Inc., "History," *Writers Guild of America, West, 2012*, **www.wga.org/history/timeline.html** (accessed July 30, 2012); Jonathon Mandell, "Recalling 1988 Strike," *CBS News*, February 11, 2009, **www.cbsnews.com/2100-207_162-3447509.html** (accessed July 30, 2012); Screen Actors Guild, "History," *SAG-AFTRA One Union, 2012*, **www.sag.org/history** (accessed July 30, 2012); Richard Verrier, "SAG and AFTRA Members Give Thumbs Up to Merger," *Los Angeles Times*, March 30, 2012, **http://latimesblogs.latimes.com/entertainmentnewsbuzz/2012/03/sag-and-aftra-members-give-thumbs-up-to-merger.html** (accessed July 30, 2012).

Chapter 11

1. Brad Stone, "The Omnivore," *Bloomberg Businessweek*, October 3–9, 2011, pp. 58–65; Stu Woo and Jeffrey A. Trachtenberg, "Amazon Fights the iPad With 'Fire,' " *The Wall Street Journal*, September 29, 2011, pp. B1, B10; Kevin Kelleher, "Amazon versus Apple? Not So Fast," *CNNMoney*, October 12, 2011, **http://tech.fortune.cnn.com/2011/10/12/amazon-versus-apple** (accessed October 14, 2011).

2. Adapted from Pride and O.C. Ferrell, "Value-Driven Marketing," *Foundations of Marketing*, 4th ed. (Mason, OH: South-Western Cengage Learning), pp. 13–14.

3. Bruce Horovitz, "Domino's Offers Gluten-Free Pizza Crust," *USA Today*, May 7, 2012, p. B1.

4. Meng Jing, "China Gushes over High-End Bottled Water," *China Daily*, October 7–13, 2011, p. 17; "$HK1.6bn Public Offer by Tibet 5100 to Fuel Tilt at Evian Market Share," *The Australian*, June 22, 2011, **www.theaustralian.com.au/business/markets/hk16bn-public-offer-by-tibet-5100-to-fuel-tilt-at-evian-market-share/story-e6frg91o-1226079779794** (accessed November 1, 2011); Tibet 5100 website, **http://hk.5100.net/** (accessed November 1, 2011); "IPO Fact Sheet: Tibet 5100 Water Resources Holdings Limited (1115.HK)," VC Group, June 20, 2011, **www.vcgroup.com.hk/CM_v2/Document/tc/IPO%20Factsheet%20--%20Tibet%205100.pdf** (accessed November 1, 2011).

5. "Beauty Queen," *People*, May 10, 2004, p. 187.

6. Michael Treacy and Fred Wiersema, *The Discipline of Market Leaders* (Reading, MA: Addison Wesley, 1995), p. 176.

7. Jefferson Graham, "At Apple Stores, iPads at Your Service," *USA Today*, May 23, 2011, p. 1B; "Apple Stores," AAPLInvestors, **www.apple.com/retail/storelist/** (accessed May 14, 2012).

8. Beth J. Harpaz, "Campgrounds Court New Visitors with Comfortable Cabins, Activities," *USA Today*, May 26, 2011, **http://travel.usatoday.com/destinations/story/2011/05/Campgrounds-court-new-visitors-with-comfortable-cabins-activities/47687132/1** (accessed August 23, 2011); E. J. Schultz, "Why Camping Evolved to Keep Up With Travel Trend," *AdvertisingAge*, June 20, 2011, **http://adage.com/article/news/camping-evolved-travel-trend/228287/** (accessed August 24, 2011); Kitty Bean Yancey, "'Glamping' Brings Creature Comforts to Outdoors," *USA Today*, August 5, 2011, **http://travel.usatoday.com/destinations/story/2011/08/Go-glamping-in-the-Ohio-Wilds/49819754/1** (accessed August 24, 2011).

9. Customer Insight Group Inc. "Program Design: Loyalty and Retention," **www.customerinsightgroup.com/loyalty_retention.php** (accessed January 4, 2011).

10. Venky Shankar, "Multiple Touch Point Marketing," American Marketing Association, Faculty Consortium on Electronic Commerce, Texas A&M University, July 14–17, 2001.

11. Brad Wieners, "Lego Is for Girls," *Bloomberg Businessweek*, December 19–25, 2011, pp. 68–73.

12. David Kesmodel, "Brewers Go Courting Hispanics," *The Wall Street Journal*, July 12, 2011, p. B8.

13. "Minority Report," *The Economist*, March 31, 2011, **www.economist.com/node/18488452** (accessed April 6, 2012).

14. Dennis Schaal, "Search Site for 'Glamorous Camping' Lays Foundation," *USA Today,* May 7, 2012, p. B3.

15. Horovitz, "Domino's Offers Gluten-Free Pizza Crust," p. B1.

16. "The Coca-Cola Company Fact Sheet," **www.thecoca-cola company .com/ourcompany/pdf/Company_Fact_ Sheet.pdf** (accessed March 30, 2010); "Growth, leadership, and sustainability," The Coca-Cola Company, **www.thecoca-colacompany.com/ourcompany** (accessed August 16, 2012).

17. Hannah Elliott, "Most Fuel-Efficient Cars For The Buck," *Forbes,* March 30, 2009, **www.forbes.com/2009/ 03/30/fuel-efficient-cars-lifestyle-vehicles-efficient-cars.html** (accessed March 30, 2010).

18. "AdWords," Google, **https://adwords .google.com/um/gaiaauth?apt%3DNon e%26ltmpl%3Djfk%26ltmpl%3Djfk&er ror=newacct&sacu=1&sarp=1** (accessed May 14, 2012).

19. Sarah E. Needleman, "Facebook 'Likes' Small Business," *The Wall Street Journal,* September 26, 2011, p. B11.

20. Emily Steel and Geoffrey A. Fowler, "Big Brands Like Facebook, But They Don't Like To Pay," *The Wall Street Journal,* November 2, 2011, **http://online.wsj. com/article/SB1000142405297020429450 4576613232804554362.html?mg=com-wsj** (accessed May 14, 2012).

21. Christine Birkner, "10 Minutes with . . . Raul Murguia Villegas," *Marketing News,* July 30, 2011, pp. 26–27.

22. "MSPA North America," Mystery Shopping Providers Association, **www. mysteryshop.org/index-na.php** (accessed April 1, 2010).

23. Piet Levy, "10 Minutes with . . . Robert J. Morais," *Marketing News,* May 30, 2011, pp. 22–23.

24. Steven Kurutz, "On Kickstarter, Designers' Dream Materialize," *The New York Times,* September 21, 2011, **www. nytimes.com/2011/09/22/garden/on-kickstarter-designers-dreams-material ize.html?pagewanted=all** (accessed December 7, 2011).

25. Mya Frazier, "CrowdSourcing" *Delta Sky Mag,* February 2010, **http:// msp.imirus.com/Mpowered/imirus .jsp? volume=ds10&issue=2&page=72** (accessed February 18, 2010), p. 73.

26. Sue Shellenbarger, "A Few Bucks for Your Thoughts?" *The Wall Street Journal,* May 18, 2011, **http://online.wsj.com/ article/SB100014240527487035091045 76329110724411724.html** (accessed February 7, 2012).

27. David Rosenbaum, "Who's Out There?" *CFO,* January/February 2012, pp. 44–49.

28. Jack Kaskey, "The Superweek Strikes Back," *Bloomberg Businessweek,* September 12–18, 2011, pp. 21–22; Andrew Pollack, "Widely Used Crop Herbicide Is Losing Weed Resistance," *The New York Times,* January 14, 2003, **www.nytimes.com/2003/01/14/busi ness/widely-used-crop-herbicide-is-losing-weed-resistance.html** (accessed September 26, 2011).

29. Bruce Horovitz, "Gum Goes from Humdrum to Teen Fashion Statement," *USA Today,* May 8, 2012, p. B1.

30. Jon Gertner, "How Do You Solve a Problem like GM, Mary?" *Fast Company,* October 2011, pp. 104–108, 148; Sharon Terlep, "The Secrets of the GM Diet," *The Wall Street Journal,* August 5, 2011, pp. B1, B4.

31. "Brewers Association Release 2010 Top 50 Breweries List," Brewers Association, 2012, **www.brewers association.org/pages/media/press-releases/show?title=brewers-association -releases-2010-top-50-breweries-lists** (accessed July 30, 2012); Cotton Delo, "New Belgium Toasts to Its Facebook Fans," *Advertising Age,* February 13, 2012, **http://adage.com/article/news/belgium-toasts-facebook-fans/232681/** (accessed July 30, 2012); New Belgium Brewing, **www.newbelgium.com** (accessed July 30, 2012); New Belgium Brewing: Ethical and Environmental Responsibility," in O.C. Ferrell, John Fraedrich, and Linda Ferrell, *Business Ethics: Ethical Decision Making and Cases,* 9th ed. (Mason, OH: South-Western Cengage Learning, 2013), pp. 355–363; "COLLABEERATIONS," Elysian Brewing Company, **www.elysian brewing.com/beer/collabeerations .html** (accessed March 27, 2012); Devin Leonard, "New Belgium and the Battle of the Microbrews," *Bloomberg Businessweek,* December 1, 2011, **www.businessweek.com/magazine/ new-belgium-and-the-battle-of-the-microbrews-12012011.html** (accessed March 27, 2012).

Chapter 12

1. Duff McDonald, "The Mastermind of Adrenaline Marketing," *Bloomberg BusinessWeek,* May 23–29, 2011, pp. 64–70; **www.redbullusa.com** (accessed August 24, 2011); John Gaudiosi, "Red Bull Treats Pro Gamers Like Dave 'Walshy' Walsh Like Real Athletes, *Forbes,* July 10, 2011, **www.forbes.com/sites/johngaudiosi/ 2011/07/10/red-bull-treats-pro-gamers-like-dave-walshy-walsh-like-real-ath letes/** (accessed August 25, 2011).

2. Narendra Rao, "The Keys to New Product success (Part 1)—Collecting Unarticulated & Invisible Customer-Needs," *Product Management & Strategy,* June 19, 2007, **http://productstrategy .wordpress.com/2007/06/19/the-keys-to-new-product-successs-part-1-collect ing-unarticulated-invisible-customer-needs/** (accessed April 1, 2010).

3. Gwendolyn Cuizon, "SWOT Analysis of Dell Computers," **Suite101.com,** March 5, 2009, **http://strategic-business-planning.suite101.com/article.cfm/ swot_analysis_of_dell_computers** (accessed March 31, 2010).

4. Nicholas Kolakowski, "HP's Touch Pad Proves a Bestseller in Its Dying Moments," **eWeek.com,** August 22, 2011, **www.eweek.com/c/a/Mobile-and-Wire less/HPs-TouchPad-Proves-a-Bestseller-In-its-Dying-Moments-373816/** (accessed April 12, 2012).

5. Associated press, "Jobs Says iPad Idea Came Before iPhone," June 2, 2010, **www. foxnews.com/scitech/2010/06/02/jobs-says-ipad-idea-came-iphone/** (accessed April 12, 2012).

6. John A. Byrne, "Greatest Entrepreneurs of Our Time," *Fortune,* April 9, 2012, pp. 68–86.

7. "Cat® CT660 Vocational Trucks Ready for Work," Caterpillar Press Release, September 2011.

8. Julia Scott, "Jamba Juice honoring McDonald's smoothie coupons," Daily Finance, August 10, 2010, **www.daily finance.com/2010/08/10/jamba-juice-honoring-mcdonalds-smoothie-coupons/** (accessed April 12, 2012).

9. Jessica A. Vascellero, "Apple Preparing Upgrade to iCloud," *The Wall Street Journal,* May 14, 2012, **http://online.wsj .com/article/SB10001424052702304371 50457740418041792743 6.html** (accessed May 14, 2012); Brian X. Chen, "4th Time a Charm for Apple? From iDisk to Mac to MobileMe to iCloud," *Wired,* May 31, 2011, **www.wired.com/epicenter/2011/05/ icloud-apple** (accessed May 14, 2012).

10. Kent German, "A Brief History of Android Phones," *CNET,* August 2, 2011, **http://reviews.cnet.com/8301-19736_7-20016542-251/a-brief-history-of-android**

-phones/ (accessed April 12, 2012); Mike Luttrell, "Android Suffers First-Ever Market Share Decline," *TG Daily,* January 27, 2012, **www.tgdaily.com/mobility-brief/61070-android-suffers-first-ever-market-share-decline** (accessed April 12, 2012).

11. Duane Stanford, "Africa: Coke's Last Frontier," *Bloomberg Businessweek,* October 28, 2010, **www.businessweek.com/magazine/content/10_45/b4202054144294.htm** (accessed May 14, 2012); Kim Peterson, "Coke Debuts Smaller Bottles," *MSN Money,* September 19, 2011, **http://money.msn.com/top-stocks/post.aspx?post=2e4eaa5c-2162-4135-81c6-6d41a02d91b9** (accessed May 14, 2012); Meghra Bahree and Mike Esterl, "PepsiCo's Health Push," *The Wall Street Journal,* July 7, 2011, p. B8.

12. MSN Autos "Good riddance! Worst discontinued cars for 2011: Chevrolet Cobalt," **http://autos.ca.msn.com/specials/buyers-guide/gallery.aspx?cp-documentid=26951603&page=7** (accessed April 12, 2012).

13. "Product Life Cycle," Answers.com, **www.answers.com/topic/product-life-cycle** (accessed March 31, 2010).

14. Bruce Horovitz, "Barbie Ventures into Online World with Stardolls," *The Wall Street Journal,* November 14, 2011, p. 1B.

15. ABC News, "Jason Wu for Target Apparel Sells Out in Hours," February 6, 2011, **http://abcnews.go.com/blogs/business/2012/02/jason-wu-for-target-sells-out-in-first-morning-2/** (accessed May 14, 2012).

16. "Private Label Gets Personal," *Shopper Culture,* **www.shopperculture.com/shopper_culture/2009/10/private-label-gets-personal.html** (accessed April 2, 2010).

17. Mona Doyle, "What Packaging Will Consumers Pay More For?" *Food & Beverage Packaging,* August 1, 2008, **www.foodandbeveragepackaging.com/Articles/Article_Rotation/BNP_GUID_9-5-2006_A_10000000000000401665** (accessed January 14, 2011).

18. Bruce Horovitz, "Marketers Capitalize on Fond Thoughts of the Good Ol' Days," *USA Today,* March 11–13, 2011, p. 1A.

19. Mike Esterl, "A Frosty Reception for Coca-Cola's White Christmas Cans," *The Wall Street Journal,* December 1, 2011 p. D1.

20. Mike Ramsey, "Ford Drops in Quality Survey," *The Wall Street Journal,* June 24, 2011, **http://online.wsj.com/article/SB10001424052702304569504576403824202399548.html** (accessed April 12, 2012).

21. "National Quarterly Scores," *ACSI,* **www.theacsi.org/index.php?option=com_content&view=article&id=31&Itemid=117** (accessed April 12, 2012).

22. "American Demographics 2006 Consumer Perception Survey," *Advertising Age,* January 2, 2006, p. 9. Data by Synovate.

23. Rajneesh Suri and Kent B. Monroe, "The Effects of Time Constraints on Consumers' Judgments of Prices and Products," *Journal of Consumer Research* 30 (June 2003), pp. 92.

24. Tim Culpan, "AUO Losses Continue as Slowing TV Demand Pushes Prices Lower," *Bloomberg Businessweek,* November 1, 2011, **www.businessweek.com/news/2011-11-01/auo-losses-continue-as-slowing-tv-demand-pushes-prices-lower.html** (accessed April 12, 2012).

25. Ellen Byron, "Little Package, Small Problem," *The Wall Street Journal,* July 1, 2011, p. B6; Kristen Heist and Heather Reavey, "A Dry History of Concentrates," *Bloomberg Businessweek,* **http://images.businessweek.com/slideshows/20110908/a-dry-history-of-concentrates/** (accessed October 7, 2011); Sarah Rich, "Almost Genius: Cleaning Products Where You Just Add Water," *Fast Company,* July 22, 2010, **www.fastcompany.com/almost-genius-cleaning-products-where-you-just-add-water** (accessed October 7, 2011); Alissa Walker, "Replenish Cleaning Products: You Provide the Water (And Help Save the Earth)," *Fast Company,* **www.fastcodesign.com/1662521/replenish-cleaning-products-you-provide-the-water-and-help-save-the-earth** (accessed October 7, 2011).

26. Emily Maltby, "Restocking the Old Vending Machine with Live Bait and Prescription," *The Wall Street Journal,* March 22, 2012, p. B1.

27. "The Sysco Story," Sysco, **www.sysco.com/about-sysco.html#** (accessed May 14, 2012).

28. "Top Threats to Revenue," *USA Today,* February 1, 2006, p. A1.

29. Brad Howarth, "Hear This, iPods from a Vending Machine," *The Sydney Morning Herald,* November 14, 2006, **www.smh.com.au/news/biztech/hear-this-ipods-from-a-vending-machine/2006/11/13/1163266481869.html** (accessed April 8, 2010).

30. "Welcome to the Future of Shopping," Zoom Systems, **www.zoomsystems.com/zoomshops/zs_index.html** (accessed April 5, 2010).

31. Piper Aircraft, "International Dealers and Sales Locations," **www.piper.com/docs/DealerMap_Intl.pdf** (accessed May 14, 2012).

32. William Pride and O.C. Ferrell, *Marketing Foundations,* 5th ed. (Mason, OH: Cengage South-Western Learning, 2013), pp. 415–416.

33. William Pride and O.C. Ferrell, *Marketing Foundations,* 5th ed. (Mason, OH: Cengage South-Western Learning, 2013), pp. 415–416.

34. Ashley Lutz, "Rivals Rush to Copy Lululemon's Yoga Pose," *Bloomberg Businessweek,* September 8, 2011, **www.businessweek.com/magazine/rivals-rush-to-copy-lululemons-yoga-pose-09082011.html** (accessed October 6, 2011); "Lululemon Athletica: Our Company History," Lululemon, **www.lululemon.com/about/history** (accessed October 6, 2011); Solarina Ho, "Lululemon Seen Growing in Lucrative Niche Market," *Reuters,* November 2, 2010, **www.reuters.com/article/2010/11/02/idUSN0116446120101102** (accessed October 6, 2011); Lululemon Compay, "Lululemon Athletica Inc. Announces Fourth Quarter and Full Year Fiscal 2011 Results," March 22, 2012, **http://investor.lululemon.com/releasedetail.cfm?ReleaseID=658839** (accessed May 14, 2012).

35. Abbey Klaassen, "Even Google Has to Advertise," *Advertising Age,* June 2, 2008, p. 4.

36. Michael Wei & Margaret Conley, "Some Chinese Kids' First English Word: Mickey," *Bloomberg BusinessWeek,* June 9, 2011, **www.businessweek.com/magazine/content/11_25/b4233024744691.htm** (accessed August 26, 2011); Malcolm Moore, "Disney Breaks Ground on Shanghai Theme Park," *The Telegraph,* April 8, 2011, **www.telegraph.co.uk/news/worldnews/asia/china/8437153/Disney-breaks-ground-on-Shanghai-theme-park.html** (accessed August 27, 2011); **disneyenglish.com/EN/home page.html** (accessed August 26, 2011); James T. Areddy & Peter Sanders, "Chinese Learn English the Disney Way," *The Wall Street Journal,* April 20, 2009, **http://online.wsj.com/article/SB124017964526732863.html** (accessed September 15, 2011); Frederick Balfour, "Disney to Expand Hong Kong Disneyland,"

Bloomberg Businessweek, June 26, 2009, **www.businessweek.com/globalbiz/blog/ eyeonasia/archives/2009/06/disney_to_ expan.html** (accessed May 14, 2012); Karen Chu, "Hong Kong Disneyland Narrows 2011 Loss to $30.5 Million," *The Hollywood Reporter,* January 11, 2012, **www.hollywoodreporter.com/news/ hong-kong-disneyland-narrows-2011- 280689** (accessed May 14, 2012).

37.   Suzanne Vranica, "Higher Prices Don't Keep Marketers Away from Ad Time for Super Bowl," *The Wall Street Journal,* January 3, 2012, p. B1.

38.   Rich Thomaselli, "National Football League Players: CBS Rejected Let Us Play Ad," *Advertising Age,* January 31, 2011, **http://adage.com/article/news/national- football-league-players-cbs-rejected- play-ad/148580/** (accessed April 13, 2012).

39.   "Best Buzz Marketing/Influencer Program," *Event Marketer,* June 14, 2011, **www.eventmarketer.com/ex-awards/ 2011/best-buzz-marketinginfluencer- program** (accessed February 21, 2012).

40.   Gerry Khermouch and Jeff Green, "Buzz Marketing," *BusinessWeek,* July 30, 2001, pp. 50–56.

41.   Andrew Romano, "Now 4 Restaurant 2.0," *Newsweek,* February 28, 2009, **www. newsweek.com/id/187008** (accessed April 5, 2010).

42.   Lauren Johnson, "Mobile Coupon Redemption Expected to Reach 8pc by 2016: Study," *Mobile Commerce Daily,* January 6, 2012, **www.mobilecommerce daily.com/2012/01/06/mobile-coupon- redemption-expected-to-reach-8pc-by- 2016-study** (accessed April 13, 2012).

43.   "Kimberly Clark: Becoming the Indispensable Partner for Retailers," *Retail Solutions,* **www.t3ci.com/pdfs/ Retail_Solutions_Kimberly_Clark_ Case_Study_2009-01.pdf** (accessed April 5, 2010).

44.   "Sweepstakes: Enter for a Chance to Win," Travel Channel, **www.travel channel.com/sweepstakes** (accessed April 13, 2012).

45.   Lauren Etter and Douglas MacMillan, "The Education of Groupon CEO Andrew Mason," *Bloomberg Businessweek,* July 12, 2012, **www.busi nessweek.com/articles/2012-07-12/the- education-of-groupon-ceo-andrew- mason#p1** (accessed July 31, 2012).

Chapter 13

1.   Zhang Jing, Yang Yang, and Meng Jing, "Micro Revolution Sweeps Nation,"

China Daily, April 22–24, 2011, p. 9; Kenneth Rapoza, "China's Weibos vs US's Twitter: And the Winner Is?" *Forbes,* May 17, 2011, **www.forbes.com/sites/ kenrapoza/2011/05/17/chinas-weibos- vs-uss-twitter-and-the-winner-is/** (accessed October 10, 2011); Loretta Chao, "China's 'Twitter' has big dreams," *The Wall Street Journal,* June 27, 2011, **http://online.wsj.com/article/SB100014 24052702304231204576405041750625026.html** (accessed October 10, 2011).

2.   This material in this chapter is reserved for use in the authors' other textbooks and teaching materials.

3.   Brad Stone and Bruce Einhorn, "Baidu China," *Bloomberg Businessweek,* November 15–21, 2010, pp. 60–67; Trefis Team, "Baidu Girds For Google Battle In China, *Forbes,* **www.forbes.com/ sites/greatspeculations/2011/12/07/ baidu-girds-for-google-battle-in-china/** (accessed February 10, 2012).

4.   "Fortune 500," *CNNMoney,* **http:// money.cnn.com/magazines/fortune/ fortune500/2011/full_list/** (accessed February 29, 2012).

5.   "Fortune 500: Amazon.com," *Fortune,* 2009, **http://money.cnn.com/ magazines/fortune/fortune500/2009/ snapshots/10810.html** (accessed March 19, 2010); Josh Quitter, "How Jeff Bezos Rules the Retail Space," *Fortune,* May 5, 2008, pp. 127–132.

6.   "Media Info," Hulu, **www.hulu.com/ about** (accessed March 19, 2010); Hulu website, **www.hulu.com/about** (accessed February 29, 2012).

7.   Bobby White, "The New Workplace Rules: No Video-Watching," *The Wall Street Journal,* March 4, 2008, p. B1.

8.   Etsy website, **www.etsy.com/?ref=so_ home** (accessed November 1, 2011); Spencer E. Ante, "Etsy Knits Together a Market," *The Wall Street Journal,* July 14, 2011, **http://online.wsj.com/ article/SB10001424052702304223804 576444042827007476.html** (accessed November 1, 2011); Max Chafkin, "Can Rob Kalin Scale Etsy?" *Inc.,* April 2011, **www.inc.com/magazine/20110401/ can-rob-kalin-scale-etsy.html** (accessed November 1, 2011); "Rob Kalin Out as Esty CEO," *Inc.,* July 21, 2011, **www. inc.com/articles/201107/rob-kalin- steps-down-as-etsy-ceo.html** (accessed November 1, 2011); "Our Mission," The Etsy Blog, **www.etsy.com/blog/en/about/** (accessed November 1, 2011).

9.   "Internet Usage Statistics," Internet World Stats, **www.Internetworldstats .com/stats.htm** (accessed March 21,

2010); "Internet Usage Statistics," **www. internetworldstats.com/stats.htm** (accessed March 1, 2012).

10.   Michael V. Copeland. "Tapping Tech's Beautiful Mind," *Fortune,* October 12, 2009, pp. 35–36.

11.   Matthew Boyle and Douglas MacMillan, "Wal-Mart's Rocky Path From Bricks to Clicks," *Bloomberg Businessweek,* July 25–31, 2011, pp. 31–33; "Free Shipping With Site to Store®," Walmart, **www.walmart.com/cp/Site- to-Store/538452** (accessed February 10, 2012).

12.   Aaron Back, "China's Big Brands Tackle Web Sales," *The Wall Street Journal,* December 1, 2009, p. B2; "The Taobao Affair from China Largest Auction Website," *PR Log,* February 7, 2010, **www.prlog.org/10552554-the- taobao-affair-from-china-largest- auction-website.html** (accessed February 16, 2012).

13.   Shayndi Raice, "The Man Behind Facebook's Marketing," *The Wall Street Journal,* February 3, 2012, p. B7; "About Sponsored Stories, Facebook, **www. facebook.com/help/?page=15450007128 2557** (accessed February 13, 2012).

14.   "2009 Digital Handbook," *Marketing News,* April 30, 2009, p. 13.

15.   Cameron Chapman, "The History and Evolution of Social Media." *WebDesigner Depot,* October 7, 2009, **www.webdesignerdepot.com/2009/10/ the-history-and-evolution-of-social- media/** (accessed April 2, 2010).

16.   "The history of social media in a blink," Windows Live, November 22, 2007, **http://mbresseel.spaces.live.com/Blog/ cns%2133234018BF280C82%21345 .entry** (accessed February 18, 2010).

17.   "CafeMom," Highland Capital Partners, **www.hcp.com/cafemom** (accessed February 10, 2012); "Top 15 Most Popular Social Networking Sites," *eBiz,* February 2012, **www.ebizmba.com/ articles/social-networking-websites** (accessed February 10, 2012).

18.   Zachary Karabell, "To Tweet or Not to Tweet," April 12, 2011, *Time,* p. 24.

19.   "It's a Social World: Social Networking Leads as Top Online Activity Globally, Accounting for 1 in Every 5 Online Minutes," comScore, December 21, 2011, **www.comscore.com/Press_Events/Press_ Releases/2011/12/Social_Networking_ Leads_as_Top_Online_Activity_Globally** (accessed March 1, 2012).

20.   Jon Swartz, "Timberlake Could Revive Popularity of Myspace," *USA Today,* July 5, 2011, p. 5B.

21. Myspace website, **www.myspace.com/** (accessed April 11, 2011).

22. "Justin Timberlake Debuts Myspace TV," *Rolling Stone,* January 10, 2012, **www.rollingstone.com/music/news/justin-timberlake-debuts-myspace-tv-20120110** (accessed February 10, 2012).

23. "Facebook: Largest, Fastest Growing Social Network," *Tech Tree,* August 13, 2008, **www.techtree.com/India/News/Facebook_Largest_Fastest_Growing_Social_Network/551-92134-643.html** (accessed January 12, 2010).

24. Nick Summers. "Heated Rivalries: #9 Facebook vs. MySpace." *Newsweek.* **www.2010.newsweek.com/top-10/heated-rivalries/facebook-vs-myspace.html** (accessed January 13, 2010).

25. Courtney Rubin, "Internet Users Over Age 50 Flocking to Social Media," *Inc.,* August 30, 2010, **www.inc.com/news/articles/2010/08/users-over-50-are-fastest-growing-social-media-demographic.html** (accessed February 13, 2012).

26. Bruce Horovitz, "AmEx Rewards Points Now Buy You Facebook Ads," *USA Today,* June 29, 2011, p. 1B.

27. Cotton Delo, "New Belgium Toasts to Its Facebook Fans," *Advertising Age,* February 13, 2012, **http://adage.com/article/news/belgium-toasts-facebook-fans/232681/** (accessed February 27, 2012).

28. Jefferson Graham, "Cake Decorator Finds Twitter a Tweet Recipe for Success," *USA Today,* April 1, 2009, p. 5B.

29. Aaron Smith, "Twitter Update 2011," Pew Internet & American Life Project, June 1, 2011, **http://pewinternet.org/Reports/2011/Twitter-Update-2011.aspx** (accessed March 1, 2012).

30. Elizabeth Holmes, "Tweeting Without Fear," *The Wall Street Journal,* December 9, 2011, p. B1.

31. Bruce Horovitz, "Marketers Step Up Their Rewards for Twitter Buzz," *USA Today,* November 17, 2010, p. 2B.

32. Zachary Karabell, "To Tweet or Not to Tweet," *Time,* April 11, 2011, p. 24.

33. Suzanne Vranica, "Tweeting to Sell Cars," *The Wall Street Journal,* November 15, 2010, p. B12.

34. "As Twitter Grows and Evolves, More Manpower Is Needed," *Marketing News,* March 15, 2011, p. 13.

35. "Social Media Summit," Harrisburg University, 2012, **www.harrisburgu.edu/academics/professional/socialmedia/index-2012.php** (accessed February 16, 2012).

36. A.C. Neilson, "Global Faces and Networked Places: A Neilson Report on Social Networking's New Global Foot print," March 2009, **http://server-uk.imrworldwide.com/pdcimages/Global_Faces_and_Networked_Places-A_Nielsen_Report_on_Social_Net workings_New_Global_Footprint.pdf** (accessed June 3,2010).

37. "Couldn't stop the spread of the conversation in reactions from other bloggers," from Hyejin Kim's May 4, 2007, blog post "Korea: Bloggers and Donuts" on the blog Global Voices at **groundswell.forrester.com/site1-16** (accessed January 10, 2010).

38. Randy Tinseth, "Randy's Journal," Boeing, **http://boeingblogs.com/randy/** (accessed January 10, 2010).

39. Drake Bennett, "Ten Years of Inaccuracy and Remarkable Detail: Wikipedia," *Bloomberg Businessweek,* January 10–16, 2011, pp. 57–61.

40. Charlene Li and Josh Bernoff, *Groundswell* (Boston: Harvard Business Press, 2008), pp. 25–26.

41. Nora Ganim Barnes and Justina Andonian, "The 2011 Fortune 500 and Social Media Adoption: Have America's Largest Companies Reached a Social Media Plateau?" University of Massachusetts, 2011, **www.umassd.edu/cmr/studiesandresearch/2011fortune500/** (accessed February 16, 2012).

42. Emily Glazer, "Who Is Ray WJ? YouTube's Top Star," *The Wall Street Journal,* February 2, 2012, p. B1.

43. Tom Foster, "The GoPro Army," *Inc.,* February 2012, pp. 52–59.

44. "Keller Williams Reality Photo stream," **www.flickr.com/photos/kellerwilliamsrealty/** (accessed February 16, 2012).

45. Bianca Male, "How to Promote Your Business on Flickr," *The Business Insider,* December 1, 2009, **www.businessinsider.com/how-to-promote-your-business-on-flickr-2009-12?utm_source=feedburner&utm_medium=feed&utm_campaign=Feed%3A+businessinsider+(The+Business+Insider)** (accessed April 12, 2011).

46. "How to Market on Flickr," Small Business Search Marketing, **www.smallbusinesssem.com/articles** (accessed April 12, 2011).

47. "2009 Digital Handbook," p. 14.

48. "About Made Money," *CNBC,* **www.cnbc.com/id/17283246/** (accessed February 28, 2012).

49. Jefferson Graham, "Mobile Apps Make It Easier to Go Green," *USA Today,* May 12, 2011, **www.usatoday.com/tech/products/2011-05-12-green-tech_n.htm** (accessed October 6, 2011); "Green Apps That Can Save You Money," *Reuters,* February 18, 2011, **http://blogs.reuters.com/environment/2011/02/18/green-apps-that-can-save-you-money/** (accessed October 6, 2011); Jefferson Graham, "GoodGuide App Helps Navigate Green Products," *USA Today,* May 13, 2011, **www.usatoday.com/tech/products/2011-05-12-GoodGuide-app_n.htm** (accessed October 6, 2011).

50. "Dominos Pizza, Second Places," **www.secondplaces.net/opencms/opencms/portfolio/caseStudies/caseStudy_dominospizza.html** (accessed February 16, 2012).

51. Brandy Shaul, "CityVille Celebrates the Golden Arches with Branded McDonald's Restaurant," *Games.com,* October 19, 2011, **http://blog.games.com/2011/10/19/cityville-mcdonalds-restaurant/**.

52. Emily Glazer, "Virtual Fairs Offer Real Jobs," *The Wall Street Journal,* October 31, 2011, p. B9.

53. Roger Yu, "Smartphones Help Make Bon Voyages," *USA Today,* March 5, 2010, p. B1.

54. Melissa Hoffman, "Mobile Marketing to Explode in 2012," *Direct Marketing News,* January 12, 2012, **www.dmnews.com/mobile-marketing-to-explode-in-2012/article/222991/** (accessed February 28, 2012).

55. "Mobile Marketing Advertising Budgets Will Increase in 2012 Due to Smartphone Sales," PR Web, January 11, 2012, **www.prweb.com/releases/2012/1/prweb9095950.htm** (accessed February 28, 2012).

56. Mark Milian, "Why Text Messages Are Limited to 160 Characters," *Los Angeles Times,* May 3, 2009, **http://latimesblogs.latimes.com/technology/2009/05/invented-text-messaging.html** (accessed February 28, 2012); "Eight Reasons Why Your Business Should Use SMS Marketing," *Mobile Marketing Ratings,* **www.mobilemarketingratings.com/eight-reasons-sms-marketing.html** (accessed February 28, 2012).

57. *Lauren Folino* and *Michelle V. Rafter,* "How to Use Multimedia for Business Marketing," *Inc.,* January 25, 2010, **www.inc.com/guides/multimedia-for-business-marketing.**

html (accessed February 28, 2012); "Motorola Powers House of Blues(R)," *PR Newswire,* **www.prnewswire.com/ news-releases/motorola-powers-house-of-bluesr-54990822.html** (accessed February 28, 2012).

58. Lauren Johnson, "Orville Redenbacher Promotes Healthy Snacks with Mobile Banner Ads," *Mobile Marketer,* October 26, 2011, **www.mobile marketer.com/cms/news/advertising/ 11321.html** (accessed February 28, 2012).

59. Nick Bilton, "Mobile Devices Account for a Growing Portion of Web Traffic," *The New York Times,* October 12, 2011, **http://bits.blogs.nytimes. com/2011/10/12/mobile-accounts-for-7-percent-of-web-traffic-report-says/** (accessed February 28, 2012).

60. Foursquare website, **https://four square.com/** (accessed February 16, 2012).

61. Anita Campbell, "What the Heck Is an App?" Small Business Trends, March 7, 2011, **http://smallbiztrends. com/2011/03/what-is-an-app.html** (accessed February 28, 2012).

62. "Half of All Adult Cell Phone Owners Have Apps on Their Phones," Pew Internet and American Life Project, November 2, 2011, **http://pewinternet. org/~/media/Files/Reports/2011/ PIP_Apps-Update-2011.pdf** (accessed February 28, 2012).

63. Jefferson Graham, "Shopkick App Knocking on Doors of Local Retailers to Offer Deals," *USA Today,* June 22, 2011, p. 3B.

64. Todd Wasserman, "5 Innovative Mobile Marketing Campaigns," *Mashable,* March 8, 2011, **http://mashable.com/ 2011/03/08/mobile-marketing-camp aigns/** (accessed February 13, 2012).

65. Umika Pidaparthy, "Marketers Embracing QR Codes, for Better or Worse," *CNN Tech,* March 28, 2011, **http://articles.cnn.com/2011-03-28/ tech/qr.codes.marketing_1_qr-smart phone-users-symbian?_s=PM:TECH** (accessed April 11, 2011).

66. Brad Stone and Olga Kharif, "Pay As You Go," *Bloomberg Businessweek,* July 18–24, 2011, pp. 66–71.

67. "Google Wallet," **www.google.com/ wallet/what-is-google-wallet.html** (accessed February 16, 2012).

68. Miriam Gottfried, "Mobile Banking Gets Riskier," *The Wall Street Journal,* July 10, 2011, p. B7.

69. Vangie Beal, "All About Widgets," *Webopedia™*, August 31, 2010, **www.web opedia.com/DidYouKnow/Internet/ 2007/widgets.asp** (accessed February 28, 2012).

70. Rachael King, "Building a Brand with Widgets," *Bloomberg Businessweek,* March 3, 2008, **www.businessweek.com/ technology/content/feb2008/tc2008030 3_000743.htm** (accessed February 28, 2012).

71. "Barkley Develops Krispy Kreme® 'Hot Light' App and Widget," *The Wall Street Journal,* December 23, 2011, **http://online.wsj.com/article/PR-CO-20111223-904499.html** (accessed February 28, 2012).

72. Li and Bernoff, *Groundswell,* p. 41.

73. Li and Bernoff, *Groundswell,* pp. 41–42.

74. "Forrester Unveils New Segment of Social Technographics—The Conversationalists," *360 Digital Connections,* January 21, 2010, **http:// blog.360i.com/social-media/forrester-new-segment-social-technographics-conversationalists (accessed April 17, 2012).**

75. Li and Bernoff, *Groundswell,* p. 44.

76. John Bussey, "Facebook's Test in China: What Price Free Speech?" *The Wall Street Journal,* June 10, 2011, **http:// online.wsj.com/article/SB100014240 5270230477830457637581035977799 64.html** (October 31, 2011); Kit Eaton, "Zuckerberg's Taking Facebook into China, But It'll Be a Baidu Beast," *Fast Company,* **www.fastcompany.com/1746392/ facebook-china-baidu-social-networking** (accessed October 31, 2011); Gordon G. Chang, "China Wants to Buy Facebook," *Forbes,* July 3, 2011, **www.forbes.com/ sites/gordonchang/2011/07/03/china-wants-to-buy-facebook/** (accessed October 31, 2011).

77. Li and Bernoff, *Groundswell,* pp. 44–45.

78. Li and Bernoff, *Groundswell,* pp. 26–27.

79. Julia Angwin, Shayndi Raice, and Spencer E. Ante, "Facebook Retreats on Privacy, *The Wall Street Journal,* November 11, 2011, **http://online.wsj. com/article/SB10001424052970204224 60457703038374551516.html** (accessed February 16, 2012).

80. Julia Angwin, "U.S. Seeks Web Privacy 'Bill of Rights,' " *The Wall Street Journal,* December 17, 2010, pp. A1–A2; Julia Angwin and Steve Stecklow, "'Scrapers' Dig Deep for Data on Web," *The Wall Street Journal,* October 12, 2010, pp. A1, A18.

81. Jon Swartz, "Facebook Changes Its Status in Washington," *USA Today,* January 13, 2011, pp. 1B–2B; John W. Miller, "Yahoo Cookie Plan in Place," *The Wall Street Journal,* March 19, 2011, **http://online.wsj.com/article/ SB100014 2405274870351240457620870081381557 0.html** (accessed July 5, 2011).

82. Byron Acohido, "Net Do-Not-Track Option Kicks off to Criticism," *USA Today,* August 30, 2011, p. 2B.

83. Larry Barrett, "Data Breach Costs Surge in 2009: Study," *eSecurityPlanet,* January 26, 2010, **www.esecurityplanet. com/features/article.php/3860811/ Data-Breach-Costs-Surge-in-2009-Study.htm** (accessed January 28, 2010).

84. "Friend Me On Faecbook," *Bloomberg Businessweek,* November 7–13, 2011, pp. 36–37.

85. Greg Hudson, "Warning: Fake Japanese Tsunami Videos Scam Facebook Users," Better Business Bureau, March 16, 2011, **www.bbb.org/us/post/warning-fake-japanese-tsunami-videos-scam-facebook-users-10529** (accessed March 1, 2012).

86. Brett Molina, "Legit Magaupload Users Cut Off from Their Files," *The Wall Street Journal,* February 1, 2012, p. 3B.

87. Derek Broes, "Why Should You Fear SOPA and PIPA?" *Forbes,* January 20, 2012, **www.forbes.com/sites/derekbroes/ 2012/01/20/why-should-you-fear-sopa-and-pipa/** (accessed February 16, 2012); "SOPA and PIPA Bills: Online Companies Win Piracy Fight," *Huffington Post,* **www. huffingtonpost.com/2012/01/21/sopa-and-pipa-bills-anti-piracy-legislation_ n_1220817.html** (accessed February 16, 2012).

88. Kevin Shanahan and Mike Hyman "Motivators and Enablers of SCOURing," *Journal of Business Research* 63 (September–October 2010), pp. 1095–1102.

89. Seventh Annual BSA and IDC Global Software Piracy Study," BSA, **http://portal.bsa.org/globalpiracy2009/ index.html** (accessed April 13, 2011).

90. Max Chafkin, "The Case, and the Plan, for the Virtual Company," *Inc.,* April 2010, p. 68.

91. "Social Media at Work—Bane or Boon?" *CNN,* March 8, 2010, **www.cnn. com/2010/LIVING/worklife/03/08/ cb.social.media.banned/index.html** (accessed July 31, 2012); Emily Glazer, "P&G Curbs Employees' Internet Use," *The Wall Street Journal,* April 4, 2012, **http://online.wsj.com/article/SB100014 2405270230407200457732414284700 6**

340.html (accessed July 31, 2012); Ethics Resource Center, *2011 National Business Ethics Survey®: Ethics in Transition* (Arlington, VA: Ethics Resource Center, 2012); Miral Fahmy, "Facebook, YouTube at Work Make Better Employees: Study," *Reuters,* April 2, 2009, **www.wired .com/techbiz/media/news/2009/04/ reuters_us_work_internet_tech_life** (accessed May 5, 2010); Sharon Gaudin, "Study: Facebook Use Cuts Productivity at Work," *Computer World,* July 22, 2009, **www.computerworld.com/s/ article/9135795/Study_Facebook_use_ cuts_productivity_at_work** (accessed May 5, 2010); Sharon Gaudin, "Study: 54% of Companies Ban Facebook, Twitter at Work," *Computer World,* October 6, 2009, **www.computerworld. com/s/article/9139020/Study_54_of_ companies_ban_Facebook_Twitter_at_ work** (accessed May 5, 2010).

Chapter 14

1. Nathaniel Popper, "For Amazon, Stakes Are High in Sales Tax Fight," *Los Angeles Times,* July 19, 2011, **http:// articles.latimes.com/2011/jul/19/ business/la-fi-amazon-taxes-20110719** (accessed September 14, 2011); Stu Woo, "Amazon Battles States over Sales Tax," *The Wall Street Journal,* August 3, 2011, **http://online.wsj.com/article/SB1000 142405311190477230457646875356 4916130.html** (accessed September 14, 2011); "Bipartisan Trio of U.S. Senators to Introduce Federal Sales Tax Collection Bill," *Los Angeles Times,* November 9, 2011, **http://latimesblogs.latimes.com/ money_co/2011/11/bipartisan-trio- of-us-senators-introduce-federal- sales-tax-collection-bill.html** (accessed January 4, 2012); Jennifer Liberto, "Amazon and eBay Brawl over Web Sales Tax," *CNNMoney,* December 2, 2011, **http://money.cnn.com/2011/11/30/ technology/onlines_sales_tax/index .htm** (accessed January 4, 2012); Marielle Segarra, "Online Retailers Feel the Heat," *CFO,* April 2012, pp. 19–20.

2. "SEC Charges Deloitte & Touche in Shanghai with Violating U.S. Securities Laws in Refusal to Produce Documents," U.S. Securities & Exchange Commission, May 9, 2012, **www.sec.gov/news/press/ 2012/2012-87.htm** (accessed May 18, 2012).

3. "Report to the Nation," Association of Certified Fraud Examiners, **www.acfe .com/resources/publications.asp? copy=rttn** (accessed March 31, 2010).

4. "About the ACFE," ACFE website, **www.acfe.com/about the acfe.aspx** (accessed May 18, 2012).

5. "Reporting," Accounting for Sustain ability, **www.accountingforsustainability .org/reporting/** (accessed October 4, 2011); "About this Book—*Accounting for Sustainability: Practical Insights,*" *Earthscan,* **www.earthscan.co.uk/?tabid =102272** (accessed October 4, 2011); Michael Cohn, "Accountants See Sustainability Practices Growing," *Accounting Today,* September 28, 2011, **www.accountingtoday.com/news/ Accountants-See-Sustainability- Practices-Growing-60332-1.html** (accessed October 4, 2011); Canadian Institute of Chartered Accountants, American Institute of CPAs, and Chartered Institute of Management Accountants, "SMEs Set Their Sights on Sustainability," September 2011, **www. aicpa.org/InterestAreas/Business IndustryAndGovernment/Resources/ Sustainability/DownloadableDocu ments/Sustainability_Case_Studies_ Final%20pdf.pdf** (accessed October 4, 2011); David Rosenbaum, "No Résumés Required," *CFO,* April 2012, p. 24.

6. Mary Williams Walsh, "State Woes Grow Too Big to Camouflage," *The New York Times,* March 29, 2010, **www.nytimes.com/2010/03/30/ business/economy/30states.html** (accessed March 31, 2010).

7. Sarah Johnson, "Averting Revenue-Recognition Angst," *CFO,* April 2012, p. 21.

8. Evelyn M. Rusli and Peter Eavis, "Facebook Raises $16 Billion in I.P.O.," *The New York Times,* May 17, 2012, **http://dealbook.nytimes.com/2012/05/ 17/facebook-raises-16-billion-in-i-p-o/?hp** (accessed May 25, 2012); Brad Stone and Douglas MacMillan, "How Zuck Hacked the Valley," *Bloomberg Businessweek,* May 21-May 27, 2012, pp. 60–67; Facebook Newsroom, **http://newsroom.fb.com/ content/default.aspx?NewsAreaId=22** (accessed May 25, 2012); "Facebook IPO Fallout Continues," *The Washington Post,* May 24, 2012, **www.washingtonpost .com/business/economy/facebook- ipo-fallout-continues/2012/05/24/ gJQAJcTxnU_story.html** (accessed May 25, 2012); Brett Philbin and David Benoit, "Morgan Stanley Revisits Facebook Trades; Investors File Suit," *The Wall Street Journal,* **http://online.wsj.com/ article/SB1000142405270230470760457 7422063685311108.html?KEYWORDS =Investors+File+Suit+Against+Face book** (accessed May 25, 2012).

9. "IFRS FAQS," AICPA IFRS Resources, **www.ifrs.com/ifrs_faqs.html#q3** (accessed September 19, 2011); Michael

Rapoport, "Accounting Move Pits Big vs. Small," *The Wall Street Journal,* July 6, 2011, pp. C1–C2; David Bogoslaw, "Global Accounting Standards? Not So Fast," *Bloomberg Businessweek,* November 13, 2008, **www.businessweek .com/investor/content/nov2008/ pi20081112_143039.htm** (accessed September 19, 2011); Marie Leone, "Comparability: Still Up in the Air?" *CFO,* September 1, 2011, **www3.cfo.com/ article/2011/9/gaap-ifrs_gaap-ifrs-migr ation** (accessed September 19, 2011).

10. Julie Clements, "City of El Dorado Receives Accounting Award," *El Dorado Times,* April 3, 2012, **www.eldoradotimes.com/features/ x586045543/City-of-El-Dorado- receives-accounting-award** (accessed May 25, 2012).

11. "Accountants and Auditors: Occupational Outlook Handbook," *Bureau of Labor Statistics,* April 6, 2012, **www.bls.gov/ooh/Business-and-Finan cial/Accountants-and-auditors.htm** (accessed August 21, 2012).

12. Goodwill website, **www.goodwill .org/** (accessed July 31, 2012).

Chapter 15

1. "Yuan Will Be Fully Convertible by 2015, Chinese Officials Tell EU Chamber," *Bloomberg Businessweek,* September 8, 2011, **www.bloomberg. com/news/2011-09-08/yuan-to-be- fully-convertible-by-2015-eu-chamber. html** (accessed November 1, 2011); Kersi Jilla, "Global Common Currency— Part 1—Understanding Convertible Currency," *Forex Metrics Blog,* **www. forexmetrics.com/blog/?p=1114** (accessed November 1, 2011); "Foreign Reserve," *Business Dictionary,* **www. businessdictionary.com/definition/ foreign-reserve.html** (accessed November 1, 2011); Wang Xiaotian, "Experts: China's Yuan Will Go Global," *China Daily,* June 27, 2011, **www. chinadaily.com.cn/china/2011-06/27/ content_12780327.htm** (accessed November 1, 2011); "New Move to Make Yuan a Global Currency," *The Wall Street Journal,* January 12, 2011, **http://online. wsj.com/article/SB100014240527487 0379190457607608217839353532.html** (accessed November 1, 2011); Stephen Elliot, "Yuan Has Potential to Become 'International Currency,'" *China Daily,* August 5, 2011, **www.chinadailyapac. com/article/yuan-has-potential- become-international-currency** (accessed November 1, 2011).

2. Paul Krugman, "Why Is Deflation Bad?" *The New York Times,* August 2, 2010, **http://krugman.blogs.nytimes. com/2010/08/02/why-is-deflation-bad/** (accessed May 29, 2012).

3. "First Annual Negative Inflation in 49 Years," *RTE News,* February 12, 2009, **www.rte.ie/news/2009/0212/inflation. html** (accessed May 29, 2012).

4. Phillip Inman, "Ireland Back in Recession as Global Slowdown Hits Exports," *guardian.co.uk,* March 22, 2012, **www.guardian.co.uk/business/2012/ mar/22/ireland-recession-global- slowdown-exports** (accessed May 29, 2012).

5. "Currency in Circulation (WCURCIR)," Economic Research: Federal Reserve of Saint Louis, **http:// research.stlouisfed.org/fred2/series/ WCURCIR** (accessed May 24, 2012).

6. "Weird and Wonderful Money Facts and Trivia," *Happy Worker,* **www. happyworker.com/magazine/facts/ weird-and-wonderful-money-facts** (accessed April 2, 2010).

7. Ibid.

8. "About the Redesigned Currency," The Department of the Treasury Bureau of Engraving and Printing, **www. newmoney.gov/newmoney/currency/ aboutnotes.htm** (accessed April 2, 2010).

9. Chris Isidore, "Obama Wants Cheaper Pennies and Nickels," *CNN Money,* February 21, 2012, **http://money. cnn.com/2012/02/15/news/economy/ pennies_nickels/index.htm** (accessed May 24, 2012).

10. Michael Zielinksi, "Cost to Make Penny and Nickel Rises, Annual Loss Reaches $116.7 Million," *Coin Update,* January 2, 2012, **http://news.coinupdate. com/cost-to-make-penny-and-nickel- rises-1139/** (accessed May 15, 2012).

11. Jessica Dickler, "Americans Still Relying on Credit Cards to Get By," *CNN Money,* May 23, 2012, **http://money. cnn.com/2012/05/22/pf/credit-card/ index.htm** (accessed May 24, 2012); Martin Merzer, "Survey: Students Fail the Credit Card Test," *Fox Business,* April 16, 2012, **www.foxbusiness.com/personal- finance/2012/04/09/survey-students-fail- credit-card-test/** (accessed May 24, 2012).

12. Roben Farzad, Mary Childs, and Shannon D. Harrington, "How JPMorgan Lost $2 Billion Without Really Trying," *Bloomberg Businessweek,* May 24–27, 2012, pp. 44–46.

13. "C40 and World Bank Form Groundbreaking Climate Change Action Partnership," The World Bank, June 1, 2011, **http://web.worldbank. org/WBSITE/EXTERNAL/TOPICS/ EXTSDNET/0,,pagePK:64885161~ contentMDK:22928707~ piPK:592 9285~theSitePK:5929282,00.html** (accessed November 9, 2011); World Bank Confronts Sustainability Criticism," *Business Ethics,* March 19, 2011, **http:// business-ethics.com/2011/03/19/1900- world-bank-confronts-sustainability- criticism/** (accessed November 9, 2011); "Benefits," Support Narmadadam.org, **www.supportnarmadadam.org/sardar- sarovar-benefits.htm** (accessed November 9, 2011); "About Us," The World Bank, **http://web.worldbank.org/ WBSITE/EXTERNAL/EXTABOUTUS /0,,pagePK:50004410~ piPK:36602 ~theSitePK:29708,00.html** (accessed November 9, 2011); "Renewables Almost a Quarter of World Bank's Energy Lending," The World Bank, **http:// climatechange.worldbank.org/content/ world-bank-renewable-energy-lending- rises** (accessed November 9, 2011).

14. "Deposit Insurance Simplification Fact Sheet," FDIC website, **www.fdic. gov/deposit/deposits/DIfactsheet.html** (accessed April 2, 2010).

15. "Bank Failures in Brief," Federal Deposit Insurance Corporation, **www. fdic.gov/bank/historical/bank/** (accessed May 29, 2012).

16. Harry Maurer and Alexander Ragir, "Brazil's New Middle Class Goes on a Spree," *Bloomberg Businessweek,* May 12, 2011, **www.businessweek.com/magaz ine/content/11_21/b4229010792956 .htm** (accessed October 12, 2011); Kenneth Rapoza, "No Major Slowdown as Brazil Consumers Still Happily Spending," *Forbes,* August 12, 2011, **www.forbes.com/sites/kenrapoza/ 2011/08/12/no-major-slowdown-as- brazil-consumers-still-happily- spending/** (accessed October 12, 2011); "FACTBOX-Bright and Troubled Spots in Brazil's Economy," *Reuters,* August 18, 2011, **www.reuters.com/ article/2011/08/18/brazil-economy- idUSN1E77E1EZ20110818** (accessed October 12, 2011).

17. "NACHA Reports More Than 18 Billion ACH Payments in 2007," NACHA: The Electronic Payments Association, May 19, 2008, **http://nacha.org/News/ news/pressreleases/2008/Volume_Final. pdf** (accessed April 2, 2010).

18. "From the Vault . . ." Ohio Commerce Bank, Winter 2012, **www. ohiocommercebank.com/PDF/OCB% 20Newsletter%20Winter%202012.pdf** (accessed May 29, 2012).

19. Federal Deposit Insurance Corporation website, **www.fdic.gov** (accessed April 1, 2010).

20. Shira Ovide, "Government Exits Citigroup: Is a Dividend Next?" *The Wall Street Journal,* December 7, 2010, **http://blogs.wsj.com/deals/2010/12/07/ government-exits-citigroup-is-a-divid end-next/** (accessed May 24, 2012).

21. Michael Lev-Ram, "A Twitter Guy Takes on Banks," *Fortune,* February 7, 2011, pp. 37–42; Jason Tanz, "Twitter Cofounder Shakes Up the Credit Card Biz," *Wired,* May 17, 2011, **www.wired. com/magazine/2011/05/mf_qadorsey/ all/1** (accessed November 2, 2011); Dan Fletcher, "The 50 Best Inventions of 2010," *Time,* November 11, 2010, **www.time.com/time/specials/ packages/article/0,28804, 2029497_2030652_2029712,00.html** (accessed November 2, 2011).

22. "CSI Pennsylvania," *CFO Magazine,* March 2008, p. 92.

23. David Reilly, "Banks Need Just One Thing to Spur Lending: Borrowers," *The Wall Street Journal,* July 29, 2012, **http://online.wsj.com/article/SB1000 08723963904448401045775532919820 01720.html** (accessed July 31, 2012); Laura Marcinek, "Biggest U.S. Banks Shrinking Loans as Regional Lenders Fill Gap," *The Washington Post,* June 26, 2012, **http://washpost.bloomberg.com/ Story?docId=1376-M5ZC211A74E901- 6TCC18E25KL8I48S7VK3O1C45O** (accessed July 31, 2012); Alan S. Blinder, "How Bernanke Can Get Banks Lending Again," *The Wall Street Journal,* July 22, 2012, **http://online.wsj.com/article/SB1 00008723963904448732045775372127 38938798.html?mod=googlenews_wsj** (accessed July 31, 2012); Bruce Bartlett, "The Fed Should Stop Paying Banks Not to Lend," *The New York Times,* July 31, 2012, **http://economix.blogs.nytimes. com/2012/07/31/the-fed-should-stop- paying-banks-not-to-lend/** (accessed July 31, 2012); Rachel Streitfeld, "Small- Business Owners, Hit by Recession, Seek Remedies," *CNN,* December 6, 2009, **www.cnn.com/2009/US/12/06/small. business.recession/index.html** (accessed July 31, 2012).

Chapter 16

1. Dan Fitzpatrick, "BofA Readies the Knife," *The Wall Street Journal*, September 13, 2011, p. C1; Candice Choi, "BofA Plans $5 Debit Card Fee," *USA Today*, September 30, 2011, p. 2B; Paul M. Barrett and Dawn Kopecki, "Can Brian Moynihan Save Bank of America," *Bloomberg Businessweek*, September 8, 2011, **www.businessweek.com/magazine/can-brian-moynihan-save-bank-of-america-09082011.html** (accessed October 6, 2011); Bruce Horovitz, "Consumer Gripes a Growing Force," *USA Today*, November 2, 2011, 1A; Maxwell Fisher, "Is it Time to Cash in on Bank of America?" *The Motley Fool*, May 7, 2012, **http://beta.fool.com/stockcroc1/2012/05/07/it-time-cash-bank-america/4278/** (accessed May 31, 2012).

2. Kate O'Sullivan, "Going for the Other Green," *CFO*, September 2011, pp. 52–57; Carlye Adler, "Thinking Big," *Time*, May 3, 2011, **http://bx.businessweek.com/carbon-markets/view?url=http%3A%2F%2Fc.moreover.com%2Fclick%2Fhere.pl%3Fr4627673218%26f%3D9791** (accessed September 26, 2011).

3. Calculated by Geoff Hirt from Apple's annual reports and website on May 27, 2012.

4. "About Relativity Media," **www.relativitymediallc.com/about.asp** (accessed November 2, 2011); Ben Fritz, "Relativity Media Deal Opens Film Door to China," *Los Angeles Times*, August 4, 2011, **http://articles.latimes.com/2011/aug/14/business/la-fi-ct-china-studio-20110814** (accessed November 2, 2011); Ronald Grover, "Ryan Kavanaugh Is Ready for His Close-Up," *Bloomberg Businessweek*, February 17, 2011, **www.businessweek.com/magazine/content/11 09/b4217024893975.htm** (accessed November 2, 2011); Ron Grover, "**Ryan Kavanaugh May Make Believers Out of Hollywood Yet**," *Bloomberg Businessweek*, February 7, 2010, **www.businessweek.com/innovate/FineOnMedia/archives/2010/02/ryan_kavanaugh_may_make_believers_out_of_hollywood_yet.html#more** (accessed November 2, 2011).

5. Joshua Kennon, "Should You Invest in an IPO?" About.com, **http://beginnersinvest.about.com/od/investmentbanking/a/aa073106a.htm** (accessed May 30, 2012).

6. Marielle Segarra, "Taking the Next Step," *CFO*, July 15, 2011, **www.cfo.com/article.cfm/14586563?f=singlepage** (accessed November 3, 2011); Dan Fitzpatrick and Lisa Rappaport, "Financial Firms' Ceiling," *The Wall Street Journal*, September 8, 2011, **http://online.wsj.com/article/SB10001424053111904103404576557100384026220.html?KEYWORDS=Financial+Firms%27=Ceiling** (accessed November 3, 2011); Kyle Stock, "Ranks of Women on Wall Street Thin," *The Wall Street Journal*, September 20, 2010, **http://online.wsj.com/article/SB1000142405274870485830457549807173213 6704.html** (accessed November 3, 2011).

7. Vincent Ryan, "From Wall Street to Main Street," *CFO Magazine*, June 2008, pp. 85–86.

8. Morningstar website, **http://corporate.morningstar.com/US/asp/home2.aspx?xmlfile57083.xml** (accessed July 31, 2012); ChicagoMag.com, June 2006, **www.chicagomag.com/Chicago-Magazine/June-2006/The-Quiet-Billionaire/** (accessed May 12, 2010); Jody Clarke, "Joe Mansueto: The Simple Idea That Made Me $1bn," *MoneyWeek*, September 4, 2009, **www.moneyweek.com/news-andcharts/entrepreneurs-my-first-millionjoe-mansueto-money week-45135.aspx** (accessed May 12, 2010); "FAQ: The Morningstar Rating for Stocks," Morningstar, **http://news.morningstar.com/articlenet/article.aspx?id 54982#anchor3** (accessed July 31, 2012).

9. Tamar Lewin, "Burden of College Loans on Graduates Grows," *The New York Times*, April 11, 2011, **www.nytimes.com/2011/04/12/education/12college.html** (accessed May 30, 2012).

10. Dennis Cauchon, "Student Loans Outstanding Will Exceed $1 Trillion This Year," *USA Today*, October 25, 2011, **www.usatoday.com/money/perfi/college/story/2011-10-19/student-loan-debt/50818676/1** (accessed May 30, 2012); "Senate Stalls on Legislation for Student Loan Relief," *The New York Times*, May 24, 2012, **www.nytimes.com/2012/05/25/us/politics/senate-stalls-on-legislation-for-student-loan-relief.html** (accessed May 30, 2012).

11. Jill Jackson and John Nolen, "Health Care Reform Bill Summary: A Look at What's in the Bill," *CBS News*, March 21, 2010, **www.cbsnews.com/8301-503544_162-20000846-503544.html** (accessed May 30, 2012); "Patient Protection and Affordable Care Act," *Federal Register 75*(123), June 28, 2010, **www.gpo.gov/fdsys/pkg/FR-2010-06-28/html/2010-15278.htm** (accessed May 30, 2012).

12. Barbara Weltman, "What You Need to Know about the Estate Tax," *U.S. News*, January 25, 2011, **http://money.usnews.com/money/blogs/my-money/2011/01/25/what-you-need-to-know-about-the-estate-tax** (accessed May 30, 2012).

Glossary

A

absolute advantage a monopoly that exists when a country is the only source of an item, the only producer of an item, or the most efficient producer of an item.

accountability the principle that employees who accept an assignment and the authority to carry it out are answerable to a superior for the outcome.

accounting the recording, measurement, and interpretation of financial information.

accounting cycle the four-step procedure of an accounting system: examining source documents, recording transactions in an accounting journal, posting recorded transactions, and preparing financial statements.

accounting equation assets equal liabilities plus owners' equity.

accounts payable the amount a company owes to suppliers for goods and services purchased with credit.

accounts receivable money owed a company by its clients or customers who have promised to pay for the products at a later date.

accrued expenses all unpaid financial obligations incurred by an organization.

acquisition the purchase of one company by another, usually by buying its stock.

administrative managers those who manage an entire business or a major segment of a business; they are not specialists but coordinate the activities of specialized managers.

advertising a paid form of nonpersonal communication transmitted through a mass medium, such as television commercials or magazine advertisements.

advertising campaign designing a series of advertisements and placing them in various media to reach a particular target market.

affirmative action programs legally mandated plans that try to increase job opportunities for minority groups by analyzing the current pool of workers, identifying areas where women and minorities are underrepresented, and establishing specific hiring and promotion goals, with target dates, for addressing the discrepancy.

agenda a calender, containing both specific and vague items, that covers short-term goals and long-term objectives.

analytical skills the ability to identify relevant issues, recognize their importance, understand the relationships

between them, and perceive the underlying causes of a situation.

annual report summary of a firm's financial information, products, and growth plans for owners and potential investors.

arbitration settlement of a labor/management dispute by a third party whose solution is legally binding and enforceable.

articles of partnership legal documents that set forth the basic agreement between partners.

Asia-Pacific Economic Cooperation (APEC) an international trade alliance that promotes open trade and economic and technical cooperation among member nations.

asset utilization ratios ratios that measure how well a firm uses its assets to generate each $1 of sales.

assets a firm's economic resources, or items of value that it owns, such as cash, inventory, land, equipment, buildings, and other tangible and intangible things.

Association of Southeast Asian Nations (ASEAN) A trade alliance that promotes trade and economic integration among member nations in Southeast Asia.

attitude knowledge and positive or negative feelings about something.

automated clearinghouses (ACHs) a system that permits payments such as deposits or withdrawals to be made to and from a bank account by magnetic computer tape.

automated teller machine (ATM) the most familiar form of electronic banking, which dispenses cash, accepts deposits, and allows balance inquiries and cash transfers from one account to another.

B

balance of payments the difference between the flow of money into and out of a country.

balance of trade the difference in value between a nation's exports and its imports.

balance sheet a "snapshot" of an organization's financial position at a given moment.

behavior modification changing behavior and encouraging appropriate actions by relating the consequences of behavior to the behavior itself.

benefits nonfinancial forms of compensation provided to employees, such as pension plans, health insurance, paid vacation and holidays, and the like.

blogs web-based journals in which writers can editorialize and interact with other Internet users.

board of directors a group of individuals, elected by the stockholders to oversee the general operation of the corporation, who set the corporation's long-range objectives.

bonds debt instruments that larger companies sell to raise long-term funds.

bonuses monetary rewards offered by companies for exceptional performance as incentives to further increase productivity.

boycott an attempt to keep people from purchasing the products of a company.

branding the process of naming and identifying products.

bribes payments, gifts, or special favors intended to influence the outcome of a decision.

brokerage firms firms that buy and sell stocks, bonds, and other securities for their customers and provide other financial services.

budget an internal financial plan that forecasts expenses and income over a set period of time.

budget deficit the condition in which a nation spends more than it takes in from taxes.

business individuals or organizations who try to earn a profit by providing products that satisfy people's needs.

business ethics principles and standards that determine acceptable conduct in business.

business plan a precise statement of the rationale for a business and a step-by-step explanation of how it will achieve its goals.

business products products that are used directly or indirectly in the operation or manufacturing processes of businesses.

buying behavior the decision processes and actions of people who purchase and use products.

C

capacity the maximum load that an organizational unit can carry or operate.

capital budgeting the process of analyzing the needs of the business and selecting the assets that will maximize its value.

capitalism (free enterprise) an economic system in which individuals own and operate the majority of businesses that provide goods and services.

cartel a group of firms or nations that agrees to act as a monopoly and not compete with each other, in order to generate a competitive advantage in world markets.

cash flow the movement of money through an organization over a daily, weekly, monthly, or yearly basis.

centralized organization a structure in which authority is concentrated at the top, and very little decision-making authority is delegated to lower levels.

certificates of deposit (CDs) savings accounts that guarantee a depositor a set interest rate over a specified interval as long as the funds are not withdrawn before the end of the period—six months or one year, for example.

certified management accountants (CMAs) private accountants who, after rigorous examination, are certified by the National Association of Accountants and who have some managerial responsibility.

certified public accountant (CPA) an individual who has been state certified to provide accounting services ranging from the preparation of financial records and the filing of tax returns to complex audits of corporate financial records.

checking account money stored in an account at a bank or other financial institution that can be withdrawn without advance notice; also called a demand deposit.

classical theory of motivation theory suggesting that money is the sole motivator for workers.

codes of ethics formalized rules and standards that describe what a company expects of its employees.

collective bargaining the negotiation process through which management and unions reach an agreement about compensation, working hours, and working conditions for the bargaining unit.

commercial banks the largest and oldest of all financial institutions, relying mainly on checking and savings accounts as sources of funds for loans to businesses and individuals.

commercial certificates of deposit (CDs) certificates of deposit issued by commercial banks and brokerage companies, available in minimum amounts of $100,000, which may be traded prior to maturity.

commercial paper a written promise from one company to another to pay a specific amount of money.

commercialization the full introduction of a complete marketing strategy and the launch of the product for commercial success.

commission an incentive system that pays a fixed amount or a percentage of the employee's sales.

commitee a permanent, formal group that performs a specific task.

common stock stock whose owners have voting rights in the corporation, yet do not receive preferential treatment regarding dividends.

communism first described by Karl Marx as a society in which the people, without regard to class, own all the nation's resources.

comparative advantage the basis of most international trade, when a country specializes in products that it can supply more efficiently or at a lower cost than it can produce other items.

competition the rivalry among businesses for consumers' dollars.

compressed workweek a four-day (or shorter) period during which an employee works 40 hours.

computer-assisted design (CAD) the design of components, products, and processes on computers instead of on paper.

computer-assisted manufacturing (CAM) manufacturing that employs specialized computer systems to actually guide and control the transformation processes.

computer-integrated manufacturing (CIM) a complete system that designs products, manages machines and materials, and controls the operations function.

concentration approach a market segmentation approach whereby a company develops one marketing strategy for a single market segment.

conceptual skills the ability to think in abstract terms and to see how parts fit together to form the whole.

conciliation a method of outside resolution of labor and management differences in which a third party is brought in to keep the two sides talking.

consumer products products intended for household or family use.

consumerism the activities that independent individuals, groups, and organizations undertake to protect their rights as consumers.

continuous manufacturing organizations companies that use continuously running assembly lines, creating products with many similar characteristics.

contract manufacturing the hiring of a foreign company to produce a specified volume of the initiating company's product to specification; the final product carries the domestic firm's name.

controlling the process of evaluating and correcting activities to keep the organization on course.

cooperative (co-op) an organization composed of individuals or small businesses that have banded together to reap the benefits of belonging to a larger organization.

corporate charter a legal document that the state issues to a company based on information the company provides in the articles of incorporation.

corporate citizenship the extent to which businesses meet the legal, ethical, economic, and voluntary responsibilities placed on them by their stakeholders.

corporation a legal entity, created by the state, whose assets and liabilities are separate from its owners.

cost of goods sold the amount of money a firm spent to buy or produce the products it sold during the period to which the income statement applies.

countertrade agreements foreign trade agreements that involve bartering products for other products instead of for currency.

credit cards means of access to preapproved lines of credit granted by a bank or finance company.

credit controls the authority to establish and enforce credit rules for financial institutions and some private investors.

credit union a financial institution owned and controlled by its depositors, who usually have a common employer, profession, trade group, or religion.

crisis management (contingency planning) an element in planning that deals with potential disasters such as product tampering, oil spills, fire, earthquake, computer virus, or airplane crash.

culture the integrated, accepted pattern of human behavior, including thought, speech, beliefs, actions, and artifacts.

current assets assets that are used or converted into cash within the course of a calendar year.

current liabilities a firm's financial obligations to short-term creditors, which must be repaid within one year.

current ratio current assets divided by current liabilities.

customer departmentalization the arrangement of jobs around the needs of various types of customers.

customization making products to meet a particular customer's needs or wants.

D

debit card a card that looks like a credit card but works like a check; using it results in a direct, immediate, electronic payment from the cardholder's checking account to a merchant or third party.

debt to total assets ratio a ratio indicating how much of the firm is financed by debt and how much by owners' equity.

debt utilization ratios ratios that measure how much debt an organization is using relative to other sources of capital, such as owners' equity.

decentralized organization an organization in which decision-making authority is delegated as far down the chain of command as possible.

delegation of authority giving employees not only tasks, but also the power to make commitments, use resources, and take whatever actions are necessary to carry out those tasks.

demand the number of goods and services that consumers are willing to buy at different prices at a specific time.

departmentalization the grouping of jobs into working units usually called departments, units, groups, or divisions.

depreciation the process of spreading the costs of long-lived assets such as buildings and equipment over the total number of accounting periods in which they are expected to be used.

depression a condition of the economy in which unemployment is very high, consumer spending is low, and business output is sharply reduced.

development training that augments the skills and knowledge of managers and professionals.

digital marketing uses all digital media, including the Internet and mobile and interactive channels, to develop communication and exchanges with customers.

digital media electronic media that function using digital codes via computers, cellular phones, smart phones, and other digital devices that have been released in recent years.

direct investment the ownership of overseas facilities.

directing motivating and leading employees to achieve organizational objectives.

discount rate the rate of interest the Fed charges to loan money to any banking institution to meet reserve requirements.

discounts temporary price reductions, often employed to boost sales.

distribution making products available to customers in the quantities desired.

diversity the participation of different ages, genders, races, ethnicities, nationalities, and abilities in the workplace.

dividend yield the dividend per share divided by the stock price.

dividends profits of a corporation that are distributed in the form of cash payments to stockholders.

dividends per share the actual cash received for each share owned.

double-entry bookkeeping a system of recording and classifying business transactions that maintains the balance of the accounting equation.

downsizing the elimination of a significant number of employees from an organization.

dumping the act of a country or business selling products at less than what it costs to produce them.

E

e-business carrying out the goals of business through utilization of the Internet.

earnings per share net income or profit divided by the number of stock shares outstanding.

economic contraction a slowdown of the economy characterized by a decline in spending and during which businesses cut back on production and lay off workers.

economic expansion the situation that occurs when an economy is growing and people are spending more money; their purchases stimulate the production of goods and services, which in turn stimulates employment.

economic order quantity (EOQ) model a model that identifies the optimum number of items to order to minimize the costs of managing (ordering, storing, and using) them.

economic system a description of how a particular society distributes its resources to produce goods and services.

economics the study of how resources are distributed for the production of goods and services within a social system.

electronic funds transfer (EFT) any movement of funds by means of an electronic terminal, telephone, computer, or magnetic tape.

electronic marketing refers to the strategic process of distributing, promoting, pricing products, and discovering the desires of customers using digital media and digital marketing.

embargo a prohibition on trade in a particular product.

entrepreneur an individual who risks his or her wealth, time, and effort to develop for profit an innovative product or way of doing something.

entrepreneurship the process of creating and managing a business to achieve desired objectives.

equilibrium price the price at which the number of products that businesses are willing to supply equals the amount of products that consumers are willing to buy at a specific point in time.

equity theory an assumption that how much people are willing to contribute to an organization depends on their assessment of the fairness, or equity, of the rewards they will receive in exchange.

esteem needs the need for respect—both self-respect and respect from others.

ethical issue an identifiable problem, situation, or opportunity that requires a person to choose from among several actions that may be evaluated as right or wrong, ethical or unethical.

eurodollar market a market for trading U.S. dollars in foreign countries.

European Union (EU) a union of European nations established in 1958 to promote trade among its members; one of the largest single markets today.

exchange the act of giving up one thing (money, credit, labor, goods) in return for something else (goods, services, or ideas).

exchange controls regulations that restrict the amount of currency that can be bought or sold.

exchange rate the ratio at which one nation's currency can be exchanged for another nation's currency.

exclusive distribution the awarding by a manufacturer to an intermediary of the sole right to sell a product in a defined geographic territory.

expectancy theory the assumption that motivation depends not only on how much a person wants something but also on how likely he or she is to get it.

expenses the costs incurred in the day-to-day operations of an organization.

exporting the sale of goods and services to foreign markets.

extrinsic rewards benefits and/or recognition received from someone else.

F

factor a finance company to which businesses sell their accounts receivable—usually for a percentage of the total face value.

Federal Deposit Insurance Corporation (FDIC) an insurance fund established in 1933 that insures individual bank accounts.

Federal Reserve Board an independent agency of the federal government established in 1913 to regulate the nation's banking and financial industry.

finance the study of money; how it's made, how it's lost, and how it's managed.

finance companies businesses that offer short-term loans at substantially higher rates of interest than banks.

financial managers those who focus on obtaining needed funds for the successful operation of an organization and using those funds to further organizational goals.

financial resources the funds used to acquire the natural and human resources needed to provide products; also called capital.

first-line managers those who supervise both workers and the daily operations of an organization.

fixed-position layout a layout that brings all resources required to create the product to a central location.

flexible manufacturing the direction of machinery by computers to adapt to different versions of similar operations.

flextime a program that allows employees to choose their starting and ending times, provided that they are at work during a specified core period.

floating-rate bonds bonds with interest rates that change with current interest rates otherwise available in the economy.

franchise a license to sell another's products or to use another's name in business, or both.

franchisee the purchaser of a franchise.

franchiser the company that sells a franchise.

franchising a form of licensing in which a company—the franchiser—agrees to provide a franchisee a name, logo, methods of operation, advertising, products, and other elements associated with a franchiser's business in return for a financial commitment and the agreement to conduct business in accordance with the franchiser's standard of operations.

free-market system pure capitalism, in which all economic decisions are made without government intervention.

functional departmentalization the grouping of jobs that perform similar functional activities, such as finance, manufacturing, marketing, and human resources.

G

General Agreement on Tariffs and Trade (GATT) a trade agreement, originally signed by 23 nations in 1947, that provided a forum for tariff negotiations and a place where international trade problems could be discussed and resolved.

general partnership a partnership that involves a complete sharing in both the management and the liability of the business.

generic products products with no brand name that often come in simple packages and carry only their generic name.

geographical departmentalization the grouping of jobs according to geographic location, such as state, region, country, or continent.

global strategy (globalization) a strategy that involves standardizing products (and, as much as possible, their promotion and distribution) for the whole world, as if it were a single entity.

goal the result that a firm wished to achieve.

grapevine an informal channel of communication, separate from management's formal, official communication channels.

gross domestic product (GDP) the sum of all goods and services produced in a country during a year.

gross income (or profit) revenues minus the cost of goods sold required to generate the revenues.

group two or more individuals who communicate with one another, share a common identity, and have a common goal.

H

human relations the study of the behavior of individuals and groups in organizational settings.

human relations skills the ability to deal with people, both inside and outside the organization.

human resources the physical and mental abilities that people use to produce goods and services; also called labor.

human resources management (HRM) all the activities involved in determining an organization's human resources needs, as well as acquiring, training, and compensating people to fill those needs.

human resources managers those who handle the staffing function and deal with employees in a formalized manner.

hygiene factors aspects of Herzberg's theory of motivation that focus on the work setting and not the content of the work; these aspects include adequate wages, comfortable and safe working conditions, fair company policies, and job security.

I

identity theft when criminals obtain personal information that allows them to impersonate someone else in order to use their credit to obtain financial accounts and make purchases.

import tariff a tax levied by a nation on goods imported into the country.

importing the purchase of goods and services from foreign sources.

income statement a financial report that shows an organization's profitability over a period of time—month, quarter, or year.

inflation a condition characterized by a continuing rise in prices.

information technology (IT) managers those who are responsible for implementing, maintaining, and controlling technology applications in business, such as computer networks.

infrastructure the physical facilities that support a country's economic activities, such as railroads, highways, ports, airfields, utilities and power plants, schools, hospitals, communication systems, and commercial distribution systems.

initial public offering (IPO) selling a corporation's stock on public markets for the first time.

inputs the resources—such as labor, money, materials, and energy—that are converted into outputs.

insurance companies businesses that protect their clients against financial losses from certain specified risks (death, accident, and theft, for example).

integrated marketing communications coordinating the promotion mix elements and synchronizing promotion as a unified effort.

intensive distribution a form of market coverage whereby a product is made available in as many outlets as possible.

intermittent organizations organizations that deal with products of a lesser magnitude than do project organizations; their products are not necessarily unique but possess a significant number of differences.

international business the buying, selling, and trading of goods and services across national boundaries.

International Monetary Fund (IMF) organization established in 1947 to promote trade among member nations by eliminating trade barriers and fostering financial cooperation.

intrapreneurs individuals in large firms who take responsibility for the development of innovations within the organizations.

intrinsic rewards the personal satisfaction and enjoyment felt after attaining a goal.

inventory all raw materials, components, completed or partially completed products, and pieces of equipment a firm uses.

inventory control the process of determining how many supplies and goods are needed and keeping track of quantities on hand, where each item is, and who is responsible for it.

inventory turnover sales divided by total inventory.

investment banker underwrites new issues of securities for corporations, states, and municipalities.

ISO 9000 a series of quality assurance standards designed by the International Organization for Standardization (ISO) to ensure consistent product quality under many conditions.

ISO 14000 a comprehensive set of environmental standards that encourages a cleaner and safer world by promoting a more uniform approach to environmental management and helping companies attain and measure improvements in their environmental performance.

J

job analysis the determination, through observation and study, of pertinent information about a job—including specific tasks and necessary abilities, knowledge, and skills.

job description a formal, written explanation of a specific job, usually including job title, tasks, relationship with other jobs, physical and mental skills required, duties, responsibilities, and working conditions.

job enlargement the addition of more tasks to a job instead of treating each task as separate.

job enrichment the incorporation of motivational factors, such as opportunity for achievement, recognition, responsibility, and advancement, into a job.

job rotation movement of employees from one job to another in an effort to relieve the boredom often associated with job specialization.

job sharing performance of one full-time job by two people on part-time hours.

job specification a description of the qualifications necessary for a specific job, in terms of education, experience, and personal and physical characteristics.

joint venture a partnership established for a specific project or for a limited time.

journal a time-ordered list of account transactions.

junk bonds a special type of high interest rate bond that carries higher inherent risks.

just-in-time (JIT) inventory management a technique using smaller quantities of materials that arrive "just in time" for use in the transformation process and therefore require less storage space and other inventory management expense.

L

labeling the presentation of important information on a package.

labor contract the formal, written document that spells out the relationship between the union and management for a specified period of time—usually two or three years.

labor unions employee organizations formed to deal with employers for achieving better pay, hours, and working conditions.

leadership the ability to influence employees to work toward organizational goals.

learning changes in a person's behavior based on information and experience.

ledger a book or computer file with separate sections for each account.

leveraged buyout (LBO) a purchase in which a group of investors borrows money from banks and other institutions to acquire a company (or a division of one), using the assets of the purchased company to guarantee repayment of the loan.

liabilities debts that a firm owes to others.

licensing a trade agreement in which one company—the licensor—allows another company—the licensee—to use its company name, products, patents, brands, trademarks, raw materials, and/or production processes in exchange for a fee or royalty.

limited liability company (LLC) form of ownership that provides limited liability and taxation like a partnership but places fewer restrictions on members.

limited partnership a business organization that has at least one general partner, who assumes unlimited liability, and at least one limited partner, whose liability is limited to his or her investment in the business.

line of credit an arrangement by which a bank agrees to lend a specified amount of money to an organization upon request.

line-and-staff structure a structure having a traditional line relationship between superiors and subordinates and also specialized managers—called staff managers—who are available to assist line managers.

line structure the simplest organizational structure, in which direct lines of authority extend from the top manager to the lowest level of the organization.

liquidity ratios ratios that measure the speed with which a company can turn its assets into cash to meet short-term debt.

lockbox an address, usually a commercial bank, at which a company receives payments in order to speed collections from customers.

lockout management's version of a strike, wherein a work site is closed so that employees cannot go to work.

long-term (fixed) assets production facilities (plants), offices, and equipment—all of which are expected to last for many years.

long-term liabilities debts that will be repaid over a number of years, such as long-term loans and bond issues.

M

management a process designed to achieve an organization's objectives by using its resources effectively and efficiently in a changing environment.

managerial accounting the internal use of accounting statements by managers in planning and directing the organization's activities.

managers those individuals in organizations who make decisions about the use of resources and who are concerned with planning, organizing, staffing, directing, and controlling the organization's activities to reach its objectives.

manufacturer brands brands initiated and owned by the manufacturer to identify products from the point of production to the point of purchase.

manufacturing the activities and processes used in making tangible products; also called production.

market a group of people who have a need, purchasing power, and the desire and authority to spend money on goods, services, and ideas.

market orientation an approach requiring organizations to gather information about customer needs, share that information throughout the firm, and use that information to help build long-term relationships with customers.

market segment a collection of individuals, groups, or organizations who share one or more characteristics and thus have relatively similar product needs and desires.

market segmentation a strategy whereby a firm divides the total market into groups of people who have relatively similar product needs.

marketable securities temporary investment of "extra" cash by organizations for up to one year in U.S. Treasury bills, certificates of deposit, commercial paper, or eurodollar loans.

marketing a group of activities designed to expedite transactions by creating, distributing, pricing, and promoting goods, services, and ideas.

marketing channel a group of organizations that moves products from their producer to customers; also called a channel of distribution.

marketing concept the idea that an organization should try to satisfy customers' needs through coordinated activities that also allow it to achieve its own goals.

marketing managers those who are responsible for planning, pricing, and promoting products and making them available to customers.

marketing mix the four marketing activites—product, price, promotion, and distribution—that the firm can control to achieve specific goals within a dynamic marketing environment.

marketing research a systematic, objective process of getting information about potential customers to guide marketing decisions.

marketing strategy a plan of action for developing, pricing, distributing, and promoting products that meet the needs of specific customers.

Maslow's hierarchy a theory that arranges the five basic needs of people—physiological, security, social, esteem, and self-actualization—into the order in which people strive to satisfy them.

material-requirements planning (MRP) a planning system that schedules the precise quantity of materials needed to make the product.

materials handling the physical handling and movement of products in warehousing and transportation.

matrix structure a structure that sets up teams from different departments, thereby creating two or more intersecting lines of authority; also called a project-management structure.

mediation a method of outside resolution of labor and management differences in which the third party's role is to suggest or propose a solution to the problem.

merger the combination of two companies (usually corporations) to form a new company.

middle managers those members of an organization responsible for the tactical planning that implements the general guidelines established by top management.

mission the statement of an organization's fundamental purpose and basic philosophy.

mixed economies economies made up of elements from more than one economic system.

modular design the creation of an item in self-contained units, or modules, that can be combined or interchanged to create different products.

monetary policy means by which the Fed controls the amount of money available in the economy.

money anything generally accepted in exchange for goods and services.

money market accounts accounts that offer higher interest rates than standard bank rates but with greater restrictions.

monopolistic competition the market structure that exists when there are fewer businesses than in a pure-competition environment and the differences among the goods they sell are small.

monopoly the market structure that exists when there is only one business providing a product in a given market.

morale an employee's attitude toward his or her job, employer, and colleagues.

motivation an inner drive that directs a person's behavior toward goals.

motivational factors aspects of Herzberg's theory of motivation that focus on the content of the work itself; these aspects include achievement, recognition, involvement, responsibility, and advancement.

multidivisional structure a structure that organizes departments into larger groups called divisions.

multinational corporation (MNC) a corporation that operates on a worldwide scale, without significant ties to any one nation or region.

multinational strategy a plan, used by international companies, that involves customizing products, promotion, and distribution according to cultural, technological, regional, and national differences.

multisegment approach a market segmentation approach whereby the marketer aims its efforts at two or more segments, developing a marketing strategy for each.

mutual fund an investment company that pools individual investor dollars and invests them in large numbers of well-diversified securities.

mutual savings banks financial institutions that are similar to savings and loan associations but, like credit unions, are owned by their depositors.

N

National Credit Union Administration (NCUA) an agency that regulates and charters credit unions and insures their deposits through its National Credit Union Insurance Fund.

natural resources land, forests, minerals, water, and other things that are not made by people.

net income the total profit (or loss) after all expenses, including taxes, have been deducted from revenue; also called net earnings.

networking the building of relationships and sharing of information with colleagues who can help managers achieve the items on their agendas.

nonprofit corporations corporations that focus on providing a service rather than earning a profit but are not owned by a government entity.

nonprofit organizations organizations that may provide goods or services but do not have the fundamental purpose of earning profits.

North American Free Trade Agreement (NAFTA) agreement that eliminates most tariffs and trade restrictions on agricultural and manufactured products to encourage trade among Canada, the United States, and Mexico.

O

offshoring the relocation of business processes by a company or subsidiary to another country. Offshoring is different than outsourcing because the company retains control of the offshored processes.

oligopoly the market structure that exists when there are very few businesses selling a product.

online fraud any attempt to conduct fraudulent activities online.

open market operations decisions to buy or sell U.S. Treasury bills (short-term debt issued by the U.S. government) and other investments in the open market.

operational plans very short-term plans that specify what actions individuals, work groups, or departments need to accomplish in order to achieve the tactical plan and ultimately the strategic plan.

operations the activities and processes used in making both tangible and intangible products.

operations management (OM) the development and administration of the activities involved in transforming resources into goods and services.

organizational chart a visual display of the organizational structure, lines of authority (chain of command), staff relationships, permanent committee arrangements, and lines of communication.

organizational culture a firm's shared values, beliefs, traditions, philosophies, rules, and role models for behavior.

organizational layers the levels of management in an organization.

organizing the structuring of resources and activities to accomplish objectives in an efficient and effective manner.

orientation familiarizing newly hired employees with fellow workers, company procedures, and the physical properties of the company.

outputs the goods, services, and ideas that result from the conversion of inputs.

outsourcing the transferring of manufacturing or other tasks—such as data processing—to countries where labor and supplies are less expensive.

over-the-counter (OTC) market a network of dealers all over the country linked by computers, telephones, and Teletype machines.

owners' equity equals assets minus liabilities and reflects historical values.

P

packaging the external container that holds and describes the product.

partnership a form of business organization defined by the Uniform Partnership Act as "an association of two or more persons who carry on as co-owners of a business for profit."

penetration price a low price designed to help a product enter the market and gain market share rapidly.

pension funds managed investment pools set aside by individuals, corporations, unions, and some nonprofit organizations to provide retirement income for members.

per share data data used by investors to compare the performance of one company with another on an equal, per share basis.

perception the process by which a person selects, organizes, and interprets information received from his or her senses.

personal selling direct, two-way communication with buyers and potential buyers.

personality the organization of an individual's distinguishing character traits, attitudes, or habits.

physical distribution all the activities necessary to move products from producers to customers—inventory control, transportation, warehousing, and materials handling.

physiological needs the most basic human needs to be satisfied—water, food, shelter, and clothing.

picketing a public protest against management practices that involves union members marching and carrying antimanagement signs at the employer's plant.

plagiarism the act of taking someone else's work and presenting it as your own without mentioning the source.

planning the process of determining the organization's objectives and deciding how to accomplish them; the first function of management.

podcast audio or video file that can be downloaded from the Internet with a subscription that automatically delivers new content to listening devices or personal computers.

preferred stock a special type of stock whose owners, though not generally having a say in running the company, have a claim to profits before other stockholders do.

price a value placed on an object exchanged between a buyer and a seller.

price skimming charging the highest possible price that buyers who want the product will pay.

primary data marketing information that is observed, recorded, or collected directly from respondents.

primary market the market where firms raise financial capital.

prime rate the interest rate that commercial banks charge their best customers (usually large corporations) for short-term loans.

private accountants accountants employed by large corporations, government agencies, and other organizations to prepare and analyze their financial statements.

private corporation a corporation owned by just one or a few people who are closely involved in managing the business.

private distributor brands brands, which may cost less than manufacturer brands, that are owned and controlled by a wholesaler or retailer.

process layout a layout that organizes the transformation process into departments that group related processes.

product a good or service with tangible and intangible characteristics that provide satisfaction and benefits.

product departmentalization the organization of jobs in relation to the products of the firm.

product layout a layout requiring that production be broken down into relatively simple tasks assigned to workers, who are usually positioned along an assembly line.

product line a group of closely related products that are treated as a unit because of similar marketing strategy, production, or end-use considerations.

product mix all the products offered by an organization.

product development teams a specific type of project team formed to devise, design, and implement a new product.

production the activities and processes used in making tangible products; also called manufacturing.

production and operations managers those who develop and administer the activities involved in transforming resources into goods, services, and ideas ready for the marketplace.

profit the difference between what it costs to make and sell a product and what a customer pays for it.

profit margin net income divided by sales.

profit sharing a form of compensation whereby a percentage of company profits is distributed to the employees whose work helped to generate them.

profitability ratios ratios that measure the amount of operating income or net income an organization is able to generate relative to its assets, owners' equity, and sales.

project organization a company using a fixed-position layout because it is typically involved in large, complex projects such as construction or exploration.

project teams groups similar to task forces that normally run their operation and have total control of a specific work project.

promotion an advancement to a higher-level job with increased authority, responsibility, and pay.

promotional positioning the use of promotion to create and maintain an image of a product in buyers' minds.

psychological pricing encouraging purchases based on emotional rather than rational responses to the price.

public corporation a corporation whose stock anyone may buy, sell, or trade.

publicity nonpersonal communication transmitted through the mass media but not paid for directly by the firm.

pull strategy the use of promotion to create consumer demand for a product so that consumers exert pressure on marketing channel members to make it available.

purchasing the buying of all the materials needed by the organization; also called procurement.

pure competition the market structure that exists when there are many small businesses selling one standardized product.

push strategy an attempt to motivate intermediaries to push the product down to their customers.

Q

quality the degree to which a good, service, or idea meets the demands and requirements of customers.

quality control the processes an organization uses to maintain its established quality standards.

quality-assurance teams (or quality circles) small groups of workers brought together from throughout the organization to solve specific quality, productivity, or service problems.

quasi-public corporations corporations owned and operated by the federal, state, or local government.

quick ratio (acid test) a stringent measure of liquidity that eliminates inventory.

quota a restriction on the number of units of a particular product that can be imported into a country.

R

ratio analysis calculations that measure an organization's financial health.

receivables turnover sales divided by accounts receivable.

recession a decline in production, employment, and income.

recruiting forming a pool of qualified applicants from which management can select employees.

reference groups groups with whom buyers identify and whose values or attitudes they adopt.

relationship marketing the creation of relationships that mutually benefit the marketing business and the customer.

reserve requirement the percentage of deposits that banking institutions must hold in reserve.

responsibility the obligation, placed on employees through delegation, to perform assigned tasks satisfactorily and be held accountable for the proper execution of work.

retailers intermediaries who buy products from manufacturers (or other intermediaries) and sell them to consumers for home and household use rather than for resale or for use in producing other products.

retained earnings earnings after expenses and taxes that are reinvested in the assets of the firm and belong to the owners in the form of equity.

return on assets net income divided by assets.

return on equity net income divided by owners' equity; also called return on investment (ROI).

revenue the total amount of money received from the sale of goods or services, as well as from related business activities.

routing the sequence of operations through which the product must pass.

S

S corporation corporation taxed as though it were a partnership with restrictions on shareholders.

salary a financial reward calculated on a weekly, monthly, or annual basis.

sales promotion direct inducements offering added value or some other incentive for buyers to enter into an exchange.

savings accounts accounts with funds that usually cannot be withdrawn without advance notice; also known as time deposits.

savings and loan associations (S&Ls) financial institutions that primarily offer savings accounts and make long-term loans for residential mortgages; also called "thrifts."

scheduling the assignment of required tasks to departments or even specific machines, workers, or teams.

secondary data information that is compiled inside or outside an organization for some purpose other than changing the current situation.

secondary markets stock exchanges and over-the-counter markets where investors can trade their securities with others.

secured bonds bonds that are backed by specific collateral that must be forfeited in the event that the issuing firm defaults.

secured loans loans backed by collateral that the bank can claim if the borrowers do not repay them.

securities markets the mechanism for buying and selling securities.

security needs the need to protect oneself from physical and economic harm.

selection the process of collecting information about applicants and using that information to make hiring decisions.

selective distribution a form of market coverage whereby only a small number of all available outlets are used to expose products.

self-actualization needs the need to be the best one can be; at the top of Maslow's hierarchy.

self-directed work team (SDWT) a group of employees responsible for an entire work process or segment that delivers a product to an internal or external customer.

separations employment changes involving resignation, retirement, termination, or layoff.

serial bonds a sequence of small bond issues of progressively longer maturity.

small business any independently owned and operated business that is not dominant in its competitive area and does not employ more than 500 people.

Small Business Administration (SBA) an independent agency of the federal government that offers managerial and financial assistance to small businesses.

social classes a ranking of people into higher or lower positions of respect.

social needs the need for love, companionship, and friendship—the desire for acceptance by others.

social network a web-based meeting place for friends, family, co-workers, and peers that lets users create a profile and connect with other users for a wide range of purposes.

social responsibility a business's obligation to maximize its positive impact and minimize its negative impact on society.

social roles a set of expectations for individuals based on some position they occupy.

socialism an economic system in which the government owns and operates basic industries but individuals own most businesses.

sole proprietorships businesses owned and operated by one individual; the most common form of business organization in the United States.

span of management the number of subordinates who report to a particular manager.

specialization the division of labor into small, specific tasks and the assignment of employees to do a single task.

staffing the hiring of people to carry out the work of the organization.

stakeholders groups that have a stake in the success and outcomes of a business.

standardization the making of identical interchangeable components or products.

statement of cash flows explains how the company's cash changed from the beginning of the accounting period to the end.

statistical process control a system in which management collects and analyzes information about the production process to pinpoint quality problems in the production system.

stock shares of a corporation that may be bought or sold.

strategic alliance a partnership formed to create competitive advantage on a worldwide basis.

strategic plans those plans that establish the long-range objectives and overall strategy or course of action by which a firm fulfills its mission.

strikebreakers people hired by management to replace striking employees; called "scabs" by striking union members.

strikes employee walkouts; one of the most effective weapons labor has.

structure the arrangement or relationship of positions within an organization.

supply the number of products—goods and services—that businesses are willing to sell at different prices at a specific time.

supply chain management connecting and integrating all parties or members of the distribution system in order to satisfy customers.

sustainability conducting activities in a way that allows for the long-term well-being of the natural environment, including all biological entities; involves the assessment and improvement of business strategies, economic sectors, work practices, technologies, and lifestyles so that they maintain the health of the natural environment.

T

tactical plans short-range plans designed to implement the activities and objectives specified in the strategic plan.

target market a specific group of consumers on whose needs and wants a company focuses its marketing efforts.

task force a temporary group of employees responsible for bringing about a particular change.

team a small group whose members have complementary skills; have a common purpose, goals, and approach; and hold themselves mutually accountable.

technical expertise the specialized knowledge and training needed to perform jobs that are related to particular areas of management.

test marketing a trial minilaunch of a product in limited areas that represent the potential market.

Theory X McGregor's traditional view of management whereby it is assumed that workers generally dislike work and must be forced to do their jobs.

Theory Y McGregor's humanistic view of management whereby it is assumed that workers like to work and that under proper conditions employees will seek out responsibility in an attempt to satisfy their social, esteem, and self-actualization needs.

Theory Z a management philosophy that stresses employee participation in all aspects of company decision making.

times interest earned ratio operating income divided by interest expense.

Title VII of the Civil Rights Act prohibits discrimination in employment and created the Equal Employment Opportunity Commission.

top managers the president and other top executives of a business, such as the chief executive officer (CEO), chief financial officer (CFO), and chief operations officer (COO), who have overall responsibility for the organization.

total asset turnover sales divided by total assets.

total quality management (TQM) a philosophy that uniform commitment to quality in all areas of an organization will promote a culture that meets customers' perceptions of quality.

total-market approach an approach whereby a firm tries to appeal to everyone and assumes that all buyers have similar needs.

trade credit credit extended by suppliers for the purchase of their goods and services.

trade deficit a nation's negative balance of trade, which exists when that country imports more products than it exports.

trademark a brand that is registered with the U.S. Patent and Trademark Office and is thus legally protected from use by any other firm.

trading company a firm that buys goods in one country and sells them to buyers in another country.

training teaching employees to do specific job tasks through either classroom development or on-the-job experience.

transaction balances cash kept on hand by a firm to pay normal daily expenses, such as employee wages and bills for supplies and utilities.

transfer a move to another job within the company at essentially the same level and wage.

transportation the shipment of products to buyers.

Treasury bills (T-bills) short-term debt obligations the U.S. government sells to raise money.

turnover occurs when employees quit or are fired and must be replaced by new employees.

U

undercapitalization the lack of funds to operate a business normally.

unemployment the condition in which a percentage of the population wants to work but is unable to find jobs.

unsecured bonds debentures, or bonds that are not backed by specific collateral.

unsecured loans loans backed only by the borrowers' good reputation and previous credit rating.

V

value a customer's subjective assessment of benefits relative to costs in determining the worth of a product.

venture capitalists persons or organizations that agree to provide some funds for a new business in exchange for an ownership interest or stock.

viral marketing a marketing tool that uses a networking effect to spread a message and create brand awareness. The purpose of this marketing technique is to encourage the consumer to share the message with friends, family, co-workers, and peers.

W

wage/salary survey a study that tells a company how much compensation comparable firms are paying for specific jobs that the firms have in common.

wages financial rewards based on the number of hours the employee works or the level of output achieved.

warehousing the design and operation of facilities to receive, store, and ship products.

whistleblowing the act of an employee exposing an employer's wrongdoing to outsiders, such as the media or government regulatory agencies.

wholesalers intermediaries who buy from producers or from other wholesalers and sell to retailers.

wiki software that creates an interface that enables users to add or edit the content of some types of websites.

working capital management the managing of short-term assets and liabilities.

World Bank an organization established by the industrialized nations in 1946 to loan money to underdeveloped and developing countries; formally known as the International Bank for Reconstruction and Development.

World Trade Organization (WTO) international organization dealing with the rules of trade between nations.

Photo credits

Chapter 1 p. 3: © The McGraw-Hill Companies, Inc./Jill Braaten, photographer; p. 5: © Amber Smith, Mommastuffblog; p. 7: © PRNewsFoto/MilkPEP/AP Photo; p. 17: Courtesy of the U.S. Department of the Treasury, Bureau of the Public Debt; p. 23: © Michael Ansell/ABC via Getty Images

Chapter 2 p. 35: © Paul J. Richards/AFP/Getty Images; p. 39: © Bloomberg via Getty Images; p. 40: © Congressional Quarterly/Getty Images; p. 42: © Chuck Hodes/CBS via Getty Images; p. 46: © Alex Mahoney/Corbis RF; p. 47: © Matthew Staver/Bloomberg via Getty Images; p. 55: © Jeffrey Mayer/WireImage/Getty Images; p. 57: Courtesy of The Home Depot; p. 61: © Paul Edmondson/Getty Images RF; p. 62: © Habitat for Humanity Manitoba; p. 69: © Bill Pugliano/Getty Images; p. 78: © The McGraw-Hill Companies, Inc./Mark Dierker, photographer

Chapter 3 p. 85: The Procter & Gamble Company; p. 86: © Chintunglee; p. 90: Courtesy of AT&T Intellectual Property. Used with permission; p. 92: © Aktion Plagiarius e.V. – www.plagiarius.com; p. 94 (left): © Ryan McVay/Getty Images RF; p. 94 (right): © Stockbyte RF; p. 99: © The McGraw-Hill Companies, Inc./Barry Barker, photographer; p. 102: © Glow Images RF; p. 107: Used with permission of McDonald's Corporation; p. 108: © Cancan Chu/Getty Images

Chapter 4 p. 119: © Eliza Snow/iStockphoto; p. 122: © Ariel Skelley/Blend Images LLC RF; p. 126: © Matthew Staver/Bloomberg via Getty Images; p. 131: © The McGraw-Hill Companies, Inc./Mark Dierker, photographer; p. 133: © Eric Charbonneau/WireImage for Showtime Networks/Getty Images; p. 134: © Stockbyte/Getty Images RF; p. 136: © Chuck Burton/AP Photo; p. 141: © Travis Long/MCT/Newscom

Chapter 5 p. 149: © Katherine Frey/The Washington Post/Getty Images; p. 153: © The McGraw-Hill Companies, Inc./Mark Dierker, photographer; p. 154: © Paul Sakuma/AP Photo; p. 156: © Ariel Skelley/Blend Images RF; p. 158: © John Foxx/Imagestate Media RF; p. 162: Courtesy of localnewsonly.com; p. 163: © Oxytouse; p. 166: © Creatas/Jupiterimages RF; p. 167: Jack Dorsey/@jack

Chapter 6 p. 177: © Dennis Van Tine/ABACAUSA.COM/Newscom; p. 178: © Giuseppe Aresu/Bloomberg via Getty Images; p. 181: © PRNewsFoto/AirTran Airways/AP Photo; p. 182: © Mario Tama/Getty Images; p. 185: © The McGraw-Hill Companies, Inc./Mark Dierker, photographer; p. 186: © Yuriko Nakao/AFP/Getty Images; p. 190: © NAN104/iStockphoto; p. 196: Courtesy of Southwest Airlines; p. 197: © Aaron M. Sprecher/Bloomberg via Getty Images; p. 199: © The McGraw-Hill Companies, Inc./Mark Dierker, photographer; p. 201: © 2012 LinkedIn. LinkedIn and the LinkedIn logo are registered trademarks of LinkedIn Corporation, Inc. in the U.S. and/or other countries. All rights reserved

Chapter 7 p. 209: © Alison Yin/AP Photo for Green Mountain Coffee; p. 212: © PRNewsFoto/TOMS Shoes/AP Photo; p. 214: Library of Congress, Prints & Photographs Division, LC-USZ62-107065; p. 215: © Bloomberg via Getty Images; p. 229: © Alija/iStockphoto

Chapter 8 p. 239: © Steve Helber/AP Photo; p. 243: © Elan Fleisher/Getty Images; p. 244: © Doctor's Associates Inc.; p. 249: © China Photos/Getty Images; p. 252: © Patagonia, Inc.; p. 253: © Corporate Traffic; p. 254: © Washington Post/Getty Images; p. 256: © Richard Vogel/AP Photo; p. 261: © Kent Knudson/PhotoLink/Getty Images RF

Chapter 9 p. 271: © Image Source/Getty Images RF; p. 272: © Ann Heisenfelt/AP Photo; p. 273: © Jason Smith/iStockphoto; p. 277: Progressive assembly of transmitter bridge, ca. 1925. Western Electric Company photograph album. Baker Library Historical Collections, Harvard Business School (olvwork278795); p. 280: © WorldFoto/Alamy; p. 285: © Jack Hollingsworth/Corbis RF; p. 287: © Chris O'Connor/AP Photo; p. 289: © Erik Snyder/Getty Images RF

Chapter 10 p. 297: © Justin Sullivan/Getty Images; p. 298: © Yuri Arcurs/Cutcaster RF; p. 300: © The McGraw-Hill Companies, Inc./Mark Dierker, photographer; p. 303 (top): © Kirby Hamilton/iStockphoto; p. 303 (bottom): © Accurate Background, Inc.; p. 307: Used with permission of McDonald's Corporation; p. 309: © Nika Dreamscape; p. 310: © Royalty-Free/Corbis; p. 315: © Mark Bowden/iStockphoto; p. 320: © Justin Sullivan/Getty Images; p. 322: © Jupiterimages/Getty Images RF

Chapter 11 p. 341: © Emile Wamsteker/Bloomberg via Getty Images; p. 343: © David Brabyn/Corbis; p. 346: Francinegirvan; p. 348 (left): © Yasuyoshi Chiba/AFP/Getty Images; p. 348 (right): © LUDOVIC/REA/Redux; p. 352: The Procter & Gamble Company; p. 355: © The McGraw-Hill Companies, Inc./Mark Dierker, photographer; p. 356: © American Marketing Association and Kasia Biel/iStockphoto; p. 357: © Mark Von Holden/Getty Images for (RED); p. 360: Photo provided courtesy of Goya© Foods, Inc.; p. 361: Photo, Gustavo Millon/Illustration, Philip Bone/FABRICA/Benetton

Chapter 12 p. 369: © Clive Sawyer/Alamy; p. 371: © Joe Raedle/Getty Images; p. 373: © www.delorean.com; p. 377: © PhotoAlto/Antoine Arraou/Getty Images RF; p. 379: GREEN WORKS® is a registered trademark of The Clorox Company. Used with permission. © 2011 The Clorox Company. Reprinted with permission; p. 380: © Kim White/Bloomberg via Getty Images; p. 382 (top): © NetPhotos/Alamy; p. 382 (bottom): © Little Man Ice Cream; p. 388: © Paul Fenton/ZUMAPRESS.Com/Alamy; p. 389: Reprinted with permission of BNSF Railway Company; p. 391: Photo provided by Spectrum Photofile. © Mattel, Inc. All Rights Reserved; p. 394: © Google Inc.; p. 395: © RetailMeNot.com

Chapter 13 p. 405: © Imaginechina/Corbis; p. 407: © NexTag, Inc.; p. 408: Courtesy of Benjamin Moore Paints; p. 411: © 2012 Wal-Mart Stores, Inc.; p. 412: The NBA and individual member team identifications reproduced herein are used with permission from NBA Properties, Inc. © 2013 NBA Properties, Inc. All rights reserved. Screen-capture taken on Twitter, Inc. September 5, 2012; p. 416: © Sharpie; p. 417: © CBS News; p. 418: © Linden Research Inc.; p. 421: © Yowza!!; p. 424: © JGI/Jamie Grill/Blend Images LLC RF; p. 428: © 2012 BitTorrent, Inc

Chapter 14 p. 437: © Micah Young/iStockphoto; p. 440: © VIEW Pictures Ltd/Alamy; p. 443: © KingWu/iStockphoto; p. 444: © 2006 Kjetil Ree; p. 445: Courtesy of Rendezvous; p. 457: © Andrey Rudakov/Bloomberg via Getty Images; p. 465: © Scott Eells/Bloomberg via Getty Images

Chapter 15 p. 475: © Photodisc/Getty Images RF; p. 477: Photo © FSM Visitors Board; p. 479: Courtesy of the U.S. Department of the Treasury, Bureau of Engraving and Printing; p. 481: © Daniel Acker/Bloomberg via Getty Images; p. 485: © Erik Dreyer/Getty Images; p. 487: © Chris McGrath/Getty Images; p. 491: © State Farm; p. 494: © Royalty-Free/Corbis

Chapter 16 p. 503: © Stan Honda/AFP/Getty Images; p. 507: Courtesy of the U.S. Department of Treasury, Bureau of the Public Debt; p. 508: © Phillip Spears/Getty Images RF; p. 512: © Jeff Greenberg/Alamy; p. 514: © The McGraw-Hill Companies, Inc./ Jill Braaten, photographer; p. 517: © The McGraw-Hill Companies, Inc.; p. 521: © Brand X Pictures/PunchStock RF; p. 536: © Brand X/Jupiterimages/Getty Images RF; p. 541: © Photodisc/PunchStock RF; p. 547: © Blend Images/Getty Images RF

Name Index

Page numbers followed by n refer to notes.

Company Index

Invesco Mortgage Capital Inc., 490
Istithmar World, 125
Ivory Soap, 374

J

J. D. Power & Associates, 259, 260
Jaguar, 108
Jamba Juice, 373
JCPenney, 324, 385
JetBlue, 243, 259
Jiffy Lube, 163
John Deere, 93, 457
Johnny Cupcakes, 220
Johnson & Johnson, 47, 183, 324, 392, 408, 413, 523
Johnson Controls, 251, 252
JP Morgan Chase & Co., 39, 68, 132, 140, 314, 321, 487, 490, 500, 523

K

Kaiser Permanente, 322–323, 324
Kayak, 407
Kele & Co Jewelers, 314
Keller Williams, 417
Kellogg's, 377
KFC, 79, 86, 384
Kia, 259–260
Kickstarter, 357
Kimberly-Clark, 396
Kirkland & Ellis, 257
Kleenex, 377
Kmart, 385
Kogi, 395
Komatsu, 86
KPMG, 257, 324, 439, 440
Kraft Foods, 140, 188, 324, 360, 523
Krispy Kreme Doughnuts, 420–421
Kroger, 220, 385
Kumon North America Inc., 106

L

La Posta, 10
Land Rover, 108
LegalZoom.com, 136
Lego, 350
Lehman Brothers, 75, 467
Lenovo, 97, 99
Leukemia and Lymphoma Society, 362
Levi Strauss, 23, 150
Lexus, 359
Liberty Tax Service, 164
LifeSpring, 166
LinkedIn, 132, 201, 297, 300, 357
Lionel LLC, 181
Lionsgate, 133
Little Green Beans, 154
Little Man Ice Cream, 382
L.L. Bean, 280, 345
Lockheed, 66, 139
Lockheed Martin, 66, 139
L'Oreal, 392

Lowe's, 315
Lululemon, 391

M

Macy's, 213, 323, 384, 385, 388, 420, 482
Manpower Group, 54
Marketing News, 356
Marlboro, 378
Marriott International, 24, 324
Mars, 131, 199, 348, 351
Marsh & McLennan, 490
Martin Marietta, 66, 139
Maryland Institute College of Art, 270
MasterCard Worldwide, 324, 481, 487
Matsushita, 109
Mattel, 121, 377, 384
Maytag, 286
Mazda, 366
McDonald's, 23, 75, 86, 95, 106, 107, 110, 150, 154, 211, 219, 220, 244, 254, 258, 307, 372–373, 377, 378, 384, 416, 418, 465–466, 475, 519, 523
McDonnell Douglas, 66
McGraw-Hill, 517
McKesson, 132, 189, 276
Medtronic, 210, 277
Menchie's, 164
Mennen, 353
Mercedes-Benz, 377
Merck, 324, 523
Merrill Lynch, 39, 75, 182, 408, 482, 487, 491, 520
Metacafe.com, 416
Method, 383, 505
MGM Entertainment, 131
Microsoft, 3, 23, 140, 150, 277, 371, 378, 520, 521, 523
MicroSolutions, 12
MidwayUSA, 155
MillerCoors, 350
Mitsubishi, 15, 101, 109
Moen, 246
Monsanto, 324
Monster.com, 185, 300
Moody's, 490
Morgan Stanley, 453, 492
Morgan Stanley Smith Barney, 520
Morningstar, 530
Moss Adams LLP, 439
Motel 6, 401–402
Motorola, 376, 418
Mountain Dew, 379
Mrs. Acres Homemade Pies, 29
MSN Money-Zogby, 356
MSNBC, 417
MTC, 79
MTV, 86
myemma.com, 247
Myspace, 356, 412, 413–414, 423, 431

N

Nakheel, 125
Namasté Solar, 282

NASCAR, 131
NASDAQ, 521
Nathan's Famous hot dogs, 213
National City Bank, 487
National Fluid Milk Processor Promotion Board, 7
National Football League, 40
Nestlé, 109, 218
Netapp, 289
Netflix, 30, 357, 383, 411, 424, 433, 464
NetJets, 348
Netscape, 431
Neutrogena, 388
New Belgium Brewing Company, 61–62, 168, 251–252, 366–367, 414
New York Giants, 243
New York Stock Exchange, 100, 521
News Corp., 34–36, 414
Nextag, 407
Nielsen Marketing Research, 409
Nike, 91, 220, 256, 274, 391, 415, 518
Nissan, 348, 361, 379
No Mas Vello, 164
Nokia, 286
Nordstrom, 220, 357
Northrop Grumman, 66, 324
Novartis, 124, 324
NPR, 417
Nucleus Research, 432

O

Ocean Spray, 138
Odebrecht, 108
Oglethorpe Power Corp., 138
Old Spice, 353
Omnicom Group, 189
One Call Now, 271
OpenWave Systems Inc., 141
Oprah Winfrey Network, 153
Oracle, 167, 521
Orville Redenbacher, 419

P

PA Live Bait Vending, 385
Panasonic, 86, 184
Pandora, 43, 132, 432, 433
Paramount Pictures, 186
Patagonia, 54, 62, 151, 192, 252
Patrick Hoover Law Offices, 433
PayPal, 426
PBS, 417
Pennzoil, 397
People Planet, 383
PepsiCo, 54, 55, 86, 106, 223, 323, 376
Peregrine Financial, 68
Petco, 382
Petroleos de Venezuela, 108
Pfizer, 392, 523
Photobucket, 417
Phusion Products, 46
Picasa, 417
Piper Aircraft, 389
Pitney Bowes, 82

Unisys, 388
United Airlines, 259
United Auto Workers, 56
U.S. Postal Service, 133, 243, 351
United States Steel Corporation, 22
United Technologies, 523
UnitedHealth Group, 189
Universal, 518
Universidad Autonoma de Baja
    California, 99
UPS, 54, 240, 257, 357
Urban Outfitters, 220
US Airways, 259
USAJobs, 300

V

Valero Energy, 132
Vanguard Cleaning Systems, 164
Verizon Communications, 132, 324,
    392, 523
Viadeo, 300
Video.Yahoo.com, 416
Virgin Blue, 108
Visa, 481, 487, 490
Vista Bank Texas, 137
Volkswagen, 242, 397
Volvo, 181, 359, 397
Vornado Realty, 189

W

W. Atlee Burpee and Co., 157
Wachovia, 487, 495
Walgreen's, 420
Walmart, 7, 23, 53, 61, 68, 91, 104, 108, 109,
    132, 151, 157, 160, 168, 179, 181,
    254, 284, 313, 370, 377, 384, 385,
    392, 398, 409, 411, 413, 415,
    509, 523
Walt Disney, 26, 61, 115–116, 121, 189, 211,
    393, 519, 520, 523
Warby Parker, 22
Warner-Lambert, 378
Washington Mutual, 487
WD-40 Company, 365, 377
Wegmans, 54, 289
WellPoint, 324
Wells Fargo, 39, 324, 444, 487, 495, 500
Wendy's, 106, 384
Western Electric Company, 276
Westin Hotels and Resorts, 218
Westinghouse, 135, 307
Whirlpool, 324
Whole Foods, 24, 54, 60, 139, 151,
    165, 220, 276
Wikipedia, 229, 415
Wild Oats, 139
Wolfgang Express, 21

Wolverine Worldwide, 518
WorldCom, 439
Wrigley, 131, 199, 348
Wyndham Hotels and Resorts, 240
Wynn Resorts, 128

X

Xerox, 15, 54, 168, 227, 228, 377
XM Satellite Radio, 139

Y

Yahoo!, 78, 406, 417, 423
Yammer, 201, 228, 413
Yogen Fruz, 106
Yogurtland, 163, 164
Yoplait, 106
Young American Bank, 8
YouTube, 41, 43, 196, 408, 416, 427, 432, 433
YUM! Brands, 104

Z

Zagat, 139
Zappos, 206, 211, 409, 413, 415
Zebco, 181
zerogate, 419
Zoom Systems, 388
Zynga, 132, 418

Subject Index

Boldface entries denote glossary terms and the page numbers where they are defined.

Cooperatives, 118–120, **138**–139
Copper inventories, 254–255
Copyrights
  lack of overseas protection, 92
  legal protections, 75, 79
  online challenges, 79–80, 427
Core work time, 286
Corporate bonds, 541
Corporate charters, **130**, 136
Corporate citizenship, **53**; *see also* **Social responsibility**
Corporate cultures; *see* **Organizational cultures**
Corporate raiders, 141
Corporate scandals; *see* **Sarbanes-Oxley Act**; Scandals
Corporations
  advantages and disadvantages, 135–137
  basic features, 120, **129**–130, 142
  creating, 130
  stock ownership, 134–135;
    see also **Stock**
  types, 131–133
Corpus Christi (TX) organizational chart, 217, 222
Corruption Perceptions Index, 44, 45
Cost of goods sold, **449**–452
Cost-of-living escalator clauses, 319
Cost reductions, 6
Costs, small business advantages, 157
Cotton gin, 20
Counseling benefits, 315
Counterfeit products, 75, 92
Counterfeiting, money's resistance, 479
Countertrade agreements, **104**
Coupon rate, 516
Coupons, 395, 419, 421
Court systems, 69–71
Cramming, 57
Creative salespersons, 394
Creativity, 195, 199, 325
Creators (digital), 422
Credit availability, 500, 510
Credit CARD Act of 2009, 482
Credit cards
  basic features, **481**–482
  personal use, 533, 536, 537–538
  smart phone readers, 496
Credit controls, **486**
Credit lines, 162, 510, 538
Credit policies, 508–509
Credit-rating services, 44, 510
Credit reports, 543
Credit scores, 500
Credit unions, **488**
Credit usage, 537–539
Credits, in accounting, 445, 446
Creditworthiness, 542
Criminal law, 69
Crisis management, **183**
Critical path, 258
Critics (digital), 422
Crowdsourcing, 424
Cuba, 9, 93–94

Culture (national); *see also* **Organizational cultures**
  abusive behavior and, 42
  impact on buying behavior, **360**
  impact on ethics, 40–41
  impact on incentives, 290
  as trade barrier, 95–97
Cumulative claims to dividends, 134
Currencies; *see also* **Money**
  common, 100
  counterfeit, 479
  defined, 476
  durability, 478
  exchange controls, 93
  exchange rates, **90**–91
Current assets, 454, **455**, 504–509
Current liabilities, 454–455, **457**, 509–511
Current ratio, **463**
Customer benefits, 345
Customer costs, 345
Customer departmentalization, 216, **218**
Customer information, online protections, 79
Customer relationship management, 349, 363
Customer satisfaction, 380, 381
Customer service
  airlines, 258–259
  at Apple stores, 3
  at L.L. Bean, 280
  top companies, 357
  Zappos approach, 206, 211
Customization, 244, **247**
Cyber crime, 425–428
Cybersquatters, 79

D

Damage awards, 73
Data types, 355–356
Databases, 79
Day care, 56
Debentures, 516
Debit cards, **482**, 504, 536, 537
Debits in accounting, 445–446
Debt crises in Euro zone, 101, 104
Debt financing, 75–76, 162–163, 515–517
Debt problems of states, 444
Debt to total assets ratio, **464**
Debt utilization ratios, **464**
Decentralized organizations, **219**–220
Deceptive business practices, 39
Decision making
  delegating, 218–220, 223–224
  diversity and, 189
  employee involvement, 185, 193–194
  ethical, 40, 49–50
  as management function, 193, 198–200
  partnership advantages, 127
  sole proprietorship advantages, 122
Decisional role of managers, 193
Decline stage (product life cycle), 376–377
Deductibles, **546**, 547
Default risk, 540
Defective products, 73

Deferred debit cards, 482
Deficits, 17
Defined benefit plans, **544**
Defined contribution plans, **544**
Deflation, 16, 477, 484
Deforestation, 59–60
Delaware County District Attorney's Office, 497
Delegation of authority, **218**–220, 223–224
Demand
  creating, 396, 397
  defined, **12**
  estimating for services, 243
  forecasting, 248
Demand curves, 12–14
Demand deposits, 480
Democracy, under socialism, 10–11
Democratic leaders, 193
Demographic segmentation, 353
Demographic trends, 166–167
Department stores, 384, 385
Departmentalization, **215**–218
Depository insurance, 486, 488–489
Depreciation, 450, 454
Depressions, **16**, 525
Deregulation, 168
Derivatives, 82
Design, 246–247, 250
Destructive testing, 262–263
Devaluation of currency, 91
Development, **307**
Diagonal communication, 229
Diamond trade, 87
Digital marketing; *see also* **Digital media**; **Marketing strategies**
  challenges of, 421–423, 428
  growth of, 408
  impact on marketing mix, 409–413
  legal and social issues, 424–428
  major forms, 413–421
  overview, 406, **407**
Digital media; *see also* **Digital marketing**
  advantages, 406–407, 409–410
  business use, 408–409
  challenges for marketers, 421–423, 428
  defined, **406**–407
  impact on marketing mix, 409–413
  legal and social issues, 424–428
  major forms, 413–421
  market research via, 408, 421, 423–424
  role in U.S. economy, 21, 22
Digital Millennium Copyright Act, 77
Digital music players, 514
Diligence, duty of, 75
Diluted earnings per share, 465
Direct deposit, 493–494
Direct investment, **108**–109
Direct marketing, 363, 387–388
Directing, **185**
Directors (corporate); *see* **Boards of directors**
Disability insurance, **548**
Disaster recovery plans, 183
Disasters, supply chain impacts, 255

Discharging employees, 310–311
Disciplinary procedures, 310–311
Disclosures (corporate), 137
Discount rate, 485
Discount stores, 385
Discounts, 384, 508, 510
Discretionary expenses, 536
Discrimination in employment, 56,
    304–305, 325
Discussion forums, 424
Dishonesty, 44–48
Disinflation, 484
Dismissals for whistleblowing, 51
Disneyland, 115–116
Dispute resolution, 69–71, 319–321
Distribution
    career opportunities, 399
    channels and strategies, 384–390
    digital media impact, 411
    in marketing mix, **354**
Distribution of resources, 13–14
Diversified firms, 489
Diversity
    achieving, 189, 190, 322–323, 325
    benefits of, 188–189, 324–325
    in finance positions, 523
    importance, **321**–323
    market segmentation and, 350
    top companies, 324
DiversityInc Top 50, 324
Dividend yield, 519
Dividends
    accounting for, 450, 453
    decision to pay, 518–519
    defined, **130**
    preferred versus common stock, 134–135
    taxes on, 136
Dividends per share, 465
Divisibility of money, 477–478
Divisions, 223–224
Do Not Call Implementation Act, 78
Do-not-track requests, 425
Dodd-Frank Act
    intent for future of banks, 496
    major provisions, 82–83, 440, 487
    purposes, 38, 78
    whistleblower provisions, 51–52, 83
Dog food, 251
Dollars, 474–475, 478
Domain names, 80
Domestic corporations, 131
Domestic system, 20
Double-entry bookkeeping, 445–446
Double taxation, 136
Dow Chemical, 359
Dow Jones Industrial Average, 522–524
Down payments, 486
Downsizing, 168, **184**–185, 311
Downward communication, 229
Drive-in restaurants, 173–174
Drive-thru service, 238–239
Drug testing, 303
Dumping, 94
Durability of money, 478

Durbin Amendment, 83
Duties of agents, 75
DVD rentals, 30, 355
"Dynamics of Public Trust in Business"
    study, 67–68

E

E-business; *see also* **Digital media;**
    Information technology
    advertising, 393
    defined, **406**
    online vendors' sales tax resistance,
        436–438
    prescription eyewear, 22
    trends, 21, 22, 167, 384
E-mail, 231
E-readers, 14, 409
Early payment discounts, 508, 510
Earnings before interest and taxes, 450
Earnings per share, 450, 464–465
Echo boomers, 166
Ecomagination program, 179–180
Economic conditions
    expansions and contractions, 15–17
    impact on marketing, 360
    impact on motivation, 289–290
    measurement, 17–19
    as trade barrier, 90–91
Economic contractions, 16–17
Economic expansions, 15–17
Economic order quantity model, 255
Economic systems, 9–12, 19–23, 103
Economics, 8
Education, 63
Effectiveness, efficiency versus, 178
Efficiency, 6, 178, 214
Efficiency objectives, 181
Egalitarianism, 11
El Dorado (Kansas) financial reports, 467
Electric cars, 252
Electronic banking, 492–495
Electronic funds transfer, 493, 505–506
Electronic media, 392–393
Electronic monitoring, 230
Electronic trading, 521
Electronic waste, 5, 211
Elements of contracts, 74
Elks Clubs, 133
Embargoes, 93–94
Emergency recovery planning, 183
Emotional intelligence, 309
Employee assistance programs, 315
Employee development, 306–309
Employee stock ownership plans, 137, 314
Employees; *see also* **Human resources**
    management; Motivation
    attracting to sole proprietorships, 124
    benefits of diversity among, 188–189
    developing, 306–311
    downsizing staff, 184–185
    empowering, 206, 209, 218–220, 227,
        268, 276
    firms' responsibilities to, 56
    importance in company cultures, 210

    involvement in decision making, 185,
        193–194
    misuse of company time, 41–42, 326
    owners versus, 5–6, 137
    recruiting and selection, 184, 299–305
    as resources, 179
    theft by, 44–45, 46, 284
    unionized, 317–321
Employer retirement plans, 544
Employment by small businesses, 150,
    152–153
Empowerment
    by delegating authority, 218–220
    at Green Mountain Coffee Roasters, 209
    of self-directed teams, 227
    at Toyota, 268
    at Whole Foods, 276
    at Zappos, 206
Energy alternatives; *see* Alternative energy
    sources
Energy calculators, 181
Energy drinks, 46, 368–369
Energy-efficient building; *see* Environmental
    concerns; Green business strategies
Engagement with work, 273
English language instruction, 393
Entertainment industry unions, 332
Entrepreneurs, 21–23
Entrepreneurship; *see also* **Small businesses**
    in aquaculture, 180
    business forms and, 142
    as career objective, 169
    defined, **150**
    dog food, 251
    economic role, 21–23
    in large corporations, 168–169
    well-known examples, 150–151
Environmental analyses, 110
Environmental concerns; *see also* Green
    business strategies
    antipollution measures in China, 91
    of electronics firms, 5
    impact on marketing, 361
    large cities initiative, 20
    major areas, 57–62
    in operations planning, 251–252
    as part of corporate citizenship, 53
    World Bank challenges, 488
Environmental Protection Agency, 71, 72
Equal employment opportunity, 56; *see also*
    Diversity
Equal Employment Opportunity
    Commission, 71, 304–305
Equal Pay Act, 305
Equilibrium prices, 13–14
Equipment depreciation, 450, 452
Equipment leasing, 512
Equity
    in accounting equation, 445
    on balance sheets, 454, 457, 458
    managing, 517–519
    return on, 462
Equity financing, 161–162, 515, 517–519
Equity theory, 283–284

Erupt-a-Cake, 227
Estate plans, **548**–549
Esteem needs, **279**
Ethical issues, **40**–41
Ethics
in accounting, 466–467
career opportunities in, 64
cultural influences, 40–41
defined, **36**
of greenwashing, 61
growing importance to business,
24, 39–40
impact on employment opportunities,
62–63
improving, 49–52
legal requirements, 80–83
major types of violations, 41–48
in organizational cultures, 36–37, 51,
211–212
overview, 36–38
recognizing issues, 40–41, 49
Ethics committees, 226
Ethics officers, 64
Ethisphere Institute, 53
Ethnic minorities; *see* **Diversity**; Minorities
Ethnographic research, 356
Euro Disney, 115
Euro zone, 101
Eurodollar market, **507**
European debt crisis, 101, 104
European Union, **100**–101
Euros, 100, 101
Evaluating performance, 307–309
Even/odd pricing, 383
Everquest, 417
Exams, cheating on, 46–47
Exchange controls, **93**
Exchange rates, **90**–91, 100
Exchange relationships, **342**–343
Exchanges (insurance), 547
Exclusive distribution, **389**
Executive compensation
ethics scandals, 39
highest paid CEOs, 189, 276
linking to performance, 188, 276, 284
major issues, 188
public disapproval, 284
Zuckerberg, 186
Executive employment agencies, 197
Executive misconduct; *see also* Ethics;
Scandals
impact on business environment, 24, 39
legal environment for, 80–83
organizational cultures and, 211–212
reporting, 51–52, 83
Executive search firms, 300
Executive summaries, 31
Exempt employees, 326
Expansions, economic, **15**–17
Expectancy theory, **284**–285
Expenses, 450, **452**, 536
Expertise, 195
Export agents, 104–105
Exporting, **87**–88, 104–105, 152

Express warranties, **72**–73
External job candidates, 300
Extrinsic rewards, **274**
Eyeglasses, 22

F

Facilities planning, 248–251
Factors, **511**
Factors of production, 8
Factory closures, 63
Factory farms, 53
Failure risk, 158–160, 169
Fair Packaging and Labeling Act, 77
Fairness, 44–48, 283–284, 310
Fake Web sites, 427
False credentials, 304
Family members, funding from, 162
Family roles, 96
Farm cooperatives, 138–139
Farmville, 418
Fast-food restaurants, 238–239
Fat Tire beer, 366
FDIC, 488–489, 525
Federal Aviation Administration, 71
Federal Bankruptcy Court, 70
Federal Communications Commission, 71
Federal courts, 70
Federal Deposit Insurance Corporation,
82, **488**–489, 525
Federal Energy Regulatory Commission, 71
Federal Highway Administration, 71
Federal Insurance Agency, 82
Federal Reserve Board
Dodd-Frank reforms, 82
intervention in 2007–2008 financial crisis,
495–496, 525
overview of role, 23, **483**–484
policy tools, 484–486
Federal Reserve system, 483–486
Federal Savings and Loan Insurance
Corporation, 489
Federal Sentencing Guidelines for
Organizations, 80–81
Federal Trade Commission
Bureau of Consumer Protection, 57
major functions, 11, 71, 72
privacy regulation, 425
Federal Trade Commission Act, 77
Federal Trademark Dilution Act, 77, 80
Fee-for-service plans, 547
Feedback, 230–231, 424
Fees
credit card, 538
franchising, 163
investment banking, 520
transaction, 481
Fiat money, 476
Fiduciary duties, 75
Figurehead role, 193
Film financing, 518
Finance, 7, **476**
Finance charges, 538
Finance committees, 226
Finance companies, **492**

Financial Accounting Standards Board, 438
Financial compensation, 312–314; *see also*
Compensation
Financial crisis of 2008; *see* Global financial
crisis
Financial health, 531–535
Financial incentives, 276
Financial industry conflicts of interest, 44
Financial management
current assets, 504–509
current liabilities, 509–511
debt financing, 515–517
equity financing, 517–519
for fixed assets, 511–515
investment banking, 519–520
securities markets, 520–525
Financial managers, **190**, 202
Financial networks, 491
Financial planning; *see* **Personal financial
planning**
Financial projections, 32
Financial ratios, 460–466
Financial resources; *see also* Funding
defined, **8**, **9**
options for startup firms, 161–163
Redbox early challenges, 30
Financial Services Modernization Act, 487
Financial Stability Oversight
Council, 82, 83
Financial statements
balance sheets, 453–458, 532–533
basic uses, 441–444
cash flow statements, 458–460, 533–534
income statements, 448–453
legal environment, 81
ratio analysis, 460–466
terminology, 448, 449
when prepared, 447, 448
Financial system
bailouts in 2008–2009 crisis, 440,
495–496, 525
banking institutions, 486–489; *see also*
Banks
career opportunities, 497
electronic banking, 492–495
Federal Reserve role, 483–486
money in, 476–482
nonbanking institutions, 489–492
overview, 482–483
subprime loan risk, 524–525
Financing activities, 460
function of marketing, 344
Finished-goods inventory, 254
Firing employees, 51, 310–311
First-line managers, **189**
Fishing practices, 15
Fitness centers, 315
Fixed assets, 454, 457, **511**–515
Fixed interest rates, 511
Fixed-position layouts, **249**
Fixed tariffs, 92–93
Flat organizations, 221
FlexFuel vehicles, 252
Flexibility of operations, 157

in marketing mix, **354**–355
objectives, 7, 397
push and pull strategies, 396
Promotion mix, 390–395
Promotional discounts, 384
Promotional positioning, 397
Promotions (job), 197, **310**
Property law, 75
Property rights, 12
Proposals, 31
Prospecting, 394
Protect Intellectual Property Act, 427
Protective tariffs, 93
Prototypes, 372
Proxy voting, 135
Psychographic segmentation, 353
Psychological factors in buying behavior, 358–359
Psychological pricing, 383
Public accountants, 439–441
Public Company Accounting Oversight Board, 81, 438
Public corporations, 131–133
Public relations, 394
Publications for small businesses, 165
Publicity, 394–395
Publishing, 409
Pull strategies, 396
Punishments, 285
Purchase decisions, 355
Purchasing, 253–254
Pure capitalism, 11
Pure competition, 14
Push strategies, 396
Pyramid of Social Responsibility, 52

Q

QR scanning app, 420
Quality
assessing for products and services, **380**
competition and, 14
managing for, 258–263
pricing to convey, 383
product recalls for, 47
reputation, 157
of services, 244, 259, 261, 380
standards for, 247, 261–262
at Toyota, 268
Quality assurance managers, 264
Quality-assurance teams, 227
Quality circles, 227, 282–283
Quality control, 259–260
Quality of life concerns, 5
Quantity discounts, 384
Quasi-public corporations, 133
Quick ratio, 464
Quotas, 93

R

Race discrimination, 56
Racial diversity; *see* **Diversity**
Racial groups, 322, 323, 352; *see also* Minorities

Radio artists, 332
Radio frequency identification, 509
Railroads, 20, 389
Rain forest destruction, 59–60
Ranking systems, 308–309
Ratio analysis, 460–466
Raw materials, 254, 374
Real estate speculation, 524
Real property, 75
Rebates, 538
Recalls, 72, 226, 268
Receivables; *see* **Accounts receivable**
Receivables turnover, 463
Recession of 2008–2009; *see also* Global financial crisis
causes, 16
government actions, 11, 440, 495–496, 525
impact on credit availability, 500, 510
impact on public trust, 67
layoffs during, 184, 325
severity, 525
Recessions, 16
Recognition, 185, 290
Recruiting, 296–298, **299**–300
Recycling; *see also* Green business strategies; Sustainability
batteries, 251
Best Buy program, 211
electronics, 5
growing business support, 61–62
Patagonia program, 192
Red Cross, 4, 62
Reference checking, 303–304
Reference groups, 359
Refill packages, 383
Regional managers (retail), 399
Regional organization, 218
Regional trade agreements, 97–103
Regulation; *see also* Legal environment; **Sarbanes-Oxley Act**
business practices laws, 76–78
under capitalism, 11
Federal Reserve role, 486
fishing, 15
impact on lending, 500
impact on marketing, 360
major federal agencies, 71–72
of partnerships, 127
safety, 56
of sole proprietorships, 122
Reinforcement promotion, 397
Relationship building with customers, 348–349
Relationship marketing, 414
Relationships, ethical, 48
Religious practices, 96
Renewable energy, 162, 488; *see also* Alternative energy sources; Green business strategies
Renters insurance, 546
Repeat business, 348–349
Repurchase agreements, 467
Reputation, 157

Research and development, 371, 372, 452
Reserve requirement, 485
Resource allocation, 13–14, 193
Resource management, 178–179
Resource misuse, 43–44
Responsibility, 218
Restricted Zone (Mexico), 92
Results Only Work Environment (ROWE), 236, 309
Résumés, 296–297, 304
Retailers, 384–385
Retailing; *see also* **E-business**
Apple stores, 2–4
career opportunities, 399
as marketing channel, 384–385
online vendors' sales tax resistance, 436–438
site to store systems, 411
as small-business industry, 154
turnover rates, 294
RetailMeNot website, 395
Retained earnings, 452, 455, **517**–519
Retention, 274
Retirement, forced, 305
Retirement planning, 543–545
Return on assets, 461
Return on equity, 462
Return on investment, 462
Revaluation of currency, 91
Revenues, 449–452
Reverse discrimination, 325
Rewards, 273–274, 285; *see also* **Motivation**
Right-sizing, 168
Rights of consumers, 56–57
Rights under free enterprise, 12
Risk assessment, 512–513
Risk in marketing, 344
Risk-reduction strategies, 345
Risk types, 540
Robinson-Patman Act, 77
Robots, 250
Rotating jobs, 285–286
Roth IRAs, 490, 544, 545
Roundup, 359
Routing, 257
ROWE (Results Only Work Environment), 236
Russia, capitalism in, 11

S

S corporations, 120, **137**–138
Safe deposit boxes, 487
Safety regulations, 56, 72
Safety rights of consumers, 56–57
Salaries, 314; *see also* Compensation
Sales, stabilizing, 397
Sales agreements, 72–73
Sales of businesses, 123–124, 128–129
Sales of partnership interests, 128–129
Sales orientation, 347
Sales promotion, 395
Sales taxes, 436–438
Salespersons, 314, 394
Samples of products, 395

Traditional IRAs, 544, 545
Training, 198, **307**
Transaction balances, 505
Transaction fees, 481
Transfers, 310
Transformation processes, 241, 242
Translations, 95
Transparency International, 44
Transportation, 20, 344, **389**
Treasury bills, 485, **506**
Treasury Department website, 17, 19
Trends, 348
Trial balances, 446–448
Trial courts, 70
Troubled Asset Relief Program, 495
Truck transport, 389
Trust
   in banking industry, 36, 37
   business efforts to rebuilt, 67–68
   ethics and, 39
Trusts, 487
Tu Mazi, 227
Tuna, 15
Turnover
   common causes, **309**–311
   low morale and, 273
   overspecialization and, 215
   in retailing, 294
Two-factor theory, 279–281, 294
Typosquatting sites, 427

U

Undercapitalization, 159
Undercover Boss, 42
Unemployment, **16**, 19, 62–63
Uniform Commercial Code, **72**–73
Uniform Partnership Act, 124
Uniformity of inputs and outputs, 244–245
Unions, 317–321, 332, 444
U.S. economic evolution, 19–23
U.S. Treasury, 495, 525
U.S. Treasury bills, 485, **506**
United Way, 62
Unlimited liability, 123, 128
Unsecured bonds, 516
Unsecured loans, 510
Upward communication, 229

Uruguay Round, 97
Usury, 74

V

Vacuum cleaners, 154
Value, **345**, 398, 477
Variable interest rates, 511
Vending machines, 165, 355, 385, 388
Venezuela, communism in, 9
Venture capitalists, 162
Vertical mergers, 139
Veterinary practices, 123–124
Video rentals, 30
Video sharing sites, 416–417
Vietnam, economic development, 103
Viral marketing, 395, **416**
Virtual teams, 226
Virtual testing, 356
Virtual worlds, 309, 417–418
Voice over Internet Protocol, 122
Voluntary agreement, 74

W

Wage/salary surveys, 311
Wages, 312; *see also* Compensation
Wages payable, 454
Warehouse clubs, 385
Warehouse managers, 264
Warehouse showrooms, 385
Warehousing, 344, **390**
Warning labels, 48
Warnings to employees, 310
Warranties, 72–73, 345
Wars, economic impact, 16–17
Washington State University School of Food
      Science, 227
Waste disposal, 60
Water pollution, 58, 59, 91
The Wealth of Nations (Smith), 11, 214
Webb-Pomerene Export Trade Act, 92
Websites; *see also* **Digital media**; **Internet**
   benchmarking tools for, 260
   for job seekers, 300
   for mobile devices, 419
   promotions on, 355
Weibos, 404–406
Weighted averages, 522

Wellness programs, 323
Wheeler-Lea Act, 77
Whistleblowing, **51**–52, 83
White knights, 141
Wholesalers
   distribution role, 354, **386**, 387
   as small businesses, 154–155
Wide span of management, 220, 221
Wikipedia, 415, 427
Wiki, 229, **415**–416
Willingness to repay, 543
Wills, 548–549
Wind power, 60, 61, 168, 251
Women
   cultural perceptions of, 96
   employment growth, 21
   employment issues, 56, 305
   in financial careers, 523
   financial planning, 548
   as market segment, 350
   in top management, 306
   U.S. businesses owned by, 152
Women's Career Strategies Initiative, 523
Word-of-mouth marketing, 403
Work groups, 225
Work-in-process inventory, 254
Work/life balance, 277, 287
Work times, flexible, 286–289
Worker productivity, 19
Workforce development, 306–309
Working capital management, 504
Workplace safety, 56
Workplace use of social media, 432–433
World Bank, 103, 177, 488
World of Warcraft, 417
World Trade Center attacks, 183
World Trade Organization, **97**–98
Writers Guild of America, 332

Y

Yelp, 380
Yoga, 154, 391
Yowza!!, 421
Yuan, 474–475

Z

Zimbabwean inflation, 15–16